PIETIST AND WESL

Editors: David Bundy and J. Steven O'Malley

This monograph series will publish volumes in two areas of scholarly research: Pietism and Methodism (broadly understood). The focus will be Pietism, its history and development, and the influence of this socio-religious tradition in modern culture, especially within the Wesleyan religious traditions.

Consideration will be given to scholarly works on classical and neo-Pietism, on English and American Methodism, as well as on the social and ecclesiastical institutions shaped by Pietism (e.g., Evangelicals, United Brethren, and the Pietist traditions among the Lutherans, Reformed, and Anabaptists). Works focusing on leaders within the Pietist and Wesleyan traditions will also be included in the series, as well as occasional translations and/or editions of Pietist texts. It is anticipated that the monographs will emphasize theological developments, but with close attention to the interaction of Pietism with other cultural forces and to the sociocultural identity of the Pietist and Wesleyan movements.

1. Gregory S. Clapper, *John Wesley on Religious Affections*. 1989.
2. Peter Erb, *Gottfried Arnold.* 1989.
3. Henry H. Knight III, *The Presence of God in the Christian Life: John Wesley and the Means of Grace.* 1992.
4. Frank D. Macchia, *Spirituality and Social Liberation: The Message of the Blumhardts in the Light of Wuerttemberg Pietism.* 1993.
5. Richard B. Steele, *"Gracious Affection" and "True Virtue" according to Jonathan Edwards and John Wesley.* 1994.
6. Stephen L. Longenecker, *Piety and Tolerance: Pennsylvania German Religion, 1700–1850.* 1994.
7. J. Steven O'Malley, *Early German-American Evangelicalism: Pietist Sources on Discipleship and Sanctification.* 1995.
8. R. David Rightmire, *Salvationist Samurai: Gunpei Yamamuro and the Rise of the Salvation Army in Japan.* 1997.
9. Simon Ross Valentine, *John Bennet and the Origins of Methodism and the Evangelical Revival in England.* 1997.
10. Tore Meistad, *Martin Luther and John Wesley on the Sermon on the Mount.* 1999.
11. Robert C. Monk, *John Wesley: His Puritan Heritage.* 1999.
12. Richard B. Steele, *"Heart Religion" in the Methodist Tradition and Related Movements.* 2001.
13. Diane Leclerc, *Singleness of Heart.* 2001.
14. Charles Yrigoyen, Jr., *The Global Impact of the Wesleyan Traditions and Their Related Movements.* 2002.
15. Laurence W. Wood, *The Meaning of Pentecost in Early Methodism: Rediscovering John Fletcher as John Wesley's Vindicator and Designated Successor.* 2002.

16. Floyd T. Cunningham, *Holiness Abroad: Nazarene Missions in Asia.* 2003.
17. Howard A. Snyder, "*Live While You Preach": The Autobiography of Methodist Revivalist and Abolitionist John Wesley Redfield (1810–1863),* 2006.
18. Fred van Lieburg, *Living for God: Eighteenth Century Dutch Pietist Autobiography,* 2006.

"Live While You Preach"

The Autobiography of Methodist Revivalist and Abolitionist John Wesley Redfield (1810–1863)

Edited by
Howard A. Snyder

Foreword by David Bebbington

Published in collaboration with the
Marston Memorial Historical Center
Indianapolis, Indiana

Pietist and Wesleyan Series, No. 17

The Scarecrow Press, Inc.
Lanham, Maryland • Toronto • Oxford
2006

SCARECROW PRESS, INC.

Published in the United States of America
by Scarecrow Press, Inc.
A wholly owned subsidiary of
The Rowman & Littlefield Publishing Group, Inc.
4501 Forbes Boulevard, Suite 200, Lanham, Maryland 20706
www.scarecrowpress.com

PO Box 317
Oxford
OX2 9RU, UK

British Library Cataloguing in Publication Information Available

Library of Congress Cataloging-in-Publication Data

Redfield, John Wesley, 1810–1863.
"Live while you preach" : the autobiography of Methodist revivalist and abolitionist John Wesley Redfield (1810–1863) / edited by Howard A. Snyder ; foreword by David Bebbington.
p. cm. — (Pietist and Wesleyan series ; no. 17)
Includes bibliographical references (p.) and index.
ISBN-13: 978-0-8108-5280-8 (pbk. : alk. paper)
ISBN-10: 0-8108-5280-2 (pbk. : alk. paper)
1. Redfield, John Wesley, 1810–1863. 2. Methodist Church—Biographies. 3. Evangelists—Biography. 4. Abolitionists—Biography. I. Snyder, Howard A. II. Title. III. Pietist and Wesleyan studies ; no. 17.

BX8495.R35A3 2006
287'.6092—dc22
[B] 2005057543

The paper used in this publication meets the minimum requirements of American National Standard for Information Sciences—Permanence of Paper for Printed Library Materials, ANSI/NISO Z39.48-1992.
Manufactured in the United States of America.

Revitalization: Explorations in World Christian Movements

This volume is published in collaboration with the Center for the Study of World Christian Revitalization Movements at Asbury Theological Seminary. Building on the work of the previous Wesleyan/Holiness Studies Center at the Seminary, the Center provides focus for research in the Wesleyan Holiness and other related Christian renewal movements, including Pietism and Pentecostal movements, which have had a world impact. The research seeks to develop analytical models in studying these movements, including biblical and theological assessment. Using an interdisciplinary approach, the Center bridges relevant discourses in several areas with a view toward effective Christian mission globally. It recognizes the need for conducting research that combines insights from the history of evangelical renewal and revival movements with anthropological and religious studies literature on revitalization movements. It also networks with similar or related research and study centers around the world, in addition to sponsoring its own research projects.

This critical edition of John Wesley Redfield's autobiography not only narrates the life of a central and controversial figure in the rise of Free Methodism; it includes as well important reflections on proto-Pentecostalism, abolitionism, revivalism and evangelical feminism, and the influence of these currents on the larger society. The volume is thus congruent with the mission of the Center and serves to advance its research objectives.

Center for the Study of World Christian Revitalization Movements
Asbury Theological Seminary

Contents

Foreword – David Bebbington ix

Series Editor's Preface xi

Preface xiii

Apparatus xvii

Biographical Introduction: John Wesley Redfield xxi

Chronology xxvii

The Text 1

I. Redfield's *Apologia* 1

II. Birth and Early Call 3

III. Redfield Resists the Call to Preach 9

IV. Assisting a Methodist Preacher 20

V. Rejection of Call; Wanderings 26

VI. Redfield's Unfortunate Marriage 31

VII. Licensed to Preach 46

VIII. Abolitionism: "Proclaim the Jubilee of God" 49

IX. Seeking Holiness: "By faith alone" 65

X. Evaluating Impressions: "Faith, fancy, intuition" 66

XI. New York City: "Unearthly power lifted me" 71

XII. "Resolved to make a business of seeking holiness" 80

XIII. Phoebe and Walter Palmer: "I feared them" 83

XIV. "A remarkable dream fulfilled to the letter" 96

XV. "If you want revival, seek holiness" 100

XVI.	"Led to review my history"	109
XVII.	Expanding Revival Ministry, 1844–1846	113
XVIII.	"New fields opening"	120
XIX.	"Jesus cures both soul and body"	124
XX.	"Ain't I dying?"	141
XXI.	Phoebe Palmer: "These strange facts"	144
XXII.	"Entering the harvest field with all my might"	145
XXIII.	Continue Stressing Holiness?	150
XXIV.	The 1846 Middletown, Connecticut, Revival	153
XXV.	Revival Ministry in the East, 1846–1850	157
XXVI.	Philadelphia: "Operations next to Pentecostal"	168
XXVII.	Newburgh Camp Meeting: "Gusts of power"	187
XXVIII.	Further Revivals	193
XXIX.	Redfield Meets Fay Purdy	195
XXX.	Prison Ministry in New York	201
XXXI.	Ministry in Bridgeport, Connecticut	206
XXXII.	Revivals in Connecticut	214
XXXIII.	Summer Camp Meetings	223
XXXIV.	Encountering Paranormal Phenomena	236
XXXV.	Return to Syracuse, New York	247
XXXVI.	Pentecost: God's Ideal Church	262
XXXVII.	Redfield Visits His Boyhood Home	267
XXXVIII.	Revival Ministry in Western New York	268

XXXIX. Redfield's "Most Splendid Mansion" 274

XL. Ministry with B. T. Roberts in Buffalo, 1853 280

XLI. The 1854–55 Burlington Revival 286

XLII. Redfield's Second Marriage 289

XLIII. Ministry in "The West" 296

XLIV. Revival in Marengo and Woodstock, Illinois 302

XLV. Ministry in Wisconsin 307

XLVI. St. Louis, Missouri, 1858–59 311

XLVII. Ministry in Illinois; Growing Controversy 332

XLVIII. Return to St. Louis, 1860 342

XLIX. Redfield's Stroke, Visions, and Decline 344

L. Pentecost: God's Ideal for the Church 352

LI. Entering into Jesus' Sufferings 354

LII. Suffering and the Plan of Salvation 357

LIII. Redfield Assesses Early Free Methodism 362

LIV. The Bible versus Rationalism and Spiritualism 364

LV. Methodism, Slavery, and the Civil War 367

LVI. Last Things 371

LVII. Final Return to Syracuse 384

Bibliography 397

Index 401

Foreword

Methodism was the most successful Protestant movement of the nineteenth century. Beginning in England in the 1730s, it spread to Ireland, America, Canada, continental Europe, Australia, New Zealand, the South Pacific and parts of India and Africa. Enjoying the organizational structure that was the achievement of John Wesley and the rich hymnody that was the legacy of his brother Charles, Methodism conquered much of the globe in the name of Christ. Its advance was specially rapid during the first half of the century, a period when in the United States it grew from some 65,000 to over one and a quarter million members.

Throughout the world, however, the movement was plagued by tensions. The most acute was between populism and social conformity.

Populism was often associated with the doctrine of entire sanctification. Upheld by the Wesleys, this was the teaching that, while still on earth, human beings could attain a state of holiness fitting them for heaven. Entire sanctification, or full salvation, was often enforced by the most vigorous revivalists. They were prepared to tolerate, or even encourage, disorderly meetings in order to foster the spread of their teaching, which they were confident, from experience, would lead to mass conversions as well as to higher spiritual attainments among those already converted. Shouting, jumping and dancing were acceptable as signs of fresh blessing. People collapsed on the floor, overcome with a sense of the glory of God. These features were common in the English denomination that was called Primitive Methodism because it was believed that these phenomena signaled a resurgence of the spirit of the earliest days of Wesley's movement. The same phenomena were also apparent in the ministry of J. W. Redfield, the author of this autobiography. He often summed up his work as a revival of "Primitive Methodism."

Redfield found himself resisted by the forces of social conformity. As Methodists prospered, especially in the growing cities, so they wanted to demonstrate their respectability. These "fashionable, fancy Methodists," as Redfield terms them, built large churches, inserted stained glass windows and added ornate decorations. They installed organs, an innovation that led to a secession from Wesleyan Methodism in England by those who saw them as symbols of social pretension. They tolerated dancing, card playing and novel reading. Their women wore jewelry. Although the notion of entire sanctification was unavoidable in the writings of the Wesleys, the respectable played it down as rather too fanatical a notion. Occasionally they even denied it, positing instead the Calvinist belief that sanctification is slow and gradual. These "pomp- and pleasure-loving people" seemed to Redfield the betrayers of authentic Methodism.

Redfield's recollections therefore form a classic account of the struggle for the soul of nineteenth-century Methodism. There is no balance, no even-handedness, here. Redfield was passionately devoted to entire sanctification, revival and all their concomitants, including dreams, revelations and being slain in the Spirit. He was constantly at war with the forces of moderation, restraint and good order. He avoided becoming an ordained preacher so that his energies should not be inhibited by officialdom.

For many years Redfield hoped that his manifest success as a revivalist would lead the authorities "to stem the tide of formalism and ungodliness" and so to reform the Methodist Episcopal Church. He also deeply desired that the church would come out as the champion of the slaves and so align itself with active abolitionists. But his hopes were dashed. Eventually he found himself, with a handful of other devotees of entire sanctification, outside the church that he had wanted to reinvigorate. He was one of the creators, in 1860, of the Free Methodist Church that stood for full salvation, revival and abolitionism. Redfield was one of the populists who was forced out of a denomination that increasingly was socially conformist. His narrative captures the central tension of nineteenth-century Methodism.

David Bebbington
Professor of History
University of Stirling

December 2004

Series Editor's Preface

Evangelist and abolitionist John Wesley Redfield (1810–1863), a significant and colorful figure in the Methodist Episcopal and later the Free Methodist churches, wrote a lengthy autobiography shortly before his death. Professor Howard Snyder, a leading author in Wesleyan studies and church renewal, has now prepared the first critical edition of this important manuscript, which is housed in the Marston Memorial Historical Center in Indianapolis. It represents an important primary source for the study of the Wesleyan Holiness tradition and of American Methodism.

The Redfield manuscript holds considerable interest in its own right, but the primary reason for publishing this edition is historical. Redfield was virtually the cofounder of the Free Methodist Church but is little known today, resulting in some misunderstandings and misinterpretations of both Methodist and Free Methodist history. The manuscript documents Redfield's contributions as an outspoken abolitionist, his stormy marriage and divorce, contacts with leading contemporaries such as Charles Finney and Phoebe Palmer, his occasional practice of medicine, and his remarkable revivals which this edition documents in some detail. Redfield gives his reflections on a variety of topics of contemporary interest, including proto-Pentecostalism and women's issues. Professor Snyder's critical apparatus makes this volume a valuable resource for scholars, and it is with pleasure that it is presented in the Wesleyan and Pietist Series.

J. Steven O'Malley
Series Editor

Preface

This book makes available in published form the 425-page handwritten autobiography of John Wesley Redfield (1810–1863), controversial American Methodist "lay" revivalist and abolitionist of the 1840s and 1850s. Redfield produced the manuscript shortly before his death. It has never been published or seriously studied, though Joseph G. Terrill incorporated large extracts (often heavily edited) in his book, *The Life of Rev. John Wesley Redfield, M.D.* (1889).

The life of Redfield provides a case study in the clash of cultures between the Methodism of the 1830s and 1840s and the quite altered Methodism of the 1850s and 1860s, especially in America's emerging cities. In a variety of ways, the autobiography documents the theological and cultural shifts occurring within Methodism in the eastern U. S. Redfield invariably cast the issues within Methodism in spiritual terms, but involved also were matters of culture and personality, of cultural aspirations and expectations.

Redfield had no descendants. His manuscript autobiography has been preserved in the Marston Memorial Historical Center for many years; probably it was in the hands of Joseph Terrill and came into the possession of the Free Methodist Publishing House (and hence later the denominational historical center) following Terrill's death, if not before. The narrative is published here in collaboration with the Marston Memorial Historical Center and the Free Methodist Historical Society. It is presented in its entirety, with critical and contextual notes, as an important primary source in the study of nineteenth-century revival and reform movements, American Methodism, early Free Methodism, and the holiness movement.

Though Redfield's manuscript is a fascinating account in its own right, the primary purpose for publishing it now is historical. In effect the cofounder of the Free Methodist Church, Redfield in the 1840s and 1850s had a broad ministry in the Methodist Episcopal Church and beyond. He is little known today, leading to some misunderstandings of Methodist and Free Methodist history. An outspoken abolitionist and advocate of women's right to preach, Redfield was controversial among Methodist leaders and in the church press. He had some occasional contact with Charles Finney, and in 1856 the two conducted simultaneous revivals in Rochester, New York.

Redfield's manuscript details briefly his early life and conversion, his stormy marriage and divorce, his abolitionist activities, his contacts with Phoebe Palmer, his occasional practice of medicine, and especially his remarkable revivals. He held notable revivals in several Eastern cities including New York, Philadelphia, and Burlington, Vermont, and later in Illinois and St. Louis, Missouri. His revivals typically were marked by emotional manifestations including people being slain in the Spirit, dramatic conversions, and opposition by some.

Redfield was distressed with the changes he saw happening within Methodism, and as a result of this and his own personals struggles, his story sometimes reads more like the lamentations of Jeremiah than the labors of Paul. At times Redfield reports dreams and visions reminiscent of Ezekiel or other biblical prophets. Most of his story however consists of remarkable revival accounts. Near the end of the manuscript Redfield gives his analysis of Methodism in relation to slavery and the Civil War, which was raging even as he wrote.

How reliable is Redfield's self-reporting of the fruits of his revivals? Fairly reliable, as it turns out.

There are two ways to check Redfield's claims: Membership statistics and independent contemporary accounts. In a number of cases I have been able to identify the churches Redfield visited and corroborate Redfield's reports by examining official membership figures. Even though it is not always possible to document the results of Redfield's revivals fully, I have found a fairly consistent positive correlation between his revivals and the membership statistics of the churches involved.

Also, in some cases I've found newspaper or other firsthand accounts that tend to confirm Redfield's description of particular revivals. (Corroborating evidence is detailed in the reference notes.) I have found that, although Redfield often rounded off, or perhaps "rounded upwards," the reported number of converts or new members resulting from his revivals, he gave generally accurate accounts and was not guilty of major exaggeration. A modest man, Redfield reported the results of his revivals as he saw them, though of course through his own lenses in the way he viewed the gospel and contemporary currents within Methodism.

This book is in some ways a companion volume to my *Populist Saints: B. T. and Ellen Roberts and the First Free Methodists* (Eerdmans, 2006). Redfield had a decisive influence on the younger Benjamin Titus Roberts (1823–1893), and his autobiography is an important source for understanding Roberts and his time. Following years of ministry in the Methodist Episcopal Church, the two men were instrumental in the birth of the Free Methodist Church, even though Redfield lived only three years beyond its founding in 1860. The role of the two in the rise of Free Methodism is symbolized by the fact that their portraits appear as frontispieces in volume one (Roberts) and volume two (Redfield) of Wilson T. Hogue's *History of the Free Methodist Church* (1915).

Readers who follow this strange and remarkable tale through to the end will doubtless come away with varying assessments. My own view is that Redfield, despite obvious feet of clay, had a good heart. His preaching testifies to remarkable gifts and power in the pulpit. Perhaps he represented the best yet at times also the most extreme elements of antebellum Methodism and early Free Methodism.

Apparatus

The following conventions have been used to make Redfield's manuscript more intelligible:

[ ] Indicates material inserted editorially for clarification.

[?] Immediately following a word, indicates an uncertain reading of a word in Redfield's manuscript.

[?] Indicates an omitted indecipherable word.

{ } Indicates corrections or alterations made by another hand. In most cases these can be presumed to have been made by J. G. Terrill.

/1/ Indicates the pagination of the handwritten manuscript (beginning of a new page). The first available page of the manuscript bears the notation "P 3," apparently indicating that an original sheet (front and back; perhaps a title page) is missing.

Strike-throughs (~~thus~~) indicate editing or altering of words, either by Redfield or someone else. I have retained these when they indicate wording which Redfield wrote but then crossed through in favor of different wording, but have deleted them when the strike-throughs were merely corrections. Redfield frequently struck through a word and then rewrote it; I have removed these strike-throughs, for ease in reading.

Redfield divided his manuscript into chapters, using the designation "Chap" and the number of the chapter. I have retained these chapter divisions. I have broken the text into paragraphs where the flow of thought seemed to justify this, even if in the text the writing is continuous, without paragraph breaks.

Although Redfield generally did not use quotation marks when quoting himself or someone else, I have supplied them for the sake of clarity (also adding the necessary punctuation).

Redfield often did not put periods at ends of sentences and frequently ran sentences together or strung them together with "&" or "but." I have supplied punctuation and capitalization where these are clearly indicated by the sense, without use of brackets, and have changed "&" to "and" or deleted the "and" or "but" and begun a new sentence when this facilitated reading and comprehension.

I have in most cases silently corrected misspellings Redfield commonly used (such as "aweful" for "awful," "whome" for "whom," and also "passed" for "past" and "alter" for "altar" when those clearly were the intended meanings). Redfield commonly spelled compound words such as "everything" and "anyone" as two words. For ease of reading I have changed these to the one-word form. I have changed the abbreviated forms "Dr" and "Bro" to "doctor" and "brother" where Redfield used these as common nouns.

An idiosyncrasy of Redfield's style is that he often begins sentences with "When," but with the meaning of "Then." In such cases I have changed "When" to "Then." Redfield was somewhat inconsistent in the capitalization of nouns. Where he capitalized common nouns I have removed the capitalization except in a few cases where the capitalization seemed to indicate personification or added emphasis.

Redfield frequently underlined words for emphasis, sometimes with a double underline and occasionally with a broken line. I have generally retained this emphasis. He almost always underlined "God," "Lord," and other words for the deity, except that he usually did not underline the first letter—so the words appear as G<u>od</u> and L<u>ord</u> (perhaps because of the way his capital Gs and Ls extend below the line). I have removed this underlining as not essential to Redfield's meaning.

Where Redfield inadvertently repeated a word, I have removed the repetition. I have followed the convention of spelling out numbers below 100 and at the beginning of sentences, though Redfield frequently used numerals in these cases. In a few cases I have corrected grammar or syntax for ease in reading.

Often words in the manuscript are nearly indecipherable and must be determined by context. The words "when" and "where," "the" and "this," and "could" and "would" are often indistinguishable, as are "He" and "The" at the beginning of sentences. In such cases I have relied on context and, where possible, also on Terrill's rendering. Occasionally where Redfield's text is almost indecipherable, my renderings of particular words are conjectural, but based on the apparent meaning. (Terrill also apparently had trouble deciphering Redfield's script. In some cases he misread words, and in many cases he simply skipped over words or phrases which he found unintelligible.)

Note on Terrill's *Life of Redfield*

In 1889 Joseph Goodwin Terrill (c. 1838–1895) published a biography of John Wesley Redfield which he based largely on the manuscript of Redfield's autobiography. It was published as *The Life of Rev. John*

Wesley Redfield, M.D.[1] Since this 464-page account is the most important single published source on Redfield, and since Terrill quoted or paraphrased Redfield's manuscript extensively, I have frequently cross-referenced to Terrill's text (using the designation JGT, followed by the page number).

As a young Methodist Episcopal preacher in northern Illinois, Terrill was strongly influenced by Redfield's revival ministry. He became a Free Methodist on the organization of the new denomination in 1860. As a Free Methodist he exercised a variety of leadership roles and was serving as general missionary secretary at the time of his death. He had hoped to write a history of the Free Methodist Church, which he probably would have completed had he not died prematurely at the age of fifty-six. His colleague Bishop Wilson T. Hogue wrote of Terrill, "The fidelity and accuracy of his memory enabled him to recall with great precision anything and everything he had ever read, as occasion demanded."[2]

In his biography of Redfield, Terrill sometimes quoted Redfield's manuscript word for word, using quotation marks but making editorial corrections. In some quoted material, however, Terrill in fact revised, condensed, or toned down Redfield's often strong and colorful language. For example, on page 164 Redfield writes, "Such a power fell upon me while I was reading that it seemed to me that every word of the hymn fell upon the hearts of the congregation with the weight of forty pounds each word." Terrill however has, "Such an unction was given that every word fell upon the congregation with great power."

In many cases Terrill used Redfield's text as the basis of his own narrative, condensing, paraphrasing, or at times amplifying the account, especially at those points where Terrill had additional information. Not infrequently Terrill silently omitted material found in Redfield's manuscript—material which would now be considered important from a historical or theological standpoint.

I note the places where Terrill made significant changes or omissions. Readers will now, therefore, get a fuller sense of what Redfield said and intended than from the Terrill book, and people familiar with Terrill's volume will learn much here that is not found there.

---

[1] Joseph Goodwin Terrill, *The Life of Rev. John Wesley Redfield, M.D.* (Chicago: Free Methodist Publishing House, 1889); reprinted in 1912; later reprints.

[2] Wilson T. Hogue, *History of the Free Methodist Church of North America* (Chicago: Free Methodist Publishing House, 1915), 2:208. See also "Experience of Joseph G. Terrill," *The Earnest Christian* 3, no. 2 (Feb. 1862): 53–57; "Rev. Joseph G. Terrill," *The Earnest Christian* 69, no. 5 (May 1895): 160.

Biographical Introduction

"The mightiest revival that Burlington ever saw, and which shook all Vermont" is the way Cassius Castle, a young Methodist in Burlington, described meetings that began in the local Methodist Episcopal Church in December, 1854. The revival started under the ministry of evangelist Fay Purdy but continued another six weeks with the preaching of John Wesley Redfield. "Never have I heard such divine eloquence as poured forth from the lips of this devoted and faithful servant of the Lord Jesus Christ," Castle reported—not even from Bishop Matthew Simpson himself.[1]

John Wesley Redfield was a sort of John the Baptist figure within Methodism in the 1840s and 1850s. B. T. Roberts called him "the most wonderful evangelist of his day,"[2] and Wilson Hogue considered him "among the greatest evangelists of the nineteenth century."[3] Yet he was a quixotic and controversial figure.

Redfield was a self-taught medical doctor and a Methodist local preacher. He was born June 23, 1810, probably in Claremont, New Hampshire.[4] As a child Redfield felt called to preach but wasn't actually converted until his teen years, as he relates in his manuscript.

Methodist preacher Willbur Fisk was a friend of the Redfield family and took interest in this unusual young man. He suggested that Redfield attend Wesleyan Academy, which had just been opened at Wilbraham, Massachusetts, and where Fisk served as the first principal before going on to become the founding president of Wesleyan University.[5] One of the imponderables of Methodist history is what would have happened had Redfield taken Fisk's advice and gone to Wilbraham, where solid learning was punctuated with periodic revivals. He didn't, and in fact never received much formal education.

Terrified at "the awful responsibility of a Christian minister" and fearful of following human rather than divine direction, Redfield turned

---

[1] C. A. Castle, *A History of the Methodist Episcopal Church in Burlington, Vermont* (Burlington: Free Press Association, 1903), 24.

[2] B. T. Roberts, "Introduction," in JGT, 3.

[3] Hogue, *History of the Free Methodist Church,* 1:267.

[4] JGT, 17. Terrill gives Clarendon, New Hampshire as the birthplace; probably the correct town is Claremont, as a number of Redfields lived there and there is no Clarendon, New Hampshire.

[5] JGT, 21; cf. Joseph Holdich, *The Life of Willbur Fisk, D.D., First President of the Wesleyan University* (New York: Harper and Brothers, 1842), 151, 164–70.

away from God and began to wander spiritually. He abandoned his faith and between the ages of twenty and thirty studied medicine (apparently on his own), dabbled in art, philosophy and spiritualism, and entered into a disastrous marriage.

After more years of struggle and eventual separation from his wife, Redfield rededicated his life to Christ and began a fruitful evangelistic ministry. He was licensed as a Methodist local preacher in Lockport, New York, and subsequently in various Methodist local churches. An 1855 letter from James Floy, presiding elder of the New York District of the New York East Conference, certifies that Redfield was "a duly accredited Local Preacher in the Methodist Episcopal Church" in New York City, having been "examined and approved at the Quarterly Conference of the Twenty Seventh St. charge" on April 13 of that year.[6]

Eventually Redfield divorced his wife and years later, in 1856, remarried. However his earlier marital difficulties were a frequent source of anxiety to him. Questions would be raised, and rumors whispered. Understandably, his later remarriage did little to stop the gossip.

During several months of serious illness in New York City, probably during the winter of 1841–42, Redfield struggled again with his duty to preach. He finally received a word from the Lord, "You may live while you preach, but no longer." He consecrated himself fully to do God's will and, as he says in his manuscript, "This single sentence has kept me moving for more than twenty years at my own expense to toil in the face of all opposition."

Redfield relates his quest for holiness as he sought to be more effective evangelistically. He tells of his encounters with Phoebe Palmer, through whose ministry he experienced entire sanctification. His experience and preaching illustrate the debates over the Wesleyan doctrine of Christian perfection at the time. He came to describe the experience of holiness or entire sanctification as the "baptism of the Holy Spirit," using that terminology well before it came into more general use later in the century.

Redfield's Revival Ministry

Redfield began conducting revival meetings throughout New York State and New England. He was actively engaged as a revivalist from the early 1840s until late 1860. The chronology of his ministry is sometimes unclear, however. Redfield seldom supplies dates (though

[6] Copy of handwritten letter, dated New York, June 5, 1855 (Marston Memorial Historical Center, Indianapolis, Indiana).

Terrill's account is of some help), and his narrative does not always follow a chronological sequence. In order to preserve the integrity of the manuscript I have not rearranged sections in chronological order. Instead, I provide a reconstructed chronology of Redfield's life and ministry, indicating uncertain dates by question marks.

Redfield was explicit about God's call to the church of his day: A return to the purity and power of primitive Methodism. His essential message was one of conversion and sanctification as understood and emphasized in the early Methodist movement. He was sure that the way to effective evangelism and church growth was to preach holiness.

Redfield had a passion for the poor and was committed to abolitionism, simplicity, and the right of women to preach. "He labored to bring all to the gospel level by noticing the poor, and especially the colored poor," wrote Terrill.[7] He was particularly sensitive to suffering of all kinds. "Suffering in others he could not witness, unless he could assist in relieving it." Killing animals bothered him so much that, if while lodging at a farm he learned that an animal was being slaughtered, he would pace his room in anguish.[8]

Redfield's revivals were often attended by such phenomena as shouting and seekers being slain in the Spirit. In this sense his revivals resembled those of frontier Methodism and of Methodist camp meetings a generation earlier. In fact Redfield was often unwelcome in larger city churches which were becoming more urbane and wanted to distance themselves from what they saw as earlier Methodist excesses.

One of Redfield's more remarkable revivals brought him into direct contact with President Stephen Olin of Wesleyan University in Middletown, Connecticut. This early 1846 revival had a considerable impact on the church, the campus, and the community, with around 400 conversions, and was endorsed by President Olin. Prof. Joseph Holdich called it "the most remarkable revival of religion I have ever seen."[9] Olin reported to his brother at one point, "Twenty of [our students] have become professed converts within the last ten days, and more are inquiring the way. Nearly fifty converts are also numbered in our town congregation. It is truly a wonderful time. About three fourths of our students profess religion, and I never saw a more hopeful company of

---

[7] JGT, 259.

[8] JGT, 11.

[9] Joseph Holdich, "Revival in the Wesleyan University" (Letter to the Editors), *Christian Advocate and Journal* 20, no. 33 (25 March 1846): 130.

young men."[10]

After Middletown, Redfield went on to conduct revivals in many Methodist churches and holiness camp meetings. Gradually his ministry extended into western New York and on to Illinois, Wisconsin, and the St. Louis, Missouri, area.

The revival in Burlington, Vermont, mentioned above, was especially noteworthy. Redfield preached in Burlington in early 1855, before going west. Although his manuscript gives only a brief summary—less than a page—this revival bore multiplied fruit and is well documented in secondary sources. It had an impact not only in the local Methodist church but also among students at the nearby University of Vermont. One of the students later described how "in a few weeks, twenty-five or thirty young men were converted, many, if not most of whom, became ministers."[11] One of these was the writer himself, R. H. Howard, who became a Methodist preacher. Another was Constans L. Goodell (1830–1886), the noted Congregational minister, who was converted during his senior year at the University of Vermont. Howard's sketch of Goodell's conversion gives an insightful glimpse into Redfield's method and manner:

> [Goodell] had become greatly interested in Doctor Redfield and his meetings, not so much on any religious grounds as on the score of his eloquence and the marvelous sweetness of his singing. The writer will never forget seeing Goodell and [another] gifted classmate . . . night after night elbowing their way to the front, and sitting flat on the carpet before the pulpit—the house being too full to obtain seats—for the sake of listening to the wonderful oratorical flights of that now long since departed, but gifted, evangelist—little dreaming, meanwhile, that he was himself so soon successfully to engage in the same glorious work of calling sinners to repentance.[12]

---

[10] Stephen Olin to J. R. Olin, March 1, 1846, in *The Life and Letters of Stephen Olin, D.D., LL.D., Late President of the Wesleyan University,* 2 vols. (New York: Harper and Brothers, 1853), 2:272.

[11] Quoted in JGT (286) from a letter (c. 1886) by Howard printed in the *California Christian Advocate.*

[12] Account by R. H. Howard, *The Congregationalist* (11 Feb. 1886), quoted in A. H. Currier, *The Life of Constans L. Goodell, D.D.* (New York: Anson D. F. Randolph and Co., 1887), 21. This account is quoted also in JGT, 286. Goodell was the long-time pastor of Pilgrim Church, St. Louis, Missouri, and a leader in the (Congregational) American Missionary Association whose major focus was ministry to Africans and African Americans. See also "Death of Rev. C. L. Goodell, D.D.," *The American Missionary* 40, no. 3 (March 1886).

Goodell was to attain national prominence in the Congregational Church. When he died in 1886 William M. Taylor, pastor of New York's Broadway Tabernacle, said of him: "When he was converted, he was converted through and through. The change in him was so marked because it was so radical."[13] Some of Redfield's spiritual genes seemed to transfer to Goodell, who had a lifelong concern for evangelism, missions, and ministry to the poor.

Some of Redfield's most stirring revivals were held in towns west of Chicago in the late 1850s. Here also Redfield's preaching proved controversial, and it is more than coincidence that when the Free Methodist Church was organized in 1860, many of its earliest "western" congregations arose in places where Redfield had held meetings in Methodist congregations.

Redfield lived only three years after the formation of the Free Methodist Church. Shortly after the new denomination was organized in the summer of 1860, he at age fifty suffered a debilitating stroke. The date was Tuesday, November 6, 1860—coincidentally, the day Abraham Lincoln was elected U.S. President. Redfield did have some limited ministry in 1861 and 1862, and during this period he wrote his autobiography, hoping to have it published. In the summer of 1862 he purchased "forty acres of unimproved land" near St. Charles, Illinois hoping, he said, to establish "a pilgrims' home."[14]

Redfield died on November 2, 1863 near Marengo, Illinois, where he had been ministering. His funeral was on November 4; his tombstone is located at lot eleven, block three, of the Marengo Cemetery.

In announcing Redfield's death in *The Earnest Christian* B. T. Roberts wrote:

> Dr. Redfield was one of the most remarkable men of the day. . . . For over twenty years he has devoted his time to the promotion of revivals of religion, receiving no compensation for his unremitting labors. As a revival preacher, he had no equal in this country. . . . Vast audiences were wrought to the highest pitch of religious excitement under his awful appeals, and wherever he held meetings the country was moved for miles around, and hundreds of converts were added to

---

[13] William M. Taylor, "Introduction," in Currier, *Life of Constans Goodell*, x.
[14] JGT, 460-61.

the church of God.[15]

Redfield's autobiography gives an inside understanding of the man that is available nowhere else.

---

15 [B. T. Roberts,] "Death of Dr. Redfield," *The Earnest Christian* 6, no. 6 (Dec. 1863): 184.

Chronology

1810	June 23	Birth, Claremont, New Hampshire
1825?	Summer	Converted in a Methodist camp meeting
1826		Struggles with call; first receives heavenly "sign"
1827		Some evangelistic ministry with Methodist pastors
1828 (approx.)		Rejection of call; wanderings
1830–1840		Medical and artistic studies
1834 (approx.)		First marriage
1836		Desertion of first wife
1839–40	Winter	Abolitionist activity in Cleveland, Ohio
1840–41?		Ministry in Lockport, New York, area
1841	Winter	Severe illness (tuberculosis) in New York City
	Spring	Begins preaching, Eighteenth St. M.E. Church, New York City
1841–42		Occasional preaching in New York City area
1842	Aug.-Sept.	Encounters Phoebe Palmer at Sing Sing, N.Y.
1843–45		Intermittent revivals; mostly unrecorded
1846	Feb. 15	Begins Middletown, Connecticut, revival
	Feb. 26	President Stephen Olin defends Redfield
	Mar. 1 or 2	Redfield leaves; Middletown revival continues
	Mar.-Apr.	Ministry in New Jersey
1847	Sept. 8	Redfield (Westhampton, N.Y.) writes to Palmer
	Nov. 4	Redfield (Pleasantville, N.Y.) writes to Palmer
1848?	Summer?	Divorce, New York City (possibly earlier)
1850	Feb.	Ministry in Goshen, New York; writes Palmers
	March	Goshen and Middletown, New York
	April?	Ministry in Long Island, New York
	Dec.	In Bridgeport, Connecticut; writes Palmers
1851	Jan.?	Revival in New Haven, Connecticut
	Feb.?	Ministry in Stamford, Connecticut

	Oct.?	Chelsea and Boston, Massachusetts
1852	Oct.?	Ministry in Syracuse, New York, area?
	Nov.	Ministry in Henrietta, New York
	Nov.-Dec.	Painted Post, Bath, and other area M.E. churches
1853	Jan.	Revival at Niagara St. M.E. Church, Buffalo
	Feb.?	Ministry in Townsendville, New York
1854		Revival ministry in western New York; mostly unrecorded
1855	Jan.	Revival, Syracuse, N.Y. Congregational Church
	Jan.-Feb.	Ministry in Albion, N.Y., with William Kendall
	Feb.?	Ministry in Bridgeport, Connecticut
	Feb.-Mar.	Revival at Burlington, Vermont
	April(?)	Redfield remarries at Keeseville, New York
1856	March	Ministry in Lima, New York
	April	Rochester, New York
	June	St. Charles, Illinois
	July-Aug.	Rest, Mackinaw Island, Michigan
	Sept.-Dec.	Ministry in Wisconsin
1857	January	Ministry in Appleton, Wisconsin, area
	Mar.-Apr.	Revivals mostly in northern Illinois
	June	St. Charles, Illinois, Camp Meeting
	Fall	Revival at St. Charles, Illinois, and vicinity
1858	January	Ministry at Elgin, Illinois
	Feb.	Revival at Marengo, Illinois, M.E. Church
	March?	Revival at Woodstock, Illinois
	Spring	Redfield and wife visit B. T. Roberts, Pekin, N.Y.
	June	Ministry in Appleton, Wisconsin
	July-Aug.	Ministry in Kane County, Illinois, area
	October	Redfield in St. Charles, Illinois
	Late Nov.	Redfield and wife arrive in St. Louis, Missouri
	Dec.	At Ebenezer M.E. Church, St. Louis

1859	Jan-Mar.	Ministry in St. Louis
	Mar.	Ministry in Quincy, Illinois
	June 23–29	Preaches at Bergen, N.Y., Camp Meeting
	July 1–5	Redfields visit Roberts family, Buffalo, N.Y.
	July 6–12	Camp meeting, Belfast, N.Y.; 4,000 attend
	Aug.	Redfields travel to Chicago
	Nov.-Dec.	In St. Louis, Missouri; suffers first stroke
1860	March?	Recovers sufficiently to resume preaching
	April	Temporarily pastors new church, St. Louis
	May-June?	Visit to western New York
	June-July	St. Charles, Illinois, Camp Meeting
	July 2	Western Convention (St. Charles) enrolls Redfield as F.M. preacher
	Nov. 6	Redfield suffers severe stroke
1861	April	Revival at Second F.M. Church, Buffalo, N.Y.
	June	Limited preaching, northern Illinois
	June	Ordained by B. T. Roberts at Western Convention of Free Methodist Church
	Fall?	Begins writing autobiography
1862	Winter	In northern Illinois; writes autobiography
	Summer	Purchases 40 acres near Geneva, Illinois, for "pilgrims' home"
	Nov.	Last visit to western New York
1863	Late Jan.?	Returns to Marengo, Illinois
	Nov. 2	Death, Marengo, Illinois

John Wesley Redfield (1810–1863) in his prime. This engraving by H. B. Hall pictures the evangelist at about age 40, when he was most active in revival ministry.

John Wesley Redfield near the end of his life. This only known portrait of the evangelist appears to have been taken sometime after his stroke in November, 1860. He died at age 53.

Redfield's portable writing case in which he kept his manuscript and in which it is still stored at the Marston Memorial Historical Center.

P3

Preface

For a long time I have purposed to give to the public, a history of my life, as I have been urgently requested to do by my friends. To whom I have related some of the very strange incidents in my experience.

Again I have thought it best to abandon the design of making public & leave the judgement of the great day to tell my history. But at last I thought it best & even necessary to meet & repel the thousand & one misrepresentations which by my silence I tacitly admit to be true. I shall state plainly & fairly all the main incidents which might by any fair deduction form a possible pretext or foundation on which to build up the falsehoods concerning me & my course. The reader may believe as little or none of my statements as he pleases, without any offence to me. I shall feel satisfied that in giving my history to the world I have done what I could to correct the wrong impressions which must seem to be doing an injury to the kingdom of Christ. I have learned pretty thoroughly one fact in my long toiling contest & that is that he who takes sides with God & the right will not only find himself on the unpopular side, greatly in the minority. But at war with the world the flesh & the devil in any practical form & I have expected all this from the world, But I did not expect to find my

Redfield's autobiography begins with this "Preface," marked as page 3. There may have been a title page, now lost.

P 6 Chap 1

To all human appearance my journey to the spirit land is nearly over And as I gaze over the past I feel instinctively to exclaim What a life I have lived! What a course I have run! What agonies I have endured!

In the language of the poet I can say

"I have felt all that anguish can feel
I have wept till my tears are all dry
My reason with dizziness reels
I would lay down in sorrow & die."

On the 23d day of June 1810 I first started on my sorrowful career through the long tedious & versatile scenes which like a map I can readily trace & call to memory as I write.

From my earliest childhood a strong impression followed me that God had designed me for the gospel ministry But so disagreeable to me was the thought that I kept the whole matter a secret from even my nearest & dearest friends and pondered it only in my own heart. What sometime after was related to me of the impressions of my mother to the same purport concerning me added much to my fears that a fate so unwelcome might possibly await me. My mother from my infancy assured her confidential Christian friends that she was sure that God would call me to the gospel ministry And when the neighbors came in & found me to all appearance dying & so stated to my mother She would assure he will not die but live & preach the gospel. So distressed was I in the contemplation of this to me abhorrent subject & so assured that I feel that this was my fate

Redfield begins chapter 1 with an account of his birth on June 23, 1810. The corrections are likely by Joseph Goodwin Terrill, author of *The Life of Rev. John Wesley Redfield, M.D.* (1889).

The Text

I. Redfield's *Apologia*

/3/ Preface

For a long time I have purposed to give to the public a history of my life, as I have been urgently requested to do by my friends, to whom I have related some of the very strange incidents in my experience.

Again I have thought it best to abandon of making [my story] public and leave the judgment of the Great Day to tell my history. But at last I thought it best and even necessary to meet and repel the thousand and one misrepresentations which by my silence I tacitly admit to be true. I shall state plainly and fairly all the main incidents which might by any fair deduction form a possible pretext or foundation on which to build up falsehoods concerning me and my cause.

The reader may believe as little or none of my statements as he pleases without any offense to me. I shall feel satisfied that in giving my history to the world I have done what I could to correct the wrong impressions which must now be doing an injury to the progress {kingdom} of Christ. I have learned pretty thoroughly one fact in my long tedious contest, and that is that he who takes sides with God and {the} right will not only find himself on the unpopular side, greatly in the minority, but at war with the world, the flesh, and the devil in every possible form and guise.

I expected all this from the /4/ critics. [But] my worst opposers [have been] among the professed ambassadors of Christ.

The very ~~act~~ {attempt} to reform the world ~~must take for granted~~ {is on the supposition} that it needs reforming. And no one as yet has ~~ever~~ had the wisdom in ~~this~~ undertaking {this} ~~to aim for such an end~~ without meeting a deadly foe at every turn. Jesus tried it and met death for His pains. The Apostles followed on the same path and paid the ~~forfeiture of~~ {penalty with} their lives. Over one hundred million of martyrs, first and last, have entered the lists for God, but their ashes tell how hazardous it is ~~to take sides~~ with God and exact right.[1] Luther and Wesley escaped death but with the skin of their teeth, {~~But not its character.~~} Did any of these martyrs or servants of the most High attempt to make the world worse? True, this accusation ~~which~~ afforded the pre-

---

[1] Redfield frequently speaks of the "exact right" or "exact truth."

texts to make their persecution a godly act {act}. ~~Here He~~ {Jesus, they said} cast~~s~~ out devils by Beelzebub, ~~or some other great crime or if the crime has not been committed it soon will or~~ His followers either had committed some great crime or were about to, or the crime would soon result from ~~such a~~ {their} course of action.

Every man must have a motive for his acts, especially if his course {course} is one of perpetual sacrifice and disaster ~~especially when his persistence is disapproved by some questioned by others~~. {to himself.} ~~I have never wrote without a motive and~~ whoever will take the pains to read my life candidly will see what motives have kept me in motion for more than twenty years, and that too amid so much disaster and agony.[2]

One thing is certain: I am either a fool, crazy, or honest. If a {~~I am~~} fool or {am} crazy, I ought to have the forbearance of the wise rather than {their} severity~~{.} practiced towards me~~.

/5/ I may ~~be~~ {have been} thought to be ambitious of notoriety. {but} The compensation I ~~get won't pay~~ {have received does not pay.} Please hear my story then. Ask yourself only if you would have done differently, ~~from what I have~~ and wherein could you mend it for the better{.} ~~what I have tried to do~~ when impressed at every step that you ~~was~~ {were} acting for the judgment and might be called for at any moment. I know I have been honest in trying to do all I could, to the best of my ability, and in such a manner that I would dare to meet it in the awful hour when God shall settle with me for my whole acts and motives of my life.

And now, hoping that a history of my life together with the accompanying circumstances may be doing services for Christ when I may cease to labor, I commit ~~this book to and send on the missionary work~~ {these lines to their mission} of trying to win a lost world to Jesus. My life has been one of sorrow, toil and conflict. I know religion to be good, and true, for I have tried it twice on the brink of the grave, and I here perpetuate my testimony in its favor and look forward to a time when I shall be at rest. I take leave of the world, not with any hard feelings, though the world and a dead church have nearly killed me by inducing a stroke of paralysis which came upon me in consequence of deep and long protracted grief and sorrow in meeting persistent persecution under which I finally surrender and must now leave the matters of difference which have so long existed to be settled by Him who sees all things as they are.[3]

---

[2] This time reference and other evidence suggest that Redfield began writing his autobiography in 1861, or thereabouts.

[3] This was the stroke Redfield suffered on November 6, 1860. Cf. JGT, 453.

/6/ Chapter 1

To all human appearance, my journey to the spirit land is ~~far passed~~ {nearly} over. And as I gaze over the past I feel instinctively to ~~pause~~ and ~~say~~ {exclaim}, "What a life I have lived! What a course I have run! What agonies {I have} endured!"

In the language of the poet I can say,

> I have felt all that anguish can feel,
> I have wept till my tears are all dry,
> My reason with dizziness reels
> I would lay down in sorrow and die.

II. Birth and Early Call

On the twenty-third day of June, 1810, I first started on my sorrowful career through the long tedious and versatile scenes which like a map I can readily trace and call to memory as I write.[4]

From my earliest childhood a strong impression followed me that God had designed me for the gospel ministry. But so disagreeable to me was the thought that I kept the whole matter a secret from even my nearest and dearest friends and pondered it only in my own heart.

What sometime after was related to me of the impressions of my mother to the same purport concerning me added much to my fears that a fate so unwelcome might possibly await me. My mother from my infancy assured her confidential Christian friends that she was sure that God would call me to the gospel ministry. And when the neighbors [on one occasion] came in and found [me] to all appearances dying, and so stated to my mother, she would answer, "He will not die, but live to preach the gospel."

So distressed was I in the contemplation of this to me abhorrent subject, and so assured did I feel that this was my fate, /7/ that when about eight years of age and just able to write a legible hand I tried in secret to write and compose a sermon. Then, borrowing a book of John Wesley's sermons to compare the merit of mine by, in great perplexity I said with a sigh to myself, "O, I never can compose such a sermon, and I don't know anything about religion, and I am sure I never can

---

[4] Terrill gives Redfield's birthdate as January 23, 1810 (17). However the manuscript clearly reads "June," not "January." In his January 1864 tribute to Redfield, B. T. Roberts also gives the date as June 23. B. T. Roberts, "Rev. J. W. Redfield, M.D.," *The Earnest Christian* 7, no. 1 (Jan. 1864): 5.

preach."[5]

So persistently did these impressions press upon me that I have been ready to account for them as the result of a mark born into my very nature.[6] But however I might satisfy myself for the moment that I was the unfortunate victim of hallucination, the impression was so inwrought in my nature that I found myself in every act or plan of my life swayed to this one dreaded and yet absorbing thought, that I must yet preach the Gospel. And yet I studiously and persistently contended against the impression and concealed the gnawing worm in my own bosom.

When I might have been twelve or thirteen years of age I was informed by a neighbor of the strong impression of my Mother concerning my future course and the detail of many remarkable circumstances. I was informed that even my name was a matter of special impressions, and on this wise. The very night on which I was born one of the very choice Christian ladies of the same society with my mother dreamed she was visited by an angel who informed her that she must go to the house of my father and there she would find a son born, and she must announce to my mother that /8/ my name must be called John W. [i.e., Wesley] and my mother would respond "Such is his name." And by that unlucky name was I baptized and have passed thus far through my pilgrimage.[7]

Between the age of thirteen and fourteen I had such a loathing and alarming view of my sinful state that I really feared I was past all hope of mercy. While thus fearing I was lost I desired to so provoke the Almighty to destroy me that without the guilt of self-murder I might go and know the worst of my case and cut short the fear of making my case worse by a farther life of sin. I felt I had only to die to begin a life of hopeless despair. I had tried to my utmost to court the pardon and favor of God but so far in vain, and giving up all hope, having tried so hard and knowing no other way than what my reason suggested, I had no farther object to live [for].

My agony and fears would make me to lie awake and sweat with fear aroused by every unnatural and to me exaggerated sound. This state of things continued till [one day I was] listening to the conversa-

---

[5] JGT quotes this as: "Oh, I can never preach! I don't know anything about religion. I am sure I can never preach" (JGT, 17).

[6] JGT (17): Redfield "was inclined to consider it an 'antenatal mark.'"

[7] JGT (17): "By that unlucky name was I baptized and have been known through life." Throughout his biography Terrill often reworks Redfield's wording to make it more readable or contemporary.

tion of some Christian neighbors who were contemplating a visit to a camp meeting, and they incidentally spoke of the probable conversion of sinners. My heart instantly took hope and I secretly said to myself, "It may be if I go there, I too may get religion."[8]

I obtained permission to go. I went in company with a neighbor, and on reaching the ground he directed my eye to the old altar where souls had been converted the year previous. At the sight of this my whole heart rose up in revulsion. I can say such a dread and hatred arose as even now astounds me at the depth of hostility to God which then existed in my /9/ heart against God.

In due time a goodly number of tents were erected. A good old gentleman came to me and invited [me] to a prayer meeting in one of the tents. He requested me to kneel, but O how disgusted did I feel to be kneeling there in sight of everybody who might chance to pass that way, and the prayers too so simple and to me even ridiculous. I was sure I could not get religion there.

In process of time the tents were well set up all over the ground, the main assembly came, and the preachers were called to the stand by the sainted [Willbur] Fisk.[9] Preaching began and closed and the way was prepared and sinners invited into the altar for prayers, and I among them.

Before long a good old gentleman who mistrusted my state of mind (the one I think who invited me into the tent) came to me and tried to instruct me in the way to seek salvation. But there were a goodly number of penitents seeking religion, and they were praying most lustily. "Well," thought I, "this is no way to seek religion. Why can they not be more calm and rational in seeking? For certainly they will never be able to think their way through amid so much noise and confusion? At least, I can do nothing without a quiet time to reason my way through. O how little did I understand that all reasoning and human planning was useless here.

But soon I saw, sure enough, this very irrational way and this vociferous manner is successful, for they are really getting saved. And after all, it may be that there is some to me unknown virtue in this apparent pell-mell confusion. And as every other effort with me has failed, I will try it, too. So I too cried out, "Lord be merciful to me, a sinner."

But I /10/ was shocked and mortified at this sound of my own

---

[8] JGT (18): "If I go, I too may be converted."

[9] JGT (18) has "Wilber Fisk"; the correct first name is Willbur.

voice.[10] I did not get salvation by loud praying nor while praying. But this one good I found to result from my vociferous effort—I was fully committed now before everyone and disqual[ified] for life, and pride was just humbling down and getting me where Jesus could begin His work, for I was no longer experimenting on the suggestions of my own reasoning. All that was given up and I [was] fully committed to go through in this way at the cost of all things.

I now left the altar and went out alone into the edge of the grove. There under a large tree and upon my knees I made the solemn vow to take Jesus for my only Savior. Then instantly as my faith ventured on Jesus my burden was gone I was filled with inexpressible delight. Before I was aware of what I was doing, I found myself on my feet shouting, "Glory to God!" But shocked at this strange and almost spontaneous utterance, I said to myself, "What does this mean? I have heard the Methodists say 'Glory to God,' but I don't know what it means. My burden is all gone."

Everything around seemed vocal with the praise of God, and as the Indian said in similar circumstances, "The trees looked glad, and the birds sung glad." The world looked glad, and I felt glad. All nature seemed in harmony, like a beautiful and well-tuned harp, and sung praises to the Most High. My heart could now beat time to such unearthly[11] music as I have heard all around, above, beneath and within.

I had not ~~the~~ most distant idea that this was religion, but thought some strange thing has happened to me. For I was sure that I should know /11/ when I had religion from the peculiar solemn gloom which would settle down upon me, and that a peculiar, desolate state of heart and of earth would attest that I at last had obtained religion. All this uncomfortable state I was desirous to obtain, that I might be saved from the terrible state of despair that hung over me like the pall of second death.

Bewildered at what had taken place and wishing [to] know what next to do, I went back to the camp and found an elderly lady, a profes-

---

[10] JGT often narrates the story using much of the language of Redfield, but without quotation marks. So here: "But he soon saw that this apparently irrational way and this vociferous manner were successful; for some of the seekers were getting saved. As every other way with him had failed, he at last thought he would try this one. So he cried aloud, 'Lord, be merciful to me, a sinner.' But he was shocked and mortified at the sound of his own voice" (19).

[11] This is one of Redfield's favorite terms. He often speaks of "unearthly power" (especially), "unearthly joy," "unearthly glory," etc.

sor of religion.[12] I asked her if she would tell me what was the matter with me. "For," said I, "my burden is all gone and I cannot feel afraid of hell, and I love God and everybody. And I don't know if I must be damned after all, but I cannot feel one fear."[13]

"Why," said she, "you are converted, and this is religion!" I told her I had thought that religion would make my feel gloomy. "O no," said she, "it makes people feel happy."

"Well," said I to myself, "if this is religion, the world will now very soon be converted! For I shall tell everyone with whom I meet, and I can tell it so convincingly that they will certainly believe and seek and find." So exalted did salvation seem, and so valuable, and so ardently did I desire the salvation of the world, that I felt I could have parted with life to impart salvation to the world.

I now found elements in my being which by their aspirings and exalted perception and appreciative powers showed me to be in family alliance with the great Father. "I am a child, an heir of God!" How astounding the thought, how overwhelming the idea. When I passed along the streets, every sound and every sight seemed written all over and vocal with "Glory to God in the highest forever!"

/12/ I now met a young man and immediately spoke to him about salvation, expecting to see his eyes flash with hope and [his] anxious voice to enquire, "Where? Where? Where?" and ready to start off in haste to get this great pearl. But he, turning, [gave] a look of scorn and an apparent disgust at my impertinence which almost seemed to ask, "What? Have you become a Methodist fool? Away with such stuff, for I don't want to hear one word about the silly subject of religion."

I was taken all aback. I had expected the same kind of reception that I might expect if I would have brought the welcome news of a gold mine or the tidings that he had just been elected to one of the highest offices of state.

I now turned steps towards home. Before I reached home, I visited the home of a relative [who had] a large family and began to tell them

---

12 The common parlance of the time was to speak of a professed Christian as a "professor of religion." This usage is frequent in Redfield's manuscript.

13 JGT quotes this whole passage, beginning with "Instantly, as I ventured" (i.e., in the original, "When instantly as my faith ventured") in considerably edited and somewhat condensed form. For Redfield's "I cannot feel afraid of hell" he has "I can't feel bad if I try." But Terrill may have had difficulty in deciphering Redfield's hand here; the scrawl is very difficult to read at times. (Conversely, Terrill's published account is often useful in deciphering Redfield's handwriting.) (JGT, 19–20.)

what great things Jesus had done for me. I seemed to them, too, like one that mocked. But I pressed the subject and finally obtained permission to pray with them, and [later] after a short time [I] had the happiness to learn that the whole house professed religion.

I met too with a young convert who found salvation at the same meeting [I did,] and I told him how long I had been praying that God would move his heart to seek religion, promising the Lord that if this young man would set out in the way of life, I would follow.

"Did you?" said he. "Well, that was just what I had been waiting for [for] a long time." That young man has long been a laborer in the gospel field.

I next reached home and set up a family altar [i.e., daily family prayers] in my father's home. This by some was /13/ thought to be going too far and showing myself too forward. But the importance of my mission and the danger in which sinners seemed to be absorbed all minor sense of propriety. Soon I had the unspeakable pleasure of having a very large number of old acquaintances to go with me. I went from house to house and from town to town to carry the glad news that a Savior had come to save.[14]

But now I began to learn what I never before dreamed—that the human heart hates God and everyone who loves God. If this friendship of the world is enmity against God, I now learned [that] to be a friend of God made all the world my enemy. I passed in my journey a house and went in to enquire about the state of religion. There I found a woman, and as I began to talk of Jesus and salvation, she bade me leave the house. [I] did, saying, "I am clear from all farther obligation to you and now shake the dust from my feet as I leave you. [I] will meet you once more, and that will be in the judgment of the Great Day."

I left, as I felt forbidden to stay. She came to the door, and as long as I was in hearing I heard her plaintive call to me to come back. But I followed my own impression and left.[15]

I next came to a place where in visiting from house to house I went into a Universalist's house. But [I] soon found that the man of the house, a very strong Universalist, was so exceedingly enraged that he

---

[14] It is not clear whether Redfield means simply that many of his acquaintances also were converted (i.e., "went with" him in following the gospel) or that these new converts accompanied him "from house to house" and "town to town." Probably the former; in the following narrative he seems to be traveling alone.

[15] This early incident is very typical of Redfield's later ministry and character, somewhat in the spirit of Old Testament prophets. (Cf. JGT, 22, which quotes this incident with some editing.)

threatened personal violence, and came to execute his threat to horsewhip me. But my age, and being small of my age (only about fifteen), I found friends who /14/ protected me [from] his violence for this time. But he showed his disposition to harm me as far as he could by sending a threatening letter to my father. The people were getting saved, and the Universalists tried to stop it, and this opened my eyes to the fact that with all their boasted religion of love, their hatred was exceedingly violent against religion which really saves men.

III. Redfield Resists the Call to Preach

Dr. Fisk, who used to visit my father's house, seemed to take great interest in my cause, and suggested that I go to Wilbraham [Academy].[16] I saw that the old subject of preaching was at the bottom of this plan, and [that] the course I was pursuing would sooner or later lead me out into the field. At once all my abhorrence of such a course came up, and I resolved to leave the [evangelistic] field at once.

The cause of my distress at the thought of preaching was this. I had contracted the most dreadful and solemn responsibility connected with the office of a gospel minister.[17] If I could know to a certainty that God had called me to this awful mission, I would not stop to contend with flesh and blood [cf. Galatians 1:16].[18] I think I felt something as a man would if ignorant of navigation to take charge of a craft freighted with human life and liable to run into danger, and hardly knowing when or where. This fearful responsibility was to me truly overwhelming.

With these views I returned home, but my peace and power with God were greatly depreciated. I began now to try to settle this matter by reasonings, which brought me into great straits. And now my many Christian friends would beset me with their impressions concerning my duty, /15/ and that was that God had called me to preach the gospel.

---

[16] One of the earliest M.E. educational institutions, founded by New England Methodists in 1818, originally in New Hampshire. It moved to Wilbraham, MA, in 1824 and was incorporated as Wilbraham Wesleyan Academy. The school "was intended both for general studies and for young men who designed to enter the ministry." Fisk was president until 1831, when he became founding president of Wesleyan University in Connecticut. Thus he would have been president at the time Redfield refers to here. Simpson, *COM,* 945.

[17] That is, Redfield viewed "the office of a gospel minister" as a "dreadful and solemn responsibility."

[18] JGT has "confer," as in the KJV of Gal. 1:16, but clearly Redfield has "contend" (JGT, 23). In this and all subsequent Scripture references the KJV is employed, as this was the version Redfield used.

This, together [with] my own impressions, my mother's presentiment, and the sainted Fisk and others whose talk had its influence upon me, now rendered me miserable.

[I] principally feared that these influences, rather than the voice of God, might persuade me to enter a work which to me without God's sanction would be downright sacrilege. My whole nature shrank with dread at the thought [of] occupying [such an exalted position]. I now reasoned thus: That so many had exerted their influence upon me, that I could trace all my own impression to this source. I resolved to go among strangers and beyond this influence, and farther, to commit myself by bonds[19] to the employment of a gentleman of renown I had heard [of] but never seen, thinking that I might create an obligation which would settle my mind at least for a time and cut off all farther trouble on the score of duty to preach.

The gentleman was reported to be somewhat of a proficient [sic] in the fine arts. I obtained permission of my father to go, but hid from him and everyone else the real object of my cause.[20] I started on my journey, and when beyond the limits of my acquaintance I felt myself rather secure from being beset with other people's impressions of duty. I called at the house of a preacher by request to leave a letter with his wife. She looked me in the face as I handed the letter to her and asked me to tell her if I was not running away from God. To which I responded, "I think, Madam, that your husband or someone else has been writing to you concerning me."

"No," said she. "I never saw or heard of you in my life. But as soon as I saw you I was impressed that you

/16/ Chapter 2[21]

was running away from duty." She then abruptly turned to me and said, "Will you not go out to a spring and bring me a pail full of water?" As soon as that was done she requested me to cut up some wood. Of course I could not refuse, nor did I know why she was thus detaining me from my journey.

But soon I saw the girl of the house in company with an old gen-

---

[19] Probably by an apprenticeship.

[20] Or "course." In Redfield's script, "cause" and "course" are often indistinguishable, and the more likely rendering must be determined if possible by context.

[21] Redfield has "Chap 2" at the top of this page, though the sentence continues from the previous page. It is not clear exactly where he intended chapter 2 to begin.

tleman, and [they] passed into the house. Then the good lady of the ~~house~~ came to the door and invited me in, and then I saw that she employed me to keep me till she could send for the good old brother. There she then introduced me to Father Liscomb, saying, "There is a revival in a little hamlet over the fields, and Father L. desires you to go in company with him and see the converts." By this means she hoped to turn me from my purpose of leaving the cause of duty.

To avoid any talk on this most dreaded subject of preaching, I instantly said, "I will go," but I fully determined as soon as a convenient opportunity offered to leave the old gentleman's company and go on my way and pursue my purpose.

We started together, and on my way I enquired of the good old brother the way and the distance to W., the place of my destination.[22] He said that [it was] to pass through the woods in a northwest direction. I could get there in going about five miles. This was all I wanted to know for my purpose, so I walked on till we reached one of the cottages. It was a beautiful afternoon in September. Sun about three to four hours high.[23] He knocked at the door and was bidden to go in. As he opened the door, I turned my face to the woods and ran as fast as I well could till I reached the timber. It might have been eighty rods. I was resolved to endure no more from the impressions and importunities of others.

But no sooner had /17/ I reached the woods than I was taken stone blind, not able to see a single thing, not even my own hand, which I tried to, but in vain. I lost my point of compass.[24] I knew not either East, West, North or South. I found myself walking in mud and water, running over logs and against trees, and every now and then scaring up squirrels and other wild game till it seemed I was surrounded with animals or reptiles, which I could hear but could not see.

Thus I wandered till late in the evening, when I felt all the horrors of being lost.

I now felt I was contending with a power that was stronger than I. So greatly were my fears aroused that I promised God if He would but lead me out of this dreadful place, I would take any course He might

---

[22] Possibly Windsor, Vermont, about ten miles northwest of Claremont on the other side of the Connecticut River.

[23] JGT has, "the sun about two hours high" (25).

[24] JGT has simply, "About eighty rods brought him into the woods, and he entered them with congratulations at his nice escape. He lost his way and wandered about until night came on" (25). Redfield seems to mean, however, that he literally was made blind temporarily.

direct as the one of duty.

In a moment I felt a gentle pull like the pull of a single hair, leading me in some direction. But which way I could not tell. I soon found however that I was out of the swamp and woods, for I no longer ran against trees, bogs, stumps, or into the mud and water. I still followed the leading till I found myself against a fence. I got over the fence and still followed the leading impulse, crossing fields and getting over fences till I found by the feeling under my feet that I had reached some road. While stopping to find out my location, I turned and saw but a few rods beyond me a light in the window of the very house from which I had started with the old gentleman.

I now thought, "If I return to that house, the lady will only distress me by pressing her convictions of duty upon me, and in my distracted state, I cannot bear it."[25]

The next thought was, "This is the direct road /18/ to the place to which I wish to go, and it is now only seven miles. There is now no fear of being lost, for the fences will guide me, and possibly by morning I may reach the place, and by going tonight I shall avoid any farther annoyance from the importunities of the preacher's wife to do duty."

As I turned to go, I saw the woman in the road, and nearly facing me, and as plainly as I ever saw her. I truly thought it to be the very woman. I said, "Mrs. B., what time of night is it?" But she gave no answer. I then told her that I had been lost and was just out of my dilemma and desired her to say no more about duty, for I was too much agitated to hear it. Still no response. I thought she was trying to frighten me into obedience to her opinion of my duty, and I said to her, "You will not frighten me, for I know it [is] you, and I am resolved I will never go to preach till I am positive that God says go. I am going this night to W., so good night."

But as I started to go, she stood right before me. I turned out to pass her, but she turned and faced me still. I turned to pass on the other side, but still she turned and faced me. I passed to near the fence on either side; still she stood and faced me. I then said, "Madam, I thought you to be a professor of religion! What do you think your neighbors would say to see you conducting yourself in this manner?" Still I could get no response. "You need not think to press me to this course by any

---

[25] JGT: "The thought came in a moment, if I return to the house the lady will only distress me by pressing upon me her convictions of what my duty is, and that I cannot bear" (26). This is one of several occasions in which Redfield when in distress promised God full obedience, and then promptly disobeyed once he was out of the immediate distress!

tricks of this kind." Still all was silent.

At length I was suddenly seized with such fear that /19/ I turned and ran to the house. As I entered, I saw the woman was waiting for my return. As she looked up, "Ah," said she, "I expected you would be back, for I prayed that God would put my image before your eyes as the ~~angel was~~ [He]did before Balaam."

"Well," said I, "I thought it was you." Thus with one sentence I exposed the facts. I now learned that it was twelve o'clock at night. The fact that I had seen what she prayed for probably reassured her that she was right. But I said to her, "Please let me have a place to rest for this night." She gave me a light and directed me to a room. There I resolved to be up and off so early that I should avoid any farther annoyance from her. It did seem as though my fate was hard indeed.

I arose, and thought to be off early enough to escape farther trouble. But in [my] passing the sitting room which led to the street, [I saw that] there sat the lady, in waiting. I spoke first, saying, "Don't say anything more to me about duty, for I am resolved that no human influence shall determine my course, but I shall certainly go to W. I cannot, I dare not be prevailed upon to enter so fearful a place as that of the gospel messenger. So good morning."

On opening the door, I felt that someone on the outside was lifting the latch. When the door opened, there stood a man who, putting his hand upon my head, said, "Stop, Jonah, for you are running away from God!"

"Well," said I, "it seems you are in the secret too!"

"Secret?" said he. "I never saw or heard of you before this moment. I live four miles from here. I am not a believer in dreams. But I had one last night in which an angel came to me /20/ and directed me to come to this house, and here I should find a young man who was trying to run away from God. He told me to tell you that unless you go and preach the gospel, you will be damned. I have [come] four miles to stop you."

I however broke away and went on my journey and found the professed artist, and found him willing to enter into a contract with me. But while I was yet talking with him, I was seized again with such horror and guilt, and for that [reason] I dared not to say a word more. I left the place, nor would I turn to see this place till I was out of sight of the place.

Chapter 3[26]

I now returned home, resolved to live religion but to abandon all thoughts about ever preaching unless God by unmistakable signs should reveal it as His will concerning me. Thus I continued restless and comfortless till the next fall, mourning over my sad lot and wondering why I should be the victim of such impressions and yet have no certain clue to settle the matter, no power to throw it off. I would allow no one to know a word of this corroding anxiety which was eating away at my vitals.

To heighten my distress and perplexity, suddenly I saw an indescribable sign hanging up in the west, the sight of which caused this sentence to be impressed upon my bewildered heart: "That sign hangs over the place where God wills you to go and labor."

The evident folly and impropriety of following [such] a sign was so distressing that I could not do it. I reasoned thus: In a matter of so much moment, and where there is a possibility of making a mistake, I had a right to expect /21/ of God that He give me reasonable and sensible evidence of His will, or He could not in justice hold me responsible for obedience in a matter so susceptible of doubt and deception. I could not stop or get out of hearing this terrible din of woe, "If I preach not the gospel!" [I Corinthians 9:16]. Nor could I on rational grounds see the propriety of being led by a doubtful impulse. I never can allow my reason thus to be violated.

I could never tell the distance, only the exact direction [indicated by the sign in the sky.] It might be a thousand miles, or it might be only one to five hundred miles. Still, there it hung, night and day. It had neither shape or dimensions that I could describe it; yet I could see it as distinctly as I could a cloud. I believe if I were to get lost, I could always know my point of compass by that sign.

My whole reason so revolted at the thought of following any such ideal phantom that I fully determined if I must obey that sign, I shall require a sign of confirmation which cannot be disputed.

Appetite and sleep forsook me, till in about two months I was worn down, weak and wasted. I asked, "Must I follow so unreliable a shadow? O God, I cannot, nor can I tell one person a word of what so distresses me." I feared I might pass to the borders of insanity, for I felt I could endure but a little more, and in deep grief have I wept and sobbed alone and when no eye but God's could see me.

---

[26] JGT follows Redfield here, beginning chapter 3 at the same point as in Redfield's manuscript (29).

I finally resolved to go to God and ask a sensible confirmation, which I did by asking that an angel might appear or a bird and tell me that that sign was to be obeyed. Or if an audible voice would speak, I would believe and obey. I felt I might ask and expect if /22/ God had really called me that He would put the whole matter beyond a doubt.

Day after day and week after week this so wore upon me as to make me most unelated[?]. I finally determined to seek the Lord's will by fasting and prayer and see if by that means this terrible suspense could not be settled beyond a dispute. I was being literally worn out and unfitted to do anything. I felt I must have this ~~terrible~~ distressing doubt settled. So I resolved to hold a day of fasting and prayer and follow it with a watch-night, and at twelve o'clock I should expect a bird of angel or voice to settle this distressing perplexity.

The hour arrived; the town clock struck the solemn noon of night. I arose and looked and listened for a testimony which should ~~settle this~~ put my doubts to rest. But no angel, bird or voice. I said to myself, "Well, I am glad that I have gone through with my fast and watch-night, and now I can go to rest and drop this troublesome subject. For the absence of the testimony which I have asked I shall regard as sufficient to satisfy me that all my impressions are unreliable, and I have been the dupe of hallucination. I will now go to bed and congratulate myself that I have now disposed of this subject."

But after all, late and dark as it was, there hung the sign still. An impression beset me, "Turn to the Bible, and see what you may get from that." In this mode of determining the will of God I never dared to trust, and therefore very seldom try it.[27] I opened my Bible at random and let my finger touch without knowing where, and on looking I found it on the words in Genesis [27:8], "Therefore my Son obey my voice according to that which I command Thee."[28] /23/ For a moment I was ~~shocked~~ disturbed, and began to feel that the absence of the signs which I had looked for was somewhat unreliable[?] as testimony. But I soon began to reason thus: "That was probably a happen-so, and I will try once more and be sure to reach far enough not to touch the same place again." And I next put my finger on the fifteenth verse of the twenty-eighth of Deuteronomy, beginning with: "And it shall come to pass, if

[27] This sentence seems to be Redfield's retrospective comment at the time of writing (probably in late 1861).

[28] Redfield does not give the verse reference. JGT has "Genesis 17:3," but that is incorrect; the verse is found at Genesis 27:8. Perhaps the printer misread Terrill's handwritten "27:8" as "17:3," which could be an easy mistake. (JGT, 30.)

thou wilt not hearken to the voice of the Lord," and "that all these curses shall come upon thee." And God and my heart only know how extensively this threatening was fulfilled, and how deeply I have drunk the cup of sorrow.[29]

I soon reasoned thus: "This also may be a happen-so. I will open once more." Then my finger fell on Jonah, third chapter and first verse: "Arise and go to Nineveh." This shook me greatly and well nigh upset all my hopes of finding relief from the absence of testimony on which I had determined to rest the subject. But again, I reasoned that we are not now living under the Old Testament dispensation, and I will venture to open once, more and be sure to reach far enough to hit upon the New Testament. My finger touched the quotation of Christ: "The Spirit of the Lord is upon me, because he hath anointed me to preach the gospel" [Luke 4:18]. I was greatly distressed and filled with fear. But [I] thought I would try just once [more]. I begged the Lord not to be angry with me, but let me try once more, and then I would not ask again. I opened and touched these words, "Go ye into all the world, and preach the gospel to every creature" [Mark 16:15].

Thus five times in /24/ succession did I accidentally touch upon the very words that reversed my opinions and put my distressed soul upon the rack. I could not rest. I could not sleep. I could not endure this pent-up agony that raged within and almost paralyzed my spirit. I wept and groaned before God. But [I] kept my thoughts to myself and, cold as was the weather, I left the house for the fields and woods and, like Balaam, [repeatedly went] to try a new place in hopes that God might speak or send an angel or bird from there to settle my agitation. But no answer, from the first place where [I knelt] in the cold snow [to the last. Repeatedly] I knelt and pled with God, as a man would plead for his life, to grant me [just] this once such an answer as would forever settle my doubts.[30]

I went from place to place, but no answer [came]. Finally I reached the top of a hill in a grove and knelt once more, and while pleading there I had such a sense of the Awful Majesty and near approach of an offended God that my agony of body and soul was so extreme I felt I could not live. It really seemed that if my whole being had instantly been crushed into a nutshell. I could not have endured more, and I in-

[29] Again this is a parenthetical comment reflecting the time Redfield was writing.

[30] The bracketed words bring out what seems to be Redfield's meaning. Here, as often, Redfield does not supply all the necessary words to complete his thought.

stantly shrieked out, "Oh God, remove this from me, and I will go!"

Immediately this sense was removed. Then my doubting heart said, "There! I have seen no angel, bird, no voice, and how can I go under these circumstances, go on such a doubtful errand?"

I then went on to a hilltop farther on and again, overlooking a swamp, I knelt down and there continued in prayer till about sunrise. Then, seeing that I was not likely to bring God to my terms, I thought [it] best to /25/ retrace my steps back to the house. But on trying to arise, I found I was frozen to the earth. So great was my distress of mind that I did not once think that I was cold. I pulled my knees loose from the frozen earth, but I could not move till I had with my hands waked my knees, one at a time. Finally I so far gained the use of my limbs that I could with some difficulty, and in a stooping posture, begin to move towards home.

I passed the spot where the awful presence of God had so distressed me, and down into a valley, and sat down upon a log, deeply grieved that I must be the victim of so much anguish and doubt when God might so cheaply and easily grant me a satisfactory sign. The thought pressed me while sitting on the log, "Stand still and see the salvation of God" [Exodus 14:13]. Instantly a bird came and lighted on my shoulder. I brushed it off, but it flew and lighted on my arm. Again I chased it off, but it repeated the effort and lighted upon me. I then thought it possible I might be in the way of the bird, so I arose and left and passed onto another hill on my way home, and knelt once more under a pine tree. Instantly I heard a sound like a stiff wind rustling in the trees which drew my attention in that direction, but I saw nothing. I arose and pursued my way home.

I entered the kitchen, where my father had built a good fire and himself gone to the barn. As soon as the warm air struck me, I felt so faint that I sat down by the door, pale, haggard, weak and prostrate. My mother, coming out of her /26/ bedroom and seeing my distressed look, in surprise said, "Why John, what is the matter?"

I made out to answer, "Nothing, Mother," but I felt I should betray my emotion, so I got up instantly and staggered out again into the cold where I could give vent to my loud sobbing rather than to allow my dear mother to say a word. I got out, but my pent-up heart burst into a wild sob and I said, "O God, is there no relief? What shall I do? Oh Lord, do hear me in my helpless and distressed state."

I wept and groaned and prayed for my signs to be granted, but all in vain. I felt that I could not endure this state of suspense. [I said to myself,] "This matter must be settled. I will hold this day also as a fast day before the Lord, and follow it once more with a watch-night." I passed the day in fasting and prayer, and at night I held my watch-night till the town clock again struck twelve. But the same ill success attended my effort.

"Well," I thought, "I will turn again to the Word of God, and as I had [earlier] refused to take testimony from the Old, I will turn far enough to reach the New Testament." I did so, and my finger fell on these words: "There shall no sign be given" [cf. Matthew 12:39, 16:4; Mark 8:12; Luke 11:29].

This one sentence upset all my hopes and plans as much as did the five passages the night previously. I could not sleep, but again I left the house for the field, and then and there I reviewed the whole ground. I said to myself, "There is that sign [still in the sky], and I feel that reason can only regard it as evidence that my mind is suffering under a spell of religious hallucination. But true or false, I never can settle the matter, nor can I shake it off. My /27/ body is wore down. I feel I can endure this agony no longer. I feel my mind is almost wrecked. As I am, I must either go deranged or die, for I can neither eat nor sleep and my body is so exhausted that I feel more like dying than trying to live.

"However there is just one more experiment which I can try, and that can have any influence on me to settle this doubtful matter. I can go and find the place [indicated by the sign], and when I have found out by positive examination the truth or falsity of the sign, that and that alone can settle my disturbed mind." As soon as I had resolved to go and put the matter to a test, cold as it was I was as happy as I could well bear and I could say in truth, "December is pleasant as May."

I did not feel that I could tell anyone a word of my impression. I went to the house. It was daylight. As I entered the house and made my way to the parlor where stood a Bureau, I began to take out a couple of changes of undergarments and to bundle them up in a pocket handkerchief. In came a pious sister,[31] her face red with weeping. Handing me a Bible and hymnbook she said, "Brother John, the victory is gained." I could contain [myself] no longer but I burst into a convulsed sobbing, yet said not a word. She afterwards informed me that she knew all about the struggle I was passing through and continued in secret to pray for me and knew the moment I yielded, though she was in the house and I some distance off. I had supposed that no one knew a word about my agony, or the cause of it, for I never uttered one word to anyone

[31] JGT has "my sister Mary, then living at home" (32), but Redfield clearly has "a pious sister." However, see a later reference to "a sister" in which Redfield may in fact mean his own sister (page 47 of the manuscript).

concerning my sorrow.[32]

I took my little bundle under my arm, and without bidding farewell was about to start in quest of the place indicated by my sign. I chose to take but a small bundle, as I must carry it and I designed /28/ to pass in a straight line to the sign and not follow the roads. The joy unspeakable and full of glory was welling up within.

I opened the door, and there stood a young man who had just driven his team up to the door. He asked, "Where are you going?" I would only answer, "I am going west," for I knew not myself where that sign [led, nor] did he.

"Well," said he, "wait a minute, and you can ride with me." Instantly I resolved to accept his invitation, designing to say nothing about the cause of my strange proceedings nor of the place of my destination. I meant to go as long as he went in the direction of my sign, and as soon as he should turn off from the road which led in that direction I meant to ask permission to get out of the carriage and go on foot.

We continued all day riding in a westerly course, and I saw that we were making a direct line to my sign in the horizon. Just about the going down of the sun, we had reached the foot of a hill when, as suddenly as a flash of lightning, my sign had totally vanished. I said not a word but thought, all in a moment, "Well, at last the mystery is solved, and now I see I have been led by a phantom," and how glad I was to find myself thus released from this distressing perplexity.

I said to the young man, "Just stop the carriage, and let me get out and take this last right-hand road which we had just passed." To which he answered, "You had better go to the top of the hill and warm yourself first."

I went to the top of the hill [with him], and to a home where lived a very devoted minister of the Methodist E. Church. The young man knocked at the door and was bid come in, and I passed [in] after him. As I entered I saw the minister, a very large man, standing up with his family around the tea table and about asking a blessing upon his food.[33]

---

[32] JGT edits and condenses the above account, and ends chapter 3 at this point with the sentence, "I had supposed all the time that none but God and I knew anything about it" (33).

[33] JGT modifies the details somewhat. For example he has, "The stranger answered: 'You had better go to the top of the hill, and stop there at the house of an old minister until morning, as it will be a long way before you will find a stopping place on that road'" (35). Also, Redfield describes the minister as "very large," whereas Terrill says he was "old" (which Redfield does not). Nor does Terrill include here the fact that the minister was of the M.E. Church.

But as his /29/ eye met mine, he sat down and began to weep. As soon as he could command his feelings enough to speak, he said to the ~~young man~~ one who brought me, "You must leave this young man with me."

As soon as the young man left, he said to me, "God showed me in a dream that you were to be sent to me, and to labor with me on my circuit. I never saw you before in my dream, and so strongly do you resemble the one that I saw that on your entering my door I could not restrain my emotions."

I took out my little hymnbook and opened on the hymn,

> Master, I own thy lawful claim,
>   Thine, wholly thine, I long to be!
> Thou seest, at last, I willing am,
>   Where'er thou goest, to follow thee;
> Myself in all things to deny;
>   Thine, wholly thine, to live and die.[34]

I now felt myself fully committed to God's will, although I kept and pondered these things in my heart. But the unearthly[35] sweetness and calmness which now took possession of my distressed heart made, by the contrast, my soul to appreciate the blessedness beyond the powers of words to express.

IV. Assisting a Methodist Preacher

He took me onto a part of his circuit where Universalism was a great injury to the cause of Christ. I went on laboring from house to house and pressed the subject of religion amid opposition and threats of dogs, and other maltreatment. But I felt that God had committed to me a dispensation of the gospel of reconciliation, and the awful importance of my themes and the condition of sinners so overwhelmed me that I believe I should have suffered martyrdom in vindication of the truth.

Sometimes I was ordered out of the house on pain of /30/ personal abuse if I did not obey. But feeling the authority of my mission, I candidly but firmly told them, "My message is from God to you, and I

---

[34] First stanza of Hymn 332 in John Wesley, comp., *A Collection of Hymns, for the Use of the People Called Methodists* (London: John Mason, 1835). Since Redfield did not use quotation marks here, it is not clear from the text whether it was Redfield or the Methodist minister who opened the hymnbook and read the stanza. JGT however interprets it as being Redfield (35), and that seems the more probable interpretation.

[35] JGT has, "heavenly" (35).

shall not, I dare not disobey, and it is at your peril if you do not give heed to it." Thus, while the tears flowed and my sobs interrupted my speech, I asked, "Will you seek God?" I insisted on an answer, nay or yea. Then amid threats I would take the liberty to kneel down and present each one to God, and then rising, take them by the hand when they would allow it and tell them, "You know I have in the name of the great God given you my message faithfully! Farewell; I will see you again in the judgment." Though I visited many a house each day and left them in various moods, either penitent or boiling with rage, yet I do not remember a single case where twenty-four hours passed till I was sent for to come back and pray for them.

One afternoon two Methodist ministers called at a house and [later] said to me, "Will you go and visit Mr. B., who lives in yonder house? He is a Universalist, and through his influence religion is kept out of this place." They both had been to him and had done the best they could to convince him of his error and get his influence out of the way. One said, "I have used up all the arguments I can think of, and then I have read Dr. Fisk on the subject, and [John] Fletcher, and have used all their arguments too, and as yet nothing has any effect to shake his faith in universalism."

I answered, "I will ask the Lord."

That night I dreamed that an angel stood by and said, "Yes, go to Mr. B. and deal plainly. But don't argue with him. These ministers have indeed plied their arguments to his mind. But ~~the~~ evil lies in his heart. Now, do you /31/ go and exhort him to flee the wrath to come. But," said the angel, "he will try hard to get you away from the heart to the head, but do keep right on just as though you knew that he believed your message and was trying to parry off the shaft of convictions."

Early in the morning I entered his house, and while I was weeping over him I told him, "Sir, I have a message from the great God to you, and that is to repent and seek salvation, or you will be damned."

Said the man, "I do not believe in your damnation doctrine."

I made no reply, but pressed him for an answer. "Tell me, sir, will you obey God and shun damnation?"

Again he would try to divert me from the heart to the head. Again I said, "My message is from God. Will you obey it?" When he could not divert me from the heart to the head, he became very angry and told me to leave his house or he would give me a beating, for he would not be talked to in such a manner by a boy.

I said, "You will strike me at the peril of God's displeasure, for that God who has sent me on this errand of mercy will certainly stand by me and defend me. So touch me if you dare while I am on God's business."

While I was thus pressing him to immediate repentance, his wife with tears asked, "O, will you pray for us?" I did not need a second invitation but instantly knelt, and both man and wife knelt, and God so far broke his opposition that his influence was now checked.

Another Universalist opened his doors for a prayer meeting. The work of God broke out and swept all over that section of country. I now enlarged my field of labor and gave out [notice] for a meeting in a schoolhouse some miles from this place.[36]

/32/ I reached this place, and learned that a mob had collected and resolved to take me out and abuse me. But a young man whom all the rowdies feared came to me and, taking me by the arm, said, "Come along with me. These fellows have threatened to abuse you but," said he [to the crowd], while he led me through the mob, "let anyone touch this young man and I will move[?] my arms with you."

I passed on without any further molestation and returned to the place where I met the Universalist, and renewed my visiting from house to house, pressing everyone with whom I met to seek God. If they promised and refused, I would say to them, in effect, "I will meet you in judgment and witness before God [and] yourselves, one witness that I have done all that could be expected of me."

Chapter 4

Continuation of Strange Events[37]

My labors were apparently mostly finished in this region.

Then my sign appeared again in the sky, directing me to another field of labor. With the appearance of my sign came the fear and dread of passing through another terrible siege of suffering, and my heart utterly sunk within me. I secretly resolved to go home and leave the work on the next day.

I inadvertently told someone that I should go home the next day, to which they replied that God would come out in judgment against me if I dared to leave the field of labor. I did not for the moment think I could go willingly to the new field of labor, and thus [hoped to] save [myself from] all the agony which I saw in store for me. Amid all their warnings I was not the least moved, for I was never to be moved by the

---

[36] Redfield does not identify the place or area of this period of ministry.

[37] Redfield begins a new chapter here, as does JGT (his chapter 5). JGT however omits the preceding incident about the young man and the mob (36–37). This is the only place where Redfield gives a chapter title.

opinions of man in matters relating to my duty to God. Nothing short of a positive "Thus saith the Lord" would stir me.[38] Not that I was stubborn, but I dared not to enter so responsible an office till I knew that God had ordered it.

/33/ Seeing my determination to leave, they I think directed me to sleep with a young man and, as I believe, for the purpose of watching me and to give warning if I should dare to leave for home. I waited for him to go to sleep, then I got out of bed carefully without waking him, and began dressing myself. It was a bitter, cold night.

While I was dressing, a severe pain took me all over, and instantly I saw letters as of fire in the form of a rainbow pass through my room, and the question was, "Will you go?" (meaning to the place indicated by the sign). In a moment the thought of passing through as much suffering as I had [experienced previously] caused my nature to shrink and exclaim, "Oh God, I can't go." Suddenly the agony of body was so great that I fell senseless on the floor.

About daybreak I came out of the paroxysm. I attempted to rise, but could [not], except with great difficulty. In my bewilderment, I began to question myself as to how I came upon the floor, and what does all this mean? Then the scene of the past night flashed upon me and I said, "O, I now remember. I fell when I refused to follow that sign."

I saw that the young man had not been awakened yet and said to myself, "I thought I should have died last night. But thank the Lord, I am not dead, and as yet no one is up in the house. I will finish dressing and be off, and thus save myself from the importunities of the people to stay."

When I had finished dressing and reached the top of the stairs, the same letters, "Will you go?" came again with the same terrible agony of body, and with [it] the assurance, "If that passes through without your committing to go, you will certainly die and be lost." Such was my distress that I told the Lord, if /34/ He would let up, I would go. Then instantly the whole passed off, and I was as happy as I could live in the body.

I left the house. It was very cold outdoors, snow very deep, but I went wading through the snow into the fields and could sing, "December is pleasant as May."

When I returned to the house, I prepared to go to the place indicated by the sign. As I went [traveling toward it,] I visited from house to house, warning the people to flee the wrath to come. But my name had [already] gone far and near, and some I saw as I was nearing their

---

[38] This trait marked all of Redfield's ministry.

house left and ran out to their barns to keep out of my way and avoid my exhortations. I subsequently learned that the people had contracted a great fear of me, under the impression that I was an angel and not a man. My singular and persistent course, together with my youth (for I was only seventeen), probably contributed to give currency to such an impression.

I finally reached the place, walking backwards against the blustering, flying snow with my coat cape held [and] drawn tight over my face to get my breath. Thus on I went, hiking my own path without any fear of meeting teams [of horses], for the weather was too rough for teams to be out.[39]

I reached the place of my destination and was led to go first to a house where lived a [Methodist] class leader. The day was so tedious[40] that the children could not get out to school on account of the driving snow. I first saluted the father and mother with the enquiry, "Are you on the way to heaven?" To which the Father replied, "We trust we are."

"Well," said I, "God has sent me to tell you that you are both on the way to hell, and will certainly be lost if you do not repent and seek the pardon of your sins." /35/ This I said not in a threatening mood or offensive manner, for my whole soul was moved, and with tears and deep emotion I delivered my message. But I had aroused a most turbulent spirit, and with vehemence the man told me to leave his house. I told him I could not leave till I had obeyed my instructions from God.

"Then," said he, "I will use means to get you out," and to appearance was about to raise a chair in a threatening manner.

I told him, "You will strike me at your peril while I am delivering God's message to you." He seemed to hesitate from his purpose. I then turned to the children and asked, "Do you wish to go to hell because your father and mother are going there?"

With tears the little ones said, "No, sir."

"Well then," said I, "will you kneel down while I pray for you? You need not fear that your father will hurt me, for God will defend me."

Down the little ones knelt, and that brought the parents to their knees, and they began in good earnest to seek God. When I arose from my knees, the man and wife began confessing their awful backslidings. I was then invited to stay for the night.

Feeling that my work was done up for that place, I left the place

---

[39] JGT omits the foregoing details about Redfield's age and his trudging through the wind and snow (37).

[40] JGT, "severe" (37).

the next morning and again returned to the place from which I came. I soon learned that this class leader, after he was readmitted, went to work and God made him the instrument of reviving his work all over that region.

After getting back to the place from whence I came, I saw the preacher, who told me that the presiding elder[41] had requested him to see me and get me to join the church on probation, and then to take me to a quarterly meeting for the purpose of giving me a license and putting me onto /36/ a circuit.[42] I thought, "This may be of God," so I went to the quarterly conference.

But before opening the quarterly conference, the presiding elder went on telling a most ludicrous and laughable anecdote, at which the conference burst into a glee of laughter in which the presiding elder joined heartily. Then in the midst of their merriment the presiding elder said, "Let us pray." This was too much for my sensitive conscience, and the devil took advantage and set me to reasoning thus: "Does this elder believe the Bible? Did Jesus set such an example of trifling over a perishing world? Are sinners now every hour passing away to the judgment, and unprepared? Would the apostles have been thus guilty? Was this like Paul, who for the space of three years night and day with tears labored for the salvation of sinners? [cf. Acts 20:31]. Am I hallucinated, or wild, or blind? Be it as it may, all I can see from my standpoint is the Savior of the world staggering under the weight of a world's salvation, and a world in proud procession on this way to eternal night. If the Bible is true, this world is on the eve of a terrible tragedy, passing to eternity unprepared. I hardly dare stop to sleep but men shall be lost while I am at rest. No," thought I, "there must be a mistake somewhere, and I am most likely the mistaken one. That elder is a man of mature years. and in all probability was while young as zealous and ardent as I am. But in all probability he has found out that religion is a sham, and now continues to preach for the profit. I will never take a license till I can go and settle the truth or falsity of the system of religion."

I did go home, resolving to live religion [privately] and in the meantime to investigate its claims by the light of /37/ reason—little knowing that I had undertaken one of the most absurd tasks imaginable,

---

[41] The superintendent over a district within a M.E. conference was called a "presiding eider." Redfield usually has "P Elder," but I render it "presiding elder," without capitalization, unless the elder's name is given. I have done similarly with "Q. Conference," rendering it "quarterly conference."

[42] The normal process within the M.E.C.

for I might as well attempt to settle questions in algebra by the rules of music, or the science of astronomy by the rules of grammar. However, I began with my method [of reason] to bring theology to my standard for investigation. But I soon found myself beset by persons who would be pressing upon me their impressions of my duty to go into the gospel field. To get away from the annoyance, I resolved to leave the country and go where I was not known, to avoid the talk of other people. For, as forever attempting to preach for any earthly consideration, or to be moved by only human advice, I never would. I would not reveal to anyone my motives or incentive to act, for I would not implicate any other one.

V. Rejection of Call; Wanderings

Chapter 5[43]

I left for a distant location, nearly one hundred miles from where I was known. But in less than a fortnight after I arrived there, I was again beset concerning my duty to preach the gospel. I left this place also and went, as I supposed, far enough to get out of any farther annoyance of this kind. But here too I found old acquaintances who plied the old lash of duty. In less than a week again I left, and the next place that I went to, I resolved to make no profession of religion nor to say anything about it, thinking that other problems would cease when I was not known as a professor of religion. But alas, I now found myself an infidel in spite of myself.[44]

/38/ I could now manage tolerably well in banishing the thought of duty by day. But nights I would dream dreams of preaching, and so awesome that I would wake in the morning and find my pillow wet with my tears. [This continued] till I was vexed by the annoyance. I would not allow anyone to speak to me concerning my duty. My own dear mother thought me stubborn and would not be advised[?]. But I could not, I dared not violate my sense of right and wrong, and I felt compelled to tell her that she must never utter a word more on that hated subject, for I would not hear to it nor allow myself to be swayed in a matter that must be settled between me and God alone. And yet I felt conscious that, could I know without a doubt that God called me to go and preach, I would suffer death [rather] than to disobey the voice of God. But the infidel notion now beset me that I had been the dupe of

---

[43] This begins chapter 6 in JGT (page 40).

[44] It is not clear how much time was spent in these wanderings, just where Redfield went, or how he supported himself.

deception through all my strange course, and I would abandon all thoughts of duty. Then, [though] tolerably clear from the impressions by day, my nights were disturbed by the same unwelcome dreams.

I now resolved to make one desperate effort to end these distressing impressions. I had heard of a man who once, like myself, distressed by such unwelcome impressions, got down and deliberately prayed that if his impressions were from the Holy Ghost, they might now and forever leave, and was instantly relieved and never troubled more. I tried the same awful experiment, and with the same result. And [I] believe that, but for the praying and sacrifices of my mother, who like Job wept and prayed before God for me, I should never [more] have been troubled, and should have been forever lost.

My soul shudders with horror /39/ at the thought of what I have passed and done in opposition to the impressions of duty. And I wonder how such a mass of testimony concerning duty could be brought to bear upon me, and [yet] without the least effect upon me. I felt the Spirit leave me as plainly as ever I felt the taking off of my clothes, and yet [was] no more alarmed than I should have been at the loss of a copper [coin].

To me infidelity was now a fact. And right in the wake came downright atheism, for as soon as I had resolved to settle all questions on theological points by my external senses, I found nothing but vague uncertainty on which to cast my troubled spirit. Nature's laws were all the God of which I could get any notion, and the bare admission that a given system of religion might possibly be true was the utmost that my reason could possibly conjecture. From the simple fear that I was the subject of hallucination, I dared not to act. And the fact [was], that reason could not settle all matters of doubt in matters above its range.

I now saw the whole phenomena of religious emotion, mental and moral changes, as due only to laws within our minds and influence, but beyond our control or comprehension. And now the funeral pall of annihilation settled down upon me, and I could see nothing but darkness and desolation. Man and earth seemed orphans or divorced, and my anxious heart would often seek in anatomy, philosophy, and physiology for testimony to clear up the fog and if possible find a single reliable point to settle my disturbed mind.

One favorite haunt was an old burying ground of an ancient tribe of Indians, where graves /40/ washed by a river were many of them washed entirely away, while the dark sand of the half-washed graves pointed to the resting place of those who had slept from two to four hundred years. Now nothing still remained to tell that they had ever lived except a few seashells and flint arrowheads, or beads and stone hatchets which had been buried with them under the superstitious notion that these implements would be needed in the spirit land. My whole soul would instinctively break out while I felt almost the suffocation of death upon me, and my prayer was, "Oh God, if there be a God, send me to the Christian hell, but don't annihilate me." I would have died a hundred deaths if that would make the Christian doctrine true, and then run my chance of heaven or hell.

I now commenced the study of anatomy for the purpose of ascertaining from the machine left [i.e., the physical body only] whether man had a soul or a conscious thinking part separate from the body; or whether a fortuitous combination of matter might not possibly, while thus arranged, cooperate with laws and produce the phenomena while [continuing in] this combination of mind or thought—and which phenomena of mind or thought would not cease as soon as the combination of matter and laws had ended this relation.

I now found, among other works *Paley's Theology Illustrated*, which gave a sober, common sense basis to my mode of reasoning, and the result was that I was cured of all speculative infidelity or atheism.[45] And, by a rational mode of investigation, with helps of philosophy, anatomy, and manual physiology, I saw the whole mystery cleared /41/ up, and the natural operation, independence, and perpetuity of the human soul redeemed from all doubt and established upon a true and solid foundation.

While I was thus suffering, my poor mother, who had heard of my infidelity and my abandonment of religion and all thought of duty, became very sad and would not be comforted. For in my fall, all her impressions concerning me and my duty from my infancy were dashed to the ground, and as a pious mother only can, she kept my case before her God. (Amen, bless her.) She pined away and nearly lost her mind in her mourning over me. With grief I learned that she pled with God for her long-lost son. I have reason to believe that this, together with her bed of afflictions, reduced her to a state of such childishness that if she saw strangers passing the house she would go out and hail them and ask most sorrowfully, "Have you seen anything of my son John? Where

---

[45] Probably *Paley's Natural Theology with Illustrated Notes,* by H. L. Brougham and C. Bell (2 vols., 1836), or possibly "Paley's Natural Theology Illustrated; Lord Brougham's Preliminary Discourse. A Review," a twenty-nine-page article which appeared in 1836 in the *Quarterly Review.* The apologetic work of the Anglican divine William Paley (1743–1805), particularly his *View of the Evidences of Christianity* (1794), was much read by Christians, including Methodists, during this period.

is he, and what is he about?"

I was all this time from one to six hundred miles from home. I must believe that the prayers of that sainted mother prevailed with God to stay with me, and that I am now in the field of gospel labor in answer to her faithful prayers.

With all my infidelity, I saw and believed that human nature needed some form of religion to restrain them [sic] from injuring society. I would attend church and read prayers, for I thought if it should happen to be true that there is a God and that the religion of the Bible is true, it is best to cultivate a moral tone of mind, and thus be fitted for any possible evil unseen by man or uncontemplated by the Bible.

My infidelity was still visiting me with a terrible retribution. /42/ Not that I was settled that infidelity was true, nor could I for a certainty see that the Bible was true. If there is no God, or only such a one as the deranged condition of nature reveals; if we have nothing to hope beyond the grave, not even the guarantee of bare abstract existence—This terrible uncertainty is overwhelmingly awful. Men may talk of annihilation as a possible fact and regard their theories as a light affair. But let them stand as I have upon the brink of the graves of the long-forgotten dead, and in imagination pass down the vista of coming time and think that, "With all my wish for life, I must yet lie down in the dust and darkness of the tomb, and let the misty centuries fold over my head till ages have passed and gone, and sleep on still as these have, who now lie mingled in the common ruin, forgotten and forever gone."[46]

Sad thought! Poor nameless dust. You once lived, hoped, feared, made as you thought ample provisions for your spirit life in the [array?] of seashells, flint arrowheads, and beads and hatchets. A hope how vain, and here four hundred years have piled their dust upon your unknown graves, and you sleep on still. I would instinctively gasp for breath and utter my cry to God to spare me at least a bare existence.

I might make or study theories on which to build a hope of life beyond the grave. But an instinctive dread of deception forbade it. I would know the truth, however unwelcome the fact. But to whom shall I go? Where shall I turn for relief from this terrible nightmare which hangs over me and sports with my agony?

/43/ I now resolved to study anatomy. My main object was to get a clue to the animating forces of life or soul as seen by the machinery which is left.[47] I left for a country village and began the study of anat-

---

[46] See JGT, 43. JGT has "rusty centuries," which may be correct, rather than "misty centuries."

[47] Here Redfield repeats what he wrote a bit earlier (manuscript page 40).

omy in the office of a practicing physician.[48] I began by reading the theories of old anatomists who used to indulge in speculations concerning the soul, and such assumptions and vague theories as they propounded convinced' me that here also I was doomed to fail of my object. Suffice it to say that I afterwards pursued a course which removed all my doubts as to the nature and perpetuity of the human soul. And by the light of my investigation I saw as possible the science of magnetism, clairvoyance, and much of what now passes for spiritualism, not knowing at the time that any discoveries had ever been made of these strange and subtle subjects.[49]

I had now become convinced that man is immortal, and that his existence must hence keep date with the coming age of God. But next: Is the Bible a revelation of truth? The confidence and wishes of men don't make it so. I procured Leslie's *Short Method with a Deist*[50] [and] gained some little light, but nothing satisfactory. Next I procured and read *Paley's Theology*, and here I learned what has always been of essential service to me: The importance of occupying a correct standpoint of stating the essential parts. Then could I clearly see that the historical part of the Bible rests upon /44/ a rational basis.[51] If then the Bible be true, and man immortal and accountable, then I have need of some kind of religion. My former experience had been banished, and of course furnished me with no help to the proper use of means to secure salvation.

In good earnest I resolved to seek religion. Among other unworthy[?] objects, I thought to seek it among a people who would not be likely [to] say anything to me about the duty of preaching. But I found

---

[48] In summarizing this section, JGT says: "His study of anatomy, under the tutorship of an eminent physician, was continued after his return to faith, and laid the foundation for his future practice of medicine" (43).

[49] JGT has, "'Questions of magnetism, clairvoyance, and much of what now passes for spiritualism,' were carefully studied by him at that early period (between 1830 and 1840)" (43)—that is, when Redfield was in his twenties. Although Redfield's medical studies had practical value the rest of his life, his manuscript makes clear that initially his studies were part of his spiritual quest. Like John Wesley in interest, though not in breadth of understanding or education, Redfield was always fascinated by the interplay between the physical, spiritual, emotional, and psychological aspects of human existence.

[50] The reference is to the widely republished pamphlet *A Short and Easy Method with the Deists* (1697) by the distinguished Anglican divine and controversialist, Charles Leslie (1650–1722).

[51] JGT does not include this part about Redfield's wrestling with the truth of Scripture.

myself mistaken. For scarcely had I obtained a little light on experimental religion before the minister[52] met me in the street and made an appointment for me to meet him at his house. But fearing the old subject of duty would be stirred up again, I did not go.

I soon met him again, when he expressed his disappointment at my failure to meet him and made another appointment. This time I met him, and what I feared was indeed the subject of his wish. Said he to me, "I have but little confidence in impressions. But I wish to know for my own satisfaction, for I have been strongly impressed that you were called [of] God to preach. I wish you to answer me direct." To which in Spirit I could only ask, "My God, am I found out here also?"

I frankly answered him, "I have." But I stated to him the insuperable barriers in my way, and the principal one, which I had just placed in my own way. This I had done by promising to marry, and one prime object I had in this /45/ was to create an obligation which would keep this troublesome subject from harassing me. This proved the great mistake of my life, and I was soon made to feel how surely God would confront me, and how intensely I could be made to suffer.

VI. Redfield's Unfortunate Marriage

Chapter 5 [sic; i.e., 6][53]

How gladly would I suppress this chapter altogether! [I] would, but for the thousand and one misrepresentations from which the cause of Christ has and will suffer if my silence any longer permits [the] enemy to gain concerning nobody knows what. But for this, I should leave all veiled till the revealments [sic] of the last day shall bring every secret thing to light.

If I say nothing, I have the enemies of the cross to make current the gossip, and then [make] what use they please of this most unfortunate affair. Yet if I state facts, I am sure that my enemies will make capital of that. At all events, I shall venture to disgorge this load of anguish which has crushed me for more than twenty years. I might have told my story long ago, and relieved myself from a thousand misrepresentations. But I preferred to suffer in silence, and now I feel glad that I have. I have buried this horrible trouble and made my heart a living

---

52 JGT adds," whose church I attended" (44).

53 This begins chapter 7 in JGT (45). Terrill begins, "The bitter and sorrowful experience occasioned by his rash marriage engagement will be related in Mr. Redfield's own words. Speaking of this matter, he says: 'Gladly would I suppress this chapter,'" etc.

grave.

I shall designedly withhold much of the worst and only state /46/ enough to give a specimen of what I have suffered, and then ask the candid reader, if he was to make the case his own, "Would you do better in the same circumstances?"

At all events, I do wish after I have lived through my whole life in this misunderstood affair that the cause of Christ may be shielded from any unjust imputation. And allow me to say: I have not borne this living death in silence and alone, refusing even to avail myself of the facts which would at once have relieved me from all suspicion, [simply] now only to make my sorrows public.[54] I say, I have not so long suffered in silence and now, to win sympathy, reveal the facts. [Rather, I do so, not] for any other purpose than to correct any unjust judgment of me and my cause and thus remove all hindrances to the spread of that glorious gospel which I have spread at the cost of all things. I must as a last act try at least to protect the cause of Christ and myself from unjust imputations. And what I now publish will be all that the world will ever get of this painful history of my calamities, unless circumstances shall compel me to make all known.[55]

I married one who, I thought, would make me a happy home. But alas, I had signed my own death warrant, and the life-long tragedy was now to begin.[56]

I hired me a house with the desire and approval of my wife, but within three weeks was compelled to abandon it. I found I had been most dreadfully imposed upon, for she was no more fit than was a child to take any interest or care of a home. I saw no other way than to board out, nor could /47/ I find [but] one place where I thought it at all proper to secure a place to board, and that was at her own father's home. But soon her father told me I must take her away, for he could no longer endure her and I must relieve him and his home of the evil.

I hired another house, and to make it possible to keep house at all, I was obliged to hire a housekeeper. This I did, [hiring one after another,] only to have them turned away as fast as I could hire them. I did one week hire six girls in succession, and yet all were by her turned away during the week.

---

[54] That is, Redfield had not so long concealed the story simply because he wanted to tell it all later.

[55] JGT condenses and paraphrases this passage, but accurately conveys the sense (45).

[56] Redfield is very vague about the details and even the date of his marriage. It appears to have been around 1834, probably in New Hampshire.

I began now to see the depth and extent of my living calamity. I next sent for a sister to come to my help that things might be managed so as to make things more tolerable.[57] But in a few days I was compelled to permit her to leave my house and take board otherwheres [sic] till she could arrange to return home.

I next tried to get along by doing the housework myself, and as far as possible to hide from the public my misfortune. But neglecting to fasten the door [one day], I was caught by persons calling doing my own cooking. When the question was asked, "Where is your wife?" I could not tell, for I did not know, as she was often away from home.

The fact that I was alone and doing my own cooking soon reached the ears of her parents who, mortified at the circumstance of their daughter's conduct, attempted to make a reform. I kept all matters to myself, not even telling her father or mother what a ~~awful~~ condition I was reduced to from /48/ this bad conduct of their daughter. Her father, learning that she was in the habit of leaving me to do my own housework, positively forbade her going home again except accompanied by me. But of this I was ignorant.

Late one night she told me she was going home, and I must accompany her. To which I answered, "It is late; your people will be abed, and I can't go and disturb them when there is no urgent need." I then locked the door, put away the key and went to bed.[58] But [I] was soon aroused by the fall of a window. I arose immediately and saw her out with a light, and going the back way [to her parents'] home. I knew now that fresh trouble was on hand, so I staid up, waiting the sequel. I soon heard a heavy thump at the door with a cane. As I opened the door I asked, "Who is here, and what is wanted?"

It was her father; said he, "I will see if you are going to turn my daughter out of doors." I had no light, and he was trying to find me, and I knew by the tone of his voice that he was greatly exasperated and designed to commit violence upon me.

I ran to the parlor, and he could not follow me except by the sound of my voice. Then I spoke, for I was bare-footed. I said, "Be quiet and calm till we can see what is the matter." As I spoke he would again press his way in the direction of the sound of my voice. He was too much excited to hearken to reason. But hearing the sound of his foot-

---

[57] JGT has "my sister" (46). Redfield clearly says "a sister," which would seem to mean a Christian woman, not necessarily a relative, but it is possible he means his own biological sister.

[58] There is an asterisk (*) after "went," but there is no corresponding note of explanation.

steps, I would keep out of his way and thus continue to avoid harm till he so far cooled down /49/ as to pass out and go home.

I then closed and fastened the door, fully resolved that I would never submit to have her return till this matter was fully understood and settled. So I cooked my breakfast when the morning came and went off to my business, having carefully fastened up the house.[59]

About ten o'clock she came and asked my forgiveness, and desired me to give her the key to the house. I told her she could not have the key till the last night's difficulties were settled.

"Well," said she, "go down home with me and I will, I will confess it all." So down we went [to her parents' home,] and found the parents in a very uncomfortable mood. I never had and never would make a single complaint to them of the bad conduct of their daughter.

I said, "Good morning, Mother."

[She replied,] "Don't you call me 'Mother' if you will treat my daughter so badly."

I said, "Let your daughter tell her own story." I then asked her, "Did I turn you out of doors?"

"No," said she.

"Did you not leave when I was asleep?"

"Yes," said she.

"Did I know you was going?"

"No!"

"Did you not get out of the window so still that I might not know you was you?" [sic].

"Yes," said she.

"Then," asked the parents, "why did you misrepresent to us in saying your husband turned you out of doors?"

She answered, "Father told me never to come home again unaccompanied by my husband unless he should turn me out of doors, and I made up the story so that father would let me stay." Then their whole indignation was turned against her, and she called upon me to protect her from the /50/ rebuke of her parents. I felt very sorry for her father, for if he had the right of a matter, he had generosity and Christianity enough to induce him to do the right thing, and never through the whole affair did I feed but that he was an honorable and right-minded man.

I now permitted her to return. But the same state of things continued.

---

[59] Thus Redfield was supporting himself, either by medical practice or (possibly) portraiture.

Next I was suddenly called upon by a committee of the church to investigate matters which could not be tolerated. I had hired another house and was trying once more to keep house. I said to them, "Go on and find out all you wish, for I am ignorant[60] of the object of your investigation."

I permitted her to tell her own story, uncorrected [by me]. When they found the whole a matter of misrepresentation, she confessed the whole to be false. She had reported that I would not make any provision for her wants, but starved her by not providing the necessaries of life. When the committee [came to our house and] found plain bread, meat, and all kinds of provision in abundance, her mother, greatly mortified, asked her how long these things had been in the house, to which she answered [that] she had never been out of them.

"Then what could you mean, thus to report what is false?"

"O," said she, "I wanted some oysters, and he said he could not find them. But I didn't believe him."

The committee knew it was the season when there were none in market, and again her mother, deeply mortified, upbraided her severely. Then /51/ she would turn again to me for defense and said she wondered, "How [can you] live with me?"[61]

I was of course exonerated by the committee of the church. One of them said to me, "No one can ever blame you if you leave that woman, for such conduct is past all forbearance."[62] But all I could do was to hold on and wait for deliverance in God's time, and nothing but the consciousness that I was suffering a just punishment for disobedience made my case at all endurable. Then again, my conscientiousness would not allow me to take legal steps to get rid of her.

I was now taken violently sick, and nigh unto death. It was the first season of the cholera, and I was the only one who [having contracted it] survived the disease in that region. I passed into what was called the stage of collapse. But I felt, "I have not yet done my duty, and I cannot die." I then felt. "I shall not die," and was shortly restored to health.

But my trouble [with my wife] still continued. Now and then she would have a religious streak. On one night, after making a great disturbance and giving me a great scolding, [she] turned suddenly upon

---

[60] JGT has "ignorant," but the word is virtually indecipherable (48). JGT omits the previous sentence, which also is difficult to decipher.

[61] Redfield has, "she wondered how you ~~I~~ could live with me," but the meaning is as I have rendered it.

[62] From this point on for a few pages the handwriting is smaller, neater, and more legible, but still in Redfield's hand.

me and commanded me to pray as her father did. To which I answered, "I can never think of mocking God by any mixture of prayer with such wicked and violent a temper." I saw she took it in ill part. But [I] thought it best to drop all and go to rest, still keeping up a disguised but vigilant watch.

When she supposed me to be asleep, I saw her come near enough to get a clear view of me and about how and where I lay. She then took the light and set it back /52/ so that it should not shine in my face, but I could see her movements all the better. She then went to the fireplace and took up a heavy pair of brass-mounted tongs, and taking a good hold with both hands, came within a few feet and then darted with great fury and began to strike heavy blows very rapidly at my head. But seeing the whole operation, I was prepared for it, and with my arms held the bedclothes over my face and head. I received the whole shower of blows on my arms through the bedclothes. I carried the marks on my arms for some time after.

I now felt I had reason to fear much more violence in some unlucky hour and kept up a vigilant watch, but unbeknown to anyone. Nor could I even inform anyone, not even her own parents, what I was suffering from the conduct of their daughter. Sometimes she would either by accident or purposely burn up two or three or more dresses, then come and demand new ones. The mother I think must have known that she burnt them ~~by accident if she knew it all~~, for she came and asked me to furnish her [i.e., Mrs. Redfield] with one or two cheap dresses. To keep peace this I did, and when her mother saw them, she made a great fuss about it and went among her relatives to get up a subscription sufficient to get a more expensive suit, declaring that I refused to dress her daughter in a becoming manner.

Some of my friends came to see me, and she would tell them to leave, for they could not be harbored there. My troubles were so great, and having no one to entrust my complaint with I said, "O Lord, my punishment is greater than I can bear." I was unfit for business and in short was so broken in spirit that [I] could not attend /53/ to business as it required, and was obliged to fail in business. I gave up all I owned to the last bed, chair, and spoon. I had nothing left. I could not hire a room, nor would my wife stay if I did. There was only one place where I could procure a shelter for the night, and that was at her own father's house.

What to do or which way to turn was more than I could tell. I might have found some employment there but no place for permanent board, as no other house would board my wife except her father, and he only till I could manage to leave town and rid them of the mortification to which they were subject while she lived in town. I believe that they felt truly sorry for me when they saw me in this most distressed condition. They advised me to take up some business with which I could travel, and the bare hope of their daughter's being among strangers might produce a salutary effect [sic].

I borrowed enough [money] to get out of town and where she was not known, and soon procured board. But shortly I saw by the deportment of the people [there] that something was amiss. But I knew my true and only way was to keep perfectly still and wait for matters to develop, whatever they might. We stayed about four weeks, when the lady of the house informed me that such had been the misrepresentations of me that they could scarcely endure me. All this I knew well enough, but thought it best not to let it be known until I was compelled to take notice [sic], for I utterly despised the /54/ man who would reveal his affliction in the shape of a bad wife.

The lady of the house now expressed great sympathy for me. "But," said she, "though you are welcome to stay as long as you please, I cannot have my house so disturbed by that woman, and you must take her away."

I left for another place and could only stay one week. Then I procured a team to take us some thirty or forty miles from the last place [to another,] among entire strangers. There again I found a very genteel family and obtained board, where I staid twelve weeks.

In a few weeks after my arrival I saw again that something was going wrong, but waited for developments to indicate my course of action. But my time was evidently coming to an end. Then the lady told me that such had been the reports of my wife concerning me that she had believed me a bad husband. "But," said she, "I have found out where all your trouble lies, and though I deeply sympathize with you in your affliction yet," said she, "we can endure her conduct no longer." Of course I expected it. I could blame no one for turning me into the streets under such circumstances.

What to do I could not tell; houseless, homeless, and almost without money, and no place to get board where ~~this woman~~ my wife was known. I must leave town or find no place for a shelter. So I took stage and traveled about fifty miles. I thought to try if I could get board in a public house and in a country village. But here I could stay only a few hours, for she positively refused to stay a day or night. And now I did not know what to do.

I could only [think] /55/ of barely one more experiment to make, and that was to take her to my own father's home, [for I thought,] "Her own father will not let her stay there, and every boarding place refuses to keep her or live with her."

I took the next stage and took her home. About fifty miles farther on my funds were exhausted and I was in great distress of mind, though I managed to conceal my real sufferings.[63] But I soon found that my good old father and mother could not endure her conduct, and they told me I should not live with such a woman. "This," I felt, "is my last experiment, and if this fails, the Lord knows I don't know what to do." I saw nothing but agony and the poorhouse as the final winding-up of my calamity. My spirits utterly sank within me, and although I was advised to leave her and get a bill of ~~divorcement~~ ~~I could not~~ divorcement [sic].

While I was in this suspense to know what to do next, all at once she resolved to go home to her father's house, and demanded the money to go. My funds were gone, but she positively insisted she would go, and actually started to go on foot over one hundred miles, and in most snowy roads. When I found she was fully bent in carrying out her purpose, I went after her and promised to see if I could in any way send her home. So I sold my watch to pay for the hire of a horse to carry her to her father's house. But I took good care not to go myself, and now felt a little relief at being free for a short time of my living trouble. But very soon a letter came from her father to me, saying that she was very sorry and penitent at having /56/ left me, and she promised to change her conduct if I would take her back. I wrote back that I had suffered enough and tried experiments enough and I could no longer endure her conduct. I felt the very last feeling of attachment that I had ever felt snap free, and [I] fully resolved that if the offence of refusing to live with such a woman should be state prison, I would sooner go to prison than to live with her. I felt a kind of dread and a repugnancy as much as I would at a rattlesnake.[64]

In the spring I started for the West. I passed through the place where her father lived and where she then was. But I could not bear the thought of seeing her, so I passed on and found me a place about three or four hundred miles west of her father's.[65] After I found a place and was settled, I wrote the old gentleman to let him know where I was and to enquire after the wretched woman who had made my life so bitter. And now he beset me and urged me to take her back, saying he really believed she was changed and would now behave herself. I again wrote

---

[63] The meaning is unclear. Redfield appears to mean that he left his wife to live with his parents and went on alone to another place.

[64] JGT omits this last sentence (52).

[65] JGT inserts, "and located in Lockport, N.Y." (52). Up to this point Redfield is very vague as to places and dates.

that I had no confidence in her reform and could not on any condition take her back. But I was finally overcome by his entreaties and thought it might be possible after all, as she had professed to become religious. So I wrote him that he might bring her about half way, and I would meet him and her there and would make one more trial.

I went in due time to the place and found him and her there and started with her back to my new place of residence. To make all /57/ as favorable as possible for a successful trial, I thought it best to take her to a first-class hotel to board, and if she was not quite reformed, she might be more likely to be held in check here than at a private house, my house.

We staid one night only, when she positively refused to stay another day. So off I went and found a private boarding house, and before the week ended she was turned into the street. The lady of the house positively forbade her to enter the house on any terms. But [she] said to me, "Sir, you are an unfortunate man and are welcome here as long as you please. But that woman must not come in at all." There I found to my cost that I could not hide or run away from duty without being visited by calamities which would turn all my cups to gall.

A lady of the place helped [me] to find another boarding house, and thus I could get her a shelter for the night. We staid here a few weeks when I was again warned to leave. I pled to be permitted to stay from day to day till I could write to her father and ask what could be done to enable me to rid them of the burden.

I must here give a sample of some of her conduct, [in order for the reader] to know what the worst of it consisted in. Instance: If she wished to make any use of the fire [at the boarding house], she would throw the food which was cooking for the boarders into the ashes or fire and usurp authority to dictate as she pleased. The lady of this boarding house told me that my wife was a bad woman, for she had seen men follow her off into by-places. I could not say much, for I had seen her in the embrace of one /58/ of the boarders, hugging and kissing. Another man who thought me to be away came in the night to my room and, [finding me there,] tried to excuse himself as best he could. But I believed him to be a man who from reports was none too pure to avoid evil.

I told her how improperly she behaved in permitting such liberties. Then she gave me to understand that she should do as she pleased, without getting my consent. I then went to her trunk and took out a bundle of letters. But she caught hold and took them all away except one, which proved to be from her brother, and from it I saw she had been misinforming him concerning my deportment, and this was a letter to advise her to leave me. So I saw no hope of any end to my troubles.

Not knowing what to do or where to go, I was nearly distracted. I did not believe she was really corrupt, nor would I ever complain of any of her conduct. But I should have felt relief if I could only die to get out of my distress.

I was again informed that she must leave the house. Suddenly she said that she would go home to her father's, and I must take her to the [canal] boat, about fifteen miles off.[66] I knew not what else to do. But when we arrived at the place, the boat was gone, and no other would go till the next week. I must take her back. But then there was no place to stay for a single night, and to get another boarding house was out of the question. I stopped at a public house and thought, "I will at least have one more night in which to contrive what course next to take."

In the morning we started back to the place which I had left,[67] and she promised /59/ to let me take a room and keep house, and she would not leave me. But just before we entered the village, she suddenly resolved that she would not stay but go home at once, and I must take her that night and go sixty miles where she could take cars and steamboat and return to her father's house.[68] I knew it was useless to attempt to persuade her to stay even for the night. So I borrowed the money and left that night on a public conveyance to the place where she could take cars for the boat.[69] I then gave her the money to pay her fare all the way home.

As soon as she left on the cars, I felt such a sudden relief from my agony that I fainted and could [only] with great difficulty stagger along to get [to] a place where I could lie down. A high nervous fever set in, and for fifteen days I was not able to be moved. A physician like the Good Samaritan attended me faithfully, and I owe him a debt of gratitude which I can never pay.

But after all the best efforts, I sank and to all appearance was near death. A couple of consulting physicians [who] came to visit me told my nurse that I must die, and they must make ready for my funeral in

---

[66] Presumably a boat on the Erie Canal at or near Lockport, New York.

[67] If Redfield's reference to Lockport is correct (52), it would seem that Redfield and his wife were boarding in a village about fifteen miles from Lockport (probably north or northwest from Lockport; otherwise they would not have had to travel fifteen miles to reach the Erie Canal).

[68] JGT has "take her that night to Rochester" rather than "take her that night and go 60 miles" (54). Lockport is about sixty miles east of Lockport.

[69] JGT has "Rochester" for "the place where she could take cars" (54).

two days. They then told the people where I was staying that my disease must have been caused by some deep trouble. I knew not their decision. But I saw them leave me to my fate, and [yet] felt most deeply that I could not possibly die. Then suddenly the old subject of duty came up again, and I inwardly felt, "God will not /60/ permit me to die, but I shall yet live to preach the gospel." I at once began to mend.

Now all my neglect to obey the voice of God stared me in the face. In three days after they left me dying, I walked into their office. Then they started[70] as if I had come from the grave, and then I learned the conclusion of their counsel.

Chapter 6 [i.e., 7][71]

When I was able to go home, I returned to the place of my late residence. But my long absence induced them to believe that I had run away, and the man at whose house I had boarded and where I had my great trouble had taken all I possessed on a writ against me as an absconded debtor. But on my return, and when they learned the cause, all of my property was returned without any cost to me.

Next I was waited upon by a committee from the church to know how my moral character stood. It seemed I had been charged with keeping a bad woman in town under the pretence that she was my wife, and that I probably was never married to her, and knew her to be corrupt. But I was able to convince that committee that I was indeed unfortunate but not criminal. That I was indeed married. I was at once restored to their confidence at the church. A lawyer, learning the circumstances of my misfortune, came to me and offered to procure me a divorce free of expense to me. But my lacerated, timid spirit could not consent to go through all the details of litigation.

/61/ Now that I was free from this great trouble, my former impressions of duty came upon me with redoubled force. I longed for an abode away from the busy world of mankind and resolved to find me a home like a hermit in the wilderness where I might serve God, commune with nature, and at last lay my bones to rest in some lonely cave, unseen [and] unknown by man. I did go into bachelors' hall and, but for neglected duty, which it seemed to me must now be forever abandoned, I should have been comparatively happy. But it seemed that my affliction must prove an everlasting obstacle in my way. [I thought,]

---

[70] JGT has "stared at me" for "started" (54).

[71] JGT here begins chapter 8 (55) with an introductory paragraph before resuming Redfield's diary account.

"Everybody will find out that I have had family trouble and will feel at liberty to make what capital they please. How can I ever preach when and where I am marked as a man of suspicion? I could set all things right in the eyes of the honest and well meaning. But I cannot bear to bring the facts in my sufferings to light. No; It must be abandoned forever, and I must meet God at last and answer for the neglect."

Night and day for a number of years I was silently brooding over my sad state and trying all means in my power to banish the scorpion stings of a guilty conscience, which was ever lashing me with the convicting thought, "You knew your duty and you did it not." A large share of my time I spent alone in the grove nearby, weeping before God and making the dells and vales vocal with the wail of my suffering.

I would sometimes go to the church on a Sabbath Day, /62/ when the sight of a gospel minister would make me to writhe with agony and I was compelled to leave the church and resort to the woods and there weep, groan, and pray for deliverance from the agony I endured in view of my long-neglected duty. Yet I kept it all buried in my heart. If I saw a gospel minister in the street, my eye would follow as long as I could see him and my heart, choked with emotion, would sigh over my own unhappy state.

I now suddenly felt impressed with the conviction that I should never see my Father or Mother again in the flesh. So strongly was I impressed with the conviction that I dared not to go to the post office lest I should find the sad tidings there that my parents had passed away. Then I would compel myself to go, and finding no letter was a relief to me. Finally I made it a subject of prayer that God would permit me once more to see them and the answer came, "You shall," and then I was easy and went as usual for my letters without fears.

The fall came around and I went to the city of N. York to spend the winter. [I] procured my winter quarters and began a course of studies in the fine arts.[72] There I met with a young Southerner in ~~great distress having~~ failed in business and unable to get a situation.[73] I freely offered to meet his wants while my funds should last. He was overwhelmed with my generosity and soon told me, "Sir, you have proved a real

---

[72] On two or three occasions Redfield studied art, for which he apparently had some gift. He learned portrait painting; occasional references in the manuscript and in JGT indicate that Redfield at times supported himself through this skill.

[73] The words "great distress having" are crossed through with large Xs. Redfield apparently means the text to read, "There I met with a young Southerner in business." JGT omits this, passing directly to Redfield's "strong impression" that he should go to his parents' home (56).

friend, and I mean to let you know that I can fully /63/ appreciate your kindness. And now I propose that you go with me south, and I will make you rich." I have no doubt that he felt it. And now to make his promise probable, he said he would reveal to me his scheme. "I know," said he, "that some do not look upon it as very respectable, but there are many who do get rich in this way and," said he, "I will relieve you from any misgivings in the matter or participation except to receive the profit.

"My plan," said he, "is this, to hire about forty mulattos and make them do work enough to pay their hire, and from them I raise mulattos enough in ten years to bring $40,000, for they shall be my own children, and I think they would sell well. Besides this," said he, "I can go onto the plantations and find a plenty of [female] one-quarter bloods at about the age of fourteen or fifteen and can buy them frequently for $300 to $400, and however squalid they may appear, I can judge of their person as well as some men can of horses. I can take them and keep them in the house for about a year, dress them in silks, get some white lady to teach them to drum on the piano and to dance, and then I can take them to New Orleans and sell them as misses to some gentleman. They frequently sell as high as $2000, for some of them are the most beautiful creatures you ever saw, with just a little tint of color."

I said, "But sir, among a large company of such women there must be culls that will be left on your hands, and how can you dispose of them?"

"O," said he, "I should /64/ sell them to some common-house [i.e., brothel] for the use of sailors."

"But," said I, "I should not suppose they could live long in following such a life."

"O, no," said he, "they cannot expect to live more than from three to five years in that course of life."

By this time I had got all the information I wished of that feature of the great southern bastard. I turned upon him and told him to stop all further talk of that matter, for I would not hear it nor bear it. "I will help you to the utmost of my ability, but such a depth of iniquity and {downright rascality is too much for me to endure. Thus I found by allowing him to go on that a depth of iniquity was tolerated beyond all that I ever supposed to exist.}[74] ~~This I saw was~~ and even tolerated in the M.E. Church.

I now felt a strong impression to go immediately to my father's

---

[74] In the journal, the words I have placed in braces are crossed through with a large looping scribble.

house. I felt perfectly at rest about the health of my parents from the witness I had received to my prayer that I should see them again.

So pressed was I to go home that I promised myself I would take steamboat and go home the last of the week, about 250 miles.[75] The impression urged me to go home, so to satisfy myself I appointed a day earlier when I would start for home. But I was just as unsatisfied with that, nor could I feel the least relief till I promised to take the first boat and go home.

I did so, and arrived at home just one day before my mother died. Her last rational words to me were, in effect, "I could die in peace if my son would do his duty." She /65/ was dying of apoplexy. I watched my chance to go to her dying bed when all were gone and tried to arouse her. I could barely get an answering[?] response when I took hold of her and said, "Mother, do speak to me once more." I wanted to tell her, "I will go and obey the call of God to preach the gospel." But she was too far gone to comprehend me. In ten days after [this], my dear father too suddenly fell sick and passed away.

I followed them to the tomb. But oh, how did my heart sink on leaving them in their last resting place.[76] Now memory with a thousand tongues spoke of the anguish I had caused that sainted mother, whose prayers I had so often heard as she used to plead with God to spare her boy and fit him for the great mission which she had believed from my infancy was waiting for me. I found myself home and around the desolate hearthstone, but so bereaved at my loss that I have never been able to call to mind any of the circumstances of our return from the funeral. I only remember the last sight of the coffins, and next I was in my now forever desolate home.

But all the funeral solemnities being passed, I thought to visit a sister who had lately become a widow.[77] She seemed glad to see me and began at once to plead with me to promise her that I would go and preach the gospel, saying, "You /66/ know, Brother John, that Mother has gone to her grave brokenhearted over your neglect to obey God. And now," said she, "this is the last time I shall ever see you on earth, and I want you to promise me that you will do your duty and let me

---

[75] Claremont, New Hampshire, where Redfield was born, was about 250 miles north of New York City.

[76] It would seem from Redfield's account that his mother died and was buried, and that ten days later his father died, though he speaks of the funerals as if they were one event.

[77] JGT: "I went almost immediately to visit one of my sisters." Redfield has "a," not "my," but apparently does mean his own sister.

carry your promise to Mother."

"But," said I, "I shall meet you next week."

"No," said she, "this is the last time we meet on earth, so you must promise." The appeals to Mother broke me down, and to get rid of her importunity I made a promise which she construed to mean all that she desired and then said, "Come, Brother, let us get down and ratify it before God." Of course I knelt, and she poured out her soul for me in tones and words that wrung[78] me to the quick. We arose and I left her house, expecting to visit her the next week. But on going to the post office I found a letter urging my immediate return some six hundred miles as an important witness.[79] I obeyed, and indeed it proved the last visit with my sister, for I heard in about one month from the time I saw her [that] she passed away to the spirit land. I was very sad at these repeated desolations in the loss of my dearest earthly friends. But conscience had me be still and know that God was dealing in mercy in allowing me to live /67/ ~~as favorable as possible for a favorable trial. I thought it best to take her to board at a first class hotel~~[80] and with the bare possibility of trying to do something in the vineyard.[81] Now [I was] back in my bachelors' hall, alone, to avoid the annoyance from those who would beset me about the duty of preaching.[82]

---

[78] JGT has "stung" (58), but in the manuscript it looks to be "wrung" or "wring."

[79] JGT has, "calling me to go immediately six hundred miles away" rather than "urging my immediate return some 600 miles" (58). Presumably Redfield was returning to the Lockport, New York, area which, though only about 360 miles from Claremont, N.H., would have been closer to 600 miles by the fairly indirect route used at that time.

[80] These stricken lines at the top of page 67 evidently were written as the continuation of page 56, but then were crossed out and Redfield began page 57 on a new sheet, using slightly different wording. Later the sheet became page 67 rather than 57.

[81] Terrill ends chapter 8 and this point and begins chapter 9 (58–59).

[82] JGT here gives a description of Redfield's room, which "must have been a curiosity shop indeed. Shelves covered the walls on all sides. These shelves were loaded with geological specimens, freaks of nature in wood and stone, Indian relics and mechanism of his own invention. Two mice, bound with delicate chains of his own manufacture, which fed and sported and slept at their pleasure, were his only companions" (59). These details apparently came through Terrill's personal acquaintance with Redfield, as they are not found in Redfield's manuscript.

VII. Licensed to Preach

One day I met the Methodist preacher in the street, [and he] pressed me to begin to work in the gospel field. I tried to argue myself out of my dilemma, to prevent him from pursuing the subject too thoroughly home. I had held an exhorter's license which had been pressed upon me, but I would not use it.

The above-named [sic] preacher desired me to let my case pass the leaders' meeting for a recommendation for license to preach. A strong and abiding conviction seized me that unless I would permit the official board to act on my case and give me a license to preach, if they would, I should be killed with lightning. The strangeness of such an impression took all my sense of rationality aback, and it seemed utter folly to allow myself to be swayed by any such hallucination in matters of so great moment. But the fear haunted me night and day for a long time. When the terrific thunderstorms which frequently passed over would arise, there was an end of all my sleep. Till it was passed over I would get up and open a window and door to give a free circulation of air and then place my chair on glass standards[83] and there sit and /68/ pray and tremble till the storm was over.[84]

This state of things continued for some weeks. Then one night my fears were so great that I promised most faithfully that if the Lord would remove this fear, I would take the first opportunity to present my case to the official board. I was answered in the midst of the covering thunder gust[?]. I then went to rest and slept as calmly as ever I did in my life.

Friday evening came when the official meeting was to meet, and I to redeem my promise must present my case. I went to the business-room at the church where the meeting was to be held. It was in the basement of the church. I stated to the board that they might act on my case and grant me a license if they chose. I was now about to retire when one asked, "How do you stand on the abolition question?"

I answered, "I am an abolitionist of the strongest kind."

"Then," said he, "I shall oppose you."

I earnestly hoped they would not grant me a license on [account of] this question, and then I should feel released. I then said, "I wish it distinctly understood that if you give me a license and that should add any

---

[83] JGT: "in glass tumblers" (60), intended as insulation from electrical shock.

[84] JGT adds, "The familiar acquaintances of the man can fully appreciate this" (60)–i.e., people well acquainted with Redfield could imagine him doing this.

influence to what I now possess, I shall certainly use it for God and the slave. So now your eyes are open and you know who I am and what to expect."

Again they said, "We shall contest that matter." But they passed my recommendation, and the [presiding] elder gave me a license to preach.[85]

/69/ Our meeting held [i.e., continued] late. When we closed, I left, but we had not closed but a very short time and left the church when the church was struck with lightning, and the very window where I sat was torn to pieces on both sides. So great was the shock as to throw a man from his bed [in his home] on the opposite side of the street. The reader may put what construction he pleases on the sanity of my mind, but I always have and still do believe that that was the shaft which would have killed me if I had not yielded to go when I did. For I should have been at the meeting, as I was a class leader, and our business meetings frequently continued much later than this one.[86]

When my license was handed to me I felt I could not use it. I was in perpetual fear that my wife would come back, and I knew I could do nothing with her nor could anyone else, and then I knew that the tongue of slander would improve upon an occasion like this to injure my influence.

I used my license [however] for a few times, and was pressed to go upon a circuit as a supply [preacher]. I continued for a short time and was pressed to continue [longer]. But I could not consent, nor would I receive [i.e., accept] anything for my services. My sensitive nature so shrank from occupying this awful ~~stand point~~ position that I gave it up

---

[85] I.e., this meeting recommended Redfield for a local preacher's license, and this was approved by the quarterly conference, under the leadership of the presiding elder, and Redfield was given the license.

[86] JGT omits the last few sentences (including the important information that Redfield was at this time a class leader in the local Methodist congregation), merely saying that the church building being struck by lightning "made a profound impression upon" Redfield. JGT then adds, "and when soon after, the quarterly conference convened, he was ready to be examined according to the discipline. The license was granted, but when it was handed to him, he felt he could not use it" (61). Redfield does not specifically mention the quarterly conference (though it is implied in his reference to "the elder.") From the manuscript one could infer that when Redfield says "When my license was handed to me" he is referring to the meeting just described. But Terrill, knowing the process whereby the license would actually be granted by the quarterly conference on recommendation from the local church, supplies the additional information.

altogether and took a journey off into the city of C. [Cleveland], Ohio to spend the winter.[87]

I gave in my church letter to the Methodist Church, which letter stated that I had a license to preach. I was called upon to preach and /70/ in conjunction with the preacher held a protracted meeting, and God owned our labors in the salvation of souls.

While [I was] there, a deacon of a Presbyterian church in the absence of the minister desired me to preach at the Seamen's Bethel on a Sabbath afternoon.[88] The hour came, and I was taken into a full house. I resolved to be honest for God and truth, and while speaking against gambling, swearing, drunkenness, and horse racing, one cried out from the congregation, "Do you mean me, Sir? Do you mean me?"

I could only say, "If this is your case, I certainly do mean you."

When the services closed, the deacon who urged me to preach said to me, "That was a very sad mistake, and you have done us a great wrong." Then, as if to mitigate my ~~rebuke~~ punishment, [he] began to excuse the matter thus: "Our minister," said he, "I don't think is quite right. He knows they will do all these things of which you spoke, and he never reproves them or speaks against such conduct, and they are all bound up in [i.e., attached to] him. Sometimes," said he, "I think he don't go far enough, but you went altogether too far, and besides this, many of them are rough sailors and then won't bear reproof."

"My God," thought I, "and is this the type of religion here?" And O how glad I was to get out of that nest of corruption. But by the help of God I resolved to go the straight way at all cost.[89]

---

[87] JGT: "He finally gave up preaching altogether, and went to Cleveland, Ohio, for the winter" (61). No reason is given for going specifically to Cleveland. This seems to have been the winter of 1839–40. Terrill ends his brief chapter 9 at this point and begins chapter 10 with Redfield's account of his experiences in Cleveland. He notes, "In Cleveland, Mr. Redfield engaged in his chosen profession— portrait painting" (62).

[88] The Seamen's Bethel in Cleveland was one of an extensive network of chapels ministering to seamen worldwide, including at ports on the Great Lakes. See Roald Kverndal, *Seamen's Missions: Their Origin and Early Growth* (Pasadena: William Carey Library, 1986).

[89] JGT tones down Redfield's language a bit: "Shocked at this, Mr. Redfield turned away with a thankful heart that he was not more closely identified with such a state of things, and resolved that what work he did for the Lord should be faithfully done" (62).

VIII. Abolitionism: "Proclaim the Jubilee of God"

Soon the M.E. preacher asked me what were my views on the subject of antislavery. I told him I was an abolitionist from head to foot.

"Well," said he, "would you be willing to give us a lecture on antislavery?" Said he, "Our preachers' /71/ hands are tied by a vote of the Erie Conference[90] forbidding them to meddle with the evil of slavery. But yet," said he, "the colonizationists[91] make it a point to create all the prejudice they can against [us abolitionists] till some people regard us as the vilest disorganizers in the land. I am not allowed to speak for the poor dumb slave under pain of conference penalties. But," said he, "it does seem that someone who dares should be permitted to speak the sentiments of the antislavery part [of the church[92]]. There are a number of strong abolitionists in the city who would be glad to stand by anyone who dares to take a firm stand. But they dare not make a bold and independent stand unless someone should take the lead and meet the brunt of opposition which is sure to come when a true antislavery society should be started."[93]

I gave a promise that I would make a trial, as I had nothing too good to sacrifice for right.

The appointment was given. But when the time came, I was informed that a mob had collected, nailed up the house, and were ready to mob me if I should dare to speak in favor of the Niggers.[94] I must be

---

[90] JGT does not identify the particular Methodist Episcopal conference (63). The Erie Conference, which included Cleveland, at its August 1838 session "adopted a resolution forbidding abolition lectures, similar to that of the Pittsburgh Conference, for violating which Benjamin Preston was suspended for one year from his ministerial office" (L. C. Matlack, *The Antislavery Struggle and Triumph in the Methodist Episcopal Church* [New York: Phillips and Hunt, 1881; reprint New York: Negro Universities Press, 1969], 116–17). The appointed M.E. preachers at Cleveland in 1839–40 were John K. Hallock and M. H. Bettis (*Minutes,* Erie Conference).

[91] I.e., members of or sympathizers with the American Colonization Society, which advocated freeing slaves and sending them to new colonies in Africa.

[92] JGT adds the clarifying phrase, "of the church" (63).

[93] The Methodist preacher reasoned that since Redfield was a local preacher and not a ministerial member of the annual conference, he would not be subject to the restrictions which the conference had placed on its appointed preachers.

[94] JGT: "When the time came, a mob had collected, nailed up the doors of the building in which the lecture was to be given, and were waiting for the lecturer himself" (63).

visited with vengeance, either with pistols, or tar and feathers at least.

I felt it was no compromise of right or of conscience to avoid an infuriated mob when I could by no possibility get a hearing or do the cause any good. So I waived my appointment for the time. My quiet retirement without a chance to give [what] the views of our antislavery [position] were, compelled as I was by a mob, called out the better part of society[95] who said they were not yet prepared to surrender the rights of free speech in a free state. They demanded that the house should be /72/ opened to me [and] if I had the daring ~~and courage~~ to represent my cause at the risk of tar and feathers, I should at least have the opportunity. The plea for me was mainly this, that the colonizationists had free opportunity to misrepresent the abolitionists without hindrance, and it is no more than right to get at the creed of the abolitionists through one who stands out to the public as an abolitionist.

Another appointment was given. By the time this next appointment came around I had had time to make myself better acquainted with certain facts relating to slavery which would give my theme a better commendation to the confidence and acceptance of those most prejudiced by the very violence by which I was deterred from giving my lecture on a former occasion. But all this violent opposition gave me to know the strength of opposition and prejudice against God's lowly poor.

I had procured a synopsis of all the slave codes in each slave state.[96] I copied enough for my purpose of setting before them the true state [of affairs], as seen in the confessions and enactments of the wicked laws of the American house of bondage. [In my lecture] I then gave them the preambles and enactments [from various states] which were passed by their respective legislatures to ameliorate the condition of the poor bondmen of the South. These enactments were pressed through by some of the more humane [people in each state].

These preambles recited the causes which called for a law to protect the poor slave. I gave page and section. One states, "Whereas some of the masters whose wanton cruelty was practiced even to the taking

---

[95] The text here seems confused, but some of the words are hard to decipher. JGT: "His quiet retirement aroused the better element of society" (63).

[96] Redfield probably secured a copy of Theodore Weld's influential *American Slavery As It Is: Testimony of a Thousand Witnesses* (New York: American Anti-Slavery Society, 1839), based largely on an exhaustive collection of clippings from Southern newspapers that his wife Angelina Grimké Weld and her sister, Sarah Grimké, had compiled. The book included excerpts from laws in slave states, but as this book indicates, there were other published sources that Redfield might have had access to.

of life: Now therefore be it enacted that whoever /73/ shall hereafter kill his slave, he shall on conviction thereof be adjudged as guilty of murder as if he had killed a white man, unless such slave shall die under material[?] conviction, and again unless he [i.e., the slave] shall by his own oath [falsely] swear himself free[?]." Another, ". . . unless such slave shall resist the will of the Master," and this last applies to all those females who may attempt to protect their virtue against the beastly passions of the monster owner. In all these cases the owner of all such slaves has a right to kill his slave.

Another preamble and enactment reads, "Whereas some of the masters do overwork and poorly feed and clothe their servants, Now therefore be it enacted, that whoever shall compel his servants to labor more than twenty out of twenty-four hours, the extra hours being allowed for cooking and sleeping and eating . . . ." The clothing demanded by law: "four pairs of tow[97] pants and one of woolen, one tow shirt and an extra amount of woolen for the year, and on conviction of infraction of this law shall forfeit five to ten shillings to go into the town or county treasury." But no remuneration to the slave for abuse. And for food: "Each field hand shall be allowed one quart of raw corn a day or one peck a week," or to forfeit a like sum to the town or county [if the owner fails to comply]. But no remuneration to the slave.[98]

I then asked, "How are these laws obeyed, and what advantage do their owners take of their legal power over their slaves?" I then read extracts from their own papers advertising their runaway slaves,[99] a sample of which I here give: "Ran away from the subscriber. My slave Sally who without doubt is lurking about the plantation of Mr. blank in Georgia, as I sold her husband to that gentleman about eighteen months ago and she has been very sullen ever since. She will /74/ try to pass herself off as a white woman as she is very white and beautiful spoken and very capable of putting on this air of a white lady. Fearing that she might run away I took the pains to mark her by breaking out two of her front teeth and branding her on the buttock with the letter S. She is likewise much scarred with the whip on her neck and shoulders. The

---

[97] Tow: Fabric made of flax, hemp, or jute fibers.

[98] It is not clear how much of the above is direct quotation and how much is Redfield's summary or paraphrase, so the quotation marks supplied are somewhat conjectural. Terrill does not include these quotations, merely saying that Redfield "gave a synopsis of the slave codes in each State" and giving some summary examples (64). Weld's *American Slavery As It Is* gives similar examples, but I have not been able to find these specific examples in the book.

[99] *American Slavery As It Is* contains well over a hundred such advertisements.

legs are torn by the dogs made by catching her fifteen months ago, about three months after her husband was gone. The left thumb has the mark of a rifle ball where I shot at her before she would surrender."[100]

I then gave them the story of poor George, who ran away and whose master followed and found him in New York and took him back, then collected his slaves into the long kitchen, compelled the slaves to build up a large fire in the large fireplace and then bring in the large chopping block. [He] bound George fast and then with ax in hand began to lecture the slaves as to their fate if they dared to run away. He then cut off one of George's feet, holding it up to let them see the fate of those who should run away, then throwing it into the fire. [He] cut off another piece of the limb, and so continued cutting and torturing till he had cut off a large share of feet, legs, and arms. Poor George faintly cried out, "O Massa, do cut off my head."

Finally, fearing that the poor creature would die too soon, [the master] cut off his head and then compelled the slaves to put the body into the fire. After it was quite well burnt, the master had the slaves take down a part of the back of the fireplace and put the burnt body in, and put up the fireplace to conceal /75/ what was left of George.

An earthquake that night threw down the chimney, and a white man passing saw the charred body of poor George. This white man compelled an investigation and the facts [were] brought to light enough to have the monster shut up in jail, and ~~that night~~ the prisoner killed himself in jail before morning.[101]

---

[100] JGT quotes this advertisement, printing the words "RAN AWAY FROM THE SUBSCRIBER" as a headline (64). While quite similar accounts are found in *American Slavery As It Is,* this specific one does not seem to be in the book. So Redfield may have been using another source, unless he created this as a composite of several accounts.

[101] JGT understandably omits this gruesome story, merely saying, "This was followed by recitals of cruelty, blood-curdling to read at the present day" (64). Such a murder apparently occurred in Livingston County, Kentucky, in 1807; the perpetrators were Lilburn Lewis, a nephew of Thomas Jefferson, and his brother. The account is found in *American Slavery As It Is* (93–94) in a slightly different version from Redfield's account. In Weld's book, George was not a runaway to New York but a youth of about seventeen who had displeased his master; the murder was discovered because the slaves "whisper[ed] the horrid deed," not as a result of an earthquake; and the perpetrator did not commit suicide in jail. Redfield may have gotten the story from this book (and embellished it), or from some other source; *American Slavery As It Is* notes that the story, contained in a letter by the Rev. William Dickey, was published in *Human Rights* in August 1837, and earlier had "been scattered all over the country,

I saw by this time that the opposition began to yield, and the mob quieted down. The congregation was very large, and crowded inside and out. I was expecting to hear or "feel" a shot from some pistol from outside.[102] But I said to myself, "This is the cause of God and humanity, and I may as well die here as anywhere."[103] I then appealed to their honor as men, and to their humanity. Drawing a picture of a similar state of sufferings among the Algerians endured by Americans stolen from this place, [I] then asked them to wait till I should finish or stay, and if they thought me worthy of ill treatment after that, I would not hesitate to abide their decision.

I then made a supposition that [they] themselves, instead of the poor Africans, were thus suffering, and that I ventured at the risk of my life to undertake their deliverance. ["What if," I suggested,] "on making this ~~investigation~~ my desperate and hazardous effort, I should finally return and hear a like message of suffering.[104] Should you then feel that I deserve tar and feathers or mobbing?"

[Redfield dramatizes:] An old lady asks me, "Did you see anything of my poor boy, nine months[?], who was stolen from me twenty years ago?"

I answer, "Yes, and [I] will [bring] him out. Here, Madam, is your boy who has been suffering among the Arabs. He has lost one eye you see, shot out while trying to run away from his cruel task; /76/ very lame from the bite and tear of the dogs which they keep to catch runaways. He is old and gray and lean from hard usage. But he is your boy, and loves his poor desolate mother."

Another mother asks, "And have you seen my poor and only daughter, who was stolen away from me, and how is she?"

I answer, "Geo Don [will] tell you," and Geo begins, "Yes, Madam, she was the slave of the planter who lived next to my master. Her master had a good chance to sell her three children. They were to be taken away the next day by the traders who bought and sold slaves, and they shut them all up together to keep them from running away,

---

south and north" (93).

[102] Redfield has a quotation mark before "feel" but not one after.

[103] In summarizing this section, JGT does not include this statement (65).

[104] This "supposition" that Redfield dramatized may possibly have been suggested by a report included in *American Slavery As It Is* by General William Eaton, U.S. Consul in Tunis, who related "his feelings at the sight of many hundreds of Sardinians who had been enslaved by the Tunisians." Eaton wrote, "[T]he Christian slaves among the barbarians of Africa are treated with more humanity than the African slaves among professing Christians of civilized America. *American Slavery As It Is,* 127.

and Lucy felt so bad to think her three fine boys were to be taken away forever from her, and she should see them no more, and then the sufferings they might endure, so that night she cut the throats of all of her children and then killed herself."

These with other like facts I related as such that had transpired in the South and [been] endured by the poor Africans, and only supposed that Americans instead of Africans were the sufferers. I then further gave a parallel of sufferings by those who held a sympathy for the suffering Americans among the Arabs by supposing the scene shifted, and that some in trying to benefit our people had been shot, hung, burnt and imprisoned. I then gave a sample of laws actually existing in Ohio, and in full force, where the law forbids anyone to give a person (suspected of being a slave) anything to eat till he should at his own expense prove himself free, on pain of a fine of $50. To give them work to do imposes a fine of $100, and to help them towards a land of freedom subjected the offender to a fine of $500 and ten years imprisonment in state prison.

I then asked, "Does that man deserve mobbing whose kind feelings /77/ press him to hazard fines, liberty and even life to carry out his kindness? This kindness for the poor lowly African leads me as an abolitionist to do what I am trying to do for them, and I would run the same hazard to help you in like circumstances.[105] Now, if you think I deserve tar and feathers, I am ready for the penalty."

Not one move was made to molest me, nor [were there] any indications of a disposition to trouble me. I then said, "If you think our cause worthy of support, we will form an antislavery society here." Then all but three persons in the house gave in their names to form the first antislavery society in that place. *[106]

I acknowledge that there is apparent force in the objection [which some make] to the narrative of these extreme facts by which to represent the wicked workings of the system of slavery. I answer that if

---

[105] JGT summarizes the imaginary scene of Americans being slaves in Algeria in about five lines and omits the references to laws in Ohio (65).

[106] There is a large asterisk here, apparently added (by Redfield or Terrill or someone else) for emphasis; there is no corresponding asterisk elsewhere on the page. Terrill says, "This was the first organization of the kind made in the city" (65). It probably was not in fact the first antislavery society in Cleveland; the *Second Annual Report of the American Anti-Slavery Society* (New York: 1835) shows that an antislavery society had been formed in Cleveland by that date, with John M. Sterling as president, whereas Redfield seems to have been in Cleveland a few years later.

these facts can only occur once in an age under the protection of law, that fact alone is enough to brand with an eternal curse the system of American slavery. And here with all the emphasis I can utter it I say that every hair of my head and every nerve of my being prays, "O God of justice, wipe out the foul bloodspots of slavery and purge our nation of the vilest sum of all villanies [sic]." And when I look at the complicity of American Methodism with slavery, and yet know that the Almighty hand put the keys of the house of bondage into her hands and that she has not only proved untrue to her trust but has actually pressed her influence into the service of sustaining slavery, and even to mask and proscribe the true antislavery spirit in the M.E. Church, I can but say her days are numbered and hereafter she will only exist as a monument of God's displeasure.

/78/ She will be known hereafter as a thing that once was. Having outgrown her heavenly zeal, power and efficacy, her stately towers and metropolitans[107] like whited sepulchres will warn the true pilgrim that dead Methodism is rattling within. For if I have any correct idea of a just and holy God, I must believe that *Mene Tekel* will be written against a system of church polity which can tolerate and sustain a system which compels its victims to break every moral ~~law of a just and pure God~~ phase of the decalogue.

There is yet one morsel of comfort for poor Africa, for assuredly she shall yet stretch out her hands to God,[108] and heaven will in sight of the universe assure the protection of the lowly. Then must the abettors of slavery hang their unholy heads. Poor Ham has fallen among thieves. Public opinion, manufactured by church dignitaries and sustained by church organizations, must yet witness the estimate in which the great God judges the poor and lowly brotherhood of Jesus. Then who shall answer to the Almighty for the great wrong mutually imposed by church and state? He will not shut out the cry of the lowly. He will remember them, forty hundred thousand[109] who have cried out of wrong to the great Father. For their many long years must be heard, or the throne of heaven must be held responsible. Should it cost our nation rivers of blood, that wrong against humanity and insult to God must

---

[107] Redfield seems to use the term "metropolitans" in the sense of the principal church edifices of a city, not in the sense of ecclesiastical office.

[108] A reference to Psalm 68:31, "Princes shall come out of Egypt; Ethiopia shall soon stretch out her hands unto God"—an important verse in the history of missions to Africa.

[109] I.e., 4,000,000. Theodore Weld in *American Slavery As It Is* gave the number of slaves in the U.S. in 1839 as 2,700,000 (7–8).

and will be settled. /79/ The church and state have plotted to strengthen each other's hands and rob the innocent, and poor Ham has felt the killing blow. The most of this responsibility lies with the M.E. Church, inasmuch as to her was committed the authority of the Almighty to proclaim the jubilee of God and the freedom of the oppressed.

Some remarkable cases of conversion among slaveholders will give a clue to the general sentiments of the Methodists in the early days of their history. [In the life of] Freeborn Garrettson occur instances. While a penitent and listening to the voice of the Spirit, [he] could not find pardon to his soul till he had called all his slaves together and proclaimed freedom, and then he found mercy and became one of the fathers and bright ornaments of American Methodism.

By and by [within Methodism,] charity for the oppressor called for forbearance [in dealing with slaveholding members] in certain cases. Forbearance was the compromise which demanded toleration, till finally church and state hand-in-hand became the protectors of cruelty and brought their combined power to bear in extending and defending the sum of all villainies.[110]

While [I was] at C. [Cleveland] in Ohio, one case of a slave who was escaped from the house of bondage I will relate, as one among many whose cases came under my observation. This city was a point from which many a slave took leave of the land of oppression and passed over to the land of Britain [i.e., Canada], whose laws know no property in man.[111]

---

[110] Terrill, working with Redfield's manuscript long after the Civil War, omitted this whole section denouncing slavery and Methodism's complicity in it, beginning with "I acknowledge that there is apparent force" to here (a little more than two pages of manuscript). See JGT, 65. Methodist pioneer and organizer Francis Asbury himself struggled with this dilemma and at times expressed similar sentiments. He wrote as early as June 27, 1780, "There are many things that are painful to me, but cannot yet be removed, especially slave-keeping and its attendant circumstances. The Lord will certainly hear the cries of the oppressed, naked, starving creatures. O, my God! think of this land." Elmer T. Clark, ed., *The Journal and Letters of Francis Asbury*, 3 vols. (London: Epworth Press; Nashville: Abingdon Press, 1958), 1:362.

[111] JGT adds here: "Cleveland was a point on the under-ground railroad . . . . It was a criminal act, according to the law of the land, to harbor or assist a fugitive slave" (65). The federal Fugitive Slave Law was not passed until 1850, but as Redfield had noted, a state law was in effect. An earlier (1793) federal fugitive slave law had been largely ineffective. See William Gravely, *Gilbert Haven, Methodist Abolitionist: A Study in Race, Religion, and Reform, 1850–1880* (Nashville: Abingdon, 1973), 67.

I remembered on one evening in our congregation to have seen a very tall, straight and well-built figure /80/ of a gentleman who, hymn-book in hand, took part in our worship. The hue of his skin and slight wavy ringlets of his hair betrayed his pedigree. But his dignified air and manly bearing with me would almost dissipate any suspicion that he could be one of those unfortunate brothers of Jesus whom our law and the unwritten creeds of the Evangelical churches had already declared had no rights that white men are bound to respect.

Shortly after, at night, came the same manly figure to my lodgings and in great agitation said to me, "Oh sir, save me. I am in great distress. Will you help me?"

"I will if I can. But tell me what is the matter?"

"O, Sir, I am a slave. A large reward has been offered for me, and I learn that a man is in the city in search of me to take me back into slavery."

"Come in to my room," said I, "and you shall be perfectly safe. My windows are all shut, fastened, and blinded, and I will fasten the door."

"But what if they break in?"

"I shall then do the best I can to defend you at all cost." I then said to him, "Be calm and sit down, and now tell me all about your ~~case~~ history. Now, why did you run away? Was you badly treated in your person?"

"O no," said he. "I will tell you the whole history of the cause of my leaving the land of oppression. In the first place, I belonged to a man who died some years ago, and the widow married again. Before the legal heirs could make their claim to a part of the property, my new master desired to sell me. But of all this I knew nothing till one day while I was working in the tan-yard, cleaning /81/ out a tan vat. (I had been hired out by master to a tanner, as I had learned that trade.)

"Well, while I was shoveling out the old bark and singing a Methodist hymn, a sudden impression came upon me, and I thought I heard a voice saying to me, 'You are sold.' I instantly arose and looked all around, to see where the voice came from. But, seeing no one, I said to myself, 'I will not allow myself to be duped by superstition.' And to work I went again, still singing a favorite hymn.

"Then again the shrill voice echoed all through my soul, 'You are sold!' Again I sprang to my feet and looked for the author of the dreadful sound, but all in vain. To work I went again, determined to banish all my fears and resume my labor.

"But the same voice said again, 'You are sold.' Again I looked for the voice, and in the distance I saw my new master in company with a stranger passing apparently leisurely around the tan-yard. In a moment

I knew by the inward voice that my destiny was sealed. And then the thought, 'I must now be torn and forever separated from my dear wife and child.' The keen sense of the great wrong about to be perpetrated upon me nerved me to resolve, 'I will die first.'

"I kept my eye out, and found that they were gradually drawing nearer to me. Soon they stood at my back. While I was lifting a shovel full of tan bark one of them asked, 'Shall I not help you lift it out?' I knew that was the signal to tie me, and I must now with the nerve of a mad man [attempt to escape,] for the agonizing thought of seeing my family no more made be blind to all consequences, and resolute to contend for my rights or die.[112] /82/ While trying to gain time I sprang to the top of the vat and raised my shovel in an attitude of defense. Then they instantly presented pistols and bade me surrender or die. I cared not a fig for death, I was so aroused to a sense of the great wrong they were doing me. But I next thought, 'It is of no use to contend. They have the law on their side and can do what they please. I must submit and, like my Savior, visit not evil, but endure.' It was my conscience and not my fear that subdued me and bade me look to the future and to God to settle all these wrongs.

"I then let them tie me with a long rope, with my hands behind me. They then gave a sharp and loud sound of a whistle, and soon I saw a man coming in the distance. When he came up, they gave me into his charge. He took the rope and bade me walk on. He was taking me to a place on the road where a ~~large~~ a coffle[113] of fifty slaves were to have me tied with them, and then [he would] take us all down to the Mississippi River where we were to embark for a southern port.[114] But when we were away from those two men, I said to the man who had me in charge, 'Please let me go home and see my wife and child once more before I leave them forever.' 'No,' said he with a terrible oath, 'you shall not go, for if your wife sees you in this fit she will only make a Dd [damned] fuss, and you will only feel a great deal worse than to go without seeing her.[115] You better make up your mind never to see her

---

[112] JGT: "Instinctively I knew that this [offer of help] meant to tie my hands while I was holding them up. Blind to all consequences, and with the nerve of a madman, I sprang out of the vat" (66–67).

[113] Coffle: "a train of men or beasts fastened together" or "a gang of slaves chained and driven along together," deriving from the Arabic word for caravan (*World Book Dictionary*).

[114] JGT: "He took me to a place by the roadside where there were about fifty more slaves, tied together, preparatory to being taken down the river to be sold again" (67). Terrill doesn't identify the river.

[115] JGT: "Your wife would make a — — fuss, and you will feel a great deal

again.'

"O," said the poor fellow while telling me, "it did seem I was so heavy with grief that my feet slumped into the ground at every step. Then with all my might I gave a sudden wrench and so far loosed my hands /83/ that I got hold of the rope with my hands, and being much stronger than the man, I pulled him right up to me, and then said to him, 'I shall go and see my family once more before we are parted.' And when he saw that I had him in my power, with another oath said he, 'Well, you may go, but it will be the worse for you.'"

While thus narrating his history, this noble specimen of a man would falter and choke and struggle to swallow down his grief, which was yet rending that manly heart. Then again he would arouse himself and seem to say by his effort, "I will put on the fortitude of a man and tell my story and conquer this seeming weakness."

"Finally," said he, "we reached the cabin of my family. And sure enough, as soon as my wife saw me in my condition, with a shriek she fell on the floor, and then my poor heart seemed to break worse than before. But as I was compelled to hasten, I picked up a few things of clothing and tied them up in a small bundle. I then kissed my wife and boy for the last time. But oh, how my brains reeled as I turned to leave my desolate cottage and sorrowful wife! I had the same sense of sinking into the earth at every step while passing from my poor family forever.

"I was now hurried along, and soon reached the coffle of slaves and was soon bound in the same gang by one of my wrists to a chain which ran the whole length of the company. The driver being in a great hurry urged us to the top of our speed, and traveling so far and so fast, with my rough old shoes, which I used to wear in the tannery, my feet became so galled that the blood ran from my shoes.

"We reached the river that night and were taken into a tavern that stood /84/ at the landing. We were all put up into the garret together, which was made like unto a jail with grated windows for the accommodation of slave traders.

"Soon the whole gang were asleep, being quite weary with the day's travel. Some had cried themselves to sleep. Some [were] sullen and [showed] a spirit of carelessness as to what did become of them, for the last tie was broken and the last hope had fled. Others were so gross and stupid that they fell asleep for want of energy and life enough to keep awake. Like the beasts, as soon as they were away from the

---

worse" (67). Redfield apparently meant to indicate "damned" or "God-damned."

goading lash they fell asleep.

"When all were sound asleep (as near as I could judge), [and while] the rain was falling rapidly,[116] I went around the garret, feeling my way cautiously. Then I happened to put my hand on a clothesline, as this place was used by the family for a place to dry clothes when not otherwise used. I then made my way to the grated [window] and with a jack knife which I brought from the old tan-yard I dug one end of an iron grate out of the wall. That made a place just large enough for me to ~~crawl~~ squeeze through. I then fastened one end of my clothesline to another of the bars. I next threw out my little bundle. I then carefully got out of the window and ventured my weight upon the cord.

"As I let myself out upon the frail rope, I heard one of the strands snap and expected the next moment to fall to the ground. But no, it held my weight, and I let myself down till I came to the end of my rope, but had not yet reached the ground by a number of feet. As I hung upon the end of the rope, I saw a door open and someone passing in. /85/ For a moment all my fears were aroused, thinking that I was discovered. But they did not see me in the dark, and I only saw them by the light coming from the open door. The rain was pouring down. I now let go my hold and came to the ground, and then carefully felt around and found my little bundle. I then found my way to a stream of water close by which came to the river from the same direction which I came. To avoid the hounds which I knew would be put on my track, I waded the stream for a long distance.

"As daylight began to dawn, I got out of the stream and hid in the woods to wait till night again. When night came, again I pursued my homeward course again [sic]. About daylight the succeeding morning I came in sight of the cottage [of] my dear wife, and for fear of frightening her or arousing some of the slaves which slept in one part of the cabin, I went cautiously to a little window and in a low tone called, 'Liza.' With a scream she cried out, 'Oh my God, that is my Thomas. O Thomas, Thomas, the patrol will kill you.' I said, 'Hush, Eliza, and keep still and we will manage some way.' I then went into the cabin and planned to get up into the little garret through a hole over a door between the two rooms, and my wife put up a box onto the door casing to hide a part of the hole through which I had passed.

"When daylight had fairly set in the patrol, who had heard of my escape, were at the cabin of my wife, supposing I would be most likely

---

[116] In place of this phrase, JGT inserts at the end of the previous sentence: "It was raining hard without, and the patter upon the roof and the splashing upon the ground, made it difficult to hear other sounds" (68).

to be found looking after my poor heartbroken wife. I heard them ask Eliza if I had got back. To which she answered no, and that she had not seen me since I left with the slave ~~driver~~ trader.

"The patrol kept such a /86/ close watch for me that I could not and dare not go out anywhere. So I thought it best if I could to shift the place of concealment, and started in the night to go to the cabin of my mother, four miles distant, as she belonged to a man there. So as not to startle Mother, I went up to Mother's window and in a low tone asked, 'Aunt, is Uncle at home?' But my mother knew my voice and knew also that I had run away and that the patrol was after me. Mother was so agitated that she cried out, 'Oh, it is my poor boy Tommy! O Tommy, Tommy, they will kill you.' She then let me into her cabin, and we together took up a board from the floor. I then lay down on the ground and Mother put the floorboard back again. Here I staid till I could with safety come out and stretch myself, as I could when the patrol were off from that beat.

"My mother's cabin as well as that of my wife was closely watched, and we continued to go into Mother's garret, as there was a ladder to it and as Mother could have my child brought over and keep it there without suspicion. Here I had the sorrowful consolation of caressing my darling boy.

"I resolved however to go to the North as soon as I could with safety and gain my freedom. But so closely was I [i.e., the cabin] watched that I was compelled to stay under the floor and in the garret of my mother for thirteen months. By this time I was so completely bleached out and my skin was so fair that Mother got me some women's clothes. I dressed in them and went out boldly and took stage as a white woman, and no one seemed to think it possible that I was a runaway slave.

"When the stage had carried me away from where I was likely to be known, I got out and went out into the woods and, putting on my men's /87/ clothes, traveled nights and slept in the daytime till I reached the free states. I lived on corn, fruits, and such other things which I could help myself to. After a long time I found myself in this state [Ohio], and then found friends.

"After awhile I felt so bad for my poor wife and child that I had left in bondage that I resolved to hazard the dangers and ~~go back after them~~ get some white man to write back to my master that if he would allow me to live with my family, I would come back and give him the balance of my labors for life. But he wrote back that he would have me anyway, and then he would do as he pleased. So when this hope also had failed, I resolved to go myself and by some means bring them both away.

"So I turned my steps again towards the land of bondage. I traveled nights and slept in the daytime in the woods till I once more came in sight of my desolate cottage. But when I went in, I found my little one was dead and buried, and here again it seemed my heart would break again. I now fully determined to take my wife and flee from this cruel land of oppression.

"We started and passed the patrol and entered the woods at night. But my poor wife had become so nervous and broken by the long sorrowful story of her wrongs that [at] every unusual sound [such] as the break of a bush under my feet while I carried her in my arms she would cry out, 'The patrol is coming, the patrol is coming!' I now clearly saw I must give up my undertaking or by her fearfulness we should both be betrayed and taken back to the house of bondage. So I must let her return while I again turned my mournful steps back to the North.

"And now," said he, "they have got track of me and are in the city after me."

Suffice it to say /88/ that I had the privilege of learning that this poor brother of Jesus was safely landed in Canada, where slaves have as good a right to take care of their families and to their own lives as any man on the face of God's free Earth.[117] I know I laid myself liable to church proscription. But I had frankly told them, "I shall act for God and humanity." The law of the state could have sent me to state prison for ten years and required of me the payment of a fine of $500 had they known of my offense and prosecuted me. But what had I to do in protecting my own rights when there stood my suffering Jesus in the person of this poor outcast? I seemed to hear his voice still ringing in my ears: "Inasmuch as ye have done it unto one of the least of these my brethren, ye have done it unto <u>me</u>." Yes, and I would do it again if I knew I must pay the whole penalty by imprisonment and fine.[118] And

---

[117] JGT: "Mr. Redfield had the privilege of learning that this suffering man landed safely in Canada, where colored people had equal rights with white people" (71).

[118] In the foregoing sentences, JGT quotes Redfield almost word for word. But for the following extended "prophetic truth" Terrill substitutes a summary paragraph concerning "the great antislavery conflict" of the time, the compromising position of the M.E. Church, and Redfield's attitude toward these matters. Terrill writes, "His sensitive soul listened with horror to the accounts of proscription against such men as Orange Scott, Cyrus Prindle, Luther Lee and others" and comments on the later organization of the Free Methodist Church (72). (Redfield does not mention Scott, Prindle, Lee, or the Free Methodist Church.)

Oh my God, what an account must Methodists give (to say nothing of other Christian churches) when the great day of God's reckoning will settle the wrongs of earth! Especially when the cry of the poor shall be heard, many of them the precious jewels whom the great God has chosen in the furnace of affliction. The M.E. Church may vindicate herself as she will, but she has given hope and succor to both church and state by her feeble do-nothing course and her proscription of those who would act. By my word for it, the Almighty will soon [remove] her candlestick out of its place.

The church and the world may pass what judgment they please on the correctness of my judgment. But I feel led to utter it as a prophetic /89/ truth when I say that the M.E. Church in all that belongs to effective power will now and forever pass away and be known only as a mummy, or a corpse laid out in state, and God will now give their mission to another people. The church will exist as a grand old family tomb to perpetuate the memory of the once-honored people whose God was the Lord. And as long as money can build and adorn beautiful whited sepulchres and hang out tablets bearing the historic fame of other days, way-marks in the shape of metropolitans and saintly temples will yet mock the land. There will be yet some prosperity in missions and frontier work. But the soul of religion, coming down to the simplicity and comprehensiveness of God's poor in the highways and hedges, has passed, and forever.

If [i.e., Though] repentance could ward off the calamity, it never will take place. Confession and retraction will cost too much, and it will never take place. Now God's wronged children who have cried so long must be redressed, and now I record this, my last protest, and utter it with all the emphasis which I can command. I insist [i.e., protest] this great wrong against man and insult to God in treading out the life of the poor. I wipe my hands and say, "I am innocent of the blood of these lowly children of the great Father. Trifle as you please with those heart-stirring appeals of the downtrodden; my heart always has and still does respond to their calls for relief. Mock as you may at those deep emotions stirred by the Holy Ghost. Put down if you can those stern truths which exact perfect obedience and conformity to the great Model, Jesus. Conform to the /90/ world if you dare. Love the world if you will, and make the cross of no offense by any or all ornaments, and accommodate the unchanged heart—and I would utter with unmingled grief my conviction: You are ruined!"

Some will say it is awful thus to implicate church dignitaries. But I think it is awful for them to displace God's authority by their own traditions. I must stand on the blessed Bible, still reeking with the blood that bought us heaven's best gift to man, and declare my eternal loyalty to God at all cost. To follow its dictates has made [me] very unpopular thus far all my life. But I accept it still, and take the consequences and bless the name of God for the precious privilege. I may yet fail by the way, but I will never yield till I am fairly put down—not by pain, for that never can conquer me. But till I am put down by right and justice.

Chapter [8][119]

I had now passed one winter in active service for God and humanity, and knew that many souls had been converted. A good antislavery spirit was inaugurated, and nearly fifty slaves had passed and been aided in their flight to the land of promise over Lake Erie. Now I thought to return to my bachelors' hall some 230 miles from Cleveland,[120] and when I had returned I was pressed to take work as a preacher to supply the place made vacant by the removal of one of the preachers who became unacceptable on account of his antislavery proclivities. I went on and soon became equally unacceptable, for I too was an abolitionist. Now I felt utterly to despair of doing my duty acceptably to God /91/ and satisfactory to myself. So I spent the summer in my lonely retreat and in studying into the works and ways of God as seen in nature, and gave up the idea of going into active service as a preacher of the gospel, especially as a traveling preacher. But [I] thought to content myself in preaching occasionally and attending to my business. I would preach occasionally but never allow myself to take one cent for my expenses, even.

---

[119] The Redfield manuscript has no numeral here, though in sequence it is chapter number 8. At this point JGT begins his chapter 11 (74), having omitted about two pages of the manuscript containing Redfield's "prophetic" denunciation of Methodism. JGT concludes chapter 10: "It is hardly possible for the present generation, though little more than a quarter of a century has since passed by, to conceive of a state of society in this country such as has been illustrated in this chapter; but many there are who have outlived the generation in which these cruelties were perpetrated, and who, vividly recalling those exciting times, will testify that the picture is in no wise overdrawn" (72–73).

[120] JGT: "an efficient anti-slavery society had been organized, and nearly fifty fugitives from bondage had been assisted in their efforts to reach Canada. He now determined to return to Lockport, N.Y., the scene of some of his severest conflicts, and where he consented to accept a license to preach the gospel" (74). Lockport is in fact about 230 miles east of Cleveland. If given a local preacher's license, Redfield was perhaps assigned to assist one of the appointed preachers in the Genesee Conference. He was never a member of the conference. The year is uncertain, but it must have been in the early 1840s.

But again the hand of disease was upon me. Still I tried to keep my conscience as free as I could from condemnation by visiting or praying with the people and exhorting sinners to come to Christ, and with some success. But so little was I satisfied with the very little I was doing that I was in great distress.

IX. Seeking Holiness: "By faith alone"

I now began in good earnest to seek the blessing of holiness, thinking that that state of grace would empower me to do my duties with some more success and with greater satisfaction to myself. In my ignorance of the true way to seek that state of grace successfully, I wept and moaned before God and wished that I could meet with someone who could instruct me.

I finally became desperate, and resolving to make a business [of it], I began by a day of fasting to seek this great blessing.[121] Then I followed up with [a] watch-night and resolved never to close my eyes or leave my knees till I could claim the blessing. But before morning nature sank under the burden, and I fell on the floor and went to sleep. When morning came I awaked to find myself exhausted and on the floor. When I remembered the vows and resolves I made the night previous, and how poorly I had kept my promise, I would chide myself for my faithless promise and then in tears I would ask, "O God, must I live another day as I did this one that has passed? What must I be? /92/ Can I be no more like God?" O, "'Tis worse than death my God to love, and not my God alone"[122] I could sing from the depth of my soul.

Again I fasted, and again I held a watch-night. I resolved not to move till I either died or should gain this great pearl. But being still more exhausted, I again sank on the floor and fell asleep. I waked again the next morning to upbraid myself for my broken vow.

All these struggling efforts only proved to me how useless were human plans and will power to gain what I afterward found must be found by faith alone.

By the Spirit I was led to make a thorough search of self to find in how far my will was in harmony with God, and then my mind was

---

[121] JGT: "I finally became desperate, and resolved to make a business of seeking it. I began with a day of fasting and prayer" (74).

[122] Phoebe Palmer (on Nov. 24, 1827) and Ellen Stowe (on Sept. 20, 1844; later Ellen Roberts) also quote these lines in their diaries. See Richard Wheatley, *The Life and Letters of Phoebe Palmer* (New York: Palmer and Hughes, 1884), 24; manuscript diary of Ellen Stowe, Roberts Wesleyan College Archives.

wrought up to settle the great question of questions with me. I thought, "I never can think of preaching after all my trouble with that unfortunate being who has blasted every hope of my life, and I cannot go and attempt to regulate public opinion by a narration of my sorrows. I shall be misunderstood, and my misfortune must always be the foundation for any amount of slander which will hedge up my way and arrest the progress of the gospel. No, no, Lord, I can never go. I might once have gone without an impediment, but that day is passed forever, and now I must meet broken obligations as best I can and abide the consequences. I will do the best I can in a private way and try to approve [i.e., please] God the best I can by doing the duties of a private Christian. But to go out and devote my life to the preaching of the gospel, I never can do it /93/ till I can be assured that I shall have an honourable discharge forever from the woman who has embittered my whole life for these years and whose conduct would, if [she were] with me, make both me and my ministration entirely unacceptable to everybody and as such impossible."

X. Evaluating Impressions: "Faith, fancy, intuition"

I resolved to spend my time in active service, so I went around to visit the sick and to pray with them and point them to the Lamb of God. I went to see a young man who was very sick and had been given up by the counseling physicians, who had just left him to die. While at prayer for him, an impression came upon me that he would not die, and I instantly gave utterance to the expression that God would raise him up. I then arose and, taking him by the hand said to him, "You will not die. Now give your heart to God and live for Him."

This he promised to do. I left the house. Then one or two of my brethren who were there and heard my expression of faith that God would heal him told me they were distressed at my prophecy and feared the consequences. So did I feel too, nor was I relieved till, a few days after, I saw the man walking the street in comparative health.

Soon after I was called on to visit another man who was given up to die by his physician, who said that he could not live through the night. The man himself insisted that I should be called, saying he would take no medicine from any other hand than mine or by my direction. I presume that he had heard of the restoration of that man who had recovered, for as soon as I approached his bed he said to me, "Don't pray for me to get well, for I prefer to die." But the impression was upon me and I said to him, "I can pray neither way, for you /94/ will certainly get well," and the sequel justified the prediction.

I was called upon by a class leader to go and visit one of his members, then apparently dying with the consumption. It was a cold night in March. We found the windows and doors open to give her breath. The physician had just left, declaring that she was dying. While I was praying, the same impression came with such force that it was with difficulty that I could repress the utterance of a prophecy that she too would live.[123] On leaving the house I stated to the leader my strong impression and the difficulty I had in checking the utterance of the impression. To which he answered, "It is a good thing that you did not, for she is certainly dying and if you had, the cause of religion would be greatly injured." To our astonishment, she was able to walk the streets in a very few weeks, and for aught I know is still living.

I will relate one more case in this connexion to illustrate the lesson which I learned by these events. One of our class leaders was taken sick, and to all appearance it was unto death. Now the suggestion came with great force to my mind that the prayer of faith would save the sick [cf. James 5:15]. I felt that we could not lose him. So I shut myself up in my room and determined if possible to prevail with God to raise him up to live. Here I continued until with merest shade of difference I could see and feel the same impression that he should not die. But after all, that exceedingly thin veil which covered my vision made me to hesitate to publish as a fact that he would recover, and sure enough, he soon died. I then saw that none of these cases were restored by /95/ faith. The first three cases were intuitively reflected upon my mind as a coming fact. The last case was purely strong desire prompting imagination. This fact has always been of great benefit in after life as a gauge by which to test strong impressions and to distinguish between faith, fancy, and intuition.

Still bent on compromising [i.e., covenanting] with God if I could, I determined to live a devoted life. I would pay up to my ability, and even nearly emptied my pockets to pay [the] minister's salary, and lived on roast potatoes in my hall that I might save all I could, and felt I was buying my time of God at a very cheap rate if by these means I could avoid that dreadful voice of woe if I preached not the gospel [cf. I Corinthians 9:16].

Two young men came to my apartments, and we three bound ourselves to do all we could for the salvation of the world. We after[wards]

---

[123] JGT does not use the word "prophecy" but records, "While I was praying with her, as in the other cases, the impression came that she would recover. It came this time in such power that it was with difficulty that I could repress the utterance of it" (76).

got together in my room and there held our special prayer meetings for a revival of God's work. One night there was a gathering in the next room of a band of music for the purpose of practicing. We would pray round and round till we got our answer. On this night we first prayed God to put out that music, and soon all stopped and we heard them pass downstairs. We then continued our prayers till each one of us received the answer that God would revive His work and save the place. The next day we learned numbers of the music band were awakened and were enquiring the way of salvation. Soon after, our minister commenced a series of meetings, and the result was the conversion of two hundred souls.

I now had my hands and heart full in laboring in prayer meetings and in personal effort, and could almost feel that I should not have to preach after all if I would only be faithful as a private laborer in the church and among the people.

[There was] one gentleman /96/ with whom I had boarded before I went into bachelor hall, and who was an infidel and Sabbath breaker, and for whom I had felt great concern and desire for his salvation. [I] had tried to win him to Christ by recommending to him the subject of religion, but still he remained without it. I now felt convicted that I had not been sufficiently earnest, and now resolved to do my whole duty at all hazards. He came into my room one day, and I took him by the hand, saying, "I have tried to recommend religion to you by my life and gentleness. But I see and feel I have never done my duty as I ought, and now I will never let go of your hand nor let you go till you either repulse me or give your heart to God."

Then with emotion he said, "The last obstacle is now removed. I was a disbeliever in religion till I became acquainted with you. I have watched you and could find but one fault, and that was that if you really felt friendly towards me as you seemed to, I could not see how you could believe my soul to be in danger and not compel me to seek religion. But this remains the last obstacle and now," said he, and with tears, "take me to some of your prayer meetings."

Another gentleman [was] a good friend and acquaintance with whom I had labored frequently to bring him to Christ, and who with his wife remained impenitent. I resolved to be in earnest and do my duty to him faithfully. So I sent word to him and his lady that I should visit them at a certain time. So as not to take them unawares, I sent word that my errand would be to talk to them upon the subject of their own salvation.

When the time arrived I went to the house and found it closed against me, and to appearance they were /97/ both gone from home.

Again I appointed a time and again went to the house and found it as before shut against me.

After this he came to my room. I stepped to the door and locked it, saying to him as I took his hand, "Now, Lyman, I will never let you leave this room till you promise to seek salvation, or utterly refuse me." To which he answered, "I appreciate your motives, but if it has come to this, I must tell you distinctly, I shall not make any such promise."

A strong impression came upon me, and I uttered it. "Very well, Lyman, God will now come to you in judgments."

Shortly after I was called in great haste to go to his house and see his poor dying wife, the violence of whose disease ended in mortification. She was in the extreme agony of passing the severest point in that dreadful disease.[124] I reached the door-yard and saw the groups of neighbors who were talking in a low tone and whose very appearance indicated that they were deeply absorbed in distressing thoughts of some fearful subject.

I passed them and approached the door and opened it into the room. There sat others in melancholy mood who in low and measured whispers emitted the impression that some scene of sorrow ruled their hearts, while now and then the sound of agony was heard through the closed doors and from the room of the sufferer. And now the door opened between me and the dying lady. Our eyes met. The eyes flashed, and with a groan never to be forgotten she cried out, "Oh, why did you not come before?"

To which I answered, "I have tried, but you closed your doors against me."

"Well then, pray for me now."

I knelt down and tried, but in vain; the heavens appeared as brass and the earth as iron,[125] /98/ and I was obliged to give up without an answer from God. She then called upon her attendants to remove her to another room, which they did by lifting her, cot and all, and when they had set her down she raised her mortifying arms towards heaven and uttered the mournful cry, "Oh, God, for a few hours to get ready for this awful change." But no; her arms fell in death, and she ceased to breathe.

---

[124] JGT: "Shortly after this I was called to go to his house to see his dying wife. The violence of her disease ended in mortification while she was yet living, and had now reached its crisis" (79). Redfield uses "mortification" in the now-rare sense of the death or decay of body tissue, as in gangrene.

[125] Cf. Lev. 26:19, "And I will break the pride of your power; and I will make your heaven as iron, and your earth as brass" (KJV).

I then approached her distracted husband and asked, "Lyman, will you now yield to God?" to which he answered, "I cannot now as well as I could before."

"Then," said I, "God will come again." And in a very few days one of his children was called to pass away suddenly, and again I was called to visit the house of mourning. There stood the father, convulsed with grief at the loss of his little one. I went immediately to him and, taking him by the hand asked, "Lyman, has God done enough, and will you now yield?" To which he answered as before.

"Well, then," said I, "God will come once more." In a few days I was called to visit him, who to all appearance was passing into the cold waters of Jordan. This time he professed to have stopped the controversy and [have] given his heart to God. But to my mind, eternity alone will clear up all doubts as to the final results.[126]

Occasionally I would go out to assist in a protracted meeting, resolved to pay my own way and thus avoid the prejudices which might arise against me should I receive anything for my services. The first place to which I went, myself and the preacher in charge visited from house to house. While in the house of one man who was an infidel, but whose wife was a professor of religion, I attempted to persuade this man to commence a life of prayer. His response /99/ was, "Go on, Sir, and attend to your business, for which you undoubtedly receive a good salary, and this is your trade."

"My dear sir," said I, "I do not ask or expect one penny for all my efforts, but it is a bill of expense to me every day I am thus engaged."

"O," said he, "you need not tell me that, for I am sure you would not thus spend your time without pay."

"Sir," said the minister, "I positively know that Bro. R. neither asks nor gets anything."

"Well," said the infidel, "if that is so, he gives away his time so that he may have the privilege of telling [about] it."

But do what I could, sacrifice as I might, there was the dread nightmare of duty hanging over me. All I could do [could] not stop the clamor of that voice ringing in my ears to "go and preach the gospel to every creature." But I deeply felt, "If I die, I must, for it is now entirely out of my power to go out and preach the gospel," and that dreadful fear [remained] that Satan might send on that woman to torment my life out of me and cause disaster to the cause of Christ. "No, no; I must give up all hope and die with my duty undone."

---

[126] JGT ends chapter 11 at this point (page 80) and begins chapter 12 (81).

XI. New York City: "Unearthly power lifted me"

Chapter [9]

In this mood of mind [I found] the hand of disease was again laid heavily upon me. To appearance I was fast going with consumption [i.e., tuberculosis], which resisted all remedies which I used. I now had but one forlorn hope, and that was if I could spend the winter in the South, I might possibly protract my life till the succeeding fall. I had my medicines put up, and with a very limited purse started for N. York, by which route I meant to make a southern tour.

But in New York I found a friend[127] who insisted that I should stay in the city, and he /100/ would keep my room for the winter at as mild and even a temperature as I would have in a Southern climate. So I concluded to run the risk and stay. But I now began to waste away very fast [with] regular hecticks and [a] hoarse cough.[128] Very much emaciated, [I was] obliged to take my bed usually twice a day.

The house where I was staying was opposite a large M.E. Church [building] which had a large cemetery within the enclosure for the use of the public at a small cost.[129] The dead were deposited there every

---

[127] JGT: "A few remedies that he still thought of using were packed with his clothing and books, and with a limited purse, he started for New York city to take a steamer for the South. On arriving at the city, and while waiting for the day of the steamer's departure, he met an old friend" (81).

[128] JGT: "Here he wasted fast with hectic and cough" (81). "Hectic" in this context is a noun meaning a flush or fever. A person with fever associated with consumption (tuberculosis) was sometimes called "a hectic" (*World Book Dictionary*). Redfield is saying, in other words, that he was often feverish.

[129] JGT: "His room was opposite a Methodist Episcopal church, with a public cemetery and vault in the rear." At this time New York City consisted of Manhattan only. The Methodist Episcopal Church which comes closest to this description would seem to be the Bedford Street Church, whose building was located at the corner of Bedford and Morton streets on the West Side. Contemporary maps show a cemetery on Morton Street, less than a block away (Paul E. Cohen and Robert T. Augustyn, *Manhattan in Maps, 1527–1995* [New York: Rizzoli, 1997], 116, 119). This may have been the church, though the membership numbers Redfield mentions later are not entirely consistent with the numbers reported in the *Minutes* (assuming Redfield was there in 1840–41; it is unclear, however, just how long Redfield participated in this church); the church in question may therefore have been the Eighteenth Street Church. (See below; cf. JGT, 81, 85, 102–3.)

The Bedford Street M.E. Church reported 750 members in 1840 and 800 in

day, often as many as two and three a day. Every funeral was to me like my own funeral knell, warning me of my approaching doom.

I would on a fine Sabbath bundle up and cross over to the church. But I would not give in my church letter, for that stated that I held a local preacher's license, and I was afraid of being called upon to preach.

But now my disease was so rapidly gaining upon me that I was sure in all reason that I should never live to see another summer. Occasionally I would cast my eye upon my hands and say to myself, "This poor body must be turning away to dust before these eyes shall greet another spring." Now I was left a prey to the goadings of conscience. The upbraidings of neglected duty stood like ghosts to confront me, and with a thousand stings to thorn my guilty conscience. [I asked myself,] "What can I do to soften the terrible punishment, or appease that God who has borne with me so long?"

Had I [had] voice to give vent to my pent-up agony, I could have made the town vocal with the note of anguish which was now filling my poor tormented heart. "I never shall be able to preach, for I am too far gone with consumption for that, and to die I cannot, I dare not," and in the bitterness of my soul I cried to God, "What shall [I] do? Wilt Thou not look with pity on my poor helpless state?" Such [was] my distress that the cold /101/ sweat would break out, and I was compelled to have a stove kept red hot to overcome my chilling.

Finally I thought, "God has raised me up from the jaws of death four times before this by my promising that I would go and preach the gospel," and I resolved to try the power of prayer once more. I went upon my knees and, weak as I was, I pled with God for my life. Long

---

1841 and was at this time the second largest M.E. congregation in New York City. Allen Street (Phoebe Palmer's church) was largest, with 1012 members in 1841, though by 1844 Bedford Street, with over 1100 members, was largest (*Minutes,* Methodist Episcopal Church, 1840–45).

On balance, it seems more likely that the church in question was Eighteenth Street (which was formed from the Bedford Street Church in 1828). Redfield later mentions James Youngs, who was the preacher at Eighteenth Street in 1840–42 (as noted below). The Eighteenth Street Church's membership, according to the *Minutes,* was 452 in 1840, 604 in 1841, 752 in 1842, 1003 in 1843, and 851 in 1844—numbers which more nearly correspond with Redfield's account than do the statistics for Bedford Street I have not however been able to find evidence that there was a cemetery in the vicinity of the Eighteenth Street Church location. (See *Inventory of the Church Archives of New York City – The Methodist Church* [New York: Historical Records Survey, Work Projects Administration, December, 1940], 65.)

days and many nights alone I wept before the mercy seat when no eye or ear but God's could witness my state of heart, broken fears, and anguish.

I now made my vows again. I said, "Who knows but that the Lord will pity my weakness and hear me once more?" I continued by the side of my bed almost all of one night, weeping, pleading and promising to go and preach if God would only spare my life. It might have been two or three o'clock in the morning when the answer came, as clear and distinct as if it had been spoken [audibly] to me: "You may live while you preach, but no longer." And it is this sentence which has kept me moving ever since amid losses, crosses, misunderstandings, oppositions, persecutions, and that too from the very quarter [from which] I had hoped to have received aid and comfort. And without something like this, I believe my timid heart would often have run from duty and tried to pacify my conscience with the excuse that others had hedged up my way and I had a right to retire. Yes, this single sentence has kept me moving for more than twenty years, and at my own cost, mostly to toil hard, meet opposition, and still hold my tongue and then let God who sent me settle up all wrongs in the final day of reckoning.

It is true that in many instances, without my desire or request, churches have paid my traveling expenses, and sometimes much more. But it is equally true that I have been compelled to pay /102/ $25 to $75 or more in a single winter's tour and never received the first dollar. But that was all right, for I neither asked nor expected it. And I have worked hard, early and late, through the summer to get the means to pay expenses for the coming winter campaign.[130]

Sometimes I have been called of God, as I believe, to pack up and go to some place and yet had not the first dollar to go with. I would then run to some of those indebted to me[131] and try to collect enough for the journey, and that too would fail. Still the voice came to me, "Pack and go," and on starting with nothing I found at every point where I expected to pay [that my needs were] provided for.

I did believe that God called me by an extraordinary call to pursue an extraordinary course of life, and that I must be careful to avoid the usual prejudices of the people who believe preaching in all cases to be a trade. This induced me to go free of charge. But in this I found myself mistaken [i.e., that he could avoid such prejudices or expectations]. I

[130] In these retrospective comments Redfield provides some insight into his normal pattern of operation during his years of continuous revival ministry: Earning money during the summer to provide funds for his "winter campaign."

[131] Perhaps from his medical practice or portraiture.

then tried to make myself so well acquainted with medicine that I could win men to Christ by kindness while they were in distress, as [I] gave away [free of charge the services of] my [medical] practice while I was preaching. God and my own soul only know how faithfully I have tried by all means to find some way to the hearts of men, and then to avail myself of the advantage [of this] to bring them to Jesus.

But I have found this also to fail of giving satisfaction as to the rectitude of my motives. One of the objects I have in leaving this book behind me is that some honest hearts who may hear only one side of my history may have something by which to make a more correct estimate of my labors and motives, and not from prejudice cast away without examination the claims of earnest Christianity. For as an honest man, I do now feel that with Paul I can say, "I fought a good fight," and there is certainly a crown laid /103/ up for me, and God, even my God, has given me assurances that I have a title to an inheritance. But if this honest avowal of my motives, cause, and faith fails to abate or moderate the hostility against me, I shall continue as long as life lasts to do the best I can to plant and perpetuate this kind of religion, for I know it is true and of God, for that sentence still hangs over me, "You may live while you preach, but no longer." Whoever reads this I would assure that the old resolve made more than twenty years ago[132] is yet fresh with me, and unless I am convinced of error I shall certainly preach, press [on,] and try to live for God in the way I have just so long as I can, and stop only when I must.[133]

Chapter [10]

I said in the last chapter that I obtained the witness that I might live while I preached, but no longer. Well, on the Friday night after I re-

---

[132] Since there are no dates in the manuscript up to this point (other than Redfield's birthdate, 1810), this reference is important for establishing chronology. The manuscript apparently was written about 1862, so his "resolve" to obey God (apparently while he was in New York City) would have come about 1841. A later reference to 1841 (see below) confirms this.

[133] JGT omits this whole retrospective section (the last four lines of manuscript page 101, all of page 102, and almost half of 103), beginning "It is true that." He continues on with the narrative without a chapter break. Terrill (or possibly someone else) has written across the face of page 102, perpendicular to and across Redfield's script, "Dissertation on the nature of his call," and similarly across the top part of page 103, "On the nature of his Call." This is a very important section for understanding Redfield's ministry and how he understood his call.

ceived the promise of life, I was able by bundling up well to cross the street and attend the love feast. I thought to give in my letter. I had been seated but a short time when the minister[134] came to me and asked me, as a stranger, "Have you not got a preacher's license?" I told him I had. "Well," said he, "you must preach in this church next Sunday morning."[135]

Thus soon was my promise to preach put to the test. My whole being so shrank, mostly from the consciousness of inability, that I pled with him to excuse me for this time.

"No, no, I cannot do that," [he said].

Here now I was in trouble enough. I thought I could not preach at all. Then the heart-distressing thought [came] that the cause of my family troubles might turn up, as I knew that some of her relatives resided in the city—then who knows what kind of capital will be made out of my calamity. ~~I was then sorry that~~ [sic] What surmises [might be] set afloat, and then the cause of God will suffer. I might indeed sue for a bill [of divorce], but in my weak and /104/ nervous state I could not bear the course of litigation and [to] be compelled at a cost I could not bear to bring on witnesses and to bring to light facts which would exhibit to the public matters that I preferred to bear in silence, and let the Judge of all the Earth in due time make the final settlement.

But then again there was the promise I made: If God would spare my life, I would go. Besides which, when the answer came from my Heavenly Father, "You may live while you preach, but no longer," there was instantly presented to my view an open coffin and the word kept ringing in my ears, "You can preach or go into that," and the sight of that coffin was perceptible to me for more than two months.[136]

"Well Lord," said I, "I will go and try." But I secretly hoped that I should make so bad a failure in the trial that I should never be called upon again; then I might feel free to desist from any farther ~~connexion with this subject of duty~~ effort to preach.[137] But I had yet to learn that the calling of God was without repentance [cf. Romans 11:29].

Saturday morning came. The awful thought rushed upon me that I

---

[134] The Eighteenth Street preacher in 1840–41 was James Youngs. The preacher assigned to Bedford Street was Phineas Rice, with Noah Bigelow, a supernumerary preacher, as supply assistant. (*Minutes,* New York Conference).

[135] Probably the pastor already had some awareness of Redfield by this time.

[136] JGT condenses this passage, omitting the reference to divorce and the vision of the open coffin.

[137] "Effort to preach" is written in above the crossed-through phrase, in Redfield's hand.

must preach in that large church tomorrow at 10 o'clock, and a tremor would seize me and then the cold sweat break out so that I had to sit on a hot stove to keep warm.

Ten o'clock of Saturday came. In twenty-four hours I must try to preach. But my shrinking heart cried out in grief and agony, "Oh God, I cannot, and why dost Thou thus pursue me?" And thus hour after hour passed and I was on the rack.[138]

At last Saturday night came. I have often thought [that at such times] I would approximate the state of the criminal to be executed the next day and hour. The very hours were given tongues to scourge his poor troubled spirit.

I went to bed, but not to sleep. As I would occasionally begin to lose myself in a dream it would almost be screamed in my ear, "Preach tomorrow!" Then I would spring [up] and the cold sweat would again start. Thus through that /105/ long, long tedious night did I pass in mental suffering. As daylight first entered my room, "Soon you must preach" like a ghost rung in my ears again, and there I lay trembling and sweating.

Soon the first footfalls of the passers-by in the early morning shocked me again. Sunrise succeeded. I could have shrieked with agony if that could have given me relief. Soon the Sabbath school bell emitted its terrible warning that I must preach.

Church bells in due time rang all over the city. The people were gathering in flocks, and our large church was evidently receiving a very large congregation. Everything seemed conspiring to make me as miserable as I could well bear.

Finally the fatal hour came, and I must walk over to the church. I started, but my bursting [heart] cried, "O God, I cannot. O, do help me in this, my hour of distress. I cannot preach." But the same voice echoed in my ear, "Live while you preach, but no longer," and there is my coffin by my side, and the prolonged echo of the same voice would utter, "Preach or go into that coffin."

I walked up into the pulpit and in my confusion mistook my hat for a spittoon. The moment of moments had come, and I stood up to read a hymn. But so weak and exhausted [was I] that I could only stand tottering and holding on upon the top of the pulpit. The hymnbook I had not

---

[138] This recurring theme in Redfield, together with other references, suggests that he was by nature somewhat timid and introverted, but that he had an unusual charism and boldness in preaching that quite contrasted with his demeanor otherwise. This seems to lie behind the great anguish he often felt before preaching.

power to hold up in my hands, nor could I stand on my feet while the congregation sang.[139] I arose and gave out my text, and then it seemed that some unearthly power seized me and held me up, and then gave me volume of voice and sustained me through to the end of my talk.

I concluded and sat down, congratulating myself that this specimen of my preaching would put an end to any more invitations. But to my surprise and sorrow, the preacher /106/ turned to me and said, "You must preach again on such an evening," naming it. Then all my troubles returned, and I begged and pled with him to excuse me for this once. But he was inflexible. Preach I must or, he said, he should lay his commands upon me. And but for just such a man to press me to it, I think I should have given up all idea of preaching and have gone down to the grave.[140]

When ~~Saturday~~ Friday night came round, he told me I must preach on Sunday night.[141] I was on the rack again all day Saturday, and at night so intense were my sufferings that I could not go to rest. But I prayed before God that if it was His will that I should preach, He would give me a text and then the subject, and then promise to go with me in the power of the Spirit. I felt there was no use of my going, and I would not, unless God should go with me.

About two o'clock on Sunday morning the answer came. But with it another of my strange revelations.[142] The substance was this: "Here is your text, and this your subject, and I will go with you in awful power. But you must open the services by announcing to the congregation that that Sunday night will be ~~one of~~ the greatest for a display of God's power that they ever saw, and further, that the probation of one soul

---

[139] JGT omits the reference to the coffin in the previous paragraph, and relates Redfield's beginning to preach as follows: "He reached the pulpit, in great distraction of mind, and made some mortifying blunders. He arose to give out a hymn, but was too weak to hold up the book. He clung to the desk to keep from falling, and had to sit while the congregation sang. The prayer over, the lesson read, and another hymn sung, he arose to announced his text" (84). JGT omits the remark about the spittoon, including it in Redfield's "mortifying blunders"!

[140] JGT: "Had it not been for falling into the hands of such a man, it is quite probable that the church would never have been stirred by the mighty eloquence of Dr. Redfield" (84).

[141] JGT: "On Friday evening, he was again at church. The minister said to him, 'You must preach Sunday night'" (84). Since the preacher had earlier, on Sunday, specified the evening Redfield was to preach, the implication seems to be that he had first told Redfield he was to preach on Saturday (or perhaps Friday) night, but then changed it to Sunday night.

[142] JGT changes "revelations" to "impressions" (84).

ends on this night, so that it is salvation now or never.

I well knew that no one could sympathize with me in this seemingly hazardous presumption. [I reasoned,] "In all probability it will only shock the church and prove a failure, and as such could only [bring] disaster to the cause of Christ." I said, "O Lord, I cannot do that!" Immediately I was thrown into distress and darkness about my text and subject and even my own relation with God. This I could not endure, so I pled with God to show me /107/ what He would have me do. I would yield my objections and plead for light, and the answer would be renewed and the same impression found home again.

Again I would revolt at so daring a stroke of presumption. But [this would be] followed by the same darkness and distress. I could see no light, feel no comfort, nor witness a single smile from my Heavenly Father. Only when I would leave the results with God and promise to obey the instructions [did I sense God's presence].

When Sunday morning service came I sat in the congregation. Dr. [Samuel] Luckey was about to preach.[143] When the congregation arose to sing, the thought came home to my heart, "Service has begun, and when it closes this night, the doom of one soul in this house will be fixed forever." I was compelled to sit down and hold my mouth to keep from wailing aloud and sending confusion all over the house. I shook with emotion and held my mouth with my hands. Again the manifest impropriety of venturing a prediction made me to shrink from the purpose, and thus I continued to alternate between light and darkness as I welcomed or repelled the impression, and thus [I] spent the day.

In the afternoon Dr. P. preached[144] and I was to be called upon in

---

[143] JGT: "The noted Dr. Luckey preached" (85). Samuel Luckey (1791–1869) was presiding elder of the district at this time. An article about him in Bishop Matthew Simpson's *Cyclopædia of Methodism* notes that he had been principal of Genesee Wesleyan Seminary in Lima, New York (1832–36) and was elected editor of *The Christian Advocate and Journal* in 1836 (Simpson, *COM,* 221). He spent his later years in Rochester, New York, where he had contact with B. T. Roberts. Luckey served as editor of the *Christian Advocate* from 1836 to 1840, and then as presiding elder of the New York District, 1840–41, and as pastor at Duane Street, New York City, 1841–42 (*Minutes,* New York Conference). Simpson's *Cyclopædia* described him as "a man of more than ordinary power of intellect, [who] was thoroughly acquainted with the history and economy of the church" (553). He was also the uncle of Joseph McCreery, a Methodist preacher and colleague of B. T. Roberts who with Roberts and others was a key figure in the "Nazarite" controversy.

[144] Possibly Dr. George Peck, at the time editor of the Methodism *Quarterly Review* and a member of the New York District (*Minutes,* New York Confer-

the evening.[145] At the appointed hour I went over to the church. The house, a very large one, was densely packed, gallery and all, and all standing room occupied, besides vestibule and all.[146] I made up my mind, "I will venture it, and leave God to take care of the results."

With a firm, clear voice I said, "You may prepare for the greatest display of God's power that you ever witnessed. And besides, there is one soul here tonight whose probation ends this night. With that soul it is salvation this night or never. I may not be able to prove it true, /108/ but that soul will tell me in the judgment that this Sunday night 1841 was the last of its probation."[147]

As soon as I gave utterance to this message, I was perfectly relieved. But the church was shocked, and so great were their fears that from their own confession I believe they prayed that God would overrule my presumption and arrest any evil which might otherwise grow out of it.

I now took my text. Then an unearthly power so lifted me up that it seemed to me that my feet, only, touched the earth but my whole head, heart, and body were above the skies and in heaven. The unearthly thrills of power which I then felt I never can describe. I can only compare it to a sense of power put into my hand for that hour which could shake a world or sway an influence that would move a nation.

I had not finished my preaching when, without an invitation, the people arose and rushed up to the altar, screaming for mercy. All within and around the altar was crowded. When there was no more room, the preacher asked all in the house who desired religion to arise. It was judged that five hundred arose for prayer, and the number soon converted justified this estimate. That night has been called "the great night" ever since.

About a month after this an old [class] leader [came] and asked me

---

ence, 1840). If Luckey preached in the morning and Peck in the afternoon, it is likely that this weekend was a district quarterly meeting.

145 JGT adds, "These great preachers occupying the same pulpit, both the same day, did not make his [Redfield's] cross lighter" (85). JGT does not identify "Dr. P."

146 This also suggests that the occasion was the quarterly conference, which could well have been held in either the Eighteenth Street or the Bedford Street Church.

147 This is only the second date so far in Redfield's manuscript, and thus is important for establishing chronology. Apparently it was late winter or early spring, 1841, before the end of the conference year. The New York Conference met on May 19, 1841 (*Minutes,* New York Conference); presumably this occasion was earlier than that.

if I remembered to have made the statement on "the great night" that one of the souls present finished its probation then. I told him I did.

"Well," said he, "one lady who was converted that night and joined my class told me that six weeks previously she dreamed three times in one night that her probation would end in just six weeks. The six weeks ended that night, but she was happily converted."[148]

XII. "Resolved to make a business of seeking holiness"

/109/ Chapter [11]

I was now called upon to preach in different churches in the city, and as my health began to return rapidly, I was to all appearance getting well. I resolved to use it all for the glory of God. But the consciousness of my utter unworthiness to occupy so responsible a place, and more than all the constant dread I had that [that] evil-disposed persons might make a bad use of what little they might know, or rather the much they did not know, of my misfortune, and the reproach that the cause of Christ might suffer, weighed me down to the dust.

When questioned concerning my former life I frankly told the whole story, at least as much as I thought would meet their curiosity. But I soon learned that a history once out was likely to grow into untruthful details. I made up my mind that this was to be my sore, and the best way for me was to endure it in silence and alone.[149] The need of

---

148 JGT ends chapter 12 here and begins chapter 13 (which is less than two pages). However he adds a brief concluding paragraph: "Though this incident is given by Mr. Redfield himself in this connection, it is not designed to teach that probation ends with conversion. He was the furtherest [sic] from teaching any such doctrine, as his experience herein would show. The account is related because of the remarkable coincidence in the events described" (86–87).

149 JGT: "But he soon learned that a story once out was likely to grow into untruthful details. At last he came to the conclusion that this was to be his 'thorn', and his best way was to bear it in silence and alone" (89). Terrill in this brief chapter first of all gives his own summary, writing, "The great awakening with which the last chapter concluded continued without interruption for fourteen months" (presumably from early 1841 through mid-1842). He writes, "Persons under conviction would sometimes fly from the house to avoid yielding to Christ, and afterwards be found lying upon the walks, helpless. At first, the policemen would take them to the station house, and lay them side and side upon the floor, and watch them until they 'came to.'" But later, when "it was discovered that such persons were neither harmed nor harmful, the officers ceased to take them to the station, but watched them where they fell, until they 'came to' and were able to take care for themselves" (88). This narrative does

grace which I knew I did not possess [distressed me]. I felt I must have [the grace of holiness] to fit me for the task which lay before me, and I looked forward once more to the acquisition of the blessing of holiness to fit me for my labors and raise [me] from sinking beneath my affliction.

I had my perverted views of what constituted that state of grace, and the way to obtain [it] was equally [as] dark to me as was the state of holiness itself. But as well as I knew how, I resolved to set about seeking it.[150] I had enquired of a number of persons who professed to know something of the matter what I must do to get possession of so desirable a state of grace. But their instructions did not in the least help me out of my difficulty or throw any light on what course I should pursue to gain the desired end. All I had done furnished me with no evidence whatever that I was making any appreciable advance toward it.

/110/ I resolved to make a business of seeking holiness, and of desperation in the effort. I had long before this time sought earnestly by fasting, prayer, and watch-nights to secure this coveted state of holiness. Thus I continued night and day, till I became utterly exhausted by the efforts. I had not yet found out the grand end to be secured to be nothing more nor less than perfect submission to and harmony with the will of God. I had yet to learn that the preparation of heart to receive [it] was to get the consent and choice of my own will that God's will should be done, and that whatever else I might do, a deficiency here could defeat my effort.

I had now fairly entered the gospel field.[151] This long-neglected and much dreaded duty I had begun, and [I had resolved] to make of it a life business, and now I began with a singleness of purpose to seek the precious pearl. Yet, fearful that one so utterly unworthy might be

---

not occur in Redfield's manuscript. Terrill then adds, "Singularly, this timid, shrinking man, who dreaded the responsibilities of the Christian ministry so much, was providentially thrown into the great metropolis of the nation to commence his work; where the people, gathered in such masses, made the responsibility so much the greater" (88). Presumably these details came from Terrill's conversations with Redfield or others.

[150] JGT begins his chapter 14 at this point, devoting it to Redfield's "experience in the matter of seeking holiness." He quotes Redfield as follows: "I now began to see and feel my need of entire sanctification. I had perverted views of what constituted that state of grace, and of the way to seek it, but I resolved to set about seeking it as best I knew" (90). At this point in the manuscript Terrill (or possibly someone else) has written, apparently in pencil, in very large script over the face Redfield's writing, the word "Experience."

[151] Presumably the year is 1842 or 1843.

denied so great a boon, I longed to lay my heart open to someone who could instruct me so that I could comprehend the thing and the means to secure it—not knowing that this state can no more be comprehended before it is attained than can justification be comprehended by the infidel.[152]

I at length heard of a good old gentleman who had enjoyed this blessing for more than forty years and that he was coming, as was usual with him, to visit his children and would be likely to stop at the house where I was then boarding. In due time he came. I took him to my room and closed the door, and then with a keen sense of my own unworthiness I modestly asked him if he thought God was willing that such an unworthy person as myself should possess so great a blessing as perfect love. The enemy [was] suggesting all the time the probability that he would say to me, "You are too young and presumptuous to think of that great and exalted state yet."

But no, with deep and tender emotions the good old father answered, "Why, bless you, dear heart. Why yes, the /111/ Lord wants you to be holy." The glow of gratitude which I felt towards the good man, to think he barely thought God was willing to indulge me with the gift of so great a grace, I can never describe.

From this I took fresh courage and I asked him, "Can you tell me how I can get possession of it?" to which he answered, "By faith." But he might as well have answered in Hebrew, for I understood not the meaning. I dreaded deception and I could not suppose it possible that a state of grace that I had set so high an estimate upon could be secured short of a corresponding valuable price or gift instead of a single cheap and worthless act of ~~faith~~ believing.[153]

If he had told me to do some great thing, or to live very faithful and expect to grow up into it by a long and tedious process, I could have thought his instruction to be more rational. I remembered the apparent soul-tearing process which I witnessed in a brother who was seeking this blessing at the camp meeting where I was converted, and I

---

[152] At this very time Phoebe Palmer was conducting her Tuesday Meetings for the Promotion of Holiness at her home near the Allen Street M.E. Church, about a mile and a half away, as Redfield soon discovered. Palmer had taken over the leadership of the Tuesday Meeting from her sister in 1840. Up to this point Redfield apparently did not yet know of her ministry. Later he had some correspondence with her. Palmer's first and very influential book, *The Way of Holiness,* was published in 1843, and the articles on which it was based began to appear in the *Christian Advocate and Journal* in late 1842. See White, *Beauty of Holiness,* xx; Oden, *Phoebe Palmer*, 11.

[153] JGT adds, "[So faith appeared to him then.—Editor]" (91).

thought that must be the true way to get so great a blessing. But I had serious doubts about my constitution being able to endure the agony necessary to obtain the blessing.

I was conversing with a brother one day upon the subject while others were standing by when one asked me, "Why don't you go across town in R. St. [Rivington Street] where they have meetings every week at the house of Dr. P. [Palmer]? They can tell you how to find the blessing." Then an elderly brother who likewise stood by and in whose piety I had great confidence, but who though he believed in that state of grace and had been seeking it about twenty-six years without success, said to me, aside from the others, "You must be very careful about having anything to do with Dr. P.'s people across town, for they will tell you to believe that you already have the blessing. Besides this, many people don't believe them to be quite so pious as they pretend, after all. They put on sanctimonious airs and dress in uniform and make great pretensions."

XIII. Phoebe and Walter Palmer: "I feared them"

From that moment I so greatly feared /112/ them that I would no sooner have received instruction from them than I would from a Mahometan [sic]. Indeed, I think I should have avoided them at all hazards if about to meet them in the streets.

I remembered once when [I was] a little boy to have heard Dr. [Willbur] Fisk answer the question of my mother as to how and what she should believe. "Believe," said he, "that you have it, and you have it." I did not then see the difference between "believe that you are receiving it, and that will bring it," or "believe you have already received it, and that will make it that you have received it." All this was utterly and alike opposed to my reason, and I could as readily have endorsed Mohammedanism as holiness secured by these irrational means.

I now thought I could see very clearly through the vagaries of this people [i.e., the Palmer circle]. Their holiness consisted in giving up all concern about the matter and then, by imagining that the end was gained, and [consequently experiencing] the cessation of this struggle, [this] would leave them quiet from all further struggle or concern in the matter. This quiet they would call the witness of the blessing of holiness. Of course I [had] abandoned all hope or effort to seek the blessing in the old long and hard way which I had so long pursued, and without success. Now I went to work with all my might, hoping that if my body could endure the agony through which I expected to pass, I might by this desperation gain the land of Beulah.

Hearing there was to be a camp meeting in the bounds of an adjoining conference, I determined to go as a stranger, and thus avoid being seen by any of my brethren of the church to which I belonged, for I knew they had confidence in my piety. I feared should they see me in great agony seeking the blessing of holiness, they might not know what to make of it and possibly might conclude that I had been committing some grievous sin, and now God had overtaken me, and I not being able to explain to their satisfaction, they would feel grieved, and I should be the cause of great injury /113/ to the cause of Christ.

But when I arrived on the campground, I was sorry to find a number of the very brethren there whom I had wished to avoid from my own church. "Well," thought I, "it is my privilege and duty to be holy, to fit me for the great work I have to do. So I shall attend to that and leave God to take care that His cause is not injured by other people's mistakes while I am doing my duty."

I was called upon to preach. But having come for the purpose of seeking the blessing of holiness, I meant to make that my business.[154] But when in good earnest I began to rein up my mind for the struggle, the devil became in earnest too and induced me to begin to inspect the external evidences of other people's piety, and it did seem to me that I never so saw the corrupt state of the church. One person's mode of dress was trim, and that was [to me] evidence of pride; another was careless, and that was equal evidence of pride of their humility.[155] I really felt grieved at such sad evidence of decline, and my tears flowed in abundance.

Then I left the congregation to walk by myself alone and sigh over this declension. But soon I met the good old man who had given me such comfort in saying that he thought God was willing I should possess the great blessing. I began telling him how I had come to that meeting to seek holiness, but that such evidences of decline in the church made me feel so bad that I could not attend to it with any hope of success.

The good old father saw this to be a device of the enemy to divert my attention and effort from the great purpose, and with one word set

---

[154] JGT: "I was called upon to preach, but as I had come to seek the blessing of holiness, and to make that my business, I declined" (93). By this time Redfield, now about thirty-two, was becoming known in Methodist circles as a revivalist.

[155] JGT: "One person's mode of dress was trim, and that to me was evidence of pride; another's was careless, and that indicated pride of his fancied humility" (93). Since Redfield uses "their" rather than "his" or "her," it is not clear whether he was referring to the dress of men or of women, or both.

me right.[156] "I," said he, "was once troubled as you are now, and I got out of it by resolving, 'If everybody else goes to hell, by the grace of God I am going to heaven.'"

This broke the spell, for I saw [it] to be one of the devil's pious frauds to stop me from earnest efforts to gain the /114/ precious prize I was after. I now thought, "If I ever gain the blessing, I must call on my New York brethren to go into a tent and there to pray for me that I might gain the blessing of sanctification, and thus risk any evil accruing through their mistake of my moral state," [and this I did]. We all knelt after I had stated to them my desire for their prayer and my purpose of gaining the blessing of entire sanctification. I had an idea that they would pray for me with all their might and possibly create a wave, so to speak, [upon which] my little barque could come to land.

They began to pray at random for everybody and everything, without touching my case at [all], just as people usually pray when they don't expect to get anything. But I was now compelled to learn that no delegated power could reach my case, and I must go to God, and alone. I while on my knees concluded that I must do my own desperate praying and struggling if I ever got through. Supposing that the successful mode of prayer must be intensely urgent, with the force of will power, I watched my opportunity to break out in vociferous tones. But I could not have uttered a loud word if it would have saved me, for my lips seemed to be sealed. And this taught me it was "not by might or power but by my Spirit, saith the Lord" [Zechariah 4:6].[157] I then turned to look into my own heart to note progress, and was overwhelmed to see nothing but to loathe and abhor. It seemed to me that I had lost all of my religion in trying to get more. The enemy now suggested, "You have lost all in trying to get holiness. You had better give up the struggle, if such is to be the success of your effort." And I, believing it to be a fact, got up and left the tent to mourn over this my last and greatest of calamities.

As I was passing along, I found the good old man again, and [told] him what a disaster I had met with in trying to get holiness, saying, "Don't you think I have done [wrong] /115/ to aspire after such an exalted state of grace? For I know I have lost all my religion in the trial,

---

[156] JGT: "The old gentleman saw this to be a trick of the devil to divert my attention and efforts from the great work, and with a few words he set me right" (93).

[157] A large X occurs here, possibly written by Redfield, or perhaps added later by Terrill (or someone else) to especially mark the preceding sentence. Terrill gives the sentence no special emphasis in his book (94).

and I certainly know I had religion when I left N. York, for I had the witness, and now I know it is all gone."

"Why, bless your dear heart and soul," said this blessed man; "don't you know the Lord is emptying you?" Thus in a word he [again] set me right. I had supposed holiness to be gained by installments, and that when a succession of blessings, combined, had filled my heart about so full, I might call it holiness—first the pardon of sins, then the joys of salvation, and then a succession of indefinite blessings which in the aggregate would make up the sum total of holiness. But now I learned that every blessing I ever had must be emptied out, for God would not fill a vessel with the wine of Canaan while it was near half full of manna.[158] I had now passed the days for relishing manna. My Father had enough of the old corn and wine, and this hereafter was to be my food. But I was seeking the last installment to complete the blessing.

I then asked him, "What shall I do?"

Said he, "You must believe for the blessing."

I went out into the grove alone and into a by-place. While in a waiting mood, and trying to believe, I then saw clearly with my inner eyes the same personage whom I saw just after my conversion, and while I was praying to be made holy.[159] It was the appearance of the Lord Jesus Christ as crucified for me, and a voice seemed to say to me, "All you can do now is to believe in this crucified man Jesus"—for His divinity was hidden from [me]. But the idea of trusting my soul's salvation in a crucified man aroused all my old infidel notions, and I dared not to risk it.[160] That image appeared as distinctly as any person's image had to my outward eye. /116/ [It appeared] at twilight, and but a very few rods distant.

But finally the camp meeting closed, and I was yet without the

---

[158] This seems a strange teaching, that God can sanctify one only after he or she is "emptied out" of every prior blessing (despite the Old Testament reference). The intended point, however, seems to be that a believer cannot receive the blessing of sanctification if he or she is *depending* upon what God has done in the past, rather than coming to God "empty" and receiving the blessing by "naked faith."

[159] JGT: "I went out into the grove alone, and while waiting upon the Lord and trying to believe, I thought I saw Jesus with my inner eye, just as I saw him at the time of my conversion" (95).

[160] JGT: "A voice seemed to say to me, 'All you can do now is to believe in this crucified man, Jesus' (for the time his divinity was hidden from me). But the idea of trusting my soul's salvation on a dead man, aroused all my old infidel notions, and I dared not risk it'" (95).

great blessing. So away I went to another camp meeting which was to be held the next week. Here again I stirred up myself to a desperate effort and so continued till about Wednesday, but without any appreciable success.

Then someone told me that the family from New York [Walter and Phoebe Palmer] were on the ground and had a tent and meetings for the promotion of holiness.[161] This family I feared more than the enemy of all righteousness. But as my success was so poor, I finally thought I would find the tent and take my seat in some corner where if I saw they were pressing error upon the people I could leave them. Strange as it may seem, an impression beset me that they might, without or against my reason or consent, fasten error upon me. So I resolved to be on the alert, and if I saw it coming, avoid it by flight.

I reached the tent and took my seat, as I had purposed. I saw a large number there, among them Presbyterians and I think [people] of other denominations. They were all sitting very composedly while one was reading the Bible. I thought, "Can this be the way to seek holiness? I wonder they don't get down and pray with all their might!" Still, I could not complain of reading the Bible, for that must be right.

After the reading a lady arose whom I guessed to be the very lady of N. York whom I most feared, and subsequently [I] found [her] to be the one. "Now," I thought, "I must be on my guard." But the first words she uttered were, "'I beseech you therefore brethren by the mercies of God that ye present yourselves a living sacrifice.' A living, that is a perpetual sacrifice," said she.

"Well," thought I, "that's Bible, and all right so far."

She then stated the preliminary step to be taken, and that was to be a thorough consecration of ourselves to God. "Very well," said I to myself; "all this I have done over and over again." She then made this entire consecration to appear as a reasonable demand.

/117/ Then [she showed] the reasonableness of believing that God

---

[161] JGT: "One day some one told me that the Palmers from New York were on the ground, and had a tent for the promotion of holiness" (95–96). This likely was the Sing Sing camp meeting held at Sing Sing, New York, on the Hudson River north of New York City, in late August and early September, 1842. According to White, Mrs. Palmer spoke at the Sing Sing camp meeting in 1842 and 1844 but at no New York City area camp meetings in 1843 (*Beauty of Holiness,* 237).
Ellen Stowe (later the wife of B. T. Roberts, who worked closely with Redfield in the 1850s) tells in her diary of attending Phoebe Palmer's meetings at the 1844 Sing Sing camp meeting. Manuscript diary of Ellen Stowe, Sept. 3–6, 1844 (Special Collections, Roberts Wesleyan College Library).

meant what He said, and would do what He had promised, and that our faith must rest mainly on the testimony of God. [She said,] "He has said, 'If I will do this,' and so He will meet me there, and my faith consisted in taking God at His word."[162]

I then saw the way of faith as never before, and I said to myself, "I have tried everything else but faith. I will now go out and make an experiment." So I went out beyond the encampment and stood renewing my consecration, to know that all was thoroughly devoted to God in an everlasting covenant.[163] Then in a moment appeared that same image of Christ crucified. But I saw only His humanity. I seemed to be standing upon the edge of a fathomless pit, and this image of Christ stood upon the opposite brink, so far that it was impossible for me to leap over. The act of faith for me to put in force was in spirit to leap off from this cliff over this bottomless abyss of error and risk that crucified Christ to catch me and rescue me from ruin. I was deeply sensible that if I made the effort and it should fail, I must from that moment bid adieu to all hopes of the world of blessedness and abandon the profession of religion forever.

This brought me to a stand[still]. I saw that everything I hoped, feared, or desired was now—with all to be expected in the world to come, all—all on a single act [was] to be lost or won forever. I was most intensely stirred at the thought of hazarding every hope of heaven on a single throw.[164] Then in substance I uttered this prayer, "O Lord, thou knowest all hearts, and that I want to be and do what I have tried honestly to know, and do all that I could to get right, and that I stand ready to do or suffer anything imposed upon be by which to secure the great blessing of perfect love. I see I have tried everything but this single and apparently inefficient and hopeless act of faith, which looks to my reason more like presumption than it /118/ does like an act that can do anything for me. And now, O God, seeing no other untried act, I shall make the venture. If this fails, on God must rest the responsibility, and if I am lost for believing Christ, I cannot help it. I shall trust to the generosity of God to cover my ignorance and run the venture which seems to my reason only like an act of presumption."[165]

---

[162] JGT puts this as a quote from Palmer: "He has said if I will do thus and so, he will meet me there and then, and faith consists in taking him at his word" (96).

[163] This echoes Phoebe Palmer's language.

[164] JGT: "I was intensely aroused by the thought of hazarding every hope of heaven like that" (97).

[165] JGT omits this sentence. The phrase, "to cover my ignorance" is written in

It now seemed that I opened converse with the Holy Ghost. [I] asked, "How shall I believe, with my head or heart?"

The answer came, "It is with the heart man believeth unto righteousness; and with the mouth confession is made unto salvation" [Romans 10:10].[166]

I now felt that in spirit I did leap off this precipice, and as distinctly as I should if I had in body sprung off. Just in that moment I felt that the man Christ Jesus caught me in His arms and held me up safely, and in that moment I felt that I could risk a world in His hands, for in Him truly "dwelleth the fullness of the Godhead bodily" [cf. Colossians 2:9]. Oh how changed did all nature seem in that awful and glorious moment! Surely, I thought, this must be heaven or like it, for it comes up to my highest ideal of heaven. But I could not remember when I had died.

But in the next moment my enemy suggested, "This is not the blessing of holiness, for you did not lose your strength, nor have you shouted aloud or made any great ado about it. But on the other hand, you do not want to speak aloud at all," for one word aloud would mar the rich spell which held me as captive. I then took my eye of faith off from the Savior to examine this temptation, and in that moment I was set back in the place from where I stood on the far side of the gulf, and there was the image of Christ on His side, as when and where first seen. Thus I stood as vacant as ever.

"Well," said I to myself, /119/ "I did feel all right while believing." Now the success of the first leap emboldened me to try again, and with [even] more daring I made the second leap, and with the same happy results.

But the temptation, "You cannot keep it," drew my eye off from Jesus again, and again was I placed back with the gulf between me and Christ. I sprang off again, but then the tempter said, "No one will believe you." [Thus he] succeeded in robbing me of my witness. And so did I alternate between faith and doubt, joy and sorrow. [But I] learned this fact, that not *for* but *while* believing I could hang upon the atonement and feel the response of God's Spirit assuring me that the work was done.[167]

---

very small script as an insertion above the words "of God," and was apparently intended to be inserted between "God" and "and."

[166] Redfield, Terrill, or someone else has added a superscript X following the word "salvation."

[167] Italics added for clarity. JGT has, "And so did I alternate between faith and doubt, joy and sorrow, until I learned this fact, that it is not for believing, but

So I determined to step off and continue in that act, and when the enemy asked, "How will it be with you tomorrow?" I answered, "I don't know; tomorrow has not yet come."

"Well, how will it be in five minutes?"

"I don't know, nor will I concern myself about it. I believe now and am saved now, one moment at a time." I never try to get but one breath of air at once; that's all I want or need, and when I want another, it is all around me and ready. So I do not need a stock of the joys of salvation for future use but take it, breathe it by a single act of faith just as I have need. A continuous act of faith brings a continuous supply of salvation.[168] Faith to the soul is what breathing is to the body. Now too I learned the philosophy of consecration: It is to make room by emptying out the heart and leaving room for storing salvation.

"Now," said the Spirit, "go and tell Bro. M. what the Lord has done for you."

I went onto the ground and found him and began saying, "Bro. M., I believe . . . ." Then the devil said, "If you tell him, he will say you must be very careful about making great professions, for sanctification is a very great blessing."

He stood gazing at me without saying a word. Then I began again, saying, "Bro. M., I believe—," but fearing he would think I was boasting, I began to qualify [my] saying, but [then] I did not do it. [I said,] "Well, I believe, /120/ if I don't keep it five minutes, that Jesus has sanctified my unworthy heart. Glory to God!"

Said Bro. M., "Now, go and tell my wife."

I gathered strength by the avowal and the confidence he seemed to have that Jesus had really done the work. So away I went to his wife and said, "Sister M., Jesus has given me the great blessing."

She rejoiced and said, "Now go up onto the stand and profess it to all the people."

I did so, which seemed to settle me and establish me in the system of confessing the exact thing done for me, and as a guard against the force of temptation to vacillate in professing the thing as it was.

---

while believing that the work is done. I hang upon the atonement, and realize the response of the Holy Spirit assuring me that the work is done" (98).

[168] JGT modifies this slightly: "'I don't know nor will I concern myself about it; I believe I am saved now.' I now saw the philosophy of faith. I breathe but one breath of air at a time; that is all I need; when I want another, it will be allowed. So I do not need a stock of the joys of salvation for future use, but take it, breathe it, by acts of faith just as I have need. Continuously acting faith brings a continuous supply" (99).

Dr. P. [Palmer] found me and, said he, "Mr. Wesley says that one sanctification is equal to ten conversions, as it will result in that."

I took my cue and resolved, "I will make that trial." Away I went into a tent and at once [began] inviting my brethren to come at once to the blood that cleanses from all sin. "Now claim your privilege," [I said]. We began a meeting in our tent[169] on the subject of personal holiness, and now [it] was the leading feature [of our meetings]. God at once began to work in awful power, and as I have always found since, the making this doctrine the main, the principal feature in our labors did not hinder the work of conversion. For unasked, one or two penitents came in and said, in substance, "I want religion." Said one, "I felt impressed to come to this tent and get it. I passed by other tents and prayer meetings, for I felt that this was the place to come and get religion." In a very few minutes they and others were happily saved of the Lord, and these conversions increased to the end of the camp meeting.[170]

Now I had an opportunity to see one strong distinction between the joys of sanctification and [those of] justification in my own experience. Formerly when leaving the campgrounds after a good meeting I used to feel sad to leave the hallowed spot, and to strike [i.e., take down] the tents to leave was like a funeral. But now it was only a matter of joy, /121/ for I felt, "I carry a camp meeting with me, for in holiness I have all the elements of a good camp meeting."

I went back to my room in the city [New York]. On going to rest the thought was suggested, "You will sleep this all off, as you have all other blessings formerly." I went to rest and the last word uttered was, "Glory to God," and when I awoke in the morning it was yet "Glory to God!" Thus I found the old corn and wine of Canaan to [be] unlike the manna of justification; hearty, solid and abiding.

Sabbath came, and I found no more shrinking from doing [my] duty. I went over to the church, and in offering the closing prayer I had special liberty and was sweetly blessed. But on [my] passing down the

---

[169] It is not clear what Redfield means by "our tent"—a tent connected with the Eighteenth Street (or possibly Bedford Street) Church, the tent Walter and Phoebe Palmer were using for their meetings, or perhaps the tent in which Redfield was staying. Terrill simply says, quoting Redfield, "I went into a tent" (100).

[170] JGT condenses this somewhat: "Here one or two penitents came in unasked, and one said, 'I was impressed to come to this very tent.' In a few minutes they were converted. The work in this manner increased until the end of the camp meeting" (100). Redfield's account gives a fuller sense of the dynamics of the camp meeting.

aisle a good old brother met me and, said he, "Do you know how you prayed? Why, you really shocked me. Why, you prayed directly to Christ! You did not even mention the name of God, but seemed to pray as if you could get anything you asked of Jesus, without naming the name of God."

"Well, Brother, it did seem to me that in Him dwelt the fullness of the Godhead bodily [cf. Colossians 2:9], and Christ himself did once say, 'Hitherto ye have asked nothing in my name. Now ask and receive, that your joy may be full'" [cf. John 16:24]. I now felt and saw the force of that text, "No man can call Jesus Lord but by the Holy Ghost" [cf. I Corinthians 12:3], and now I saw it was no risk to hang a world's salvation on the merits of Christ.[171]

In this light I saw the sin of unbelief to be the great soul-destroying sin of the world. In point of criminality, murder and robbery and every hateful crime appeared comparatively innocent when ranked with unbelief, which makes God a liar. Unbelief is a positive insult to God in the abstract[?] and the root of every evil and hateful crime.[172]

Chapter [12]

My pastor [was] a good man but [was] not enjoying the blessing [of holiness]. /122/ But like an honest M.E. preacher, [he] stood by it although he did not possess it. He told me that many years before, he was seeking that blessing and when the power began to be felt by him, he was tempted to believe that it would take his life. [So] resisted it, and from that time he had thought that he must pass through the world without [it], as a punishment for resisting it. But he told me to go on, and I should have his approval. With a full heart and good purpose did I set about the work of inviting my brethren and sisters to claim their privilege and seek the great blessing of sanctification.

I kept up my own [Methodist weekly] class [meeting] and visited most of the others and all of the prayer meetings, besides preaching often. I also appointed one meeting each week for the promotion of holiness. God worked in great power. The work of holiness was the theme all over the church and neighborhood, and in a very short time did we listen in love feast to the testimony of more than one hundred at a time who could say, "I know that God has fully saved me." All those

---

[171] This strongly christological (rather than primarily pneumatological) accent is significant, as is Redfield's vivid perception of the humanity of Jesus Christ.

[172] JGT omits Redfield's last sentence and ends the chapter here, beginning his chapter 15 where Redfield begins his next chapter.

thus saved became laborers for God both in and out of season for the conversion of sinners, who now filled our meetings and were soon converted and then sanctified, and added their labors to carry on the work.

One sister who was fully saved kept a school. [She did] up her own housework, took care of her children, prepared all the meals for her husband, and yet found time to bring from six to twelve sinners to Jesus every week.

The work of conversion broke out with great power and extended rapidly, till the church numbering five hundred came up to nine hundred and [the members] were obliged to swarm and build up another new church, and still again furnish a large number to make up a congregation in a third church.[173] A heavy church debt was rapidly running down by the free-will offering of the people. Visitors from other

---

[173] JGT: "The work of conversions at last broke out with great power, and extended rapidly, until the membership ran up from five hundred to nine hundred, and the society had to be divided, and then again the second time, and furnished a large number for a third church" (102–3). Note that Redfield does not actually say that the second and third churches were started at this time as a result of this revival or solely from the church Redfield was attending, as JGT implies; Redfield does not say that the church "had to be divided." When he says, "build up another new church," does he mean found a new church from the existing congregation, or build up an existing church that had recently been founded? Probably the latter. The New York Conference *Minutes* show that, in fact, two new M.E. churches were started in 1842–43—Asbury Church and the Sullivan Street Church, both of which first appear in the *Minutes* in 1843, with memberships of 330 and 200, respectively. Presumably these are the churches Redfield means. Both probably received some impulse from this revival, but the revival apparently was not their source.

The figures Redfield cites fit better the Eighteenth Street Church than Bedford Street. Eighteenth Street had 604 members in 1841 and 752 in 1842; this jumped to 1003 in 1843, then declined to 851 in 1844. Bedford Street had 800 members in 1841, 900 members in 1842, and 1196 in 1843. This dropped to 1107 in 1844 and 1056 in 1845, perhaps in part because of the founding of the nearby Sullivan Street Church (*Minutes,* New York Conference). If the church in question is Eighteenth Street, as seems probable, Redfield's assessment of the numerical impact of the revival was roughly accurate.

While the Sullivan Street Church first appears in the *Minutes* in 1843 and was organized as an M.E. Church in 1842, the *Inventory of the Church Archives of New York City* says this church "Originated in the Sullivan Street Methodist Protestant [rather than Methodist Episcopal] Church, established in 1833." Historical Records Survey, Division of Professional and Service Projects, Works Projects Administration [WPA], *Inventory of the Church Archives of New York City The Methodist Church* (New York: Historical Records Survey, 1940), 68.

churches and from the country, some from sixty miles distance, came to gain a knowledge of full salvation and then returned to spread the holy fire.

I wish the [situation] /123/ did not exist requiring statement of some facts which operated this early to hinder this great and glorious work. But I feel I cannot in justice to the cause of holiness avoid such a statement as will show the honest-hearted that the final slow movements, and lastly the almost entire extinction, of that blessed doctrine was by no means due to any weakness in the blessing itself. It began to wane under the combined hostility of a few who would not pay the cost of getting right with God.

Some of [these] could and did have dances in their houses. Some said, "We want no more revivals in our church, for it is too dirty [a] work. If sinners want to get religion, let them go somewhere else. We have enough members for our church." And again, "We must begin to have order and neatness and taste if we mean our children shall not, as they grow up, go off to the more fashionable churches." So they had the church newly and fancifully painted in the inside and then got up instrumental music for the choir. Then [they] sold the seats and then God quit them, [the] congregation ran down, church debt ran up, and the last end was worse than the first. And then [it was said that] Redfield had done more harm than he could ever do good.

Some who professed to believe in holiness began a settled warfare against the good cause. They would even go to some who professed to have experienced the great blessing and begin thus: "You say you are sanctified, do you?" In great modesty they would answer, "I do believe that Jesus has wrought that great work in my heart."

Then the opposers would say, "You must be very careful how you profess anything like that, for some people get excited and call it holiness. But I have been praying for it a good many years and I have not got it yet, and [I] don't know how long before I shall get it. And besides, we don't think you who have /124/ only [recently] been converted treat us old professors with due consideration, to step in before us even if you do, so early in your experience, get the great blessing we have been seeking so long without success."

One of them who made this complaint to me I asked, "Well, good Father, how long have you been seeking that blessing?"

"Twenty-six years," said he.

"Well, how much nearer the blessing are you now than twenty-six years ago?"

Then he hesitated and finally answered [that] he could not see he was any nearer.

"Well then, how long will you have them wait, and how much longer will it take you to get the thing after twenty-six years [of] fruitless efforts?"

This stopped his cavil with me, but not his hostility to the thing.

With these arguments against the possibility of young converts so readily entering the haven of perfect love, they, the converts, would give up their faith and instantly the witness would depart.[174] Then the opposers would say, "There now, do you feel and know you are sanctified?"

The answer would be, "Well, it may be I am mistaken."

"There," said the opposer in triumph; "if you really had the blessing, I could never get it away from you."

I of course was deeply grieved, and hardly knew what to do. I felt so sure that I had found the great philosopher's stone that would convert the world. I had the belief that the Methodists, and Methodist preachers, needed only to see the workings of their own doctrines applied, and with such success, and they would at once return to them in preaching and practice, and then the world would soon be redeemed.

But I thought, "This church proves only an exception. These doctrines of Wesley, Fletcher, Bramwell,[175] Abbott[176] and Fisk will yet succeed,[177] and I will not abate but keep on preaching and pressing that doctrine, which I know from the experiment so far will work wonders [in] /125/ saving sinners." I felt to say, "I know this is the right kind of

---

[174] JGT: "Such arguments against the possibility of young converts entering into the experience so early, caused many of them to give up the doctrine and the testimony, and then they lost the witness to it" (104).

[175] William Bramwell (1759–1818), noted British Methodist preacher and revivalist. "His memoir and life have been read by thousands to their comfort and edification" (Simpson, *COM*, 132).

[176] Benjamin Abbott (1732–1796), born in Pennsylvania, "one among the earliest [Methodist] laborers and pioneer preachers in New York, Pennsylvania, and Maryland" under whom "many thousands were awakened and added to the church." At his death he was called "an uncommon zealot for the blessed work of sanctification [who] preached it on all occasions, and in all congregations; and, what was best of all, lived it" (Simpson, *COM*, 10).

[177] JGT: "I had felt so sure that I had found the secret of how to convert the world, and believed that Methodists and Methodist preachers needed only to see the practical workings of their own doctrine, and they would at once return to it in preaching and practice, and their methods and polity would enable them to take the world. I believed, though, that this manifestation of opposition was exceptional and that this doctrine of the Wesleys, Fletcher, Bramwell, Abbott and Fisk would yet succeed" (104–5).

religion, and [even] if everyone fights, it I know it is of God, and I will stand if I stand alone."

XIV. "A remarkable dream fulfilled to the letter"

At this time I had a remarkable dream which I have seen fulfilled to the letter since, and which my after life will prove. I dreamed that I stood upon the rocky shore of a river, and it became my duty to walk down to a great distance and then to return. But I must go alone with my feet bare and my pant legs folded neatly up to my knees, and then I must walk on the rocks, which were like very large saw teeth, and my feet rested on their points at every step. [At] every step I took I felt the squirming of rattlesnakes and copperheads. But regardless of all, I kept to my purpose and finished the end of my journey, and then returned from whence I had started.

And now I came upon a most beautiful white sand beach. Though my road continued, it was now very smooth and easy, and perfectly free from serpents. I stepped off from the pointed rocks and onto this beautiful pathway and took a look at my feet. So greatly was I astonished that in my sleep I broke out, "Well, if this doesn't prove there is a God, I don't know what can! For I have trodden every step in this long journey with my bare feet upon venomous reptiles, and [I have received] not a single scratch or bite, though they have tried it at every step."

I had passed but a short distance on this white beautiful path when I saw a wall before me of solid masonry, and I knew it to be just fourteen feet thick. So far did it reach to the right and left [that] I could not go round it. So high and smooth, I could not scale it, and [there was] no place beneath it to pass. And yet my path, and my only path, lay right through. Although no one was near, I knew that an enemy had put /126/ that wall there secretly to arrest my progress.

"Well," thought I, "I have gone to the utmost of my powers, and still my journey is not completed." I would but commit[?]. I then stood and looked up steadily for a moment, [and] then I was lifted up and [I] glided over like a bird.

[I had] another dream about this time, equally remarkable and significant, and now fulfilled, although it has taken over twenty years to fulfill it. I was with this preacher of whom I spoke (who was my pastor and who, under God, has done more than any other man to get me out into the field)[178] on board of a steamer, and we were slowly but surely

---

[178] James Youngs, the appointed preacher at Eighteenth Street M.E. Church,

passing up North River. The water was very muddy, and the sun streamed down only upon one spot through the dense, dark fog. That place where the sunbeam struck the water was at the bow of the steamboat.

I looked over and, lo, it was swarming with a vast school of small fish. I turned to look at the engine, but it was entirely concealed from view, but I could just hear the most gentle puffing of steam from within a room which stood on the deck.

I took a look at Bro. Youngs, who was the preacher, and there was such an air of cleanliness about him.[179] Especially his feet were perfectly clean.

I took a look on the left side of the steamer, and there was another little steamer being towed by the large one, and at the bow of that [swam] another very large school of small fish.

Soon, and without my knowing when, how, or why, I found myself out of the vessel, which was now beyond my reach. I was in the muddy water with sharks and all kinds of dirty, filthy substances in the shape of rotten stones[?]. [I] went on, expecting to feel the deadly bite of some of these ferocious monsters of prey, who I knew to be after me. But all these I too escaped without a single scratch or injury. In the /127/ fulfillment of this dream, I am positive that none but a God could have carried me through safely.[180]

I now felt my commission to the world was renewed and extended, and regardless of all difficulties and warnings, I made up my mind: "I will go as far as I can and stop only when I must. And if I never get through, I will try, and die if I must trying, and at my post." But I would cry with the old Syracusan,[181] "Eureka! Eureka! I have found it, I have found it! If some oppose, [yet] some will endure this blessed doctrine, and the results will give them confidence, and then Methodism will fulfill its utmost mission to the world.[182] But sustained or countenanced by any man or not, I do know, bless the Lord, that Jesus approves me in my purposes and course. Whatever becomes of me,

---

New York City.

179 James Youngs served the Eighteenth Street Church for two years (June, 1840 to May, 1842; *Minutes,* New York Conference).

180 JGT (105) omits these two dreams, which take up two pages of Redfield's manuscript. Thus Terrill also omits the specific reference to Bro. Youngs.

181 Citizen of Syracuse, Greece.

182 JGT: "and like the old Syracusan, when he had discovered the power of the lever, I'll cry, 'Eureka! Eureka!' I have found it, I have found it. For if some oppose, some will embrace the blessed doctrine, and the results will give them confidence, and Methodism will fulfill its mission in the world" (105).

heaven shall have it to say, 'This is one man who will either prove true to God or die trying.'[183] If I find some who will pull down the work of God, I must work harder and faster to build it up."

I was soon to be put to my first serious test. I continued thus to work till one day a brother came to me and said, "You must not go to your class tonight but to the official [board] meeting, for there is trouble about to come on you and you must not wonder if your class-book is taken from you and your meetings on holiness stopped."[184]

"What," said I, "is the matter?"

The answer was, "Some of the official board very much dislike your talking so much about holiness. They say you have already done more harm with it than you can ever do good."

But with all this wonderful work of God before me, I of course failed to see the evil I was doing. Honestly believing that God bade me go on, I told him I could not go to the official meeting, but should go to my class.

/128/ Another and another came to me with the same tidings and urged me to go to the official meeting and defend the cause, saying, "If you don't, I shall."

I said, "Brother, I feel that God calls me to my class, and He will defend His own cause. And if not, then let it fall, for I don't want to be found contending for a cause that God don't want to stand. If God won't defend it, the sooner it falls the better. It is clear that if God calls me to my class, I am not called to go to the official meeting."[185]

---

[183] JGT has, "Whether I am countenanced by men or not, I do know, bless the Lord, that Jesus approves of me, in my purposes and course; and whatever becomes of me, the world shall have it to say, that there is one man who will either prove true to God or die trying" (105). In the manuscript, however, the word before "shall have it to say" is not "world." It appears to be "heaven," though the writing is quite contracted.

[184] Apparently Redfield was conducting his holiness meetings through his role as a class leader—probably still at Eighteenth Street Church. The impression is that he had an assigned class (or possibly more than one), and that either the class meetings had become open meetings for the promotion of holiness, or more and more people had experienced holiness and been enrolled in his class or classes. However it is possible that (as a class leader) he was leading special open meetings for the promotion of holiness outside of and in addition to his own class.

[185] JGT: "Another and another came to me with the same message, and one of them said, 'If you don't go, I shall.' I told them all, 'God calls me to my class, and he will defend his own cause. If not, I don't want to contend for anything he will not stand by'" (106). JGT omits the rest of the sentence and the follow-

Then came the good old preacher and advised me to go to the official meeting. To whom I answered, "With due deference to you as my pastor, I must decline, for I feel that I must go to my class, and leave [the] consequences to God."

When I went into my classroom, I found it all filled as thick as they could sit and stand, and then the passageway from the street well filled, and our door being closed, we had two congregations, one inside and one outside the classroom.[186] In opening the meeting by prayer in a low calm voice, I said in substance, "O Lord, if we are engaged in a work that pleases Thee; if this is Thy cause, give us a token in the shape of such a blessing as we have never had or known." Then instantly fifteen or twenty were slain by the power of God, and I among the rest. To me it seemed I could appreciate some of the power that Enoch felt, for I felt my feet were lifted upwards, and I sought to get hold of the stair legs to keep myself down by.[187]

There was a great commotion inside and outside the classroom, for the blessing was not shut off from the congregation outside by the closed door. As soon as I could speak, I said, "Go on, for you have a greater Leader than man tonight." One sister who had recovered strength arose and said, "I have /129/ been powerfully tempted this day, hearing that there was going to be an attempt made to stop these meetings and to take Bro. R.'s class-book from him. I have been praying all day, and just before night [I] got the witness that God would not let it be done."

Then arose another, and still another, till some twelve to fourteen stated that they had the same temptation, and the same answer before sundown that it would not be done. Not one of them knew what was going on in the official board, for all that matter was confined to a few who were members of the board.[188]

Our meeting closed, and the next day we had a report from the official meeting, the substance of which was that an effort was made to get up and pass a resolution to arrest the farther work of holiness and of these meetings. Then the preacher interposed, saying, "While I am in

---

ing sentence.

[186] JGT: "When I went into the class-room I found it filled as full as it could be, while the passage way was full out to the street" (106). JGT omits the rest of the sentence.

[187] JGT omits this sentence.

[188] JGT, after relating the several testimonies, emends the last statement to read: "Of course they could not know beforehand what the action of the official board would be" (106).

the chair I shall assume my prerogatives, and whatever resolutions you may pass, I shall act upon my authority and tell you that you cannot interfere with those meetings or abridge Bro. Redfield's liberties." One or two of the members of the board who were our warm opposers immediately arose and stated that they felt that their own opposition was wrong and that they were contending against God. And so the opposition for awhile subsided, and the work went on.

One evening I shall never forget in the body of the church,[189] after [I had been] urging the church to seek holiness as the best mode of promoting a revival, and that sinners would be convicted while the church was seeking holiness. The church came forward, filling the altar and the three large aisles to a great distance towards the doors, as thick as they could kneel. While [I was] looking towards the door, I saw it pushed open and in came a man walking through the mass of those who were kneeling in the passageway, till he reached the altar. Then extending out his hand /130/ and taking mine, said he, "I was passing the church but a few minutes [ago] and knew not what was going on here. But I was suddenly impressed that I must come in here—but for what, I could not tell. But now I know why, and I ask, is there any salvation for me?" Soon [he] was among the seekers of religion.

XV. "If you want revival, seek holiness"

A deputation waited upon me from another church and informed me that they had come to invite me to labor in their church, stating how they thought if I would go, they could have a revival. I said, "Brethren, if you want a revival, let your church seek holiness, and God will work among sinners at the same time."

I was however persuaded to go, and I preached as well and faithfully [as I could] to sinners outside of the church. Then to show the church how fruitless would be our labors in that direction, I urged and invited sinners to come out and seek religion, but without any success. I then said to the church, "I did not expect to succeed. But now, if you as a church will seek holiness, God will work among sinners." Then, stating the cost and conditions of securing holiness, I asked the church to come to our altar, barely saying, "If any sinners want religion, you may come too." Then eleven sinners followed the church to the altar.

I went home. In a week or ten days the brethren came to me again and said, "We want you to come right back, for the revival has all

---

[189] JGT: "One evening I shall never forget. We were in the main audience-room" (107).

stopped."

"But were not those eleven sinners converted?"

"O yes, and then [it] all went down."

"Let me ask," said I, "has anyone of the church found the blessing of holiness?"

"O, no," said they; "we so rejoiced to see sinners get religion that we forgot all about that."

"I thought so," said I. But again I was persuaded to go and preach once more. I did so, and with the same poor success with sinners. I then said, "Brethren, you know what God did do when I was here before, as soon as the church began to do what God bade you. Now try it over again, and hold on till God saves you. [They did so,] and then nine more sinners followed them /131/ out and sought religion.[190]

While I was there laboring, with my hands full, our [annual] conference came and our preacher, whose time was up, was removed. We had a young and I believe ambitious man who I think tried to please the party at our church who were determined to put down holiness, as they were the fashionable ones of the church.[191]

When the last quarterly conference for the [conference] year was about to sit, at which time all local preachers' licenses must be renewed or run out, I was hard at work in a glorious revival some ~~eight~~ miles up the city.[192] I went to the new preacher to ask if something could not be

---

[190] JGT: "'Now try it over again, and hold on until God saves you.' They came forward again, and nine sinners followed them to the altar; and the meeting went on for some time with great success" (108). Terrill ends his chapter here and begins chapter 16 as follows: "The annual conference came on, and there was a change of pastors" (109). Redfield does not specifically say that the meeting referred to "went on for some time with great success," but perhaps Terrill inferred that from the beginning of the next sentence ("While I was there laboring with my hands full"), which he omits.

[191] JGT says the new pastor "was evidently ambitious, and tried hard to please the party opposed to holiness, as that was the predominant party in the church" (109). Thus Terrill substitutes "predominant" for "fashionable." If the annual conference referred to was that of 1842 (which seems likely), the new pastor probably was Davis Stocking, who was appointed to Eighteenth Street in 1842, replacing James Youngs. (There was no change that year at Bedford Street). This further confirms that the church involved was probably Eighteenth Street. The following year (1843) Laban Cheney was appointed to Bedford Street, replacing Benjamin Griffin. So if the year was possibly 1843, the church could have been Bedford Street.

[192] JGT: "When his [the new pastor's] first year was drawing to a close, and the time for the last quarterly conference was at hand, Mr. Redfield was laboring some eight miles up the river above the city" (109).

done to pass my character and renew my license in my absence, as the work where I was laboring seemed to require my stay.

"O yes," said he; "You go on to your meeting, and I will see that your license is renewed."

I went back and to work, and soon learned that this preacher took advantage of my absence to lay my license over, and I was virtually stopped, for I was charged with heresy. But the presiding elder sent to me not to mind it but go right on, and he would sustain me.[193]

So I continued on. When the next quarterly conference came, I was greatly tempted not to go at all but to take this as a providential release and let those settle with God for my stopping, if it was now wrong to stop. I felt greatly grieved to think I had been so badly whipped till God had got me into the field, and [I thought], "Now for doing just what I know God tells me to I must be whipped, for being in the field and doing my duty. I don't try to make anybody bad or miserable, and I have a constant increasing testimony from good men who say they have become better, and of bad men that they are trying to become good."

But when I thought of stopping that word rang in my ears, "Live while you preach, but no longer," [and this] kept me preaching on at my own expense, and alone with God. But heaven's approval was a rich reward for the loss of all riches, and my soul fills with joy at the /132/ remembrance of His approval twenty years ago. And yet I felt very bad to see my way hedged up by the very men who ought to have stood by me. I could but say, "If they only knew how much it has cost me in suffering and sacrifices to do what I am now trying to do!" I wonder that Christian men and some ministers don't stop and ask, "What can be the [i.e., Redfield's] motives?" and let that guide them in their decisions.

If they look at the work, there is a large army who will say, "Holiness has done wonders for me in changing my nature, so the work must be good, of a truth." But [each of my opposers should reason,] "What motive can move Mr. Redfield? Certainly not money, for [he] asks nothing and is at perpetual expense to keep moving, and labors with his own hands to get his supply. And it cannot be fame, for a man must either be a fool, crazy, or honest who will persist in such a thankless[?] effort. If a fool, [he is] not responsible, and wise men show folly in beating a fool. And if crazy, I have pity [on him]."

[193] The presiding elder (in effect, superintendent) of the New York District of the New York Conference at this time was Phineas Rice (mid-May 1841 to mid-June 1844). He had previously been the appointed preacher at the Bedford Street Church (1839–41). *Minutes,* New York Conference.

But I know before God—whoever may call it boasting—I know I am honest in my motives. So conscious am I every hour of my life of this fact that, with my hand on my heart, I can face the judgment and say to the Judge of all the earth, "Thou knowest I am honest."[194]

I told some of my brethren [that] I thought I would not go to the quarterly conference, but they urged me to go. I went, and we had a full board [sic; i.e., conference] numbering about forty-five or fifty. Conference opened. The elder called upon me to answer to the charge of heresy on two points. The first was my views on the character of the millennium, and the second on the doctrine of Christian perfection.

I said, "I wish anyone present to correct me if I do not tell the truth, and prompt me if I don't tell all." And when I had finished [explaining my views on the millennium],[195] the elder said, "We must accept that from Bro. R., for he is with Dr. [Adam] Clarke in his views. Now about the doctrine of holiness."

Then again I called /133/ upon them to correct or prompt me, and thus get the exact truth. I told them so much of my experience as had any special bearing on the doctrine of specific holiness and of my teaching, preaching, and belief. When I had finished the elder again interrupted [the discussion]: "Well, brethren, we must accept that, for his is exactly with Mr. Wesley."

The call was then made whether I should have my license renewed. Forty voted for and five against it.

I then told the conference that I had [a] little business, and asked to present it. I told them that during the three months past the report had been kept in circulation that my own church would not renew my license, and the public knew not the cause. Even some preachers with whose charges I was called to labor had to ferret out the facts and then satisfy their own official boards of the true state of affairs before they could commit to allow me to labor. I now wished them to pass a vote, and give me a copy, stating that I had been examined on the points of heresy on which my license was suspended[196] and was found to be a

---

194 JGT deletes most of this self-defense. He writes, "He [Redfield] could but say, 'If they knew how much of suffering it costs me to follow this path, and would ask themselves what motive must it be that governs him, they would not do so'" (109). JGT then omits the following sentences.

195 Implied. This was the time of the Millerite excitement, with many people expecting the imminent return of Christ.

196 That is, not renewed. Redfield's account suggests, not that he was formally suspended but that the quarterly conference had failed to renew his local preacher's license—which of course amounted to a *de facto* suspension.

sound Methodist.

Then the preacher who had thus far played the innocent arose and said he could not vote me a sound Methodist because, said he, "We as a church do not believe with either Clarke or Wesley on those points, but with Benson."[197]

One of the official board [members], most grieved that I was let off so easily, arose and said, "If any man says there is anything in the doctrine of sanctification, he is a liar."

The elder cried out, "Stop, stop! Bro. Redfield is a Methodist, but you ain't. I did not know that this church would tolerate such anti-Methodistic doctrines as you do."

Finally the vote was modified to the liking of the [objecting] preacher to read: "That this board [sic], having examined Bro. Redfield, found nothing against him." But O, how my soul felt to see such quibbling and dodging. Now I saw that we had an element even among the preachers /134/ who were not Methodists.[198] But my confidence in the ultimate success of these particular doctrines to save the world was not in the least impaired.[199]

One brother came to me as I left and with deep emotion congratulated me on the final triumph of my case. But how greatly was I disappointed to learn that this same brother who so rejoiced that my impediments were removed would follow me to camp meetings, and while I was laboring in the tents would tell those who were strangers to

---

[197] JGT: "At this his pastor arose and said, he could not vote Mr. Redfield a sound Methodist, because, said he, 'We as a church do not believe with either Clarke or Wesley on these points, but with Benson'" (110). The reference presumably is to Joseph Benson (1749–1821), British Methodist and close friend of John Fletcher, whose five-volume Bible commentary, *Notes, Critical, Explanatory and Practical* (1811–1818) was issued in an American edition in 1820 and, according to Chiles, "was widely used by Methodists" (Robert E. Chiles, *Theological Transition in American Methodism: 1790–1935* [New York: Abingdon, 1965], 41). It is not clear, however, why this pastor (probably Davis Stocking) would appeal to Benson against Wesley and Clarke, as Benson's doctrine was essentially that of Wesley. See Marsh Wilkinson Jones, "Pulpit, Periodical, and Pen: Joseph Benson and Methodist Influence in the Victorian Prelude" (Ph.D. Diss., University of Illinois, Urbana-Champaign, 1995).

[198] JGT: "Of these proceedings Mr. Redfield says, 'Oh, how my heart was pained, not only to see the unsoundness as to the truth, but such quibbling and dodging when it came to the issue. I also saw that among the preachers there was an element that was not Methodistic" (111).

[199] JGT: "Still, my confidence in the ultimate success of the doctrine of holiness was unshaken" (111).

the facts that the church refused to ~~license~~ renew my license at home, without stating the case as to the cause and the farther fact that I had been approved after examination.

I now began to see that if the M.E. Church was to be redeemed and reinstated to do its heaven-charged business, that holiness must be put forth with untiring effort. I do not make these statements to retaliate for the unjust opposition with which I have had to contend, but to give those who care to know some of the facts which will enable them to form a just opinion of both the cause and motives of one who feels he is working for eternity and [is willing to] take the consequences [from those who oppose holiness]. Certainly they cannot be very selfish motives which will keep one laboring under those circumstances, and for naught.[200]

I soon learned that this hostility was not against me but [against] the cause, and farther, that he who dares to declare himself on the side of God has virtually declared war against earth, hell, dead formality, and especially ambitious ministers of the gospel.

A friend of mine, an uncompromising champion for God and truth, was so much feared that the preachers in his own conference sought his ruin. Like the accusers of Daniel, they were compelled to find cause in his religion. So they appointed a preachers' meeting where each one was expected to give a specimen of his preaching abilities by reading a sermon or essay, and then the preachers present should criticize it. /135/ They appointed this man to preach on the subject of holiness. Of course he must [comply] with [them], which he did, waiving his scruples against written sermons.

The time came. and he arose and read off his written sermon. When [he] finished, "There," said one, "I have often heard that this brother was anti-Wesleyan on the doctrine of Christian perfection, and now we have heard with our own ears the heresy." Then followed so severe a criticism that some felt that the brother was being too roughly handled, and [one brother] interrupted by saying to the supposed heretic, "Brother, you have a right to defend your points."

"Well," says the brother, "never mind that, but go on and say all you have a wish to."

Then another arose and took the poor brother's sermon all to

[200] JGT omits this paragraph. At the beginning of the next sentence (which starts a new line and apparently a new paragraph), Terrill or someone else has placed a large superscript X. This may have been Terrill's mark indicating that the book manuscript should continue here, after omitting the previous several sentences.

pieces, showing up the [supposed] anti-Wesleyan heresies in his sermon, and then another and still another. Finally the elder was called upon to make his remarks. But he only said that he thought the items of heresy so flagrant that he felt he must take a disciplinary course of first reproving the brother in private before he should bring his heresy out before the public. [He] intimated that he might arraign him before the coming conference and have him disposed of as an anti-Wesleyan preacher.

"Well," said the [accused] brother, "if you have all got through, I will tell you I have copied every word, from the first to the Amen of that sermon, straight out of John Wesley, and there you will find it quoted, volume and page on the margin. And now I only ask, who is Wesleyan, you or I?"

This was a pass, and some began to excuse themselves that they had not refreshed their memories by lately reading the works of Wesley. Another complained of the unfairness of picking out such isolated portions of Wesley and reading it to them as if it were the production of the poor heretical brother.

When I heard this, I saw that the hostility which I had met with was not against me, but [against] the cause of holiness. /136/ Now I began to see to some extent some of the oppositions of Methodist preachers to the Methodist doctrine of holiness, and [that] in all probability I should yet be made to feel its force upon me and probably shall be compelled to stop altogether. But, [I resolved,] "I will go to the last link in my chain for God and purity and stop only when I can go no further."[201]

---

[201] JGT here adds two summary paragraphs before closing the chapter. Terrill says first, "With a clearer understanding of what it meant, [Redfield] now more fully than ever committed himself to the work of spreading scriptural holiness over the land." He then summarizes what Redfield says in the next paragraph about his hope that holiness would still have considerable success within Methodism. Finally Terrill adds a closing paragraph (not in Redfield) concerning Bishop Leonidas L. Hamline: "About this time, also, Rev. L. L. Hamline was elevated to the episcopacy of the church, a man whose experience and preaching, and holy life, made him one of the brightest examples and witnesses of the doctrine [of holiness] in the annals of the church. For many years after this he was a confidential adviser of Mr. Redfield, and, to a great extent, guided his labors, as to place and time" (113). Hamline (1797–1865) was elected bishop at the May-June, 1844, General Conference which met in New York City—the conference at which prolonged debate over slaveholding led to division and the formation of the Methodist Episcopal Church, South. Hamline resigned as bishop in 1852, due to ill health. His wife, Melinda, was also a

Chapter [13]

I was now fully committed for life. [I resolved, "Even] if everybody contends against me, I know the cause is right and I will never abandon it, but hope on." And I did most religiously believe that the workings of this precious doctrine would win its own way to the acceptance of the preachers who would by the success of holiness in saving the world arise in the night and reassert it as a Methodist doctrine, and back it by a reference to our published works of standard authors.

Some advised me to join conference, but I foresaw that I should be circumscribed in my labors and be put where this growing hostility to Methodism would be felt in all its crushing power.[202] So I resolved never to commit myself with that body of men. I knew that many of them were right, but timid. Some with whom I was laboring had confessed to me[203] that they once enjoyed the blessing, but that the conference proscription was such that they avoided any farther definite labor on that subject. [They] then lost it [i.e., the experience of holiness] and then became inefficient. I then saw that my true place was in the local ranks; that was the only place where I would be permitted to follow the dictates of my own conscience. But I honestly believed that in this place, [as an unordained local preacher,] I could do something which with the blessing of God would bring our church back to its primitive simplicity and power.[204]

---

leading holiness advocate (Simpson, *COM*, 424–26). JGT's comment about Hamline tends to confirm the chronology; the year now is about 1844.

[202] Redfield was advised, in other words, to begin the process toward becoming an ordained preacher in the M.E. Church (probably in the New York Conference).

[203] Syntax modified for clarity. Redfield has, "Some had confessed to me with whom I was laboring."

[204] JGT begins his chapter 17 here, summarizing the above two paragraphs and also adding two paragraphs on the general state of evangelistic work: "At this time there were but few evangelists in the field. It was the beginning of a new era of evangelistic effort. James Caughey [1811–1891; Methodist evangelist] had just commenced his great work, and was going like a flame of fire over England and Ireland." Terrill also mentions "John Newland Maffit, one of the most eloquent preachers of this century," and "the eclipse of his brilliant career," perhaps "the result of his own indiscretion" which "produced a public sentiment in regard to evangelistic work which was embarrassing and unfavorable to others who would enter upon it." He adds, "Finney and Burchard of the Presbyterian Church, and Knapp among the Baptists, were the leading men, if not the only ones in this particular department of church work, except Mr. Red-

As a local preacher I could go where I pleased and depend on my own resources. And now the field opened to me as an evangelist, and I deeply [felt] that God called upon me in this strange manner to pursue this new path and become a kind of pioneer [so] that other local preachers, seeing the result, might go too where no /137/ organized church existed, or where the arduous labors of the regular preachers were too much for them.[205]

I had been invited to go up the [Hudson] River about twenty miles from N. Y. and add my efforts to the labors of other local preachers who had broken ground and begun to see some hopes of good. I learned that the people [there] did not hear a sermon but twice in a year, and that in the afternoon of a weekday by a very rank predestinarian.

On my very first visit, a beautiful Sabbath, we had benches set out in a grove. The people came for miles around, and we had a large congregation. Evening meetings were held in a private house. God was with the people to save. I was greatly interested while listening to the simple tales of the people relating their experience in no borrowed phraseology, having as yet never heard the cant phrases of converts.

One [testimony] I well remember at a meeting in a private house, [given by a woman] while sitting with a child in her arms. Her face whitened out and she sat swaying to and fro with deep but suppressed emotion. Then a sister sitting nearby, seeing about the state of things, offered to take her child.

Then she [i.e., the mother] arose and said, "I don't know as I have got this good 'ligion what I hear you talk about, but I do feel so good and warm all along up here," at the same time passing both hands over her heart.[206] I needed no learned doctor of divinity to tell that she was

---

field, who represented the Methodist Episcopal Church" (114). Maffitt was a preacher and conference missionary (1822–23) in the New England Conference of the M.E. Church. In 1830 the Board of the Methodist Missionary Society voted to request Bishop Elijah Hedding to appoint Maffitt as "an Agent for the Missionary Society." However, Wade Crawford Barclay reports, "For some reason the Bishop did not see fit to make the appointment." Wade Crawford Barclay, *Missionary Motivation and Expansion* (New York: Board of Missions and Church Extension of The Methodist Church, 1949; Vol. 1 of *History of Methodist Missions*), 261, 297–98.

[205] Although in early Methodism local preachers were to some degree evangelists beyond the local Methodist congregation, in the M.E. Church of Redfield's day their ministry was confined largely to the local church. Redfield means that his (in effect) itinerating widely as a local preacher was something of a new precedent that might extend Methodism's evangelistic outreach.

[206] JGT: "she arose and said, 'I don't know as I have got this good religion

happily converted to God.

When forty (or fifty it might be) were converted, [they were] formed into a class. The people set about building a church [edifice] in good earnest, and in eleven months from the time that the first man was converted the house was finished, paid for, and embraced in the bounds of a circuit, and I was sent for to come and preach the dedication sermon.[207] It was in the evening. I said to Jacob, who was the first convert, "Now, when I close preaching, I want you to give an exhortation from the altar and then invite the people to come forward and seek religion." Such another exhortation I never heard, and its effects convinced me that God's tools were adapted to, and far more efficient when selected from among, the people to be saved /138/ than all the labored and scientific productions could be.

His exhortation ran like this: "Now, sinners, I tell you, look a here. I tell you, you don't know how good this good 'ligion is. O, I wish you would come up heres, kneel down and get it. You know I used to drink rum like anything, and swear and play cards. But O how good this good 'ligion is. O, do come and kneel down and get it." And to my astonishment, stout-hearted men as well as others flocked up to the altar of prayer.

When our meeting closed, I said to Jacob, "Now you and I must go all over the place from house to house and exhort the people to get religion. We will begin tomorrow morning."

In the morning we started on our mission. The first house we entered [was one] where two families lived. In the first room sat an elderly lady who had been out to our church the previous evening, and she was weeping. Jacob left me to converse with her and went into the other part of the house to exhort the family there. When Jacob left, this old lady broke out and with emotion said to me, "O, that sarmint that Jacob preached last night made me detarmint to get this good 'ligion."[208]

XVI. "Led to review my history"

I was sometimes led to review my history, ~~and to remember~~ and [to] draw the contrast between my sufferings before I entered the field

---

what I hear you talk about, but I do feel so good and warm along up here,' at the same time putting both hands on her breast" (115).

[207] I have not been able to identify what church this might have been.

[208] JGT ends his chapter 17 here and begins chapter 18, "Mr. Redfield was now invited to a church in one of the suburbs of New York city" (117).

and the present approval of God and the unearthly glory that ravished my soul. [I thought, "There is] but one thing to mar the otherwise perfect felicity in the consciousness that I am just where God wants me," and that one evil was the perpetual dread that that player in my life might yet turn up and destroy all my usefulness.[209]

O how many a time have I gone to my rest and thanked God that He counted me worthy to put into the ministry, and [I often reflected,] "One more day has passed and I am yet free from that terrible affliction [caused by my wife], by whose bad conduct I used to suffer so much." I regularly thanked God as I went to bed for every day's freedom from my living[?] trouble. But even after all, [I thought,] "How much better is my present state than to be put /139/ back [to the days] when in fighting against duty [I] was compelled to contend against God." How great were my troubles about the matter. My anxious heart has often been the most desolate of all around me, and yet I thought, I was willing to go if I could only know for a certainty that it was the will of God [that] I should go and preach.

To put my impressions [of my call] to the test [in those days], I have approached the most deficient and unpromising ones I could find and asked them, "Did you never feel it your duty to preach the gospel?" And when they would answer "Yes," I tried to gather consolation in making myself believe that my impressions were only a phantom like theirs, as I was sure that theirs were founded in fancy. But my comfort was of short duration, for the impression [of my call] would be doubled, and at such times I would hunt up some lonely retreat out of hearing of mortals and for very grief sob and weep aloud to think I was thus pursued by impressions which I could not reason away nor shake off. I felt like howling. I would stand it among men as long as I could, but when my grief made my heart to ache, a good wailing time alone would take off the pressure and give me relief.

Sometimes my anguish and distress was so great, especially when I would survey myself and ask, "What, must these hands, feet, and head go into the gospel ministry? Oh no, Lord, that is asking too much. I never can. I know I am totally unfit." To be pressed into a work to which every feeling of my nature revolted seemed to me an act of injustice. I was sure if all men were of my mind, not one could ever be forced into the ministry by any earthly consideration. Money, position, or honor would alike fail to bring them into the gospel field and to dare

---

209 This sentence begins a long, several-page digression in which Redfield "review[s his] history," reflecting on his call and the struggles he had over it. JGT omits this whole section.

to take the awful responsibility of preaching the will of God to man. I can say for years "my tears have been my meat /140/ day and night" [Psalm 42:3], and my plaintive voice cried out to God and besought that I might be excused. In graveyards and groves and other by-places, and in bachelors' hall I have spent many hours in complaints, for years together weeping and praying that God would settle this distressing dilemma and let me know that I was free.

At such times the sight of a gospel minister would send me off to some lone retreat where I would indulge my grief and weep it out. I once went in the morning to a large city church and took my place in the gallery, and when I saw the minister walk up the aisle to the pulpit I was so distressed [that] I would not stay. To hide my tears and anguish [I] left the church, hunted up a grove and spent the day in loud wailing and lamentation over my hapless condition. God and my own heart alone have any idea of the sufferings I have passed through in getting out into the field.

But O, how changed now! Since I have obtained the blessing of holiness all fears, all hesitancy is gone. I feel so honored of God in being permitted to preach the gospel that any amount of suffering from opposition would not move me.[210]

Since I have been out [in ministry, I have had] to stand amidst opposition, sometimes expecting bullets or tar and feathers and threatened with dogs and, worse than all, [opposition from] professed gospel ministers [who] would so far forget their calling as to stoop to very questionable means in trying to arrest my influence, [or to divert] me for a moment, or raise one desire in me to turn aside from the track on which I had started. I have indeed often wished they could know what I have passed through in getting out [into gospel ministry]. But now I rejoice to be counted worthy to be misunderstood by men, [and at] the unearthly joys which arise at the thought that if I keep my holy unction and finish the race and fight in this war to the end, I can /141/ then say with the apostle, "I have fought a good fight" [II Timothy 4:7]. I am yet sometimes tempted that I shall never be able to finish this race. But I have made up my mind I will get as near the mark as I can, and if I fall, it shall be so near the goal that I will not give the resurrecting angel a great deal of trouble to come far after me.

It was so strange that religious men did not see and acknowledge that when the work of God prospered so gloriously under the preaching of holiness, and they endorsed it by receiving the members, that at the

---

[210] Since these last couple of pages largely repeat what Redfield had said earlier, it is understandable that JGT omitted them.

same time they did not at least let me alone. I once enquired of a presiding elder, "What is the matter? Ain't the work good?"

"Yes," said he, "and when you have preached this doctrine in our very best churches on the district, I will tell you," said he, "the doctrine is right, the results are right. And yet where these doctrines are preached it does us great harm, for we cannot find preachers among us who can satisfy the people in the wake of this kind of work."

I asked another, "Why do you find fault? You know, or ought to know, that I preach Methodist theology after Wesley's model."

"O," said he, "there are many of us Methodist preachers who don't believe with John Wesley on holiness."

O my God, I never could have stood this but for the precious perfect love which casts out all fear, and O how sweetly has my heavenly Father whispered in my heart, "I will settle all these matters, but do you go on as I have commanded you."

I said, "I will, Lord," and the question came, "Can you drink of the cup that I shall drink of, and be baptized with my baptism?"

I said, "Lord, I accept it. I can but die, and I will [persist] or die trying." Then appeared [before me] the life of Christ. His bloody footprints. One only thought, wish, and purpose consumed Him, and that was to do the will of God and then [endure] misunderstandings, jealousies, opposition, persecution, and final death.

/142/ "Well, Lord," [I said,] "give me his spirit to do it with, and I accept the task."

"But his best deeds were imputed to the power of the devil."

My heart says, "All right, Lord, I take it."

"But He stood up for the rights of God when no others dared confront the opposition and [he] was compelled to stand alone and suffer alone."

"Well," [I reflected,] "He would [not] defend [himself] or speak a word in self justification, but like the lamb in the hands of the butcher, [He] opened not His mouth. Well, Lord, give me Christ's spirit to do it with, and I will make the trial every hour."

I was fully committed, but little did I dream where all this would lead me, and with what heart anguish I must redeem my vows! I knew that the Almighty and one poor man was a majority and would in the end triumph, and my course was safe. But I had directly taken sides with God in spirit and saw myself alone with the blessed Jesus, committed to try to win the lost world and dead church to Jesus. So of course I could consult no man, and this was thought to be rash, stubborn, and opinionated. But God owned me, and sinners by hundreds and sometimes by the thousands got salvation; new churches [were] built and many an old one about to be lost by the foreclosure of mortgage or executive over judgment[211] were saved. But men did become godly, and good men became better, and then God smiled, and that was enough. I shall keep on till I cannot take another step.[212]

XVII. Expanding Revival Ministry, 1844–46

Chapter [14]

I was now invited to go to a church in the suburbs, to [a] church sustained mostly by the home missionary society.[213] When I reached the place I learned that there was a formal church of another denomination who were in the habit of keeping this little Methodist [church] reduced in numbers by proselyting[214] away the fruits of their revivals and offering a premium to our converts /143/ in the shape of a more fashionable church. I found that these old proselytes were sent out to get around our new converts and do up the proselyting.

I knew too well that it was not a superabundance of piety that made these formal churches of the dead attractive to our converts, and by the help of God I resolved to plant our foundation on holiness so hot as to spoil our converts for their use. But our revivals were too superficial, and that made our converts an easy prey to those who could offer worldly advantages to the young converts (or rather I should say convicts). Yet I found one advantage in this fact, that their fashionable church had so far kept our church pruned of fashionable, world-loving performances that the sharp doctrines of holiness found no opposition, and [in my meetings] God was allowed to work in power, without any hindrance.

So we took the strongest stamp of thoroughgoing religion. But we soon found we had waked up a plenty of opposition in two clergymen who were now favored with an opportunity to make, to them, some interesting charges against the Methodists, quite to the edification of some of their most fashionable church members. They advised the people to keep away from these meetings, adding that the Methodists were

---

[211] Meaning, apparently, a legal judgment.

[212] An X following this last sentence, likely added by Terrill, indicates the point at which Terrill begins again to quote Redfield's journal. JGT omitted about four pages of manuscript and here begins his chapter 18 (page 117).

[213] JGT begins the chapter, "Mr. Redfield was now invited to a church in one of the suburbs of New York city. This church was sustained mostly by the Home Missionary Society" (117).

[214] Redfield (and JGT) used "proselyte" as a verb (as well as a noun), rather than "proselytize."

"going to have another excitement," but it would soon blow over.

I found that as soon as some of the choice ones [i.e., choice new converts] began to get excited, one of their preachers would be after them to join his church.[215] God worked among us in great power, and I was resolved if possible to stop this unhallowed work of stealing converts and making them twofold more the child of hell than themselves [cf. Matthew 23:15]. I soon learned that two persons, a man and wife (he converted and the wife not), [were] going to join the Dutch [Reformed] church. The brother was seemingly converted, and came into the altar to labor.

I said to him, "I hear /144/ that you are going to join the Dutch church, and that your wife is, [also,] as soon as she gets religion."

"Yes," said he, "that is our design."

I said, "Don't you do it, Brother, for they will press your religion out of you and final perseverance into you, and you be sure to be lost. You won't join them, will you?"

"No," said he, "I will not."

I next got down [by] the altar where his wife was seeking and asked, "Why is it you don't yet get religion? Do you give your whole will up to God?"

"O, yes."

"Well, would you be willing to join the Methodists, if God will convert you?"

She started back, and I saw her will was up against it. Fully believing that to join that [other] church was to surround herself with influences which would make her final salvation an almost impossible thing, I said to her, "You may rest assured that God will never touch your case until you are willing to join the Methodists."

"Do you think so?" said she.

"Yes, I know it."

"Then," said she, "I will be willing."

"But," said I, "will you join the Methodists?"

Again she started back. Here I saw [it was that] the trouble lay, and I said, "You will never get salvation till you make up your mind to join the Methodists."

---

[215] JGT: "He [Redfield] had scarcely commenced operations, before two clergymen of the other church commenced to war against him. At first they advised the people to stay away, because the Methodists were simply going to have one of their usual times of excitement. When the meetings began to get hold of the people, and particularly of some of the more choice in the community, one of their preachers began to visit them and to coax them to join his church" (118).

"Well," said she, " I will." And instantly she shouted, "Glory to God! I have got it!"

Various plans were adopted to drag our people away from us, but without success, and of course we saved the whole, to a man and woman, to our church, who so swelled our numbers that our church no longer asked missionary money to help but now paid for the help of other churches. So much for preaching and pressing full salvation, the primitive doctrines of the Methodists!

After the ill success of the two ministers either to stop our revival or proselyte from us, their own people dismissed them. The one, an Episcopalian minister, /145/ was so much displeased at being dismissed that he exposed the people whom he served, saying that there was but one real ~~member~~ communicant of his church and that one was a Roman Catholic, and the balance were a set of would-be genteel people [who] only sustained the church as an item in the luxuries of upper-tendom.[216] The other minister, for drunkenness and stealing church funds and night-reveling and horse-racing, was soon silenced.

Thus have I seen time and again that the people who can persuade their minister to enter the field and contend against the work of God, will soon contend against him. I have also learned that the main opposition to the work of God is from professors of religion who have never been converted through and through, or those who have backslidden—and most of all from the professed ministers of the gospel. But whatever others may think, do, or say, there is but one way for me, and that is at all risk and expense to maintain God's rights and call in question any and every thing that doesn't bear the seal of God's approval. Nothing short of this will give success to the church or preserve it from downright formalism. The supposition that there are redeeming traits in human nature which only need discipline rather than a change, and the use of appliances to polish and adorn what must be rooted out, will run heartfelt religion out of the world.

The work of God was not only powerful but extensive. Our revival continued till into May. Here too I learned that God will demand of us harmony and purity among ourselves. Likewise [I learned] how great a hindrance to success will one Achan make [cf. Josh. 7], and how God refuses to work amid unbelief. One night when the altar was well filled we came almost to a dead halt, and my soul was crushed within me. I cried to God to remove the hindrances, and I was instantly impressed that we had those present of whom God would say, "Remove from before me the vile, and then offer your sacrifice."

---

[216] That is, the desire to rise in social standing.

So impressed was I that this was our hindrance that I arose and called the attention /146/ to the fact of my impression. [I] then desired those present who were conscious of wickedness in their own hearts, and opposition to this very work now going on, to have the goodness to leave the house. Then three persons, all members, arose and in high spirit left.[217] But no sooner had they left than the converting power of God fell upon the people, and souls were immediately brought into the light.

What made this so remarkable was the fact that for twelve to fourteen nights after, we could not move till we could succeed in getting them to leave the house. And what made the case still more remarkable was the fact that two of them were soon expelled for gross immoralities. One was proverbially deficient in Christian spirit and the other was a hypocrite—playing the part of friend to our faces, and when with infidels joining with them in talk against the work of God.

While we were holding our meetings with success, the colored people held meetings in a private house. The power of God was with them in awful glory. One night a young woman who had become deeply awakened arose and ran to the door, determined to get away from the leadings of the Holy Ghost. But before she reached the door, she fell. In an agony [she] would just rise onto one elbow and cry, "O Lord, have mercy, Lord have mercy, Lord have mercy," and then sink down, to all appearance senseless. In a few minutes she would rise as before and utter the prayer and then sink away again.

This she continued without a moment's intermission for seven days and eight nights. Some thought she would die, and called upon me to go and see her. I did so after she had been in this condition for a number of days. I tried to offer her Christ and if possible to find out the particular trouble in her way, and though I persisted and called to her in a loud voice to tell me what was the matter, she paid no kind of regard to my voice. She seemed to hear nothing and to see nothing. But still at these short intervals she would arise and utter the prayer /147/ again and again. She obeyed no call of nature, except once they put a few drops of milk into her mouth.

She was laid on a bunk on the floor, and there she continued day and night. Two sisters slept in the room to watch her. On the eighth night, when all were gone to rest, this poor sinner continuing as she had for the seven days previous. These two sisters went to rest in the same room, and [they] having put out the light, the poor sufferer was heard again to rise on one elbow and cry, "O Lord, have mercy, Lord have

[217] JGT: "Three members of the class immediately left" (120).

mercy, Lord have mercy." And [then finally], "There, Lord, I give myself away; it's all that I can do." Then instantly the room was flooded with flashes of light, and she was bounding and jumping and praising God in the midst of it.[218]

As soon as the first gust of glory passed, she sank down from weakness through her long fasting and want of rest. They fed her by teaspoons-full till she could bear a more hearty meal. When she fully came to herself, she said in substance that she had seen the awful state of the damned, and it was this dreadful sight which had so distressed her and kept her in this agony for so long a time, but that the awful state of the damned was beyond the power of language to describe. She proved to be one of the very clear as well as remarkable specimens of the converting power of God.

Chapter [15]

I now felt myself fully committed to stand up for primitive Methodism, seeing that it would win and work so powerfully and successfully.[219] I left there to go to another church in a neighboring city and met with another preacher of one of the city churches. Probably hearing how greatly God was at work where I had just been, said he, "Now, Brother, this is a Godsend, and you must go to my church and help me, for we have been holding a meeting for six weeks, and not one soul is converted."

I thought I might stay a few nights and still [at the same time] serve the church to which I had been engaged. Following the leadings of God's Spirit, I tried to preach that class of truth which the Holy Ghost inspired /148/ me to preach to that church and then call upon them as Methodists to seek the great blessing of holiness as the sure way to a revival among sinners. But they would not move a step. The preacher then expressed his surprise that they would not respond to that invitation. But he failed too in his effort to move them.

---

[218] JGT: "At last she changed the wording of her prayer to, 'Here, Lord, I give myself away. 'Tis all that I can do,' and instantly began bounding, and jumping, and praising God" (121). JGT omits the reference to flashes of light.

[219] JGT here begins his chapter 19, as follows: "The success of the meeting described in the last chapter, deepened Mr. Redfield's convictions that the preaching of holiness would conquer the world for Jesus, and that it was his duty to follow the same course wherever he went, since it had proved successful in every instance heretofore. In conscience he could choose no other course." JGT then relates Redfield's going to help in the neighboring city (122).

After meeting, they gave him some sharp reproof for pressing them to take the objectionable stand of seeking holiness before the world. To save himself, he threw the blame upon me, and the next day told me plain that he did not like such preaching and thought that I was probably backslidden and thought everybody else to be so, too. But how was I astonished a few years after to see this very man, after I had been to a place of great importance. The dignitaries of the church were paying special respect to me, and here he could not do enough in words and affability to show himself friendly. But O how my soul did feel that I wanted grace to endure such tokens of friendship which go with the popular current. If I ain't right, I thank nobody to stand by me. I should feel amazed at the tokens of approval to me while wrong, and I value no man's friendship who cannot stand by me when I become a mark of disgrace and scorn because I stand identified with an unpopular truth.

I now left this place and went to the one where they were expecting me. There I found people and preacher all right in theory and in effort, and the first night fifteen professed to have obtained the blessing of holiness. The work of God among sinners broke out in great power, and about three hundred souls were among the saved.

And now I was sure that the Methodist Church would rapidly return to their primitive power and glory, and the world will soon be redeemed. The redemption of the world through the M.E. Church was the theme of my day labors and night dreams. And now, [I thought,] I can /149/ at last count on one man who will exert all his power and influence in the conference to win our church authorities back to primitive power.

But I was again doomed to disappointment as I learned little by little [that there was] a deep-seated hostility to holiness, and that too in Methodist preachers, and an evident leaning in them towards a system of worldly policy and a desire to prune Methodism of all the features that were objectionable to the pomp- and pleasure-loving professors.[220] I had heard that the argument had by one of our preachers been plied to the world thus: That the time had come when a man without a profession of religion could not find access to genteel society, nor do business. I could only regard this as a slander, had I not the proof that a worldly policy was gaining ground in many places, showing how greatly a time-serving spirit swayed the councils of the powers that be.

Of course I was thought to be an old-fashioned man who could not keep up with the progress of the age. But I was somewhat relieved while in company with one of our bishops, one who has since learned

[220] Syntax revised slightly for clarity.

how hazardous a thing it is to take a part with God against all sin. He told me of things showing the downward progress of Methodism to an extent I never at that time knew, and he greatly grieved over it but feared the final results. He then and there gave me such counsel and such encouragements as led me anew to hope and vow before the Lord that I would undauntedly pursue the thorough way. I could now say, "I know of one preacher and one of the bishops, and they will stand for God and right."[221] I believed that the most of them were, as they thought, in favor of a high-tone of piety. But I was equally sure that they had more confidence in their own ideas of propriety and consistency than they had /150/ in the leadings of the Holy Ghost. But in charity to them I did believe that, taking a rational standpoint, they did the best they could. And I thought, "With these accessions of preachers (for I knew of a goodly number of them and one bishop), the cause of primitive Methodism will certainly be revived, and we shall now see our Fletchers and Bramwells and Abbotts, blessed men whose writings and memories are still as ointment poured forth."[222]

But again I was doomed to disappointment, for I found not only hostility to the doctrines but successful efforts put forth to put down these revivals. When successful [opposing ministers would] sneeringly say, "Here too is one of Redfield's revivals, and you see what it has come to," then I would have spells of discouragement till I would sink so low that it seemed I could never try again, and [I felt,] "If the world is lost, I cannot help it." I seriously thought I would now and forever abandon this life of disgrace, toil, and sorrows, and settle down. Then the word once more rung in my ears, "Live while you preach, but no longer."

Then I arose once more and vowed, and would have signed it with my own blood, if I could: "O Lord God, the Father, Son, and Holy Ghost, I am nothing. But such as I am, I am thine, and I will go straight for Thee if I go alone and with the fearful odds of the world, the flesh, the devil, and ministers against me. I may fall but, God help me, it shall be at my post." And the rich unearthly joys which at such times filled

---

[221] Redfield does not identify this bishop. It may have been Bishop Hamline.

[222] JGT clarifies this passage as follows: "But in charity to them I believed that, taking a rational standpoint, they did the best they could. I thought that with the accession of new preachers who were clear and straight (and I knew a goodly number of them that were about to enter the work), and with one bishop who could be relied upon, that the work of holiness would certainly be revived, and we should again see our Fletchers and Bramwells and Abbotts, blessed men, whose influence would be like ointment poured forth" (123–24).

my whole being are beyond words to express. It is worth a life of toil and disgrace to feel that God approves, and none can know the sweetness of it who has not tasted it.

Again, with God's approval I felt my courage and hope revive that the end I seek will be gained some day. I may die without witnessing the glorious triumph of old Methodism once more. But someone must be [the] pioneer and meet the rebuffs, and even my failure to see primitive piety again restored to our church will furnish notes by which some capable one may be /151/ able to escape the rocks on which I founder and carry the grand achievement to a successful end. What am I, that I may not be used like one of the [soldiers of Napoleon's] Grand Army who, [the army] having no bridge to pass [over], allowed themselves to be shot in the river till bodies enough could fill up and form a bridge of human bodies so that the reserve army could pass over and conquer. I have more hope for the M.E. Church, for I find an accumulating number of ministers who are trying, some it is true but feebly, but they are trying to "know no man after the flesh," and their influence will be felt.[223]

XVIII. "New fields opening"

But now new fields were opening to me by the invitations of preachers to come to their help where a church was mortgaged and soon to be sold, and nothing but a revival could save them.[224] In such cases I have found the churches in such a feeble-spirited state that I have been compelled to allow the preacher to be shocked at the bold stroke of putting the Bible standard right up where, in the contrast, the real state of the church was [seen to be] exceedingly depressed. [Only] with difficulty could I sometimes persuade the preacher to suspend judgment till God should redeem his own cause by unwonted success.[225]

---

223 JGT deletes this section, beginning with "Again, with God's approval."

224 JGT: "He found new fields of labor were opening before him, and calls came on every hand; but, usually, they came from mortgaged churches, and nearly extinct societies" (124).

225 JGT: "To succeed in such places it was necessary for him to raise the standard of piety to where the Bible puts it, and this would greatly shock both pastor and people. The piety and even the morals of the membership were generally of so low a type, and the contrast between the standard he presented and the characters they manifested was so great that it was with difficulty sometimes that he could induce the pastor to suspend judgment until God could redeem his cause by giving unwonted success" (124–25).

The results of course would follow; God's Holy Ghost will work amid truth. Then the preacher, seeing the result, would [generally] say, "I never thought that your course would result so gloriously. I shall know what to do at my next station." Said one to me, "I once saw things in this light, and tried to pursue the same course as you do, and with like results. But I found that influential ministers in the conference began to look upon me suspiciously and to utter murmurings against me as an 'unsafe man' and 'injudicious,' 'behind the times,' 'old fogy,' 'not a good representation of our church.' Besides, I knew what they did to other men who took the course you do, and the same which I used to do. They were proscribed, sent out onto starvation appointments, or /152/ located."[226]

Sometimes they would ask me, "What system do you adopt which works so successfully? Do you have a regular course of sermons?"

"O, no. I feel I have nothing to hope or lose, and I take the rough, unpopular, old class of Methodist truth which you who hope to be bishops or [presiding] elders dare not use." Though I would leave in the best of feelings, thanking the Lord that one more preacher was won back to primitive Methodism and could be counted on as an addition to the thoroughgoing ministers of Jesus, how greatly have I been shocked in less than one year to learn that the same preacher had returned to his former state of cowardice and inefficiency and indifferent moral state and, more, had entered his protest against these "Redfield revivals."[227]

Though compelled with sorrow of heart to give up any further hopes of these men, still my hopeful heart would say, "I know this is God's cause. Though all men forsake it, by the help of the Lord one man shall be found true to God's right at all hazards, and I shall yet see the thing a success, and old apostolic religion shall yet rear its head. I will leave a clear track for some honest and capable one to follow, and [thus I will] make it [i.e., my ministry] in the end successful while I am passing back to dust. But fail or not, I shall certainly never waver a hair from what I know is the exact thing, right or nothing—and on this issue my fate is sealed." I thought I had no reason to fear for my own personal safety if the cause was put down, and I could in reason expect that the worst I had to fear would be only a cool turning away from me.

I pursued my own way, and God was certainly with me. Church af-

---

226 Along the left margin of page 152, perpendicular to Redfield's script, someone (presumably Terrill) has written, "views of the state of things, his labors etc."

227 JGT omits the next few sentences, picking up the account again with the preacher who slandered Redfield.

ter church had been saved and become a paying institution and, [I thought,] "Some of them will reap the benefit." But no; I was compelled to learn a far more bitter lesson than that. For when nothing else could /153/ effectually discourage my influence and put me down, my moral character would be slandered. In one instance the preacher reported me as having abandoned a very excellent woman, making no provision [for her].[228] When he had forged this slander and handed it over to those who wished to put down this straight way, I said to someone, "If that man is a preacher or even a member of the Methodist Church in five years from to day, call me a false prophet." In a very short time he was called to account for bastardy. Report said there were two cases, and he was compelled to run away. Although these preachers knew these facts, yet his case was bunked and his slander against me [was] thrown in as truth all over the land.

If I had been trying to persuade men to be wicked I could hardly have waked up a worse hornet's nest. This same man, who was in charge of a church and sick when I entered the neighborhood, sent for me to come and see him. Said he to me, "Now this is a Godsend, and you must go right into my church and labor."

Soon some of his members came to him and said, "O, Brother, we have got the right man to help us. Why, he preaches the pure old doctrines of Methodist holiness."

"O, I am so glad," said the hypocritical preacher. "Only let me get well, and I'll stand by him."

When they left, in came some of the cold, formal [members] with quite a different story and made their complaints that I was doing great harm in going against little things such as jewelry and fashions of the world, and they could not and would not endure it.

"Well," said he, "just hold on till I get up, and I'll stop him." Thus would he have a face for everybody, and while thus opposing the work [he] was doing the iniquity which compelled him to run away.[229]

---

[228] Terrill (presumably) has written in the left-hand margin, perpendicular to Redfield's script, "Fate of one who slandered him."

[229] Terrill condenses (and somewhat alters) this account to read as follows: "In one place to which he went, the preacher was sick and unable to attend the meetings. The work broke out in glorious power. Some of the members immediately began to seek and obtain the experience of perfect love, while others opposed it. 'When the former would go to the pastor,' says Mr. Redfield, 'and speak favorably of the meetings, he would fall in with them and approve of all. When the latter would complain to him of my preaching on dress, etc., he would fall in with them and promise to stop me when he could get out. After a little he began to circulate slanderous stories about me. These came out after I

One of the leaders [in this church] had enjoyed the blessing of holiness, [but] had been persuaded to stop his profession of it so as not to annoy /154/ those who would not make the sacrifice to get it. The professor of that state of grace was a standing reproof to them. He was finally persuaded not to introduce the disturbing element of holiness, and the result was that he lost it out of his own heart. Then they accused him of being backslidden. But when I began to preach the doctrines of holiness, he was the first to receive the truth, seek for and obtain it in power. And then, repairing to a large factory in which he worked, [he] asked permission of the foreman to address the workmen, which he did with great power. Catholics and infidels stood before him and wept on account of their own state.

But dead professors who found out how zealously he had been exhorting the people in a factory found great fault with him. He went home, and God so blessed him that he could do but little, only shout the praises of Jesus. Then in great haste came one of the dead brothers [to] where I was staying, and in great haste urged me to come immediately and see Bro. V. From the manner of the brother I supposed that the good brother must have had an apoplectic fit or some other sudden seizure of disease, and what was to be done must be done quickly. So I caught up my case of medicine[230] and found my way to the brother's house. On opening the door where he was, there sat the good brother, face all whitened out, just filled with smiles, clapping hands and shouting, "Glory, glory to God!"

In an instant I saw the cause of the poor dead brother's fright. But I joined with the happy brother in giving praise to God. "But," said the offended brother, "I don't like it at all."

"Well," said I, "it is none of your business. This brother is not your property; he belongs to God, and God has a perfect right to bless him as much as He pleases."

"But," said the other, "what if he never gets over this? What will become of him?"

Said I, "He will never be fit for another horse race as long as he lives."

"Well," said the other, "I would not have that spell on me for five hundred dollars."

---

left. I remarked to some one that I would not be surprised if he was out of the ministry in less than five years. In a very short time he was called to account for a scandalous crime, and deposed from the ministry'" (125–26).

[230] Redfield was at this time practicing medicine to some degree, as he did throughout his revival ministry.

"Well," said /155/ I, "make yourself perfectly easy about that matter, for I assure you, you are in no danger of that calamity, for God will keep clear enough of you while you are in this mood."[231]

XIX. "Jesus cures both soul and body"

I was, not far from this time, called to go and visit a poor sinner dying with the consumption. She was reduced to a mere skeleton, and to all appearance might die that night.

I tried to point her to Jesus as the great physician of souls, and besought her to cast her soul on Jesus at once—thus to encourage her that though so very low with disease, there was nevertheless hope. I said to her, "I have just been to see a man dying with consumption, and without hope. On [my] trying to lead him to Jesus, he tried to get onto his knees in bed, but was so weak that he would fall over at every attempt. But he got salvation and died in peace. But," said I to her, "there is no use of your trying to get onto your knees, for the Lord can hear you just as well while you are lying down."

But when I left she directed the lady who was watching with her to leave the room and close the door. Then she managed to get her bones out onto the floor, and by the side of her bed [she] sought and obtained salvation and was healed of the consumption at the same time. In one or two Sabbaths after that [she] was at our church giving glory to Jesus who had cured her, both soul and body.

I was now called to see a brother who had lately been converted but was just then dying with consumption, and [who] desired me to call on him before he left. I found my way to his house and there found him apparently breathing nearly his last. There stood his wife and sister weeping around his bed, and there [also] his child, just old enough to know that Father was sick and that Mother and Aunty felt bad. The man himself was gasping and rattling and writhing in agony from suffocation. He was rolling his head from side to side and throwing his arms about. Yet in the midst of all this terrible suffocation I saw his face was filled with smiles. I said, "Dear Brother, /156/ when you can speak again, if you ever do again, tell me if you can feel that Jesus sustains you in these agonizing suffocations."

Again he seemed to be putting forth a last desperate struggle amidst the death rattle. Finally [he] succeeded in monosyllables to answer back, "O — No — I — am — so — happy — I — don't feel it —

---

[231] JGT recounts this incident (126–27) but rewrites it some, condensing and leaving out some details.

and — if — this — is — to — be my — heaven — forever, it's — enough —."

I soon went to see a good old sister who had enjoyed much religion for many years. I went in company with her [class] leader. As we passed up the hall stairs, there stood the consulting physicians close by the head of the stairs. They had given their opinion that the good old saint was then dying.

We were invited in, and her daughter stepped to her mother and told her we had arrived. The daughter would put her ear down close to her mother's mouth and catch the whispers and then convey to us the wishes of her mother. We prayed, and left.

But scarcely had we left when her spiritual vision caught a full sight of her coming Lord, and so great was the strength granted by the sight that she sprang up in bed and, raising her hands in triumph, declared that she saw Jesus. Clapping her hands and with loud shouts [she] continued to triumph till she passed behind the clouds.[232]

A goodly number of others I visited who gave more or less clear testimony of the power of their religion in this awful and trying hour of dissolution.

When spring came, I went to Long Island to spend the summer and recruit.[233] I preached in the villages on Sabbaths and attended prayer and class meetings. I used to go into the woods before I was about to preach and there continue until I could get an answer that God would go with me and help [me] to preach the awful law and gospel, and while strung up in preaching I was often led to see and preach a class of truths which put my own religion to the test.[234] And I can say that I have profited more by trying to practice the truths which I saw while

---

[232] JGT tones down Redfield's language a bit: "'scarcely had we got outside the door when her spiritual vision caught a full view of her coming Lord, and so great was the strength imparted by it that she raised to a sitting posture in the bed, and waving her hand in triumph, declared that she saw Jesus; and continued thus to triumph until she passed beyond the clouds'" (128). JGT ends his chapter 19 here and begins chapter 20 on the next page.

[233] JGT begins chapter 20 here: "When the spring came Mr. Redfield went to Long Island to spend the summer and recruit" (129). By "recruit" Redfield probably means "recover my strength." Apparently this was the spring and summer either of 1844 or 1845.

[234] JGT: "Before preaching he would go into the woods and plead with God until he received assurances of divine help." Beginning a new paragraph, JGT continues: "Referring to these times, he says: 'While under the Spirit's influence and power in preaching, I would often see and proclaim truths that put my own experience and piety to test" (129).

/157/ preaching to others than from the preaching of others.

The fall came, and I went to a camp meeting. Meeting the [presiding] elder, [I] was persuaded by him to go to a place made vacant on his district by one of his preachers who had abandoned the place. I promised to go and stay until the season of protracted meetings [began]. Then an old preacher came to me and said, "I cannot advise you to go to that place, for in all my labors of twenty years in the ministry I have never seen a place that was so hopeless."

But I was resolved to go and make the trial. When I arrived, I found that this once flourishing church, raised by Jesse Lee, who was sent there in answer to prayer, was now in a most deplorable condition.[235] Three or four classes were now reduced to one. Many members had not visited their class in three years. One of the leaders had not met his class for a year. Some of the members were claimed as Universalists. Some [were] in the habit of drinking, and besides [there remained] an old unsettled quarrel of over twenty years' standing.

My heart was made sad. I began visiting, and one of my first visits was to the house of the old man who was the principal in the quarrel on one side. He asked me if I had come to be the preacher for them. I told him I had.

"Well," said he, "there is no use, unless you first bring up these people and put them through a course of discipline." Then he began in a rapid and zealous manner to bring their sins to light and to show me how much he had suffered by them.

"But," said I, "Hold on a moment."

"I tell you," said he, "they ain't worthy of church fellowship."

"Wait a moment," said I.

"O, it's no use of your trying to do anything here amid so much wrong, and everybody knows it."

I let him go on till he got almost out of breath, then I repeated my request to hold on one moment until he heard me and waited for me to say what I wished to. I then said, "Now, Brother, you are a great deal older than I am, and I don't feel myself capable of entering upon the settlement of this affair till I have asked God for wisdom." Instantly [I] dropped upon my knees, and he followed. I then determined not to move till God should melt his heart all down. I continued my struggle with God till the old gentleman /158/ began to break and cry out, "O

---

235 Jesse Lee (1758–1816), originally from Virginia, was a prominent early American Methodist preacher. He is said to have introduced Methodism into Boston. He was a close friend and associate of Francis Asbury and wrote the first history of American Methodism (1809). Simpson, *COM*, 535.

my God, what have I been about? Lord have mercy on me. O, how wickedly have I sinned against Thee."

We arose and the old gentleman said, "Now, I want a meeting called so that I can confess my wrong and sin, for I am the one to be blamed." A meeting was called, and the offended members readily received the confession and forgave the old man, and the breach was healed.

I went around visiting, and went to the house of one old Father V., who was one of the first members in society and at whose house the few pious ones used to meet in olden times and pray God to send them a minister after His own heart, and Jesse Lee was sent to them. The old man, who used to be a very efficient leader and exhorter, was now only a wreck of his former self, mind and memory all in ruins. His good old lady said to him, "Pa, here is the preacher who is sent to us."

The good old saint raised up from his stooping position in the chimney corner [and] with a vacant, wavering stare said, "Why — how — is your Mother? Well — why — you look good."

I had heard that pious old people, however broken, would sometimes remember well matters concerning religion, and after fully satisfying myself that he was so far lost as only to converse in a very incoherent manner, I abruptly said, "Father V., do you know one Jesus of Nazareth?"

Instantly his whole demeanor changed, and with an intelligent air he answered, "Why yes, I have known Him a great many years, and He is my Savior, and He will not turn me off." Then [he] repeated appropriate texts and hymns so clearly and well-adapted to the case that I started back from him and put on my best enquiring look to assure myself that he had not been [earlier] trying to play a deception upon me.

Sabbath came, and away I went to the church, and of course curiosity led the people in good numbers out to see the new preacher. Regardless of all persons and conditions, I resolved to deliver my own soul, [though I] /159/ could see no favorable indications.

After a few efforts in the work to bring about a change, and finding it all in vain, I went out to visit sinners and to exhort them to "flee the wrath to come," and got for a response, "Go and look after your own ungodly members."

Sabbath again came, and I delivered my message for the judgment. When I left the church I was met by the principal member of the official board, who accosted me thus: "We don't like your preaching here at all, nor the chapters which you select to read. Hell ain't very popular here."

"Well, you tell me, Brother, what I have preached that ain't Bible truth."

"Well," said he, "I believe it is true."

I simply retorted, "Shall I preach lies?" I then went weeping through the streets till finally I saw if I was going to do anything, it must be with all my might. So Monday morning I started for the grove, and there I got down and struggled in prayer against the power of darkness until I felt I was in spirit rising, until my spirit had struck a rock, and instantly it crushed me down. I arose and sought another place to plead with God for souls, and after the same intense struggle my spiritual head struck a rock, which sunk me in spite of every power I could put forth to rally. And so I continued day after day till the week was ended. I would go to the house once in awhile to get something to eat, then [go] right back to my wrestling ground. Sometimes in an agony I felt I could rend the heavens, for sinners must be saved. "If I can succeed, they will be," [I thought]. "But if I, because the contest is so agonizing, yield, they must be lost."

When Saturday night came, my brain was so sore that the jar of my step on the ground was very painful, and I could perceive a kind of bewilderment coming on. But though I had got no answer, I had got up a resolve: "In the name of God I will either see a break and salvation come to this church tomorrow, or if God will help me I will try to put an end to /160/ it so it shall not stand here as a representative of Christ's church on earth and yet remain such a stench in the nose of God and the world."

Sunday morning came. My eyes [were] sore with weeping, and my head tender from long-continued agony for the church. I walked but softly and carefully and went into the pulpit.

In opening the service I told them, "With this day's labor my services end in this place.[236] You don't want me here and I don't want to stay, for I am heartily tired of pouring water onto rocks. But if God will help me, I will either see a break today or see this ungodly apology for Methodism annihilated. I have asked no man's money. I go on my own expense. But I shall go the straight way for God."[237]

I went into the pulpit again in the evening and announced that we should redeem our pledge. Of course this threat but aroused their hate to a pretty high pitch. As God helped, I laid out the track of an acceptable disciple, and the only one that could possibly pass the gates of

---

[236] Presumably Redfield was planning to leave soon in any case to hold protracted meetings elsewhere during the winter.

[237] JGT adds here the sentence, "Nothing seemed to move in the morning" (132).

Paradise. After preaching I asked those and only those who meant it and would take this track and, where needed, go to their neighbors and confess and pray with them, and then seek till they should know they had the blessing of holiness, just to arise. For, [I said,] "I don't believe I could get you to come forward to the altar."

Two persons only arose, and these were among the most lowly, and of course of no great account [in the congregation's eyes].

"Well," said I, "there seem to be only three of us, counting myself as one, and God besides. But I think we will try to have a prayer meeting." These two and myself were all that would kneel, I in the altar and they in their seat about halfway down the aisle. I opened with a short prayer, and as I began to rise in spirit, I felt my spirit head strike the rock and bring me down again. I then said, "Amen. Now let someone else pray," but no one /161/ offered to pray. I broke out again and with the same sense of striking a rock, and then I called the third [sic] time for someone to pray, and finally the fourth and fifth and sixth time.

While I was praying the sixth time in succession, I felt assured that "This is the last time, and if that rock brings me down this time, God will say, 'Now let them alone,' and this will be the end of the church, and that forever." The case was a desperate one. "What can I do?" [I thought]. "The world and devil against me, and all the church members too, and so much offended that they refuse to kneel. But O God, I will go to the last possible step."

But this time when I felt my head strike the rock, it flew into ten thousand fragments. Instantly the house was filled with the glory of God. The two who were kneeling fell under the power. Then the shouts and screams were so loud as to alarm the village, and they came running into the Methodist church to see what was the matter. As they crowded up the aisle and saw there two [lying] under the power of God, their tears began to chase each other down their cheeks, and the poor tempted members began to arise one after another and confess their hostility and ask pardon, and promise to take the track.

I staid one more week, and forty-five sinners were converted. Then their old preacher returned to town, and the work continued to go with power. And what is best of all, I heard from that church some ten to fifteen years after and learned that they were still doing well.

I was now waited upon by a preacher some seven miles distant who said, "I want you to go to our church. We have been holding a meeting for three weeks, and not one soul is yet converted and," said he, "I have had the counsel of the Baptist and the Presbyterian ministers, and they think I ought to get you to come, if you will."

I went to the place, but never consulted the preacher about my course [of preaching], but followed as I believed the leadings of the Spirit.

/162/ The first night I preached I saw that some would get up in great haste and run out of doors and slam the door very loudly as they went. But I observed that the same persons would soon come back again, and then repeat the same ceremony. I learned after meeting that they were members who took that way to show their dislike to me. They went to the preacher and told him that he must send me away, or I should ruin the Methodist Church. The Baptist and Presbyterian ministers gave the same counsel.

Again I went and preached as God directed. The house was still better filled, although my opposers said that my course would drive everyone out of the house and likewise that I had broken up their revival. Some two or three had been forward before I came, but after I came they would not come to the altar again. I sent someone to go and seek them and see how much they designed or desired religion, and learned that they did not design to change their lives but thought if any benefit could be derived by allowing the Methodists to pray for them, they were willing. But [they] did not mean to change their lives nor do the duties of Christians.

So I saw I had not harmed the revival, and of course kept right on in the track I had begun. Now they became very angry and went out and began to counsel people not to come again to our church, for that man was not fit to [be] heard and was no proper representative of a Methodist preacher. A prominent infidel met them face to face and said to them, "You need not oppose that man who is preaching for you, for he is the only honest man among you who dares to tell you the whole truth. He cuts me up fore and aft, but I shall still go, for I like to see a man who is honest for his God." And he did keep on, and got salvation.

But now the war began in good earnest. Ministers of other /163/ denominations entered their counsel, and their deliberate conclusion was that to allow me to stay on longer would ruin the M.E. church. The opposers who were members of our church were greatly emboldened and I think were determined to stop me, saying, "Nobody will be at our church again if he ain't stopped." Well, the Baptists and Presbyterians left their churches, and [these two churches] appointed a meeting on each side of us to draw their members off.[238]

---

[238] Redfield appears to mean that Presbyterians and Baptists began to abandon their own churches and attend the Methodist meetings, so as a defensive measure both churches sponsored their own special meetings to attract ("draw off") their people back. The phrase "on each side of us" probably means that the

I went home to the house where I was staying and laid the matter before the Lord. I felt to say, "O Lord, Thou knowest that I don't know what to do. Now, Lord, give me help for this once, and tell me what is the message."

A text and subject were then presented [to my mind]. My reason said, "O Lord, that will never do! The people are so much offended now that to preach that subject will produce a perfect tempest and break up our meeting in disorder." But the moment I hesitated to go with this message I was in the dark, and so distressing was this state of affairs that I could not endure it. I would cry again, "Lord, show me, and I will follow," and again would this text and subject come with force. Finally I thought to ask the Lord to direct me to some appropriate text as a counsel.[239] Opening the Bible at random, my finger touched the words, "Be not afraid, but speak, ~~bold~~ and hold not thy peace but speak, for I am with thee."[240] I said, "Lord, I will venture it at all hazards, although I am sure in all reason that I shall be stopped before I can possibly deliver my message."

When I went to the church, I found that instead of a small congregation, the house was so crowded as to make it necessary to use the unfinished galleries, which had never before been called into use.[241] And the two meetings, one on each side, to draw off the people were deserted, and our house filled.

But now was to come the tug of war. One thing /164/ encouraged me, and that was that the preacher was a very devoted man of God. Though he said but little, I knew he was ready to identify himself with the right, and rise or fall with it. But I did expect trouble with the people, and especially with the official members.

When I went into the pulpit, I thought, "Certainly they will order me out of the pulpit before I can read the first hymn. But I will proceed till they do stop me." I opened [the hymnbook] and read:

> Shall I, for fear of feeble man,
> The Spirit's course in me restrain?
> Or, undismay'd in deed and word,

Presbyterian and Baptist church buildings were located to the right and left of the Methodist building, perhaps along the same street.

[239] JGT has, "as corroborative" (135).

[240] Terrill (apparently) crossed out "bold" and inserted above the line, "not afraid, but speak," correcting the reference from Acts 18:9–10 (135).

[241] This was a frequent pattern in Redfield's meetings. Though (or because) his preaching was controversial, crowds often substantially increased.

Be a true witness of my Lord?[242]

Such a power fell upon me while I was reading that it seemed to me that every word of the hymn fell upon the hearts of the congregation with the weight of forty pounds each word.[243] I finally finished reading the hymn and said to myself, "I have read my hymn and have not been ordered out yet." But the temptation came, "If you pray as you feel, you will be collared by some of the official members and ordered out of the pulpit, and home." But unflinchingly I had resolved to pray up to the last word that I might utter, just as the Holy Ghost prompted.

I said again to myself, "There, I have prayed and have not been collared yet." I finished my preliminaries and then took my text, "I Am hath sent me unto you" [Exodus 3:14]. And as the Spirit gave utterance I tried to array before them my authority as from God, and then the message as from God and the unbending character of that message, which could not be trifled with but must be obeyed.

I felt an unearthly thrill charging me from head to foot, and the awful power of God upon and all around. The house, which was greatly crowded, I soon saw in spirit were[244] in great commotion, and the tide of emotion would sway from side to side till finally in one mighty wave I saw the wave of emotion start from both /165/ sides of the house at the same instant, and like two waves they met in the center of the house. Then the power of God broke like a thunderclap upon the people.[245] Such screaming, falling, shouting, and crying for mercy I had not thought of ever seeing in that congregation. All denominational distinctives were obliterated in an instant, and then Baptists, Presbyterians, and Methodists took each other by the hand and with deep emotion declared this God to be their God. Now the work went on gloriously.

One brother after meeting said to me, "I now see what was the matter with our revival five years ago. We did not go deep enough. It

---

242 First stanza of a hymn by Johann J. Winkler, translated by John Wesley. It is No. 655 in *Hymns for the Use of the Methodist Episcopal Church* (New York: Lane and Scott, 1849).

243 JGT: "Such an unction was given that every word fell upon the congregation with great power" (136).

244 "The house" here in the sense of all the people in the congregation—thus the plural verb.

245 JGT: "I felt an unearthly thrill charging me from head to foot, while the place was filled with a sense of the awful presence of God. I soon saw that the minds of the congregation were in great commotion; and in a few minutes the power of God broke like a thunder clap upon the people" (136).

was for the want of the strong doctrine of holiness that it all fell away, for out of five hundred converts we have barely one left who has not backslid."

I was invited by a good old preacher to come to his help about five to seven miles from here. This good brother had been doing his best to start the work without touching the heart-stirring doctrine of holiness.

I felt like telling the people how gloriously the work of holiness would move the work forward, and called upon all the church to begin the work of seeking holiness. [I] then offered the sinners who would pledge themselves to seek to stand up, and fifteen made a move at once.

The next day myself and the preacher went around visiting from house to house. [At] the first family we visited we found the lady of the house rejoicing in the fullness of salvation. She was at work around the washtub and, to use her own language, she said she came from the church the night before after pledging herself to seek the blessing of holiness, and at it she went that night, and before morning God came in power and gave her the great pearl of perfect love. Said she, "It does seem that I never found it so easy to get along. I tried to sweep out the house this morning, and it seemed as though the broom moved of itself. My children never seemed so obliging and good as this morning. O, glory to God in the highest!"

My calls were so many to /166/ go to the help of the preachers that I could only stay [in each place] a short time.

I had met with a preacher on the campground in the fall who came and pressed me to go to his charge about ten to fifteen miles distant—a very large church where they had enjoyed an extensive revival the winter previous. I went, but not without many fears to come under his influence, for I greatly feared that he was disposed to be too superficial.

I had hardly begun our meeting before the preacher told me that an invitation had been sent for us to go out to tea. This I greatly feared was a trick of the devil to dissipate my communion with God. I frankly told the preacher I dared not go out to any afternoon parties, for I had only time and strength to do the bidding of God, and I felt the need of keeping closeted with God every moment when not at church or on my way from place to place. He told me I need not fear any irreligious tendencies. So I was over-persuaded to go, for once.

When I arrived I found the suit of parlors filled with the bright, gay, and intelligent ladies of the city, some of whom were members of the M.E. Church. My heart sank within me. I wanted to leave. But the preacher assisted in giving a religious tendency to our gathering. Yet all this kind of forced apology for religion but pained me.

Tea was soon passed around on servers. I soon paid all the compliments I designed to to the tea and eatables and [then] began to sing a spiritual hymn, then knelt down. We continued in prayer till God broke up all the nice and shaped-up order, and the power of God began to slay in great power. This good beginning was the sample after which we patterned and held social meetings every afternoon in private houses, and thus [people] were fitted for the labors of the church, where God saved a multitude of sinners. Yet I must say, I think it is hazardous to try to carry out a system of fashionable visiting in connexion with religious meetings.[246]

I now received a letter from a brother to whom I promised help in the /167/ winter, if possible. I had seen him at the aforesaid camp meeting, where he came seeking the blessing of perfect love. He inquired of one of the preachers if he could tell him what to do to gain the precious blessing. The preacher sitting on the stand said to him, "There is Bro. R., a local preacher. You go and ask him, and he will tell you."

He told me afterwards that his heart revolted at the idea of asking a [mere] local preacher. "What!" said he to himself. "What does he know more than I do about sanctification?" But finally [he] concluded to come to me. When he asked me if I could tell him what to do to inherit so great a blessing, I felt to begin with deep humility and meekness and said to him, "I am but a poor, unworthy creature. I am only a local preacher. It is asking a great deal to ask me to give you counsel. But with your leave, I will tell you some part of my experience and then ask you a few questions." And when I had finished my experience I asked, "Brother, can you say to begin with, 'The will of the Lord be done'?"

He answered, "I ought to."

"But do you say, 'O God, thy will be done'?"

"I do," said he, with emphasis.

"But hold a moment, Brother," said I. "Let us see what may possibly be the will of God, and then see if, when you comprehend it, you can still say, 'Thy will be done.' God's will is comprehended in two tables: What you must do, and what you must suffer. Let us try it," said I.

"Now, it may be the will of God that you should be put down as a very inferior preacher and be sent out onto the frontier as unfit to represent Methodism in any populous town. Now do you say, the will of God be done?"[247]

---

246 JGT ends his chapter 20 here (page 138) and begins chapter 21.

247 Redfield is warning the preacher that if he experiences and professes holiness (as Redfield taught it), he might well be marginalized due to the decline of the emphasis on and acceptance of entire sanctification within Methodism.

"I do."

"Stop again. It may be God will cause you to go to Africa and spend your life there, leave home and country and let your bones sleep in the hot sands of Africa. Now can you say, the will of God be done?"

"I do," with promptness he answered.

/168/ "But Brother, that may not be your track, for God wants [i.e., needs] poor-house preachers, and I don't know but that you can, in poverty and rags in the poor-house, show the power of grace to triumph there. It may be that your suffering there will so preach the power of the gospel that someone will by this means be persuaded to get religion, and would not by any other. Can you now say, 'Thy will be done'?"

"I do," was the prompt reply again.

"But it may be, Brother, that God wants you to testify by the triumphs of grace over pain. Your calling may be to suffer distress of body, and the power of grace may so happen to shine out in your case as to win some infidel, and that man may prove to be a successful gospel minister. Thus you may do more than you could do in any other way. Now do you still say, 'Thy will be done'?"

Again he said, "I do."

"Well, Brother, you have got just halfway through, and by this you know you have got the consent of your will to suffer the will of God. Now, about doing the will of God. You may have duties to do at which your heart up to this hour has shrunk. The low and little duties, those which will put you at variance with everyone who is not in harmony with God. 'Who is deaf as my servant and blind as he that is perfect' [cf. Isaiah 42:19], says God. Take sides with God and never allow yourself to set up a defense for self. Be thorough, straight, and honest to vindicate the rights of God as you would in five minutes of the judgment. You can stand for God when protected by men of position in your conference, but will you be as tenacious for all of God's right, wish, and will when all shall turn against you?

"Remember, you will pass for an 'ascetic old fogy,' 'unsafe,' 'imprudent,' 'in want of charity.' You need not abuse men to win a bad name; only be unflinching for God, and your name is worth more now /169/ than it ever will be again. If a man of wealth should pick you up out of the ditch in a starving condition and take you under his care, provide for you and make you one of his heirs on condition you keep watch of his interests, would you then think it is right to allow men to come and steal his property, and fear to try and stop it for fear of making enemies of those thieves? No more can it be right to allow others to move[?] the gospel, which has been painted in blood. [You must] watch God's interests and protect against the wrong with all your heart. God has called you to be a watchman, and you must on no condition allow in silence an infringement upon God's rights.

"You will find a plenty of ministers who will regard it as [a] small thing to be so particular. But no man is too particular in protecting against a matter which is not too small for the Almighty to protect against. The world, the dead church, and the time-serving minister will enter their protest against you and resort to all kinds of means more or less dishonorable to humble you. But do you, can you, will you say, 'O Lord, I will do Thy will, if I stand alone'? Can God count on you as one who can be trusted to do the exact right thing when His back is turned and the whole church and world conspire to outlaw you for your fidelity."

"I do," said he. "The whole will of God shall be done in me and by me, at all cost."

"Well now, then, you are all the Lord's, are you not?"

"O," said he, "it seems there is something that I have not yet comprehended in this surrender."

"Well, Brother, tell the Lord when that something is made apparent that you will then give that, too."

"I do," said he.

"Well then, you have given all to suffer and do the will of God, have you not?"

"O Yes."

"Well then, you are the Lord's. /170/ Well now, Brother, who has required all this surrender at your hands?"

"Why God has, has He not?"

"What, everything?"

"Why yes, has He not?"

O yes," said I. "Well then, if God has demanded all this and you have given all, do you think He will ever accept it?"

"O yes, if he has required and I have given, for He cannot be trifling with me."

"Well, if He will accept, when will it be?"

"O," said he, "I don't feel."

"Well, you ain't ready to feel. You are now just ready to believe[248] —not that you have the witness, for you have not, but believe on the bare promise of God that, having complied with the conditions in giv-

---

[248] A large X has been inserted in the manuscript here, between "believe" and "not."

ing yourself to Him, God now finishes the work by accepting [you]."[249]

"Why must I believe before I feel?"[250]

"Well, Brother, do you tell sinners when seeking religion to wait till they feel, or to take the promise of God for the face of it?"

"Why," said he, "I tell them that God is to be trusted, and they must credit His word."

"Well," said I, "is not the promise of God to the sinner just as good for the preacher? Do you want better security than the sinner that God will keep His word?"

"Why, I ought to ask no better security, and I will try to believe. But," said he, "I don't feel yet."

"Well, [you] have not done all yet. Now finish the condition, 'with the heart,' not simply the assent or consent of the head. But 'with the heart' you believe 'unto righteousness' [Romans 10:10]. You finish the work of doing right in your compliance with the conditions. But now it is 'with the mouth' that 'confession is to be made unto salvation.'"

"What, confess that I feel what I don't feel?"

"O no, that would be telling a lie. But confess what you believe, and that is, you so believe that God is true to His Word that on the bare say-so of God you do believe that He accepts what you have given."

/171/ Immediately he went to a tent and confessed, not to what he felt but what he believed simply because he had complied with the condition. And sure enough, in the very act the witness came. To use his own language some eight weeks after, he said it seemed to him he was like a vessel lost at sea beyond bottom or shore, until he prayed God to stay the hand of power and glory.

"Now," said the brother, "I want you to come to my charge and help me in a protracted meeting this coming winter."

I said, "I will go, if the Lord shall permit. But Brother, you go home and persuade all of your church, if possible, to seek the blessing of sanctification, and I will guarantee to you that in the meantime God will work upon sinners. Nothing can surer." He said he would do it.

About two months after this came a letter from him saying, "I wish you to be here next Tuesday to begin a protracted meeting." I took public conveyance and reached his place on Monday evening and went to his house, and learned there that he was gone out to a private house to a meeting which was held for the promotion of holiness. I found the house, and on opening the door found it well filled, and the faces of the people shone. They went on giving in a good and strong testimony to

---

[249] This was a point often emphasized by Phoebe Palmer.

[250] JGT: "'What, must I believe before I feel?'" (142).

the fact that they were in possession of the blessing of holiness, or were hard pressing after it. The glory and power of God was indeed rich.

The meeting closed. I went out in company with the preacher and I asked, "How long have you been holding these meetings for the promotion of holiness?"

"About two months," said he.

"Well, how many of the church now enjoy it as a distinct blessing?"

"I think," he answered, "that the largest proportion are in the possession of it, and almost the entire balance are pressing hard after it."

"Well," said I, "do you remember that I told you at the camp meeting that if you and your people would keep at work on holiness, that God would work /172/ in awakening and converting sinners?"

"O yes," said he, "Very well."

"Well then, do you know of any cases of awakening?"

"No," said he, "not one."

Then, calling upon one of the leaders who was walking nearby, [I] said to Brother H., "Do you know of any sinners who are serious?"

"No," said Brother H., "not of any."

"Well," said I to the preacher, "all this beats me, for I never before knew it to fail, and I must believe yet that you will find that God has been doing something."

Tuesday afternoon came and we met at the church. But there was no sign of any stir among sinners, and so [also] at the evening services. This [continued] till the next Thursday afternoon, when it seemed as if we had come to a perfect halt, and could not stir. As a last resort we called upon the church to come out to the altar and to renew our consecration, and others to seek the blessing of holiness. We finally came to a point where it seemed as if the powers of darkness were let loose upon us. The preacher would cry out, "Hold on, steady faith, steady faith!" Soon the power fell, the work broke out in power, and sinners in the congregation cried aloud for mercy. One or more came up to the altar screaming for mercy and soon was hopefully converted to God. From this moment the work went on in great power.

The next morning a [class] leader came to the preacher's house and said, "Bro. O.,[251] my cousin who is an Infidel and never goes to any

---

[251] "Bro. O." apparently was the Methodist preacher whose experience Redfield had just related. This may have been Thomas G. Osborn, who was the appointed preacher at Southampton, Long Island District, New York Conference, 1844–46. This church first appears in the *Minutes* as a separate appointment in 1844. It reported 55 members (including 3 "Colored") in 1845, 68 (including 6

church don't seem to act as bad as usual but goes with his head down, and I would not wonder if you might be able to talk to him about religion. Will you and Bro. R. go with me down to his house and see him?"

Down we went, and were introduced to his lady and sat down to wait for the brother to go to his shop and call him in. Soon he came in at the kitchen door. But the moment he caught sight of us he wailed out, "O God, O God, what shall, what shall I do? O, O, O God, what shall I do?"

I felt like getting the Bible and directing him to read for himself a promise to the broken-hearted sinner. I asked his wife, "Have you a Bible in the [house]?" /173/ She went to a short cupboard over the fireplace. As he caught sight of the forthcoming volume of God's blessed Word he broke out again, "O, that poor neglected Bible!"

I took the precious book and turned to the invitation of Christ, "Come unto me all ye that are heavy laden. Take my yoke upon you." "Ask and ye shall receive. Seek and ye shall find." I then held it to him and said, "Look at that, and read it."

He brushed his long hair from his eyes by a single wipe with his hands and gazed through his tears upon the previous word. I said, "I want you to read it for yourself." Then with great emphasis he said, "I am reading it."

"Well," said I, "I want you to believe it."

"I am believing it!" Here he broke and could say no more, but burst into such a perfect tempest of shouts as made the whole house to ring.

His wife immediately shrieked, "O God, O God, have mercy," and [began] wringing her hands, walking the floor and crying, "What shall I do?" The little children who were too young to appreciate the matter with the parents burst into a fit of loud crying. In a moment or two more the wife was happy in God.

As soon as the first gust of glory had passed over and the man became so far recovered from his frantic state of joy [as to be able to speak], he said, "I now know what all this means. I now know what all this means." And then deliberately [he] said, "I have not been to any church in two years. But about two months ago I felt sadly impressed that some great calamity would soon befall me, and I thought it prob-

"Colored") in 1846, and 75 (including 5 "Colored") in 1847. This identification is not at all certain, however, either as to preacher, place, or time. It seems likely that the church in question was in the New York Conference and that the year was 1844 or 1845. However there were at this time several conference preachers whose surnames began with O.

able I should either die or lose some of my family. But now I see it was the Holy Spirit convicting me, and now I have got religion."

The preacher went down through Main Street to visit the people, while I returned to his house. After a long while [he] came back with the glad tidings that God had indeed broken up the entire place /174/ for, said he, "As I was passing the first store one of the partners called me in and, standing over the counter weeping, asked me if I could tell them what they must do to be saved. I directed them as well as I could and started on down the street. [As I was] passing the court house, the jailer asked me to come in and pray for him, for he wanted religion. I left here and, passing a lawyer's office, he accosted me there, 'Sir, can you tell me what I must do to be saved?'"

I continued a few weeks to labor with this preacher. But the work was going well enough without me, and I left for other more pressing calls. Just before I left I counted about forty who gave in their testimony for God in one of our meetings, and they all spoke of the instrumentation which brought them to Christ. Without one exception, the forty which I counted would begin in about this strain: "About two months ago while in my field (or store, or office or about my business), I felt that the awakening Spirit of God had got hold of me, and I sought and obtained mercy." But no one was there among them all that referred to any preaching or any meeting whatever as operating in awakening them.

Chapter [16][252]

I now went at the call of a brother to a small city where the Methodists had been kept pruned of all [evangelistic fruit] that was of any financial benefit to a church. The very churches who would make cormorants of the Methodists to fish for them began their usual tirades against our church when our meetings began. Twenty long years had they lived off from Methodists' revivals to keep up their membership. Of course as soon as our labors began, they must widen the distinctives and increase the contrast in the cost, which their own reason told them must be kept up if they should succeed in taking in our converts.[253]

I saw the wickedness of this ungodly trick and resolved to stop it if

252 Though Redfield here begins a new chapter, JGT continues the narrative uninterrupted.

253 JGT condenses this to: "He now went at the request of a minister to a small city where the Methodists for many years had been robbed by systematic proselyting of all who would be of financial benefit to a church; and this by open hostility" (146).

I could. So I told them publicly, "You must either [sic] get religion enough to stop your /175/ wicked proselyting and then quarry out sinners for your own church, for your success in picking the Methodists is now ended. For I warn all who get religion here to keep clear of you or they will most likely lose their souls under your treatment."

One of their ministers preached directly against us—and soon after his church dismissed him. Another preacher attempted it, and his church told [him] to let that be the last, or they would dismiss him. We had five or six ungodly establishments to pick at us. But God enabled us for once to hold our own and save our converts from going into a wolf's den under the supposition that they were going into a sheepfold.

But a poor drunken Universalist preacher who had once been a Methodist, and [was] expelled and then turned Episcopalian, and [was there] dismissed and then [became a] Universalist, was not so easy to get along with. He went off to New York and tried to get something against me out of which he could make up a probable story which would shake the confidence of the people in me and stop me. For he was likely to lose his members, as some of his most staunch ones were converted, and his church which he was building was stopped from further progress. He was [so] foolish [as to] to lay open his plan before some persons who knew me, and they sent me information of his plans.

I paid no regard to it. I had happened to take the last stage from New York before the steamer navigation was opened after a great freeze, and was the only passenger. Of course but few knew when I came into the city. This gave [this preacher] a chance to get up the slander that I came to the city on a stolen horse and that I had lately run away from a city some two hundred miles distant under great disgrace. But, poor fellow, I left him in the hands of God, and shortly after he died of delirium tremens.[254]

XX. "Ain't I dying?"

I continued to labor with all my might. So greatly had I become reduced in health that I expected to die, and every time I preached it did seem that I never could preach again. I would /176/ [have attacks of] vomiting, which seemed to indicate that I had a cancer of the stomach.[255] As soon as I had finished my sermon I was compelled to lie

---

[254] JGT ends his chapter 21 here and begins chapter 22 (on page 148).

[255] JGT: "Mr. Redfield's extreme and incessant labors now began to tell severely upon his naturally frail constitution. For some time each effort to preach had greatly exhausted him, and sometimes it had seemed as though he would

down in the pulpit and let others attend to the prayer meeting. After the close of our meeting, weak and distressed I would go to the preacher's house, and by the use of strong mustard plasters would drain so much to the surface as to recuperate enough to preach once more. But when mustard could no longer relieve, I would burn it in with a hot iron and compel enough counter-irritant to rise [to enable me] for one more effort.

Thus I continued every night till I could stand no longer, and now went home to die. I did not preach again in eight months or go to church in six months. The customary pains now seized me, which would convulse me and send the cold sweat out of me and wring from me agonizing groans. But in the midst of it all my soul was so full of God that I cried out, "O Lord, I would not have one pain less." O how happy I felt with the consciousness that I had fallen with my armor on. I was suffering for my zeal for God and not for any wickedness.

I now found a place in a very kind family who would do all they could for my comfort. To all appearance I could not live but a very short time, and yet I would not allow anyone to sit up with me. Then they would come in to look at me in the night. I did not know but that I should die alone, but I would not allow them to take so much trouble as to come to me in the night. So one night I locked my door so that they would feel themselves excused from watching me in the night.

I went to my bed and lay down. But scarcely had I lay down when I felt a wave pass over me from head to foot, and with it an impression clear as a voice saying, "This is death!" In a moment I realized my condition and thought, "They will find my door locked in the morning, and after awhile will force upon the door and find me dead.

"Well," thought I, "if this is death, I /177/ will go singing." So I sang, "I am on my way, passing over." I sang the first verse and began the second when my voice was hushed, and I finished it in a whisper.

I tried the third verse, but my breath stopped. I then tried to move a hand or foot, but could not. I then felt a sensation all over as if my spirit was just going to leave the body, but it seemed to stick about the shoulders. My eye was turned up and, O, the sight of myriads on myriads of angels [who] were hovering all over me and waiting to take me home! I never before had any idea of the innumerable host. All my previous notions of the multitude of angels in the heavenly world were eclipsed. How utterly bewildering must be the number of angelic beings, if the little escort that came to welcome me were so far beyond count!

---

never be able to preach again. Severe attacks of vomiting had now set in that indicated cancer of the stomach" (148).

But with the same suddenness, that wave of death was removed and I was entirely out of this state. My heavenly visitors were all gone. I had often prayed before this that I might have some testimony which would be reliable and prove that the frequent sights which the dying declare they have are indeed so, and not hallucination. I saw two sisters in quick succession follow each other with consumption to the grave. Both professed to find the blessing of perfect love in a revival where I was laboring. The first one that died raised her arms while dying and gave me with her dying lips a kiss of love, and passed away saying she saw angels and heard them, and children were mingled with them. She then called upon her watchers to listen and to look. But they pronounced her as out of her right mind, to which she responded, "O, no I am not. Now look there, and now listen." But the scene and sound was only for her eyes and ears.

Soon after I was called in company of the attending physician [to] make the last sad visit to the other sister. On [our] approaching the sick-room, as we entered she asked, "Who has come?"

"Your physician."

"Well, let him come in. And who is the other one?" They told her.

"Well, let him come in, too."

I approached the bed. /178/ There stood her weeping mother and husband and other friends. Her eyes were already glazed with the clouds of death. She then asked the physician, "Doctor, ain't I dying? I think I am, and have been all day."

Her doctor, who knew not the supports of grace in the trying hour, feared to answer. But the more he hesitated, the more she cried, "Say, Doctor, ain't I dying? You must tell me."

He touched her pulse and then her temple and finally said, "Yes, you are now dying."

Words must fail to paint the inexpressible smile which passed over her face. "And now," said she, "Let everybody come in, that I may testify to them of the power of salvation in death." Then she would sink into a gentle doze of half a minute, and then again arouse herself and with a heavenly smile say, "O yes, bless the Lord, I am dying."

She then reached out her hand and took mine. The chill of death was on [it]. "O," said she to me, "do [you] see those beautiful stars? I want once more, if I can, to testify to the power of this great salvation. O," said she, "do continue to preach holiness, for O how it saves. I want the whole world to hear my testimony for once." She had felt quite offended at my pressing her so hard to give up all conformity to the world to get this blessing, and now she seemed eager to encourage me to press it on others with all my might, as the glorious results were so rich.

I had prayed that I might know, and the answer came that I should, and the suspended animation when I saw the vision of angels was the fulfillment of the promise.[256]

XXI. Phoebe Palmer: "These strange facts"

I shortly went to one of the large city churches to preach one Sabbath, as my health would allow. Going to the house of Sister P. [Palmer] at noon, I thought to exchange some thoughts with her and related some of these strange facts.[257]

[Phoebe Palmer said,] "I believe we should have much more of these than we do, if we would not make a bad use of them." Then [she] said, "I wish Sister B. was here; I would like to have her tell you some facts concerning her mother."

The doorbell just then /179/ rang and in came Sister B. Turning to her, [Mrs. Palmer] said, "I wish you would tell Bro. R. about the remarkable death of your mother."

"Well," said Sister B., "My mother enjoyed the blessing of perfect love for more than forty years. When she came down with the sickness which ended her life, myself and sister watched with her by turns all through, till on the last night Mother said, 'Now daughters, you must go to rest, for it will disturb me to know that you are so much broken of your rest.'

"But," said Sister B., "[I told her,] 'O Mother, you don't know how sick you are,' and [Mother said,] 'I now feel quite easy. But I cannot rest and know that you are so wearied out as you must be by this time.'"

The mother was so anxious that one of the sisters left the room. But Sister B. made up a little bed for herself [at] one side and out of

---

[256] JGT interprets this somewhat obscure sentence as follows: "These incidents had made a deep impression upon his [Redfield's] mind, and the vision described at the opening of this chapter he always thought was the fruition of the desire that was created by them" (150).

[257] JGT: "While recovering from his sickness, he was invited to preach in one of the New York churches. After service he went to Dr. Palmer's to dinner. When he had an opportunity to do so, he related some of these incidents to Sister P— and asked her views in regard to them" (150–51). This was likely the Allen Street M.E. Church, where the Palmers attended. Probably the Palmers heard Redfield preach and invited him home for dinner. This seems to have been Redfield's first direct conversation with Phoebe Palmer, though he may have spoken briefly with her at the camp meeting mentioned earlier.

sight of her mother, then took the light and hid it behind the fire-board in the fireplace, and then carefully lay down. But, said she, "As I lay down, all at once the room was flooded with light, as light as day. I could see all the furniture and [on] the bed covering on my bed the duct[?] and stitches."

I asked, "But were you not dreaming?"

"O no, that could not be, for I thought the same, and I raised up and felt of myself, and tried various experiments to assure myself of the truth or hallucination of the existing scene. And so I continued, till I thought I would turn around and look at the bed where Mother was. Then I saw a perfect crowd of angels who hovered all around, and over her bed, and with most heavenly but sedate faces they were intently looking right where I knew the face of my mother was. I gazed and gazed, and I greatly wondered that I felt no fears. Thus I continued till I thought, 'Well, I must have some sleep, and will now lie down.' But the instant I closed my eyes, my mother called, 'Daughter.' I sprang up and ran to her bed. Daylight had come, and as I approached her, she raised her hands and said, 'O Daughter, what a night, what a night I have spent!'

"Why Mother," said I, "was you in pain? Why did /180/ you not call me? I did not leave the room."

"O no, Daughter, I was in no pain. But as soon as you left, the angels have been here and staid with me all night." She then gave her charge to the family and passed away.

Sister P. [Palmer] then related a circumstance of interest concerning a young lady who was very pious and who, when she was dying, [she] herself and all around heard most delightful music over their heads. And what was more strange was that when the funeral was carrying her to the grave, the music followed and then returned to the house, and for months it was heard occurring over the place where she had died. The vision which I had but confirmed me in the fact that these things were so.

XXII. "Entering the harvest field with all my might"

Chapter [17][258]

As my health recruited I began again to enter with all my might into the harvest field. The promise to me was kept ever fresh, "You may live while you preach, but no longer." I had tested this course on a

[258] JGT also begins a new chapter here (chapter 23, beginning on page 153).

dying bed and found it right, and now [I determined,] "I shall use every returning[?] power to carry out the designs of God concerning me." My courage was greatly renewed in the final reform of the M.E. Church, as I could now count on four or five more ministers who were committed to the great work of spreading scriptural holiness over the land not only, but were in possession of the blessing and were beginning to see the fruits in the conversion of sinners.[259]

I was now invited to go to a place where one of these preachers had been appointed and where God was blessing his labors to some extent. But while [I was] laboring there and a goodly number had been converted, all at once the work of conversions stopped. I was in an agony, and not knowing the cause of this check to the work, I resorted to prayer. Again we met in church and my distress was so great I felt I could not contain it. When I ought to have borne it and given vent to the struggle before the people, I deliberately cast it off. /181/ Then the word was impressed [upon me,] "Let them alone," and then such a view of destruction passed before me as showed that Death would now do its work, and I prayed it right out, and then left the place.

The preacher after some time saw me again and said, "Do you remember with what an awful prayer you closed your labors at our place, in which you declared that Death would now sweep the place? Well, a disease that affected no other place around did sweep many to their graves." And then I learned what stopped our revival—a ~~large~~ number of young men banded themselves together not to seek religion, and to hinder the work.

Again I was invited to go to a place where I had before been. I did not feel called of God to go, but went, as it was early in the season. But this visit opened the way for me to go to a place where the Methodists had never as yet got a foothold, and I had an opportunity to know a little of the opposition which our pioneer preachers had to contend with where the standing order, as they were called, claimed all the rights of the church and state.

About ten miles from G., where I was called to visit,[260] there was a church occupied by one of these old bigoted men. He had likewise an-

---

[259] JGT adds, "His [Redfield's] views of the doctrine and the experience, and his methods of advancing them, had undergone a new test to him—a thorough and solemn review on the brink of eternity. He now entered the field with stronger faith, and courage, and determinations than every before" (153).

[260] JGT has, "It was about ten miles from G— (probably Goshen)" (154). Goshen is about fifty miles northwest of New York City, near Middletown, New York. The M.E. Church there was part of the New York Conference.

other flock about three miles east, and still another about six [miles] off to whom he used to go and preach once in six months, and [he would go to] attend weddings and funerals.

A short time before, I visited the village three miles east of his main church. A Methodist man attempted to have a prayer meeting in a schoolhouse. But the opposition was so great that they got the house nailed and locked up to keep the Methodists out. When I arrived in town I found an Episcopalian lady who knew some of the power of salvation, and she invited me to make her house my home. The husband was an infidel, and I believe made so by the unholy type of religion which surrounded him.

When I arrived, the [school]house had been opened, [so] I gave out an appointment to preach in the evening. Though the weather was warm,[261] yet the people who were /182/ daring enough to come out of curiosity to see a Methodist meeting either came veiled, and if [i.e., some] even took their stations outside and looked in at the windows. I had to do my own singing, praying, and kneeling as well as preaching.[262]

During the day I visited from house to house. I will give a few instances. I went into a deacon's house.

"Good morning, Deacon. How are you prospering in the good way to heaven?"

Deacon: "We don't want any of your fanaticism here."

"Well, but I suppose you love God and his ways."

Deacon: "I tell you we don't want an element of discord introduced here."

"I suppose," said I, "Deacon, that you have often prayed for the salvation of your children. Shall we pray for them now?"

Deacon: "You ain't wanted here, Sir. We want none of your disturbance, for we are all at peace now."

"But I think, Deacon, we will pray for your children now."

"I want you to leave my house."

"Well, I think I will pray first." So down I knelt and prayed for the old man and family.

I then went to another deacon's house. As I went in and found him alone, his face was white with rage. I tried to charm him into some religious conversation, but he would not answer me. After a long fruitless

---

[261] JGT has, "the weather was severe," but in the manuscript the word appears to be "warm," not "severe" (154).

[262] JGT: "The women kept closely veiled, or stood outside and looked in at the windows, and he had to do his own singing and praying" (154).

effort to get him to say something, I at last said, "May I have the privilege of praying with you before I leave?"

"Pray if you want to," was the very short and gruff reply. I needed no further permission, and I knelt down and thanked God for the kind and Christian-like deportment of the deacon who was so willing to let me pray in his house, and then left.

The next day afternoon I saw the old deacon in the schoolhouse, seated as regularly as anyone. He soon got up and wanted to speak. I said, "Go on, Brother." So he told the congregation that I had been to his house the day before and how mad he was at the sight of me, and how roughly he had treated me, and then that I had prayed for him like a Christian. "But," said he, "after Mr. R. was gone, I began to reflect, and at night I went to bed but not /183/ to sleep, for I could not. Finally so great was my agony that I got up and got down on my knees before God. I thought I must die before morning. I dared not sleep. I remained all night on my knees praying for my soul, and about the break of day God spoke peace to my soul, and now I have got religion."

This was like a thunderclap upon the ears of the people, to hear an old bigoted and staid deacon so agitated and so changed.

I did not feel called upon to put any great task or cross upon the people, such as coming to any particular place or bench. I could tell the ladies who were sufficiently awakened to make a right move, for they would come in and sit with their fans unmoved, and the men would take seats. So all I had to do was simply to ask all who wished to be saved just to stand up. The work broke in great and glorious power.

An old lady now sent for me to call on her. Two of her daughters had come out very clearly, and their bright testimony put the old lady's hope in the shade. When I reached the house and was introduced to the woman, I saw her face as the picture of despair. She broke silence and with emotion said, "O Sir, my daughters tell me they know their sins are forgiven and that they are the children of God, and I don't know what to think of myself."

Not to shock her too badly, I thought best to accommodate her prejudices by the use of those terms by which her church was accustomed to speak of the religious state. So I said, "I suppose, Madam, that you already entertain a hope."

"O, no," said she with evident horror at such presumption. "I would not dare to be so presumptuous!" Then in very measured sentences[263] she said, "I do – think – I – can – say – that – I – have – a de-

[263] JGT has, "in a nervous, sententious manner." However, the words he interprets as "nervous, sententious" appear rather to be "measured sentences."

sire – to wish that – I might have a hope." This was about the type of most which passed for religion in this place.

I found one, however, who knew the power of /184/ salvation. She was in the last degree of suffering from suffocation induced by the asthma. Her minister had been sent for to visit her, but he did not come. When I entered the room I was greatly moved to see her gasping for breath. She was bolstered up, as she could not lie down, her face swollen and her breathing very short and panting. She could say nothing which I could understand, a few feet from her. But her sister would put her ear down to her lips and catch the whispered answers to my questions. I asked her if she found religion to satisfy her in the midst of this great distress. The answer came back, "I am so filled with comfort and joy that if this agony of dying is to be forever, I am perfectly content and happy."

I started to the afternoon meeting and there saw the minister, who had been persuaded to come out and give this poor flock an extra sermon. He was almost opening religious services, so I took my seat and listened. After a formal opening he began his sermon by stating to the people that he was "set for the defense of the gospel" [cf. Philippians 1:7], and while he was upon the walls of Zion he must protect his flock from ravening wolves. He then opened his batteries on John Wesley and the Methodist Church and warned his people to keep clear of them and not to forsake the religion of their fathers.

He then in substance told them that he should now relate a matter which he had read in one of the New York papers. "But," said he, "I shall not call names." (I had happened to read the same, so I knew what was coming.)

"Yes," said he, "there was a man—but I shall not call his name—who came from New York and went into a village some thirty or more miles from N. York. [He] told the people that they had the devil in them and they must take an emetic which he had prepared for them, and vomit up the devil. But I ain't going to speak the man's name. Well, he got some to take it, and it was feared that /185/ they would die, and the constables were after this man—but I shall call no names."

The meeting closed, and one of the principal men of the place said to the minister, "Mr. E., you better stay and hear this man preach tonight and see if you think you have treated him right."

"No," said the clerical gent, "I cannot stay with you."

"But Sir, you have implied some very hard things against Mr. R., and I think it is no more than right you should be at some pains to learn what you now evidently know nothing of." But away he went.

One of his members stepped up to me and said, "Mr. R., I have hated the very sight of you, and when I have seen you passing [in] the street, it has been with difficulty that I could restrain myself from whipping you. But I won't see you so abused, and if you will build a Methodist church here, I will give you fifty dollars." Another said he would give a lot; another, fifteen dollars, and so it went on, and soon we had a church up and dedicated, and the last I heard from them, it was in a flourishing condition. The minister's opposition laid the foundation of three new churches and built one, and this work [now] forms a good appointment and is regularly supplied from conference.[264]

XXIII. Continue Stressing Holiness?

I went off to a camp meeting where [I met] a few of my old preacher friends who had promised to follow the old track of holiness. But they had all backed down and did not know it. They took me back where they could counsel me and began in this way: "Now, Bro. R., you know that everywhere you go revivals break out in great power, and the people are counted by the hundreds and sometimes by the thousands."

"Yes," said I, "I know it, and I know too it is only the legitimate workings of holiness in the hearts of the people."

"Well, well," said one; "that's all granted. But Bro. R., are you willing to take advice?"

"Most certainly I am, if it is good."

"Well now, if you could adopt any way by which thousands would be converted where you /186/ now see only hundreds—"

"Most gladly do I desire to do all I can."

"Well," said he, and they all concurred in it, "if you will not say so much about holiness, perfect love, and sanctification, and don't press anyone up to these things—for that makes many people mad, and many of our preachers are getting afraid of you. Some say you never can do good enough to overbalance the harm you have already done, and you get so many prejudiced against yourself, and it must be very uncomfortable to you to have to meet so many prejudices."

"Well, what would you have me do?"

"Why, I would have you cease to use those terms which barely to

---

[264] JGT: "'The minister's opposition laid the foundation for three new churches and built one, and made a good appointment for a preacher, and has been regularly supplied from conference ever since.' (1863.)" (158). Thus Terrill identifies 1863, the last year of Redfield's life, as the time of the writing of Redfield's manuscript.

speak them arouses the prejudices at once. But, Bro. R., you can preach up Bible religion as high as the Bible warrants, but drop these objectionable terms."

One of the preachers then said, "I am now at the church in F. where the people were so offended at you when you was there that they would not allow you to stay. But," said he, "I have preached the doctrine of holiness up very strong and have done it up so cautiously that no one knew what I was preaching about. They have endured it, and now they are willing to have you come back." (I afterwards went back and found they were worse than ever before and a stench in the nose of God and all good men.)

Well, this counsel was the exact thing to take with me, and I thought, "What a Godsend that these good brethren have helped me out of my difficulties. I certainly do find all the opposition I can possibly stand up under. I am willing to go free of charge. But my nature shrinks when called unflinchingly to stand for God and either in word or tacitly tell the time-serving preacher that he is an enemy of God. I don't ask any office in the church higher than local preacher, but I dare not do otherwise.[265] But now I have found out an easy way, apparently, to accomplish much more for God and thus to be for once and forever free from the /187/ slanders and misunderstandings which follow me all over the land."

So out I went as before. As soon as our protracted meetings began [I] attempted to preach the best I knew how, and yet avoid any objectionable term.[266] But I felt my power with God and man were gone. After two or more weeks barely one person [was] moved at all, and that one so slightly [that] she did not stand a week.

"Well," thought I, "my mission is ended. God has got through with me, so I think I can now go home and attend to business and bid farewell to this rough, toilsome and heart-aching cause. And how good it will be once more to feel that I am not an Ishmaelite, my hand against every man and every man's hand against me [cf. Genesis 16:12]. But before I go and abandon this course of life, I will ask some counsel."

In casting about for someone to whom I could open my whole soul, I thought of a pious old colored man.[267] So I went to see him and

---

[265] JGT clarifies, "I don't ask any office in the church higher than that of a local preacher, but I dare not do otherwise than take that" (159).

[266] JGT: "So out I went as soon as the season for protracted meetings began, and attempted to preach the best I knew how, and yet avoid the objectionable terms" (159).

[267] It is interesting that Redfield did not seek out the Palmers for counsel.

told him I would like to have a talk with him. I took him out into a grove and, when seated, I told him in short my experience on the subject of holiness and the awful power of God manifested in the conversion of sinners when that doctrine was preached. "But," said I, "that mission which God gave me is now with all its power gone from me, and I think God has got done with me, and doesn't now require me to keep on preaching."

"Ah, my brother," said this good old man, "and hain't you neber compromised?"

"Compromised?" said I. "Why no, dear brother, I would as soon cut my arm off. I dare not do that." But recollecting myself, I said that I had been counseled by good preachers to avoid the use of the terms perfect love, sanctification, holiness because the people's prejudice was so strong against it they would be angry at me and then I could do them no good. "But I try to preach the Bible truth as high as ever."

"Dat is it," said my good friend. "Dare all de trouble lie. Now, what God call sanctification you no business to call anyting /188/ else. It ain't you dat de people hates; it is de Lor'."[268]

God so let the light shine through this old black diamond that I saw [that] there was the very place where I lost my mission and power. "But," said I to myself, "I will go right back and preach those doctrines right in the notch where I used to, and in the meantime seek it over again."[269]

Scarcely had I touched the old key when the power came. God did not condemn me, but [had] dropped me. But I learned this lesson, and that is, that we can by no means keep right with God unless we obey in all things, great and small.

Chapter [18][270]

I now went to another place where the minister of the parish not only cautioned his people against the Methodists but brought to light an old law which gave the minister of the parish authority over the people, especially the minors of his parish. He might compel them with the rod, and he threatened to make use of it. This [however] moved the hearts of the people in the right direction, and a Methodist Church was built and

---

268 JGT exaggerates the dialect a bit: "'Dat is it. Dare is just where de trubbel lie. Now what God call sanctification, you no bizness to call anysin else. It isn't you de people hates; 't is de Lor'.'" (160).

269 JGT: "and in the meantime seek my power over again" (160).

270 Though Redfield here begins a new chapter, Terrill continues his chapter for two more paragraphs (161).

supplied as the result of this oppression.

I then went to the church where the preacher had won the people over to love holiness by preaching it in such a guise that they did not know what he was at.[271] But I found the state of affairs bad enough. There again I had one of my awful burdens, and this time it seemed to me that I must be fainting away. So I got up to the window and raised it, and when I found the fresh air did not help me, I knew it to be a burden [from God]. So intense were my sufferings I felt I could not endure it, and the suggestion came, "Cast your burden on the Lord." I got down and gave vent to my pent-up agony in sobs, groans, and tears, and as it passed off I felt, "God has left this place, and your labors are now done." So it proved, and I left.

XXIV. The 1846 Middletown, Connecticut, Revival

I was now called to visit a large place where we have a college.[272] But my heart dreaded the /189/ conflict which I knew must follow on if I did not lower the standard of gospel truth, unless I could find men willing to take sides with God. If I had been going to state prison I could hardly have felt worse, except from the disgrace of being a criminal. But I had promised to go, and I made up my mind to meet the worst that could come.[273]

---

[271] Since the next incident Redfield records is his ministry in Middletown, Connecticut, which began on February 15, 1846, this incident presumably occurred in late January or early February, 1846.

[272] JGT: "Mr. Redfield was next called to visit Middletown, Conn., the seat of a Methodist university [i.e., Wesleyan University]" (162).

[273] Here JGT adds, "Rev. B. T. Roberts, now [1889] General Superintendent of the Free Methodist Church, but who, at the time of Mr. Redfield's labors in Middletown, was a student in the university, describes the state of the work there at that time as follows," and then quotes a long paragraph from B. T. Roberts' account of the Middletown revival, part of Roberts' article, "Dr. Redfield's Labors," *The Earnest Christian* 7, no. 2 (Feb. 1864): 37–38. This passage begins, "The state of religion in the church was extremely low. Professing Christians were chiefly distinguished for their conformity to the world." Roberts says that "Dr. Redfield's preaching created a profound sensation. His deep-toned piety, his fervent, moving appeals to the throne of grace, and his unearthly, overpowering eloquence disarmed criticism, even in that congregation of critics, and prepared the way for the reception of the truths he uttered." Roberts adds that "Dr. Olin seconded the effort in the university" and that "Nearly all the young men in the college were converted" (quoted in JGT, 162–63).

Redfield began the series of revival meetings at the Middletown M.E. Church on Sunday, February 15, 1846. He preached almost daily for two

At our first meeting there were numbers who took a decided stand against me and declared that this type of religion should not get in there. But while they were getting their forces ready to put me down, Dr. O. [Stephen Olin], the president, and three or four of the professors told the right ones that "Bro. R. is a Methodist and preaches the genuine Methodist doctrine," and they should stand by me. This brought the opposition to a dead halt.

One of the professors in the college [i.e., university] was the first to take a public stand to seek the great blessing of holiness. Soon the whole place, college and all, was moved, and holiness was the grand theme. The sinners flocked from the city and over three hundred were converted. At the same time the work was going on in the college, promoted there principally by the labors of the tutors and professors who had obtained the blessing of perfect love.[274]

They began on this wise: They made the ringleader of all the rude young men a special subject of prayer, having selected one of the small rooms in the college for the purpose. They continued till they felt they had got a hold on God, and very soon they heard the young man running and rollicking through the lower hall as if possessed of evil spirits. Believing this to be an indication that prayer was heard, they held on, and the next night this young man came down to the church and obtained religion. They then informed him how they had made him a special subject of prayer, and /190/ he should now enter the plan and assist in praying for another. They picked the [next] young man, and he too soon came out in the enjoyment of religion.

They now divided the praying company into two and occupied two rooms. [They] selected [other students] again and again, and it was a very remarkable fact that just in that order these young men were convicted and converted. They had found a secret mine of power, and that was with holy hands to pray for particular persons, and that was pretty sure to succeed.

Elated with this new discovery, they could not keep it secret. Soon the very feelings of some of them [who were converted were] accounted for by themselves as resulting from the answered prayers of the

---

weeks, addressing the church in the afternoons and sinners in the evenings. The church building was located on the same property as Wesleyan University, and many of the university students attended the services.

[274] JGT has, "More than three hundred were converted at the church. At the same time the work was going gloriously forward in the college. The tutors who had experienced entire sanctification entered into it heart and soul" (163). However, Terrill omits the earlier part of the paragraph.

students. As an instance, one of the students went to one of the praying band and asked him, "Have you got my name down as a subject of prayer?"

The answer was, "We have."

"Well," said he, "I thought you must have, from my feelings, and I may as well give up now." So they went into a science room and prayed for him, and I had the happiness of hearing him testify in church that night what great things God had done for him.

The president [Stephen Olin] took a lively interest in the work at the college and desired, though in ill health, to speak ten minutes to the converted students in a large recitation room. But his ten minutes swelled into hours, and that famous speech was published and passed for a remarkable effort of the president.[275]

The [conversions during the] revival all told numbered nearly four hundred souls, city, college and all. And out of the collegians twenty-six became preachers of the gospel.[276] The sainted [William Case] Kendall probably took his cue on the subject of holiness from seeing the results there, and preached it with great success through his short but shining track.[277] He too found himself as much opposed and oppressed as I did myself for daring to take a stand for the exact right. When he entered his labors and tried to carry out the grand scheme of re-laying the foundations of primitive Methodism on the cornerstone of holiness, he found he /191/ had waked up an unrelenting hostility in the Methodist ministry, who tried in many ways to arrest his influence and put an end to the fanatical doctrine of holiness.

---

[275] This exhortation of Olin's is documented in several sources—e.g., in Joseph Holdich, "Revival in The Wesleyan University" (Letter to the Editors), *Christian Advocate and Journal* 20, no. 33 (25 March 1846): 130. See the narrative in Snyder, *Populist Saints,* chapter 10.

[276] This was one of Redfield's most remarkable revivals.

[277] JGT: "The result of the revival in the city and at the college, all together, was nearly four hundred conversions. Twenty-six of the college students became ministers of the gospel. Here the sainted William C. Kendall learned the art of soul saving, and went from here to preach the same gospel for a short season with great success. His was a short but a shining track" (164). Interestingly, Terrill changes "took his cue on the subject of holiness" to "learned the art of soul saving." No doubt Terrill means that Kendall learned from Redfield that the way to win sinners to Christ was to preach holiness. Kendall, a close friend and colleague of B. T. Roberts, died in early 1858 at the age of 35. See Charles Canon, "B. T. Roberts' Supporting Cast: Rev. William C. Kendall (1822–1858)," *Free Methodist Historical Society Newsletter* 2, no. 1 (Summer 2001): 1.

He once asked me, after [his] entering the field as an itinerant: "Why," said he, "do you always pursue this straight course?"

"Yes, Bro. K., I dare not do otherwise."

"Well," said he, "I should think they would sometimes run you under, don't they?"

"O yes, but I have this to console me, and that is, if they run me under while I am unflinching for exact right, Jesus always goes under with me, and I shall rise with Him if buried with Him, for He will certainly have a resurrection."

This dear indefatigable warrior for God labored some ten to fourteen years amid opposition of the worst kind, yet faithful to his trust to the last. He died at his post, declaring with his latest breath, "I have fought a good fight. I am going home. The angels are now all through the house." So great was the glory when the angels took him that his wife fell under the power beside his dead body. The converts came in and, taking hold of his dead hand, they vowed to follow their leader.

Strange as it may seem, while he was dying in such triumphs one of the ministers of his own conference was getting up charges to have him silenced or expelled at the coming conference.[278] But when his spirit had left, another faithful brother minister who was finally expelled said to this persecuting preacher, "You will have no more trouble with Wm. C. Kendall in worrying or cramping him in his appointments, for he is stationed on Mount Zion in the City of the living God."[279]

Strange as it may seem, this wicked preacher, who probably felt some compunction of conscience, went up to the funeral and, taking up the hymnbook, read, "Servant of God, Well Done." The notorious B. T. Roberts, a man who could not be swayed from what he believed to be right, likewise left the study of the law at fifteen[?], received[?] and became a minister /192/ of the gospel and has already made his mark all over the land.[280]

---

[278] Kendall died at West Falls, New York, on February 1, 1858. B. T. Roberts wrote an eight-part account of his life and death, including the charges that were brought against him, for *The Earnest Christian*. It was published in the 1861 *Earnest Christian* in March (85–89), April (117–19), June (181–85), July (204–05), August (229–31), September (277–81), November (335–36), and December (373–77). The account of his death is given on page 377.

[279] This presumably is a reference either to B. T. Roberts or Joseph McCreery, Jr., both of whom were expelled from the Genesee Conference in 1858. The quoted remark would have been characteristic of McCreery.

[280] JGT ends the reference to Kendall with "He too found himself much opposed, for daring to stand for the right" (164), omitting the account of Kend-

Chapter [19]

On leaving M. [Middletown], I felt confident that holiness would now win its way and I should probably live to see it pushing its victories all over the land, for I could now count on high names. But I had yet to learn in the deportment towards W. C. Kendall, that blessed man, and [in remarks by] one of our bishops, that we had yet much to fear.[281]

XXV. Revival Ministry in the East, 1846–1850

I was invited to visit a church in N. J. [New Jersey]. Arrived on Saturday night; met the church on Sabbath morning.[282] It had just been built, and in a most grotesque and gaudy manner, gilded and ornamented with showy lamps standing all around the gallery and with rich and gay carpets and sofas. My heart was grieved.

The preacher had told me, as he wished to be in New York and desired me to take his place, that he hoped I would not preach on holiness. When I saw the inside of the church, I saw the reason why. I felt that I must do my duty. But I was sure the people would not endure it and I must in all probability seek shelter in a tavern.

I took the money I had from my pocket to assure myself that I had enough to stay at the public house. When I saw I had, I felt whole[?] and resolved, "For once the people shall have the doctrine of holiness."[283] I went on regardless of all fears. When I had finished I met some in the aisle who grasped my hand and said, "Well, Brother, I believe in holiness and mean to have it."

---

all's death and the references to B. T. Roberts (a little more than a page of the manuscript). As indicated, two words here in Redfield's manuscript are virtually indecipherable. Roberts ended his study of law at the age of twenty-one.

[281] JGT restates this as follows: "Such was the success of this meeting, and the glorious stand taken by President Olin and his faculty, that Mr. Redfield began to hope again for the cause of holiness in the Methodist Church. He felt sure that such an endorsement would silence opposers and give that doctrine the right of way through the land" (164–65).

[282] JGT: "Mr. Redfield was now invited to a church in New Jersey to spend a Sabbath. He arrived on Saturday night, but did not enter the church until Sunday morning" (165). In adding the word "now" Terrill's account could be interpreted to mean that Redfield went directly from Middletown to this New Jersey church. That may be the case, but it is possible that some weeks intervened between the two engagements.

[283] JGT: "When I saw that I had enough, I was at rest, and resolved the people should hear holiness for once" (165).

I went to a prominent city in the same state and preached holiness. God came in power. The people fell under the power while [I was] preaching, all over the very large church. I could hear them dump, dump from their seats, away to the entire back of the church. But I found the preachers very much afraid of holiness, and [they would] hardly dare give it their approval.

And now someone asked me about my family. I answered, "That is a subject I very much dislike to talk about, for I have been /193/ unfortunate." This was enough to start surmises, and not long after, some bad stories came out, and again I was called to an account. I requested to select a committee of two of their presiding elders, and my wish was granted. When I had related the ~~terrible~~ great misfortune of my whole life, one of them, good Dr. B. [Heman Bangs], putting his hands on my head, said, "God bless you, Brother, you have my sympathies."[284] I told him how I had frankly told my troubles to some, and then the false details which soon appeared, and now I had simply requested to remain in silence on the subject of my misfortune. But that don't stop it.

"Well," said the good Dr. B., "I would not say anything to anybody about it." But it seemed after this that every place I visited the first question was a leading one on this to me now distressing subject. So I have often and often tried to keep ahead and in the lead in conversation so as not to allow this annoying theme to be introduced. But they would get it in somewhere and if I answered not at all, they would make what they pleased out of it.

Finally this became so distressing that I resolved to go and get legal counsel and know what it was best for me to do. So I went to a very reliable Christian lawyer in the City of N. York and told him my whole

---

[284] JGT: "Here, he again was asked in regard to his family. He told the inquirer that it was a matter he disliked to talk about, but that only made the matter worse. At last he was obliged to ask that he might meet two of the presiding elders, to whom he could tell the whole story. His request was granted, and they coincided with his view of the matter, that silence in regard to it was his best course" (165). JGT later identifies "Dr. B." as Heman Bangs (167), younger brother of Nathan Bangs, who was presiding elder on the New Haven (Conn.) District for some years in the late 1840s. The New Haven District was part of the New York Conference until 1849, when it became part of the New York East Conference when that was formed. The New Haven District did not include Middletown, which was part of the Hartford District. If Heman Bangs was at this time a presiding elder, this incident must have occurred after June 1848, more than two years after the Middletown revival, because Bangs was serving local churches up to that time. *Minutes,* New York Conference, 1846–50. However, Redfield's recollection of the chronology may have been faulty.

story. He told me what course to take and that [if I did so, then] no law on earth could annoy me. I took his counsel and was pronounced legally and forever free from all legal obligation to that bad woman.[285]

I had not seen or heard a word from her in more than five years, but I had frequently had rumors of her death. Yet I could not credit it so as to feel that I should never suffer again, for I had no means of silencing the inquisition, for I did not positively know she was dead. But I did know that I was [now] legally free from her, and [I] thought it best for me to bear as well as I could the silent grief over my misfortune. But I scarcely went to rest from day to day for a long time but [that] I thanked God [that] one more day of my life [was] gone and still [I was] free from that dreadful plague of my life. And in the morning [I would say], "Thank God [I have] /194/ been free another night."[286]

Chapter [20][287]

I was now confronted again. The preacher, who was a very tyrannical man, tried in open quarterly conference to wrench my license from me, saying he could not believe that I should have a local preacher's license to go beyond the bounds of my own church. But if I must, he would have me join every church where I preached.[288]

"But," said I, "I only preach two and three to five or six weeks in a place."

"Well, join those churches then for the length of time you do stay."

Here again good Dr. B. [Heman Bangs] came as presiding elder to my relief and said, "Bro. R. is a very useful man, and he must have his standing somewhere. He must, if he wishes it, have it here, and have his license renewed." And so it was.

---

[285] The year of Redfield's divorce is unclear. The immediately preceding narrative would suggest it was probably in 1848, but Redfield is somewhat vague as to the chronology.

[286] JGT summarizes this account in two sentences: "But from this [time] on the matter grew worse and worse, until after counsel and advice he put the matter in the hands of a lawyer and obtained a divorce. Mr. Redfield had not seen nor heard directly from her for over five years, but had heard rumors of her death several times" (165–66). JGT omits the detail that the divorce was (apparently) granted in New York City.

[287] JGT also begins a new chapter here (chapter 25, beginning page 167).

[288] JGT begins the chapter, "Mr. Redfield, about this time, met with opposition from the preacher in charge of the society where he held his membership. The issue was made on his license, the preacher taking the position that he should belong to the society where he labored. This was done on the floor of the quarterly conference" (167).

"O," I thought, "if these men only knew what it costs me in feelings to go without home and carry the masked[?] candor[?] which I do from my misfortune, and how hard I labor in the summer to get means to go with, they would not try to make my course any harder than it is." But I knew just where the pinch lay. These men were bent on making the M.E. Church a successful rival of the surrounding popular churches of the land. Wherever holiness gains ground the poor will come and crowd our congregations, and then our emotional meetings cannot be regulated, and every effort to rise into esteem among the proud will fail.[289]

I now went to R. M. to labor with an old preacher who had always been a very good representative of the primitive character of Methodism and himself had been one of the most successful of traveling preachers.[290] He gave me a number of interesting anecdotes of his la-

---

[289] JGT expands this passage, adding some of his own comments. He says that those opposing Redfield were men "who were laboring to make the church take rank in culture, splendor and influence with other churches. They could but see that the preaching and experience of holiness were attended with a renunciation of earthly pomp and glory that was fatal to what they were struggling for" (167). He adds, "One marked feature of the holiness revival was that the churches were filled with the poor, who gladly listened to truths from which the proud turned away" and explains, "Mr. Redfield at this time busied himself during the summer in earning the means by which he could pay his expenses during the revival season. His laboring without fee made it possible for him to get into places where otherwise he could not have gained admission" (168).

[290] JGT: "About this time he was invited to go to the assistance of Caleb Lippincott, a preacher of the primitive stamp, and one of the most successful in the church" (168). Redfield does not identify the preacher by name, so Terrill must have gotten the name through conversation with Redfield. Caleb A. Lippincott (born c. 1802; died July 26, 1871) was a preacher in the New Jersey Conference of the M.E. Church (*Minutes,* New Jersey Conference, 1845–49; Vernon Boyce Hampton, ed., *Newark Conference Centennial History, 1857–1957* [Historical Society of the Newark Annual Conference of The Methodist Church, 1957], 455). He would have been about 46 at the time of Redfield's encounter with him.

Probably "R. M." was Red Mills, the only appointment in the New Jersey Conference at that time with these initials. Red Mills was a rural church, part of the Paterson circuit. "The white frame church building of the Red Mills Methodist Episcopal Church was dedicated in September, 1843"; in 1849 this congregation became the mother church of the Hackensack M.E. Church (Hampton, *Newark Conference,* 485–86, 513). Caleb Lippincott was not the appointed preacher at Red Mills anytime between 1846 and 1850, but by "labor with" Redfield may mean that Lippincott was already conducting a revival there, and that he went to assist him.

bors—one of which was that when the country was new and he had to ride large circuits, he frequently passed over large tracts where there were no Methodists, and he was compelled on one occasion to stop at a public house. His gentlemanly bearing and cleanliness were at once seen, and he was treated with the respect due to a tidy, smooth-faced and healthy-looking /195/ stranger.

A ball was soon to be in operation. The people gathered, and as a matter of curiosity the stranger was invited up into the ballroom. He accepted the invitation, determined to do something for his Master if possible. When he was introduced, they according to custom invited the stranger to select his partner and lead off in the dance. He told me that he picked out a young lady that he thought would answer the purpose best and, [on his] walking onto the floor, the fiddler called to him to know what kind of a figure[?] he would have, and at the same time started the bow across the fiddle.

"Hold on, hold on a moment," cried the preacher. "I ain't quite ready," then saying, "As I must meet God in judgment for all this, I must pray first." Dropping upon his knees, [he] began to plead with God to come in awful power upon their hearts.

The young lady trembled. All was brought to a stand. Soon sobs and cries for mercy filled the ballroom, and that night twenty-three of them were converted and formed into a class and laid the foundation of a new church.

One year he was sent from conference to a circuit where a bad state of feeling had been engendered in the building of a new church some four miles distant from the first appointment, which was in a hall over a horse shed at a tavern. He went into the hall on Sunday morning and preached his first sermon and then, as was usual in those days, began to lead the class. He began with the leader. When he had finished his old stale story, the preacher turned upon him. "Well, Brother, that's an old story, I know, and you will have to get something more fresh than that or this place will get too hot for you."

"What," said the Leader, "and do you mean to insult me?"

"O no," said the preacher, "but I mean to tell you that you have not one bit of religion." He then took the next and next, and so on till he finished the class. They all in high wills told him not to show his head there again, for they would not put up with such rough and vile treatment. /196/ His only reply was, "I shall be around again in four weeks, and I shall then take into society more than forty members."

"But no," said they, "you must not come here again, for we will not stand it, and we won't have you here." But his cool and only reply was, "I shall be here again in four weeks, and then I shall take more than forty members into society."

When the time came round, he was on hand. This strange deportment created a great interest all over the region, and the hall was densely filled. The weather [was] warm and the windows open. The stairs went up to the hall from the outside, and a pump-stand [stood] at the bottom of the stairs. From the windows[?] of the hall and the position of the preacher's stand, all they [i.e., all the people] could be seen very well.

He soon began his sermon, and in due time the Spirit and power of God fell upon him. While he was yet preaching the people began to fall like men slain in battle. Many became affrighted and ran down the stairs and fell under the power at the foot of the stairs, near the pump. Some persons passing soon after and seeing some ladies in this condition, and supposing they had fainted away, began to pump water onto them.

He then engaged in a prayer meeting which continued till two o'clock in the morning. He then thought he would go out and get some refreshments. When he left the meeting for that purpose he was met by someone who told him that in a certain house there were a number of ladies who came to his meeting on the Sabbath [and who] just now [had] passed [by], and that they had fainted away. The doctor had been called and could not help them at all, and the doctor told them to go and find the Methodist minister, who would be more likely to know what was best to be done. So away he [i.e., the preacher] went and finished the night in prayer with them, and God saved them most gloriously. He then took the names of forty-three probationers and went on his way rejoicing.

Under his truly primitive stamp of preaching there have been fourteen or fifteen hundred slain at camp meeting.

The reader can see that I now had the benefit of laboring personally with one who was yet a member of conference and one whose /197/ type of labor harmonized with my views. I could but regard this as a favorable circumstance to keep in check the whisperings about my being unsound in the Methodist faith and measures. I was now at home, and thought I had no fear from the Methodist preachers to trouble me, for I was under the shelter of one who knew well what it was to go the straight way.[291] But alas, it seems that the Fates could not leave me, for

[291] JGT omits the long account of Caleb Lippincott (over two pages of manuscript) and continues here, "Mr. Redfield now thought, as he had found a preacher who was not afraid of the power of God, they would see a glorious work" (168).

when let alone from this class of people [i.e., opposition from Methodist preachers], the Universalists took up the work of trammeling me and arresting my influence. We had been laboring for some little time. The work of God broke out in great power, and great numbers were added unto the church.[292]

This revival made great horror among the Hicksite Quakers, and some very promising young men were among the fruits.[293] One old lady one night, whose daughter-in-law was soundly converted, was greatly enraged, and so far forgetting herself began to storm about the house and with violent gestures told the people she did not like it at all and was mad at them. No one who should look upon her face and gestures would be likely to call in question the truth of her statements. The meeting closed, and the old lady went home, but in the night [she was] in great distress of mind, and some of our sisters were called in to pray for her. While they were thus engaged she gave all up and believed to the saving of her soul, and her first utterance was, "O how I love everybody!"

The work continued in great power, house crowded and the altar filled and many rejoicing in the heat of their first love. Then all at once I saw our congregation begin suddenly to run down. After a few days there were so few out and the interest [was] so low that I concluded the main part of the revival had passed, and thought it was now best for me to go to my next place, about fourteen miles distant. So I got a private conveyance and made my journey to my next place. This I think was about Tuesday of the week.

On my arrival, I learned by the preacher that he had /198/ advertised the meeting to commence on the next Sabbath. "But," said I, "I can't let three or four days go unemployed, and I shall go right back and stay till Saturday morning."

In my absence the secret of our declining congregation came to the ears of the preacher. Papers by a prominent Universalist had been put in circulation describing me as a most notorious villain connected with the

---

292 I have not been able to correlate this claim with any particular church in the New Jersey Conference. It does not fit the Red Mills church.

293 JGT: "Among these [who were added to the church] were some promising young people from among the Hicksite Friends" (168). The Hicksites were a branch of the Quakers who followed a Quaker preacher-farmer from Long Island, Elias Hicks (1748–1830). The Hicksite schism began in Philadelphia in 1827–28. Hicks denied Christ's substitutionary atonement and physical resurrection. Daniel G. Reid, ed., *Dictionary of Christianity in America* (Downers Grove: InterVarsity, 1990), 524.

unfortunate J. N. M. and J. G. in matters of which I knew nothing, and in charges which did not even exist against them.[294] I was moreover accused of going about in this manner for the purpose of making money and winning a name. I read it all over carefully and then told the preacher I should meet that affair at once.

On the same night of the day I had left I was back and in the pulpit, to the no small astonishment of my enemies, the Universalists. I got right up and prepared to preach. I began by saying, "I verily left this morning not expecting again to return. But on learning at the next place that I must lose a number of days, I thought it best to come right back and spend them here. And I am glad from what I have learned that I did come back, for I find that while I have been laboring for the people's good, someone at my back has been returning me anything but good for my kindness. I hold in my hands a paper with a pretty large story adverse to the moral character of one J. W. Redfield, and when there is a congregation sufficiently large, I will tell you a story worth two of this." I then dropped the paper and went on preaching as if nothing had happened.

The next night a pretty good congregation assembled. I barely said, "I promised last night [that] when the congregation should be large enough, I would tell you a story worth two of this against me in this paper," and again [I] dropped my paper and went on preaching.

On the next night our house was crowded to a perfect fair. It being a warm night late in the fall, we had to have the door and the windows all opened. The people came for miles around. There were so many that I could see nothing but a sea of heads in all directions, in and out of the /199/ house.

I then said to them, "I will now tell you my story." And then, taking up the paper and reading the item charging me as [an] accessory with J. N. M., I simply said, "This is a matter that I can prove by such and such a man [that] I could by no possibility know [these charges] to have existed against the man J. N. M. Next, [concerning the charge

[294] JGT: "A Universalist paper had been circulated in the community in which Mr. Redfield had been published as a notorious villain, connected with John Newell Maffit, the noted evangelist, who was at that time under a cloud of dishonor. Of the matter charged in this paper Mr. Redfield had never heard" (169). Earlier Terrill refers to this Methodist evangelist as "John Newland Maffitt" (114). The second set of initials appears to be "J. G." or "P. G." Terrill does not identify or mention this person or include the initials. However, based on a later reference, it seems likely that Redfield intended "J. C." and that he is referring to James Caughey. Terrill refers to Caughey earlier (114).

that] I had been closeted with the said man in an iniquitous plot, this I can prove [by] such and such one to be false, as I was never alone with this man five minutes in my life. Next, I was charged with being in secret conclave with J. N. M. and J. C.[295] in a plot to divide the church. This I can prove by such and such an one to be entirely false and that [not] till I saw the charge here stated did I even know that such charges existed against these men.

"I am then charged with going about in this manner to make money. But I say to you, I never in any way negotiated with any church or persons for one penny for all or any of my traveling expense. I will allow, however, that when I left here last Tuesday morning, a brother of this church came to me and put two dollars, [equivalent to sixteen shillings,] into my hand and compelled me to take it. Now, it cost me twenty-one shillings to come here by public conveyance, and this brother paid sixteen shillings. So you see I have not made anything here, nor did I ask or expect it.

"The next charge which I will notice is that I go about to win a name. Now I will tell you, this is the name I get for my labors and pains, and I will sell out to any man for three cents. I am aware [that] the curious want to know why I am thus going around, and what can be my impelling motive. You yourselves must know that I am either a fool, or crazy, or honest. If a fool, don't be too hard with me. If crazy, I need your pity.

"Now everyone knows that no man in his senses will keep on the track on which I go without a motive, and I will frankly own up for once, although I do not make it a practice to dwell on these minor matters. First, then, I am where I am and doing as I am because I dare not do otherwise. Four times I have been brought to the verge of the grave /200/ and then let off on the promise that I would go and preach the gospel, and the last time the word came to me, 'You may live while you preach, but no longer,' and I dare not disobey.

"Now," said I, "I want to suppose that the president of your temperance society were to be thus treated because he tried to win your drunken husband, brother, or son back to the paths of virtue." (The president was the very man who circulated the papers.) "Do you think he would deserve it?

"Now I will tell you a little of my history. While I have been in your place, every day that the weather has been pleasant enough to bear I have spent the most of my time out in yonder grove on my knees, sometimes on my face, pleading with God to spare this place—to save

---

[295] Presumably James Caughey.

your husbands, wives, sons and daughters. And you yourselves will bear me witness that I have not tried to persuade anyone here to lie, steal, swear, fight, get drunk, or do anything wrong. On the contrary, all I have tried to do has been in the direction of trying to make them good, kind, gentle, loving, happy, and comfortable, and to get fit for the heavenly world. And this I do at my own expense and in the face of slander and persecution." Then my feelings overcame me and I could only say, "I do not think I ought to expect this kind of treatment."

The whole tide turned, and God's cause was once more redeemed.

This was the only instance where I felt called upon to say one word in self-defense. The editor of [the] paper in which this matter was published against me was kept in jail more than half of his time, suffering the penalty for slander. The character of the paper was so notorious that no honest man would allow it to influence him.

I was now invited to go back to the city and hold a meeting in one of our larger churches. We began on a Monday or Tuesday, and the Lord did work gloriously and at once in the conversion of sinners while the church was untiringly engaged in seeking the blessing of holiness.[296] The first night I think there were some fourteen conversions, the next eighteen, the next twenty, and so [it] increased through the week. When the Sabbath opened the house was greatly crowded, and on /201/ Sunday night we were [again] greatly crowded.

I went on and preached, and felt that God was with me in great power. But just as I finished and was going to call for penitents and engage in a prayer meeting, the preacher said, "Wait awhile, for I am going to marry a couple before the prayer meeting."

I said, "O, Brother, don't do that, for if you do I fear you will divert this interest from the point."

"O," said he, "I can make it very solemn, and besides, I have promised to do it."

"For the Lord and souls' sake, don't do it, for you will crush out this interest," [I said].

"Well," said he, "I shall do it."

I said, "Take the couple into your home or into the basement, but don't break us up here." But in spite of all entreaties, he arose and with a nasal singing tone began to make his matrimonial ceremony by saying "It's a solemn thing to get married; it's an awful thing to get married." I saw the day was lost and let him go on and finish his sacrile-

---

[296] JGT: "Soon after he was invited to go back to the city of New York to hold meetings in one of the large churches. He says: 'We began on Monday. The church immediately commenced to seek the experience of holiness'" (171).

gious affair and then tried to rally for a prayer meeting. But the Spirit fled and our revival stopped there.[297]

I went to another church to preach for one [night]. They had had quite a large number converted, but the revival interested seemed to wane. I think about three hundred had been converted. God helped me to preach, and the minister followed and called upon sinners to vote whether they would have the meetings stopped, or would they pledge themselves to seek religion if the meetings were continued. Then between four and five hundred arose, and as the minister afterwards told me, about that number more were converted.[298]

Chapter [21]

While I was taking courage at the sight of the success of the old doctrines of holiness and the occasional accession of a minister, I learned that one of the preachers of the conference had gone so far as to publish a pamphlet against our doctrine of holiness. But when the conference was again assembled he was required to renounce it, and then [he] took a transfer to another conference, making the promise that he would not propagate his errors. "Well," thought I, "we shall after all see the church return to its pristine purity and passion."[299]

/202/ One of the D.D. [doctors of divinity] was appointed to write a standard work on our Wesleyan view of holiness, and a very able

---

[297] JGT: But in spite of my entreaties he arose and commenced the ceremony by a brief lecture on the nature and solemnity of marriage. In a few minutes I saw our opportunity for getting people saved that night was lost. He finished the ridiculous affair, and we tried to have a prayer meeting, but the Spirit had been grieved, and the effort was a failure. The revival came to an end right there" (172). Terrill changes "sacrilegious" to "ridiculous." He might have misread the word in the manuscript, though clearly it is "sacrilegious."

[298] JGT here misreads "minister" for "minutes." He has, "About five hundred arose. The meetings went on for some time, and the conference minutes showed afterwards that about five hundred additional ones were taken into the church" (172).

[299] JGT recasts this paragraph as follows: "These successes were very assuring to Mr. Redfield of the wisdom of preaching the doctrine of holiness. He was also much encouraged by the promptness and thoroughness with which a minister was dealt with in an eastern conference for publishing a pamphlet opposed to the Wesleyan view of the doctrine. He was required to renounce his pamphlet, and to promise not to preach his peculiar opinion. This minister then took a transfer to another conference" (172).

minister soon after wrote *The Central Idea of Christianity.*[300] "Now," thought I, "we are safe, and the tongues of the opposers of our Zion will be stopped." I had yet to learn that hostility to right never ceases.

XXVI. Philadelphia: "Operations next to Pentecostal"

I went up to P. [Philadelphia] to spend the winter; labored for a while in the first old church and the cradle of Methodism in that city.[301] God was with us in power, and the preacher had lately come into possession of perfect love. But here again came up the opposition to holiness from the very man who had been cashiered in another conference. God however gave the blessed doctrine favor in the eyes of the people.

I then visited another church by request and was only permitted to preach once.

I then went to Eighth St. by request of the preacher,[302] who said to me, "We have been having a great work. Three hundred and over are converted, and I want you to come and preach a few times to our church to assist them in recovering the spiritual state which they must have to some extent lost in laboring for others. I think it will do them good to preach to them on the subject of holiness."

I had a tolerable idea of the moral state of his church and knew it to be good and in the condition to take hold of the doctrine of holiness with a good relish. "But," said I, "Brother, do you know what you ask, and are you prepared to allow the doctrines of holiness to be pressed upon your people?"

"I don't know what I have to fear," said he.

"Well, let me tell you that my impression is from the present spiritual state of your church that the introduction of that doctrine will be accompanied with a work beyond your conception. You think you have a tolerable idea of what God can do. Why, sir, this work has but just

---

300 Jesse T. Peck, *The Central Idea of Christianity* (Boston: H. V. Degen, 1856).

301 JGT: "He went to spend the winter in Philadelphia. He labored for a while in St. George's Methodist Episcopal church, the oldest church of that denomination in the city. It had been the cradle of Methodism" (173). St. George's M.E. Church had a total membership of 1025 in 1845 and 800 in 1849 (*Minutes,* Philadelphia Conference; cf. Simpson, *COM,* 711–13).

302 JGT says, "He the visited another church," but doesn't identify the church (174). In the manuscript, the designation appears to be "8th St." There was at the time an Eighth Street and a Fifth Street M.E. Church in Philadelphia. The Eighth Street Church had 887 members in 1849, including 140 probationers (*Minutes,* Philadelphia Conference).

begun."

"Well," said he, "I shall risk it."

The doctrine of personal holiness was made the theme of our labors, /203/ and in a few days we were compelled to close the church and lock the doors after the congregation had filled it comfortably full or we should be so crowded that it would be impossible to do anything. The slaying power of God was felt and seen in its operations to an extent next to Pentecostal—jumping, shouting, falling. Sinners unasked would run over the tops of the pews, wading through the masses of people, and rush to the altar of prayer. Two or three seats entirely across the church would be filled with penitents, and so great was the press of seekers that the preacher became alarmed at the violence of the commotion, and prudently (as he thought) brought the meetings to a close.[303]

I then went to two other churches and was permitted to preach once in each, and then [we] held our meetings in private homes each afternoon on the subject of holiness. On the last afternoon which I spent in the city there were fourteen sanctified at the home of J. B. L.

I now visited many places in quick succession, spending one or two weeks only in a place, and seeing many souls converted. But I saw my mistake in leaving just as the work began.[304] So I went to N.Y. or L.I. [Long Island] and learned that our church was compelled to contend for a bare existence against other churches, and especially [against] a Dutch Reformed minister whose violent opposition was a public [or: published] town's talk. He specially warned the people to keep clear of the Methodists, as the notorious disturber was coming to the place.

Our preacher was a good and had been a very successful man, but was now nearly broke down, and the labors were too much for him. When I arrived, curiosity led the people to come out and see the man who was the subject of such special notice from the ruling minister of the place. Among them was an infidel school teacher, and the next day he told the scholars to go home and tell their parents that he had been

[303] JGT renders this long sentence as follows: "The scenes of power were most remarkable. The saved would shout, jump, fall, so as to block the aisles. Sinners in the midst of this would crowd their way through and sometimes climb over the seats to get to the altar, and when that was filled, they would sometimes fill a row of seats clear across the church. So great became the press of seekers, and the violence of the commotion, that the preacher became alarmed and abruptly closed the meetings" (174).

[304] JGT here ends chapter 25 (page 175) and begins his chapter 26 on page 176.

out to hear this proscribed man preach and, said he, "Tell your people that he is the only honest preacher in this place, and if that which he preaches is religion, it is worthy of their fullest confidence. /204/ Do you tell them to come out and hear for themselves." They did come, and God owned the truths. A revival spirit broke out in different places, and many souls were saved.

One of our most holy ministers was holding a meeting about three miles from where I was, and souls were coming to Christ. The wife of one man, a retailer of whiskey, told his wife, "If I hear of you going to that altar to seek religion, I will come in and pull you out by the hair of your head." But fearing God more than man, she resolved to seek Jesus. Someone who saw her went out and told the husband that his wife was among the seekers.

The meeting closed, and when she returned home, he compelled her to take a cold room without fire or bed for the night, and here she spent the long hours in pleading with God for mercy. When morning light came she was yet without pardon, but resolved to let her husband know that what she was doing would not in the least make her a poorer housekeeper. So she to conciliate him went out of the room, built up a fire and cooked a good breakfast, and then stepped to his door and told him in all kindness that breakfast was ready. He finally came out, but with a most disagreeable and wicked look. She said to him in kindness, "Come sit down to breakfast," and he did so, and took but one mouthful into his mouth and then arose and, stepping towards her, said, "You witch, you have been to that altar," and then raised his hand as was supposed to strike her. [But] he fell dead at her feet.[305]

Not far from this time I heard of another remarkable case which I will report, although I have it from other hands. There were four young men who resolved to stop a revival which was in progress, if possible, and finally hit upon the plan to go all four to the altar and let the Methodists make a great fuss over them, and then to turn on them and to make so much sport that nobody would dare to be caught in that place seeking religion.

When the /205/ time came, the preacher, having finished his preaching, invited the people forward. The four young men came up the aisle promptly. But when within a few seats of the altar, one of them took, a seat and the remaining three were soon kneeling at the altar of prayer. The prayer meeting commenced, and one after another of the brethren inside of the altar tried in vain to find out from them what was their real state of mind, for they would not answer.

---

[305] JGT omits this incident.

Then [some]one said to the preacher, "There is something strange about these young men, for they will not answer a word." The preacher stooped down and found they did not or would not answer, and then thought he would turn up the face of one enough to see who he was. But in lifting him up so that he did not lie on the rail, he saw the young man was dead, as he fell on the floor. Startled at this, he looked at the second and the third, and all were dead. "My God," said the preacher in astonishment, "these young men are all dead." At this the young man who stopped short of going to the altar jumped up with a scream and went to the altar, asking the prayers of God's people, and then related the fact that the three others with himself were about carrying out the plan above stated.[306]

I went now to the place of the former residence of one of the old pioneers of Methodism, Freeborn Garrettson, and found his devoted widow still on the shores of Jordan but ripe for her passage to the better land.[307] Some fifty or sixty were brought to Jesus.[308]

[I next] went to C., fifty miles distant, where we had a very power-

---

306 JGT omits this incident also, no doubt because it was a secondhand report not involving Redfield's own ministry.

307 JGT: "From this place Mr. Redfield went to the former home of Freeborn Garrettson, one of the pioneers of Methodism. Here he found the widow of that soldier for Jesus still living, and in readiness for her summons to the mansions of the blest" (176). Freeborn Garrettson was born in Maryland in 1752 and died in New York City in 1827. His widow, Catherine Livingston Garrettson, was the daughter of Judge Robert Livingston who had a large estate on the Hudson River north of Poughkeepsie, New York, probably in the vicinity of Rhinebeck (Simpson, *COM*, 390–91). Mrs. Garrettson died in late 1848 or 1849, so this incident probably occurred in 1849. She was the aunt of Julia Lynch Olin, the wife of Stephen Olin. During the 1846 Redfield revival at Wesleyan University Julia Olin had corresponded with her cousin Mary Garrettson (Catherine Garrettson's daughter with whom the widow Garrettson resided in Rhinebeck), telling her of the revival (Stephen Olin File, Wesleyan University Archives). Thus Mrs. Garrettson would probably have known of Redfield's successful revival at the university in Middletown. In August 1845 Phoebe Palmer had also visited Mrs. Garrettson at her home in Rhinebeck (Richard Wheatley, *The Life and Letters of Mrs. Phoebe Palmer* [New York: Palmer and Hughes, 1884], 273).

308 JGT: "Among the tokens of friendship he received here was a set of Benson's Commentaries from Mrs. Garrettson. These had belonged to Mr. Garrettson, and had his autograph upon a blank leaf. Here some fifty or sixty were saved" (176). Redfield does no mention the gift of the commentaries.

ful work among sinners resulting from the work of holiness.[309]

[I] went to another church in [the] suburbs of N. Y. The work was not great, as the work of holiness was not so thoroughly received or embraced. But it being early in the fall,[310] I found the people were not at liberty from business to attend to salvation. But while I was here, and asking the Lord where I should go for my winter's campaign, suddenly I saw one of my /206/ strange signs appear, pointing the direction. I took a look at a map and found it pointed towards Cincinnati ~~or St. Louis~~, and as I had been invited by one of our bishops to make it in my way to visit that city, I resolved to enter any door which seemed to ~~thrust~~ help on in that way.[311]

Soon came a brother from the city of P. [Philadelphia], inviting me to return for the winter [to that city] where I [had] spent the previous winter. I resolved to go now because it led in a direction which might possibly or probably facilitate my journey to the point where my sign lay. But at night I had my track to my sign laid out in a dream, and I must begin at Goshen rather than from New York, and in the morning came a preacher from Goshen to ask me to go and help in a protracted meeting.[312] In looking over the map I saw that my sign and dream harmonized with this track. So I told the Brother from P. that I would go to G. and write to him from there. Yet I told no one what induced me to change my mind and go to G. rather than P.

---

[309] JGT: "Mr. Redfield next went to C——, about 50 miles distant. Here there was a powerful work among sinners, resulting from the church entering into the experience of holiness" (176). The location of "C." is uncertain. "C." probably does not refer to Connecticut, the border of which is only about twenty-five miles from Rhinebeck.

[310] Probably of 1850, though Redfield's narrative is not always strictly chronological.

[311] JGT: "While here he was constantly waiting upon God to know where he should spend the winter. One day there came before him the peculiar sign that had indicated the will of the Lord many times before. He got a map of the United States and found the sign to point in the direction of Cincinnati. He had before this been invited by Bishop Hamline to visit that city, and he now resolved to enter every open door that led in that direction" (177). Terrill thus identifies the specific bishop involved. Hamline had been based in Cincinnati for a number of years. (In light of Redfield's later ministry in St. Louis, it is interesting that in the manuscript he crossed out "or St. Louis." Since both Cincinnati and St. Louis lay in the same general direction from where Redfield was then located, there was perhaps some ambiguity in the "sign" itself, and the invitation from Bishop Hamline became the deciding factor.)

[312] Goshen, New York, about sixty miles northwest of New York City, in Orange County.

I went to Goshen and began labors.[313] This was a half-shire town[314] through which one of our bishops passing some years ago and finding it destitute of a Methodist church, resolved to lay the case before the Home Missionary Society and have a man sent there who should try to build up Methodism. Goshen had a bad name, for fifteen years before a Methodist preacher was whipped out of the place. [This treatment was] said to be induced by a prominent member of a Calvinistic church. They [i.e., the Methodists] were not allowed to use the [?] till a new one had been built, and then they were allowed the use of the old one, which was in so bad a condition that the people felt it to be a dangerous thing to venture up the crazy stairs. Such was the ridiculous farce of professing religion, and yet contending and even trying to put down the /207/ Methodists, that the honest-hearted worldlings became infidels. Drunkenness and infidelity ran riot. But our preacher had been sent on and was successful in building a church. Yet when he wished to get a lot to build on, he was crowded off and not allowed to purchase one except a frog pond. But he saw the metre[?] of the land and that by an expense of twenty dollars it might be perfectly drained, and then it [would be] a very desirable lot. So he bought it. When the people saw the proportions of the frame [of the church building he was raising], they thought the Methodist a wild man. It was however built, and we soon opened our meeting.[315]

The preacher in this place was a true gentleman and Christian and seconded my efforts in trying to go the straight way, though some of the poor frightened members were fearful of losing caste in the place if they should venture a still higher type of religion than what they now enjoyed, and which was far from being tolerable.[316] The deacon of one

---

313 According to two letters from Redfield to Phoebe and Walter Palmer (February 26, 1850, from Goshen, New York, and March 12, 1850, from nearby Middletown, New York), he began ministry in Goshen early in February 1850 (probably Sunday, February 3) and left there on Sunday, March 10. John Wesley Redfield Letters, Methodist Collection, Manuscript Division, New York Public Library.

314 JGT says, "Goshen was a county seat, and had a very bad name" (177).

315 JGT condenses this: "The Methodist preacher finally raised money to build a church, but when he came to purchase a lot, the only one he could buy was a frog pond. Undaunted by this, he had the pond drained, and built his church. The new church was to be the scene of Mr. Redfield's labors" (177–78).

316 Redfield probably means "tolerable" in a positive sense. JGT: "Some of the poor members were badly frightened, at the thought of losing caste with the established church of the place if they should obtain a higher type of piety than they now enjoyed" (178).

of the churches, and an editor, began his squibs for awhile in his paper to bring us into disrepute. The rum sellers were violent. One of them said I had proved myself to be a hard man, for my operations were cutting off his trade and he had lost by my means sixty dollars the first three ~~or four~~ weeks, and this in the end would compel him to let his family suffer for want of support, saying the people will [i.e., would] no longer patronize him. I should think that part of his story true, for I think there [were] not more than two or three who died with delirium tremens during my whole stay of about five weeks. He sent word to me that he would give me sixty dollars if I would leave town. I sent word back, if he would get religion and go to work and do what I was trying to do, I would leave town.[317]

When the Presbyterians found they could not drive us out of town, they tried to make capital out of us for their own aggrandizement.[318] [They] sent on /208/ two or more men who should feign themselves just [ordinary] men and come into our meetings and sing with the converts and put their arm around them very lovingly, and then track them off. In their first haul they took off sixty to ninety to go before their officers and be propounded for church fellowship. And then the deacon turned his tune. Before they had proselyted, he gave out that the Methodists were having quite an excitement. When they had raked us of sixty they published that the divine sovereignty had graciously revived his work in the Presbyterian Church.[319]

The infidels who had been made infidel by the ungodliness of this and other dead churches now thought to make their trial to put us down. So, to bring odium upon us, they got up a mock prayer meeting. The wife of the ringleader at whose house they had this blasphemous meeting was frightened and left. The man of the house was then smitten by the hand of death before all his wicked company and declared to them that he was lost and should soon be in hell. He lived a few hours raving like a mad man, declaring that he knew he was forever doomed and

---

[317] JGT has, "if the meetings went on, their families would soon suffer for the necessaries of life," and omits the remainder of the paragraph.

[318] JGT: "When the other churches found they could not drive the Methodists out of the town, they tried to build themselves up by proselyting" (178).

[319] JGT interprets this as follows: "Some of their members began to come into the meetings and to sing with the young converts, and to make much of them, and at last to lead them before their church officers to be received into church fellowship. When about sixty had been received into the church to which the village editor belonged, his paper changed its tone, and instead of saying anything more about the unhealthy excitement of the Methodist meetings, it spoke of the gracious revival in the —— church" (178).

could see the awful place to which he was going, and then died.[320]

This put a stop to all such wickedness, and the work of God triumphed gloriously. The next Sabbath this man's funeral sermon was preached by our minister in the very church [where] he had tried to hinder the work of salvation.

A new tack was now taken, and that was by one of the old deacons to go to the most influential among the converts and try to prejudice them against the Methodists. He and others whom I saw publicly trying to proselyte I told in the public congregation, "Go on and proselyte all you can among the rich. But if I catch you trying to proselyte any of the colored people or ragged poor, I will try to stop /209/ you if I can."[321]

One of the converts was a rich old man who twenty years before that time was serious minded and went to a deacon to enquire what he should do to be saved. The deacon asked him, Mr. Thompson,[322] tell me the prevailing sins of which you are guilty." When he had told the deacon, "Ah," said the deacon. "I see, Mr. T., that you are a reprobate, and Christ never died for you."

Mr. Thompson said, "I then thought the deacon knew [the truth], and that as I was a reprobate, I might as well try to enjoy myself as well as I can. But eight years ago I had a dream of seeing a man who would tell me how to get religion, and so sure did I feel that I told my wife in the morning that I now knew I was not a reprobate, for I have seen a man in my dream last night who will tell me the way to get religion. And," said he, "as soon as Mr. R. came into the church I knew he was the man whom I saw eight years ago. And he has told me how, and I have got it, and I shall join the Methodists." This man was a very rich man and of course a great loss to the Presbyterians.

Another [convert] was one of the largest merchants [and] had been a president of the village and occupied a very prominent position. The old deacon could not bear to lose this man. So he followed him to his house, and [then] came one morning very early, and as he saw me [there, he] started back and said, "I hope I don't intrude." I knew in a moment what he came for. When assured by the gentleman that he

---

320 JGT: "Her husband went insane before their meeting closed. He declared he was lost forever, and in a few hours he was dead" (178).

321 Terrill's rendering here masks the force of what Redfield actually wrote. JGT has: "An attempt was made, soon after, to proselyte the more influential of the converts. Mr. Redfield finally announced from the pulpit that he was aware of what was going on, and threatened if he found them trying to proselyte the colored people or the ragged poor he would expose them" (179).

322 JGT does not give the man's name (179).

might feel perfectly free, he began, "Well, Mr. C. R., how do you feel?"

"O," said he, "I don't have any evidence that I am converted."

"Evidence?" said the deacon. "Why, you know Deacon Blank. Well, he never had any evidence. Everybody thought he was a good man, but all the evidence he ever had of his conversion was that he felt his heart as hard as a stone."

"But," said Mr. R., "if I could only know that God heard my prayers, I should take some hope."

"Hear your /210/ prayer?" said the deacon. "Why, we have been praying for a revival for more than twenty years, and you see it has come."

"Well," said Bro. R., "I feel anxious to have Mr. T. to go with me."

"O," said the deacon, "you need not trouble yourself about Mr. T., for if the Spirit should begin with him, he will have to come."

I here felt that by the help of God, Brother R. should be pressed to go through so straight that when he was converted he should be spoiled for the Presbyterian church. He had been seeking earnestly for a number of days, and when night came he was forward for prayers. But the meeting closed and he [was] not yet converted.

I said to him, "Brother, what can be the reason you are not yet converted?"

"I don't know," said he.

"Do you make a full surrender to God of all you are and have?"

"I do," said he.

"Will you give to God every dollar you own and let Him make a draft upon you to any amount and at any time?"

"I do," was the very prompt and honest reply.

"Will you begin at once to pray in your family?"

"Why, would it be right until I should get converted?"

"Certainly. God commands all men to pray."

"I will," said he.

"Farther, Brother, will you go out and exhort sinners to come to Jesus?"

"Would it be right to do that before I get religion myself?"

"Yes, for God says, 'to everyone that heareth, not only come, but let him exhort others to come.'"

"I will," said he.

The meeting closed, and he went alone to his store. The clerks were all gone and, getting upon his knees, [he] gave all his entire property to God. (He was reported to be worth $30,000.)[323] He next went home and set up family prayer. In the morning early, he went to the house of a gentleman for whom he felt an interest and said, "Mr. T., I have come on a strange errand to you this morning, and that is to ask you to go with me and seek religion."

Mr. T. in a flood of emotion said, "I will, Mr. R.; pray for me."

Bro. R. said, "I have never tried that yet, but if you will kneel down, /211/ I will try." And while Bro. R. was praying for him, God converted his own soul.

The deacon heard that Mr. R. was converted, came again, and insisted that he should go for once up to a meeting before the session at the Presbyterian church. He did go, and they pressed him hard to give his name for church membership.

"I think not," said he.

"Why, you won't think of joining the Methodists, will you? It will greatly injure your standing if you do."

"O," said Bro. R., "I may be too zealous and hot, but I am sure if I were to join the Presbyterian Church you would freeze me to death."[324] So he joined the Methodists and became one of our leaders.[325]

The work of holiness was made the prominent theme, and converts were in a few days clearly enjoying the clear witness of perfect love.

One young lady who had thus come out in the clear light, on trying to fill a fluid lamp, the fluid took fire and bursting around her face, in a moment she was in a blaze. The family got her to the pump as soon as possible to put out the fire. But she, while literally frying in the flame, jumped up and down and sang that hymn in triumph, "Am I a soldier of the cross, a follower of the Lamb?" When the fire was extinguished a physician was called. On examining the wounds, [he] said, "the burn is not dangerous."

"But," said she, "I know I shall die, and my soul is so full of glory, I long to go and be with Jesus." On dressing her arms, [the doctor found that] the flesh fell from the bones. She lingered a few days and testified to all who came to see her, infidels and all, that Jesus could make a dying bed feel soft as downy pillows are, and then [she] died in

---

[323] JGT: "He went alone to his store; the clerks were all gone, and going down upon his knees, he gave himself up to God—person, property, and all" (181). JGT omits the reference to $30,000.

[324] JGT: "'I may be too zealous for your church. I must go where I can save my soul alive'" (181).

[325] As with many of the incidents Redfield records, this one highlights the issue of the relative social standing of the Methodists.

triumph.

Four hundred were converted in this revival, and the church paid instead of receiving mission money.[326]

Chapter [22]

I next went to a place [Middletown, New York] seven miles from this where a protracted meeting had been in progress among the Congregationalists till it was broken up by the mob. The Methodists were [even more] intolerable [to the mob]. But I went, and on beginning to operate I found we were indeed in an /212/ enemy's country, for all the bad and even vile conduct of the wicked. It was too shameful to name, and no decent person would be caught unprotected there a second time, and meanest of all, a Baptist deacon set up a young infidel to take the lead in this conduct.

After meeting, I said to some of our brethren, "Why do you allow such conduct when the law protects you?"

---

[326] Redfield wrote to the Palmers after about three weeks in Goshen, "We have adapted the old Methodist Apostolic plan of personal effort, pulled off all our gloves and entered the harvest field as journeymen for God. I was never more sensible of the great fact that all is of God than in this revival. Fanatical as it may appear we have made up our minds that God can manage his own cause well enough, that the old rough cross is smooth enough for rebels[?], that the plain gospel is fashionable enough, and in the dust is high enough for anybody. O we may well be thankful if we can be permitted to pick up crumbs among the dogs. We try to keep our work free from the mark of human tools and now God seems determined to show under these circumstances that some things can be done as well as others. Our house is packed every evening before dark, from 40 to 70 are identified as seekers every night; 232 up to last night profess to have found Jesus. It is thought there may be about 700 more old enough to be converted, and if God helps, we think it not best to stop till we see Jesus finish the job. Pray for us." Redfield to Phoebe and Walter Palmer, February 26, 1850 (cited above).

New York Conference *Minutes* tend to substantiate Redfield's report. Goshen first appears in the minutes as "Goshen Mission" in 1848 and 1849, reporting in the latter year only 34 members (including six probationers). The 1850 *Minutes* list Goshen with a total of 200 members—significantly, including 140 probationers and 30 "Colored." The statistics thus show clear signs of a revival. Given the fact that some converts probably were not brought into membership, some joined other churches, and some may already have been nominal members, 400 converts is probably a fairly accurate report. (The Goshen membership declined to 150 in 1852 and 121 the following year—a not uncommon pattern in the aftermath of revival, particularly among the Methodists, where typically not all probationers became full members.)

"O, they always do so whenever we attempt a protracted meeting, and they have just broken up the Congregationalists."

"Well, brethren, you must top it."

"We dare not meddle with it."

"Well," said I, "before you put that burden upon me, one thing is certain. If you don't break them up, they will you. And brothers, if you don't take this matter in hand, I shall."

Night came, and the house was becoming quite crowded. The congregation was singing, and soon the deacon's infidel in the gallery threw missiles at the ladies as they were coming in. I instantly called out, "Stop singing." I then, pointing him out, said, "I hope that young man in the white overcoat[327] will be civil enough to cease throwing things at the ladies."

He made a taunting reply, and I instantly told him and all others that a Methodist church was not a tavern or grog shop, and they must understand that our rights are respected by law as well as the Episcopal Church or [the] other one which they never dared to disturb. "And now I tell you upon the honor of a man, I shall see that the ladies who venture out here shall be protected by law. Our law makes it a fine of twenty-five dollars for each and every such offense, and it is jail till it is paid. I will meet you tomorrow and see that the whole force of the law is brought to bear, and break up this indecent and outlandish conduct." I then assured all that they might say to all their friends, "You can come hereafter to a Methodist church and you shall be respected." Then addressing the rowdies, I /213/ said, "Now, Sir, if you dare, take names."

All was still that night. But in the morning one of the rowdies with some of his companions were near the church, and he in great wrath began to curse us, the church, and myself in very blasphemous language. Then the hand of God smote him to the earth. His comrades thought he was dead. They took him up and carried him into a tavern and pulled off his clothes and got him to bed, and after awhile he began to come to. His first utterance was, "O God, what have I been doing?" He confessed his wrong. God spared him. The rest of the rowdies were affrighted, the opposition ceased, and in ten days from the day we began operating, over 110 were converted and the work was going on.[328]

---

327 JGT (183) has "white cravat." While Redfield's scrawl could possibly be rendered "cravat," comparison with other words suggests the reading "overcoat."

328 The fruit of this revival appears to be reflected in the New York Conference *Minutes.* Middletown reported a total membership of 84 in 1849, and "Middle-

The Baptists tried to turn the converts into their own church while I was there, but our converts were too clear and zealous to be made an easy prey.[329]

After I was gone I learned that the Baptist minister gave out that he would have a revival. When the people had gathered, he told them what he designed to do, and what regulations he wished them to observe. First, he said, he desired to have the meetings so conducted as not to offend the most fastidious ear, and first [sic] he would say he wanted no shouting or singing of those hymns which the Methodists had sung. And finally, he did not want anyone to faint away (as he called the losing strength). But he thought it might be well for those who had a desire to become pious that that fact might be made manifest by some sign, and he would propose that they should merely stand up upon their feet. One only arose, and he one who had been a seeker in our church, and with this one demonstration of this one man began and ended this genteel revival.

Some said, "I am sorry that Redfield has gone, for now [that] these uncouth rabble have been mostly converted, some of the respectable people would like to get a share in religion." But having no message for the genteel, I could not and would not return to them.

/214/ I visited P. J. on L. I. [Long Island], and with the preacher tried once more to present my special message to the world.[330] Here again I found a set of rowdies determined to break us up. I told the preacher we must command order when God gives us the benefit of the law. To which he replied, "Our people always get broken up, and we are afraid to touch the case, as some of them are children of our members."

---

town and Bethel" (reported as one) reported a total of 332 members in 1850, including 62 probationers. Middletown reported only 94 members in 1851, but Bethel is not included nor listed separately. Several new churches do appear in 1851, however, suggesting that one or more new congregations may have been organized due (in part) to the Redfield revival. The 1850 New York Conference met in May, so there would have been time to report some of the fruit of the Middletown revival, about two months earlier.

329 JGT says, "The church that had inspired such opposition now tried to gather the young converts into their communion," but does not identify the church as Baptist (183).

330 JGT: "His next meeting was in P— I—, on Long Island" (184). If the initials Redfield uses are P. J., not P. I., the church may have been Port Jefferson, which in 1850 had a total of 152 members (*Minutes,* New York East Conference, 1850). There was no appointment on Long Island with the initials P. I. Port Jefferson is on Long Island Sound across from Bridgeport, Connecticut.

"Well, Brother, I shall then do my duty and stop this."

I went again in the evening and found the element was getting very boisterous. I tried but in vain with kind words to quell the disturbance. Our afternoon meetings we kept distinctly for the benefit of those seeking holiness.

A good sister whose husband was a captain of one of the boats sailing to N. York was herself anxiously seeking holiness. In making the consecration, she could give up all but her husband, for it was suggested to her, "If you give him up, God will probably take him, and if you ever see him again, he will probably be dead, brought home drowned." But finding that she could not make progress in seeking, and stating her [decision] hastily, wound up by saying, "Well, if I am left a widow, God shall have his rights. Here goes my husband, too." The power came, and she fell onto the floor, and soon rose to testify that God had fully saved her.

The work now opened with great power. When the evening came, the rowdies began in a very boisterous manner to disturb us. I got their attention and finally told them to make one more demonstration if they dared, and I would see the law faithfully executed the next morning. All hushed up at once, and the next night seventeen of the rowdies were among the seekers of religion.[331]

Chapter [23][332]

I was sent for by the preachers of B [Boston] to come and spend the winter. In a day or two more I received a letter from a preacher in C. [Chelsea], a city joining B., who said to me in his letter, "The preachers in B. have your time all farmed out for B. and left me no chance. Now /215/ if you can, come a week or two before you enter upon your engagement in B. and spend it with [us]."[333]

So I did. When I arrived I found him in a large hall, as they were a new congregation and their church was not yet built. I found him to be a man who dared to take a straight stand for God and then risk the consequences.[334] So I ventured to open operations by putting the standard

[331] JGT rearranges this account, putting the account of the young woman seeking holiness after the account of quelling the rowdies (184–85).

[332] JGT also begins a new chapter here (his chapter 27, beginning on page 186).

[333] JGT: "Mr. Redfield was next sent for to spend the winter in Boston. But before he started he received a letter from the preacher in Chelsea, near Boston, asking him to spend a few days there before commencing in Boston" (186). Chelsea is northeast of Boston, across Massachusetts Bay.

[334] JGT: "He found the preacher a courageous, faithful man" (186).

of religion where John Wesley and [John] Fletcher and our fathers put it. God owned it. A large congregation crowded our church or rather hall and a good representation of various orthodox people came over to our help and joined heartily with us.[335]

I had not gone [on] a great while before I was waited upon by a committee, among which was one preacher of the M. E. Church. They opened this meeting by telling me they had come to labor with me and if possible to disabuse my mind of some misapprehensions which they were sure I must entertain.

I said, "Brethren, go on and do your duty."

"Well," said the Methodist preacher, "by your strong stand and sweeping declarations against all that don't come up to your standard, you tacitly reflect upon the Unitarians and Universalists, and you evidently don't know them. Besides, you offend some of our members who have friends belonging to these communions and," said the preacher, "I regard them as a good people, especially the Unitarians, and if there is any choice between them and the Methodists, it lies in favor of the Unitarians."

I was astonished to find that a Methodist preacher had the dishonesty to enter in and defend infidelity and yet publicly claim to be a Methodist. I said however to the delegation, "Your good Unitarians and Universalists have got the devil in them."

I was interrupted by one saying that I ought to know that this kind of rough deportment would never go down in a place as refined as the city of C.

"Well," said I, "if you know the doctrines of the Methodists, as you ought if you are members as you claim to be, I will this night prove to you that what I say is /216/ the truth. As Methodists you know that our doctrine of holiness is love and nothing but love. I think matters are now ripe enough, and I design this night to present perfect love to the people, and if it don't smoke out devils, I will give up that I am wrong."

I that night preached on holiness as a ~~thing~~ state to be gained now, and while [I was] preaching, one of the first converts, a very large and youngish man, fell like a dead man upon the floor. The people were alarmed, not knowing but [that] he had fallen in a fit, and they went to him and carried him out of the house. As soon as he could speak he cried out, "Glory to God! You need not hold me. God has given me the great blessing." And then, walking up the aisle, [he] gave in his testi-

---

335 JGT: "The hall was crowded nightly with a congregation made up from various orthodox churches" (186).

mony thus: "While the brother was preaching, I said, 'O Lord, I never heard about getting the second blessing. Now, Lord, if it s a true doctrine, let me know by laying me out on the floor.' Then instantly I fell as if I had been shot, and now I know I have got the blessing, and I love God with all my heart."

Then arose one of our leaders and said, "If that doctrine has got in here, I am done with the Methodists. I am a Universalist."[336] Then another leader arose and said, "I have no more to do with the Methodists, for I am a Unitarian."

Our work now went on in great power till soon near one hundred were converted, and my time was out and I must go to my first appointment in the city of B.

So over I went and presented myself at the parsonage of the preacher in C. St.[337] I told the good old preacher who I was and that I came to obey the request made some time ago. But he was frightened for, as I learned, he had heard frightful stories of my measures in C. by the preacher who brought me and the infidel Methodists who in great indignation left our church for their more congenial homes among the Unitarians and Universalists. So the good old man, to make /217/ it as easy as he could, began to excuse me as well as he could by saying they had had some [revival] meetings and he did not think the brethren would be willing to open them again.

I saw his fears and dilemma, and to save him from all possible embarrassment, I as quickly as possible withdrew and went back again to C. But the preacher in Chelsea of who [sic; i.e., the preacher at Church Street,] instead of standing aloof, came over to C. and saw for himself, and he persuaded his people to barely let me come for once [i.e., one service] and let them find out who and what I was.[338] A good number of his members were old Methodist preachers, superannuated or doing

---

336 JGT: "One of the class leaders arose and said, 'If that doctrine has got in here I am done with the Methodist Church. I am a Universalist'" (187). Redfield does not identify this person as a class leader, though that may well be what he meant.

337 JGT: "He now went to Boston, and presented himself at the parsonage of the church in which he had engaged to labor" (187). "C. St." probably was the Church Street M.E. Church, which was located in central Boston, south of Boston Common.

338 The text is confused here, or omits words. Redfield may have mistakenly written "Chelsea" for "Church Street," intending to say, "the preacher in Church Street of whom I spoke." JGT: "But the good man went over and saw for himself, and, when he returned, persuaded his people to let Mr. Redfield come and preach once, that they might know him for themselves" (188).

business in the Methodist Book Room in B., and of course they had heard such reports of me that they were afraid of me. But the preacher had prevailed with them to let me come just once, and to please him, they did.

When I arrived I was taken into a classroom, which to put some importance upon they called the little lecture room. I saw at a flash the whole thing from beginning to end, but went about my business as if all was right.[339] At the close of the meeting, one or two of the old Methodist preachers said, "Brother, you must stay tomorrow night, and we will open the large lecture room."

I was on hand in due time and took the strongest stand I could for primitive Methodism. God redeemed His own cause, and the body of the church [building] was now opened and I continued some two weeks or more, and it might be forty or fifty were converted.[340]

I was now bound for another place some two hundred miles distant. They [i.e., the Methodist preachers in Boston] tried to prevail on me to stay. The preachers in B. who had once found out my service[?] for the winter had now learned how they had been deceived by listening to the false reports, got their official boards together and sent [an] invitation [for me] to stop and labor with them summer and winter for a year. These old preachers had reported to them that all the [?] and objections to me were on account of my being a genuine old Methodist. The Unitarian Methodist preachers soon left us. /218/ Professor T. of the W. [Wesleyan] University took a stand here for my course and doctrines and said to the people that Bro. [Redfield] was a genuine Wesleyan Methodist, and this complete recitation gave my despairing heart once more to hope that Methodism would yet be redeemed. I could only get away by promising if I could I would soon return, but that time has never yet come.[341]

---

339 JGT: "When the time came for the appointment, the meeting was held in what was called the small lecture-room of the church. Mr. Redfield perceived what this meant, but went straight forward about his work" (188).

340 JGT: "God blessed the truth, and in a few days the main audience-room was opened, and in a fortnight forty or fifty were converted" (188).

341 JGT: "About the same time Prof. ___, of the Wesleyan University, came to Boston and bore testimony to Mr. Redfield's soundness as a Methodist. This so broke up the opposition that the ministers of the city endeavored to engage him for a year. Greatly encouraged by this, Mr. Redfield promised, if it was possible, he would return. But the opportunity to do so never came" (188–89). Who was the Wesleyan University professor? The initial appears to be "T"; if so, it may have been Charles True, a Methodist preacher who in 1849 went to Wesleyan University as professor of Moral Science and Belles-Lettres. See

I went now to U. I.[?] Again our peculiar doctrines were the main apparent means under God of arousing the minds of the people to a religious interest, and the people in great numbers were converted.[342]

One night I observed a goodly number of people full of interest in the front seats, watching the people as they came forward and looking very much pleased to see the good work going on.[343] After meeting I asked one of our brothers, "Who are these people who occupy the front seats and seem to be very much pleased to see the work go on, and frequently smile their approval?"

"Why, don't you know?"

"No," said I.

"Well, they are Baptists and Congregationalists and Presbyterians."[344]

"Well, what are they doing here?"

"O, they are watching to see if we have anyone come forward to our altar that will weigh more than four ounces. For they never allow the Methodists to string a fish that weighs more than that.[345] They say they can do better by the upper class than we can, and we can do better by the lower classes. They are very willing to help us financially, and do so, for they say we are a great blessing to them in filling up the church with members, and they are willing to give us of their money to

---

Frank W. Nicolson, ed., *Alumni Record of Wesleyan University,* Centennial (Sixth) Ed. (Middletown, Conn.: Pelton and King, 1931), 10; Carl F. Price, *Wesleyan's First Century: With an Account of the Centennial Celebration* (Middletown, Conn.: Wesleyan University, 1932), 78–79. (Redfield, or perhaps JGT or someone else, placed two large X marks at this point in the manuscript.)

342 JGT: "He now went to U___, as he had promised. Again the doctrine and experience of holiness was the theme and the apparent means of arousing a great religious interest, and many were converted" (189). Redfield's script could be read "U. I" or "U. A." It is probably not possible to identify the place, because a distance of two hundred miles from Boston would take in all the New York City area, much of upstate New York, and most of New England.

343 JGT has, "One night he observed a youngerly man sitting in the front seat who appeared to be interested in the work. Others sitting with him manifested the same kindness, though none of them took part in the altar work" (189). Terrill reads "a goodly number" as "a youngerly man," and omits the words "of people," but the sense seems to be "a goodly number of people" (though the word I render here as "number" is nearly illegible).

344 JGT: "'Why, don't you know them? They are ——ists, and ——ists, and ——ists'" (189).

345 JGT translates this colloquialism as follows: "Oh, they are watching those who come forward, to see if there are any that they want. If any of influence come forward, they will soon be after them" (189).

keep moving.

"Our preacher once asked one of their ministers, 'Suppose the Methodists should have all of [their] own converts, how would you fare?' 'O,' said he, 'we should have nothing, for we have all our members from the Methodists.'"[346]

I saw one night that these watchers were greatly elated, and I was put in mind by their maneuvers of a cat that was just fixing for a leap at a bird.[347] I asked one of our Brethren what /219/ that meant.

"O," said he, "that man who knelt at such a point they got their eye upon, and in their estimation he is a fish that weighs four ounces."

Sure enough, the next evening I heard the great Baptist bell [go] ding dong. "What?" said I to a Brother present. "Are the Baptists going to begin a series of meetings?"

"O, no, they are going to have an experience meeting."

"What, have then [they had] a revival?"

"No. But you remember such a man who came forward to our altar last night."

"Yes."

"Well, he is going to tell his experience."

"His experience? Why, but he ain't converted." But it seemed they did not dare to wait, and so got him into the water as soon as possible. But I learned that he was in the gutter drunk before the year passed.

I met one man, a local preacher and school teacher, whose wife opposed his preaching. If he did not preach as often as once or twice a week, [however,] he was sure to go into a deep sleep and in his sleep go through all the services of revivals and begin [to] call upon someone to pray, and then taking a text, [to] preach. But this so annoyed his wife—as he preached very loud, and the people would collect around the house—that she gave consent to let him preach, and this put an end to his sleep preaching.

This brother told me the remarkable case of a child three years old whose mother used to take him out and lead him by the hand. One day while walking the road, the little [one] said, "Ma, let me go catch that little bird on the fence." The mother, to see him waddle off, let go of his hand. Then sure enough, he did catch it and, bringing it to his

---

[346] JGT: "One of our preachers once asked one of theirs, 'If the Methodists should hold all their converts what would be the result?' The answer was, 'Our growth would be comparatively small'" (189). As usual, Redfield's language is more graphic and colorful than Terrill's.

[347] JGT: "Mr. Redfield saw one night that these watchers were greatly elated over something that occurred" (189). JGT omits the reference to a cat.

mother said, "Ma, Jesus Christ sent me this little bird, and it tells me I am going to heaven." Strange to relate, the little one in less than six days was numbered with the heavenly hosts.[348]

XXVII. Newburgh Camp Meeting: "Gusts of power"

Chapter [24][349]

[I] visited Newburgh before camp meeting and tried to /220/ preach the pure doctrines of Methodism.[350] Some Episcopalians in our church, shouted and some of our members ran.[351] The preacher did not like it. But the old presiding elder got up and endorsed the doctrines which I preached.

A brother with whom I staid related the following circumstance. This city was once totally controlled by the infidels. Many years ago a pious deacon of the Presbyterian church came here and was looking around to find a place where religious services could be held, and one of these infidels met him in the street and, with awful blasphemy, told the deacon to be off, for his religion would not be tolerated there. Instantly the infidel fell dead, and the brother who informed me pointed out the spot where he died.

After this a club of infidels numbering about thirty resolved to lay a plot to prevent religion getting in. A Methodist had begun, or soon was to begin, religious services. A last resort of these infidels was to get up so much action[?] on the Christian religion that no one would dare to embrace Christianity in that place. So they took a dog and cat, and about fifteen of them went out in procession to a spring where they in mockery performed the two sacraments upon those two animals,

---

[348] JGT omits this incident. In Redfield's manuscript it is crossed out with a large X.

[349] JGT also begins a new chapter here (his chapter 28, beginning on page 191).

[350] JGT: "Mr. Redfield visited Newburgh just before the camp meeting held near there that year" (191). Presumably this was Newburgh, New York, seventy miles north of New York City on the Hudson River and in the same general area as Middletown and Goshen. Phoebe Palmer spoke at the camp meeting there in 1842 (White, *Beauty of Holiness,* 237). Redfield's visit probably was in the summer of 1850 or 1851.

[351] JGT elaborates: "Some Episcopalians who had united with the church, entered into the experience of holiness, and shouted in their new-found liberty; while some Methodists who had never belonged to any other church, became angry and opposed the work" (191). By the words "some of our members ran" Redfield may mean, however, that some of the Methodists got blessed (ran the aisles).

baptizing the one and giving the sacrament of the Lord's Supper to the other, and in high glee returned to the city. But before they reached home Dr. H., the ringleader, cried out in agony, "I am burning up!" And himself and two others died that night in great agony. In less than three years every soul who participated in that blasphemous conduct died violent deaths—some drowned, some shot, and some hung, and some by other accidents passed away to their final account.

The brother who related these facts to me told me farther that the judgments of God seemed still to mark the very tomb of the /221/ ringleader, Dr. H., for though they had put up a beautiful marble table on his grave, they had never been able to make it stand. It had been put up on marble pillars and then with brick, but it would not stand. The marble pillars would be broken and tumbled down, and the brick would crumble to pieces.

I found my way to the graveyard and saw an old man digging a new grave. I passed him at a distance and hunted up the fallen marble and read the inscription. I then went to the old gravedigger and asked him if he had taken notice of the condition of the marble table set up in memory of one Dr. H.

"O, yes," said he. "I dug that grave myself."

"But," said I, "why don't they keep that beautiful marble table in its place?"

"O," said he, "I don't know. It has been put up with marble and brick, but somehow it don't seem to stand."[352]

We went on to our camp meeting. The preacher for whom I preached on Sabbath was there, so I did not feel at liberty to be very offensive in trying to do anything, but to bide my time.

They went on till Thursday afternoon, trying to make things go, but in vain. Finally one of the preaches who had just exhausted his skill in trying to make a move turned to me said, "Bro. R., can you do anything?"

"No, Sir," said I, "but I know of one that can. The Lord Jesus Christ will take the whole matter into His own hand and no man can stay it, if you will begin at the right end by getting holiness."

I was permitted to go on, and as clearly as I could I stated the conditions of thorough consecration and then called upon all who would meet the conditions to come to the bench and kneel. (We were now in a very large prayer-meeting tent.) A large number knelt, evidently closely understanding the import of the vows they were making. But scarcely

[352] JGT condenses this incidental account down to six lines, leaving out many of the details (191).

had we engaged in this work before the slaying power of God fell upon us.

/222/ Then sinners rushed up uninvited, and kneeling at the bench, begged us to pray for them. The tent was fifty feet long. A continuous row of seats ran the whole length through the center, and during the whole balance of the camp meeting, that bench was filled from one to three deep on each side, the men on one side and women on the other.[353] As soon as a lady was converted, we requested the sisters to take her away so as to have room for others, and as soon as one was removed, some weeping penitent who stood watching her chance would fill the place made vacant. And so [also] of the men. Nobody had to exhort or labor to persuade the penitents to come forward. God was there in awful power, and the people felt it and only wanted the opportunity to take their places, and they would instantly act.

A remarkable fact in many cases was related by them on this wise: "I live over two or three miles from here. An awful sense of my sinful state pressed me down, and something said to me, 'Go to the camp meeting and get religion.' When I came, I felt drawn to come to this tent, and when I came, I saw this was the place to get religion, and now I have got it, bless the Lord."

I saw many of the young ladies who, following a foolish fashion prevalent in that region, had their bonnets filled with artificial flowers. [Although] as yet nothing had been said to them personally about the matter, they would struggle hard and cry loud for mercy and, finding no relief, they would put up both hands and grasp the artificial flowers and tear them out, and then, with beams of sunshine smiling through their tears, [they] would make the place vocal with their joyful notes of praise.

We were so crowded with penitents that we were compelled to open another smaller tent for the accommodation of those seeking holiness. Then these two tents /223/ became the God-honored brotherhoods[?] of the ground. When night came the work went on in great power till ten or eleven o'clock in both tents. Then the camp meeting committee of regulators resolved to stop the meeting in the tent where holiness was the theme, and they appointed one of their number to go

---

[353] JGT: "The tent was eighty feet long with a row of seats running the whole length through the center. During the remainder of the camp meeting, without cessation, that bench was filled with seekers, and sometimes two and three rows on each side, the men on one side, and the women on the other" (192). Though Redfield says the tent was eighty feet long, Redfield's manuscript clearly says fifty.

to the tent and tell the people that the meeting must close for the night. One brother said, "O, don't stop us! You see God is at work."

"I tell you," said he, "I have orders to say this meeting must close." Then instantly the power of God [fell] upon him, and he lay prostrate on the earth. Such was the gust of power that then all fell, and all in the tent feeling it, a spontaneous burst of victory arose louder than before. The balance of the committee said, "You see, brethren, that brother can't stop them, for they are going on more than before."

"Well now, send Bro. W. Do you tell them, Brother, that the committee say their meeting must be brought to a close." On he went, resolved to bring the meeting to order, and with vehemence he cried out, "I tell you, this meeting must and shall be stopped." Someone remonstrated, but he vociferated, "You must stop!" Then another gust of power fell, and down he went, and so great was the power that one or two sinners passing the tent at the right moment fell under the power.

The remaining balance of the committee at a distance heard the new note of triumph. Then they appointed another very resolute brother to go and do what the other two had failed to do, and still that meeting on holiness. But when the third man came and saw the condition of the others, he left and reported to the committee the fact that the other two lay prostrate under the power of God, and he thought it best not to venture to interfere again.

So that meeting on holiness, which I believe fed them /224/ by keeping God so near as to keep a good supply of penitents, was kept up all night without hindrance. Various were the estimates of the number of conversions that night. But I think it would not be too high an estimate to say one hundred were converted in the big tent that night, possibly many more. And all this from an almost dead state the day before when nothing could be made to stir. I regard [this] as a direct endorsement of God upon this our blessed doctrine of holiness.[354]

When afternoon came again, in addition to all other meetings, there was another tent in which were gathered a large number of persons who were seeking the blessing of holiness, and they sent word desiring me to come and help them. I had just been conversing with an old Method-

---

[354] JGT: "When we consider that this wonderful work commenced immediately after Mr. Redfield took hold of the meeting in the circumstances of the afternoon previous, we cannot but conclude that it was a demonstration of the correctness of his method." Terrill then adds this paragraph: "This incident gives a clue to his [Redfield's] wondrous power to break through to victory on occasions like that; and also illustrates the close alliance of the two phases of revival work,—sanctification and pardon" (193).

ist[355] who was taking strong exception to all I did and trying to mar the work in which I was engaged. When I would state the unbending exactions of God's demands and the minute details of perfect obedience, he would say, "You impose too heavy a burden upon the people as a condition of holiness." And when I would offer the final connecting out of simple faith, he would say, "You make the way too easy. Now," said he, "if I could only see this course accompanied with demonstrations of power, I should think more favorably of it."

"Well," said I, "Brother, I have just had an invitation to go into a tent where a number are seeking holiness. You go with me, and it may be that God will show you something there." When we went in I saw a large number sitting, and some of them, I saw by the wet and swollen eyes, were deeply moved. But among them I saw one large masculine lady whom I could tell at a glance was not very nervous, but still she was wringing her hands and swaying to and fro and repeating in resolute manner, "O Lord, I must have it, I shall die without it. I cannot any longer live in this manner."

I saw at a glance that her consecration was very /225/ thorough, and further that she was now putting forth a very large amount of will power, as if that would complete the work. I did not doubt but that all present expected me to get down and by vociferous praying to help heighten the emotion, and by this tempest ride into harbor.[356] But instead of this, I sat down by her and said to her, "Sister, Sister, hold on a moment.[357] Let us see, what do you want? Say, say, Sister, stop one moment and let us know what you want."

"O," said she in rather a subdued tone, "I want to be sanctified."

"How much do you want that blessing, and what are you willing to give for it?"

"O, I would give all I have."

"Are you sure of it? Would you be willing that I should now before these people turn your heart inside out and let all your real motives and wishes and desires be seen, just as they are?"

"Yes, I would," said she.

"Well, I cannot do that. But, for your own benefit, you now know that you are honest. This is the first starting point, honesty. So don't let the devil drive you from that point. Now, with that honesty, can you, do you say, the will of the Lord be done?"

---

355 JGT says "an old minister," but Redfield does not say he was a minister.

356 JGT weakens the metaphor: "and by this tempest to help them all" (194).

357 Redfield's script can be read either as "sister, Sister," or, perhaps, "Sister Suter," a proper name.

"I do," was the prompt answer.

"Will you say, and then let God take you at your word in one moment, 'The will of the Lord be done'?"

"I do," with emphasis, was answered.

I then held out a sample of suffering and asked, "Remember, God may take you at your word. But in view of any or all, do you say, 'Thy will be done'?" Again she answered yes.

I then held up a sample of duties, the hardest kind among which was the duty of going from house to house in N. York, where she lived. This also she accepted and said she would do that when she had the grace to do it with.

"Well, Sister, is God at fault? Is that the reason your have not had the grace of perfect love up to this time?—the possession of which would fit you to do that class of duties."

"O no, God is not at fault."

"Well, can you and will you say, 'Blessing or no blessing, /226/ visiting and exhorting from house to house would be my duty if I had the blessing, and I will not let my disobedience in one thing be my excuse for disobedience in another. So I will go and do that duty.'" [She replied that she would.][358]

"Well, Sister, who has ever required all this at your hands?"

Enquiringly she looked up and said, "Why Jesus, has He not?"

"O, yes," said I. "And now I ask, Sister, if Jesus has required all this and you have surrendered it, do you believe He will ever accept it?"

"Most certainly," said she, "as He is not trifling with [me]. He will, won't He?"

"O, I don't doubt it," said I. "But the only question is, Sister, when do you think He will accept what you have just surrendered?"

She stopped as if a new thought struck her, and her face changed, and in the next moment she shrieked out, "Now!" And [she] fell on the ground and made the woods ring with the loud hallelujahs.

But I do not think that this exhibition satisfied the old gentleman who wished to be convinced that this mode of seeking holiness was orthodox. For he shortly after preferred complaints to the preacher in charge against certain ones who were so wicked as to fall down under the power of God while, as he thought, they were irreverently repeating the doxology. Just after [this], three or four were converted and about that number sanctified in a single gust of heaven's breath.

The good sister who came out so brightly went home, lived faith-

---

[358] JGT similarly inserts, "'Yes, I will,' she replied" (195).

ful, and finally she sickened and died a most triumphant death.

XXVIII. Further Revivals

Chapter [25][359]

Our camp meeting closed and I was invited to go and spend the next Sabbath at a village some six to ten miles from the campground. On reaching the place, I learned that our people had a church built and given to them by a number of gentlemen residents who had retired from business and made the little quiet village of B the place of their residence. The preacher sent by our conference was one of those [who] would be [a] great man, but it was on a very small scale. When I saw /227/ him and was introduced to him, he began to make excuses for nonattendance at the camp meeting, as he had been requested to preach a controversial sermon on the subject of baptism and should deliver it on Sabbath morning, and he staid home from camp meeting to write it. This excuse formed a good basis for a reason for not inviting me. I told him he need put himself to no inconvenience about me.

Our people would have a prayer meeting on Saturday evening, and the preacher was present. God led me to begin to make some points preparatory to a call upon those who would seek holiness to make known their pledge by standing up. The preacher anticipated what I was at and abruptly got up so as not to have to get up when the call was made. But God owned the meeting, and the next day one of the leaders went out a few miles and began to work on the subject of holiness, and fourteen or fifteen sinners started on the first move.

On Sabbath morning I went to our church and saw and heard our little great man take out his long written copy of extracts on the subject of baptism. He tried to appear learned while flourishing his Baptizos Apos.[360] But O my God, sinners on the road to hell, and this solemn trifler helping the devil to direct men's minds from their personal salvation. This much for the forenoon.

In the afternoon he had a funeral sermon to preach, and that was a good excuse for keeping me out of sight. So I listened to his very commonplace remarks at the funeral. He could do no less than to ask me to close. Feeling the Spirit of God upon me, I took that occasion to

---

[359] JGT also begins a new chapter here (his chapter 29, beginning on page 197). Five large Xs are written on the page to the right of the designation "Chap," presumably added by JGT (or possibly someone else) for emphasis.

[360] Presumably Redfield is referring here to Greek terms or a book which the preacher used in his sermon. (JGT omits this.)

open a chapter on religion that saves men from sin, that changes our manner, our natures, and supplies all our spiritual wants. The poor little preacher [was] in great agitation behind me but dared not make any demonstration.[361] Upon when church closed [i.e., When the service ended], one of the gentlemen who gave the neat little chapel to the Methodists stepped up to the preacher and in an earnest tone (which the /228/ [preacher could not] comprehend whether it was a tone of disapproval or of approval) demanded of him, "Say, Mr. T., who is that man who closed the meeting?" Then in great trepidation, as I was told, [he said,] "O – He – I don't – He –"

Again he demanded, "Who is he, and where from?"

"Why, he is a local preacher from N. Y."

"Well," rejoined the querist,[362] "if that is the Methodist doctrine, why do you trifle with us as you have in giving us this bosh? Why not like an honest man tell us the truth?"

The poor preacher was momentarily humbled.[363] When conference came round, he wished to go back for another year's trial to make out as good a report as he could of the "spiritual prosperity" of the charge. And someone said, "Bro. T., what prosperity [is there] in B.?"

"O, pretty good."

"How much of a revival?"

"Well, something of a revival."

"Well, how many converted?"

"Well," said Bro. T., "General R. has been onto his knees once."

I saw how such men could be tolerated in the conference, and such men as Bro. V. were kept out of full connexion in the conference for years, kept out on the frontier on the plea, as was told me, that he could not pass his examination on geography. He knew enough to find his way to his appointments and would get more souls converted than would a regiment of these men whom we accrue to our cause and will in the end conspire against all of the genuine stock of old Methodists.

Already I see they are trying to oust or check the very spirit of Methodism, that which has made Methodism what it is. Asbury, Bramwell, Abbott, Nelson, and a host of worthies could not be tolerated, and I could only say, "How blind or dishonest must our ruling officers in the church [be] who will continue to sell and send out to the

[361] JGT: "An invitation to conclude the service gave an opportunity for a brief exhortation, in which Mr. Redfield set forth the type of religion that would save. The minister was very restless, but did not interfere" (197).

[362] Questioner; one who asks a query.

[363] JGT ends this incident here, omitting the extended account.

public the lives [i.e., biographies] of men whose cause would not be tolerated in these days.

I see /229/ the end is surely coming, and with my might I have tried to sound the note of alarm. I had hoped before his time to see such a return to our primitive power and simplicity that our church would be winning its victories as never before. For with all the odds against [us], and when short of applause[?], poor, few and despised, Methodism was a power, a giant to be faced by those who were constantly for numbers and popularity. But now what might not be done if, with all our resources, the entire power of this mighty marching [army], charged with the Holy Ghost, were to aim with the favor and might of God, and march like a tempest, grand, sublime and victorious over the land!

I believed it. I preached it. I felt it, and thought I could now point to the fathers and to the success of the doctrine of holiness and make the case clear. But instead of this I was met with the continuous cry, "Old fogy, fifty years behind the times." "Sour godliness," "unsafe." I knew I had the confidence of a class of old worthies who stood by and told me to go on in their track.

But in looking the matter all over, I thought it might be possible that I had seen so much of the dark side [that my views were skewed]. For my labors when at all tolerated would be most frequently in churches which were about to be closed or sold, and to get up a revival they would sooner endure me than to let their church property go by the board.[364]

XXIX. Redfield Meets Fay Purdy

While I verily thought I was the only one who saw things in the light I did, and the only one who felt called upon to rally our flagging forces, I heard by way of Sister P. [Palmer] of a Brother P. [Fay Purdy] in W. N. Y. [western New York] who felt the same and was trying to do the same work there. I then felt I would give almost anything to see

---

[364] JGT clarifies, and both condenses and amplifies, Redfield here: "He saw that Asbury, Bramwell, Abbot and Nelson would not be tolerated by such ministers. He saw the lives of these worthies on sale at the book rooms, and sometimes peddled among the membership of the church by these ministers who took pains to hold up to ridicule those who strove to walk the same way." JGT adds, "This caused him seasons of great depression of spirits. At these time he would be greatly tempted to give up the battle. Sometimes he would conclude that he had looked on the dark side so much, that he might be deceived as to the real state of things" (197–98). This last sentence in fact summarizes Redfield's reflections in the next several lines.

such a one. When she said he had heard of me and wished me to come out to H. camp meeting, I did not require any urging but in due time was ready and on my way to the camp meeting,[365] /230/ full of many conjectures as to the personal appearance and spirit of a man who was becoming as odious is his locality as I was in mine. I knew there were some Congregationalists and Presbyterians who had adopted the Wesleyan view of holiness and said, "Since the Methodists have given up their peculiar doctrines, our churches have adopted them." But to hear of a live Methodist who saw, felt, and labored as I had and did was indeed to me a treat to be remembered for a lifetime.

On [my] reaching the ground, Sister P. introduced him to me. He was very laconic but courteous and hearty in his deportment. The next moment he was gone, and I knew not where.[366] I soon however heard a voice of someone leading a meeting on holiness, and I listened for awhile and then said to myself, "Then I know I am not alone in my preaching views of holiness. I am not an old fogy. That has the right sound, and but for the tone of voice I should think that was myself, for whoever he is, he sees things clearly and he sees things as I do."

I felt a great interest in the meeting, and on going so that I could look in, there was the very man, and I loved him as my own soul.[367]

---

[365] JGT: "Just at this time Sister Phoebe Palmer informed him of a brother in Western New York who felt the same as he did, and was engaged in the same kind of work. He determined to find this brother and by his aid settle the question that troubled him. It was also made known to him that this strange brother desired his attendance at a camp meeting about to be held, and he needed no urging to accept the invitation, and in due time was on his way to the place" (198).

[366] JGT: "On reaching the campground, Sister Palmer introduced him to me. He was very cautious, but courteous and hearty in his deportment. The next moment he was gone, I knew not where" (198). The year and exact place of this camp meeting are uncertain, though it was in western New York.

[367] JGT: "I drew nearer, where I could see as well as hear, and found the speaker to be the very man whom I had come so far to see—Fay H. Purdy" (198). Redfield does not identify Purdy by name. Purdy was a young Methodist lawyer-evangelist from western New York. B. T. Roberts described him as one who "had received a mighty baptism of the Spirit" and in the 1850s was working "for the awakening of formal churches . . . with remarkable success." B. T. Roberts, *Why Another Sect: Containing a Review of Articles by Bishop Simpson and Others of the Free Methodist Church* (Rochester, N. Y.: "The Earnest Christian" Publishing House, `879) 53. See also Walter W. Benjamin, "The Methodist Episcopal Church in the Postwar Era," Chapter 19 in Emory S. Bucke, ed., *The History of American Methodism* (New York: Abingdon, 1964), 2:350–51. Benjamin describes Purdy as a "Nazarite sympathizer" (350).

And though in after years from a pure misunderstanding which I tried once but in vain to explain he has caused my much suffering, yet I have [seen] and still do see the hand of God in this matter. For on looking over the past, I can see how he would be [i.e., would have been] likely to sway me in matters where I ought to know no voice but God. My heart takes consolation in the hope that when we both pass away, all these matters will be seen in a light which will not in the least tarnish the heart-felt esteem which is due to honesty and purity.[368]

A short history of his conversion and sanctification will not be tedious to the lover of an honest, thoroughgoing man who can surrender all for God and rejoice at the privilege. He was one of /231/ [those] fashionable, fancy Methodists whose position in society won for him the indulgence of the preachers in charge, where[as] others of another grade would possibly be labored with. But at the church where he belonged, a very thoroughgoing man (of whom I had heard but never saw) was laboring. The work took a turn that virtually took [i.e., required people to take] the stand of right or nothing.

Though my friend took great exception to the commotion, yet something reached an honest spot in his heart as he examined his own state in the light of truth. He started for the altar—some thought, to enter his protest to the proceedings. But soon it was discerned that he meant to take a stand for right and to get right [himself]. Then they proposed that he kneel at a very comfortable place at the altar. "No, no," said he, "I cannot kneel." But he lay down on the floor with his face to the floor, and then they would try to console him.

"I know," said he, "what I must do." And then, as he said, he settled it forever to take a stand for the exact right.

He remained till late at night, but received no comfort. He then left for home and found his agitated wife in waiting when he entered. She asked, "And where have you been all this time?"

"Why, what's the matter?"

"O, how you look."

"Well," said he, "I have been to the Methodist church."

"Well, what have you been about?"

"Trying to get right," was the reply.

"Well, I hope you won't get fanatic and think you must give up following the practice of the law."

"I have given it up," said he. "God would not touch my case at all till I gave that up."

---

[368] JGT omits these two sentences about the misunderstanding between Redfield and Purdy.

"Well then, I expect you will be likely to turn Methodist minister."

"I shall do what God tells me to, let it be what it will."

"Well," said she very decidedly, "I never married a Methodist minister, and I will never live with /232/ one, so if that is your purpose, you may as well get papers of separation out, for I never will live with you, and you may take me right home." So home he did take her, and returned to his own home. But [he was] still settling with God.

Not long after, word came to him that his wife was very sick, splitting blood, and wanted him to come to see her. He went, but just as unbending as ever, and gave her to understand [that] at all cost he should now obey God. Some professors of religion took up a labor with him, telling him his wife's health was such that he must unbend a little. "I shall obey God at all cost," was the decided reply.

"Then your wife will die or go to the insane asylum, as a sister has before her."

"If she dies or goes crazy because I obey God, I cannot help it. I never shall stray one hair from what God requires, let the consequence be as it may." And home he went again.

But soon she sent for him in great alarm, thinking she should die. On [his] entering her room, she told him, "I see I am contending against God. Now, will you forgive me?"

"Of course."

All was settled, and she became a devoted laborer with her husband in the harvest field of God.[369]

But to the camp meeting. God did work most gloriously. I went into the stand sometime after public services, and in the back part of it I saw a pale, sickly man in deep emotion confessing to this brother [Purdy] that he had done him wrong. Said the sick man, "I expect to die, and I want to die in peace with all men. I have tried to injure your influence, and I ask your pardon." Of course it was granted.

I took a walk with my friend [Purdy] and said, "Now, Brother, that confession was noble, and I think you ought never to let it be known, but let it die with you." He consented.

But how greatly was I shocked very soon after at seeing in the public prints more severe criticism, and worse than ever before, from this same once-confessing sick man against this brother to whom /233/ he had confessed.

The same sickly man opened fire upon Sister P. [Palmer] of N. Y.

---

[369] This account of Purdy, not included in JGT, is valuable as one of the few extant sources of information on him.

and this brother [Fay Purdy] and myself.[370] I never made a reply and he dropped me. But Sister P. and/or someone for her returned the fire, and a paper war against holiness here began which to my knowledge was a prime cause in awful backslidings, for after that I found places where confessions would come out of this stamp: "So many years ago I enjoyed the blessing of holiness. But when I saw in one of our most[?] trusted[?] papers articles against the doctrine of holiness, I first was shocked. I then began to reason, if ministers who ought to know more than I do say it ain't true, it may be I am mistaken." Giving up their faith, [they] would lose the witness till finally [in one case, as] one man owned up, "It brought me to the gutter, a drunkard."

Those preachers who pampered him [Mattison] and encouraged him, some years after were glad to get rid of him.[371]

I went from this camp meeting to another. [I] found this sickly gentleman there who, I learned, had been trying to put the elder on his guard against me, knowing that I should be there. On my arrival however he [Mattison] met me and very cordially shook hands and said he desired me to go to his tent.

A gentleman who was designing to go into the ministry among the Congregationalists, who saw all this, came to me and told me of the two faces which this clerical gent put on. And said he, "I had made up my mind to join the Methodists and to ask your elder for employment, but the deportment of that man and his opposition to holiness has in-

---

370 This "sickly" Methodist minister was no doubt Hiram Mattison, D.D. (1811–1868) who suffered from ill health for many years, though he was a delegate to the M.E. general conferences of 1848, 1852, and 1856 and wrote several books (Simpson, *COM,* 569). Mattison was an abolitionist and a controversialist on several subjects. White gives a good summary of his controversy with Phoebe Palmer: "Mattison was a Methodist elder and professor of astronomy and natural philosophy in Falley Seminary in upstate New York" and for awhile assistant editor of *The Northern Independent.* "Mattison began to write about Mrs. Palmer's theology in 1861. Most of the articles were carried by the *New York Christian Advocate and Journal,* but others were scattered in different periodicals. Mrs. Palmer replied directly to Mattison only three times, but several others came to her defense" (White, *Beauty of Holiness,* 53).

371 What Redfield means by "get rid of" is unclear; it may refer to Mattison's being superannuated (for the second time) in 1852. Simpson writes, "In 1852 declining health compelled [Mattison] to take a superannuated relation, and removing to the city of New York, he filled several appointments, and was chiefly instrumental in erecting Trinity M. E. church" (Simpson, *COM,* 569).

duced me to change my intention."[372]

I went to P K L [Peekskill, New York], and in a few weeks about forty or fifty were converted.[373] There I met with an old physician who told me his experience, and this is about the substance: "When I was a lad of about sixteen, I was attending school at some little distance from home. While there I was greatly alarmed on account /234/ of the state of my soul. So badly was I concerned that I could not attend to my studies, and thought I would return home and get the counsel of my father, who was a rigid Calvinist. When my father saw my spiritual state, he seemed to be gratified at the sight. I asked, "What shall I do, Father?"

"O, nothing, my son."

"Would it be wrong to pray?"

"O yes. But if the Spirit of God should convert you, then you might pray."

"May I go to the schoolhouse where the Methodists hold meetings?"

"O no, my son. These are the deceivers prophesied who should come in the last days and if possible deceive the very elect."

"Then," said the old doctor to me, "I thought, 'Surely I am a reprobate, and hell is my portion, and I may as well kill myself and know the worst of my case.' So going out to the stable with a razor, I unbuttoned my shirt collar, and putting one hand on the manger I raised up my razor to cut my throat. But an unseen power pulled my hand away every time, and I thought, 'Well, I must give it up.'

"But soon after I heard that a Methodist preacher would preach in a schoolhouse some three miles off and I thought, 'I will not ask Father, for he will refuse, but I will go without asking and then I shall not be guilty of disobedience to my parents.'

"So on I went and took my seat in the schoolhouse. Mr. Freeborn Garrettson was the preacher, and while he was preaching my burden was so great I cried out aloud for mercy. Mr. Garrettson came to me to

---

[372] In Redfield's manuscript the preceding paragraph has a large X drawn through it, plus three smaller Xs at the end, encircled. In place of the X-ed out paragraph JGT has: "From this camp meeting Mr. Redfield went to another, and there found that the sickly minister, whose confession he had heard, had so cautioned the presiding elder, who was in charge, against him, that he was not allowed to labor much" (199).

[373] JGT: "From here he went to Peekskill, where forty or fifty were converted in a few days" (199). Peekskill, New York, is about forty miles north of New York City, less than ten miles from West Point and about five miles east of the Hudson River.

console me and to direct me to Jesus. I asked Mr. Garrettson if it would be wrong for me to pray. "O no, God calls upon you to pray."

"And," said the good old doctor, "you don't know how thankful I felt towards [him, or God] to hear him say I might pray.

"Well, home I went and went upstairs, it being dark, and I went without a light and knelt down by my bed. And while there /235/ the burden left me, and I felt myself happy and thought, 'Surely this must be heaven, and I am in heaven. Well, I don't know, but this must be heaven, and yet I don't know when I died.' So I got up and went feeling around, and felt up the windows. 'What,' said I, 'windows in heaven? Well, the Bible does speak of windows in heaven.' On looking out of the windows, I saw by starlight the old barn, but it looked so light and pale, I said, 'Yes, it must be heaven, and there's a [?],' and catching a glance at the ice, which put me in mind of the sea of glass, I was for a while confirmed that I was in heaven."[374]

XXX. Prison Ministry in New York

Chapter [26][375]

I went by invitation of Navy chaplains to the Marine Hospital.[376] Not knowing my congregation, I ventured to preach as led, and was led to treat them with all the kindness I could possibly command. The main drift was to offer hope. They would break down like whipped children and come out clearly in the enjoyment of religion, live and die happy.[377]

Some of them said to the matron, "Do get Mr. R. to preach to us, for nobody understands us as he does. The ministers who come to preach to us think we are a hard sell and they preach hell-fire and damnation to us. But that don't do us any good; we are used to that. But let anyone come and preach kindly, it breaks us all down."

I felt an interest in knowing who these broken-down mariners

---

[374] JGT omits this account.

[375] JGT also begins a new chapter here (chapter 30, beginning on page 200).

[376] JGT: "From Peekskill Mr. Redfield went, on invitation of the chaplain, to visit the Marine Hospital of New York city" (200). Opened in 1800, the Marine Hospital on Staten Island was established as a public health measure and is part of the story of the development of the U.S. Public Health Service. Edwin G. Burrows and Mike Wallace, *Gotham: A History of New York City to 1898* (New York: Oxford University Press, 1999), 358.

[377] JGT: "The main drift of his preaching was to offer hope, and they would break down and cry like whipped children. Many were clearly converted, and some of them died soon after in the triumphs of the Christian faith" (200).

could be who had come here to die, and learned that many of them were originally out of state prisons and had changed their names and enlisted in the U. S. Service. By this I learned a lesson, and that is that men who feel themselves degraded and beyond hope do not put on their real character, and need a helping hand. [Preaching] the terror of the law does not reach them. Hope only can rouse them to feel /236/ that there is something still left about them worth saving.[378]

I was by the chaplain of S.S. [Sing Sing] prison invited to come and preach to the prisoners.[379] Again I followed what I believed to be the impulses of the Holy Ghost. I saw in them nothing different from the great mass of mankind, only they were caught and the rest were not. I would most significantly ask, "And what have I that I did not receive? Let my training be what theirs was, and who can tell but that we should have changed places, they preaching and I serving out a sentence."[380]

In preaching to them I felt they needed someone to address the better part of their nature and rouse it, if possible, to respond. I tried it by stating the fact that God regarded crime as such in its incipiency and before it had worked out. Law takes cognizance of crime acted, not meditated. Men are disgraced with man only where the crime has worked [out], but with God, when it though latent [is] excited in tendency. I then tried to convince them that each one, if he knew it, had redeeming traits that might be reached. Regardless of the opinion of men, their true value and wisdom lay in disciplining and training themselves for the higher walks of a life which yet lay before them in the

---

[378] JGT: "This made a deep impression upon him, and taught him that these men were not hypocrites; that the terrors of the law do such no good for they are already in a hopeless state of mind. Hope only can reach them" (200). When Redfield says these men "do not put on their real character," he apparently means: They show their real character; they do not put on airs.

[379] JGT records this account, but rewords it somewhat (200). Sing Sing, the state prison at Ossining, on the Hudson River about thirty miles north of New York City (now called the Ossining Correctional Facility), was opened in 1828 to replace the deteriorated and crowded Newgate prison in New York City. Sing Sing "almost instantly won an awesome reputation, potent enough to draw Tocqueville and Beaumont across the Atlantic to investigate its workings. . . . They were astonished to find nine hundred completely unfettered prisoners, overseen by only thirty guards (who meted out merciless floggings with a cat-o'-nine-tails for the tiniest infractions), laboring assiduously in open-air quarries, digging up marble to grace the Greek Revival homes, banks, and churches of New York City." Burrows and Wallace, *Gotham,* 506.

[380] JGT omits these two sentences, which are quite revealing as to Redfield's character.

uncreated[?] eyes of the world to come. And however depressing might be the thought that men looked upon them as degenerate, [I told them:] "There is yet a lineament of Jehovah's image left, and it is struggling within you now to assert its destiny[381] and [prompt you to] aspire in holy rivalry to imitate the moral beauties of the great parent. With men you appear criminal and unfortunate. With God all men are criminal. But you and all [of us] are fortunate if you and we avail ourselves of the helps we all have to rise to our native dignities. What if men do write against your names disgrace and blot them out altogether, [and] if that name be chiseled in the monuments of human remembrance. What if you die and, unhonored in yonder prison grave, leave your bodies to ash back /237/ to atoms, and no stone tell where you lie—if watchful angels stand sentinel over your sleeping ashes, ready to pick up your dust at the summons of the resurrection angel!"

I did not apologize for their sins nor cover up their crimes or soften the coloring of the turpitude of sin. But [I] tried to transfer the matter of difference between them and mankind to its true place of adjustment between them and God.[382] It was becoming them[selves] to say to the Almighty, "Father, against Thee only have I sinned" [cf. Psalm 51:7, Luke 15:21]. It was wonderful to see the magical effect of kind words addressed to their hopes! The dropping tear, the anxious [look] and, I would imagine, the flash of gratitude in the eyes of these poor culprits as they gazed and gazed upon a poor mortal like themselves who instead of upbraiding them would try once more to set them up in the business of living for themselves again and [i.e., but now] with the high aim of aspiring to an exalted caste in the society of heaven, which was denied them here.[383]

The next day as I would pass from one part of the prison to another, I think I must have known some of the emotions which stir the heart of the Angel of Mercy. I was allowed to converse with the prisoners, and found true penitence. Some I believe were genuinely converted

---

381 JGT has, somewhat less positively, "yet they were capable of bearing the image of God" (201).

382 JGT: "'I did not attempt to apologize for their sin, or to soften the color of their crimes, but tried to refer the question of the difference between them and the rest of mankind to the judgment day, the proper place for the settlement of the question'" (201). But Redfield may simply mean that the key perspective in which the inmates should see themselves is in their relationship to God, not to other humans.

383 JGT: "who instead of upbraiding them was endeavoring to induce them to try once more to rise to true manhood, and to aspire to the society of heaven" (201).

to God. I was greatly astonished to see the deep depravity of some hearts and the entire alienation from God among some. [However, I found some] awakened ones who desired me to go [to] one side and even tried to hide their own faces from their fellow prisoners while they opened to me the desire they felt for salvation. One man came to me whose sentence was for ten years, and five were served out, but he had sought and found peace in Jesus. While the tears ran down his face he told me his sentence was just and that God in mercy had allowed him to become an inmate of a prison. Said he, "I have no friend or relation to come near me in my disgrace. No one who would be willing to own me in my prisoner's garb. But," said he, "since I have given my heart to Jesus, I am so happy and so contented that I cannot bear the thought of leaving this place /238/ lest the snares of the world should entrap me again. When I go to my cell and sit down upon my bunk, it seems to me that Jesus comes and sits down with me, and I have such sweet communings with Him that I don't want to leave this place. Should anyone offer me the prison yard full of gold, I would not sell out my prize[?] for the whole."

The head keeper told me he had here men who were so violent [that] they were compelled to keep them [shackled] with a ball and chain to their legs. They had once taken a stand in a cell and, armed, held possession [of it] in spite of all the power they could bring to bear.

"May I see them?" said I.

"I don't know as it will be safe for you."

I said, "Just give me permission to go to them."

I went to them and walked up to them as unconcerned as I could to approach any friend and sat down just as leisurely as I could to show how perfectly composed I felt. I then began in the utmost spirit of kindness to open communication, and I soon found that they felt themselves very badly abused. But I persisted in plying the words of kindness and appealing to their sense of right and wrong, regardless of others' wrongs, and found they were indeed ready to listen and promise a change of behavior.[384]

Among others I found one man, a foreigner who, not understanding our laws, committed an offense in kindness to one person and at the expense of another and was finally shut up here for a term of five years.

---

[384] JGT: "But I appealed to their sense of right and wrong; that it was their duty to do right whether others did or not. My kindness of manner and speech, and my treating them as though they were reasonable beings touched them, and soon they consented to change their course and submit to the discipline of the prison" (202).

The keepers were all interested in his fare and desired someone to use the means to get him pardoned. I undertook the case with one other person, and it was accomplished. But to do what I wished, I must see the man and get a clue to the facts in his case, which would enable me to lay his case in a favorable light before the governor. But to have access to him, I must hire him of the state, and to prevent him from becoming a bill of expense must furnish him some kind of employment.

The only employment which I could give him and which he understood required a better hand to work than he was. So I was compelled to hire the two, and the other man was indeed a great curiosity. He was a great genius and was now serving out his fifth sentence in state prison. /239/ [He was] very ambitious to excel and to be appreciated, and withal very affable and agreeable. But such a passion for stealing I never before witnessed. The other prisoners told me I must keep on my guard or he would pick my pockets. [They] told me that this man kept an old bag in a by-place and would steal pieces of coal, and rags cut off from the prison garments when they came to mending, and pack all such things away in his bag.

I saw another sample of the fidelity of female love and attachment when [in contrast] the males [who had wives in prison] would not at their own expense suffer and still love. I did indeed see one instance of brotherly love in the case of two brothers who came to claim the dead body of a brother who had committed suicide in prison. I never saw one man come to visit his unfortunate wife in prison. But I have seen the female come to see her still-loved husband, and one or two such scenes exhibiting female fidelity in the face of disgrace are stamped upon my memory and cannot be effaced.[385]

I attended a series of meetings in the village and tried again to press home the doctrine of holiness. The opposition was sharp, but God so far conquered as to give us a goodly harvest of souls.

---

[385] JGT rewrites this paragraph to make more sense of it, but omits the reference to the suicide. He has: "While engaged in the effort to procure this pardon, I saw several instances of the fidelity of woman's love in the face of disgrace brought upon the family. Wives came to visit their husbands who were prisoners, but though there were several married women in the prison, there was not a single instance of a husband coming to visit his wife during all the time I was there" (203). This and other references in Redfield's manuscript seem to suggest that Redfield had some involvement at the Sing Sing prison over a period of weeks or perhaps months.

XXXI. Ministry in Bridgeport, Connecticut

Chapter [27][386]

[The Methodist] preacher from Bpt. [Bridgeport, Connecticut] came to N. York to invite me to go to his help, saying, "We must have a revival to save our church.[387] Our people," said he, "have been kept gleaned of all that would do much for us financially by the proselyting system of other denominations, and they [the Methodist congregation] finally determined to build a church which should overtop all others and try by this method to gain a position among the churches which will command respect. And now," said he, "we must lose it, for we are owing upon it $12,000, and we can't pay it. Now, can't you come and help us?"

"I am sorry," said I, "that your people have been trying to win a name by this worldly policy, and I dread the spirit which I am sure such a state of things is most sure to foster." I well knew that state of things would most certainly militate against the faithful preaching of the old and pure doctrine of holiness.

He acknowledged the error of the /240/ people in building so gaudy and so costly an edifice. "But," said he, "we have it and cannot afford to throw it away, and what can we do? Must we give it up and let Methodism be ruled out of the place, or shall we try to save it?"

I finally said, "I will go, Brother." But O how I did dread it, for I well knew that God would hold me responsible for faithful dealing, and I as well knew that I should meet with terrible opposition.

On arriving at the place I saw, sure enough, a stately edifice eclipsing all of the [other] churches in the city in exterior splendor. Two great towers with a bell in one and clock in the other, and the inside with its stained glass, antique architecture and massive as well as very somber ~~hued~~ colored appearance generally, gave me the heartache.[388] But I thought, "What can be done? This state of things will yet quench the

---

[386] JGT also begins a new chapter here (his chapter 31, beginning on page 204).

[387] JGT: "About this time the preacher from Bridgeport, Connecticut, came to Mr. Redfield and invited him to assist him in revival services at that place. He said: 'We must have a revival or lose our church'" (204). This apparently was in late November, 1850.

[388] JGT: "When I arrived I saw a stately edifice, eclipsing all others in exterior splendor. Two great towers, one bearing a bell and the other a clock, reared their massive proportions in front; the whole of antique architecture and 'loud' appearance. My heart ached in view of the prospect" (204).

last gasp of vitality in the M.E. Church, and to arrest it, some giant hand of influence must grapple with it. I see none who dare to risk their reputations and hazard their chance of rising to dignified position [in] the church who will do it. Somebody must enter as pioneer and fearlessly take sides with God, and possibly be crushed out for his pains. I know it is a daring stake and I am a very feeble instrument. I may not be able to do anything. But in the name of God of right and the ghost of Methodism, I can but die in the effort, and I will do it if it ruins me forever." And when I thus resolved, I felt an unearthly nerving of soul and the sweet assurance that God approved of my vow.

I tried to bring that class of truth to bear which would arraign the conscience before the bar of God's truth [as] kindly but clearly as I could, and persistently. When I left the church [edifice after the service,] the minister took a walk with me and took up a labor with me and desired me to adopt a less objectionable class of truth.

"What?" said I. "Brother, ain't it truth which I have thus far [preached]?"

"O, yes," said he, "it is all true. But I don't know as the truth should be spoken at all times."

I then asked him if he thought Jesus could moderate the truth and tacitly give men to think He had preached the whole truth /241/ when He had not touched the real evil.[389]

"Well," said he, "I am afraid that your course will ruin us."

"Well brother," said I, "what time does the train leave town?"

"Why," said he, "you must not leave."

"O my Brother, I certainly shall if I can't go the Bible track. I will allow you to call me to an account at any time if you find me outside of the Bible or the Methodist Discipline."

"Well," said he, "you must stay, and we must have a revival or lose our church."

"I feel no interest in you saving your church [building] in the present condition of things. It would be no calamity to religion to lose it unless it can better represent Methodism that it does at present."

"Well," said he, "you must stay, and do be as easy with us as you can."

I said, "I will be as easy as God will let me, but no more so. And I wonder that anyone could even ask me to lower the only standard of

---

[389] JGT: "Do you think Jesus would mutilate the truth, and tacitly give men to think that he had preached the whole? and this when he had not touched the real evil of the case?" (205). (The word in Redfield's manuscript which JGT interprets as "mutilate" appears to me to be "moderate.")

religion that can possibly save." So on I went in the name of [the] God of right and truth, till in one of our afternoon meetings one person fell under the power of God. The husband of one of the members, who paid well but was without religion, in high affront apparently left the house.[390] At this the preacher took alarm. By and by one of the sisters arose and began confessing to dancing, card playing, novel reading, and conformity to the world. The preacher wiggled as if on nettles and finally got up and said, in effect, that we must not look too much on the dark side, adding that an old prophet once complained of the few in number who served God when he was answered that God had reserved seven thousand who had not bowed the knee to Baal.

I saw the drift was to stop this kind of exhibition of the real condition of the church. I arose and admitted it [was] true in the case of the prophet. But I insisted that if these members had danced, played cards,

---

[390] JGT supplies some additional information here: "Mr. Redfield went on with his work in the name of God and truth. In one of the afternoon meetings Fay H. Purdy, who was assisting him, fell to the floor while Mr. Redfield was praying. This was something new to the congregation, and unexpected to the minister.* The husband of one of the members, a man who paid well, but was without salvation, arose, apparently in great anger, and left the house" (206). Corresponding to the asterisk, JGT inserts at the bottom of the page: "*Rev. Clement Combes, who was present." Presumably Combes was Terrill's source of information here.

Bridgeport, Connecticut, was at this time on the New Haven District of the New York East Conference. The appointed preacher in 1850–51 was J. B. Stratton. I have not been able to find any preacher named Combes or Combs in the *Minutes* of the New York or New York East conferences. He could possibly have been a local preacher or a preacher from another conference or denomination.

A December 8, 1850, letter from Redfield to Walter and Phoebe Palmer suggests that these revival efforts were in late November and early December, 1850, and confirms Fay Purdy's participation. Redfield writes, "How or what the results here will finally show doth not yet appear. The work of holiness has gained some ground. The reflex influence is felt upon the hearts of sinners, about 30 of whom went forward for prayers last night. My fears are that the balance of the church will not take that decided stand for holiness which I believe necessary to enable them to run rather than to ride. My opinion is that we could not reach the present state of piety in the church for weeks to come, if at all, but for the valuable labors of our Brother Purdy, whose manner and class of truths, with the results, have convinced me more than ever that the salvation of Methodism depends on that thorough, honest return to first principles." John Wesley Redfield Letters, Methodist Collection, Manuscript Division, New York Public Library.

read novels, and behaved in general in a manner not becoming a disciple of the /242/ meek Jesus, it was due to God and truth that they as publicly as they have sinned before the world, just so publicly ought they to confess and restore themselves back to the confidence of the world as representatives of the religion of Christ. "The cause of Jesus is slandered and in disrepute on account of your lives," [I said,] "and I think that common honesty dictates that the wrong should be placed where it belongs. If Jesus has not disgraced his own cause, don't compel Him to bear the odium. But if we have, we ought to act the part of honor and tell the world that neither Jesus nor the gospel is at fault for your conduct, but you alone."

This hurt the preacher still worse. But soon God came in awful power to convict, convert, sanctify, and reclaim His own cause.

Next came in other denominations as previously to get a hand in. [They] complained that I was too bigoted in not inviting them to participate.[391] I well knew the motive, and that was to gather up the converts. So I took special pains to invite them to come and take hold, and to make all [things] right because, [I said,] "You [must] confess your real state, for if you don't and any of the skeptics of religion should intimate to me that they had no confidence in you on account of your ungodly lives, I shall not hesitate to make that fact known as a reason for not asking you to take a part—namely, that your Christian character is not appreciated by the penitents."

One of the ministers still cried out against me for not inviting him by letter to take a part. I well knew his motives, for he was one of the very men who most of all had gleaned the Methodists of their converts in days past. When this was all hushed up, the infidels held up their wing of the battalion to stop us. Then the strong arm of the law was invoked to come to our aid. The next time [they tried] by petty annoyances to trammel us, till one Sunday night while preaching I told our brethren not to fear /243/ opposition, for our success was just as certain as that God was the Author of our gospel. [I said,] "God might allow us to be annoyed and persecuted, but when we have taken a stand for God and right and should succeed but for opposition," then God would come to our rescue and give success to the gospel, even though He had to take life. I then related a number of anecdotes to illustrate the position where I had known God suddenly to take life, and the poor victim

---

[391] JGT: "When victory began to seem certain, the other churches began to accuse Mr. Redfield of bigotry, because he had not invited them to participate in the meetings" (207). Terrill rewrites the ensuing account in his own words, for clarity.

cried out in his extreme agony, "I am lost and shall now go to hell."

On the next day, [the following occurred.] In a house on the opposite corner lived a reputed Universalist. His daughter at the dinner table amused those present by saying in substance that Redfield had been trying to frighten the people last night by lying to them, for he said that God would kill people if they dared to oppose and ridicule religion. "Now," said she, "I would like to know who will be the first one who will be knocked down here. Come, let us try it." So, clapping her hands in mockery, she shouted, "Glory, glory," and instantly fell upon the floor in an awful agony. Word went out that J. K. was dead, and that she dropped down dead at the dinner table while she was trying [to see] if God would kill folks for ridiculing religion.

This poor girl lay four or five days in this agony. But her mind remained permanently impaired.[392]

Word came to a large boarding house where the wicked were seated for dinner. It was said by one who witnessed it that when they heard of the fate of this poor girl, they dropped their knives and forks and looked as though they had just heard their own death warrant.

The work broke out in greater power, and in a very few weeks there were over five hundred conversions. The church was saved and another new one built.[393]

I was now called to go to another place. But the preacher [at Bridgeport] said, before you go you must take in the probationers. "Very well," [I said.] I thought I would, and on the last Sabbath /244/ of my stay I desired all in the house who would, to come near the pulpit and be seated in the first pews. A large number came forward. I then took the *Discipline* in hand and said to them, "It is your duty to join

---

[392] In Redfield's manuscript, these two sentences are written along the left-hand margin. JGT renders it: "The young girl who was so suddenly stricken down lay four or five days in that condition, and then was restored, but with a permanently impaired mind" (208).

[393] JGT omits this sentence here, but at the end of the account has, "Soon after this, the debt that hung over their church property was paid, and a second church had to be built to accommodate the congregation" (210).

The *Minutes* of the New York East Conference provide some statistical evidence of the effects of this Redfield revival. The Bridgeport M.E. Church reported 217 full members and three probationers in 1850. A year later it reported 255 full members and 170 probationers. The following year full membership had jumped to 384, with 20 probationers. By 1854 full membership had reached 395 (with 35 probationers), and in 1854–55 the East Bridgeport M.E. Church was formed, Bridgeport reporting 333 full members (plus 18 probationers) and East Bridgeport 60 full members (plus eight probationers).

some church to be under its watch-care. I don't ask you to join the Methodists, nor do we want any to unite with us who are not in every essential point a Methodist. I don't know as anyone here wants to join the Methodists, but if there should be anyone who desires to united with us, I will tell you what we shall expect of you. If you cannot meet our expectations, we don't want you at all. We don't want anybody who will proselyte, and may God forbid that the Methodists should ever become so inefficient as to be compelled to keep up her number of members and hang around the Baptists and Presbyterians and watch their chances to toll off their converts into the Methodist Church."

I then read over the rules and commented on them one by one. I told them, in substance, "If you join the Methodists, there can be no more dancing, novel reading, afternoon parties, wearing of jewelry, or conformity to the world. This may seem hard to you. But there are a plenty of formal churches here who will open folding doors to let you in. So that is the place for you, and not with the Methodists, for you will only be a curse to us by your example. I know we have had to deal faithfully with some here who have thus lived, and kept the church dead and powerless. We now kindly ask all such to go as soon as possible to our preacher and demand their letters, and then join those churches which allow of this loose living.

"But so far I have only told you what you cannot do and remain a Methodist." Then the preacher gave a significant sound, and I expected the next moment to feel my coattail pulled and to be requested to stop.

"Now I will tell you what we shall expect, and that is faithful living; attendance upon all the means of grace; class, prayer, and preaching [meetings;] and family religion and active labor for the immediate conversion of sinners by personal labor for them and with them. Never allowing /245/ in a single instance a favorable opportunity of exhorting a sinner to pass unimproved, but literally to carry on the business of winning souls to Christ and [to] let all worldly matters be regarded only as the chores to be done at leisure.

"If you cannot make this pledge, you can go where you will not be expected to do anything for God at all, but remain as sleepers, except in terms of proselyting. Then you must be kept like on ice, [and will] have to freeze up all of you proselytes in order to preserve them, for you will have no salt that will save, and for want of salt you must have ice.[394]

"I will farther read your history—whichever choice you make. If you join some one of these dead churches to get the premium of, first,

---

[394] JGT, who rewords this passage somewhat, omits the reference to ice and salt (209–10).

not doing anything for God, and of doing as you please in loving and dressing like the world, you will by and by come to death. How long before, no one knows. Join one of these churches or none, and still you may live only a month or week longer. Now, join a fashionable, formal church, for this premium of a month or a week, and then come to death and let your eyes be open to see that you have exerted an influence which is still felt and is turning souls out of the way, [and thus] to ruin. Now follow on to the judgment and meet those souls which your preponderating influence, which like the last grain of sand turns the scale, and [see that] those souls are now lost.

"Or, on the other hand, join the Methodists and live like one, and not like these shows who have nearly ruined Methodism in this place. Then your influence will be felt, and will tell upon the salvation of souls. And though your probation may be short, you may pillow your head upon the bosom of Jesus and recount the souls who through your influence will be doing a work for God while you are sleeping in the dust, and [who] at the great settlement day will stand among the redeemed and report your instrumentality as the deciding influence which put them upon the road that led them up to the home of the redeemed."

The church seemed /246/ (and the preacher in particular, if I could translate the indications) to be in great fear that I had given the last blow which must fix the doom of Methodism. But when I asked them to give in their names, over one hundred gave their names at once, and the entire balance amounting to about five hundred [eventually] joined our church. And what was singular, no other church gained one. I felt that honest people loved to be thoroughly dealt with, and none but [the] honest would make good Methodists.

Some thought this a very hazardous and imprudent measure of mine, and regarded me as the only Methodist who would be rash enough to adopt it. But I learned such severity of a [i.e., from the] course pursued by Elijah Hedding before he became bishop—what to my mind deserved as severe criticism as did my course. While in or near Boston, and while he was comparatively a young preacher, a wealthy lady of the Hancock family, an Episcopalian, had a servant girl who was a Methodist, and at one [this girl] time brought home a volume of Wesley's sermons. The lady got sight of the book and began to read. God got hold of her honest heart, and on enquiring of the girl where she procured that book, the girl told her that they had a minister who preached just like that every Sunday. "Who and where is he?" said the Lady. The girl told her. Then she had her carriage harnessed and her driver took her to the plain Methodist parsonage to see Mr. Hedding.[395]

It was a novel sight in those days to see the splendid Hancock family carriage stop at the obscure and despised Methodist parsonage. Having alighted, she left the man in care of the horses and went up to the door and rapped or rang at the humble door of the Methodist preacher. Elijah Hedding, I think, answered the call. Then the lady asked, "Is this the house of Rev. Mr. Hedding?"

"I am the man you enquire for."

"Well," said she, "Mr. Hedding, I have come /247/ to join your church."

Mr. Hedding at a glance saw the person he had to deal with, and from the appearance of the carriage at the door and the rich attire, as well as the lady-like appearance of her person, and thinking there must be some mistake, [he] asked her, "Madam, can you tell me to what circumstance I am indebted for this call and proposal?" Then she told him how she had been favored with the present of a volume of Mr. Wesley's sermons and that she had made up her mind to come out herself with a people whose doctrines came so near her ideal of what Christianity ought to be.[396]

---

[395] This incident, which occurred in 1815, is recorded in *Life and Times of Rev. Elijah Hedding, D. D.* This biography was published in 1856, and since Redfield presumably was writing in 1862 or 1863, he could have gotten the story from the book. A number of details are different between the two accounts, however, suggesting that Redfield received the story by word of mouth well before the book was published.

According to Hedding's biography the woman, "the niece of Governor Hancock," was a Unitarian, not an Episcopalian. She had chanced to pass "the Methodist Church in Bromfield Lane" on a Sunday and went in and heard Hedding preach and it was this, together with reading the volume of Wesley's sermons that her servant girl had, which led her to go visit Hedding. Otherwise the two accounts are essentially the same, and make the same point. In the biography Hedding is quoted as saying that this women subsequently lived a "devout, pious, uniform, and rational" Christian life. See D. W. Clark, *Life and Times of Rev. Elijah Hedding, D. D., Late Senior Bishop of the Methodist Episcopal Church* (New York: Carlton and Phillips, 1856), 248–51.

[396] JGT quotes Redfield as follows: "She then related to him the incident of the volume of sermons, and the remark of the servant girl, and then added: 'Those so fully accord with my views of what a Christian life should be that I hasten to identify myself with the people who hold to those views'" (211). Clark's biography of Hedding says, "She had recently read a volume of Wesley's Sermons, which belonged to a servant girl in her house, into which she had first looked from curiosity; but as she continued to read, they brought her to a sense of her sin and danger, and gave her a knowledge of the way of salvation, and ulti-

"But Madam," said Mr. Hedding, "do you know our discipline and rules, and could you conform to them?" Then opening a *Discipline* he read over the rules and asked her if she could make up her mind to live up to those rules. She promptly answered she could and would.

Still desirous of dealing faithfully, and [of] getting rid of her if she was not really fully resolved to pay the whole cost, and [wanting to] give her a chance to withdraw her request if she could not in heart live so as to be an honor to the cause of Christ, he said to her, "Well, Madam, you are a stranger to me. But as we are to have a love feast at such a time, I will see some of our official board about this matter, and if you will come to our love feast, and should there be no objection to you, we will take you on probation for six months."

Suffice it to say that she was received, and proved to be a worthy member of the M.E. Church. On opening her will after her death, [the executor discovered that] the following was the substance of one clause: "I give and bequeath $500.00 to Rev. Elijah Hedding for his faithful dealing with me when I joined the Methodist Church."[397]

XXXII. Revivals in Connecticut

Chapter [28][398]

My next place to visit was N. H. [New Haven, Connecticut]. Some had been to this last place [Bridgeport] in the night of our triumph, and [they] thought, "If this is the fruit of Br. R's labors, we want him to come to N. H."[399]

But how little did they know the hard toil and many conflicts before a dead church could be /248/ brought into a spiritual state where it could become a successful working power for God. I dreaded the heart-aching times I must have. I knew that nothing but fidelity to God and

---

mately led her to the experience of that religion that Mr. Wesley taught." Clark, *Life and Times of Rev. Elijah Hedding,* 249.

397 JGT omits this last sentence. Clark, quoting Hedding, says that when she died this woman "left in her will $2,000 to the Methodist Church in Boston, to be funded [i.e., invested], and the interest to be paid forever for the poorest members of the Church; and $500 for brother [Rev. Daniel] Fillmore [Hedding's colleague at this Boston church], and $500 for myself" (250–51).

398 JGT also begins a new chapter here (chapter 32, beginning on page 212).

399 At the time there were two M.E. congregations in New Haven, First Church and a newer, smaller congregation, St. John's Street. The invitation probably came from First Church, which had a fairly new (1848), substantial building at the corner of Elm and College streets. First Church had 305 members in 1850 and St. John's Street had 228. See Simpson, *COM,* 650.

truth would do for me, and as I well knew that my already rent character would receive new wounds and my [way] would be proportionately closed up. But [I was impelled by] the thought that there are so few who will risk their own reputation for God, and that somebody must take their stand or let the cause of Jesus go by default. And farther, I felt I might as well be the one who shall fall first in battling for God's rights. It may be that my calamity may draw attention from some honest heart who will be daring enough to follow, and truth may finally triumph. So I said to them, "Brethren, I will be at your place on such a night."[400]

One of their brethren, to forestall public prejudice, gave a flaming account of the work in B [Bridgeport] and called upon the people to suspend means till they should ~~first~~ see the kind [of] workings, and all this but too clearly showed how fearful they were of the final results.[401]

The time came for the [railroad] cars to start [from Bridgeport], and with a sad and very heavy heart I took my place in the car. I knew from the distance about how long I should be in reaching the place. Taking out my watch, I said to myself, "Only so long to live, and I shall probably be warned off the first night, but if I am not allowed to stay more than one hour, that one hour shall be spent for the exact right." From reports, I knew the city to be a bad place for deep, zealous, humble piety to find a foothold. A large number of churches which once opposed real Methodism now had suspended hostilities, only because the Methodists had ceased to be a power and had been become popular like others.[402]

---

[400] JGT: "next Thursday night" (213). Terrill rewrites this passage and adds: "Reader, would you call this cowardice? True bravery does not shut its eyes to the dangers that surround it, and then go forward blindly. He is the bravest man who is most conscious of the danger and still goes forward. Some natures less finely strung than Mr. Redfield's would have gone forward easily and readily, but their work would have been more crudely and less thoroughly done."

[401] The meaning seems to be: This brother advised the church not to schedule a series of special meetings ("means") until they had some initial taste of Redfield's ministry among them. But some would see this advice as a red flag.

[402] JGT elaborates: "New Haven was the seat of Yale College. The influence of this institution was hostile to Methodism, and had been from the beginning. It was a city of many churches, and these likewise all hostile to Methodism. At this particular time there was no manifestation of opposition, for Methodism had ceased to be a power in the city. The membership had cowered before the lofty claims to superiority of these churches, and had contentedly settled down in a subordinate position and almost ceased to have an independent life" (213). Redfield does not specifically mention Yale College.

On arriving at the depot I found a number of brethren in waiting, with a nice carriage. I felt grateful for their kindness, but O how deeply did my heart feel distressed with the thought, "I know God will hold me responsible for fidelity to right, and I as well know I am /249/ destined to have a most hazardous and sorrowful time."

[I] went into the church that night. People collected, probably many of them through curiosity. The preacher arose and said, "Bro. R. has finally come, and will preach tonight and tomorrow and next day night," and then sat down.

I immediately arose and, feeling the power of God upon me, I said, "It may be so, and maybe not. You may not desire me to stay after tonight. But by the help of God I mean so to preach that if I am called to the judgment in five minutes after I get done, I am ready. And it makes no difference with me whether I stay one day or six weeks. I shall certainly go for the straight judgment truth of God, the same truth we must die by and be judged by, if it takes the last brick from the foundation of the church."

God did help me define that form and degree of religion which alone could ever pass the gates of pearl. The church was frightened, and the preacher too. But one good old father of primitive Methodism took me by the hand and bid me Godspeed.

One of the leaders met me and told me I had altogether mistaken the people, and that this kind of preaching would not take in that place. "Besides," said he, "you tacitly reflect upon the other denominations, whom we regard as a pious people."

Meeting closed, and the ex-mayor, who was there, relieved our preacher by saying, "Sir, that is the kind of preaching we want [i.e., need]. We have not a minister in the city who dares to risk his reputation, and that is the reason why the churches here have been so inefficient for the last twenty-five years. Here," said he to the preacher, "give him that as a token of my approval," handing him a twenty dollar gold piece.

Soon a lawyer met the preacher and told him, "That's the kind of truth we want [i.e., need] here." When some of the great and influential men gave their sanction to this class of truth, the fears of our preacher were somewhat allayed.

Next, the rabble began their address to me by serenading me at night by singing doggerel verses, /250/ then sending me ball tickets through the post office, by hooting and bawling after me in the streets, and by holding mock meetings and trying to imitate me in a prayer meeting. Here again my careful friends were disturbed and brought the sad intelligence to me as a matter greatly to be dreaded.

"Well thank God," said I. "The devil is getting disturbed, and these are good omens. The devil must soon exhaust his resources, and then we shall see many of theses very persons happy in God."

We continued our labor with the church, to get it sanctified. In some seven or eight weeks I was met by one or two of the official board who had the frankness to tell me that my course would injure the church if not soon changed, saying they knew of more than fifty sinners who were waiting to be called forward for prayers, and this perpetual labor for the [sanctification of the] church [members] would become stale and offensive. "And," said one, "there are many of us, and I am one of them, that shall never get out [to spiritual victory] till we can pray ourselves out by laboring for sinners."

"Well," said I, "I know of many who want religion, and they have sent word to me to know if they can have a chance to come out for the prayers of the church. And I tell them, we ain't ready for them, and we cannot do them any good yet. And now, Brethren," said I, "you want to get on the wrong side of the altar and get your old rheumatic joints warmed up by a little exercise, and then call that a revival."

"Well," said they, "what will become of sinners if we spend all our time in praying for ourselves, and don't pray for them?"

"I will ask, Brethren, what are your prayers worth for sinners when you know you have not had a blessing in answer to your prayers for six months? If I was going to ask anyone to pray, I would ask the penitents to pray for the church and not the church to pray for penitents."

But finally I saw that nothing but a failure in the effort would convince them, so at our next evening meeting after sermon I said, "If there /251/ are any who want religion enough to come and kneel at this altar while we sing just one verse and no more, you may come." I struck a short metre and sang fast, and before I could finish the verse the altar was crowded.

I said, "Now hold on, we have enough at the altar," and I felt we had more than we could do any good for. I then said, "Now, Brethren, come into the altar and pray for these." The altar, a very large one, was well filled and in quick time, too, and [I said,] "Now pray, Brethren." One broke out, "O Lord, we thank Thee for these prosperous times. Lord, have mercy on us. O bless the world and the church. Send the gospel to the heathen, and bless the Bible and missionary cause." This is about a specimen of the broken, disjointed, and inappropriate form of prayer which they went through with. I could not say "Amen" to a single petition, for I knew they did not mean or appreciate a word they uttered.

In due course of time I arose and said, "It is now time to close, and before we close, if any of these penitents have been blessed, let them confess it to the people." I held on and urged and tried to encourage them to report all that God had done for them at the altar, but not one word could any one of them say—and for the simple reason that they had nothing to say. I then said to the congregation, "I will never again while I am here ask penitents to come here for the benefit of such dead, meaningless, and formal prayers."

The next night the very ones who were so anxious to warm up by praying for others began in good earnest to pray for themselves, and one or two had such a sight of their corruption as almost to appear to be in despair.

I now appointed two meetings to go on at once in two of the classrooms for the benefit of those who desired to seek a clean heart. At the [appointed] time I went into one and opened it, and then went into the other. So I tried, for want of someone to help to keep them both going, [to lead both meetings] by going back and forth from one room to the other. And now God gave us one or more victories of perfect love. These meetings /252/ in the classrooms we held about one hour before the evening preaching.

But soon the witnesses of perfect love increased till a power was accumulated so potent that the great mass of the city was stirred.[403] We had frequently over one hundred at our altar seeking religion at once. Other churches availed themselves of this interest and in good earnest went to work in their own way. At one church, I learned they had as many as four hundred anxious [i.e., salvation-seeking] persons at one time.[404] At the college, too, the work was very prosperous. And now as far as I could learn all hostility from other churches ceased, though the Baptists as usual were proselyting at every opportunity.[405]

A good deacon came to me to inform me of a few facts which he thought I ought to know, and [to permit me to] repair the evil, if I could. First, one of the ministers was preaching to the people against my cause and doctrines and telling them it was no matter how people

---

[403] JGT: "In a few days God gave us a few witnesses to the experience. The number of witnesses then began to increase faster and faster, until soon their aggregate power moved the entire city" (216).

[404] JGT: "In one of these churches it was reported there were received above four hundred persons" (216). This is not what Redfield said, but perhaps it is what he meant.

[405] JGT: "The revival got into Yale College, and many of the students were converted. All hostility in other denominations, for the time being ceased, except the proselyting to gain members" (216). JGT does not mention the Baptists specifically.

lived in love with and conformity to the world if they only kept their hearts right. [The minister] himself would go to the social gatherings and parties where dancing and vain amusements were the order of the day and gloss over these world-loving gatherings with a prayer.

The other matter was that the report was current that I had prayed the Lord to come down right through the roof, and I would pay for the shingles.[406]

As to the first, I only could and did say publicly that God's requirements were unbending, and God said, "Love not the world" and "Be not conformed to the world." And now I warned this congregation of this fact, that though a minister might tell them there was no harm in disobedience to all the requirements of the Bible, they must settle with God after all and [they would be viewed] not from the standard which men may erect but from the Bible standard.

To show that I was not wholly guilty of sour godliness or carrying things too far in my zeal against conformity to this world, I will give one sample of a Methodist women who saw the wickedness of her /253/ example and took off three or more hundred dollars' worth of jewelry, and then went around from house to house confessing the wrong of her fashionable life and asking pardon on her knees. She then tried to do away her bad influence in her family, and in less than two weeks her family were converted to God.

Another sister, whose husband had been regarded as a model of a Christian, saw him one night in such agony before God as to arouse the block where he lived. She saw, "If my husband sees himself in this light, O Lord, where am I?" She sought in the most thorough way and means to be a Bible Christian and when she did come out [in spiritual victory], so great was the light and power of God upon her that she could not rise from her bed, and remained over one week under the power. When Christian people came in to see her, with an unearthly radiance glowing on her face and with words which carried rebukes to the soul she declared that she could now see that the church did not believe the Bible.

This type of power soon had its influence. In a few weeks from the time that the work first broke out, some seven hundred were converted, and the results in all denominations first and last has been reckoned at

[406] JGT includes the report about this minister who was saying "it made no difference how people lived" as long as their hearts were right, but omits the remark about the roof and shingles (216–17).

about 1,500 conversions.[407]

This was indeed a great work. And here I found the preacher a man who in former days had known much of the power of God, but becoming frightened had lowered his standard, though he was one of the clearest, straightest preachers of the law and stood by this type of the work. I thought, surely here is a man of fidelity, a man that is right and a man of might who will leave his mark for God and primitive Methodism. [But] I with deep grief learned that he too in less than two years would speak disparagingly of the work and call it "one of Redfield's revivals." So all my hopes for /254/ God and genuine Methodism from this quarter vanished.[408]

The revival however resulted in filling our church to overflowing, and some thirty families could not find a seat at all. So our people built a new chapel in another part of the city for their accommodation.

While the work was going on so gloriously a deputation from S. [Stamford, Connecticut], a city of about thirteen to eighteen thousand people about fifty miles distant, called upon me to invite me to come to their help.[409] I did so, and on being introduced to the preacher I asked, "How many inhabitants have you?"

He told me, and the number of churches. Our people had three churches, though one was closed.[410]

"What is the prevailing tone of religion?"

"Unitarian."

"How long since the Methodists have had anything like a revival?"

"About thirty years. But," said he, "we have become a respectable

---

[407] New York East Conference statistics suggest a very significant revival in New Haven in 1850–51. First Church nearly doubled, from 305 to 560 members (including 235 probationers), and St. John's Street went from 228 to 335 members (including 85 probationers). The next year (1852) a third New Haven M.E. congregation appears in the *Minutes,* Fair Haven, with 136 minutes—perhaps substantiating Redfield's later remark about another congregation being formed as a result of the revival.

[408] JGT rearranges the material here a bit and condenses these two sentences to: "Yet strange to say, the pastor afterward became an opposer of Mr. Redfield and spoke disparagingly of this revival" (217).

[409] JGT here begins a new chapter (Chapter 33) and renders this sentence as follows: "While the work was moving in great power in New Haven, a deputation from Stamford waited upon Mr. Redfield and invited him to that city" (218). Stamford is forty miles southwest of New Haven on Long Island Sound, near the New York State border.

[410] The 1850 *Minutes* of the New York East Conference indicate one Stamford M.E. church but with two preaching points, Norwalk and New Canaan.

people. Why," said he, "the time was when one man, Rev. Dr. O., exerted so much influence that we could not have the privilege of having a church in the city but were compelled to build some miles out. But," said he, "there is a great change come over the Doctor, and he says now that the Methodists have become so respectable that they ought to have the same privilege as do other churches. And now we have this very good edifice in this eligible part of the city."

Though I said nothing, I felt quite sure in my own mind that the Methodists had become tolerated and respectable only because they were dead and inefficient.

In due time we went to the church. God gave me a message to the church, which was the reestablishment of the primitive standard of Methodism and denying the validity of all others.[411] The meeting closed. I went home with the preacher, who enquired of me if that was the way I designed to pursue.

"Why?" said I, "What's the matter?"

"O," said he, "I don't think that course will do here at all in this city. But," said he, "I think I can give you some valuable advice, if you are willing to receive it."

"Very good, my brother," said I. "I am willing, and want good advice. Tell me now, just where you think I can mend /255/ my course?"

"Well," said he, "I would have you take the course that our conference ministers do."

"Well, give me a sample."

Then said he, "There was the Rev. Mr. Blank who preached here ~~twelve~~ some years ago."

"Well, how did he do?"

"Why, he was a perfect gentleman, and the people were all bound up in the man, and everybody thought well of him."

"Well, give me another."

"Well," said he, "the Rev. Mr. X., who followed him."

"Well, what course did he pursue, and what was the result?"

"Why, he pursued essentially the same course and was very much appreciated by the people, and had no enemies." So he continued to give a history down to his own administration, and in his gentlemanly maturity said he thought he himself looked upon the people as true friends who seemed to appreciate his effort to please.

---

[411] JGT: "In due time he proceeded to the church for the first service. The message was to the church; the theme—the New Testament standard of religion, and the unlawfulness of all others" (218). It is interesting that JGT changes "the primitive standard of Methodism" to "the New Testament standard of religion."

"Then, you think I ought to take pattern after those men, do you?"

"I do," said the worthy clergyman.

"Well," said I, "can you tell me at what hour I can leave town on the train?"

"O," said he, "you don't think of leaving, do you? We have sent for you and want to have a revival."

"Brother," said I, "God has made me a very rough man with a rough gospel for rough hearts, and I shall leave, for you think that a little more of the same stuff which you acknowledge has done nothing for thirty years will work now. You have all the tools, so you go ahead, and I will go where the people will allow me to use God's only tools for saving men."

He thought this matter all over and finally said, "Well, my time will be out in a few weeks, and this is my last year. So I shall venture to allow you to continue preaching."

I went on for two days more. Then in an afternoon meeting an old Methodist man got up and began thus: "I went home from meeting last night," said he, "and went to bed, but I could not sleep. I felt so bad and sick that I thought I should die before morning. So I dared not sleep, but I got up and then got onto my knees, and I struggled all night. But about the break of day /256/ God spoke peace and power to my soul." Then, raising his voice very loud, "Why brethren," said he, "it is the same kind of religion which we used to have thirty years ago!"

Then up got a sister who said, "Brethren, when I heard what a great revival was in progress in N. H. [New Haven] where Bro. Redfield was laboring, I thought, 'If he could only come here, what a good time we would have.' But when he came and began to preach, I said, 'O Lord, I can't have it come that way.' I thought he would put it on to the sinners, but when he preached so sharp to us, I thought I never could endure it. But last night I went home, and I felt so bad I could not go to bed. So I sat up all night and prayed God to have mercy on me. And about the break of day, God spoke in power to my soul. Why," said she, "it is the same religion we used to have thirty years ago." And as she said that she fell under the power.[412]

Then another arose and gave in substantially the same testimony. By this time Dr. O., who came out of curiosity and who had become afraid of the Methodists, left the house in great wrath and said to someone as he left that such things ought not to be tolerated, and that that man Redfield ought to be shut up at once. But the work went on for

---

[412] JGT: "'Oh, this is the same kind we used to have years ago!' and she fell, as though dead, to the floor" (220).

some time in great power.[413]

XXXIII. Summer Camp Meetings

Chapter [29][414]

In due time I visited F. [Fairfield, Connecticut?] camp meeting.[415] Here I saw such a specimen of God's grace in the conversion of a man as took all my notions of mercy and forbearance entirely aback. He was a man who had become so abandoned and vile that he was several times a candidate for state prison, but somehow escaped. To appearance, his mind was but a wreck of his former self. Sometimes he would go around peddling fish, yet if he could find anyone who would gamble with him, he would let the fish decay in his cart. So wretched and vile had the man become that some said they thought it would be wicked to pray for him.

I think a sight such as I had of him some months after his conversion must be a very graphic description of /257/ the monomaniac of Gadara. A miracle of grace. His body in ruins; his mind stupid to appearance to the last degree of imbecility; his person yet filthy and every external appearance very forbidding. And yet there was such a charm in the artless and yet emotional testimony (to use his own words) "of my blessed Jesus," uttered by a mouth overflowing with drool [which was] running down upon his dirty clothing, [that it] gave me a vivid picture of the triumphs of grace in overcoming the devil and [producing a Christian who was] shining like a diamond set in the mud.[416]

At this camp meeting I saw an Indian preacher who gave us a history of his experience which ran as follows:

"I was greatly alarmed and sought the religion of the white man, but apparently to no purpose. Then I heard that there was going to be a camp meeting among the white people, and I resolved to go.

"When I got onto the ground I went from place to place and from

---

413 Interestingly, Matthew Simpson wrote in *COM* that that Methodism in Stamford "had not made much progress until within the last twenty-five years" (828–29). Since he was writing in 1876, that would mean that the significant Methodist growth in Stamford began about the time of the Redfield revival, and tends to corroborate Redfield's assessment of Stamford Methodism.

414 Terrill here begins his chapter 34 (page 221). Terrill or someone else has marked a large X before Redfield's "Chap."

415 JGT: "After his labors in Stamford, Mr. Redfield visited the camp meeting at ____." (221).

416 Someone, probably Terrill, has placed a large superscript X after the word "mud," apparently to indicate a paragraph break.

tent to tent and looked in, but saw nothing to help my case. So I wandered over the ground all through the meeting in a most distracted[?] state of mind. Finally the meeting closed and I had found no relief. But I came to get religion, and I determined never to leave till I had obtained it.

"Soon the people began to leave. At night the tents and all were gone, and there I was alone, and no hope yet. So I got down to pray, [resolved] never to leave till I had got religion. But where I lay down to pray was in a dry run which in times of rain or spring was a runway for the water. In the night it came on to rain very hard, and by and by the water began to run down the ravine. But I felt so bad I would not move. But after awhile I found the water moving so fast as to run all over me. I managed to get and keep my head out of water, but I would not get up nor leave the place, and about the break of day (I think it was) salvation came, and my burdened heart was made happy."[417]

Another Indian, son of a chief, told me how concerned he felt for his people. [He said,] "God gave me success in /258/ bringing one of my relations to God. I had procured a [New] Testament in the Chippewa language, and having found Jesus myself, I wanted to see my red brothers enjoying the same. So I asked my friend to go out into the woods with me.

"I took my seat on a log, and he sat down with me. I then took out my Testament and began to read, I think about the crucifixion of Christ. I read on for awhile, then he laid one hand on me and said, 'Just stop there,' so I stopped, and he started to leave me. I knew by his looks what the matter was with him but thought it best to say nothing to him nor to follow him. I saw him go over a little knoll, and soon he began to pray in good earnest. He continued to cry for mercy till, just as the sun was going down, he bounded like a deer. God had saved him most powerfully."[418]

He now started for his father's wigwam, and going in, knelt down and began to pray. Soon his mother came along and knelt down by his side, then came one sister after another, and finally the father came in the same manner. By the next morning the wigwam was dedicated to God.

The father was so elated with his new-found religion and so anx-

---

[417] JGT includes this testimony but rewrites and condenses it (221–22).

[418] The following paragraphs continue the story of the second Indian, told by the first. But since the voice of the first Indian at this point in fact disappears from Redfield's narrative, I have not continued the use of quotation marks to indicate the first Indian's voice.

ious to spread it, he started off in the morning for the store of the white man who had sold the firewater to the tribe living there. On entering with his usual "Good morning," he began his labor with the proprietor in this manner. "Now, you and I have lived near together for a long time, and we have been good friends all the time. We have never had any quarrel."

The white man admitted the fact.

"Well," said the Indian, "I want you to do one favor for me as a friend. You know I never asked one before."

"Well," said the liquor seller, "I will grant you the favor if I can."

"Then," said the Indian, "don't sell any more firewater to the Indians. You know of many who [have] come here and bought the firewater, and some of them when drunk have tried to cross the ice and have fallen in and got drowned, and some have fallen in the cold /259/ snow and frozen to death, and our people have been made wretched by the use of this firewater."

The white man made the promise, and the Indian returned home to pray for the white man. Next morning he went near enough to see that the store was closed all up. So back he went to wait still longer and let the rum-seller have time to think the matter all over.

The next morning he went out again to see, and still the store was shut up. On the third day, finding the same state of things, he thought he would go in and see how matters were. And now he found that the poor fellow was in despair, and on trying to give him some consolation, "No, no," said the white man. "It is true that I have been the means of the death of those who have probably perished in hell, and there can be no mercy for me."

The Indian tried to find a place where he could offer the poor fellow hope. When finding all to fail, he finally said, "There must be hope in your case, for if the Lord could have mercy on an Indian, He certainly can save a white man." This took effect, and the man cast his soul on Jesus and was saved, and then went out as a successful missionary among the tribe of Indians nearby.

I spent the season as far as possible in attending camp meetings. At one of these I saw a converted Jew, son of a rabbi who among other items of interesting information told me how God often came to the rescue and salvation of the faithful Pharisees. As a specimen, he told me of the death of his own father who, when he was drawing near to death and while uttering the usual cry of such persons. "he called for me," said the son, "and said, 'O my son, I have tried to live in good conscience all my life and have honestly tried to serve the God of my fathers. But now in this very great extremity, I do not feel prepared to die. /260/ I have done everything I could think of to prepare me to meet God, except to have a sacrifice made for me. But then, that is now impossible, for we have no more a temple nor a high priest.'"

And now his fellow members of the sect, as was usual when one of their number was dying, came to visit him and to exhort him while dying as a last act of fidelity to God to curse Christ and thus deny all fellowship with idolatry. Just then the dying man broke out, "God forbid that I should deny my only Savior!"

This young Jew told me that this was of frequent occurrence among the very strict Jews, and O how it did give me rest from the fears I used to entertain concerning the faithful and sincere Jews who walked up to the light of their own conscience but had been trained from infancy to repudiate idolatry.[419]

I went to visit S. H. again and was passing the house of a good old man whose wife asked me to come in and see her husband. I found him almost in a state of despair induced by the doctrine of election[420] and reprobation which had been taught him in his youth. Although he had been a member of the Methodist Church for many years, yet he could never get the entire victory over the false teachings of his youth.

I asked him how long he had been in this state and found it to be ten years. His wife told me that he would go and shut himself up and pray and groan for hours together.[421]

"Can you tell me," said I, "what is the matter?"

"O," said he, "I am afraid that I am a reprobate and that Christ never died for me. Sometimes," said he, "I feel my heart a little softened and I can weep a little, and then I take comfort and hope that I am not lost. But the hardness returns and I am in distress again."

"Well," said I, "I am not going to use one word of argument against that false doctrine. But I do want you in your heart to say, 'I believe that Jesus died for me.'"

"O," said he, "I would not dare to do /261/ so wicked a thing, for if

---

[419] JGT rephrases Redfield here as follows: "This incident afforded Mr. Redfield much comfort, for the thought of missionary work among the Jews, and how to do it, had been much upon his mind" (224).

[420] JGT: "During the summer, while visiting in Stamford, as he passed a house one day a lady called him in to see her husband who was in despair over the doctrine of election" (224). Redfield appears to have "S. H.," but the second letter is difficult to decipher; perhaps Redfield intended "S. F.," for Stamford.

[421] In JGT, Redfield asks the man, "How long have you been in this state of mind?" and the may replies, "For twenty years" (224). In Redfield's text the number appears to be 10, not 20, but a later reference to 20 years apparently was the reason for Terrill writing twenty here.

he did not die for me, I should then be believing a lie."

"Never mind that," said I, "for according to this miserable and false doctrine, if Christ did not atone for you, you are lost anyway, and to be in one more lie cannot make your case a great deal worse, and you better risk it."

But instead of saying it in silence in his heart, he began to repeat it aloud, and in measured time, "I – believe – that – Jesus – died for – me – O glory, glory to God! I have got it!"

Thus I saw that one act of faith could accomplish what twenty years of prayer had failed to do.

I went to another place and met with a man who lived [in an upstairs room] in the home with another family. It was here [in the home of this family] that we had meetings on the subject of personal holiness.[422] One evening when God had taken possession and some five or more were sanctified, and a goodly number converted, this man began to raise up overhead, to stamp and make a great noise, and finally came down into the hall and commenced howling and swearing and barking or growling as if a number of dogs were fighting in the hall. He then burst in the door, his eye flashed, and shaking his fists in my face [he] demanded of us to stop. I stood still and let him flourish his fists in my face but would not move for him.

The next day our brother in whose apartments we met went to this man and asked him if he was not gentleman enough not to disturb a religious meeting.

"Sir," said he, "I do not wish to make any disturbance. But I cannot help it. I know, Sir, that I am forever lost, and for years I have known this fact, and ever since that time I cannot endure the voice of prayer, nor a song of praise. It totally unmans, me and I cannot help howling and making all the opposition I can to all religious worship."[423]

In another place I heard that a discussion was in progress between a learned Baptist and Universalist, and a desire was expressed to have me go and listen. /262/ The great Universalist, they were sure, would triumph gloriously and vanquish the learned Baptist.

"Well," said I, "suppose he may make it all appear that universalism is true and orthodoxy is false. What becomes of the real truth? A lone victory on an assumed basis may be triumphant in accordance

---

[422] JGT: "In another place, that season, he [Redfield] attended a holiness meeting held in a private house, where a room overhead was occupied by a gentleman boarder, whose strange conduct is recorded below" (225).

[423] JGT here ends the chapter and begins a new chapter (his chapter 35, beginning on page 226), omitting the next incident recorded by Redfield.

with that basis. But if the assumed basis is in error, all the talk and argument in the world will never change the facts involved in the truth of a doctrine. And to be plain, I will tell you that I do not feel the most distant interest in a discussion which can by no means settle the claims of error. And Universalism being only a myth, I know that nothing can be gained. It is nothing to begin with and will remain a nothing after all the discussion.

"When I hear people talk, I like to hear them talk about something. Universalism being nothing, I have no interest in hearing its claims discussed."

Of course I was called a bigot and dishonest if I would not go and listen to its [i.e., Universalism's] claims to confidence and [would] still denounce it in my ignorance as a nothing. "Now don't be so bigoted, and just go and hear them," [I was told].

I finally thought I would go. After the close I was met by one who said, "There now, Sir, what will you say? Didn't our preacher whip the Baptist all out? What do you think?"

"Why, just what I did before."

I then went to the post office, when one of the champions who had heard of the indignity with which I had treated Universalism before a large gathering stepped up to me and said, "Ain't you the man that has said there is no foundation for Universalism?"

"It may be I am, for I have said that it had no foundation in truth or reason."

"Well then," said he, "I challenge you to a debate."

"I shall not argue with you, Sir."

"Well then," said he, "it is because you dare not."

"No, Sir, it is because there is nothing in it to talk about, and when /263/ I talk, I like to talk about something."

"Well, Sir," said he, "I think you stand out to the world as one of the worst kinds of bigots, and dishonest to deny the sacredness of our doctrines, and then skulk away and will not give your reasons."

"Now, Sir," said they (for many had gathered together), "you ought to be held responsible for your assertions, or else defend them."

"Gentlemen, this man would not argue the case with me if I were to try it."

"Sir," said he, "that is just what I want, and I promise you that I will, if you will only argue with me."

"No you won't," said I. "And moreover, Sir, I tell you that you dare not answer me three simple questions which only admit of a yes or no without quibbling and assessing and changing the issue."

"Well," said he, "I know I will," and said I, "I know you won't."

All cried out, "Why don't you try it?"

"Because I know he does not risk the issue of his doctrine on plain open facts."

"Well," says the man, "you try it or else be branded as a dishonest man."

"Well then, Sir, I will venture the first question, and that is: Is there, was there, will there ever be a place of torment or punishment for sinners in the world to come?"

"O," said he, "I will explain. Men are punished as they go along."

"Hold, hold, Sir. I told you that you would not and dare not answer a simple question which only admits of a yes or no, and after all your assertions, you are at it. Now there either is or ain't a hell, or state or place of retribution, and now you are trying to change the issue to lay the place in question and get around a question you can neither meet nor settle."

Finally said he, "I answer No, there is not, was not, and never will be a hell or retribution."

"My second question: Do men sin, and are they punished equivalent to their sins in this life?"

"Sir, O Yes. But you /264/ must let me explain a little," and he began to rattle off a long and rapid harangue on the righteous being recompensed in the earth, and much more the sin of the wicked.

"Hold, hold! Again you are getting up a new topic. We are not now settling by-questions. But the simple question is whether our sins in this life are fully punished up to their demerits—not the mode or manner of it, but the bare abstract question, is it so or not. And the settling of these premises by a yes or no is only the preparatory step for the argument which is to come after, as I told you, provided you wish to argue the case after we have settled the bounds or limits within which we are to confine ourselves."

Finally he came out with the direct answer. "Yes, men do sin and are punished for them up to their true demerits."

"Well then," said I, "I will ask you the last question, and if you wish to enter upon an argument we shall have something to talk about. My third question is: Is Christ a perfect Savior, and what does he save men from?"

He saw it could not be from hell if there was none to be saved from, and he had equally cut himself off from the second as [well as the] third question, and [so he] said, "You answer for me."

"But," said I, "that is the very thing I must expect of you, or [else for you] to abandon all claims of Universalism to a foundation in fact or common sense."

But another Universalist was resolved to put me on a different issue and confine me to the Bible. "Very well," said I, "if you can give me the light I need, I want you to explain some passages in the Bible that I cannot reconcile with Universalism."

"Well, what are they?"

I turned to the nineteenth chapter of Revelation, twelfth verse [sic; should be Revelation 20:12] and read, "And I saw the dead small and great stand before God, and the books were opened, and another book which is /265/ the book of life, and the dead were judged out of the books according to their works."

"O, that is the very essence of Universalism. Yes," said he, "'dead in trespasses and sins'; [from 'the] book of life,' our life as we have lived it, we are judged and punished."

"But hold, friend, I want to read the next, [the] thirteenth verse: 'and the sea gave up the dead which were in it, and death and hell [. . .] and every man was judged according to their works.'"

"Why," said he, "we want nothing better than that, for it is a great foundation for Universalism. Yes, 'death and hell,' that is, the grave."

"But hold, let me read the next verse. 'Death and hell were cast into the lake of fire. This is the second death.'"

"Good," said he. "This is the quintessence of Universalism. This is the total end of death and the grave. Burnt up. Now where is your future hell?"

"But just one more, the fifteenth verse: 'And whosoever was not found written in the book of life was cast into the lake of fire.'"

"O," said he, "we as Universalists don't believe a word in the Book of Revelation."

Now this man was not an irresponsible man to represent his doctrine, for he soon after was appointed county clerk.

Chapter [30][424]

When the season came around favorable to the holding of protracted meetings, I was invited to go back to S. [Stamford, Connecticut] where the old members had found out the old religion they used to have thirty years ago. On reaching the place I found a new preacher in the church in which I had labored, and he set up his authority and will that I should not be allowed in that church. But the preacher of another Methodist Church came to me and invited me to come to his help. He

[424] JGT here begins his chapter 35, having omitted the nearly four-page narrative of Redfield's encounter with the universalist.

was in a church which was to make one more effort to revive religion and get a [?] which would sustain itself, and if it failed to do that, the church must be /266/ left without a supply at the next conference.[425]

Some three miles distant one church had been abandoned for three years, one about one and a half miles off was to be closed in the spring, and one two miles off had been shut up for years. One in a neighboring city they tried to close the spring previous, and the preacher told me he had to beg them to allow him to stay and make a trial.

The preacher in charge of the church where I went to labor was a truly devoted man of God who with kindness tried to check the downward tendency, rather than to arouse the Methodist churches to come back to life and carry out the original design of God in an aggressive warfare and in spreading scriptural holiness over these lands.

God began here also to save. Then an influence from other quarters adverse to the spirit of Methodism was sent in here to protest against my being permitted to get up so much stir and fanaticism. We not only worked in his charge but reopened the old chapel nearest, and God began to save them [i.e., people there]. But soon the opposition from other Methodist churches was so great that I had to go into the colored people's church to be permitted to preach and press holiness.

God stirred the Muses[?], and many important men of influence and of property came out. Then God so moved some of them that they came and declared that they had been infidels, and the grand reason was that they had seen nothing but this sickly formality for more than twenty years. "But," said they, "this is right," and they stood by like men.[426]

Soon however someone came to me and told me that a subscription of $3,000 had been made to build up a new church, if I would stay and supply it. I went to my presiding elder to ask his advice. But he told me it would be a very hazardous undertaking and would create great jealousies among the conference preachers. So I told them I would not /267/ [accept their] kind invitation. I knew I had all I could contend against in filling the calls of those preachers who dared to stand by

[425] JGT simply has, "As winter approached Mr. Redfield was invited to return to Stamford to one of the forsaken churches in that place" (226).

[426] JGT: "The African Methodists then opened their doors, and the revival went to them. Here God wrought mightily, and some of the most wealthy and influential people of the city came to the altar and were saved; some of them that the deadness which had reigned in the churches had well nigh made infidels" (226). It is not clear however that Redfield meant the revival was centered in or confined to the African Methodist church.

me.[427]

I went with the preacher to hold one more meeting in the old church [in Stamford] which had been closed for years. I observed a young man who appeared to be very attentive to all that we did. When we tried to get together those who were seeking the blessing of holiness, he took no equivocal stand and after meeting came to me and said, "I want you to go to my place about five miles from here and preach for me.[428] My church tried when the conference sent me last spring to refuse to receive me. I pled with them to let me stay awhile and try.[429] Now, will you go?" said he.

"Well," said I, "Brother, do you believe in the Methodist doctrine of sanctification?"

"O yes, I do."

"Do you enjoy it?"

"I do not."

?Will you seek it with all your heart?"

"I will," said he.

"But," said I, "I will tell you something which you little suspect now. I want to know if you can, in view of all the cost, answer, 'I will seek, obtain, live, and then preach holiness.' Now if you get and then preach holiness you will see a living, active church, and sinners will be converted in great numbers and they will know it in power. Then when conference comes around again, somebody else will be sent in your place, and the church and converts will injudiciously speak in great love of yourself as their former pastor. And if your new preacher has not the grace to endure to be eclipsed by the stronger love of the people to you rather than to himself, he will become jealous and will try to injure you in conference by giving you the name of an 'unsafe man,' a 'party man,' and 'one poorly calculated to keep up the dignity of

---

427 Instead of this sentence, JGT explains that Redfield "was now having all the calls he could fill" and that his "many friends among the more spiritual of the ministry" would "question the propriety" of his accepting the invitation to pastor a new church (226).

428 JGT has, "When the invitation was given for seekers of sanctification, he came forward boldly. He was a Methodist preacher, and after the service closed he invited Mr. Redfield to go to his charge five miles away to labor with him for a season" (227). Redfield neglected to mention specifically that the young man was a Methodist preacher, though clearly that was the case.

429 JGT (or someone else) has placed a large X at the beginning and end of this sentence. JGT renders the sentence as follows: "He said the church was not inclined to receive him when he was appointed the spring previous; but after pleading with them for some time, they yielded, and let him stay" (227).

Methodism.' And then you will find yourself crowded out of all prominent paying appointments, /268/ and [sent] out onto frontier work. Now, can you stand it to lose caste and standing among your brother ministers, and know that you must pass on alone, and no one in conference to appreciate you, and to be regarded as a preacher of whom the whole conference will feel ashamed, and know only that God appreciates you and that you are useful, and then let the great day of settlement adjust all these matters?"

With emphasis said the good honest brother, "I shall accept the conditions."

"Very good," said I to him. "Brother, I will go. And farther I tell you, if you ever get into a hard spot because you take the honourable cause for God, just let me know, and I will come to your help."

I then went to his place and without any trammels felt I could go the straight way for God and exact right. As soon as I had preached the first sermon, the minister took his stand and said, "It may seem strange to my congregation that I have never preached this doctrine to you. But as an honest man I could not preach to you about a matter that I knew nothing about. When I joined the conference I told them that I believed in this doctrine and would seek it, and now I ask you to forgive me and come forward here and pray for me." This he did like an honest man, freely, frankly.

The people came, and the power of God came down upon the people. Then the work of God took a type of power that was felt all through the place. Some infidels who had not been inside of a church in more than twenty years were so convicted at their homes as to be unable to leave the house, and one to leave his bed. I have seen them leave the church [building], which stood on a lot that nearby joined five streets, and the people would make that part of the city vocal with the voice of triumph.

But I finally [i.e., later] learned that the preacher saw [fit] /269/ to leave his conference to transfer as one of the first installments in remunerating him for fidelity to God. In due time we shall hear from this blessed man again.[430]

I was now called to go to the aid of one of the conference preachers who had made himself offensive by his plainness. He had been sent out into a very by-place, a village which could boast of a tavern, two churches, one blacksmith shop, and I should think as many as five or

---

[430] JGT: "This young minister, soon after, thought it best to take a transfer to a Western conference. We will not consider his case further at present, but shall hear from him again" (228).

six painted houses. But the people rebelled at the imposition of having a preacher sent to them who was so far behind the improvements of the age as to talk and preach against fashionable amusements. I staid but a few days and found, as far as I could discern matters, [that] God had quit them, and I left too.

In due time I went to a camp meeting at T. C. in W.N.Y. [western New York].[431] There I found the opposition to the doctrine of holiness among the preachers taking a type which alarmed my fears for that blessed soul-saving power. One man was called upon who in preaching flatly denied the doctrine as contained in the Bible. Another preacher sitting by quoted one or two passages in point, when the [presiding] elder called upon him to stop and yet permitted the preacher to continue to preach down the Bible doctrine of holiness.

The people in very large numbers began to prepare to leave the ground. A number of us went over the ground and persuaded the people not to leave. Then H. M. [Hiram Mattison], the first great antagonist of holiness who would be permitted to oppose Methodism, then took the stand as a pacification. It was thought that he was the real man behind the smear who [i.e., and that he] picked out the other preacher to lead the way in opposing holiness as a distinct work to be received by faith, and [thus] that gave him the chance to appear to come as a peacemaker. So he pursued about /270/ this course.[432] Said he, "The doctrine of sanctification ~~holiness~~ is a true doctrine, and I will tell you my experience. First I would say that the orange tree is a good illustration of what I am about to say. On that tree you will find blossoms, green fruit, and ripe.[433] Now, when I was converted I was a little sanctified, and when I

---

[431] JGT: "A short time after he went to a camp meeting in Central New York" (229). The initials Redfield gives appear to be "T. C." but could possibly be read as "H." Since JGT places this camp in central rather than western New York, presumably he knew which camp meeting Redfield was referring to. Given the reference (below) to Hiram Mattison, who was a member of the Black River Conference in central New York, the camp meeting may have been within the bounds of that conference. Phoebe Palmer attended a camp meeting at Theresa, New York, in the Black River Conference in 1854 (White, *Beauty of Holiness,* 238); conceivably that could be the camp meeting to which Redfield refers.

[432] JGT: "Rev. Hiram Mattison, who at this time was the leader of this opposition to the doctrine of holiness, was present, and attempted to allay the excitement by speaking somewhat as follows" (229).

[433] JGT begins the Mattison quote as follows: "The doctrine of sanctification is true and good. There are various opinions in regard to some of the details of it.

joined the church I was a little more sanctified, and when I took a license to preach I was sanctified a little more. So you see, we keep getting a little and a little more, and that's the way that the work of sanctification is to progress."

This made the matter no better with the people, who saw the transparent fraud which he tried to practice upon the people.[434]

My old friend came to the rescue and took this course to meet the false theology which had been preached to us.[435] He got up a very large prayer meeting in an unoccupied part of the ground. He then said he thought it best to make a test of experience to aid in correcting any false notions of theology. "Now," said he, "I would like to know how many of this company know by a heartfelt experience the doctrine of holiness. Please to arise." It was judged that about three hundred arose.

"Now," said he, "as many of you as received it by faith instead of growing up into it like the orange tree, please to arise." All arose again.[436] "And now, as many as grew up gradually into it, arise." But nobody responded.

This was thought [by some] to be a very unfair way of appealing to the people [as it was done] in a manner calculated to underrate the preacher. I could but think, "If Methodism has come to this, when preachers may publicly put it down and a presiding elder can back it up and yet check a man who shall try to stand by the old landmarks, we are in a bad state, and the Methodist Church must soon run out, and surely another people /271/ must be raised up to take its place. I shall probably be numbered with those who are gone before that day. But God helping me, I will do all I can to save what of spirituality remains and so far check the waning progress of Methodism as to keep it as efficient as possible while I live."

I had a faint glimpse of a something in my own personal experience to be attained to which I had not yet reached, and made up my mind to labor for God to the best of my ability and at the same time to

---

I can best express mine by using an illustration: On an orange tree you will find blossoms and green fruit and ripe fruit. My experience is similar to that" (229).

434 JGT: "He said much more, but this was the substance of it all. This made the matter no better with the dissatisfied brethren" (230).

435 JGT identifies this "old friend" as Fay Purdy: "Brother Purdy was present, and in his inimitable manner tried his hand upon the storm" (230).

436 JGT: "'Now, how many of this company know, by a heart-felt experience, that entire sanctification is distinct from justification and regeneration, and that it is received instantaneously by faith? Arise and stand upon your feet.' About three hundred arose" (230).

gain all I could [in my own spiritual experience].[437]

XXXIV. Encountering Paranormal Phenomena

I left the camp meeting at its close and went with some friends to the City of S. [Syracuse, New York] and to an evening prayer meeting, called by some a camp meeting prayer meeting.[438] On leaving the church I had one of my strong revelations of a coming revival for the City of S. and I broke out, "Bro. H., I tell you, God is going to visit this city in awful and glorious power."[439]

"Yes," said he, "a good number of us have been praying for that, and we feel that God has answered our prayers, and we are now looking for a revival."

They then wished that I might be with them, but said they had an idea that their preacher was far from being friendly to this blessed doctrine. I had never before had such revelations of a coming revival without being identified with it, and yet I had now no certain impression that I should be here. So without waiting any opening, I immediately took cars for home.[440]

But before a great while I received a letter from a preacher about three miles from this place to come to his aid.[441] So I thought, "Well, I

---

[437] JGT: "These circumstances led him to see the necessity of a greater degree of spiritual power than he had ever known, that he might be more efficient in the Master's service" (230). JGT here begins a new chapter (Chapter 36, page 231), though Redfield does not.

[438] JGT: "At the close of the camp meeting mentioned in the last chapter, Mr. Redfield went to Syracuse, N. Y., in company with a Brother Hicks and wife. While tarrying there for a few days, he attended a prayer meeting with them at the church where they belonged" (231). Charles T. Hicks, an attorney and justice of the peace in Syracuse and a member of the First Methodist Episcopal Church there, later with his wife figured in the rise of Free Methodism in Syracuse—largely in consequence of this encounter with Redfield. See Hogue, *History of the Free Methodist Church*, 1:374–77.

[439] JGT is more specific that Redfield here. He has, "On leaving the church there came to him his old sign which had always tokened to him a great outpouring of the Spirit. He said to Brother Hicks, 'I tell you God is going to visit this city in awful and glorious power'" (231). Redfield doesn't identify Hicks by name, but only by initial.

[440] JGT says that since Redfield had no direct "indication that he would be connected with this" revival, "without waiting further he started for his home in New York city" (231).

[441] JGT identifies the place as "Salina, now a suburb of Syracuse" (231). Salina and Syracuse were in the Black River Conference.

will go to this call, and it may be that this will open the way to S. [Syracuse], where my revelation was laid." So on I went, and on my way up North River in a night boat it did seem to me that if the heavenly hosts had been let loose on me and had done this but to comfort and cheer me, I could not have felt more of the /272/ power of God and the glory of heaven this side of Jordan. And all the way by the [railroad] cars I was wrapped in contemplation of God and the work of God which words of earth can never utter.[442]

When within six miles of S. [Syracuse], again on the cars there was the same cloud of glory, and [the] sign of the coming storm of salvation settled over the place.[443]

I reached the city and then went to the house of Brother H. [Hicks], at which house my heart took courage. For he had a heart to appreciate the strongest type of salvation and his house, like the temple of God, had its altar fires burning all the time. So great was the power of salvation that I have felt it on reaching his gate, and on going in [I] might often find some of the precious disciples who liked to run under his wing when pursued from without, and some of them under the power on the floor [i.e., slain in the Spirit]. I heard that complaints were made against him by some of the citizens that he was guilty of having prayer meetings all night long, to the annoyance of the people.[444]

Bro. H. took me to the brother's house about three miles off who had sent for me. On [my] crossing the bridge which separated the two places, the same cloud of power and glory rested over that place.

When I found the brother, I learned that he was in poor health. The state of religion was very low, so low that for a small assessment which the church could not pay they were about to lose their church edifice. Nor could they keep or pay their preacher. Of course the Methodist preachers could have no objections to my laboring there, as it was a doubt whether any means could be used at all which could possibly save the church.

Someone said to me, "It is a great matter of doubt about starting a revival here, for this place has been entirely overrun with mesmerism,

---

442 JGT says simply, "On his way while traveling up the Hudson river on a night boat, he began to have a wonderful manifestation" (231).

443 JGT: "As he approached Syracuse, there came to him again the same token of the coming revival" (231–32).

444 JGT: "[Hicks' house] was a sanctuary for the oppressed and the persecuted. For years one could not enter it often without finding there some one who had made it a refuge. Seasons of prayer there often lasted all night, and sometimes complaints of this were made to the magistrates" (232).

psychology, spiritualism, and from that it has gone into Unionism, that is the discarding of all sectarian distinctions, and /273/ from that into Unitarianism.[445] Now if a revival should happen to come and the emotional features of primitive Methodism should again start, it will be called spiritualism, mesmerism, or something besides religion.[446]

"Well," said I, "I believe that the old gospel has just as much power in subduing the heart now as ever, and I think that God will come to our rescue in the end. Although the tricks of wicked men and Satan may imitate the work of grace, yet as in the days of Moses, God's rod will at last swallow up their rods and they will confess there is a God in this matter.[447]

We had not gone a great many days [in conducting revival services] before a good sister from another place felt constrained to come to this place, and greatly desired to come and see me. I was at the house of Bro. P.[448] When she was introduced to me, [she] reached out her hand to shake hands. She gave two sudden screams, so sudden and loud as to start[le] me. Both her hands shot out and grasped at me at the same time. This was totally new to me, and I knew not what to make of it. But I thought it best to wait till I could satisfy my mind as to this queer voice before I allowed myself to be disturbed.

I started down for the church [building], and she with others were following on the sidewalk. But now and then I heard the same sister give the same two screams.

I went up into the pulpit and, looking towards the door, I saw the same sister coming in at the door, holding onto her mouth with both hands. She came pretty near to the front seats, and as she turned to go into the seat, the two screams came again so loud as to shock all in the house. Then she clapped both hands over her blushing face and appeared greatly mortified. But yet she could not control it.

In a subsequent conversation [I had] with her upon the subject, she

---

[445] JGT: "He also found that this place had been overrun with mesmerism, spiritism, and finally unionism; that is, the discarding of all denominational distinctions. The next step was to Unitarianism" (232).

[446] Mesmerism (named for Austrian physician Franz Mesmer, 1734–1812) was an early form of hypnotism. It became something of a craze about this time; often it was associated with spiritualism and magnetism. Mesmer thought hypnotic states could be induced through the use of magnets.

[447] Redfield may be referring to magnetic rods or wands used by mesmerists and magicians. (Terrill or someone else has placed a large X at the end of this sentence.)

[448] Possibly Fay Purdy, though Purdy at this time apparently lived in Palmyra, about sixty miles east of Syracuse.

told /274/ the history of this strange exercise. She said [that once] while [she was] conversing with an honorable gentleman, a member of the Methodist Church, he was complimenting her on the sober, staid and ~~formal~~ quiet form of her religion and that he very much approved the unostentatious deportment of her form of religion. While she was admitting to him that she felt gratified with her quiet form of religion, a power seized her and she was compelled to utter these two screams. In vain she tried to suppress them, for she had no control over herself when that power was upon her.[449]

When all was brought to order, I began to preach. Yet every once in awhile the two screams came. The people were all eager to know what this new thing could mean.

As I closed and called upon the church to come forward and seek the blessing of holiness, the altar was well filled, and we began our prayer meeting. By and by one at the altar uttered two or three sudden and short screams, so sudden and loud as to startle everybody, and soon another, and yet another. Then one came out so varied in the scream as to make it totally different from all that had gone before. Her screams sounded as if a knife had been driven right into the heart, and how[?] shrill. A sister of hers came up and took hold of her and shook her, commanding her to stop. But all to no purpose, for she continued right on. I think not far from six to eight that night were seized in this strange manner.

My old friend [blank space] happened to be there and, stepping to me, [he] said, "Ain't the devil getting in, and had you not better put your hand onto it?"[450]

"No, no," said I. "I think God has given me good sense enough to know when if ever to try to stop it."

"Well," said he, "what do you make of it?"

"I don't know," said I. "But I should not wonder if God is not even now preparing to /275/ meet and conquer the magicians who would fain imitate and put down the work of God. And you see, Brother, nobody could possibly make this noise [on their own]. Besides that, there

---

[449] JGT: "She said, 'Once while conversing with an honorable gentleman, a member of the Methodist Church, he complimented me upon the quiet and unostentatious character of my piety. I replied, "It is a source of gratification to me that I am not as demonstrative as some." Instantly a power seized me that I could not resist, and I uttered those two screams. Since then I have found it in vain to resist when that power is upon me'" (233).

[450] JGT: "In the midst of this, Mr. Purdy, who was assisting in the meeting, asked, 'Don't you think you had better check it?'" (234).

is no fear of any hypocrites as yet, for there is nothing very smart in the sounds, and no one would be likely to wish to make themselves conspicuous by making noises like these."[451]

Meeting closed, and I went to the house where I was staying. The sister of the lady of this house, then staying there, being one of the persons thus operated upon, I hoped to make myself better acquainted with this strange demonstration. She was a married lady of something more than thirty years old, and she as well as all the rest who were thus exercised, I noticed, were among the very best in the society. We knelt for prayer before retiring, and she was thrown into a spell in which for about five minutes, I should judge, she kept up her screams so steadily [and] rapid as no person could possibly imitate. Then we closed prayer and went to rest.

In the morning I arose and left my bedroom, taking a chair in the parlor where a good fire had been prepared. Soon she came in, looking very solemn, and in a very subdued voice asked me, "Can you tell me what all this means?" saying, "When I went to bed last night it all stopped, but as soon as I awoke this morning it has begun again. And," said she, "you know what a spell I had at family prayers last night. Well, I then saw my dead sister who died so triumphantly a few years ago, and I saw my father's house, and mother is very sick, and they want me to come home." And so it proved, for a letter soon came calling her home. And she [later] told me she found everything as she then saw it.

"Now," said she, "what does this all mean?"

"Well," said I, "how do you feel when you scream so sharply? Are you in great pain?"

"O no," said she, "but the glory is so unearthly, it does seem that if it did not pass off as /276/ soon as it does I could not live in such an agony of joy and glory. O, I never had an idea that the joys of the redeemed heart in heaven could bear anything like it."[452]

Just then in came her sister, a very tall, large woman who in a very anxious mood asked, "Bro. R., what do you make of all this?"

I said, "I cannot tell, and yet my opinion is that this is something that God has permitted or sent to put a silence on cavilers."

"Well," said she, "do you think it would be right for me to pray

---

[451] JGT quotes Redfield as saying: "You perceive no one can possibly make such a sound of themselves. Besides, there is no fear of hypocrites attempting it, for it is too humiliating" (234).

[452] JGT omits this exchange, going from "they want me to come home" to the incident of the sister coming into the room (which follows).

against it?"

"I do not, Sister. My impression is that you are not to court it nor fight it, but let it alone. Seek only to get right with God, and if it is allowed to come, there is an end that it will serve. Let it come or go upon you."

"O," said she, "I would not have it come upon me for ten thousand worlds."

With a scream the [other] sister said, "It will come upon you."

Then I saw her [i.e., the first sister] trembling all over. She sat down and was holding a wash bowl and pitcher in her lap, and so violently was she shaken that I expected to see them hurled upon the floor. So I ran to her and took them out of her hands. Then, with a shriek sharper than anything I had heard, she was thrown upon her hands and knees on the floor. Then with another scream she was caught up and carried to the kitchen chair, and then another and another, and a power would carry her at every scream.

After the great gust had passed over so she was able to converse, I thought I would see what I could learn from her which would enable me to form a more satisfactory opinion concerning this strange affair.

"Well, Sister, what do you think of this matter now?"

"O," said she, "I would not have this taken away from me for ten thousand worlds."

"Are you in pain when you scream?"

"When I first screamed I felt some. But the unearthly joys are beyond anything I ever dreamed could be known this side of Jordan."

"Well, Sister," said I, "do you feel such joy that you put forth the effort to scream, and is the scream the result of your effort to [scream]?"

/277/ " O no, I put forth no effort. But a power takes hold of me and compels the scream, and I cannot resist it."

Of all the other cases which I examined, only one I found in which the screams (and jumps, and in some cases dancing) all were produced by an unseen power over which they had no control.[453] In one case the

---

[453] JGT: "Of all the other cases which he examined, and there were a large number of them, some of screaming, some of jumping, and others of a kind of dancing, in every case they testified the same; that is, it was produced by an unseen power, unexplainable by them, that took hold of them, and over which they had no control" (236). Terrill further comments on such phenomena and affirms Redfield's advice neither to encourage nor forbid: "Whatever the reader may think of these incidents, if candid, he must admit the wisdom of Mr. Redfield's advice: 'They are not to be courted, or fought'" (236). He adds, "An-

person prayed it might leave, and it did. She went into spiritual agony and prayed it might return, and when it did, she was relieved. Another fought against and resisted it, and it left and she was almost in despair till it returned. And I learned years after that these screams became the highest keynotes of these persons to express the excess of their religious joys.

One sister at whose home I visited in company with others would dance all over the house and run over the tops of high stairs and behind objects which stood near the seating[?] of the house, and although her head was cast upwards and her eyes closed, she never stumbled against anything. At one time she danced around the house, giving often a scream which though very shrill was to me most sweet and musical. Then suddenly she fell at my feet and cried out to her husband, "O, there I see your mother. Had she black eyes?"

"Yes," said he.

She then went on asking him minute questions concerning the personal appearance of his mother, and to every question as to the personal appearance he answered yes.

"O, now," said she, "I see Br. Redfield's crown, and I see you crown there. But it ain't as bright as Brother Redfield's."

The place seemed awful while she went on describing the heavenly world.[454]

One sister who was converted would be the autistic, a state in which the eyes though opened put on all the appearance of death. Such an expression of the beginning of decay, and especially so perfectly soulless as to arrest the attention of everyone. At such times she would reveal and declare the moral state at those present. I give an instance or two: /278/

"Bro. B., I must tell you that you are not in the state you think you are. You are fearful and timid and do not take up the cross as you have felt it your duty to. Bro. G., you must be more faithful and exhort the people to turn from their evil way, especially the one [whom] you went by impression to see twice, and then your heart failed you and you left your duty undone."

This sister in telling her experience said she was perplexed to decide whether this was the right kind of religion, and while I was preaching, and she desiring to know, she saw an unearthly flash of light pour

---

other thing is also true,—as yet mankind knows but little of mental science, and probably many of the strange phenomena of mental operation are yet to be explained" (237).

[454] JGT omits this incident.

from my eyes. She thought, "This must be hallucination." On looking again and again and seeing the same lights, she yielded her heart to God and then obtained the blessing of perfect love and became one of the most remarkable instances I had ever known of the power of discerning of spirits.

I ought to have stated a little of my own experience just before this strange affair was developed.[455] When I began to preach in that place, I tried to put up the standard of holiness to work up to, and pressed the people to seek it.[456] Of course I found a great many, and some woefully backslidden, seeking it, but unsuccessfully.

After awhile I saw we might begin to enquire after the cause of our failure. I tried to ferret out the sins which had hitherto kept us outside of the gate, and then I proposed that with honesty we examine our own lives and make a humble confession of our delinquencies and sins. But this I found to be a hard matter, and I likewise saw brought to light very clearly the fact that a large share of them were backslidden from God. So I led off by confessing my mistake in preaching holiness, whereas it was justification they needed. Then I went on preaching justification, and when again we were brought to a stand, I saw or learned that the corruptions of the people were lowering their morality. /279/ So I confessed again the mistake of preaching justification when they needed the first principles of morality first.

After awhile I had one of my old burdens again. I have often been so burdened while laboring for a revival as to be thrown upon a bed of sickness and kept there till the victory would come. Every burden was different. In this case I could not compare it to anything but fire shut up in my bones. I was not conscious of any heat but [experienced] an untold agony which made me to writhe like a worm upon live coals. O what a relief it would be to me if I could only have howled as the prophets used to do, and thus give vent to my pent-up agony. But this I could not do. I felt as if I must die if I did not get relief. So I said to myself, "I can shake all this off by leaving the church," and I turned to the table in the altar to look for my hat. But like a voice, [the recollec-

---

[455] Following the word "developed" is what appears to be the word "any" and part of another word, which seems to be crossed through. The thought however appears to end with "developed." JGT omits this sentence and here begins his chapter 37 (page 238).

[456] JGT has, "When Mr. Redfield began his work in Salina, as usual he tried the best he was able to set forth the standard of holiness in view of having 'something to work up to,' as he expressed it. He pressed the people to seek this experience" (238).

tion of] the two burdens which I once had in other places and which I prayed off came up fresh and the impression was now, "If you cast off this burden by leaving, here will end all hopes of a revival."

"Well," I said, "O Lord, I will try to hold on half a minute longer." And then, as if another turn was made of the screws which held my bones like a vice, I was almost crushed, and [was] in agony. I said, "O Lord, I cannot endure all this. I must give it up and run." So I turned again to look for my hat.

But again the voice to me was, "If you run from this, all is lost, for this is a part of God's method to wash and save this place, and somebody must suffer inasmuch as suffering must accompany the work of revival." So again I said, "I will endure a half minute longer. But O Lord, save the people. But if I die, well, die it is. But oh my God, this people must be saved, and here I am to perish at my post and battling for God."

When I had /280/ reached this point, I was instantly and perfectly relieved. But the whole church was in a perfect commotion, screaming for mercy or rejoicing in God. And here the spell broke, and soon these strange screams and other manifestations began. Although I was never in the least moved by them, they have followed me ever since, whenever the degree of salvation was up to a given point. I leave the wise to form their own opinion or jump at conclusions. But I have my opinion of this matter.[457]

When this work got fairly into motion, sure enough, the curious were out to witness the strange things. One night came some up to the altar and asked, "Can we be permitted to see this strange matter?" I said. "Yes."

"Well," said one, "I see through it all; it's nothing but hysterics."

"But friend," said I, "do you know anything about physiology?"

"Yes, enough to know that's nothing but hysterics."

"Are people happy when they have hysterics?"

They knew not what to answer. Some cried out, "O, it's nothing but psychology or spiritualism, and it's easy enough to produce it all." I was told they did try to imitate it and even tried to make instruments to mimic the screams, and were unsuccessful. They said, "Like the magicians of old, this is the finger of God," and then in large multitudes they sought and obtained salvation.[458]

---

[457] JGT substantially condenses this account (238–39).

[458] JGT puts this a little less exuberantly: "Mr. Redfield was afterwards told that some of these men held meetings in which they tried to imitate these phe-

Among the rest, came forward a Unitarian woman of good and high standing for her benevolence and position in society, who in years past used to come to the church and became very active in persuading people to come forward for prayers. When she came forward there was to my mind an excited stir among the Methodists, and I thought it indicated about this spirit: "There, Mrs. B. has come forward herself to a Methodist altar, and now we shall be more respected than we have been and our church may possibly rise in its esteem."[459] I meant however, if God would help, to make /281/ a point for God and right in her case, [a point] not soon to be forgotten. So I knelt down inside of the altar close by her and asked aloud, so that the whole congregation might hear, "Madam, what is your wish in coming to the altar?"

"O, I want religion."

"Well," said I, "then pray right out loud for salvation."

"O," said she, "I cannot pray for myself."

"Well then, I cannot pray for you."

"Why," said she, "I have said I would go to hell before I would ever pray raising my voice."

I repeated, "[You] said you would go to hell before you would pray for yourself. Well, Madam, you will either eat your words or go to hell. You need not hope that you will succeed in your hostility to God."[460]

"Do you think," said she, "there is any mercy for me?"

"I don't know," said I. "Your case is indeed a hard one, and it may be you have already passed beyond the limits of mercy. But I would try."

"Well," said she, "I will pray."

"But Madam, will you pray [also] in your family?"

"O," said she, "I have said I would sooner be damned than to pray before my husband."

"Well," said I, "you will take that back or be lost forever."

"Well," said she, "I will."

---

nomena, but failed. They then declared it to be supernatural. Many of these men were soon after converted to God" (239).

459 JGT: "The expression on their faces seemed to say, 'Now, she will give our church character, and we'll be thought something of'" (239).

460 JGT renders the dialogue as follows: "'Why, I have said I would go to hell before I'd ever pray in such a place as this.' Raising his voice, he repeated her words, and then said, 'Madam, you will either take that back, or you *will* go to hell. You need not think of succeeding in your rebellion against God'" (240). In the manuscript, someone (perhaps Terrill) has inserted a large X at the end of the sentence.

"But," said I, "you have exerted an influence against God and Christ among the Unitarians and Universalists. Now will you go to them and cut your acquaintance and tell them why you do it?"

This was indeed a hard one. But I pressed her and opened before her that all this was hostility to God and right, and if she wished to make a clear thing of it, she must do it.

"O," said she, "I will."

"One thing more. Will you exhort them to seek Jesus and pray with them as you leave them?"

This was indeed as some would think too hard, and she felt it a dreadful thing to require of a female. But I thought it a dreadful thing for a female in high position to use her influence against Jesus of Nazareth, so I insisted, "Make the thing right with God or you are damned forever."[461]

"Well," said she, "I will." Instantly she fell under the power while asking one to pray for her of /282/ whom she had said she never wanted him to pray for her. Suffice it to say, she did obtain salvation, and with such a power would she exhort as to make everybody feel she was indeed helped by the Holy Ghost.

Next came one of the Unitarian ministers to the house where I was staying and desired an introduction to me. With all the blandishments of a hypocrite and the soft air of a very demon [he] said to me, "I am happy to make your acquaintance. I have attended some of your meetings and desire to say to you that I extend to you the right hand of fellowship. But," said he, "I think you might adopt one suggestion which I will make, and to your advantage."

"Well, what is it?" said I.

"O," said he, "let us win our way to the hearts of sinners by showing charity and love among ourselves. Just let them see how our religion unites us all together, and thus recommend the benign religion of Jesus."

"But," said I, "how far will you have me go in giving the right hand of fellowship, and to whom?"

"Well," said he, "whoever takes the name of a Christian is entitled to our charity and brotherly love."

"But," said I, "suppose a man tells me that there is no more merit

---

[461] JGT makes Redfield's language a little gentler: "Some may thing this was carrying the matter too far, and she felt it was a hard thing for her to do. But Mr. Redfield thought it a wicked thing for a woman in high position to use her influence against Jesus of Nazareth, so he insisted upon her making the thing right with God and man" (240–41).

or virtue in the blood of Christ than in the blood of a hog" (a thing which had been preached in his own church unrebuked).

"Well," said he, "it will do no good to hold a man off and deny him your charity for opinions' sake."

"Farther," said I, "suppose he tells me he cannot believe in God, heaven, hell, Christ, or a future state."

"Well," said he, "it is a free country, and everyone has a right to believe what he pleases. We can do no good to a man by prescribing what he shall believe as a condition to receive our charity."

"Well," said I, "let us pray," and down I got and prayed for him as a poor deluded man.

I went to church that afternoon and lo, there was this Unitarian minister sitting in the back part of the house. In due time he arose and said, /283/ in substance, [that] he desired to say to the church there that he felt a great interest in these meetings and would say that these meetings met with his most hearty approval.

When he finished I arose and said, "I want this congregation to understand that we have no fellowship with infidels or atheists, and I know this man to be such from conversations I have had with him this day. But," [I] said, "God calls upon us as one [i.e., as well as] upon the angels to worship Jesus. Worship Jesus!"[462] Then instantly the power of God filled the whole house. Our revival progressed[?] a short time longer. The church was saved, the debt paid, the minister was received back and provided for, and a first-class parsonage built, and besides a very large addition to the church [building],another new church was built, paid for and in full blast in a very few months.

XXXV. Return to Syracuse, New York

Chapter [31][463]

I now went back to the City of S. [Syracuse] to see if I could find a chance to labor there where the Lord first showed me the coming revival. Going to the house of Bro. H. [Hicks], [I] sent for the preacher in charge to come, as I wished to talk to him. So I said to him, "Brother, I will be frank and tell you what is the motive inciting me to come and ask you for the first time in my life the privilege of laboring for a revival in your church. I am a Methodist. I had intuitions last fall that God was certainly coming to S. to save sinners, and I think God means

---

462 JGT: "'God calls upon us and angels, to worship Christ,—to worship Jesus'" (242).

463 JGT also begins a new chapter here (chapter 38, on page 243).

to identify me with this work.[464] Now, are you willing to allow me to labor in your church?"

"O," said he, "if God has sent you, He will open the way."

"But may I labor in your church?"

"It will cost too much," said he, "for expenses."

I then said I had anticipated that, and I had brought money enough to pay expenses for a few months. I would labor free of charge if he would allow me only to come into his church to labor.

/284/ "Well," said he, "you cannot be allowed to come into my church."

Then said I, "Well, Brother, you will not feel afflicted if a way should open in some other denomination [and] if I should labor there."

With a sneer as if that would be impossible he said, "O no, of course not."[465]

He left, and I asked Sister H. [Hicks], who was deeply experienced, if she could tell me what had happened to me. For I had seen with an inner eye some to me strange sights.

Sister H. said to me, "You ask Bro. Stearns."

I soon saw that man who told me he felt desirous of having a little conversation with me. So without any explanation I asked Bro. S., "Did you ever see lights in the form of stars?"

"O, yes, for eight years I have seen them."

"Do you know what they mean?"

"O, yes. For four years I have seen them as spirits of the redeemed."

"Well, what are these with a white halo around them?"

"Angels of mercy," said Bro. S.

"What are these, very bright and very large, and yet I can gaze upon them without dazzling my eyes."

"Angels of mercy."

"What are those which come in groups and seem arrayed[?] like clear lightning?"

"Forever [?]."

"What are those dark clouds which move past me?"

"The smoke of their torment," said he.

---

[464] JGT: "He [Redfield] said: 'For the first time in my experience, I ask for an opportunity to come here and hold a revival meeting. I am a Methodist; and I have had a wonderful experience with regard to this matter; and I am sure God has designs of great mercy for this city; and from my feelings, I think he designs that I shall be identified with it'" (243).

[465] Someone has inserted a large X at the end of this sentence.

He then opened before me some of his own experience, which has ever since been of great service to me in determining these matters, and from which I see that Redemption is the great word which expresses more than any one [i.e., than any other word] and is the grand work of Jesus Christ, and [this insight] opens before me the plan of Salvation as a system of scientific developments.[466]

I was now invited to go to P. [Palmyra, New York], the home of the old friend [Fay Purdy] of whom I have spoken, whom I first met at the camp meeting.[467] Though I knew not the direction, yet while on the cars I saw my sign hanging over the place. When I came to the place where the [railroad] cars were to leave me, I saw I was left some distance south of /285/ the place where the sign lay. I soon found that I must now take stage and go north some nine miles. The stage was ready, but a gentleman who saw me as a stranger and probably wished to make a few shillings, having a private carriage, came to me and asked if I was going to P. I told him I was.

"Would you as leave go with me in private conveyance as to go in the stage at the same price?"

"Certainly, and prefer it."

I took a seat with him and we started.

"Do you live in P.?" asked the man.

"O no, Sir," said I. "I am a stranger here." And in my turn I asked, "Do you know a man by the name of P.?"

"O, yes, very well."

"Well, what of him? I hear a great many things about him by different people. What is he?"

"O," said he, "the man is in bad repute among the people where he is best known."

"He is a Methodist and labors in revivals, I believe."

"O, yes, but then the people have no confidence in him," said he.

"O." said I, "He is probably a man who swears."

---

466 JGT omits this rather obscure conversation with Stearns (or perhaps Stevens; the person is not otherwise identified). What Redfield seems to mean is that while conversing with the Methodist preacher mentioned earlier (or perhaps on some other occasion), he saw the strange phenomena he mentions. Not knowing what to make of them, he asked Brother Stearns, who gave an explanation based on his own experience. This showed Redfield the grandeur of salvation, including the fact of a presumably rational scientific explanation for such spiritual phenomena.

467 JGT: "The next mail brought to Mr. Redfield a request to come to Palmyra, the home of his friend, Fay H. Purdy, to hold a meeting" (243). Palmyra is about sixty miles west of Syracuse.

"O no, I don't think anyone accuses him of that."

"Well, he probably lies."

"O no, not that either."

"Well, he must be a great cheat, a dishonest man."

"Oh, no."

"Well, what is it?"

"I will tell you," said the man. "I am a Methodist, but it is the world's people who find fault with him."

"Well, can you tell me what the matter is with him?"

"Well," said he, "the world says, 'If he will be so zealous for religion, why don't he stay at home and work where his work is needed?'"

"Well," said I, "you have a new preacher since conference."

"Yes," said he.

"Well, how do you like him."

"O, not at all."

"What's the matter with him?"

"Why he is too old a man, and he don't look tidy about his neck, and he is no honor to Methodism. He lets his shirt collar hang down."

Said I, "Brother, I know where your difficulty lies. You are all /286/ backslidden from God. I am going to the house of Brother P."

When I got there and had a proper opportunity, I asked Bro. P., "What is the matter with your new preacher from conference? I understand the people dislike him."

"Well," said he, "I will tell you. He is a good man, but our church has got backslidden and formal, and they think he is not up with the times. We have had no revival in sixteen years. In spirituality the Congregationalists have far outstripped us, for they have revivals but we don't.[468] Our church has been mortgaged and foreclosed and is to be sold in a few weeks. Spiritual worship has been turned out of doors and an organ has been put into the gallery to make up the deficiency and to pander to the tastes of the world. The preacher is not received from conference, and the [presiding] elder has been denounced as a pope because he don't remove him.

"The dandy preacher who was here before him used to wear his gold spectacles and carry his gold-headed cane and act the fop, and now the contrast is too great for them to abide. They have not, and say they will not, pay him one cent of salary or make any provision for him either in house or provisions. So I have given him a shelter in my home and am supplying his wants."

---

[468] Here again spirituality and revivals are equated, and the having of revivals seems to be considered normative and necessary for a vital church.

I saw the whole evil at a glance.

I was then taken to the home of Brother T. and allotted my room. Then a Brother B. was brought in and introduced to me. He was a good brother who lived some seven miles distant but felt he must come to P. [Palmyra] and spend the next day, which was Sabbath.

[Sunday morning] I arose early and went downstairs. But soon I heard the groans of Brother B. from the room adjoining mine. [He was groaning] in awful agony, and around[?] us[?] [I saw] the citizens who came and stood around the front yard fence to listen.[469] I asked the family of Bro. T. what all this meant.

"O," said they, "it is Brother B. at his devotions."

"Well, /287/ what for [i.e., what sort of] a man and Christian is he?"[470]

"O, he is one of the very best of men. Everybody knows Bro. B. to be an excellent Christian."

I had told the preacher that he must preach at the eleven o'clock appointment, so I did not go to church till a few minutes before the time. When I went in I saw the preacher in the pulpit, and I walked up to him. In the basement I heard a very great outcry. When I sat down with the preacher, he said to me, "We have been having awful times downstairs this morning. Awful times."

"Why, what's the matter?"

"O, Bro. B. fell down and kicked and made so much fuss as to scare the people, and they have run out of the house, and my wife got mad about it."

"Well, I suppose your wife must have an evil spirit in her to get mad."[471]

"Hark, Brother, hear Bro. B."

"O God, I shall, I shall die if this church is not saved."[472]

"Well," said he, "I think I better go and shut him up in a classroom."

"Brother," said I, "the spirit that would interfere with that brother would drag Christ from the Garden of Gethsemane."

"But," said he, "I am afraid he will come upstairs."

---

469 JGT: "Soon he heard Brother B—— groaning loudly in the room adjoining, and a glance through the window revealed a large number of people standing on the walk who had been attracted by the noise" (246).

470 JGT: "'What kind of a man and Christian is he?'" (246).

471 JGT omits this sentence (246).

472 JGT: "And there came up from the basement a cry of anguish, and the words: 'O God! I shall die if this church is not saved!'" (246).

"Well, let him come," said I.

"Oh, he makes such an awful noise!"

"Well, you need an awful noise. But if you will get salvation enough to endure it, you will yet be able to hear a hallelujah without fainting away at it."

Then, "There he comes," said he.

"Well, let him come."

And sure enough, he did cry out in an agony that moved my heart.[473] Bro. P. [Purdy] was there, and as the man came up near the altar and in an agony fell upon the floor, Bro. P. said, "Amen!"[474] Then one of the old members said sharply, "What did you say amen for?"

"Because I am glad to see God get one more chance in this church to breathe."

"Well," said the preacher, "I will go and put him into a pew."

"Very good, do so if you please," [I said,] and when he had shut /288/ him in he went back to the pulpit and began to preach. But soon the suffering brother again broke out in an agony, fell off the seat and, straightening himself out, pushed open the door and raised up both his arms over the pew door.[475] He cried, "Oh God, I shall die if this church ain't saved."

The people rushed to the doors to get out with all speed, and I gave them the sheet for cowards. "The wicked flee when no man pursues them" [cf. Proverbs 28:1].

The preacher finished his sermon as well as he could and called upon me to close.[476] I took occasion to endorse the whole demonstration. But seeing the preacher in great distress, I thought it best to go home with him. When I got there I found one of [the] lady members of society almost in a hysteric fit, and the preacher began to plaster her up.[477] I said to the preacher, "Hold up, don't patch up that woman, who is fighting God."

After some time she told me how tempted she had been on my ac-

---

473 JGT: "And sure enough he did come, and crying out in great agony as he came" (247).

474 JGT: "As he reached the altar he fell to the floor, and Mr. Purdy cried out, 'Amen!' at the top of his voice" (247).

475 JGT says that the preacher tried to "put him into a pew" but that "soon Brother B— rolled off onto the floor, and made more noise than ever" (247). One would not know from Terrill's account that this was a church sanctuary that had pew doors.

476 JGT has, rather, "The old minister tried to preach, but the struggles and cries of Brother B— made it almost impossible for him to do so" (247).

477 JGT: "The preacher tried to soothe her" (247).

count and how hard it seemed to her to come out and do right as long as she felt so bad on account of my wrongs.

"Well, what are they?" said I.

"Why, I heard that you was worth $30,000, and I could not believe you could be a good man and not help the poor. But," said she, "I have found out that you are poor, and now I forgive you on that matter."[478]

Soon the preacher told me he should send Bro. B. home the next day.

"What," said I, "you will? Well then, I tell you, I shall go, too."

"O," said he, "you must not go. We must have a revival or we shall lose our church."

"I don't care about your church [building], and it would be no calamity to lose it. They have managed to keep God out for sixteen years, and it is now ruled by the spirit of the world, and [they] will go to hell anyway if they don't get saved."

"But," said he, "they won't pay me one cent of my claim and want to drive me off, and I am dependent on the charity the brother here for shelter /289/ and the necessaries of life.[479] Well, our church is to be sold in a few weeks."

"Let it go. It's a curse to the place in its present condition."

"Well, don't leave us, and I will let him stay."

"But," said I, "Brother, I must [add] another item to the conditions, and that is, if you believe that man to be a good man, you must give him the right hand of fellowship and thus stop what I know will follow and that is, you will have two parties in your church over that matter. For the people saw that you was greatly tried with the good brother, and unless you settle that matter at once you will have sympathies with your side. But you can stop it now."

"Well," said he, "don't leave, and I will do it."

"Very good," [I] said. "Do it tonight after I get done preaching."

At the time appointed he stood in the altar and confessed before the congregation to Bro. B. and then said to him, "I give you the right hand of fellowship. Come into the altar, Bro. B." Then instantly the preacher fell under the power, and making a great commotion said as soon as he could command himself, "If I had allowed the full tide of my feelings to rule me, I should have made a great deal more noise than Bro. B.

---

[478] JGT omits the woman's comment and has only, "After a little she began to confess that she was not right" (247). By "after some time" Redfield may mean, "Some time later."

[479] JGT has, "'I am dependent on Brother Purdy for shelter and for the necessaries of life'" (247–48).

did. Why, I have not had so great a blessing in twenty-three years."

And now began the war. One infidel to get customers hired a seat in the Methodist Church and paid ten dollars a year [pew rent], and the same thing he did for other churches. But now himself and wife left in great wrath, and reports said he went through the streets swearing he would not have anything more to do with the Methodist Church. His wife tore up the cushion from their seat and left.

But all this rang the bell, and people who heard large reverberations[?] came out of curiosity from ten, and some over forty, miles.[480] Our house /290/ was so crowded we had to open the basement at the same time and [thus] have two prayer meetings going on at once. One night I think there were thirty conversions.

I staid some two or three weeks. Some[thing] over five hundred were converted. The preacher was taken into favor, provided for, and the liabilities of the church edifice removed and Methodism took a stronger start than ever.[481]

I now got a letter from the city of S. [Syracuse] from the Congregational Society to come and labor for a revival in their church.[482] I obeyed the call at once. When I arrived I called on one of the deacons and asked, "Is it true that your church wishes me, who am a Methodist, to hold a protracted meeting?"

"Yes," said he, "we passed such a vote." He then went with me to see another of the deacons who [also] told me it was true.

I then asked, "How long since you have had a revival in this city to amount to anything?"

"O, we had a kind of a stir about fifteen years ago, but nothing to amount to much in twenty-five years."

"Have you put forth no effort?"

"O, yes, we have had Finney, Lansing, and Knapp, and still it amounted to nothing.[483] There are five churches now without a minister

---

[480] Redfield apparently is speaking metaphorically about the bell ringing. JGT has, "But this only created the more stir, and curiosity brought the people out from near and from far" (248).

[481] Someone has inserted a large X at this point in the manuscript. It may be Terrill's mark indicating the end of a chapter, as he here ends chapter 38 and on the next page (250) begins chapter 39. In the manuscript there is no chapter break.

[482] JGT identifies "S." as Syracuse (250).

[483] JGT: "'Oh, yes; we have had Finney, and Lovering [sic] and Knapp, but nothing scarcely was accomplished [sic]. There are now five churches in the city without pastors, and the place is given over to the Unitarians'" (250). Redfield has the spelling "Phinney" (and also "Lansing," which Terrill apparently

and the place is given over to the Unitarians."

"Well," said I, "Deacons, you had better put this matter to vote again, and with your eyes open. For I am sure that the old gospel is fully potent as ever to work wonders. I can do nothing, but that will. But you must prepare yourselves for a great conflict, and many things to shock all your ideas of order and propriety. I will tell you what I will do: If any fighting or setting the church on fire takes place, I will do all I can to regulate that. But if God comes—and that he will, in awful power—and the people should get to shouting or falling or anything else that God owns by working in the midst of it, you /291/ must not interfere."

One deacon said, "I have taken my stand." The other [said,] "The devil has had full swing for fifteen years without let or hindrance, and I think it no more than right that God should be allowed one chance more."

"Very good. I will go on."

I went to a Methodist preacher who lived at a little distance and asked him to take the superintendence of the meeting. Then he could take care of the work when I was gone.

"O," said he, "my health won't allow of it."

"I won't ask you to do any of the hard labor."

"Well, I ain't able."

The Methodist preacher who lived the nearest to the Congregational church was the one who would not allow me to labor in his

---

misread). The references are to Charles G. Finney, Dirck C. Lansing (1785–1857), a noted Presbyterian minister in New York State and a leader among the New School Presbyterians, and Jacob Knapp (1799–1874), fiery Baptist evangelist from 1832 on. Finney held revival meetings in Syracuse in late 1852 and early 1853 which began in the Congregational Church and then continued in the Presbyterian churches. Finney had not ministered in Syracuse previously. Redfield's meetings on this occasion seem to have been in late 1854 and/or early 1855. See Garth M. Rosell and Richard A. G. Dupuis, eds., *The Memoirs of Charles G. Finney: The Complete Restored Text* (Grand Rapids: Zondervan, 1989), 527, 531; Charles E. Hambrick-Stowe, *Charles G. Finney and the Spirit of Evangelicalism* (Grand Rapids: Eerdmans, 1996), 275–76. Finney wrote that "The Methodist brethren had held a protracted meeting; and the kind and degree of excitement that had been manifested among them had excited opposition on the part of the professors of other denominations, and a very unpleasant state of things had resulted as a consequence" (Rosell and Dupuis, *Memoirs of Charles G. Finney,* 527). The meeting referred to was in the winter of 1851–52, but it is not clear that the reference is to meetings in which Redfield was involved.

church and who sneered at the idea of my being invited into any other church. So of course I could not invite him to come in. But he rendered us good service, as I learned, in either getting up or circulating the report that I had come to S. to make war against Methodism and had run up a flag on another church where I held forth. Some came from a distance and told me that they came to look at my flag, but finding none, found our meetings, where God saved a great multitude of souls.[484]

I had not been preaching but a few times when in one of our afternoon meetings one old deacon got up and [protested] most vehemently against allowing the Congregational Church to be desecrated and abused by calling on the people to confess. I allowed him to finish his say and then stated to the congregation that I had been invited to come and labor with the understanding that I should not be trammeled in my measures. "I labor for nothing." [I said]. "Other churches are calling, and I have no time to waste in these contentions. Now, I want /292/ to know if I am to be allowed to proceed or not."

On [the church's] taking a vote, the old man was put down. I went on a few days more, and he again vented his wrath in bitter language. Again I called for a vote and he was put down. In a few days more he arose all broken and began to confess to lying, stealing, and drunkenness, and public rumor gave him credit for things much worse than this.[485]

Suffice it to say, God did come in awful power. One or two Presbyterian deacons or elders from a distance one night fell under the power. A Presbyterian who came in and came up to me said, "You Methodists get greatly excited."

Said I, "Do you know that man under the power on the floor yonder?"

"No," said he.

"Well, Sir, that's a Presbyterian deacon."

"What? Can that be possible?"

"Yes Sir, and you all have got a Methodist heart if you will only give God a fair chance at them."

Among the confessions, one young lady who had just come out in great triumph said, "For ten years I have been a member of the Methodist church but deceived, for I never knew what religion was till this

---

[484] JGT condenses this a bit, and thus leaves out the humor: "Yet the minister was soon active in circulating the report that Mr. Redfield was making war on Methodism" (251).

[485] JGT: "In a few days more he arose in a meeting all broken in spirit, and made a most startling confession to the church and congregation" (251).

night. But now I have got religion, and I know it." Another lady, a Unitarian, came as she said to prevent a friend of hers from getting religion, but on her way home, passing the Unitarian Church, she fell down in the street and cried out in great agony for mercy. It was dark, but some hearing the voice of a female in distress followed by [sic] the sound, and when they found her she cried out, "Can anybody pray for me?"

One of the men who went to her relief was a relative and a backslidden Baptist. They took her home to her own house and went to prayer, and the Baptist got reclaimed that night and the Unitarian woman was converted.

So great was the work of God, and still spreading, that the Unitarians who had lost some of their members /293/ sent off for Theodore Parker, the great Boston infidel, to come to their help.[486] He did come, and I saw his handbills posted up in various parts of the city reading thus: "The Rev. Theodore Parker will preach this night in the Unitarian Church (Subject: The Devil)." From this caption you will know his cause and drift. But [I] thought it best to mind nothing about it.[487]

He had not preached a great while before a whirlwind laid the Unitarian[?] house level with the ground. It was a strange sight to see the large church, so well protected by standing in a hallowed square, and yet nothing [left] but that damaged steeple [and] the corner of a man's house near the church against which the steeple struck as it went over.[488]

---

[486] JGT: "So great was the religious interest, and the danger to the Unitarians, that they sent to Boston for Theodore Parker to preach in their church for a season" (252).

[487] Theodore Parker (1810–1860), Unitarian theologian, reformer, and longtime pastor the Twenty-Eighth Congregational Church in Boston (for years the largest church in the city), traveled and lectured broadly beginning about 1844 and on into the 1850s; "some 50,000 listened to him lecture every year, in lyceums from Main to Illinois" (Dean Grodzins, *American Heretic: Theodore Parker and Transcendentalism* [Chapel Hill, NC: University of North Carolina Press, 2002], ix). He lectured on a number of social issues, including war and poverty, as well as "a great variety of theological and philosophical" questions (John Weiss, *Life and Correspondence of Theodore Parker, Minister of the Twenty-Eighth Congregational Society, Boston,* 2 vols. [New York: D. Appleton, 1864], 1:265). Like Redfield he was an abolitionist, but on different theological grounds.

[488] JGT summarizes: "He came, and flaming handbills were posted through the city announcing his arrival, and the themes of his discourses. But a violent

I now had to go to A. [Albion, New York] as soon as I could to the help of the blessed and sainted [William] Kendall, who was just then passing a very hot fire.[489] This afflicted band, or many of them, were resolved not to put him down. He had become very obnoxious [to some] by his stubborn adherence to the Methodist rules and discipline. They tried hard to mould him over and finally to compel him to lower the standard of religion to meet their wishes. But that he would not do. He would cry and groan, pray and starve, but he would not trifle with God's right or lower the standard of Bible truth. They however received me and the truth. But I am sure they would not [have], had he not prepared the way.

The work of God broke in great power, and then one or two in the back part of the house (one of whom was a Baptist) fell under the power. Those who knew nothing of this type of religion hurried them out and some, supposing it to be a fit of fainting, began to break out glass from the windows to let in air. Then the opposers hated me as heartily as they did Bro. Kendall and began to report that I had come there and had mesmerized some of the people.[490]

---

storm which swept over the city a few days after he came so damaged their church that he returned to Boston" (252).

Terrill here adds a long paragraph beginning, "Some of the fruit of this revival remains" and containing the recollections of Rev. M. V. Clute of the Illinois Conference of the Free Methodist Church. Clute reports that he was "a lay member of the Congregationalist Church in a neighboring town" at the time of Redfield's ministry in Syracuse and went to hear Redfield. The auditorium was full to capacity. A few minutes into Redfield's sermon a man cried out, "O God!" and ran to the altar. "As he reached the pulpit, he screamed and fell to the floor. During the time Mr. Redfield, in perfect silence, stood leaning on the pulpit watching him with great interest. For a few moments after he fell there was perfect quiet through the room, when suddenly from eighteen to twenty persons sprang to their feet and ran, praying, to the altar" (252–53).

JGT closes his chapter 39 with this incident and begins a new chapter on page 254.

[489] JGT: "Mr. Redfield was now invited to Albion, N. Y., by Rev. W. C. Kendall, of blessed memory" (254). Kendall served the Albion M.E. Church during the 1854–55 conference year only (*Minutes,* Genesee Conference, 1853–55). A February 3, 1855, Kendall letter reproduced by JGT on pages 259–60 and also B. T. Roberts' diary indicate that Redfield began his ministry at Albion about January 25, 1855. Roberts went to Albion on Monday, January 29 and reports that "Bro. Redfield preached from 'The words that I speak they shall judge you at the last day'" (B. T. Roberts Diary, 29 Jan. 1855).

[490] JGT: "Some ran for water to resuscitate the prostrate ones, while others broke window-lights to let in fresh air. Now some cried out that Mr. Redfield

After this the people would fall under the power in the streets and at their homes distant from me. When the devil was in want of more formidable forces, J. F. [James Fuller], member /294/ of the same conference with Bro. K., came from a distance with his slanders ready prepared, which were a rehash of the slanders uttered by the preacher who had forged them and then was compelled to leave, run, and evade a trial where one or two illegitimates were involved[?]. He [i.e., James Fuller] stated before leaving for A. [Albion] that he had heard that Kendall had begun a protracted meeting at A. and had got Redfield with him and he, J. F., was going down to stop him. A good man hearing of the plan brought us word.[491]

Soon J. F. was on hand, his face filled with smiles. He talked all kinds of platitudes to disguise his wicked design to my face, and then went behind my back to deal out his slanders. I heard of the whole matter, but he did not know that I had been informed.

When an afternoon meeting began, this man came in. Knowing his object and his hypocrisy, I was so overcome with grief I went up into the pulpit and got down out of sight and thought, "O my God, why hast Thou sent me out at the loss and cost of all things and then allowed such corrupt men to make my way so hard? He lives on the fat of the land and is pampered with a large salary, and I go unpaid and must meet the brunt of battle, fight the devil, the world, a dead church, and preachers besides." O, I felt as if my case was too hard, and my bursting heart was so full that I was compelled to hold both hands upon my mouth to keep from bellowing aloud. I cried, "O Lord, I can go no farther." And the voice again rang in my ears, "You may live while you preach, but no longer."

O how I wished those ambitious, wicked men could only see how God is pushing and pressing me and how they are trying to stop me from obeying God. But at such times I saw the need that someone

---

had mesmerized these people, until many in the church became alarmed and others angry" (254).

[491] JGT has, "Rev. J. M. F—, a former pastor of the church, was overheard to make the remark, in the Methodist Book Room, in Buffalo, that 'Kendall has got Redfield to help him in a revival at Albion, and I must go down and attend to matters there.' The word was brought to Albion by Rev. Brother T—, who heard J. M. F— say it" (254–55). The reference is to James M. Fuller (1807–1891) who this conference year was the appointed conference agent of the Methodist Tract Society (rather than serving a church). He had served the Albion church in 1850–51. *Minutes,* Genesee Conference, 1850; Allen, *Century*, 87. Fuller was an influential preacher in the Genesee Conference and a few years after this a principal opponent of B. T. Roberts.

should stand up and contend for the faith, especially when I saw the enemies in the persons of preachers [who were acting] against the cause of God.

J. F. did /295/ not succeed in his efforts to put me down by his backbiting, for God had got hold of the hearts of the people and the whole tide of influence was on the side of God. He next came to Bro. Kendall and put himself in the way to be asked to preach. But Bro. K. had too much regard for God's rights to ask a man [simply] out of courtesy to attempt to preach when he knew his moral character to be wholly unfit for it.[492]

Next J. F. went around to utter complaints against Bro. K. to some of the most influential members, among others an ex-senator who was a member of our church, and soon this brother came to the house of Bro. K. to labor with. He said to Bro. K., "I feel very much grieved and tried with you, for you preach to us that we must treat our brethren with Christian courtesy, and now Bro. F. [Fuller] feels that you have behaved towards him in [a] manner unbecoming a fellow minister of the same conference."

"In what particular?" asked Bro. K.

"Why, you pass by Bro. F. and don't ask him to preach or take any part in your meetings."[493]

"Well now, Bro. H.," said Bro. K., "I can now say what I should

---

[492] JGT gives a fuller account of what was involved here. He writes, "In the evening, as the congregation were seated after singing the second hymn, the house being very crowded, this man [apparently James Fuller] entered and made his way down to the altar. He looked up into the pulpit, and, as he was not invited to enter that, he seemed embarrassed, his face reddened, a pew door opened, and he was provided with a seat. That night Mr. Redfield preached one of his most awful sermons, from the text: 'And for this cause shall God send them strong delusions, that they should believe a lie that they all might be damned, who believe not the truth, but have pleasure in unrighteousness.'—2 Thess. 2:11, 12" (256). Terrill goes on to describe the sermon and its "electric" effect. He concludes, "The minister referred to, fled as if in consternation, as soon has he could make his escape. Before he left the place, by the circulation of slanders against Mr. Redfield, he alienated many of the members of the church, who finally withdrew from the meetings, and at last became bitter opposers of the work" (257). Terrill does not give the source of his information, but it seems to be an eye-witness account.

[493] According to B. T. Roberts diary, James Fuller did preach at Albion on Friday evening, January 5. This apparently was before the revival with Redfield. Roberts reports that Fuller "preached from Mat 11.28, Come unto me etc. The Church is in a very cold state. He held on till most 11 o'cl." B. T. Roberts Diary (5 Jan. 1855).

not if you had not driven me to it. And I will ask you, how could I invite him to take a part or to preach when I knew that he came to A [Albion] to put a stop to this revival?"

"What do you mean?" asked the senator.

"Just what I say."

"And how do you know?"

"Bro. T., a preacher, came here and informed me that he heard J. F. say before starting for this place that he had heard that Bro. K. was holding meetings for a revival and that Redfield was with him and he, J. F., must go down and stop him."

"Is that so?" inquired the senator.

"Even so," said Bro. K.

The senator went home and saw J. F. at his house and said to him, "I am greatly astonished at you, to learn that your business was to stop this revival and that you felt grieved at not being invited to preach."

"It [is] all a lie," said J. F., "let who will say so. I have never intimated any purpose of the kind."

The preacher who brought the report was there and, said he, "It is so, for I heard you say before you left [Buffalo] that you must come down and stop /296/ Redfield and Kendall." So he had to pocket the affront as well as he could and soon left town.

I saw in all this the fidelity of Bro. K. and thought, "Well, there is one Methodist preacher who will stand for Methodism and God against all opposition." But my final hope for Methodism was fast waning, as I saw the formidable foes we had to combat. This J. F. was the man who was laying his plans to crush Bro. K. while Bro. K. was dying in great and glorious triumph[494] and who as soon as he heard that he had passed to the heavenly land tried to atone for his ~~wickedness~~ opposition by speaking highly of him as a minister and a Christian.

Many were saved and the saints [?], and WCK [William C. Kendall] is held in the highest esteem in A.[495]

---

[494] William Kendall died (apparently of typhoid fever) in West Falls, New York, on February 1, 1858. Allen, *Century,* 99; B. T. Roberts, "Rev. Wm. C. Kendall, A.M. Labors—Death," *The Earnest Christian* 2, no. 12 (Dec. 1861): 375–77.

[495] JGT omits this paragraph but includes further comments on the Albion revival and two letters, one from W. C. Kendall to "Brother P——" (probably Purdy) dated Feb. 3, 1855, and one from Redfield to "Brother Hicks" in Syracuse, dated Albion, Jan. 31, 1855. Terrill also writes, "He [Redfield] labored to bring all to the gospel level by noticing the poor, and especially the colored poor. . . . In the Albion church there were some who set themselves against the colored people strongly. Mr. Redfield told them several times that he never saw

XXXVI. Pentecost: God's Ideal Church

I now took the [railroad] cars and made my way to D. in Ct. [Connecticut], about three hundred miles, to attend my last protracted meeting of the season.[496] There I found the preacher to be a man of clear head and pious heart and unflinching for God's rights.

I had not begun my labors but a short time when I was attacked by what I call another and terrible burden. This time it took me in the head, and so violent [was it] that I thought I was going to have a fit of apoplexy.[497] I thought I would endure it, if I could, till I could leave the meeting. I was sure that a remedy which I had in my case of medicine would remove it. I tried the medicine, but it had not the slightest effect upon me. I then saw it was one of my burdens, and resolved to endure it till the victory should come.

When I went into the prayer meeting after preaching in the evening this pain, like apoplectic pain, took me with great violence, and at the same time I saw with my spiritual eye large lights as big as my hand. But believing it to be a burden which must be borne if I would see the results in salvation, I determined to hold on. Then I felt the grasp of a hand and could count four fingers and a thumb clutch my brain, and with it an impression as clear as a voice saying to me, "I will now take

---

a revival that was complete until all such feelings gave way." Terrill relates the story of a colored woman who found salvation in Redfield's meetings (at Albion, apparently). When "some received her testimony with disdain," Redfield "made his way through the crowd until he reached her, and taking her by the hand, began to sing an inspiring salvation song. The colored sister became very happy, and jumped and shouted aloud. The Spirit of God very evidently endorsed the action of Mr. Redfield, for the power of God came upon the people in a remarkable manner. One family refused afterward to kneel at the altar with such trash, but a score of families from among the poor came and found salvation" (259).

[496] JGT: "At the close of his labors in Albion, Mr. Redfield went directly to Bridgeport, Conn., for the last protracted meeting of the season" (262). Terrill here begins a new chapter (Chapter 41). Although the initial in Redfield's manuscript appears to be "D," not "B," Terrill apparently knew that the place was Bridgeport (though Redfield may also have visited "D.," perhaps Darien or Danbury, both in the general area of Bridgeport). Redfield had held meetings in Bridgeport in 1850, as previously noted. If Redfield's (and Terrill's) chronology is correct, this second visit to Bridgeport occurred in 1855.

[497] JGT: "But the meeting had scarcely commenced before he felt one of his old burdens coming on. At first, as usual, he misread the feeling, and concluded it was preparatory to an attack of apoplexy [i.e., a stroke]" (262).

your life." I believed it to be the devil, and in heart [I] said, "I shall hold on for the victory."

/297/ Then I felt a sensation as if this hand [was] starting [to] draw my brain up and then suddenly chuck it down with great force upon my neck bone, and it stunned me by the shock [sic]. I would then rally, and again I felt the drawing up preparatory to another shock, [and] with [it] the word, "I will kill you this time."

I said in heart, "You can do so, but I will not shrink from the blow [even] if I die on the spot." And again with great force I felt the same stunning shock. But when it came again with utmost thrusting and even alarming force, with all my power I cried out in spirit, "You can do your worst, but I shall risk all on Jesus Christ." Instantly the whole pain and burden left me and I saw the church filled with large lights, bright and glowing, and the power fell upon the people in a wonderful manner.[498]

One Baptist deacon arose from the altar, his face white as a ghost. But an unearthly radiance of pure and heavenly light shone all over his face, and he began reeling and tottering all around and professing to have just received the great blessing of perfect love.

Some reported to the Baptists what had happened. They could not believe it. In their opposition they had been saying that there could be nothing in this Methodist notion of sanctification, saying, "There is Deacon O., who will turn out against any of the Methodists for piety, and he don't say anything about the blessing of holiness." But when word came to them that Deacon O. was really at the Methodist altar and did profess that blessing, "Well," said they, "we have always had suspicions of Deacon O."[499]

I did not yet know what had been done for me but supposed that my victory had only to do with the work of God upon others. But then I went into the preacher's home and, taking the Bible, I saw that a wonderful change had come over my perceptive powers to see and comprehend the spiritual meaning of the Word of God. It was then that I saw how little faith the church has in the Word of God, and I felt to say, "The Church don't /298/ believe the Bible." I saw too that German rationalism was in better repute than the Word of God. One single passage, "Have faith in God," filled up the lids of the Bible and assumed a dignity, power, and glory above my highest ideas of the whole Word of

---

[498] JGT condenses this account, makes it less graphic, and does not mention the devil (262).

[499] An X has been inserted here, perhaps to mark a new paragraph; the writing continues on the same line.

God. I saw over certain persons stars and lights, and have seen these lights ever since in places where revilers soon follow.

I went to my bed, and I was just as conscious that my mother and dear sister were in the room as I ever was in my boyhood. My mother came to me and arranged the bed clothing around me.

I leave others to make what capital they please of this confession, and they may hold me in what esteem they please. But I shall take this opportunity to say, and put it upon a lasting record, that I believe in a God who manifests Himself to man and that we live much nearer the innumerable company of the redeemed than the most of us suspect.

I had now a light by which I saw the great plan of salvation as a perfect system, and that God works after [i.e., according to] a plan. I saw that every state of grace is preceded by a death. In conversion, first men must die to actual sins. To confess Christ will kill our pride. To believe on Him is a death blow to our philosophy. Our next step is to get the tendency of our nature changed, and so changed that it is no longer a burden or drudgery to obey God but we spontaneously obey God because we love to. But this state of grace is preceded by a consecration of all our appetites and attitudes[?], likes and dislikes, and then faith in Christ reanimates us with the life which is of God.

I then saw that we have spiritual senses which can see spiritual things, if we can get those eyes open. We undoubtedly were created with these. Sin has closed them up. The burden which /299/ I once felt was the death which prepared me for the opening of my spirit eyes, and I saw those stars and light. The suffering which I endured which seemed like the precursor of apoplexy I found to be [a] death which preceded the redemption of my perceptive powers. Since then I have never wanted [i.e., needed] a commentator to enlighten me upon the spiritual meaning of the Bible.

I am moreover convinced in my own mind that God desires us to follow in the Bible track of those who have gone before and aim at reaching the highest demonstration as revealed on the day of Pentecost. I am strongly impressed that Pentecost is God's ideal of what a church ought to be, and as led and enlightened by the Holy Ghost I shall take the liberty to follow, [even] if it should lead me up to translation.[500]

The work of God [at the aforementioned church] was established

---

[500] An important statement of Redfield's theology, not found in JGT. The above reflections, beginning with "I did not yet know what had been done for me," following the X on page 297 and constituting two pages of the manuscript, are omitted by JGT. By "translation" Redfield means bodily removal to the spirit realm (cf. Heb. 11:15 KJV).

upon the basis of holiness as the great foundation ~~of Bible salvation~~ of the ~~work~~ church, and the members so greatly increased that a large new church was erected to take the place of the old one. The Universalists took occasion to misrepresent me and my cause, and this had effect upon the tastes of the people, whose sense of politeness was greatly violated.

I will give one of the strongest cases of the effect of this salvation in correcting false hopes. A lady member of the Baptist Church [who] attended our meeting and was convinced that she had not the saving grace of God was, unbeknown to me, brought into great distress.[501] Her mother came to me and asked, "What shall I do in the case of my daughter? —for she is in despair. She has been a member of the Baptist Church for ten years, and the minister has been to see her and tried to persuade her not to give up her hope. But she told him she had been deceived ten years and had now found out that she had no religion, and she wished him to let her alone and not try to deceive her again. The deacons too have been to comfort her. But she tells them the same story and refuses to be comforted. Now," said she, "ought I not to try to comfort her?"

"No, Madam, by no /300/ means, unless you want her to be deceived. Now, when she yields up her will to God, she will probably find relief."

"But," said the mother, "I fear she will become deranged."

"Better be deranged and die so in trying to be honest and get right rather than go on as a deceived person and die in that condition."[502]

"But," [she] said, "She has eaten nothing in three days."

"Well, some spirits have to be starved out."

"Well, what should I do?"

"You can pray for her, deal faithfully in pressing her to yield to God. But for her soul's sake, don't speak peace, but let God do that."

On the next or second night, about twelve o'clock at night God appeared in peace and power to her soul. And what strength my soul did take to sustain me in this cause as she related her experience in the next afternoon meeting and told how mad she was at me for mulling with

---

[501] JGT: "A lady member of one of the city churches came and was convinced that she was without the saving grace of God" (262). JGT does not identify this lady as Baptist either here or later.

[502] The manuscript, which has Redfield's handwriting on both sides, is torn here at the corner (lower right of page 299 and upper right of page 300), so that some words are wholly or partially missing. The missing words or characters are supplied by the obvious intended sense and by reference to JGT (263).

her firmly.[503] "But O how glad I am that you dealt plainly with me, and do let me exhort you to be faithful wherever you go."[504]

I had for a day or two missed a brother who had taken a very strong stand for holiness. But one day he and his wife came to the preacher's house in great distress of mind and desired to know what to do. He related his case, and his wife confirmed it. It was substantially this:

"When I went home some three days ago, I fully made up my mind to follow the leadings of the Spirit. When I got home, the Spirit told me to lie down on the floor and prophesy that I should now die."

"But you did not die, it seems."

"O no. Well, then the Spirit told me to prophesy that the man in the house opposite would die before morning."

"Well, did he die?"

"No. But then the Spirit told me to go through the streets and sing 'pink and seney' and go into the drug store singing it, and call for a given amount and make a decoction and give [it] to my children to guard them against illness. I did so, but did not give it to them.[505] And next the Spirit told me that I had once loved a lady /301/ before I married my wife. That lady is now married. But the Spirit next told me that I must go and confess the worst of crimes to her, although I knew it was not true. But the Spirit then told me I must now part with my wife."

"Well," said I, "was you all the time led by this Spirit?"

"O, no."

"Let me ask you further: When this spirit was upon you, did you not feel wretched?"

"I did, and it seemed I must die with the agony."

"Did you not feel crushed in, and a great weight sinking down? When this spirit left you, did you feel another influence inflating and lifting, and was you then very joyful?"

"Yes, exactly," said he.

"Well now, Brother, when any spirit attempts to impel you, how-

---

503 JGT: "She told the congregation, that at first she was very angry at Mr. Redfield for disturbing her peace of mind" (263). Redfield apparently uses the verb "mull," which can mean "to grind," in the sense of meddling with or disturbing.

504 Here four Xs have been inserted between the lines of the manuscript.

505 JGT: "Then the Spirit told me to go into the streets and sing, 'Pink and senna'; and to go singing it into the drug store, and call for a large amount of it, and give it to my children, to guard them against sickness. I did so, all but giving it to the children" (264). "Pink and senna" refers to herbal remedies, and possibly also to a song.

ever light it may be, if it is not also love, if it crushes you in and sinks you down, resist as you would the devil—for it is the devil. God's Spirit never distresses anyone except those burdened with guilt. But it leads by light, love, and peace."

I have occasionally met with similar cases, and to my sorrow [have] found that the church was ignorant of the tricks of Satan. Such inconsistencies as we exhibited left the impression upon the spiritual novices that insanity was beginning to appear, and they must stop the work of God to save the people from becoming crazy. I saw that in following the track of Jesus [we] must pass His temptations, too, and if we have not the spiritual discernment to distinguish between temptation and insanity, we shall be liable to do an irreparable injury to the work of Christ.

XXXVII. Redfield Visits His Boyhood Home

I went again for a short time to H., and to C. where I was born,[506] and attempted to preach the old Methodist gospel which was preached when I was a boy by such men as Willbur Fisk, A. D. Merrill, and John Lindsay.[507] But the church had become dead, and as soon as the old power began to be manifest /302/ the preacher put his hand upon it and arrested the work.

I went to the graveyard and visited the tombs of the faithful whose voices I had heard when young, and the grave of my sainted mother whose ashes and memory I could but venerate. And now to know that in so short a time, not more than thirty years, the house of God which their prayers and labors had erected was now desolate. The once spiritual singing is now all done up by monitoring[?]. The God of their fa-

---

[506] If the first initial here is "H.," as it appears to be, it presumably refers to New Hampshire. Thus the meaning would likely be, "to New Hampshire, and to Claremont where I was born."

[507] JGT: "From Bridgeport Mr. Redfield went to the scenes of his childhood. There he attempted to do his duty in the fear of God. He preached the same gospel that he had heard in the same pulpit from the lips of Wilbur [sic] Fisk, A. D. Merrill and John Lindsay, all of precious memory" (265). A. D. Merrill was probably Abram D. Merrill, a New England Methodist abolitionist and an associate of Orange Scott (Martin Duberman, ed., *The Antislavery Vanguard: New Essays on the Abolitionists* [Princeton: Princeton University Press, 1965], 81). John Lindsay (1788–1850) was a Methodist preacher in the New England Conference and with Fisk "was active in founding the Academy at Wilbraham and the Wesleyan University" (Simpson, *COM,* 539). As the dates indicate, Lindsay had died a few years before the visit that Redfield here records.

thers [is] now dishonored in the house of prayer, and in spite of the inefficient church the great mass are on the open road to hell. I have been trying to stem the tide of formalism and ungodliness for fifteen or sixteen years. I have had strong hopes that I might once more see the dry bones of Methodism arise and [the church] do its first works. I have like the widow put in my two mites and done all I could to call our people back to the work and spirit of the fathers. But now, near the bones of the fathers and mothers of Israel in my native town, I am compelled to give it up.

I was greatly distressed as I saw the interest manifested by old men whom I knew when I was a boy and who saw in the contrast the difference of primitive Methodism from the formal stuff [now] called Methodism. I would help them if I could. But the die is cast. I must leave the bones of the dead worthies, and the almost dead in formality, [a church] which has been christened in the name of Methodism but is now dead. And this shadow of a tombstone is all that is left to tell where once the grand old ark of God and the shekinah were resting.[508]

XXXVIII. Revival Ministry in Western New York

Chapter [32][509]

The next fall I went by invitation to visit H. [Henrietta], near R. [Rochester, New York]. The preacher, J.K.T. [Joseph K. Tinkham], was indeed one of the remaining preachers who sighed over the desolation of Methodism and of course was "an unsafe man" and put onto a charge that had entirely run down—only eighteen members left out of what once was a flourishing society.[510]

---

[508] JGT condenses this last section to two or three sentences (265). Both JGT and Redfield's text seem to suggest that Redfield's parents were buried in the cemetery of, or near, the M.E. Church building in Claremont, New Hampshire.

[509] JGT also begins a new chapter here (chapter 42, beginning on page 266).

[510] JGT: "In November, 1852, Mr. Redfield was invited to Henrietta, Monroe county, N. Y. The preacher was J. K. Tinkham, known for many years through Western New York for his powerful singing, and who passed to his reward in 1885" (266). According to Allen, Joseph Keith Tinkham was born in 1811 and died at Lima, New York, Sept. 30, 1884 (Allen, *Century,* 124). Thus he was about a year younger than Redfield. The East Genesee Conference *Minutes* indicate that Tinkham served the Henrietta church for two years (1852–54), beginning in late August 1852. The church reported a total of 70 members in 1852, at the beginning of Tinkham's ministry, 100 members a year later, and 79 members in 1854, though attendance in 1852 may have been well below the number of official members and closer to the number Redfield reports. Since

I called on the presiding elder on the way to the /303/ place, who asked me where I was going.[511]

"To H. to help Brother T.," said I.

"Well, I am glad you are going there, for you can do no harm there."

I thought it quite complimentary to suffer and sacrifice all I do, and labor for nothing, and then [receive such] encouraging consolation from the elder. "I am glad you are going there, for you can do no harm," and sure enough, I found that matters could not well be made worse. My old friend had been there a few days, and Bro. T. [Tinkham] was doing good service to prepare the way.[512] And I must say, it has seldom been my lot to find a more pleasant and agreeable minister of the Methodist Church. He saw the waning tendency of the church and I believe tried to do all he could to bring back the church to its primitive power and glory.

We had not long labored before we found we had come to the tug of war, and few though the numbers were, yet the contest was sharp. Finally we reached a point where the Holy Ghost pressed home the truth, and they began to confess their delinquencies. One man confessed that although he was one of the very first of the official members and had tried to carry out the duties of family religion, yet so formal and powerless [was he][513] that, [he said,] "my two boys have grown up as infidels." Then going back to one of the boys, in a loud and lamentable tone he said, "O my boy, do forgive me my unfaithfulness." The boy was mortified and tried to hush his father. But the distress of a troubled conscience urged him on and he literally cried out in distress, "O my boy, my boy, do forgive me, and do come out and get religion." But the son resisted.

He then went for the other son and was equally unsuccessful in his efforts. Then with a wail of despair he came and threw himself upon the altar, crying, "O God, must we be parted?" There was such an unearthliness to the wail as to make many hearts feel the place to be in-

---

Redfield's meetings at Henrietta were in late 1852, they actually preceded the revival with Kendall at Albion, narrated earlier.

511 The presiding elder of the West Rochester District of the East Genesee Conference this year was John Copeland (1800–80). East Genesee Conference *Minutes,* 1852; Allen, *Century,* 79.

512 Redfield does not identify the "old friend"; probably it was Fay Purdy.

513 JGT: "One night, an official member of the church confessed that although he had tried to keep up the forms of religion, yet he had been unsaved" (266).

deed awful and solemn.[514] That was the prayer of agony, and it reached /304/ the ear of heaven, though no evidence of an answer was apparent.

But that night at about midnight one of the boys was heard by the father and mother on his way downstairs, crying for mercy and then calling out, "O Father and Mother, do get up and pray for me. I fear I shall be lost before morning." His parents were soon by his bedside. After praying awhile he cried out, "O, call Samuel," and on looking for Samuel [they found that] he too was in great distress upstairs and crying too for mercy. He was soon downstairs by the side of his parents, and the prayer meeting by the parents for the boys was continued all night. But as morning dawned the blessed Comforter spoke peace with power to their souls. They were so thoroughly converted and with the harness on that they were at once prepared to go to work for others.

When our afternoon meeting was opened, the two happy young men were there. With a fearlessness and determination they went out into the congregation and laid hold of others and tried to compel them to come to Jesus. So importunate were they that sinners to get out of their way ran out of the house. But the power of God followed them. One fell under the power as he got out of the house, and another jumped over the fence into a field and fell there and crying for mercy was soon set at liberty. [The boys then] came back to testify to what Jesus had done for them.

The work now took a most powerful turn. But strong efforts were made by a minister of a sister denomination to moderate the tone of the work, as the degree of heat at which sinners were converted rendered them so hot that he could not handle them nor proselyte them.[515] I then felt called of God [to] speak with authority against any form of religion that did not pay the cost, and his opposition soon ceased. He got salvation himself and then confessed his opposition, and [he] would get happy and shout in his own pulpit, declaring that he had now found /305/ out the religion that made the Methodists shout.[516]

---

[514] JGT omits this sentence and somewhat condenses this account (266).

[515] JGT: "The work now went on in great power, and awoke the opposition of the minister of another church. He tried first to proselyte the converts, but this failed, because of the thoroughness of their conversion" (267). Here again Redfield's rendering is more graphic than Terrill's.

[516] Here Terrill inserts about two and a half pages (267–70) that are not found in the Redfield manuscript and that give further details about the meetings at Henrietta. He relates first an account from "The man who had the charge of the church in which this revival was held" who at first opposed the meetings but later repented and found mercy. Terrill states, "Mr. Purdy was present part of the time, and assisted in this meeting, with his usual liberty and power" (268),

An elder [i.e., Methodist presiding elder] from another district came for me to go with him onto a point of his district that needed a revival. On reaching the place I had to begin with his own family and one or two of the members who were present and rebuke them for setting the example they did in wearing jewelry. Of course I greatly offended them the first night, and before I had been to the church at all.

The preacher in charge had no influence in the place, for he was regarded as one of the boys.[517] But a good old preacher who had no appointment but who had been on the straight track for thirty years I found [there], and in him I had found the first man of any age who saw matters as I did and who dared to grapple with fashionable wrongs and then take the consequences, and my soul was greatly comforted. I had before known many who in the heat of a powerful revival which had been induced by holiness would promise purity, but when they came to conference [and] found themselves in the minority, and with families to take care of, dared not risk it to take sides with God and go up or down with Jesus. But at last here was one who had passed many a fiery ordeal, and still he stood.

We began labor at the church and soon found we had struck snags of no ordinary difficulty to plow through. I felt I had nothing to lose. "I am in bad odor among all the careful ones and I have none but God to please, and though in all probability I shall sometimes strike a rock that will wrench me, yet by the help of God I will go the straight path[?] of God's[?] truth till I get stopped." As I told the sainted Kendall, "I will practice what I have preached, and that is, never [to] swerve one hair's breadth from exact right and be as honest and thorough as I would if the judgment horn had just sounded to get ready for judgment in five minutes." When /306/ he asked me if I did not sometimes get run under, I said "Yes, but if I am under while in my fidelity to God and truth, Jesus will always go under with me, and Jesus will have a resurrection

---

and then includes a fairly long letter from Redfield to "Brother Hicks and Co." of Syracuse, dated "Henrietta, N. Y., Nov. 11, 1852." Redfield's letter, which helps fix the chronology, gives more details about the revival ("About twenty have been converted, which in my judgment is equal to one hundred in Syracuse"), mentions his upcoming itinerary, and states his hope that "Dr. [Elias] Bowen, or someone of his standing, would form a plan and lay it before one of our bishops for approval" for a more general "movement" of revival in the M.E. Church. "It seems to me that such is the condition of the churches, that some unusual effort must be made to check the progress of approaching ruin, and extend the borders of Zion to fields as yet unoccupied" (269).

[517] JGT: "He found that the preacher in charge had no religious influence, because of his trifling manner among the people" (270).

and I shall come up with Him." I felt I could wait to have my case adjusted when Christ settles up with the world.

I soon saw that we must find our saintship [sic] and restore ourselves to the confidence of the world by humble confessions of our real moral state.[518] I urged the necessity of making clean work for the judgment so that the world may have a correct idea of the standard of genuine religion.

On finishing my sermon, up got an old local preacher and told the people that Redfield had insulted them bad enough, and he said that church would never disgrace itself enough to make confessions at the dictation of one man. Then, straightening himself up and in a defiant tone said the old man, "He need not come here and accuse [us] of having no religion. I know I have got religion, and O, Brethren, what a glorious time we will have when we all get up yonder." (I interrupted, "Yes, if you ever get there.")

His son, who was like him a preacher, arose and gave me his spewed venom, to which I made no reply. I saw we were coming into the tug of war, and that very soon, too. But if I fall in my tracks, [still] I will never yield a hair of God's rights.

The meeting closed. Then one of the dead members went to the old man and told him, "I know the reason why you are so bitter in your opposition to this confessing business. You know that you are guilty of crimes that would make any decent man blush."

Not knowing that his life was so well known, he tried to deny [it], and asked for the proof. This man called out to another, "Say, come here. Don't you know this old man to be guilty of such and such a crime?"

"Yes," said the young man. Then, [as the questioner began] calling another and another who asserted the same, this /307/ corrupt man left the church, and did not come again.

I then put to a vote whether we should have the truth by which we must die and by which we must be judged, and called upon sinners to vote. They gave an overwhelming vote for the exact right and truth In all its severe exactions.

The next night I saw we must come to a point to act. I said to the people that I had gone to my utmost extent in preaching the Word of God but, [I said,] "all fails to do anything. I will now try one more effort—not to apply truth to the conscience, for that is all in vain. Conscience you have none. Bible truth has nothing sacred in your esteem.

---

[518] JGT: "He saw that representatives of Jesus must do something to restore themselves to the confidence of those outside the church" (271).

But you may possibly have some sense of honor left, to which I can make an appeal.

"Now, when you joined the M.E. Church, you either did or did not know the rules. If you did not, here they are. [You subscribed to a discipline] which forbids doing harm and requires [you] to do good [and which] denies conformity to the world. In all its features which takes [i.e., require] carrying on of a holy life, you are deficient.[519] Now make up your mind. Can you, will you conform to these rules? And if not, do have the honor to go to your preacher and tell him that either you did not know the rules, and it was a mistake which you committed in joining the church. Or if you did know, you can tell him you thought you could keep them but you see you can't, and say like an honest person, 'I want you to drop my name, for I can't keep those rules and I will not injure the character of your church by remaining a member.'"

One man, and a principal man, went and got the preacher to drop him and then said, "There, I have withdrawn from the Methodist Church, for I am resolved to die an honest man." Then [he] said to me, "I have been kept in this church because I was reputed to be wealthy, and that too when the preachers knew I would swear and that I was at the head of all rowdyism. But I am now out of the church."

"Well, well said. I thank God that you have religion enough to get out of the church."

I know this looks severe. But I know too that it is no worse to deal thus thoroughly than to let Jesus suffer crucifying again /308/ in the house of His friends, and the church to become a stench.

But this raised a tempest about my ears, and a principal man got up before the congregation and said to them that they had borne with me long enough and would not submit to such abuse. When he had finished I asked, "Will the brother please tell me and this congregation what I have preached here that ain't God's Bible truth?"

"We believe it is true," said he, "but we won't stand it here, anyway."

The meeting was broken up in great tumult, and a large number got around me and began most vehemently to accuse me of the disorder. I think that five to ten voices were clamoring so furiously that I could not be heard. But I turned to God and could say, "O Lord, Thou knowest I have not swerved one hair from the right. I have gone to the utmost of

---

[519] JGT: "Now, when you joined the church you either did, or did not, know its rules. If you did not, here they are [holding out a copy of the Discipline]. They forbid doing harm, and command to do good. They forbid conformity to the world. Yet, in all that you are deficient" (272; brackets in Terrill).

my power to gain the end, and now I must stop. I must give it up into Thy hands." And I left, expecting to leave matters in this state and to suffer a farther reduction in other people's estimate of my impolitic course. [I thought,] "Well, I cannot help it. I know I am right and have done the right thing for God." It is impossible for me in language to describe the right consciousness that God approved my course.

I then left the church and went to the [presiding] elder's house and went to bed. I heard that two of the best men in the church fell under the power with a great burden for the church, and especially for the man who tried to stop me.

About two o'clock I heard a rap at my door. "What is wanted?" I asked.

"Why, the preacher's wife is in despair and says she is afraid she shall be in hell before morning, and they want everybody that can pray to come and pray for her."

She had requested them to bring Bro. F., one of the men who had fallen under the burden. But he was perfectly stiff, so they had to carry him by main force. She had been slyly counseling the sisters not to mind me at all but to keep on their jewelry, and [now] she was greatly distressed.

They had not prayed long for her when a rap came to their door and a messenger said, "There are members of the church in such a house and street, /309/ and they want everybody to come who can pray, to come right over, for they are afraid they will be lost before morning. And they want you to bring Bro. F." (who again was carried as he was, stiff with the power).

Soon a rap came again, and a messenger said that a number of sinners were collected at a certain house and were afraid they should be doomed, and wanted everyone to come who could pray. But especially they must bring Mr. F. So it was found out that God had awakened the whole place at night, and salvation took the place.[520]

XXXIX. Redfield's "Most Splendid Mansion"

I next went to a place but a few ~~Chap~~ miles distant from the last place.[521] I saw the preacher on Sunday morning in the church. "Well,"

---

[520] JGT: "Before daylight it became evident that the whole place was under awakening; and the result was a glorious ingathering of souls" (273). Terrill ends the chapter here and begins a new chapter (his chapter 43) on page 274.

[521] Redfield wrote and crossed through "Chap" in the middle of the line, apparently intending to start a new chapter at this point (as JGT does) but then not actually doing so. Terrill relates this account but does not identify the place. It

said he, "we are looking for you to begin today. Now," said he, "do you object to a melodeon in the gallery? For if you do, we won't have it used."

"Well," said I, "don't let it sound a single note."

"What then of the choir?"

"Bring it down to the front seats and let the whole congregation sing in Methodist style."

We again began at the foundation stone of holiness to build up the cause of Jesus. When the doctrine of holiness had taken a deep hold and the prospect of a revival was very promising, I was waited upon by a committee who announced their business in this way: "Now, Brother, are you willing to be dealt with and if possible remove all hindrances to a revival?"

"Most certainly I am."

"Well, we have heard some reports concerning you which are greatly injuring the cause of God."

"Well, what are they?"

"Well, we have heard that you are worth $300,000 and that you own a most splendid mansion in N. York, and that it is carpeted with tapestry carpeting from the top all the way down. That you have a splendid livery and carriage and waiters, and that you carry a splendid gold watch. And then you come out here and pounce upon us for our paltry two- and six-penny gold rings. We think this ought /310/ to be corrected."

"Well," said I, "I do not hold myself responsible to use up my time in trying to settle all the lies which may be invented, for I should soon have my hands full and no time to work for God." Pulling out my very plain silver watch, I said, "That is all the watch I have." They admitted that to be all right.

I then said, "About that mansion, that is true, only they have not located it in the right place. And about the $300,000—I would not sell it for that sum. Indeed, I do not think I ought to be blamed for the possession of that, for I did not build it nor purchase it; it was willed to me by my Elder Brother when He died. And as for my describing it to please the fastidious, I shall not do it. Only this much I will say, that the fences around it are walls made of diamonds, amethyst, beryl, topaz, and other like precious stones, and the walks are all paved with gold. And you may judge from that what the mansion must be."

---

may have been Corning, New York, as Redfield later says he next went to "B. [Bath] some twenty or more miles from C." Bath is about twenty miles northwest of Corning.

Suffice it to say, the committee dismissed themselves, and I heard no more of that matter.

The work took a deep and extensive track, and near five hundred were converted. Some of the converts had the work so thorough [i.e., experienced salvation so thoroughly] that they immediately went to work in a very successful manner.[522]

One young lady, who to appearance might be sixteen years old, came out one evening and, standing by the altar, turned to the congregation and said, "Farewell to you all. I am going to seek religion, and I will have it." And then dropping upon her knees, she called upon God most determinedly for salvation. Soon she arose and, clapping her hands, she gave glory to God. Then turning a moment to the faithful old preacher and calling him by name [she] said, "O, Brother, this is good!" Then said she, "O how I want Jane to come get this good religion," and running into the congregation she soon brought Jane to the altar.

"And now," said she, "I want Mary," and she brought her. "And now /311/ I want Susan." But Susan ran out of the house, and she after her.

"And now I want Harriet." She went to Harriet, but Harriet refused to come. She then dropped upon her knees for a moment and took Harriet by the hand, and [soon] led her to the altar. Thus she continued, and I timed her by the watch and saw that [this] girl had not been converted ten minutes before she began to work. In less than one hour she had brought eleven sinners to the cross, a work immensely beyond that of multitudes in a whole lifetime.

I felt that God had perfect possession of the entire house. One sister arose and, said she, "O, what shall we do for a preacher to lead us on when Bro. Redfield is gone?" Then turning to the preacher she said, "O, you must get the great blessing of holiness, or you cannot lead us on."

The preacher arose and, instead of feeling insulted and commencing a course of fighting against the work as they often do, said, "Well, I

---

[522] The Corning M.E. Church showed a jump in membership from 152 in 1852 (140 the previous year) to 259 in 1854, including 43 probationers—an indication of revival. It declined over the next two years to 167 members (*Minutes,* East Genesee Conference). While an accession of 107 members (net) is far less than the "near 500" conversions Redfield reported, commonly not all converts became members, and the conversions may have included some nominal members and some who joined other churches. It seems likely that the revival described was at Corning, though this is not absolutely certain.

will have that blessing. And I ask you all to pray for me." And he did get it. And then he said to me, "I have had this blessing before, and preached it, and just such revivals used to follow me. But then I saw how some in the conference treated the good Brother [Purdy] who is with you, and I was afraid I should get into disrepute as he has.[523] So I lowered the standard and then lost the power, and was contemplating to locate next conference. But now I shall take my old track and risk the consequences."[524]

But I think he too failed to keep his promise, for I heard of him no more. But I heard that the conference sent a man whom I knew to be an enemy of holiness, and who tried to put down Redfield's revival (if what I heard was correct). Not long after I heard of a member [there] who had been gloriously saved and who had died in the triumph of faith, and I thanked God they [sic] had been taken away before the preacher could kill them spiritually. My heart was greatly distressed to know that after I had /312/ labored, groaned, and wept[525] before God till salvation came, to know that after I go, grievous wolves in the person of preachers will enter in not sparing the flock, and from this time out I would continue to labor and then my heart was made to again to know that the converts soon died and were safely landed out of the reach of those who would ruin them by helping them to backslide from God. Then those facts [would be used] to injure my influence abroad.[526]

I next took cars for B. [Bath, New York], some twenty or more miles from C., and again erected the standard of Bible holiness.[527] Soon the work began. Among others, one lady who took a strong stand for

---

[523] JGT: "He did get it, and afterwards said to Mr. Redfield, 'I had it once before, and I preached it; and I had just such revivals as this. But I saw how some in the conference treated Brother Purdy, who is with you, and I was afraid I should get into bad repute among my brethren, as he has'" (276).

[524] "To locate" meant to cease being a conference-appointed preacher and instead move one's membership from the conference to a local church—thus ceasing to serve as pastor but continuing as a local preacher.

[525] At the top of page 312 in the center, above these words, Redfield (or possibly Terrill) has written three large Xs. It is not clear what they are intended to signify, as there is no break in the narrative at this point.

[526] Redfield frequently mixes verb tenses this way in one sentence, alternating between an incident in the past and his present situation. While the grammar is awkward, the meaning is clear.

[527] JGT: "Having closed his labors in this place, Mr. Redfield next went to labor in Bath, Steuben county, N. Y. Here again he raised the standard of holiness" (276). Bath is about sixty miles south and a bit east of Rochester. The M.E. Church there was at this time in the East Genesee Conference.

holiness resolved to be right or nothing and made a promise to follow the leadings of God's Spirit wherever it [sic] might lead.[528] In time of one of our after-meetings [in a home] the spirit said to her, "Now, go up to the Methodist Church." So without cavil she went up about half-way, and then the same spirit said, "Now go home again," so home she went. "And now," said the spirit, "go right up to the Methodist Church." So up she came to the church.

"Now," said the spirit, "kneel down in the end of the seat so that those coming into the seat will have to step over you, and that will put them in mind of their stumblingblocks." So she did as instructed. "And now," said the spirit, "this church is very proud. Now, get down in the aisle and hop like a frog to humble them." So she obeyed. "Now, call that good old lady nearby you a hypocrite, and now go after your daughter and pull her along to Christ." So over the top of the seats she went. When her daughter saw her coming, she ran screaming over the seats to keep out of her way. The confusion was such that our meeting was brought to a stop.

She went home, and the spirit said, "Now try your faith in God by building up a large fire in the Franklin stove near the wall, then sit between it and the wall. It won't burn you if your faith is strong enough."

While in this state her husband, who was a physician, came up to the house of the preacher with the sad tale that his wife had been raving crazy, and as proof related all these facts. I saw at once she was only passing, in the track of Jesus, some /313/ temptations which He passed through. Christ was more than conqueror in resisting, but poor human nature is frequently so far affected that those who are ignorant of deep spiritual exercises mistake it for insanity.[529]

"Now," said the doctor, "I would not have this happen on any consideration, for the cause of Methodism's sake, and we must stop these meetings."

"Well, Doctor, don't you know that she is only passing a sharp temptation? For all the deciding symptoms which determine a case of insanity are wanting."

"Well," said he, "what shall I do?"

---

[528] JGT: "Here again the devil undertook to hinder the work by subjecting a woman, who experienced the blessing of holiness, to severer temptation. In her earnestness she promised the Lord she would follow the Spirit wherever it might lead" (276).

[529] That is, Jesus recognized and resisted Satan's temptations (e.g., turning stones into bread), but this woman in her spiritual ignorance failed to recognize and resist the temptations.

"Be quiet and pray for her and let her alone, for she will surely soon come out of this, and then she will see and will tell you that all this is of the devil."[530] I finally persuaded him to let the matter drop and not interfere with our meetings. Sure enough, the next morning she came out into the clear light, and such an experience of the power of saving grace is seldom seen. Then she said that all those strange influences the day before were of the devil.

But the devil that went out of her I think went into others, for years after, the first part of this matter was industriously circulated against us as [being] a result of my labors, and she was called insane. But as far as I ever heard, they never told [the full story,] that she came out right and owned this to be temptation. These false representations were put in circulation by Methodist preachers.

The work went on in power. Soon one of our brethren who came out into the clear light saw that he could not be justified and continue to make, mend, or sell any more jewelry, so he gave it up and attended only to the useful branch of his trade. But soon a distant brother came and, seeing him in his usual health, accosted him thus: "Good morning, Brother, and how do you do?"

"Pretty well, bless the Lord."

"Well, have you not been sick?"

"O, no."

"Well," said the brother, I heard that you had become deranged on the subject of religion and [that] they were soon to take you to the madhouse at Utica."

"Well," said our good brother, "I don't know as I am deranged. I only know I ain't going to sell any more jewelry."[531]

When I saw how professed ministers /314/ of Christ in their ignorance of the wiles of the devil would seize on such cases as this and make capital against me, I more than ever felt that the glory of the Methodist Church was fast passing away. Somebody must soon attempt to call back the people to their old paths. My labor, I supposed, would have its effect to show ministers who have influence where our only hope lay, and they would by the examples of powerful revivals see and return to the gospel simplicity of primitive Methodism. Yet I could not from my experience see that it would be a final[?] success, but, [I thought,] probably when I am gone God will raise up another Wesley,

---

[530] At this point someone has written a large superscript X in the manuscript between "devil" and the next word.

[531] JGT condenses this account of the jeweler to just one sentence, with which he concludes the chapter (278).

and a church will yet be raised whose main aim will be to bring sinners to God rather than to exhaust their energies and funds in building up metropolitan churches to win a name among the ungodly world.[532]

XL. Ministry with B. T. Roberts in Buffalo, 1853

I now took cars and went to N. [Niagara] Street in B. [Buffalo] to help Brother [Benjamin T.] Roberts.[533] I had enquired of a good old preacher about him and learned that I had nothing to fear in trying to go straight, for he was a man who dared to identify himself with right, however unpopular. I found him to be one of the students whom I saw but made no acquaintance with at M. [Middletown, Connecticut, in 1846], and his wife a very unassuming lady but very conscientious.[534]

I learned from Bro. R. and the principal man in the church that this once flourishing cradle of Methodism was almost run out, and that it had been a hard matter to sustain prayer meetings for a year or two. Bro. R. was at his post and ready to remain in.[535]

In due time the work of God took deep and thorough course. Soon among others came a poor drunken local preacher whom Bro. R. [had] found sick with delirium tremens. But God restored him. Then came another L. [local] preacher from the horse races in Canada and was reclaimed. And now the work of confession, reclaiming, converting and sanctifying grace [continued]. The work looked very promising, for many of the people were taking a stand for Bible Methodism.[536]

One of the strongest instances I will give. A Sister B., one of the most fashionable Methodists of N. St. Church, was covered /315/ over with jewelry. She took off a large amount of ornaments and then went from house to house among the fancy Methodists and upon her knees

---

[532] This passage, which is significant for Redfield's view of Methodism and of revival, is deleted by JGT. JGT here begins his chapter 44 (page 279).

[533] JGT: "After closing his labors in Bath, Mr. Redfield went to the city of Buffalo, where he held a series of meetings in the Niagara Street Methodist Episcopal church. Rev. Benjamin T. Roberts, now senior General Superintendent of the Free Methodist Church, was the pastor of the Niagara Street society" (279). B. T. Roberts' diary shows that Redfield arrived in Buffalo about January 1, 1853, and stayed until January 28.

[534] JGT omits this sentence, which is important in establishing the significant relationship between Redfield and B. T. and Ellen Roberts.

[535] Roberts, recently appointed to Niagara Street, had begun his ministry there on September 19, 1852.

[536] JGT has "reforming, converting and sanctifying of souls" (279) but in the manuscript the word appears to be "reclaiming," not "reforming." The course of this revival is narrated in detail in Snyder, *Populist Saints,* chapter 14.

confessed her great wrong in following their example. Then she came out a flaming simple disciple of Jesus.

But word soon reached the ears of the men who have been known as the [Buffalo] Regency, and they came on in mass to hold a missionary meeting, and appointed one meeting at the N. St. Church.[537] I saw the bishop [Edmund Janes], and to gain his influence in favor of Methodism I asked him if he could give a word in favor of Methodism, for we had already[?] an opposition to contend [with]. To prepare him to appreciate our wants, I told him how God had saved some of the people with power, and [about] the two local preachers who had been reclaimed. I then told him what the principal members told me of the low state of the church. He turned upon me and abruptly said, "I shall not believe a word of it."[538]

I saw he had [already] been engaged for the other side, and of course I must now prepare myself for trouble. When the bishop preached, he must needs go out of his way to make his flings against sour godliness and leave the people to infer that he was giving me a special benefit.[539] Then A. S. [Abel Stevens], the editor of the *Christian Advocate*, made his hits by giving the straight way his special note of rebuke, declaring to them that Christianity is not inconsistent with the luxuries or the elegancies of life.[540] [Some] old ministers sat nearby and seemed to enjoy the fun of hearing old Methodism put underfoot.

There was too J. F. [James Fuller], the persecutor of the sainted

---

[537] JGT says, a bit more even-handedly: "In the midst of this revival the meetings of the General Missionary Society came on, and one service was appointed to be held in the Niagara Street church" (279–80). JGT omits the term "Regency." Two opposing parties had developed within the Genesee Conference, one labeled "the Regency" by those who (like Roberts and Redfield) wanted to see a return to and revival of earlier Methodism; this reforming group became known as "Nazarites." See Snyder, *Populist Saints.*

[538] Edmund Janes (1807–1876) was elected Methodist Episcopal bishop in 1844. He was generally supportive of the holiness movement.

[539] JGT: "When the bishop preached he seemed to take especial pains to impress the congregation that he did not approve of Mr. Redfield's work" (280).

[540] At this time Abel Stevens was actually the corresponding secretary of the newly organized (or reorganized) Tract Society of the Methodist Episcopal Church (William Crawford Barclay, *History of Methodist Missions,* Vol. 3, *Widening Horizons 1845–95* [New York: Board of Missions of The Methodist Church, 1957], 108). Stevens was editor of *The Christian Advocate* however at the time Redfield was probably writing, having been elected to a four-year term in 1856 (Simpson, *COM,* 831).

Kendall, now gone to the army where all such ministers belong,[541] and J. B. S., another officer of the army,[542] and last though not least was T. C. [Thomas Carlton], the book agent who I was informed went among the people and told them not to regard what Redfield was doing but to put their foot on it and stop it.[543]

And last of all Lawyer V.[544] came into one of our afternoon meetings to carry out the wishes of these opposers of Methodism. /316/ He got up and said in substance that this [church] has long enough been annoyed and disgusted with this man Redfield, and now we shall have an end of these matters, for this meeting can no longer be endured.[545]

I was most wonderfully sustained and felt a peculiar and unearthly power resting upon me.[546] As soon as he sat down, I asked, "Will the

---

541 Redfield is probably referring to Fuller's year of Civil War service during the 1861–62 conference year (see Simpson, *COM,* 385; Sandford Hunt, *Methodism in Buffalo From Its Origin to the Close of 1892* [Buffalo: H. H. Otis and Sons, 1893], 79), which may have been the time when Redfield was writing. Since the reference is ambiguous it could possibly refer to Kendall's joining the heavenly army, but the ensuing reference to J. B. S. being an army officer suggests the former interpretation is more likely.

542 Not identified, though Redfield may have meant John B. Wentworth, a prominent M.E. pastor in Buffalo. There was at this time no ordained preacher in the Genesee Conference with the initials J. B. S.

543 Thomas Carlton (1808–1874), an influential member of the Genesee Conference, had since 1852 been serving as denominational book agent (publisher) in New York City. He was associated with the "Buffalo Regency" and was a principal agents in the events that led to B. T. Roberts' expulsion from the Methodist Episcopal Church in 1858.

544 Presumably Judge Peter Vosburgh, a leading member and trustee of the Niagara Street Church.

545 JGT rewrites this section, leaving out the reference to "T. C." but explaining that there was at this time "a sharp conflict in the Genesee Conference . . . over the question whether the modern innovations upon Methodism should prevail." "Now there crowded into the Niagara Street church the leading opposers" of "the Wesleyan doctrine and experience of holiness, and the simplicity of Methodism." These opposers "mingling among the membership, who were being graciously moved by the revival in progress, . . . circulated scandalous reports that had a tendency to stop the work" (280). It is not clear from Redfield's account, but the sequence was this: Redfield's meetings at Niagara Street began on Sunday, January 2. Then the area Methodist missions rally was held at the Niagara Street Church (principally, with some services at other churches) on Saturday, Sunday, and Monday, January 22–24. The confrontation with Vosburgh and others occurred on Thursday, January 27, and Redfield left the next day for New York City. See Snyder, *Populist Saints.*

546 JGT has, rather: "Mr. Redfield was kept perfectly calm and sweet amid it

brother be so kind as to tell me and this congregation what I have preached here that is not God's Bible truth?"

He retorted, "It is all true enough, but we won't endure it here, anyway."

So I was compelled to leave. And then I was followed with all the [i.e., with all kinds of] garbled ~~distortions~~ accounts of extravagances and impropriety and even gross falsehoods.

When the meeting closed, or rather was broken up, I was consoled by one sister who had come out so plainly and obtained full salvation who said to me, "When that man was putting it on so hard upon you, I saw a great light descend and cover you up, and I said to myself, 'Can this be real?' So I looked again and again, and still I saw it, and I was convinced that God was standing by you."

"Well," said I, "I saw nothing, but I felt an unearthly glory and power settle down upon me and that God approved of me."[547]

I left the place ~~and was soon followed~~ and learned that J. R. [John Robie], who printed the organ of the Regency, gave me special marks of disapproval.[548] My heart now utterly sank within me, and all my hope for poor Methodism was greatly humbled, for I saw the anti-Methodist spirit from the bishop down to the lowest [?] in the ministry. But I felt sure that God would take that church in hand, and so He did, and it has finally failed and gone down. But I had one forlorn hope even then, and that was that B. T. R. [Roberts], the pastor, would by his merits fill the episcopal chair. I was sure he would dare to speak favorably of salvation that saves. I was sure, and so stated when I returned to N. York, that I had seen one man who I believed would if raised to his true stand in the church be one of our bishops. I did not then know what wire-pulling was practiced in making /317/ bishops and how utterly impossible it would be for so fearless and honest a man as B. T. R. was, ever to get to a position which was gained not so much by merit as by management.

I would not give up in despair but that the time would yet come when primitive Methodism would rise and do its heaven-appointed work. And if it did not, and all fails and I with it go down, I can at least

---

all" (281).

[547] JGT omits this last incident and conversation.

[548] John E. Robie (1811–1872), a Methodist preacher, owned and edited the independent *Buffalo Christian Advocate* (later the *Buffalo Advocate*), which he founded in 1850. It was the principal literary opponent of the "Nazarite" group. (JGT omits this sentence but adds more details about the Niagara Street Church.)

have the consolation of knowing that I would not be swayed by any consideration to the right or left from the exact line of right.

Little did I then dream that even B. T. R. would dare in after years to beard the lion in his den. To be put to the worst indignities that could be heaped upon him, humbled and crushed and to all appearance buried forever and beyond the power of doing any more harm to the devil's kingdom. But a man of his sterling principle can never be held by any manmade tombs, and in due time B. T. Roberts makes his appearance above ground, and here is B. T. Roberts, still faithful to God and right. I know he saw the wants of the church when I left him. But I dared not tell him how my heart was moved towards him, and how I felt myself called of God to try and show an example of what Methodism could do and by that means enlist Methodist preachers to take the work in hand of trying to return to the old paths.[549]

I went to T. Ville [Townsendville] to the help of my special friend J K T. [Tinkham].[550] We had a glorious time, a powerful revival, and [witnessed] some of the deeper developments of the phenomena of salvation in redeeming our inner senses. One sister, while enduring a burden so agonizing for the cause of God in that place, was so greatly distressed that it seemed to require all the faith and prayer of a number of persons to keep the breath of life in her. But when see had passed the suffering, her spirit ear was opened to hear the music of the redeemed.[551]

I went now to P. B. to assist Bro. P. in a church which once belonged to /318/ the Presbyterians but was sold by the minister to recover the pay of his salary.[552]

---

549 JGT omits Redfield's reflections here on B. T. Roberts. He, or possibly Redfield or someone else, inserted two Xs at the end of the sentence. Here JGT includes a letter from Redfield (dated "Buffalo, N. Y., January 4, 1853") to "Bro. Hicks and Company" in Syracuse (281–82).

550 JGT: "From Buffalo Mr. Redfield went to Townsendville to the help of his especial friend, Rev. J. K. Tinkham" (283). According to East Genesee Conference records, Tinkham was never the appointed preacher at Townsendville. Thus both Redfield and Terrill seem to be in error here, unless Tinkham was at Townsendville simply as evangelist. Tinkham served the Bloomfield church, 1854–56, and membership statistics don't suggest a revival during that time. A surge in membership in Townsendville from 1851 to 1853 (from 72 to 126) does suggest revival during that period, which may reflect Redfield's ministry.

551 JGT: "A glorious revival occurred, and many were converted" (283).

552 JGT: "From Townsendville Mr. Redfield went to P— B— (probably Port Byron), to assist Brother P— (probably Purdy), in a church which once belonged to the Presbyterians, but had been sold to pay the preacher's salary"

Chapter [33][553]

I now went again to the city of S. [Syracuse] to see the brethren. We concluded to have some meetings, and finally elected to build a church of plain rough hemlock boards and put one coat of plastering on (inside) it.[554] We had then a power among us that savored largely of the Pentecostal type. Such power and such unearthly demonstrations I never saw as a whole, and such conflicts with the power of perdition.[555] We built a church and were organized as Third Methodist E. Church amid great opposition from Methodist preachers. But the [presiding] elder was favorable and took it into his charge, and thus removed the matter of controversy to [i.e., from being] between us and the conference and put it between the elder and conference. But conference sent on man after man who tried to destroy them and even to disband them. But they continued to hold up their heads against the odds of a whole conference. But God gave our people a man for the times, Bro. H. [Hicks], who has stood firmly ever since, and a remnant will yet be saved and a light emanate from that spiritual Sodom which will emanate to bless the world.[556]

---

(283). Port Byron, New York, is eight miles north of Auburn and about twenty-five miles west of Syracuse, New York.

553 Redfield here begins a new chapter, though JGT does not.

554 The word "inside" is written above the line, between "on" and "it."

555 JGT has: "A cheap building of rough hemlock boards, and plastered with one coat, was erected and dedicated to God. An engraving of it, that heads a letter written from this place to Rev. W. C. Kendall, shows it to have been the extreme of plainness and simplicity. From the beginning of the effort their meetings were attended with great manifestations of power and success" (283).

556 JGT has, "After some years an effort was made by the preachers to disband the society; but God had raised up a layman of deep experience and determined spirit, who could not be coaxed or driven from what he thought was right. This was Charles T. Hicks, to whom the letter in this chapter is addressed. He was a man of fine business abilities, which kept him in the recorder's office of the county, either as head officer or deputy, for more than forty years" (283–84). Terrill provides more details, noting that the congregation Redfield organized later affiliated with the Free Methodist Church. He adds, "How long Mr. Redfield remained at Syracuse after the organization of the Third church, or where and how he spent his time after leaving there cannot now be told, but the next trace of him is found in 1855, where, in Burlington, Vermont, he was engaged in one of his most successful meetings" (284). Other sources show that in January 1855 Redfield was in Syracuse and went from there to Albion to assist W. C. Kendall in revival efforts and was there for a week or two. This is the meeting at Albion that Redfield in fact narrated earlier (pages 293–96 of the manuscript), as noted above. See Benson H. Roberts, *Benjamin Titus Roberts,* 108–9;

XLI. The 1854–55 Burlington Revival

I was next invited to go to B. [Burlington] in Vt. where a revival had not been seen in twenty-on years.[557] My old friend P. [Purdy] preceded me, and through his labors under God a great work began.[558] The preacher [Chester F. Burdick] was favorable to old fashioned Methodism and stood by us like a man of God. Opposition from the standing order was as of old set in motion against us, but God conquered.[559] Many remarkable conversions took place and the work spread all over

---

[B. T. Roberts,] "Rev. Wm. C. Kendall, A. M. Labors," *The Earnest Christian* 2, no. 9 (Sept. 1861): 279–80.

[557] JGT here begins a new chapter (his chapter 45), stating, "In February, 1855, Mr. Redfield was invited to visit Burlington, Vermont, and assist in a protracted meeting" (285). Burlington at the time had a population of around five thousand and just one Methodist Episcopal congregation. The Methodist preacher, 1853–55, was a young man named Chester F. Burdick.

[558] JGT: "Mr. Purdy had preceded him two weeks, and in his characteristically thorough manner had prepared the way for Mr. Redfield's coming" (285). An April 26, 1855, report from Fort Edward, New York (about one hundred miles south of Burlington, Vermont), mentions Fay Purdy's ministry in the area just subsequent to this: "A series of meetings was commenced early in the winter, during which many were awakened and converted. We were favored with the services of F. H. Purdy, an exhorter, from the western part of the state, and brother S. Coleman, of Troy; and their labors were greatly blessed to the good of souls. As many as 60 have professed religion thus far, over 50 of whom have united with us on probation." J. E. Bowen, report in "Home Intelligence" section, *Christian Advocate and Journal* 30, no. 18 (3 May 1855): 70.

[559] A prominent figure in this revival, and in Burlington at the time, was the Methodist businessman Samuel Huntington, who owned a successful bookstore at the corner of Church and College streets. An 1891 report on his retirement noted, "In 1854 Burlington had a crisis in financial affairs and [Huntington] was chosen constable, overseer of the poor and tax gatherer," a position he held for twelve years. (The financial crisis may have been a factor in the revival which began at the end of 1854.)

The 1891 report notes, "President Lincoln appointed [Huntington] postmaster a short while before the latter was assassinated," but President Johnson removed him for political reasons. Huntington also served briefly as a state senator. "Over Half a Century," *Burlington Free Press and Time* (1 July 1891), photocopy from Special Collections, Bailey-Howe Library, University of Vermont.

Redfield maintained a correspondence with Huntington (whom he called "Sammy"), as noted below.

till more than a thousand souls were converted,[560] and our people saw the need of building a second church.[561] But this met with great opposition from conference ministers who now thought that Methodism had become numerically so strong that they could build a splendid church which would vie in stateliness with the dominant denominations. /319/ I advised our people to keep clear of that unholy ambition, which sets position [i.e., social standing] by elegant and expensive church edifices, and by all means to build a new church and let the active salvation party have an opportunity of going in for salvation without being compelled to contend against the metropolitan party.[562]

---

[560] The Methodist preacher R. H. Howard and the noted Congregational minister Constans L. Goodell, D.D., were part of the fruit of this revival (as noted above, in the Biographical Introduction). "The influence of [Goodell's] conversion upon his character and conduct was immediate and very remarkable. The change wrought in him profoundly impressed all who knew him. It is still remembered and spoken of by them as extraordinary." Shortly after his conversion Goodell "made a public confession of his faith by uniting with the First Congregational Church of Burlington," along with "fifty-four others . . . among whom were Mrs. George F. Edmonds, wife of the distinguished U. S. Senator, Rev. Lewis Francis, Rev. E. E. Herrick, Rev. John P. Torrey, Rev. W. W. Livingston, and Prof. H. A. P. Torrey" (Currier, *Life of Constans L. Goodell,* 22, 24). Since George F. Edmunds (the correct spelling; not Edmonds) was U.S. Senator from 1866 to 1891 (thus at the time Currier was writing) and would have been only in his twenties in 1858, the persons Currier mentions here were probably young people at the time, and likely some or all were the fruit of the Redfield revival. Thus the titles indicated refer to the time Currier was writing, not to the time of these professions of faith.

[561] Chester Burdick reported in the *Christian Advocate and Journal*: "There has been and is still in progress a revival in this place, such as has not been known here for twenty years. We have had meetings every day for seven weeks, and there is no prospect of the work stopping very soon. From 60 to 90 are enquiring the way of salvation at the altar every evening. The work has embraced all classes, from the Sabbath-school scholar of ten summers up to the gray-headed sire of sixty. About 230 have been converted, and 150 have united with the M. E. Church on probation, and others will soon join. The work of holiness is going on in the churches here, and is the grand central idea of all our success." C. F. Burdick, report dated Burlington, March 23, in "Home Intelligence" section, *Christian Advocate and Journal* 30, no. 14 (5 April 1855): 54.

The Troy Conference *Minutes* clearly register the impact of this revival. The Burlington M.E. Church had 152 members in 1854 and more than doubled to 324 a year later, including 177 probationers. A second church was formed as a result and is first listed in the *Minutes* in 1856, reporting 99 members. Most of these came from the first congregation, as explained below.

[562] This revival in Burlington is documented in numerous sources. Cassius A.

The next preacher who came from conference was a self-conceited man, vain of his imaginary skill to manage, yet feeble in those many parts which constitute the efficient pastor. When he came, he in a boastful manner said, "I hear that the people talk of building another

---

Castle, who as a young man participated in the revival, later described it in his *History of the Methodist Episcopal Church in Burlington, Vermont* (Burlington: Free Press Association, 1903). He reports that in December 1854, the official board of the M.E. Church invited Fay Purdy to conduct revival services there. Purdy ministered for three weeks and was followed by Redfield, who preached for another six weeks—apparently from early February to late March. Castle writes that the result of the Purdy-Redfield efforts "was the mightiest revival that Burlington ever saw and which shook all Vermont. [Purdy] was a man of great spiritual power—so great that one felt it instantly on coming into his meetings. . . . many were converted and many believers were sanctified. . . . he was succeeded by Rev. John W. Redfield, another noted revivalist, . . . at the end . . . there had been so many conversions that the small church edifice we then had would not suffice to seat our own members. . . . never have I heard such divine eloquence as poured forth from the lips of this devoted and faithful servant of the Lord Jesus Christ. At the close of nine weeks of protracted meetings at the church, the revival went on in cottage meetings, in various parts of the city during the entire summer and away into the autumn," after Redfield had left. The Methodist church building was too small to accommodate the mushrooming congregation, and the church debated what to do. "The official board met and discussed the situation from week to week. In the meantime opinion was crystallizing and developing two parties. At length a resolution was passed in the board, of which the writer was then a member, declaring it expedient that a new Church should be formed and requesting the Troy Conference to send two preachers to Burlington." The conference complied, but tried to discourage the formation of a second congregation. A second congregation was formed, however, with76 members (mostly new converts) from the existing congregation. It met temporarily on the third floor of the Burlington Concert Hall and became known as Pine Street M.E. Church when at the end of 1855 it moved into its new building at the corner of Pine and Cherry streets. The new church developed a Sunday school that soon became the largest in the city, "reaching a class which had never been reached before." Twelve years later the two churches merged to form one congregation. Castle, *History of the Methodist Episcopal Church in Burlington,* 23–27. See also T. D. Seymour Bassett, "'The Mightiest Revival That Burlington Ever Saw' And Its Consequences. The Pine Street Methodist Church 1855–66," *Chittenden County Historical Society Bulletin* 30, no. 2 (Spring 1996): 7–12; T. D. Seymour Bassett, *The Gods of the Hills: Piety and Society in Nineteenth-Century Vermont* (Montpelier: Vermont Historical Society, 2000), 161–63; *Programme of the Celebration of the One Hundredth Anniversary of the Organization of the Methodist Episcopal Church, Burlington, Vermont, October 20, 21, 22, 1923* (1923), eight pages.

church. But I shall put my hand on that thing." But it went on in spite of him, [a new church was built,] and many are the souls who have been converted within its sacred walls.[563] I well knew that if they [i.e., the Methodists in Burlington] could get up a great grand palace, that salvation in all probability would be a scarce article in the organization. And I did say all I thought was proper to say in vindication of a mere chapel, plain, neat, and substantial. But I found my foes bitter in the extreme.[564]

XLII. Redfield's Second Marriage

I soon learned that a story was current that I staid at a house of bad repute, had one wife in N. Jersey, another in N. York or Brooklyn, and another in a public house in the place. Of course I paid no regard to it. But soon learning [i.e., I soon learned that it was rumored] that I had two more [wives] who came to town with children, complaining that I had only given one of them and two children $9.00 for a year and the other with three children that I had given her only $7.00 for a year. [It was further rumored that] one of my daughters was urgent to find me and said she must yet see her father that night.[565]

---

563 Castle reported that "among the converts" in the 1855 revival were a number who were "especially called of God to the work of ministry," including Rodney Howard, Joseph Austin, "Revs. Freeman, Wicker, Casavant and others whose names are not now remembered" (Castle, *History,* 29.

564 JGT has, rather, "The next pastor, who came soon after the revival, endeavored to carry out the policy advocated by the preachers at conference, but failed, and the new organization was effected. An effort was now made to counteract Mr. Redfield's influence and build a fashionable church" (285).

565 JGT has merely, "An effort was now made to counteract Mr. Redfield's influence and build a fashionable church. To do this, slanderous stories were circulated about him, in regard to his wife, who had deserted him nineteen years before" (285). Terrill then includes nearly six pages further documenting the 1855 Burlington revival, including three letters from Redfield to W. C. Kendall and R. H. Howard's account (quoted above in the Biographical Introduction).

JGT also quotes Redfield's May 7, 1855, letter to William Kendall as follows: "We had great times at Burlington. Brother Purdy as usual, under God, put things in their right places, and laid a foundation [for me] to build upon. How many were converted, as a result of his labors, I cannot tell, and probably it cannot be known this side of eternity. But if we may reckon on the reflex influence, as manifest in the many extensive revivals round about, that grew out of his labors here, I shall not go wide of the mark when I say that the number is about 2,000. Revivals sprang up in almost every quarter, from ten to one hun-

I finally made up my mind that I would put an end to these repeated slanders and marry a suitable woman if I could who should be a protection against this perpetual slander.[566] It had now been nineteen years since my troubles came to an end by the desertion of that ~~unfortunate person~~ person whose name I have never but once pronounced since, and fourteen years since I was released by /320/ law.[567] Since that time I had frequently heard that she was dead, and finally [I heard it] from various sources, especially from a minister where she used to live. But I would not act on this as it was only a rumor, and I had had no word from her directly in nineteen years.

I however took the precaution to ask advice of a minister, stating the whole fact, and to get further counsel concerning the law in all these matters, and found that no laws existed but such as recognize me as fully released, even if she was living.[568]

---

dred miles away, as the result of Brother Purdy's labors" (JGT, 289–90).

JGT concludes, "Several important things may be learned from these letters"—first of all, "The absence in [Redfield] of anything like rivalry, or vainglory. The letters of Rev. Mr. Howard show that Mr. Redfield was the principal figure in that great revival, but he gives the honor to his friend, Purdy" (291).

JGT notes that about this time Redfield "was connected with another physician in starting a medical infirmary at Syracuse, with a branch at Burlington, Vt.," apparently largely as a means of financial support for Redfield's ministry (288). In his May 7 letter to Kendall, apparently written from Syracuse, Redfield says, "I must go back to Burlington for a season to take charge of a department in a large infirmary. I spend only part of my time here, and I may be compelled to be there at the time of your camp meeting. I wish I was able to devote all my time to the work, but I am compelled to use part of it for the meat that perisheth." He adds, "Our terms, for board, washing and treatment, are $10.50 per week. This includes nursing, hydropathic and homeopathic treatment, and everything else pertaining to the good and comfort of the patient. But until we can get ready the great establishment we have in contemplation, we shall charge but $7.50. Our large establishment will cost from fifteen to twenty thousand dollars" (290–91).

[566] JGT here begins a new chapter (his chapter 46, page 292), noting, "While Mr. Redfield was engaged in the work of a physician at this time, he began seriously to consider the question of marriage."

[567] These calculations suggest that Redfield's first wife deserted him in 1836 and that the divorce was finalized in 1841. His earlier narrative however suggests the divorce occurred about 1848.

[568] JGT summarizes the matter as follows: "Nineteen years had gone by since his wife deserted him, and fourteen since the courts had given him a legal separation from her. Several years had also gone by since he, by two ministers of the church, heard that she was dead; and nothing to the contrary had ever come to his knowledge. A careful consideration of all the facts and of the law in the

I went to K. V. [Keeseville, New York] to hold a meeting, and about the close I thought fit to get married to one that I then believed and now know was in every respect a helpmate to me in the gospel field.[569] But having been slandered so long, I became annoyed at the pursuing[?] course of slanders, and farther believing that if my wedding was known that I should be still more annoyed, I resolved to have only enough [people] present to make it a legal wedding and then to pass off to my next appointment as noiselessly as I could. If I were to be married very publicly, I knew I should be greatly afflicted with the rowdies. But when it was found out that I really was married, and [with] only enough witnesses [present] to meet the requirements of the law, that of course was [viewed as] a great wrong—like the drunkard who said, "If I find my wife up when I go home I will hit her, for she has no right to sit up and burn out candles when I am gone away. And if I find her abed I shall certainly hit her, for she has no right to show me such disrespect as to go to bed while I am gone." I felt myself incapable of doing right [in people's eyes]—like the poor wounded porcupine; if one is so unfortunate as to get wounded, the other porcupines will fall afoul of it and tear it to pieces.[570]

I decided[?] it was hard that I could not be allowed to do a right thing without its being /321/ esteemed a crime. I had been once married unfortunately and had been released by law fourteen years, and someone finding out just enough to make any fabrication which they could

---

case, convinced him that there was no legal nor moral barriers in the way; and he determined to marry, if a suitable opportunity presented itself" (292).

[569] JGT quotes this as, "'I went to Keesville, to hold a meeting, and about the close I saw fit to be married to one whom I then believed, and now know, to be in every respect a helpmeet to me in the gospel field'" (293). JGT explains on the previous page, "Among the many who came to the infirmary for treatment was a lady of more than ordinary intelligence, and who had had some experience in city mission work. She, like himself, had been unfortunate in her married life, and was now separated from her husband. Mr. Redfield finally proposed marriage to her, and his offer was accepted. Immediately after closing a revival at Keesville, N. Y., he was quietly married to this lady by a Methodist minister in the presence of a few witnesses" (292). Neither Redfield nor Terrill give her full name; her first name apparently was Martha, and Redfield called her Mattie. Surprisingly, Terrill does not say whether this woman had been divorced or whether her husband had died. Keeseville (not Keesville) is in northern New York, directly across Lake Champlain from Burlington, Vermont.

[570] JGT omits this aside, but gives more information about the marriage.

most appear probable.[571] So now, as it was my right legally and morally, I thought it best to put a stop to further slanders. But this only formed a foundation for other equally malicious lies.

One thing I always have regretted, and that was that I did not take the first opportunity to inform some of my wife's acquaintances of the fact [of our separation], and I had been requested by my wife to allow her that privilege.[572] So there again I had done a great wrong. Perhaps[?] I never had done right, but I never knew a person who in marrying could please everyone. I never allowed myself to interfere with other people in making their choice, and thought I had the same privilege, and I took it [i.e., the decision to marry] independently. Had I thought one moment, I might have known that when I espoused the cause of God I was in a quarrel with the world at once, and when any man is your enemy on account of one thing, it is very hard for them to see aught but evil in everything else.[573]

I left my wife to go to her father's, and I went immediately to another field of labor where again I saw the power of God displayed.[574]

I then took my wife and went home and made but a few days visit, and having a call, went to L. [Lima, New York] where I had been desired to go for a long time.[575] I went and again I found I had run against a snag, for the Methodist preachers were hostile to what they called "Mrs. Palmer's holiness," and they began to oppose. Nor did I look at is as a wonder when I learned what a stand they had taken in the college [Genesee College, at Lima] where numbers had been compelled to leave on account of this zealous tone of religion, and one preceptress finally left. One fact brought to my ears was this: One of the students

---

571 I.e., people would take what little information they discovered and on that foundation invent plausible rumors.

572 Redfield seems to mean: He did not inform his (first) wife's acquaintances of their legal separation, granting her the option or "privilege" of doing so. But now he felt it would have been better if he had informed them—perhaps because they were not informed or ill informed, thus providing a possible basis for rumors.

573 JGT omits this further reflection of Redfield's about his marital situation.

574 JGT: "Mrs. Redfield, after a few days, went on a visit to her father's, while he went to fill an engagement to hold a meeting. The name of the place of this meeting he does not give, and the writer has no means of learning it. Of the effort put forth at this place he makes this brief record: 'I again saw the power of God displayed'" (293).

575 JGT: "A few days' visit among his own people with his wife, and then they were away to Lima, N. Y., where he had been expected for some time" (293). Terrill places this ministry at Lima in March, 1856.

got salvation and was happy in God. Then one of the professors, a D.D., sent for a medical doctor to come and see what was the matter, and the medical man attempted to physic[576] /322/ the young man.

Some of the students better acquainted with the operations of God's Spirit went out and reported that the doctor was trying to physic the power of God out of one of the students. "Well," said I, "I am glad to learn at last what a Methodist Doctor of Divinity is good for, and that is to know when to send for medical men to come and deplete those who are too much inflamed with the love of God." Of course this with other like criticisms were [viewed as] a great crime in me, and I was called a slanderer of the ministry. God worked in power, but the priests and Levites finally managed to make Jesus take ship and leave their coasts.[577]

We now went to R. [Rochester], where I had for years felt I had a work to do. Now for the first time the way was open. It was in the First [M.E.] Church, and we had a minister who dared to stand up alone where principle was involved. Although I have reason to believe he was prejudiced against me, yet at the time I was there he took the ground of a noble man. When the presiding elder to get this stripe of religion out appointed a special meeting in this very church and at the hour we were using it, Bro. W. [Watts], like a staunch Methodist preacher who knew his own rights as a pastor in charge, dared to stand up and refuse to allow the work of God to be stopped by a presiding elder.[578]

---

[576] To treat, often by means of a laxative.

[577] JGT omits this account of Redfield's ministry at Lima. Instead he provides two and a half pages of additional material (293–95) further elaborating on Redfield's ministry generally and the situation within Methodism. He notes, "At this time a severe conflict was raging in the Methodist Episcopal Church, in the Genesee Conference, between those who were preaching and professing perfect love, and those who were opposed to the same. Charges were being brought against Mr. Kendall, Mr. Roberts, Mr. M'Creery, and others among the ministry, while many among the laity were also passing through severe persecution from the worldly element in the church" (294). Terrill also gives a brief account of the controversial Bergen, New York, Camp Meeting. See Snyder, *Populist Saints.*

[578] JGT identifies the Methodist preacher at the First M.E. Church as "Rev. Jonathan Watts, [who] was one of the corresponding editors of the *Northern Independent,* a brave man who dared to stand alone where principle was involved" (296). Jonathan Watts was the preacher at Rochester First Church, 1854–56. The presiding elder at the time of Redfield's meetings was Augustus C. George (West Rochester District, East Genesee Conference). At the end of

But when the power reached a culminating point and some began to fall under the power, the real clinch began. Bro. M. began to show some of [the] demonstrations of primitive Methodism, and then the work must stop.[579] The city preachers began in good earnest to utter their protests. One of them said to his charge, "If you don't keep away from the First Church, I will vacate this pulpit." The only answer was, "Then give us something to eat."

When these efforts failed, the city preachers, I was informed, collected together and entered into a discussion about the propriety of allowing me /323/ to stay, giving a catalogue of my ~~crimes~~ improprieties, inconsistencies, and the results in insanity[?]. When the war became too hot and I began to feel the pressure and hardly knew which way to turn next, I was waited upon by one who said, "We have about $3,000 pledged to build a church, if you will stay and be the pastor." I too well knew the nest of hornets that would buzz about my ears, and felt it would be impolitic to do so, and told them I could not accept. But my forebodings of the final ruin of Methodism was truly grievous to me. For I now saw what to me appeared something like an organized plot to put down this kind of religion.

Just at this time a letter came to me from St. Charles [Illinois], about seven hundred miles distant, from the preacher who years ago promised if I would go to his place he would take the stand for holiness.[580] He had been crowded out and finally went to Illinois to get into a field where he could carry out his vows of a Methodist preacher to obey the Discipline, and he had got into great trouble.

I regarded this as a Godsend, and resolved to obey it at once. I was sorry to leave the little band in R. [Rochester] among so many enemies. But how was my heart cheered a few years after to learn that the sisters had formed themselves into a body and were organized into a church. They had tried to live their religion in the church in R. till they found they could not, and then [they] swarmed.

This [i.e., in Rochester] was where I saw the sainted Kendall for the last time, and I then felt, in him under God I can say I see the element of a faithful Luther who will stand by the work of God in the

---

the 1855–56 conference year, First Church had 189 members. The previous year it reported 154 members.

[579] JGT omits these two sentences.

[580] JGT: "Just at this time he received a letter from Rev. David Sherman, of St. Charles, Illinois, inviting him to come there and hold a meeting. In the next chapter we shall see the beginning of his work in the West" (296). St. Charles is about thirty miles west of Chicago, on the Fox River.

East, and I will go West, when I sometimes felt an impression saying to me that "In the West you shall find a people prepared of the Lord."[581]

I took cars and went about twenty miles to Bro. K.'s house, from which to start in the early morning train for St. Charles, Illinois. /324/ When I arrived I found the notorious J. McC. [Joseph McCreery], since expelled for fidelity to his solemn conference vows. In him and Bro. K. I saw true spirits, pure in intention, indefatigable in energy and unconquerable in obstinacy for God, and felt, "I can now go West and feel that some are left behind who will do the work of Methodist preachers." And when not long after I saw what is called the "Nazarite Call" and saw in that the outspoken design simply to pledge Methodist preachers to sustain Methodism, I thought I saw in that instrument not only the master mind of J. McC. but the feasible position and the almost certain success of the scheme. I was sure in my own mind that this very tenable position must be at once a rallying point, and that a concert of action would follow and of course succeed.[582] But this con-

---

[581] JGT here inserts about four and a half pages of additional material (297–301) concerning the Rochester meetings, Redfield's remarriage, and the conflict within the Genesee Conference, including B. T. Roberts' ecclesiastical trials of 1857 and 1858 and his expulsion (1858) from the M.E. Church. Terrill notes, "During the time of his labors in Rochester, Rev. Charles G. Finney, the evangelist, was also holding meetings in the city, and occasionally came to the afternoon meetings conducted by Mr. Redfield. . . . The two men seemed to enjoy each others' society, and to bid each other Godspeed in their mission of calling souls to Christ" (297). Redfield was in Rochester for only about two weeks, while Finney's efforts went on for some months. See Rosell and Dupuis, *Memoirs of Charles G. Finney,* 547–56; the Methodist revival with Redfield is mentioned on page 548, n. 52. See also Snyder, *Populist Saints.*

[582] Redfield here is probably referring to the anonymous forty-page pamphlet, *Nazarite Documents: Comprising the Obligations, Practical Propositions, Lamentations, Recommendations, &c. of the Nazarite Union, of the Genesee Conference of the M. E. Church* (Brockport, N.Y.: Wm. Haswell, 1856) which significantly sharpened the crisis within the Genesee Conference. (Possibly he is referring to a shorter, two- or four-page part of this document entitled "Nazarite Union. Historic Circular" which appears to have been initially published some months earlier.) It is interesting and significant that Redfield immediately recognized the document as coming from McCreery's hand. Although the pamphlet is anonymous, on page 11 "J. McCreary, Jr." is listed as "Chief Scribe" at the end of the section entitled "Practical Propositions," and McCreery later indicated that he was the chief source. (In the earliest sources the name is spelled "McCreary"; later, "McCreery.")

Terrill omits Redfield's account here, but he does refer to Redfield's visiting Kendall before Redfield headed west. "The visit was made, and again blessed

clusion I afterwards learned to be caused by my ignorance of the extent of the departure from Methodism, for even this instrument was made a matter of offense.

XLIII. Ministry in "The West"

Early the next morning we [i.e., Redfield and his wife] started, and on the following day in the afternoon arrived at St. Charles and saw our dear persecuted brother. I subsequently learned that a band of sisters made it a subject of prayer that God would send a minister who would preach the gospel in all its length and extent. I learned that our brother had been subject to a fiery ordeal in having the [presiding] elder called to dismiss him. Indeed, he was shut out of [the] Geneva [Illinois] church. and an unctuous Methodist preacher put there who afterwards was caught in a bad affair and had to leave the country.[583]

Before the opposition could get rallied to put me down, God had conquered and salvation in awful glory began. So great was the interest that prayer meetings were continued in private houses till late at night after the church was dismissed. But a few members who were proud and /325/ vain felt themselves greatly aggrieved to be connected with so outlandish a church. They could dance all night but could not ~~allow~~ endure ~~themselves~~ to be so annoyed by the voice of prayer so near their own house.

One instance I will give of what to me was a remarkable incident. One young man who is now one of our first preachers arose in one of our meetings and in a very deliberate manner said. in substance, "Brother – I – think – if – this – is religion, I – never – knew anything about it – and yet – I – have been – a member – of – this – church – for – three – years." He soon obtained religion and became an efficient preacher of the gospel.[584] And now I began to hope for the West. Bro.

---

in prayer, with and for each other, [and thus] they parted in the early morning the next day, never to meet again on earth" (299).

[583] Terrill, whose home was in this area of Illinois and who experienced Redfield's ministry at this time, gives additional detail about Redfield's time in St. Charles. Regarding the St. Charles preacher, David Sherman, Terrill notes: "He had been transferred to the West a few years before, and in the fall of 1855 was appointed to St. Charles and Geneva, in Kane county, Illinois. . . . for some reason he had failed to make much of an impression upon either the church or the world at St. Charles, and in his extremity he sent for Mr. Redfield," whom Sherman had known in New England (302).

[584] JGT identifies this person as "Charles Elliott Harroun, now and from that time a preacher of the gospel" (303). The experience of Charles E. Harroun,

S. [Sherman], the pastor, took courage, and to all appearance we might look for a permanent standard of Methodism to be erected here. The [presiding] elder too approved of the work.[585] The next quarterly meeting was held in Aurora, and a large number of our people paid them a visit. So the good work of holiness took a start there.[586]

I labored on till the middle of June, and I became so exhausted, and the change of climate together made it needful for me to make a summer tour on Lake Michigan and spend the season on Mackinaw Island.[587] Here we hired a house furnished and had a goodly company with [us]. We kept up our family altar and I was greatly amused at the developments of moral character. In one case a lady living close by, hearing the voice of prayer, came in and tried to make herself religiously agreeable. She began by telling us what a bad neighbor she had living in the next house south of us. She said that the woman of the house allowed her children to throw stones at her children, and that she went out and whipped the woman in the street and, to use her own language, said she, "I hurt her as bad as I could." (Report said it was feared she would kill her, and the people had to part them).

"Well," said she, "after I whipped her it did not seem to do her any good. So I went down to her house and talked religion to her, /326/ but found she could not appreciate it."

I found old backsliders on the Island. [There was] one Roman Catholic Church, and one high Episcopal Church at the barracks, and this constituted all the religious privileges of the place. On the other hand, a plenty of whisky shops, drunken Indians, and gambling sa-

---

Sr., is narrated in Hogue, *History of the Free Methodist Church,* 1:270–71. He became a leading preacher in the F.M. Church.

585 JGT here inserts a long April 30, 1856, letter from Redfield (in St. Charles) to Samuel Huntington in Burlington, VT (304–8). Terrill then begins his chapter 49, starting with a June 1, 1856, letter from Redfield to Mr. and Mrs. William Kendall (309–10). In this letter Redfield says, "I think the pilgrims will yet have to organize a new church, and yet that will fail, if they do not guard every part of the Discipline against hard feelings against their oppressors" (310).

586 JGT: "After this meeting closed, Mr. Redfield spent a few days in Aurora, a young and flourishing city twelve miles south. Some of the St. Charles pilgrims went with him, and were a great help in the services. Here quite a number, also, entered into the experience of perfect love" (310).

587 JGT: "The next trace we have of Mr. and Mrs. Redfield is at Mackinaw Island, recruiting their strength for the next season's campaign" (310–11). Terrill omits the incident related next by Redfield but inserts a July 27, 1856 letter from Redfield (addressed "Mackinaw, Mich.") to the Kendalls (311–12).

loons. The Catholics ruled the place and broke up the Protestant school. So ignorance reigns, and irreligion becomes the standing order of the place.[588]

Early in September we left and came down to Wisconsin. We had a very fine visit with an old friend, and soon went to a camp meeting and from that point were invited to visit F. Du L. [Fond du Lac], where a good and glorious work began. But the preacher, a poor jealous man, could not endure it, and although he would take ~~any~~ special pains in pretending to be a warm friend, yet at my back he was trying by slanders to bring me into disrepute.

One sample I will give. He went to one sister who was deeply interested in the subject of personal holiness, and hearing her speak favorably of me, he could not endure it. So he came to me and in speaking of her told me of some misunderstanding which had sprung up between this sister and another since she had begun to seek the blessing of holiness. Then he pretended to ask my opinion as to why persons should on attempting to seek holiness find misunderstandings to spring up so easily.

"Well," said I, "don't you know that whenever anyone attempts to seek so great a blessing that every devil who can find a point to attack will be aroused to oppose?"

This was enough for his purpose. So away he went and told her that I had told him that she was full of little devils. This had the desired effect. He then sent letters off East to know if nobody knew of any evil about me. One of these letters I heard from [i.e., heard about], and in that learned that he who wrote the answer gave the poor jealous man to know that he knew nothing.

But he had got some clue to some of the slanders about my [alleged] many wives, and he was very industrious in /327/ spreading all he knew and adding enough to make his stories interesting. A good friend told me of the hypocrisy and slander by this man, and I went to see him. I found that when I met him with a charge of his wickedness, he was ready to put on his airs and assume a dictatorial air. I saw he was in so bad a mood that I left and told my friend, "I am now going to prophesy that that preacher, if he has his desserts, will be turned out of the M.E. Church in less than three years." And in less than two years he was arraigned under a vile charge. But his [presiding] elder saw the man who made the charge and got him to cover it up.

I went off to A. [Aurora, Illinois?], and on my way I looked for a house to live in. I thought, "If I am to be pursued by such wicked men,

[588] JGT omits this description of Mackinaw Island.

and when their iniquity leaks out they can find those who will help to cover their wickedness, I would rather locate and quit the field." I had now [for] nearly twenty years spent my time, money, and labor to build up the Methodist Church, and [I thought,] "This is my compensation, and it is more than I can endure." But then the old voice rang in my ears, "You may live while you preach, but no longer."

I paused[?], and these pauses[?] looked more than precious to me. My wife too felt she would prefer to die rather than to be compelled to meet these jealous men. I had hoped and believed that, although I found Methodism in so hopeless a condition on account of this new wave of corrupt, ambitious men, that I should find it very different in the West. I believed [that,] like everything else, the theology would begin in the East and travel West.

We arrived at A., and God gave us true friends. We had a good and glorious revival, and our hearts took courage to go on in our mission.[589]

We went to N. L. [New London, Wisconsin] and found a good, kindhearted preacher with whom we labored. We had but a small society; but one female to pray, and she was a Quakeress.[590] /328/ I used to request all seekers of religion to come forward who would do up their own praying. They did come, and God blessed them with salvation, and in great power.

We then went to Jefferson and met with one of our old friends, a preacher from the East, and had a good and profitable time.[591]

---

589 JGT: "He was engaged for a short time in A___ (probably Auroraville), where he found kind friends, and where God came to his help in old-time power, and many were saved" (313).

590 JGT: "From here he went to New London, where he found a good, kind preacher, but a small society, and only one, a Quakeress, to pray at the altar" (313). New London, Wisconsin, is about fifty miles north of Fond du Lac. The Methodist churches in New London and Fond du Lac were part of the Wisconsin Conference. This was still a pioneer area for Methodism; the Wisconsin Conference was organized in 1848, the year Wisconsin became a state.

591 JGT: "From New London Mr. Redfield went to Jefferson, Wisconsin, at the invitation of a preacher whom he had known in the East, Rev. G. H. Fox. Here the Spirit of God had free course, and blessed were the results" (313). Here again JGT refers only to Redfield himself, whereas Redfield has "we." Jefferson is about fifty miles west of Milwaukee. (Someone, perhaps Terrill, has inserted a large X at the end of this sentence.)

JGT inserts some additional material at this point. He writes, "While here he [Redfield] received the news of the grievous fall of one who had been a strong advocate of holiness. Several allusions in some of his letters which follow are explained by this" (313).

Terrill then includes a letter from Redfield to William Kendall and his wife,

We went to Little C. [Little Chute, Wisconsin] and again met with an old friend from the East and had a grand time.[592]

The season came round and we went to St. Charles to a camp meeting.[593] The people were glad to see us. Soon a preacher from the East who had been a member of four or five [Methodist annual] conferences there had found his way West, [at appeared at the camp meeting]. He was the man who broke up a camp meeting [back] East in preaching against holiness. Seeing me present, and the people apparently glad to see me, [he] used up the most of his sermon in flings at favorite evangelists and in preaching against Methodist holiness. One preacher told me that was the fifth time he had heard that sermon against Wesleyan perfection.

After preaching, he went on with a tirade of falsehoods against me to persons in private, saying he knew me East and had heard me, while

---

dated "Jefferson, Wisconsin, December 20, 1856" (313–16). In the letter Redfield comments on the situation both within the M.E. Church and in the nation. He says, "We expect to go to Appleton about the first or the fifteenth of January" and adds, "My wife is being greatly blessed. She is trying to do her duty" (315).

The fallen minister referred to was probably John H. Wallace, a Genesee Conference preacher who had cooperated with Redfield in the Niagara Street, Buffalo, revival in 1853. In December 1856, word came that Wallace had been charged with adultery. The 1856 Genesee Conference *Minutes* list him as superannuated, and he was expelled by the Michigan Conference in 1857. See Allen, *Century,* 127; James Arnold Reinhard, "Personal and Sociological Factors in the Formation of the Free Methodist Church 1852–1860" (Ph.D. Diss., University of Iowa, 1971), 67.

592 JGT says, "On leaving Jeffersonville, Mr. Redfield went to Waukesha, where he found another old friend in charge of the work, and who was willing to let the truth of the Holy Spirit have free course. God came in glorious power, and many were saved." JGT says that Redfield then "made his contemplated visit to Appleton, Wis., the seat of Lawrence University," a Methodist school (316). Terrill then gives an extended account of the meeting at Appleton (316–18). In his manuscript Redfield does not mention Waukesha or Appleton, but Little Chute is near Appleton.

593 JGT: "When the summer came (1857), Mr. Redfield made his way to St. Charles, Illinois, again. He came in time to attend a camp meeting, held in June, near that place" (318). This meeting proved to be the forerunner of what became the well-known St. Charles Camp Meeting, an annual institution born largely out of the fruit if Redfield's revivals which continued for several decades. See J. G. Terrill, *The St. Charles' Camp-Meeting, Embodying Its History and Several Sermons by Leading Ministers, with Some Practical Suggestions Concerning Camp-Meeting Management* (Chicago: T. B. Arnold, 1883).

[I was] operating in prayer meeting to make this a test of those who were ready for the blessing of holiness: That they must kiss my great toe.

Soon the [presiding] elder said to me, "The people are clamoring to have you preach."

"Well," said I, "if I do, I must meet the false theology of B. against Methodism."

"O, no," said he. "A camp meeting is no place to set up any such defense."

What, thought I, Methodism can unrebuked be preached down but not defended at a Methodist camp meeting? But at night I accepted the invitation to preach in one of the tents, and God gave us a good time while praying for the blessing of holiness. One of our preachers' wives was sanctified in that meeting.[594]

I went again to [the M.E. Church at] St. Charles. A new preacher was appointed to St. Charles and proved to /329/ be a very good and kindhearted man, and we had a glorious revival.

About New Year's Day [1858] we went to Elgin where, after some hard conflict, the work of holiness broke out openly and God and holiness became very popular.[595] The preacher took a stand with us and

---

[594] JGT omits this account and instead gives a different account of Redfield's ministry at the St. Charles camp meeting, based apparently on other sources or his own recollections (318–19). Terrill speaks of revival breaking out and says, "This was the beginning of better days for the people of God in this section of the country. In the following winter—1857–1858—memorable as that of the great revival, these [revived Methodist] preachers, all aflame, entered into the work with a zeal born of the Holy Ghost, and many were the victories for Christ, strong and permanent. The work in what was called the 'Fox River region' took on a type of thoroughness and clearness that made the converts marked and distinct wherever they went. Some were called Redfieldites who had never seen or heard of Mr. Redfield" (319).

[595] JGT says on page 329, "About the first of January [1858] he went to Elgin, Illinois." In the intervening ten pages Terrill narrates more of Redfield's ministry and related developments, mainly through quotations from Redfield letters of July 4 and December 21, 1857, and from William Kendall letters of August 21, September 16, and November 5, 1857. The September 16 letter is from Kendall to B. T. Roberts. In this section Terrill refers to Roberts' first Genesee Conference trial and to William Kendall's death. On page 328 Terrill begins a new chapter (chapter 51) with the statement, "In December, 1857, we find Mr. Redfield in St. Charles, Illinois, again, endeavoring to break through the crust of which he spoke in a former letter; but for some reason, never explained, he was unable to reach the signal victory here, which he experienced in other places."

promised to keep up this old Methodist standard.[596] But he soon failed to keep his promise, and those who were my warmest friends could not endure me in a very short time. One said to me on [my] leaving [Elgin,] "Anytime you want money, say $50, send on to me, and it shall be forthcoming." But the Methodist preacher had so far poisoned his mind that in a few months he did not want to see me or know me.

At this place some eleven Jonahs were routed and partially revived and promised to go to work in the vineyard, but [they] soon fell back again into slumber.

XLIV. Revival in Marengo and Woodstock, Illinois

From here I was invited to go to M. [Marengo, Illinois] where a revival was in progress and some sixty were the fruits thus far.[597] I listened to the testimony of some and found it about [like] this. "Well," said one lady, "I have not yet made up my mind to go back to the world," and another said, "I am much pleased to know that some of my friends are getting to be religious." I saw that a great part was indeed superficial.

My first sermon, which was to show the privilege of believers to go over and live in the Land of Beulah, so shocked them that some of the old members could not endure me and wished I would leave town again. Out of the sixty, not more than twelve, it was said, but what banked the cause. But soon our house was filled, and frequently long before the hour of preaching. The spirit of revival swept the place. Almost the entire whisky shops were closed [sic], and the worst of the

---

[596] JGT identifies the preacher as "Rev. C. M. Woodward, who knew many of the ministers in the Genesee Conference, of which he had been a member" and gives more details about this meeting (329–30). According to Ray Allen, Charles M. Woodward was admitted to the Rock River Conference in 1854 after having served in the Genesee Conference and died at Mt. Carroll, Illinois, September 1, 1862 (Allen, *Century,* 130). Allen spells the name "Woodard."

[597] JGT: "While engaged at Elgin, Mr. Redfield was visited by Mr. M. L. Hart, of Marengo, a village twenty-five miles away, at the instance of the official board of the Methodist Church, to request him to assist in a revival at that place" (330). M. L. Hart was the father of E. P. Hart, who was converted subsequently to Redfield's revival in Marengo and eventually became the second general superintendent of the Free Methodist Church. See JGT, 332–33; Edward Payson Hart, *Reminiscences of Early Free Methodism* (Chicago: Free Methodist Publishing House, 1903). Hart narrates Redfield's revival in Marengo, noting, "On the evening of Wednesday, February 3, 1858, Doctor Redfield began his labors in the Methodist Episcopal church at Marengo, Illinois" (10).

people were converted.[598] So great was the interest that people came from five to twenty miles distance, and some of them would get converted in their sleighs on their way home.[599]

Could the Methodist Church have been persuaded to take care of this work rather than to contend against it, they might now have spread this work and have reaped a glorious harvest. The [presiding] elder told me that though this was the right kind of work, "But," said he, "it will harm us, as we /330/ cannot supply the kind of preachers who will be acceptable to the people after they have been interested in this."[600]

Bro. F. of W. now came to invite me to go to W. [Woodstock, Illi-

---

[598] The Rock River Conference *Minutes* provide some evidence of this revival. Marengo reported a total of 116 members in 1857; a year later the total was 222, including 100 probationers. The church's decline over the next three years (to 115 in 1861) presumably reflects in part the formation of the Free Methodist congregation there in 1860.

The *History of McHenry County* refers to a winter 1856–57 revival in Marengo as "one of the most remarkable revivals ever known in the West. . . . It commenced in the fall and lasted till spring with no decrease of interest. . . . From far and near the people gathered, filling the house to overflow. The result of this revival was the conversion of over 400 souls" (*History of McHenry County, Illinois* [Chicago: Inter-State Publishing Co., 1885], 743). Both this description and the Marengo M.E. membership statistics (as well as Terrill's description; see below) suggest this was more likely the 1858 Redfield revival than one a year earlier, though this is uncertain. The Marengo M.E. Church was organized just twenty years earlier, in 1838. Some of its early members in 1860 became members of the new F.M. congregation.

[599] JGT: "Many were converted in their wagons on their way home. The number converted has been estimated at from four to five hundred. Every whisky-shop in the place was closed, and many of the worst of people were converted" (333). JGT gives more details about this revival.

[600] JGT: "The presiding elder could but endorse the character of the work, but thought in the end it would work harm, as it would be impossible to supply it with preachers who would be acceptable to the people—that is, it was unfortunate to have such a revival, because there were so few preachers in the conference who were in sympathy with it" (337). On pages 334–36 Terrill gives more information about the Marengo revival. He notes that in the Marengo M.E. Church "there were a number of deeply experienced Christians" who supported Redfield. "One of these was 'Mother Cobb,' who for many years was the only living witness to the experience of perfect love in all those parts. She had then walked in the steady light of it for more than forty years." See Mary Weems Chapman, *Mother Cobb or Sixty Years' Walk with God* (Chicago: T. B. Arnold, 1896). In this book the Redfield revival at Marengo is narrated on pages 63–65, based partly on JGT.

nois], about twelve miles distant.[601] I found a hard people. Presbyterians, Baptists, and Universalists tried what they could to put us down. We had our meeting in a hall. One of the deacons of another church would come to the outer door and ask the people when they left if they did [not] feel ashamed to be seen in a Methodist meeting. But this did not have the [desired] effect. They then sent off for an able minister to charm off our congregation, but that would not do. They next sent me a threatening letter, saying if I did not leave town in two days, I should be blessed with a coat of tar and feathers and ridden out of town on a rail.

The mob collected a number of times, and it was currently reported that one or more clergymen were in [on] the secret, and of the abettors. One night they [i.e., the mob] got too drunk for their work and then got to fighting among themselves. I saw them a number of nights in a sly place, and to appearance they had the very means to carry out their threat of giving me a coat of tar and feathers.

One night while passing out I managed to keep so near to the ladies that the mob would not attempt it. I went home guarded for near a fortnight, although they probably thought my company to be merely accidental.

Among the outsiders I was accused of gambling, and it was currently reported by one man that he saw me lose $100 in Chicago in playing a game at cards; by another that as I was leaving M. [Marengo] to go there [to Woodstock] I stopped at a gambling saloon and won $40, and that I [had] made a bargain with those who came to invite me to go to W. [that] I would first have them pay me $50 and then $5.00 a head for all converts.

When in spite of all this God was with us, the Congregational minister and the Baptist people with some others got up a union prayer meeting and invited the Universalist /331/ preacher and then asked me if I would not go. I said "No, I have no fellowship with infidels, and I believe this to be a plot to compel me to show my colors." When they had put in that Universalist, I doubt not it was to put an odor there that would keep me off, and then [they would] make capital out of what they would call my bigotry.

---

[601] JGT: "From Marengo, Mr. Redfield went to Woodstock, the county seat, twelve miles distant" (338). Woodstock, in McHenry County, is about twelve miles northeast of Marengo and about twelve miles south of the Wisconsin state line. With this Terrill begins a new chapter, his chapter 52. Here again Terrill provides additional information not in Redfield's text and does not follow Redfield's text closely.

For awhile they were distressing our converts, one of whom [was] the high sheriff, who came to me and said he felt afflicted to learn that I would not patronize the union prayer meeting. I told him it was all a plot to create a prejudice against me, and I desired him to suspend his judgment for a short time and he would learn that it was all a trick to upset what they could not direct nor contravene, and [thus] ruin this revival.

I then took occasion to preach to the people and tell them my reasons for withholding my countenance to that union plot. I said, "I have known the Presbyterian and Baptist people for many years and in many places," and I knew that as a people they had no fellowship with Universalists. "But," said I, "it seems that they are all married together here and are in harmony."

When I thus publicly advertised the marriage between the Universalists, Baptists and Presbyterian people, they tried to shake off their new spouse. But they [i.e., the Universalists] would not be shaken off and complained bitterly that the Presbyterians and Baptists were so bigoted.

All of this failed to break us up or drain off our congregation. Then the Universalist preacher talked to his people, saying, "Why do you go up into the hall to hear Redfield preach holiness? If you want it, I can preach holiness for you" (and I added to someone, "Yes, or race horses, dance, or playing cards, as well!")[602]

Before leaving W., one of my old signs again appeared and I said to [my wife] Mattie, "We must spend next winter in St. Louis." I had felt more than twenty years before that I had a work to /332/ do in that region, although I did not know the [precise] location, having never been there. I knew nobody there.

I had had another sign some twelve or fourteen years before and followed it to two places and found great success. But I then knew that I had not reached the limits [of where God was directing me]. But

---

[602] On pages 339–42 JGT provides a considerable amount of additional information about Redfield's ministry during this period, some apparently from Terrill's own recollection. He writes, "The revival swept the town and the surrounding country. Every county officer, includ[ing] the sheriff and the judge, nearly every lawyer, and many other prominent men, were converted. One lawyer became a traveling preacher in the Methodist Episcopal Church, and the sheriff became a useful local preacher" (340–41). This was a fairly new M.E. church; it first appears in the Rock River Conference *Minutes* in 1857, with 98 members. A year later (August 1858) it reported 166 members, including 69 probationers—presumably the fruit of the Redfield revival. It then declined over the next three years.

[now] taking a map and finding the range, I found that all three of my signs must have a point of a destination at or about St. Louis, [Missouri].[603]

But not feeling that I must go till another winter, and learning that the brethren in the East had taken a good and strong stand, [I decided to return there for awhile]. Although Bro. Kendall had passed beyond the flood, yet God had raised up the very man on whom I had had my eye as one that would yet leave his mark for God. I mean BTR [B. T. Roberts]. I learned moreover that with his usual daring to identify himself with right, however unpopular, [Roberts had reached the point of no return. I learned] the further fact that he now with Bro. McC. [McCreery] [had] passed the Rubicon and, as I saw, had taken down the bridges, although they thought not.[604]

I [therefore] went to Pekin [New York] General Q M [general quarterly meeting], the first I ever attended. I found a band of brethren and sisters who, having the awful power of God in their souls, presented a bold, firm front, and with a vigor of purpose [were] prepared to open the fire upon all ungodliness.[605] I listened in a transport of joy and hope as my mind ran over the past and the many conflicts I had passed. I had so often, like one of the old prophets, complained to God that "the altars of God were tumbled and the prophets slain and I am left alone, and they seek my life." But here I saw a little band, and they gave me a good report of the balance of "the seven thousand who had not bowed the knee to Baal" [cf. I Kings 19:10, 18].

I then gave [this small band] a little history of my efforts in the West to bring Methodists back to Methodism, and of the toil and opposition and how disheartened I felt at the prospect of doing anything

---

[603] JGT omits this section.

[604] Redfield so runs clauses together in this paragraph that it can be made intelligible only by rewriting it or by inserting the bracketed words. I have opted for the latter in order to preserve Redfield's actual language.

[605] JGT here begins a new chapter (his chapter 53) stating, "Soon after the St. Charles camp meeting, Mr. Redfield made a visit to Western New York. At Pekin, in Niagara county, he found a general quarterly meeting, the first of the kind he had ever attended. Here he met with preachers and laymen from afar, who had gathered to wait upon God for baptisms of power for the Lord's work. His heart was cheered with their boldness and freedom, and unction" (343). This apparently was in the summer of 1858, for Terrill says, "That very fall, but a few months after this, the work of expulsion commenced. Mr. Roberts and Mr. M'Creery were expelled from the conference and the church." Terrill says that in August 1858, however, Redfield returned to Illinois (343), as Redfield notes a bit later.

more. Then Sister R. [Ellen Roberts] reported how God had enabled her to hold on. Some from Syracuse and a goodly number of other places reported [spiritual life] where I had feared that all were killed out.

I then tried to urge upon Bro. R. [Roberts and Bro.] McC. [McCreery] the need of a firm, bold stand for vital godliness, and to keep within the /333/ rules of our Discipline, to organize bands and in them work to the end of re-establishing primitive Methodism. They had for a good while been operating in this way.[606] I then told them, "If you continue in this thing, you will surely be cut off from the church. For I am convinced [that] without a change in the powers that be in a spiritual point of view, you must either win the people back to Methodism in such numbers that they will fear to disturb you [or else you will be forced out]. Now, you labor on here, and I will go back and finish my labors there."

XLV. Ministry in Wisconsin

We came back [to Illinois] by way of Green Bay and Appleton.[607] When in Appleton I met with an old friend, a Methodist preacher whom I had befriended.[608] I saw he looked confused and hung his head and appeared strange. I did not know but he might have heard the news from my enemies East who, when it was told that I was going to visit the East [i.e., West?] said, "That cannot be, for Redfield is in state's prison in New Jersey and has been for three years."

Well, when this preacher hemmed and hawed, hung his head, and left the house, the good sister [where we were staying] said, "Did you see how strange and confused this preacher was?"

"Yes," said I, "and what's the matter with him?"

"Well," said she, "he has been reporting that Redfield was caught at last in passing counterfeit money in Iowa and was in jail, and he must feel very bad to see how soon his falsehoods are being brought to light."

---

[606] JGT: "He [Redfield] found that the work had been kept alive in some places, by the organization of bands, made up of those who enjoyed perfect love and were contending earnestly for real Methodism" (343). Redfield's point is that such "bands" were provided for in the M.E. *Book of Discipline.*

[607] Redfield probably means that he and his wife traveled by steamship from Buffalo (or another port) through the Great Lakes to Green Bay, Wisconsin, and then from there by train.

[608] JGT omits this reference to ministry in Wisconsin but provides more information about Redfield's ministry in Illinois, mainly through Redfield's letters to Sister Kendall (343–50).

I went on to another place where a friend said, "Why, I heard you was caught with a gang of horse thieves and was now shut up in jail!"

So I saw [that] in my absence from the East the enemies of God [there] and some of the preachers took the occasion to report me as in state's prison. My absence from the East gave currency to the report that I was in two jails, one for horse stealing and the other for passing counterfeit money! And I heard of another Methodist preacher who said he only wished he could get a clue at me and make a charge stick, and he would gladly have me shut up in prison. I saw full well that I had a host of deadly enemies who would ruin me if they could. I [?] since I am glad to get these items /334/ in my history, for I shall note them in my life.

In all these matters I began to learn how great and violent were my enemies. O how I wished I could unfold to them my heart, my motives, and my sacrifices in trying to build up the cause of God under the name of Methodism. I sometimes tried to inform them of the strange means by which I was moved, and then I was called a fanatic, a crazy. And yet [they] spoke of me as if they believed me to be in my right mind, and purposely doing wrong. The true fact was, they knew that old-fashioned Methodism would take with the people, and they were jealous of me. Yet in the midst of all this opposition I still clung to the hope that Methodism would be reformed and that the plan East and West would yet win its way to the heart of the people.[609]

I went to M. [Marengo, Illinois?] on my way to G. Am., and of all the agonizing times which I ever endured the night before we went [to a new place], this was the worst.[610] My wife said she was sure the devil

---

609 An important point, in terms of Redfield's perspective: True Methodism would win the people's hearts if it was faithfully presented, but opposing preachers would not allow this to happen. Here Redfield cites the motive of jealousy; in other places he cites motives of pride, popularity, and social acceptance as reasons for Methodist preachers' opposition to "old-fashioned Methodism." (JGT omits this reflection.)

610 It is difficult here to correlate Redfield's manuscript with Terrill's book because in this section Terrill relies little on the manuscript, basing his account mainly on Redfield's letters, his own recollections, and other sources. However, the struggle Redfield describes here seems to be what Terrill refers to on page 347: "Soon after this camp meeting Mr. Redfield began to get ready to go to St. Louis. At the same time he became greatly tempted about going. For several days this lasted, during which Mrs. Redfield advised against going, and finally determined she would not go. But during a season of prayer at the house of a friend, they both obtained the victory, and went forward cheerfully to their work." It is not clear what "G. Am." refers to; "M." may be Marengo.

was in the room, for she could see him. But the awful horror of darkness which overwhelmed me, I then thought I never knew its equal. In my mind I could see a flood of trouble which would forever make an end of me and of my future usefulness. But what, I could not tell. I might be mobbed. I might be made to feel the cruel power of falsehoods, or at best wear a coat of tar and feathers. Mattie was in the same fearful mood of mind, and so were our friends who were there.[611]

Mattie said, "Now, I think this is a friendly warning, and we ought not to go."

I said, "I shall go, for there is a still voice back of all saying this may be of the devil, who knows that we are going to have a triumph if we go and is taking this course to stop us. And I shall go."

"Well," said Mattie, "I cannot go."

"Yes." said I, "Trusting in God, I shall go, and you must go with me."

With two heavy hearts we started, and reached the house of Bro. O. J. [Osgood Joslyn], who likewise [was] deeply sympathetic with us in our awful temptation. We had a little prayer meeting at his house, and God gave /335/ me power to shed a few tears. O the relief which I felt, for it did seem that I had endured all that I could live under without going distracted. With this trifling relief, I felt that it was more than probable that the devil, seeing what would follow, made this terrible assault to prevent us from going.

We reached the place and in the name of our God we set up our banners, and such demonstrations of power I have scarcely ever felt and seen before. And in the midst of our greatest gust, I distinctly saw and read my name written in blood, and knew it to be in the Lamb's Book of Life. I was so overwhelmed at the sight that I could but cover my face and sob with emotion. I stated to the congregation what I saw, and my wife declared that she saw hers at the same time. The mystery of our conflict with Satan was now revealed. The triumphs of that hour will never be forgotten by many who were present.[612]

We now went back once more to St. Charles on our way to St.

JGT says earlier, "About this time [August of 1858, apparently] was held the last quarterly meeting for the Elgin charge [M.E. Church], and in the quarterly conference, of which the writer was a member and present at the time, the license of Mr. Redfield as a local preacher was renewed without any opposition. He was also given a written recommendation as a revivalist. Mr. Redfield was not present when this was done" (345).

[611] Probably in Marengo, Illinois.

[612] It is not clear where these meetings were held.

Louis.[613] We found a new preacher sent from conference, and our friends were anxious to have us stop and hold some meetings in company with the preacher. But he evidently felt unwilling, and that I was in his way. His wife asked someone, "If Redfield must preach, why could he not go off among the heathen?" I answered the one who told me that I could hardly find a more appropriate field for such a purpose than St. Charles. They [sic] further said I had no right to stay in that place. I said, "I must live somewhere."

The official board asked to have me invited ~~to help~~. The preacher did not like to have me invited, and when the vote was taken the majority favored my staying. But the preacher recorded the votes as a tie and then cast his own against me. The next I heard was that someone who favored the views of the preacher had said to the rowdy boys that if they would tar and feather me and my wife, that /336/ they would see them screened from all harm.[614] I well knew that I had outside friends among sinners who would never allow an indignity like that to be perpetrated without contending for me by manual force, and I feared that blood might be unluckily shed. Then in addition to all other slander I should bear the name of a disturber of the peace. So I said to my wife, "We will leave at once," and [we] did so.

We had a little prayer meeting at the house of Bro. O. [Osgood] before leaving[615] and I was so impressed with the saying of Paul. I go bound in spirit to St. Louis, not knowing what shall befall me save that

---

[613] JGT: "On their way to St. Louis they stopped for a few days at St. Charles" (347).

[614] Terrill's account is slightly different: "When the vote was taken on granting the petition [to have Redfield minister at the St. Charles church], nine were in favor if it, and five opposed. But such was the opposition of the five that the majority offered to leave the matter to the pastor, and he decided against it" (347).

[615] Someone has placed an X before "We" and another after "Bro. O." These may be Terrill's marks; he here begins a new chapter (chapter 54), stating, "Just before the time came to start for St. Louis, a few of Mr. Redfield's friends came together for a season of prayer" (351). In the intervening pages (347–50) Terrill includes letters from Redfield to Sister Kendall, dated "St. Charles, Ill., October 7, 1858" and October 31, 1858, also from St. Charles. The second letter is signed, "J. W. and Mattie Redfield." In it Redfield comments, "If the church here does not take the stand for the straight way, we shall leave soon for our southern tour. We expected to have been off before this time, but Mattie's health and some unfinished business have hitherto prevent. But we hope by the 10th or 15th of next month, at most, to be on our way." By "southern tour" Redfield apparently means traveling to St. Louis.

the Holy Ghost witnesseth, saying that in every city bonds and afflictions abide me [cf. Acts 20:22–23]. I wish I could have quoted the balance and say that none of these things move me. But I could not, for if I had dared to run, I would not have gone. I was confident that God said, "Go to St. Louis," and yet I knew no one there, and besides I had not money enough to run the hazard of a long and expensive journey. But I dared not do otherwise than to start.

We rode on the cars about one hundred miles and had to stop. Then a good friend said to me, unasked, "I have a little money for you." This I felt was indeed a Godsend.[616]

The next day we rode to Burlington, [Iowa] on the [Mississippi] River, and again had to stop nearly a week to get a conveyance down the river, as it was late in the fall and only now and then a strolling[?] boat could be expected.[617] Then a boat came along bound for St. Louis. We were soon on board and on our way down to the place I had so much dreaded, having an ill omen and presentiment that I was going into a pitfall.

XLVI. St. Louis, Missouri, 1858–59

We first put up at a public house where we had to pay $4.00 a day. I knew we could not endure that but a few days, so I spent the day in hunting up a boarding house where the charges varied from $30 to $60 a month.[618] I did not know but that I must leave the city and go into the country at once. But before /337/ the day ended I found one place where I could get board for $12.50 a week. I must pay in advance, but

---

[616] JGT: "They stopped at Princeton, in Bureau Co., Illinois, about one hundred miles on the way, to visit Rev. Charles French, with whom he had labored in St. Charles, the winter before. While here, a friend said to him, unasked, 'I have some money for you,' and handed him enough to take him to his destination and a little more" (351). Terrill here inserts a Nov. 18, 1858, letter from Redfield to Sister Kendall, written in Princeton (351–53). In the letter Redfield says, "God held me responsible for fidelity, and not for success" (353).

[617] JGT: "The next day after receiving the money from his friend, they took the train for Burlington, Iowa, where they expected to take a steamer for St. Louis. Here they had to wait a week, as it was late in the season, and many of the boats had stopped running" (354).

[618] Redfield provides more details than does Terrill, who writes, "On reaching St. Louis they put up at a hotel, at great expense. In a few days he began to look for cheaper quarters" (354). Although JGT says, "In a few days," Redfield's text gives the impression that he immediately began looking for a cheaper place after spending one night in the public house.

it was the best I could do so I paid a part down, got my trunks removed, and then went in pursuit of a North Methodist preacher.[619]

Having seen quotations from the *Central [Christian] Advocate* saying that the south church [i.e., M.E. Church, South] would impose on strangers by pretending to be the North Methodists,[620] I took the precaution to get letters of introduction to a North Methodist preacher so as not to be caught in a slaveholding church. I found it quite difficult to find anyone who knew anything about such a church or preacher as my letters referred to. I however [eventually] found it and the preacher, and gave in my letters of church membership.[621] We reached St. Louis in the latter part of November 1858. Our letters were read before the society, giving day, date, and church from which we came, viz., Elgin, Illinois.

I was invited by the pastor on the fifth of December to preach in his church, and I preached twice or three times more. Then someone of their official board called for a vote of the official [board] requesting the pastor to invite me to assist him in a protracted meeting. But the pastor refused to permit any official action to be taken, saying that he held the reins of that pulpit and should do as he pleased about inviting me to help him. "And," said he, "if you are dissatisfied with me and want Dr. R. to take my place, I will pack my carpetbag and leave."

I at the time knew nothing of the matter, as I did not go to the official meetings. But perceiving that I should make something of a stay, and feeling unable to pay so enormous a sum for board, and farther learning that the house I was in was not free from suspicion, I went in quest of another boarding house. What I found [was a place] where I could get board for $5.00 a week, and some credit on that.

But on [my] going to leave the house where I was, in which I had staid about four days, the woman demanded $12.50, nor would she let my trunks leave till it was paid. In the meantime I found my [dollar] draft to be imperfect and was compelled to send it back by mail to get it

---

[619] I.e., a preacher of the M.E. Church, not of the M.E. Church, South.

[620] JGT: "There were plenty of southern Methodist churches, but he desired a northern church, as he did not feel free to become identified with a slaveholding people" (354).

[621] JGT adds details: "He had letters of introduction to Rev. Dr. Williams, but no one seemed to know his residence. Sunday morning came, and he found the Ebenezer church and Dr. Williams its pastor. At the close of the morning sermon, he handed the pastor his letters of introduction, also their church letters" (354). Thomas Williams was appointed pastor of the Ebenezer M.E. Church in May, 1858, but served only one year. In 1859 he became president of the University of Missouri, Jefferson City. *Minutes,* Missouri Conference.

perfected before I /338/ could make a draft upon it, and I had to pawn my watch as security for the odd dollars yet due. I had paid all I could well spare in advance, and $7.00 was yet due. But before my draft came back perfected, an honest Jew, knowing the circumstances, went to the woman, paid my bill and took up my watch, for which I have been very grateful.

Soon my draft came, and I redeemed my watch and felt whole for awhile. But now news came to me of the proceedings of the official board and of the protest of the preacher against being advised by them about inviting me to help him. I said nothing to anyone but my wife about the matter. But I felt a presentiment that trouble was brewing, for I knew that jealousy was doing its work. So I said to my wife, "Mattie, we must leave St. Louis, for I am sure that trouble is brewing, and if it has already begun this violently, there is no knowing where it will end."

All this time the preacher would put on his best airs to me personally. But I had seen such things before. The worst enemy through jealousy I had as yet had would speak highly of me to my wife and very smilingly to me, and yet to my back was doing his worst to put me down.[622]

When I told my wife that we must leave, she said to me in a decided tone, "I shall not leave, and you shall not. God has sent us here, and we must and will fulfill our mission."

So we made up our mind that if we were going to have trouble in the church, we would go to the houses of the people and try in that way to fill our mission.[623] I was so overcome that I could not help weeping

---

[622] About this time (in January 1859) Joseph Brooks, editor of the *Central Christian Advocate* in St. Louis, visited the Ebenezer church (probably Sunday evening, January 16) and commented on the congregation and its pastor. He wrote, "The house was crowded to its utmost capacity; much of the larger portion, consisting of young men. A more intellectual looking, and attentive congregation, it has seldom, if ever, been our privilege to address. To the most casual observer, it must be apparent tat the church at Ebenezer is not accustomed to a namby pamby gospel; but are fed with substantial food." He added, "The intellectual ability and profound attainments in divinity which characterise the pastor, Rev. Thomas Williams, D. D., are producing their wanted fruits in his congregation. Quite a number of souls have been happily converted, the membership have been greatly advanced in holiness of heart and life, and many valuable accessions to the Church have been made." Editorial, "A Prosperous Congregation," *Central Christian Advocate* 3, no. 2 (18 Jan. 1859), 2.

[623] Terrill or someone else has inserted large Xs in the text before "mind" and after "we." These occur at the beginning and end of a line of manuscript.

in the streets. I felt so heartbroken to be pushed so hard by the Lord to go, and at my own cost, and then to be met by opposers in the ministry who would do all they could to crush me and ruin my influence. But here I was, and there was no telling how long I should be permitted to do anything. So I must work the best I could. We made some visits, and God began a good work which still lives. But this was called sowing dissension.

I then heard that there was an invitation for me to go over to the /339/ colored people's church and preach to them. I enjoined upon them secrecy and told my wife to say nothing about where we were going, lest the white people should find it out and some of them would go there, too. Then I knew that I should be charged with drawing them off from Ebenezer Church.

The first night God came down in power. Not a large congregation, but all the sinners among the colored people but one came out and got religion that night. Of course this could not be kept a secret, and I doubt not [it was] made one of the facts to prove that I was an abolitionist and was drawing our people off from the M.E. Church.

I was permitted occasionally to preach in the [Ebenezer] Church, to which I [now] belonged, but it was after a great deal of outside pressure had been applied. All this was due to the interest which the people felt in the (to them) novel and interesting doctrine of holiness as held and preached by our fathers. The people, and many from other churches, would try to find out when I was going to preach, and then would fill the house.

Then the pastor would resort to tricks to get a congregation. The sexton told me he had requested him to say to enquirers as they came to the door that Dr. Redfield was going to preach, and [thus] getting a good house full would preach himself. Of course that kind of trick was short-lasting indeed. At such times the pastor would evidently try to direct the minds of the people [away] from that class of truth which was producing a wonderful work in the salvation of souls.

[While] in company with the preacher one day, I felt desirous to convince him of my honesty and sincerity—especially as I had heard that he called me a fanatic. Other preachers said that I was an impostor pretending to be a Methodist but was [really] a Campbellite. And yet there [among the Methodists] I had my licenses regularly renewed for over twenty years.

But without adverting to what I had heard, I said, "Well, Dr. [Williams], I get so burdened for St. Louis, it seems I must see salvation come or I cannot endure the agony."

"Oh," said he, "I never allow myself to get such burdens. If they do come, I go to bed and sleep them off."

So I /340/ should not awake any chord of sympathy from him. I then said, "Well, Dr., I know that I am a sound Methodist and that even yourself cannot find in any of my preaching anything at variance with John Wesley."

"But," said he, "there are many of us Methodist preachers who do not believe with John Wesley."

When the quarterly meeting conference came around [at the Ebenezer Church], a vote was called for again. The vote stood unanimous (except [for] one man) inviting me to stay and hold meetings from one to three weeks, as I could. When the pastor saw the unanimity of the vote, "Well," said he, "you give us a good collection [on Sunday], and after next Tuesday he may go on and preach. (The vote was taken on Friday. I was not present, but it was reported to me by one that was).

The night before [the] turn for me to begin, according to vote, I felt a kind of presentiment that something would happen to trammel me. So I went in good season [i.e., a bit early, and found that] the preacher had praised a presiding elder who was a great foe to the doctrines of Methodism. As was afterwards told to me, [he] was in the habit of ridiculing our rules. He would sometimes go out into promiscuous assemblies [i.e., gatherings of men and women together] or parties at the houses of the people and try to interest them by singing Negro songs, [and] then go on and preach in sport and mimic some old Christians by interlarding his preaching with shouts.

When I arrived and went in at the door, this elder had passed the preliminaries and was hunting up his text. The pastor, seeing me and probably supposing I was not prepared to preach, demanded of me that I come forward at once and preach.[624]

I had felt an impression that I had better take a *Discipline* with me and a copy of J. Hartwell's collection from John Wesley on the subject of sanctification. I went on with my discourse, and in the midst of it I thought it best to say to the congregation that the official board had invited me to stay and preach from one to three weeks. "But," said I, "if

---

[624] JGT: "'But when I arrived at the church, a presiding elder, who was known to be an opposer of the doctrine of holiness, was in the pulpit, and had commenced the service. After the singing and prayer, Doctor W___ said to me, "Come forward and preach." I went into the pulpit and commenced'" (356). At services where he was scheduled to preach, Redfield often arrived just a few minutes before the preaching time, not at the beginning of the service. In this instance, it is possible that Redfield misread the situation, and that the presiding elder was about to preach simply because Redfield not yet arrived.

I do, it is due to you to know what I am." I then said, "I am a Methodist," and drawing the *Discipline* from my pocket [I] stated the rules to which I had subscribed and tried to live up to. Again I said, "You may want to know what are my views on the doctrine of holiness." Then drawing the /341/ extracts from Wesley [I] said, "Here are my views, straight out of Wesley's *Works*" (giving page and section). "And now," said I, "if I stay I must preach the same class of truths which I have been preaching since I have been here. And," said I, "I think it is due [you] to make this frank statement, that if I stay I must so preach the whole law that I can meet it again [at the judgment]. And I think it is due to me to know whether you want and will abide Bible truth. So I would ask all saints and sinners to say by vote whether you—" —and then the preacher caught me sharply by the arm and said to me, "Stop, sir. I am responsible for this pulpit."

I felt calm and turning to him said, "Dr., I was not going to transcend the proprieties of the pulpit."

"Stop, stop, Sir," said he. "I am responsible for this pulpit."

I tried again and again to make an explanation, but he forbade it and then commanded me to go on and finish my sermon. And this was reported to be an effort on my part to take a vote of the congregation whether I or the pastor should occupy the pulpit! As I had been accused of being unsound in the faith and an impostor, I felt I had a right to ask if that congregation desired and would sustain that class of truth which demanded the heart. And while I was shaken and stopped, I felt unearthly power and glory sustaining me.

The preacher bid me go on and finish my sermon, and such a sustaining power as I felt was truly rich indeed, beyond description. I had all through my preaching felt that God was very nigh and [that he] said to my heart, "I want you to preach the straight truth for once. Will you?"

My heart said, "I will."

"But if you do, you will be stopped."

"Well," said I, "I will go on till I am stopped."

"Well, you will probably never be permitted to preach again."

"Well, I will go the straight way for this once, if this is the end of my preaching."

Among others, Mary F. took a bold stand for the right. [She] went home and stripped her hat of all ornaments and took off her jewelry. One of those preachers[625] heard the facts and went to her and exhorted with her, [trying] if /342/ possible [to] persuade her to put on her orna-

---

625 Redfield does not specify what he means by "those preachers."

ments, saying "There is no religion in dress," and if there was she might bring her dress to church and stay at home herself.

"Well," said she, "you have well nigh [ruined] me by your example and teaching. But I thank God that one man has been found who has dealt faithfully with me, and I am now undeceived[?] and have got salvation."

Some others got up in church and said they felt called of God to stand up in defense of the truth which they had at last got a taste of. All of this but added to the fury of the prejudice which already existed against me. But poor Mary was already a marked victim for consumption. Before she died sent word to have me visit her and then said to me, "I am going to die, but O how glad I am that you have done your duty faithfully. I feel that I am going home, and I shall be a star in your crown of rejoicing, and will come to meet you when you cross the river." O how this one assurance more than a thousand times compensated me for all my suffering and sorrow in St. Louis.[626]

The next night was the time for me to begin to preach. I went in season, feeling impressed that I was going to see farther trouble. On [my] passing up the aisle the pastor stopped me, saying, "I have had a strange letter sent to me from the official board and," said he, "let us go into the parsonage and read it."

I opened it and read:

> St. Louis, January 20th, 1859.
>
> To Rev. Dr. [Thomas] Williams
>
> Dear brother: The undersigned members of the official board of Ebenezer charge have witnessed with regret the unprecedented conduct of Dr. Redfield since the commencement of his labors, and more especially on last night. Shocked at his proceedings, and believing that his labors are calculated to do more harm than good by creating schism and disunion in the church, and feeling an abiding interest in

---

[626] JGT omits this incident regarding Mary but inserts the following two paragraphs:

"C. H. Underwood, at that time a business man in St. Louis, but who was afterwards converted and became a minister of the gospel, once told the writer, that Mr. Redfield's sermon that night was awful, in its arraignment of the unsaved and particularly the unsaved of the church, before the bar of God.

"In the pulpit and around it, were seated, two presiding elders, one church editor, and several city pastors. While the sermon was in progress, these men seemed to listen in breathless amazement. Many were smitten by conviction that night, among whom was Mr. Underwood" (358). C. H. Underwood became the Free Methodist pastor in St. Louis in 1862 (Hogue, *History of the Free Methodist Church,* 2:81).

> the welfare of the church and prosperity of the cause, [we] earnestly request /343/ that you quietly tell Dr. Redfield that he cannot occupy the pulpit any more.
>
> Yours respectfully,
> J. W. Heath
> D. Caughlin
> J. W. Hathaway
> Wm. Schurman

For my life I could not see how so few of the board could reverse the vote of the whole [quarterly] conference. It appeared strange that all this change could take place in so short a time. The [same] complaint [had been] made against me for my conduct before the quarterly conference, and yet they voted me to stay.[627] I said to Dr. Williams, "Can you tell me why there are so few names on this letter?"

"O," said he, "it was the board of trustees, and you know that the trustees can control me and the pulpit. I am sorry," said he, "but I cannot help it. You and I are good friends."

"Well," said I, "Doctor, what do you think I better do? Should I go into the church tonight?"

"I think," said he, "you better not."

I then left the parsonage and asked someone to go in and call out my wife. Then I was met by one who asked me, "What's amiss? Are you going to leave?"

"Yes."

"Well then, something is amiss."

"No," said I, "only the board of trustees have requested the Doctor to shut me out of the pulpit."

One said, "That is a trick of Williams and a friend."

"No," said I, "it cannot be, for I saw the letter and read the names of those who signed it."

Someone whispered it in the church that I was shut out of the pulpit, and when Mr. Williams arose to give out his hymn, a stampede left the church.[628] When I got to my lodgings at an old leader's home, he enquired of me about the matter, and I told him.

"I saw the identical letter. But," said the leader, "I would not sign

---

[627] The meaning of this sentence is obscure, but the intent seems to be as indicated by supplying the bracketed words.

[628] Someone, perhaps Terrill, has placed a large X at the beginning of this sentence. Terrill rewords this as follows: "It was soon whispered through the church, that Mr. Redfield was shut out of the pulpit, and a large proportion of the congregation arose and left the house" (359).

that letter for all Saint Louis, and I believe that Dr. Williams is at the bottom of all this."[629]

The next morning I called on Dr. Williams and requested to see that letter, and took a copy of it. When /344/ I had taken a copy, I asked him to give me and my wife our church letter and incidentally said I thought I should either go into a free state or join one of the North Methodist churches [in St. Louis]. I saw he was glad to get rid of us so quietly. I then took [with me] this copy of the letter sent to Dr. Williams in order to refute the charge of his being the author of that letter.

I then saw one who had charged Mr. W. with the authorship of the letter. Said I, "Brother, this is a copy of the identical letter, and this shows that you were mistaken."

"Who are they [who signed the letter]?"

I read the names.

"Well," said he, "only one of those is a trustee, and now I know that Williams is at the bottom of this whole affair."

This opened my eyes to see that this was a mystery which looked bad indeed. Four names out of nine trustees to [over]rule the whole [quarterly] conference, and to find that but one trustee attempted to rule a whole conference.[630]

I now found that after I left the church on the last night seventy-two persons, and subsequently [a total of] ninety-four, left and proposed to organize, and sent in the following declaration to the official board, setting forth the reasons for doing so:

> To the Members of the Official Board of the Ebenezer charge of the M.E. Church.
> Brethren:
> Whereas by the uncalled-for exercise of official power by a few individuals (our people knew the letter to be a fraud but acted as if it was a genuine official act)[631] at Ebenezer charge in the City of St. Louis has lately taken place whereby a large proportion of the members of said church have been deprived of rights and privileges guaranteed to us, as we believe, by the Word of God and Discipline of

[629] JGT omits these last two sentences and ends the chapter here. He begins his chapter 55 (page 360) with what follows.

[630] Terrill interprets this obscure sentence as follows: "Here, then, were the names of four persons who attempted to rule the whole congregation, and one trustee to rule a whole quarterly conference" (360). It may be in fact that Redfield meant "the whole congregation" rather than "the whole conference."

[631] JGT includes this document but omits Redfield's parenthetical aside (360–62).

said Church;

And whereas we deem it our duty to state the causes which have induced us to separate therefrom as well as to /345/ assure our brethren from whom we have thus separated that in doing so we have no other motive than the promotion of the cause of our Lord Jesus Christ and the exercise of those privileges of which we have lately been deprived by the unlawful exercise of a power never intended to be vested in four men holding official stations in such church;

And whereas we do not believe in the one-man power nor the unlawful exercise by four men of authority never intended to be abused or brought to bear for the accomplishment of an unholy purpose such as the one lately enacted by the four officials in Ebenezer charge, and which act we deem oppressive, unjust, and unjustifiable before God and man;

Therefore, resolved, that we ask the privilege, as we claim the right, of adhering to and continuing in the Methodist Episcopal Church, both from principle as from a firm belief of the doctrines taught therein.

Resolved, that we have the utmost confidence in the Christian character, the holiness of purpose, and unblemished reputation of Rev. Dr. Redfield, a minister of the M.E. Church, and that his close-pointed style of preaching the gospel is the true apostolic way to bring sinners to a saving knowledge of the truth as it is in Jesus Christ.[632]

Resolved, that we hold the mandate issued by the four officials in Ebenezer charge excluding Dr. Redfield from the pulpit, thereby denying him the privilege of preaching to a congregation who assembled for that purpose, as unjustifiable, unauthorized by the Discipline in its object, and ruinous to the church in its results.

Resolved, that this unjustifiable and highhanded breach of trust by the said four officials /346/ deprives us of the social and religious privileges we have heretofore enjoyed in said church. And being thus deprived by the arbitrary act of those four men from the privileges aforesaid, we felt there was no other alternative left us but to separate

---

[632] JGT: "'Resolved, 2. That we have the utmost confidence in the Christian character and the holiness of purpose of Rev. Dr. Redfield, a minister of the Methodist Episcopal Church, and that his close-pointed preaching of the gospel is in accordance with the usage of the primitive church in bringing sinners to a saving knowledge of the truth as it is in Jesus Christ'" (361). Redfield was not, of course, an ordained minister of the M.E. Church but was a local preacher. It is interesting that Terrill omits "unblemished reputation" (perhaps in light of the rumors that continued to be circulated about Redfield) and that he feels free here to modify the language of the document he (i.e., Redfield) is quoting. It is possible, of course, that Terrill had the actual document before him, but more likely he is quoting from (and editing) Redfield's text.

> from and dissolve all connexions with said Ebenezer Church, which we now have done in the fear of Almighty God, who will judge our action and motives in the great day of accounts.
>
> Resolved, that we do hereby solemnly protest in the presence of the Great I Am against the course pursued by the official power in Ebenezer charge towards our worthy brother, Rev. Dr. Redfield, as also against the known wishes of a large majority of the members of said church and congregation.
>
> Resolved, that a committee of three of our number be appointed to attend the next official meeting of Ebenezer charge and lay before them the preamble and these resolutions and ask to have the same entered on record.

To this was attached over ninety names of members.[633]

The people now went in large numbers and demanded their letters. Dr. W. tried to dissuade them and told them that he was not to blame and he was very sorry, but the trustees had done this, but that he and I were [yet] good friends. After giving some less than twenty letters he utterly refused to give any more. When he saw the blame thrown upon the four men named, he to screen them confessed that he was the author of that letter. When I learned that fact I was so shocked, and [I] grieved for the man. I thought, "Poor man, he is ruined," and I lay awake and wept and grieved and prayed for him. I have often felt to pray, "Father forgive, for he knew not what he did."[634]

---

633 Ebenezer M.E. Church had 177 members and 54 probationers (officially) at the time of annual conference in late April, 1859, though it had been quite a bit larger (246 members, 40 probationers) two years earlier. A year later (annual conference in March, 1860), the numbers had dropped to 108 members and 10 probationers—a loss of 113. Most of these presumably became a part of the new congregation formed as a result of Redfield's ministry. The Ebenezer Church recovered somewhat the following year (125 members, 7 probationers), though the church was listed in 1860 as "to be supplied." Joseph Brooks was appointed pastor in 1861. *Minutes,* Missouri Conference, 1856–1861.

634 JGT omits this last comment about Redfield's reaction. He however adds this comment: "There is in this document, addressed to the official board, an evidence of haste. Probably a delay of a few days would have made a great difference in the character of that paper. But there was strife in the air that affected this movement, which was not clearly apprehended by some of the actors" (362). He adds, "The following letter to the *Northern Independent,* written about this time, will make this plain." Here Terrill inserts a letter dated April 20, 1859, and signed "The Spy," entitled "Great Secession in St. Louis" that comments on the above events and on a report that appeared in the *Central Christian Advocate* (JGT, 362–64). Terrill then adds further commentary, placing the events surrounding Redfield's ministry in St. Louis in the larger context

/347/ Chapter [34][635]

A committee now waited on me to desire me to take pastoral charge of the new organization, or at least to preach for them. To which I answered, "I cannot do that unless you are regularly organized and recognized by the [presiding] elder."[636]

They then went to see the [presiding] elder, S. Huffman, who told them he was glad of the move and would recognize them. They next drew up a petition and sent a committee to wait on him and ask to be organized and connected with the Mo. Conference. But Mr. H. had changed his mind and would not do it.

In the meantime many of our people were demanding an organization or they would join other city churches. Some had already joined. But all said they would not go back to Ebenezer. Dr. Williams then came to me and commanded me to bring the people back, or he would expel me and then publish me all over the land.

I said, "I cannot do that. I never sent them away, and I can never bring them back."

"You have split my church all to pieces," said he.

"You know better than that," I answered.

Next came a letter dated St. Louis, January 26, 1859:

> To Rev. Dr. Redfield.
>
> Dear Sir and Brother:
>
> We are pained with the disruption of our church which has occurred recently in this city. With the present light upon the subject, we are persuaded that the responsibility of this unhappy movement rests chiefly with you. That a more perfect understanding may be reached and the schism if possible healed, we respectfully ask an interview with you this afternoon at 3 o'clock at the office of the *Central Christian Advocate,* 97 N. Fourth Street.
>
> We trust you may not fail to meet us.
>
> Signed, Thomas Williams, pastor of Ebenezer Church
> Werter R. Davis, pastor of Hedding Church[637]
> Joseph Brooks, Editor, C. C. Advocate[638]

---

of current controversies within Methodism (364–65).

[635] Terrill also begins a new chapter (his chapter 56, beginning on page 366).

[636] Marston gives a brief summary in *From Age to Age,* 215, 230–31.

[637] Werter R. Davis was professor of natural science at McKendree College and about this time became the first president of Baker University in Kansas (Simpson, *COM,* 278). The appointed pastor in 1858 was John Hageman, but he died in February 1859 and Davis served as interim pastor. The 1859 Minutes list Hedding Church, "to be supplied." *Minutes,* Missouri Conference, 1858, 1859.

[638] The *Central Christian Advocate* became an official M.E. paper by 1856

In a note at the foot of the above letter, the time was changed to ten o'clock next day.

/348/ I did not feel willing to meet these men, especially Dr. Williams, who could be the author of that fraudulent letter, and Mr. Brooks, whom I too well knew from report and otherwise, to be willing to trust myself with them. So instead of going to meet them, I thought it best to answer the call by the following letter:

St. Louis, [Wednesday,] January 26, 1859
1/2 past 11 p.m.

To Rev. Dr. Williams, Brethren Rev. J. Brooks and Professor Davis.

Dear Brethren: Your note of today received after church greatly surprises and grieves me.

I know that Bro. Brooks intimated to me last night that I was the principal cause of the disaffection complained of (I was sure he must know that T. Williams was the real cause). But I could not make myself believe that the sober second thought with him after a fair investigation would at all warrant such a conclusion. I claim to be a North Methodist and have tried to build up the cause of Wesleyan Methodism, and am confident that all of my teachings in this city will bear a comparison in their orthodoxy with our standard authors. I have acted conscientiously and trust your charity will award to me the apparent consistency of this statement.

I cannot see that I am blameworthy if others should show an attachment as Methodists for Methodist doctrines. (I was accused of heresy.) It is thought [that] I could heal, by correcting all the causes of the state of affairs complained of. I honestly believe I am not the cause, and I feel just as sure that I cannot heal what I have not wounded.

I am willing and will do anything consistent with right which you may prescribe to reach such an end. When I took my letter, I did design quietly to change my relation, either to another charge North or go to a free state, hoping to get away from so troublesome a state of things. I knew not /349/ that another person besides myself had any design of taking letters from the chapel.[639] Neither did I state to anyone that I had so done till I learned that others had done the same. Fearing that it would be construed into hostility to Ebenezer Church, I designedly refrained from expressing opinions and likewise from attending preliminary meetings having in view steps of separation. But when it was announced that a new organization was a fixed fact, and

---

general conference action, with Brooks as editor. Simpson, *COM*, 182–83.

[639] JGT: "'I knew not that another person besides myself and wife had any design to take letters'" (358).

the papers were duly made out to petition the [presiding] elder to perfect their organization, and the unanimous desire expressed that I should preach for them till proper officers should make provision for them, I accepted of the invitation and believed in so doing that I was violating no obligation as a good and loyal member of the M.E. Church. If others think I have, and will convince me of the same, I will correct that error if in my power to do so. I know I mean no harm, and trust your generosity will make all due allowance for any mistake, if I have made one.

Now, if you can find one person who has taken a letter and who will state that I by word or act directly or indirectly have incited them to such an act, I will quietly retire out of your midst into a free state. Or if you can find a majority of two-thirds, or one quarter even, who will state that if I were gone out of the city [they] would go back and return their letters to Ebenezer, I will then leave. But will you permit me to ask you, brethren, if your united wisdom cannot devise some way by which the cause of Methodism may be so extended that we all can work without this to me very unpleasant state of things? I am ready to serve the church free of charge. And I ask, will you not try some plan to meet the increasing demands of this great city? Now, will you not try in your wisdom to husband the present tide of religious influence? Are we not brethren, and shall we not harmonize in /350/ the great battle for right? I will do anything that is right at your suggestion to reach so happy an end. God knows I desire to see St. Louis saved and a fair proportion of the people gathered into our beloved North church. And you will, I trust, weigh my motives in an even balance when I state to you that I have no personal interests to serve in the part I act in trying to promote this end.

I have chosen to write what I had to say to you, that I might be able to say all deliberately and that you might review at any time what I have said in making up your mind and in giving your mature counsel.

Yours most respectfully,
J. W. Redfield

The respect paid to the above letter was the following letter:

St. Louis, [Thursday,] January 27, 1859.

To Dr. Redfield.

Dear Brother:

As you have declined to meet with the pastors of the M.E. Church of this city this morning according to our request to endeavor to heal the unfortunate disruption that has taken place since you came to this city, we feel compelled by a stern sense of duty in the fear of God, as pastors of the M.E. Church, to seek an adjustment of this painful affair in another form, so far as your responsibilities are involved in the matter. Therefore at the request of these pastors it becomes my painful duty to request in accordance with the *Discipline* of the M.E. Church that you deposit your letter without ~~fail~~ delay in one of the charges of this city and have your name enrolled on a class book.

Yours respectfully,
Thomas Williams

I had a warning not three hours before, and I believe from the Spirit of God, that trouble was ahead, and said to my wife, "Something is coming, and I feel impressed that I must send /351/ our church letters away at once." So I had a letter written, and our church letters enclosed, and sent off to the Post Office. I then went to church, at the close of which I received the above letter. The pastor, Mr. Williams, then came to me and told me he should now go war to the knife.[640] Others said a plan was in vogue to compel me to leave the city and that a course would be pursued to shut me forever out of all M.E. churches. Nor would I be allowed to preach in a schoolhouse even. Another friend came to me and said he had reason to believe that the preachers would get up a mob by calling me an abolitionist and, said he, "in one hour you may see trouble enough."

"My God," thought I, "is it possible that so much iniquity can exist in M.E. preachers, and especially with those who are raking the [M.E.] South Church with their artillery against slavery, and now can they try to get me mobbed out of this city by the cry of 'abolitionist'?"

The preacher, Mr. Williams, came to me and finally said, "If you will go tomorrow to our church for once, I will then let you off." I promised him I would. My friends finding it out stoutly opposed it, as they were sure there was a plot for me. But I thought I should risk it and keep my word. But I was taken suddenly and severely sick and could not get out in near three weeks, and oh, what I suffered from fear and from grief. Every noise at night seemed to me like the noise of the mob, and I almost expected to see the windows burst in at any moment during the night. [I felt] grief to know that such corrupt men had gotten into the Methodist ministry and would certainly ruin the church.

I became so sick I felt I would not long live without relief. I told my wife, "If I don't get better soon, you must leave my bones in Mis-

---

[640] JGT has, "He came to me soon after, and said, he should now go 'war to the knife'" (370) and at the bottom adds this footnote: "The writer [i.e., Terrill], when a pastor in St. Louis in 1866, was told by a lady that she heard Dr. Williams make that declaration in front of the church where Mr. R— was then laboring."

souri."

I was able in about three weeks to be taken in a closed carriage to our church. When I came in, the singers sung a voluntary,

Jesus look with pitying eye
Savior help me or I die.

On attempting to read a hymn, I found that my eyesight was gone, and I have used glasses ever since.

/352/ Oh how I felt the force and meaning of every word.

I was again able to resume the care of the infant society. I thought it best we should form ourselves into a Methodist Church and take the *Discipline 1844*, minus the episcopacy but adding a rule against slavery. But in lieu thereof [i.e., in lieu of episcopacy] we would adopt a congregational kind[?] of government and wait for [the annual] conference to examine into and adjust our difficulties. To this end I forwarded a copy of the fraudulent letter.[641]

"But," said someone, "there is no use in sending these charges up to conference, for there will nothing be done."

"Nothing be done?" said I. "How can they help it, when they know that a fraud has been committed? What if $5.00 had been the interest involved, and the law should take its course? [It] would send a man to the penitentiary."

"O," said they, "that will be regarded as justifiable diplomacy."

But I did not believe it, so we held on to wait for relief from conference. But sure enough, it was voted out and not allowed to be examined into.[642]

Our work was now extending. We had quite a number of new preaching places, and besides this we had visitors from Richmond, Va., New Orleans, Natchez, Baltimore, Chicago, and other places who, hearing so much said about us, came out of curiosity and said, "This is what we want in our place." "If you will come," said one man from Richmond, "you shall have a chance to build a church free from slavery."[643]

---

[641] Presumably to Bishop Levi Scott, who would preside at the annual conference.

[642] The Missouri Conference held its 1859 annual sessions April 27—May 2.

[643] The implication is that people in these places found out about Redfield's ministry in St. Louis through the Methodist press. Joseph Brooks wrote an editorial in the April 6, 1859 *Central Christian Advocate* in which he mentioned Redfield and commended the Ebenezer M.E. Church for weathering the recent storm. "But a very small number of the old reliable members have gone off with the faction," he wrote. "The Ebenezer charge is left in a sound and healthy state" (Editorial, "Ebenezer Church, St. Louis," *Central Christian Advocate* 3,

While this opposition was raging, a sister U, mother of[644] one of our first preachers, with Sister C., about four hundred miles distant,[645] was led out to pray for us. Though they had not heard a word about us, yet they were impressed that we were in trouble. Knowing me to be a strong and thorough antislavery man, [they] feared it was on that account, and sent a letter to know what the matter was, and if I was not shut up in jail as an abolitionist.

I was now beset by these enemies who tried to annoy me as badly as they could. I felt so heartbroken to think I must be so hard-pressed by the Spirit of the Lord to go in this thorough way, and then to meet /353/ with such furious opposition from M.E. preachers was more than I could endure. I could but examine my whole course and motives and then ask the Lord, if I was right, why are these things permitted?

I was complaining of my doubts to Sister M. She told me (to use her own words), said she, "We came from Cincinnati about three years ago, and I told Thomas (her husband) that I never could join any church here. I was a strong abolitionist and went to the Ebenezer Church, but found it so dead that I could not think of joining it. I felt so bad to see so little of real religion [that] it seemed as if I could not stay. So I went to ask the Lord about it, and the Lord told me to hold on, "for I shall send a man here who will preach the true gospel."

"But," said she, "when you came to town, I never heard a word about it. But I felt something saying to me, 'The man has come who will preach the true gospel,' and I said to Thomas, 'I feel that the preacher has come that God promised to send, and I must go out to meeting and to the Ebenezer Church.' Thomas said my health was so

---

no. 14 [6 April 1859]: 2). A week later Brooks denounced Redfield in an editorial titled "Anti-Methodism." More articles and editorials followed in following issues. The story increasingly became not just Redfield himself but the broader issue of "Nazaritism," connections being made between Redfield and the controversy in western New York. This was also a newspaper battle with charges, countercharges, and reprinted articles appearing in the *Central Christian Advocate,* the *Northern Independent,* the *Buffalo Advocate,* and other official and unofficial Methodist papers.

644 Someone has placed a large X after "While" and another after "mother of" (which are the beginning and end of a line in the manuscript). These may be Terrill's marks, indicating a point to insert additional material, for here Terrill includes several letters from Redfield (pages 371–79), the first dated, "St. Louis, Mo., Dec. 25, 1858" and the last dated March 2, 1859, also from St. Louis.

645 Possibly Sister Harriet Coon in Marengo, Illinois, which by train would have been about four hundred miles from St. Louis.

poor that the doctor would be displeased with me if I did. But I felt I must go, although I had not heard one word about you, and the Ebenezer Church was about two miles off.

"I finally got Thomas to go with me. And sure enough, as soon as we opened the door and saw you in the pulpit, I said to Thomas, 'That is the man that the Lord showed me was coming to St. Louis to preach the true gospel.'"

This was indeed a note of encouragement to me and allayed all my fears for the time being about my being out of the way of duty.[646]

I now heard that B. T. Roberts and J. McC. [Joseph McCreery] were acting in a more independent manner for God, and although both were expelled, yet they worked for and in the M.E. Church for the salvation of souls.[647]

I now had a call to go to Quincy, Illinois, and had so many calls to go to so many places. And withal I felt so strong an impression to send for B. T. Roberts to come to our aid.[648] I felt to say to him, "If God calls upon me to go out as pioneer to rebuild the walls of Methodism, He calls on you to come and take care of them." I now saw why it was that I was so impressed on my first acquaintance with /354/ him when at Niagara St. Church, that he was a man bearing the mark of a high commission from God to do a great work. He came [to St. Louis] and helped to perfect an organization and to make a rule against slavery, and this [one] that could not be evaded.[649]

---

646 JGT here ends the chapter and begins a new chapter (his chapter 57) on page 381.

647 JGT: "Information now came to Mr. Redfield that Mr. Roberts, who had been expelled from the Genesee Conference [in 1858], was laboring under the auspices of a Laymen's Convention held in Albion, N. Y., during the first part of the winter" (381). JGT gives more details about the Roberts and McCreery cases. The story is told in full in Snyder, *Populist Saints.* This was an interim period between Roberts' and McCreery's expulsions from the Genesee Conference of the Methodist Episcopal Church and the organization of the Free Methodist Church in 1860.

648 JGT: "As Mr. Roberts' relation to the Methodist Episcopal Church, at this time was similar to that of their own, the new society in St. Louis now sent for him to come and take Mr. Redfield's place for a season. This would leave Mr. Redfield free to go to Quincy, Illinois, where a field had awaited him for some time" (381). Quincy is on the Mississippi River, about 140 miles northwest of St. Louis.

649 JGT adds: "One of the members, Joseph Wickersham, who for conscience' sake, when seeking perfect love, a few years before, had set at liberty $30,000 worth of slaves, was one of the most eager for such a rule" (381). JGT elaborates on the antislavery sentiment among this group in St. Louis (381–82).

In the East, proscription was doing its worst in turning [M.E. Church] members out of the church and then declaring that they had withdrawn, whereas they knew nothing of the matter. In one instance the preacher forbade them the use of the church [building] when he was not preaching, even to hold prayer meetings, and finally set a guard of men with clubs, dogs, and other weapons to guard the church doors and not allow them to hold a meeting there.[650]

We were expecting our [annual] conference to set our matters right and then to admit us into conference. But when that failed, we had but one forlorn hope left, and that was [in] the general conference, [which was] to sit in about a year. It was expected that they would begin a system of correction which would eventually reach us. But with that failure, we were compelled to setting off independently for ourselves.

The threatenings and slanders were increasing around us in order to put me down. Then our people, to head it off, and without consulting me, got up the following:

> At a meeting of the (at present) congregational Methodist Episcopal Church on Sixth St., the following resolutions were unanimously adopted as an endorsement of the course pursued by Rev. Dr. Redfield in the late difficulties at Ebenezer.
>
> Resolved, that we deem it due to our worthy brother Rev. Dr. Redfield to state that amid all the difficulties, as well as the causes which resulted in the division of the M.E. Church at Ebenezer in this city, he has stood aloof, neither advising or counseling us as to what course we should pursue in relation to said division. But like a man of God, full of love for the salvation of souls and the prosperity of our common Zion, he appeared to weep over the apparent calamities

---

B. T. Roberts received Redfield's letter on February 26, 1859, and arrived in St. Louis on March 16. Redfield was "almost overcome at seeing me," Roberts wrote. Redfield left for Quincy by boat two days later. Roberts organized Redfield's congregation into a free (i.e., non-slaveholding) church on Friday, March 25 (B. T. Roberts, Pocket Diary, 1859; cf. Snyder, *Populist Saints*). Early Free Methodist *Disciplines* carried the statement, "The first Free Methodist Church ever organized was in St. Louis, a slave-holding city, and at a time when slave-holders were freely admitted to the churches generally. Yet they made non-slaveholding a test of membership, prohibiting, as they have ever done, 'the buying, selling, or holding a human being as a slave.'" *The Doctrines and Discipline of the Free Methodist Church* (Rochester, N.Y.: The General Conference, 1870), v–vi.

650 JGT omits this paragraph and inserts an account of the Laymen's Convention in western New York "under whose auspices Mr. Roberts was now laboring" (382–83).

brought upon us by the unwise conduct of those assuming to have authority over is.

/355/ Resolved, that as our brother is about to leave us, we commend him to all the churches in our beloved land and pray that the great Head of the Church may shield and protect him and his devoted wife from the persecutions of their enemies as well as the slanders which the ungodly may send after them.

Resolved, that the *Central Christian Advocate, North Western, Western, Western Advocate and Journal,* and those journals favorable to the cause of religion are requested to publish the above.

St. Louis, February 28, 1859.

This was signed by ninety-four members of our church and taken to the office of CC Advocate [*Central Christian Advocate*] and desired to have it published [sic]. But they said, "Don't ask us to publish that, but drop all matters and be still, and we will be still. You publish nothing and we will publish nothing." Mr. T. Williams came to me and desired me to use my influence to stop it, and they would publish nothing. I said to him, "I will." And the way they redeemed their this pledge may be seen in the following. This is the review of following.[651]

Special Request[652]

I then wrote the following, but did not send it:

To S. Huffman
Review of your article headed "Special Request":[653]

---

[651] These five words are crowded in after the previous sentence, marked off by a vertical line before "This" and a horizontal line above. He means, this was my response to the printed notice—i.e., his letter to Samuel Huffman.

[652] The notice appeared in the *Central Christian Advocate* 3, no. 11 (16 March 1869):2. The notice begins, "Early in the past winter, a Mr. J. W. Redfield, a local preacher, claiming to be directly from Northern Illinois or Michigan, and more remotely from New York or New England, came to this City. Being properly endorsed by the authorities of the Church, he was invited to aid in a series of religious services at Ebenezer Church." The notice then reviews and criticizes Redfield's ministry in St. Louis, accusing him of "evasion, unmitigated duplicity, and contempt of the authority, order, and Discipline of the Church," and requests anyone "having knowledge of where he holds his membership, and is ecclesiastically amenable," to notify the writer. The piece is signed, "Samuel Huffman, P. E., St. Louis District, Missouri Conference." Redfield does not quote this "Special Request," but Terrill prints it in its entirety (385–86), with only a couple of very minor inaccuracies (e.g., "endorsed by the authority" instead of "endorsed by the authorities").

"Claiming to be from": You know that my letter stated just where I came from.

"Properly endorsed": I wonder at this admission, amid all of your strange proceedings.

"Succeeded in sowing dissension": It is strange to me that the preaching of Methodism should be seditious in a Methodist Church. Hundreds will testify that I preached the doctrines of our standard authors, to which I referred publicly.

"Proposed to take a vote as to who should have the pulpit": Will this go down with those who know that the official board voted /356/ to request me to occupy the pulpit and hold a series of meetings from one to three weeks? And I ask, who could know the purport exactly of a proposition but half stated, and arrested by the preacher in charge? I did design to take a vote as to whether these people (in and out of the church) wished me to continue to preach the same class of truth which I had hitherto done. If so, I would accept the invitation of the official board, and if not I would quietly leave.

"Kindly invited me to desist": —by shaking me by the arm and in a commanding voice calling upon me to stop before I [could] get my proposition out.

"Got his letter by promising to unite with another church or going to Illinois": I did expect to join another. But finding that the same power that ruled me from the pulpit ruled them likewise, and farther learning that the letter charged upon the trustees was a fraud of the pastor, I was fearful to put myself within the grasp of a man capable of so great a fraud.

"Giving assurances that I would in no case have anything to do with separate services": How could I know anything about a separate organization before a word had been uttered about a separation?

Someone in kindness got a paper for me as it was just printed containing the "Special Request," and I took it with me to Quincy. I thought it best not to take my wife, not knowing but that I should be so hard pressed by these wicked men and I might have to return, and did not feel able to pay the expense.[654] So I went in advance, and with a

---

[653] In the review, Redfield quotes phrases from Huffman's notice and comments on them. For clarity, I have placed in quotation marks the phrases which are quotations (or paraphrases) from the "Special Request" notice. Terrill omits this and instead reprints a piece from the *St. Louis Christian Advocate* implying some criticism of Redfield, and a defense of Redfield (apparently published in the *St. Louis Christian Advocate*) signed by "H. Wickersham, Leader," seven others, "'and one hundred members'" (386–90). This defense of Redfield covers many of the same points Redfield does in the section below, but in more detail.

[654] JGT: "Before Mr. Redfield started for Quincy, a friend handed him a copy

heavy heart. I thought, "I might as well keep moving till I am compelled to stop." And Satan now beset me, [tempting me to ask,] "What am I about, and if I am right, why don't God stop this great wrong?"

"Well, I cannot see, I don't know, I am a rock of offense," [I thought]. /357/ "I cannot help it. I feel that I am like a poor, hunted animal dodging the shots and still trying to work for God as well as I can."

XLVII. Ministry in Illinois; Growing Controversy

I reached Quincy the next day. But the reports had got ahead of me, and I was waited upon to know if I was willing to join their church and come to trial. I said, "I am not willing to allow my case to be acted upon by such men as those who know of the fraudulent letter and connived at it. I can show you papers which will attest to the truth of the whole matter. Now," said I, "you can do as you please. But I do not feel it to be my duty to suffer all I have from these men and then to begin a series of meetings here after allowing myself to be tried for a crime of other men."

They [i.e., Methodist leaders in Quincy] finally concluded to let me stay awhile.

Just then the good old lady at whose house I stayed came to me and said, "Brother, I have lived here for seventeen years. I have felt it to be my great business to labor for God. I have seen one church among the Germans built up and become a Bethel for souls, and we have two American [i.e., English-speaking] Methodist churches. Well, about five years ago I got to feeling so bad at the low state of religion that after meeting I took a by-street so that I could bawl aloud on my way home and ask God what could be done. And that night God showed you to me in a dream and told me that you would come and preach the gospel in its power. As soon as I saw you this morning I remembered my dream, and knew you to be the very man. And I saw your wife, but she did not come at the same time with you. But," said she, "I think I shall know her."

When she did come some week or ten days after, she did know her. One remarkable fact was that she [i.e., Mrs. Redfield] came just about the time for family prayer, and the old lady taking me aside said, "Oh, I heard that prayer five years ago."

---

of the paper with the article his enemies had published. This induced him to leave his wife, for the present, in St. Louis, as he did not know the reception he might receive in that place" (390).

All this was very consoling to my wounded heart. But for these occasional instances of revelation to God's people, I should /358/ sink. How it was that I could be right in pursuing this course, and yet so many against it, was more than I could divine. I never asked the Lord to make my track one shade lighter or my task one grain lighter. But to reconcile the fact that God should allow me to suffer so much when He knew that every motive of my heart was honest! I go to labor because I dare not hesitate, and the voice still rings in my ears, "Live while you preach, but no longer." But why don't God give these opposers to know that their opposition is against God, and that I am only doing the bidding of the Lord?

I offered to show papers and allow the brethren to examine the case. But the president of the college and the agent said, "No, we will go to St. Louis and find out the facts." When they returned they said, "We saw only the men who are pursuing you, and we knew from their own mouths that the whole matter of disturbance is with and [was] caused by them. So you have our confidence and may go to work."[655]

This was some relief to me. So on I went, and God did work in a glorious manner in the salvation of souls.[656] One case I will relate of a Baptist clergyman, an honest and earnest seeker after what he pleased to call the higher life. God did indeed grant him a great and glorious blessing. But I doubted about his being able to carry out and preach it in his own denomination. If I am called to suffer what I do among the

---

[655] JGT: "But the president of the Methodist college, and the agent of the same, said, 'We will go to St. Louis and find out all the facts.'

"They returned in a few days, and said to Mr. Redfield, 'We saw only the men who are pursuing you, and we knew from their own mouths that the whole matter of the disturbance is with, and caused by, them. So you have our confidence, and can go to work'" (391).

Quincy was the home of Quincy English and German Seminary, founded by the Methodists in 1856; "a few years later it was raised to the grade of a college." In 1857 Quincy had an English-speaking M.E. church of 184 members, a substantial German Methodist congregation, and an African M.E. Church. Simpson, *COM,* 741.

[656] The Illinois Conference *Minutes* do not show any remarkable growth in the two Quincy M.E. churches, 1858–60. Since annual conference met in September and Redfield visited Quincy in March, any impact from his ministry should have registered in the 1859 *Minutes.* The Vernon Street M.E. Church actually lost members that year (from 204 to 176) though it bounced back to 200 (including 40 probationers) in 1860. The Fifth Street Church grew 24 percent from 1858 to 1859 (91 to 113 members) and another 24 percent the following year (to a total membership of 140). Redfield does not indicate which church he preached in; perhaps he preached in both.

Methodists, who were raised up with this special mission, certainly I fear that my good brother Baptist will be put down before he can accomplish much.[657]

God did a great work in the church. One sister's case I will relate. I was out visiting till late one morning when word came to me to come home to the place where I boarded in great haste. When I got back, I saw a Sister D. in great distress of mind, walking the floor, wringing her hands and crying, "Oh, do, do pray every moment, for I cannot live."

My dear wife and others had been praying for her until they were exhausted, and wanted [i.e., needed] fresh hands /359/ to renew the struggle. I was impressed on entering the house that she had not wholly surrendered her will to God. She would walk the floor and often fall flat upon the floor, crying, "Why don't you pray? O, don't stop one moment, but do pray, pray for me—"

I said, "Hold on, Sister. You aren't ready for prayer. Now, Sister, do you say, if God will bless you, 'Any way, Lord'?"

"O," said she, "that is the difficulty. I am not willing to be singular."[658]

"Well, if God will save you, do you say, 'Any way, Lord'?" I then urged and urged her to say, "Any way, Lord." And soon she broke out, "Any way, Lord."

I said, "Say it louder," and she did. "But," said I, "say it louder." Soon she repeated it [several times], raising her voice each time, "Any way!" And in a few minutes she was so filled with joy as to raise the whole block with the high tones of praise.[659]

---

[657] Possibly a reference to William E. Boardman (1810–1886) who in 1858 published the influential book, *The Higher Christian Life.* See Daniel G. Reid, ed., *Dictionary of Christianity in America* (Downers Grove: InterVarsity, 1990), 169–70. Though Boardman was Presbyterian, not Baptist, his writings had considerable influence among Baptists and other non-Wesleyan groups, and his writings popularized "the higher life" terminology.

[658] I.e., this sister wanted salvation without any emotional outbursts or manifestations or having to adopt plain dress.

[659] JGT: "In a few minutes she was so filled with joy that her shouts of praise aroused the people of the entire block" (392). Someone has inserted a large X at the beginning and end of the line of manuscript that begins "with the high tones" and ends "While I was thus." It may well have been Terrill, for at this point he inserts a March 30, 1859, letter from Redfield to "Brother and Sister Foot" (392–95). Terrill prefaces the letter, "In the following letter, written at this time, Mr. Redfield opens his heart and mind to our gaze." In the letter Redfield relates his experiences in St. Louis. JGT then begins a new chapter on

While I was thus laboring for God the said [Thomas] Williams and [Samuel] Huffman had brought two of the local preachers to trial. Two had left and were beyond their jurisdiction. Two others remained, and at the last quarterly conference were called up before renewing their license and asked, "Where do you design to worship."

One said, "Where I hold my membership." And as they would not give him a letter, he [later] joined our new church. But they, supposing [that] as he had a name with them he would stay, passed his character. But after that he said, "Now, as you have passed my character, I want a letter to go to the new church."

They then reviewed[?] his character and cited him to trial. The next [local preacher] they [also] cited to trial. A third was a great drunkard, and they asked him where he should worship. He said, with them. They then passed his character and promised to renew his license, but required of him to sign a temperance pledge, which he did. But they had to steady his hand to write his name. His wife told me they [had] promised to renew his license.[660]

/360/ The two local preachers who were cited to trial filed their exceptions and appeared. But they [i.e., the leaders] dare not proceed, but adjourned. They [i.e., the local preachers] appealed [to] the E. [presiding elder], but time and again the elder and T. Williams adjourned. The suit was adjourned [up] to five times.

On the fifth adjournment one preacher said, "If you are going to worry me out in this way, I shall not come again." This was just what they wanted. The other was taken sick and could not come. So they took the snap judgment and expelled them both, and then it was told me that S. Huffman, the presiding elder, had the face to go onto the [annual] conference floor and declare that these [had] men never come near their trials, but treated the court with contempt.

I was sure that had I allowed such corrupt men to act on my case, they would have done the same unjust and wicked thing and then [would have] published me as an expelled man and [would] stop my influence as far as they could. Williams did send me a letter demanding of me to tell where I had deposited my letter. Seeing my way so pursued, I left my letter with a minister of the [M.E.] Church, South so that if I was called to an account I had the testimony right there, and by that testimony I could prove the iniquity of the North M.E. preachers.

This [however] gave a good opportunity to fabricate new falsehoods, such as that I had become a slaveholder, "gone South," and was

---

page 396 (his chapter 58).

[660] See JGT, 396.

a member of the South Church. I well knew they did not want to come in collision with the South Church. They knew that their rascality would be exposed, and farther that I had on the ground the very men who could by their testimony prove me to be the victim of malice. So I put my letter where they would know, if they began, [that] they would be unable to bribe the court.

But this was evading a trial, they said, and compromising my anti-slavery principles. To which I answered that I thought it honorable to run into a skunk /361/ hole to escape a rattle snake.[661]

Our people at St. Louis procured the publication of the correction to S. Huffman's slanders. [They] got at the mail-books of the C C A [*Central Christian Advocate*], by the kindness of the printer and agent, for which kindness towards us they were removed. These papers, with the corrections, were sent to all the *Advocate* family. But not one of them would correct their wrong statements, although they would continue to republish all fresh slander against me.[662]

I must mention one exception; The [editor of the] NWC Advocate [*Northwestern Christian Advocate*], who put the brakes on a little. My impression is, though I have never seen the man, that he years ago felt it to be his duty to take the stand which I have, and battle for primitive Methodism, but that he saw the cost and dared not to risk his reputation in so hazardous an undertaking.[663] I feel confident that he has had a severe conflict to pass through in finally deciding not to risk his fame and fortunes in so heartless[?] an enterprise as that of standing single-handed and alone in the gap to stop the world, the flesh, and the devil from running away with Methodism. If he will be honest, I venture my reputation, my honor, and what character is left that had Mr. Eddy taken the stand that God indicated to him years ago, he instead of my humble self would now be in the forefront of this battle, and the toughest[?] for every battle. Again I say, I have never seen the man and

---

[661] JGT omits this vivid metaphor. See 396–97.

[662] By "the whole *Advocate* family," Redfield apparently means the offices of the various Methodist papers which used the name *Christian Advocate,* such as the *Northern Christian Advocate, Western Christian Advocate,* and the *Christian Advocate and Journal*, the official denomination-wide weekly published in New York City. Redfield appears to be saying that his friends printed a sheet of corrections to (or a response to) the material Huffman had published and mailed this to the editorial offices of the other *Advocate* papers. It seems unlikely that he means the correction was sent to the entire mailing list.

[663] Thomas M. Eddy (1823–1874) was editor of the Chicago-based *Northwestern Christian Advocate* at this time. He survived Redfield by more than ten years. Cf. Simpson, *COM,* 326.

should not know him, but so sure am I that I am right that I would venture this whole cause on the prophecy that if T. D. Eddy [sic] had himself[?] done as God intimated to him years ago, that T. D. E. [sic] instead of J. W. R. would now stand in my place enjoying the scandal and glory of trying to clinch[?] the cause of primitive Methodism. If he is alive when this is published, he can answer for himself.[664]

/362/ Letters now came to us from a great distance, asking what is the matter, and what was all this stir? I said to my wife, "It will not do to tell all the facts, for had anyone told me six months ago that Methodist preachers could be found who would do all we know they have done, we should call it slander. So we will let everyone find out for themselves."[665]

We went off East and gave out opportunity [to be invited to preach], but were met by handbills stating [i.e., alleging] that we [in St. Louis] welcome [slave]holders and members of the [M.E.,] South, Church and [that we] were unwilling to meet the charges against us.[666] So I found my way closed up by Methodist preachers. I now saw what it was to be misinterpreted[?] and hated of all men.[667]

We came back in due time to work for God as the way might open, and knowing we had perils in St. Charles, the place where we first entered Illinois, we went there, and found a new preacher.[668] Our friends

---

664 JGT omits this long paragraph.

665 JGT has, "This drew letters in large numbers from all parts of the country, asking for explanations. But what was painful to him was that some staunch friends for this cause now forsook him. Among these was ex-Bishop Hamline" (396).

666 JGT: "During the summer following, Mr. Redfield went East, on a visit, and met with handbills, stating that he and the new society in St. Louis were slaveholders, and belonged to the Southern Methodist church" (396–97). At this point JGT adds several pages of material (397–412) concerning Rev. Seymour Coleman (to whom Redfield later refers) and Coleman's and Redfield's ministry in Aurora and other places in Northern Illinois in 1859. Much of these seems to be drawn from Terrill's own recollections.

667 B. T. Roberts' diary shows that Redfield and his wife were in western New York from about mid-June to Aug. 2, 1859. Redfield participated in a number of meetings including the Bergen camp meeting (June 23–29) and another camp meeting where on Sunday afternoon, July 10, according to Roberts, "Dr. Redfield preached one of the most powerful sermons I ever listened to from 'Whence once the door is shut'" to a crowd estimated at between four and five thousand (B. T. Roberts, Pocket Diary, 1859).

668 JGT: "On returning to St. Charles, Mr. Redfield found that the preacher in charge had taken a decided stand against his holding a revival meeting there" (413). JGT here begins a new chapter (his chapter 60).

asked him if I might preach.

"No," said he; "he cannot enter this pulpit. Well," said the preacher, "I have been sent here to guard the pulpit against Redfield and Coleman."

"And what have you against these men?"

"O, nothing," said he. "I believe them to be good men, and they are doing good, but they must be sacrificed for the good of the church."

Just then I had a letter from Brother J. [Joseph] Terrill[669] a promising young man [who] embraced religion at Elgin and who was now ~~ablaze~~ a local preacher at Ogle, asking me to visit there. I learned that the opposition of the men at St. Louis was known by them [i.e., the Methodists at Ogle], and [so] I thought it best not to incur the expense of taking my wife with me. So I went alone and determined, if the way was open, to send for my wife to come, too.

We found the work in a good state, and then for the first time [I] began to learn the worth of Bro. T. [J. G. Terrill]. I had often wept and prayed before God to send out laborers. I had thought that we must have men of experience /363/ who have been in the ministry. But God's ways are not ours. He was raising up men who should grow up in sympathy with this work, and J. T. [Joseph Terrill] was one of them, and [was] to be one of the fathers of this new movement.[670]

The preacher in charge was a great curiosity. I could not tell from what he said what he could mean. I learned however that his conduct and opposition was a main cause in inducing some of the finest members of the church to mistrust that there was another side to all this tirade about me. [They] were determined if possible to have me come out there. As one said to me, "I know the whole [case] to be your faithful course for right and against this formality which is filling our church."

Bro. H. and S., two men of God, had taken a stand at Clintonville,[671] which had been abandoned by the Methodists years before, and God was blessing their labors in a most wonderful manner. And now the M.E. preachers were desirous of taking the fruits. But they had seen

[669] The two initials here appear to be J. T. Someone (perhaps Terrill) has written in small letters after the T., apparently completing the name, "Terrill."

[670] I.e., the Free Methodist Church. Terrill omits these references to himself, though in earlier pages he relates some of his own ministry.

[671] Clintonville, a village near St. Charles, not Clinton, in central Illinois, where the M.E. Church had a substantial congregation. JGT: "Three miles south of Elgin, on Fox River, was a village of about fifteen hundred inhabitants, then known as Clintonville. Years before, it had been a Methodist appointment, but long since had been abandoned" (420).

and heard enough to know that some M.E. preachers could and did sometimes say and do some things of which they could not approve. So they wrote to ask me what it was best to do.

I well knew that we must now show our hand if we meant the Methodist Church to see the need of permitting Methodists to enjoy Methodism. So I wrote to them: "For the first, keep everyone and organize under the [M.E.] *Discipline* as we did at St. Louis."[672]

Next came a letter from Bro. Fairchild, the man who induced me to go to W., where we had a glorious work of God. When the opposition was known in St. Louis, the preacher here partook of the Spirit, and Bro. F. had the foresight to see it was now time to save all that could be gained for God. Having labored very efficiently, he asked me by letter what was best to do with the fruits, and I wrote him too to save all, but organize as Methodists. I could not see any other way, from the conduct of the Methodist preachers both East and West, than to hold ourselves aloof as hostages, /364/ hoping that we might dictate the conditions on which we would wheel into line under the existing M.E. power, and that was, that we might have our rules reinstated and be sustained in preaching a living Methodism.[673]

I soon found that Madam Rumor had made some large stories concerning my St. Louis affair. Knowing that all of our *Advocates* [i.e., Methodist newspapers] had retailed the slanders of S. Huffman against me, and none of them would correct the same after being [petitioned by a letter[674]] issued by 109 names that it was false (nor would they allow what every putative journal feels bound to do, and that is correct a misrepresentation), I saw we had nothing to hope until general conference should sit [in 1860] and reverse some of the Eastern decisions against

---

672 JGT omits this account but inserts other material about Redfield's ministry, including two Redfield letters, dated October 20 (Wayne Station) and October 24 (St. Charles, Illinois), 1859 (416–18).

673 In other words, Redfield was advising people who were converted or who had experienced holiness, if they were not welcomed within existing M.E. churches, to organize as independent congregations, but according to the M.E. *Discipline* (as the group in St. Louis had done after B. T. Roberts arrived), in the hope that in exchange for their agreeing to be integrated into the M.E. Church they would be permitted to follow strictly the Methodist disciplinary rules and practices. Terrill says, "This advice was accepted, and three societies were organized; and waited the action of the General Conference in May," 1860 (422). (Note references to the upcoming general conference, below.)

674 This seems to be Redfield's meaning, probably referring to the special mailing mentioned above.

such men as Roberts, McCreery, and [Loren] Stiles.[675] But with that failure, I knew we must stand alone, and in the language of B. T. Roberts, to "appeal to God and the people."[676]

We soon saw a glorious time at Ogle. But the preacher, as usual with such men, was very kind to our face but slandered us to our backs.

Back we came to St. Charles, where our friends were urgent that I stay and preach. But knowing the hostility of the preacher and the presiding elder, who had a face for every society, I did not feel it safe to accept, even should I have been invited. The Baptist people learning this state of affairs sent word to have me occupy their pulpit, as they had no pastor, and Bro. Coleman was in the same odor[?] with myself at Aurora and was invited by the Baptists there.[677]

I went to the Baptist church and preached and was asked to do so again. But the Baptists were waited upon and requested to shut their doors against me, or it would injure the harmony existing between Methodists and Baptists. So they informed me that my appointment must be taken up. My friends then went to the Universalists and hired their church, and I preached a number of nights.

When the preacher who was sent to guard [the] St. Charles pulpit against Redfield and Coleman heard that some of his members had been to hear me preach, he got up a sham official meeting and pronounced fourteen of his members as having withdrawn. In a few days were twenty-four more of them /365/ summarily dealt by. He declared that he was carrying out the instructions of Bishop Simpson in doing this.[678]

Our people thus expelled under the misnomer of "withdrawn" collected and organized, and were then called seceders.[679]

---

[675] Redfield consistently spells the name "Styles."

[676] Cf. JGT, 421–22.

[677] JGT: "When it became known that he [the Methodist preacher at St. Charles, referred to earlier] had refused the pulpit to Mr. Redfield, some of the Baptist people suggested that he could have their pulpit, as their preacher was away" (413).

[678] See JGT, 413–14.

[679] JGT here adds a considerable amount of material concerning the organization of the Free Methodist denomination in 1860 and concerning Redfield's ministry in St. Louis. He includes a number of Redfield letters.

Redfield served for some months as pastor of the new First Free Methodist Church of St. Louis (as it was called, though the new denomination had not yet been organized) in early 1860 before returning to northern Illinois. The group decided to buy a lot at the corner of Carr and Twelfth streets costing (according to a letter in JGT, 430) $10,000. In April Redfield printed up a number of circu-

We went on now [in 1860], regardless of all slander, and went to work for God. We had a most powerful time at our first St. Charles camp meeting, with B. T. Roberts as our general superintendent, and at our first Western Convention [of the Free Methodist Church], organized at the same time, and sent out nearly twenty preachers to begin to spread again the doctrines of Scripture holiness over these lands.[680]

---

lars, soliciting dime contributions, and sent them to many of his contacts in Illinois and elsewhere. The circular was headed "DIME CHURCH" and read:

> The First Free Methodist Church of St. Louis, organized in 1859, now occupying the Baptist Church, on Sixth St., between Franklin Av. And Wash St., have secured a lot . . . and propose to erect a cheap, plain and large brick Church. Free seats forever, and a free Gospel for all.
>
> Our people, up to their ability, have subscribed from one to ten dimes, to be paid each week till the Church is finished and paid for. The Church will be about 50 to 55 feet by 80 to 85 feet, and capable of seating 800 to 1,200 people, at a cost inside of $6,000.... We beg of no one out of the Church, but would thankfully receive what is freely offered to build a free house for the long neglected poor. ("Dime Church" Circular, Marston Memorial Historical Center.)

In an April 6, 1860, letter printed in Terrill (which accompanied a batch of the circulars) Redfield wrote, "We want to build two more [churches] to meet the wants of this great city. But we are poor, and need help" (JGT, 430).

[680] The "Western Convention," held July 2, 1860 in conjunction with the St. Charles camp meeting, was the *de facto* formal organization of the Free Methodist Church in Illinois and St. Louis, preceding the denomination's official founding at Pekin, New York, in August. The M.E. General Conference had ended just four weeks earlier, and since it had not taken action to redress the concerns of Redfield, Roberts, and their compatriots, Redfield's followers and associates in Illinois and St. Louis felt they must organize as a separate denomination. Marston says, "The convention proceeded to transact business much as though it were an annual conference" (Marston, *From Age to Age,* 250).

For the first few years the Free Methodist Church used the term "convention" rather than "conference" to identify the annual business sessions of its various districts, reflecting the language of the series of "Laymen's Conventions" held in 1858 and 1859. Terrill gives an account of this Western Convention (448–51). He gives the date as July 1, but the minutes indicate the sessions were actually held on July 2 (a Monday). See also Snyder, *Populist Saints,* chapters 23–25.

At this convention "Redfield's character was passed, and he was appointed superintendent of the Western work," Terrill notes, quoting the minutes (JGT 450). It was probably just shortly before this that Redfield and his wife Mattie became two of the founding members of the F.M. society in Marengo. Thus Redfield ceased being a local preacher in the M.E. Church and officially be-

And now the Methodist *Advocates* gave me the splendid benefit of their ill will. Brooks of the C C A [*Central Christian Advocate*] at St. Louis called loudly for the watchmen to look out for me. It was interesting indeed to see now and then in a Universalist paper articles quoted from Methodist papers giving the same severe strictures against us as the Universalists used to wield against the Methodist Church.

XLVIII. Return to St. Louis, 1860

In the fall [of 1860] I was again sent for to visit St. Louis. On arriving there, [I] learned that it was currently reported that I was in jail in Virginia with J. [John] Brown! I found a man who was demanding $1,100 a year [as preacher's salary], and our people were paying $1,200 more for church rent. This man had distracted our people and so far disgusted them that many had left, and [he] now spent most his time in a very exceptionable way for a minister of the gospel. My heart was broken to see that little band once numbering about 275 reduced to less than 100 members.[681]

I could only weep day and night at the desolation. I tried as long as I could to stem the disaster, and used to walk my room and rub my forehead and cry to God, "Why, Oh Lord, is it that I must witness this desolation? Was I not led by a phantom to come here at all? [sic] I have watered this vine with my tears. I have lost my character in this effort, and now must I witness this desolation? Oh God, I cannot endure it." My brain felt to reel in a maze until I sat down and told my wife, "I feel such a paralysis of will power and spirit that I could not say 'Amen'[?] if it would save all St. Louis." I felt I had put forth my last /366/ effort, and [said,] "I can do no more, if the world is lost." Add to this the fact

---

came a member and then a preacher in the F.M. Church. The following year he was "elected to Deacon's Orders" and ordained (presumably by B. T. Roberts) at the Western Convention (Hogue, *History of the Free Methodist Church,* 1:353).

681 Terrill explains: "On their arrival at St. Louis, he [Redfield] found that disaster had overtaken the new society, and its membership reduced from two hundred and seventy-five to about one hundred. After he left them in the spring, they employed a man by the name of Dunbar to preach for them. . . . He came, and for a season his sensational style drew large crowds. He insisted upon the society going into larger quarters, at an expense of $1200.00 per year, and their paying him nearly as much; besides which he rented a theatre for a Sunday afternoon appointment. Altogether, the financial burden became so great, that soon murmurs began to arise. . . . The enthusiasm was checked; the revival spirit was lost" (420).

that this wicked man had completely turned to an enemy the main man who stood by like a man in the hour of trial, and but for whose assistance I think I should have left the field when these cruel slanders began this work of death.

I went into the street and thought to walk it off, but I was conscious that I staggered, and soon all of a sudden my left hand dropped. I now saw that my mental sufferings were inducing a stroke of palsy and that my only safety was in shaking this whole affair off. I immediately took a course of medicine and so far righted up as to be able to leave the city. But Oh, what a heavy heart I carried with me. As far as I could see, all I had done and suffered was now to be put out forever, and what could I think of the impressions which guided me to St. Louis?[682]

It is true that Bro. Roberts had enlisted to help us, but then the claims upon him as the general superintendent of East and West were such that I could not hope much of that kind of attention which was necessary to keep the little church moving. I had carried that church as a millstone upon my heart for more than a year, and [I thought,] "Now it is gone, as far as I can see. Well, I can console myself with the reflection that I have done and suffered all that I have passed through honestly and conscientiously for God."

I now went up to Quincy, but there the new preacher had taken the field and used[?] a special guard to keep me out. But then calls at a distance were many and urgent. I went East, and there learned that many of our people had run into the wildest of fanaticism. I tried to ferret it out, and found to my satisfaction that they were greatly misunderstood.

I went to R. [Rochester] and saw those blessed sisters who had taken it upon them to raise a church in R., and found likewise a goodly number of new societies and churches, and took some hope. Before I left Bro. Roberts at Buffalo, he incidentally remarked that he was greatly concerned by his fears that the preachers in our new connection would /367/ not feel the same anxiety to push the work as he did. I felt sorry for our superintendent and secretly resolved that he should have no just occasion to find fault with me. So I started to make a visit to all of our [new Free Methodist] societies within a circumference of some-

---

[682] JGT summarizes: "When Mr. Redfield saw the desolation this man had caused, he was nearly heart-broken. It so wrought upon his mind as to induce a slight stroke of paralysis. He was now obliged to cease entirely from all public labor for a season, and put himself under medical treatment. By spring he had so far recovered as to be able to preach again" (420). JGT explains, "But the work in other parts was prospering" (420).

thing like two hundred miles.[683] Now the story that I was in state prison at Attica was current with some.[684] One night I would be organizing in one place and the next preaching in another place.

XLIX. Redfield's Stroke, Visions, and Decline

I had nearly completed my round; preached on Sunday, [November 4, 1860] and organized at Aurora, and on Monday met [the] official board. On Tuesday morning at about eleven o'clock [I] felt the same old staggering as at St. Louis and suddenly fell in a fit of paralysis. I was taken to the home of Bro. Mead.[685] When I was taken, my mind was perfectly clear and I knew my case well enough to know that I could not expect to breathe longer than from three to ten minutes. And then my inner eyes were opened, and I saw Jesus as distinctly as I ever saw a human being, and he was preparing and arranging to resist[?] the devil. I saw the two circles[?] there[?],[686] and eternity like two great

---

[683] I.e., apparently, in northern Illinois. JGT: "In September a convention was held on a campground at Aurora, Illinois, by which the new [Free Methodist] Discipline was adopted. The preachers who had taken work [at the Western Convention] in June now went forth to organize Free Methodist churches wherever opportunity could be found" (451). He further notes, "After the Pekin [New York] Convention [in August 1860, at which the Free Methodist Church was officially established], Mr. Redfield returned to the West [i.e., Illinois], and commenced his labors for the winter with great zeal and encouragement. He undertook the visitation of all the points where societies had already been organized, and where there was a desire to organize" as F.M. congregations (453).

[684] This sentence Redfield inserted in tiny script between the lines, beginning after the words "One night I." The rendering "current with some" is partly conjectural, as Redfield's script is nearly illegible. I have sequenced his statements according to what seems to be his meaning.

[685] JGT: "He preached for the new society on Sunday, met the official board Monday night, and while sitting in the rooms of a friend, Tuesday morning, was suddenly smitten to the floor with paralysis. He was taken to the house of Rev. Judah Mead, a local preacher, where he lay for weeks in terrible physical and mental anguish" (453). Apparently Redfield had suffered a serious stroke on Tuesday morning, Nov. 6, 1860. Terrill gives more details about Redfield's condition but omits the vision which Redfield next recounts. Though Redfield subsequently went through severe spiritual and mental battles, the clarity and eloquence of many of the passages in his manuscript show that for the most part his mind remained sharp.

[686] Alternatively, the correct reading could be "the two Wesleys there." The second word looks more like "this" than "there," but "this" does not fit the context.

concaves, forming one shell. I saw the untold heaps of human dust filling this whole lower world, and not one foot of earth that had not human dust in it. Then I saw Jesus pass over an eminence and disappear out of my sight, and then I knew that I should see Him no more till I had passed around to another point where I knew I could see Him. Then I saw a long passageway through which I had to go. It was then revealed to me that I should not die but live. Then rushed upon me in great force, "You may live while you preach, but no longer." Knowing that I had not given up preaching, I felt sure that I should not then die.

Not long after, Sister T. [Terrill?] came in and, said she, "[I] felt so strongly impressed to pray for Dr. Redfield that I asked, 'Why should I feel so pressed on his account?' Then an answer came: 'Remember, he has a wounded spirit and the affliction of his body, and then the care of the churches.' And," said she, "it was then revealed to me that your sickness was not unto death, but for the glory of God."

My pains were most agonizing, and with them [came] the power of the tempter to array my whole life before me, and what I had suffered—accident, /368/ opposition, and disgrace. "And now," said the tempter, "this is all you get for your pains. Oh, your enemies will call this a judgment against you for your disturbances of the churches."

I now felt that the hardest trials, pains, and persecutions which [had] cost me the most grief were the brightest spots in my while life.

Just before the assurance that I should live, and while I thought I must die, I made my will, verbally. Then, in view of the glory which would burst upon me, I gave them all what I supposed was my dying testimony—that was, that I now saw this to be the right kind of religion. The gusts of glory were so perfectly overpowering that it did seem that it would take my life. I prayed the Lord to withhold, for I could not endure the awful glory which seemed to lift me up and would [threaten to] tear the soul out of my body. I could use one hand and one foot [due to my paralysis], and I could stomp and pound and scream, "Glory to God!" My wife would beg of me to moderate down, for fear of hurting myself. But I told her, "Someone must praise God, and if they would not, I must."

The whole Book of Job came up before me and was the language of my heart when my paroxysms came on. I suffered enough in the first few months to die twenty times. When the worst of the paroxysm was on, I would stuff my mouth with the pillow and bedclothes so as not to annoy others too much and then scream with all my might.

A good sister P. was with me, who told me that she saw a long time since that I was going into a dreadful place and then [would] pass from that into an untold glory and power. I never before knew the power of the devil nor the power of salvation. A remarkable fact was that Sisters C. [Coon] and Call of M. [Marengo] and Bro. Joslyn saw me months before about to pass through a terrible ordeal. When Sister Coon saw me [in premonitions or visions months before] she cried out, "My Lord, what are they going to do with Dr. [Redfield]? Will they kill him?"

Bro. Joslyn said he saw me as nearly [having] come up to an immense wall. The track behind as far as the eye could see was perfectly smooth and clear as glass and without an obstacle. But [he saw] that I was now just up to an unprecedented obstacle, and he asked, "O Lord, how will he ever get through?" Then it came to him like a vision: Jesus is going /369/ to take him through. I saw too that this was the wall to which I came in my dream more than twenty years before, when I promised the Lord to take the thorough track.

Bro. O. J. [Osgood Joslyn] heard of my sickness when about fifty miles distant. From the report, it was thought that I must be dead. He went right to the Lord, and he said that God gave him the assurance that I should not die, but he must come to see me. When he did come, it was revealed to him that this was the spot where he saw [me] stopped by the great wall to which he saw I had come, when he got such a view of my track and of the difficulties in my way.[687]

As near as I can, I will give a description of one paroxysm and one spell of temptation. These spells were numberless during my first three months of suffering.

First, a heat so severe that I could not endure but a single sheet over me and then must frequently have the door opened in midwinter to cool off, and likewise to be moistened with alcohol. Then would come

---

[687] JGT explains: "Brother Osgood Joslyn, who had been converted under his ministry, was impressed while praying at home, that Mr. Redfield was in great trouble, and that he must go to his assistance. He immediately went to Aurora, and found him in the condition described above. From this time for three years this brother, with all the fidelity and sympathy of a son for a father, nursed, and traveled with, and cared for, this afflicted man of God, until he saw his remains laid in the tomb" (454).

Osgood and Mary Joslyn, together with the Redfields and a number of others, were founding members of the Marengo F.M. congregation in 1860. Among these first members were "Auntie" Harriet Coon, Mr. and Mrs. M. L. Hart (parents of E. P. Hart, later Free Methodist bishop), and the Bishop family, some of whom were influential in the extension of Free Methodism to Michigan and California. One of the Bishop daughters, Martha, became the wife of E. P. Hart. Hogue, *History of the Free Methodist Church,* 1:269–72; *History of McHenry County,* 742.

such a severe cold spell that fourteen or fifteen quilts around me would not warm me. Then such awful sensations [would] go from my back clear over my head, and my limbs [would] cramp, and in the midst of these cramps I would scream to my utmost. Then the devil would say, "You do not very much like your Master, don't you?" And then it would come with such a force to me, "You vile hypocrite, you had no need of screaming as loud as you did. If you make those around you believe that your groaning and screaming is only an index of your sufferings, you have lied to them." Then I would confess that I had lied, and next came the temptation, "Now you [really] are a hypocrite, for you are trying to make them believe that you have a very tender conscience." And then my heart would break and I would weep like a whipped child, and next fall to praying that God would not take advantage of me and of my weakness and ignorance.

Then came the temptation, "God never does wrong. Therefore you are suffering for crimes." Then I would hunt for the crimes and ask the Lord to show me, /370/ "Wherefore Thou dost contend against me with Thy great power?" [cf. Lamentations 3:1–10]. Then I would beg of the Lord to show me what He had against me, and then in grief [I said], "O, He won't show me, nor take this agony away from me."

The last and only thing I could light upon was this, that I had unwittingly violated a law by going out to preach so strict a form of religion. Then I thought: "It may be after all that God, who has created man, designs him to foster and practice the use of all his tastes and appetites." I had preached against gambling, but how do I know but that God is willing that men should develop all these passions and tastes for such [things] as novel reading, dancing, and the whole round of frivolities, and I have taken sides against the whole of this stuff. If I am compelled to change my views of the moral tastes and character of God, as I must to admit this, I felt I was [i.e., would be] cut loose from anything reliable on which to rest.

When driven by these awful temptations to the last extreme of endurance, I would beg of the Lord to let me have just one token of His power. Then the floods of glory that filled the room and [were] felt by all Christians [present] was truly unearthly. I have known Bro. O. J. [Osgood Joslyn] to declare that he had felt such a power that sometimes it seemed that the very sofa on which he rested was electrified. But it was with an unearthly glory.

After these spells I could sleep for awhile, but then awoke [i.e., would awake] to a sense of my most pitiable condition and go the same rounds over and over again. In the severest part of my rage I lost all control of myself and would bite myself and tear my clothes. But in a very few minutes, if I chanced to think of those men from whose conduct I was suffering, I would feel such a commiseration as to burst into tears and weep and pray for them.

I once had it shown to me how this matter would appear in the judgment. I saw the principal man who had broken up his church and then accused me of it.[688] We both stood at the judgment seat of Christ and the question was put to him, "Why did you harass and persecute my servant as you did at St. Louis?"

He answered the Judge thus: "O Lord, I thought he was /371/ disturbing and ruining my church."

"Yes," answered the Judge, "but you did not stop to learn the truth of your imaginings. I," said the Judge, "sent him to St. Louis. I stood by him and pushed him to take every step which he did take, and he dared not to falter, for I was pressing him all the time. You was not opposing him but me."

This sight so overwhelmed me, and my grief for the man was so pungent, that I said, "O Lord, if it be possible, let me suffer for him"—[even] though my agony had been such that I would have taken my life if I dared, and really meditated it if I could be convinced that God would allow it and not condemn for it.

O, how clearly I saw that none of these men had the least idea that they were doing a wrong and were really arrayed against God. I could no more have felt hard towards them or injure them than I could the poor culprit on the way to the gallows, and I soon found a luxury in praying for them that I never could have known, had I not been made to suffer on their account.

The cause of my paralysis was the mental suffering which I endured at St. Louis, and of course it was all in my brain. My nerves became so sensitive that all my senses were very much exalted. My memory was so clear that almost all the minutia in detail of any circumstances long past was [as] clear and fresh as at the time of occurrence. In [anyone's] reading to me, I could detail the least misspelled or misprinted word or sentence.[689] In taste, it was so exalted that I have distinctly tasted the weakest attenuation of homeopathic medicine, such as a few pellets of the 30th potency of aspirin dissolved in a tumbler nearly full of water.

---

688 Apparently a reference to Thomas Williams.

689 Redfield seems to mean that whenever anyone read to him, he could detect even tiny errors or misprints on the printed page, by a kind of clairvoyance or insight. But perhaps "to me" is an error in his writing, and he is referring to his own reading.

I knew too the mood of other people's minds, and could see just about the moral state of any, whatever they might profess as to religious attainments. But [I] never felt allowed to tell them. My hearing too was acute, and my imagination was either morbid or I had an open /372/ view of the spirit land. I had only to be quiet and look within and the scenes would come up before me, and I gazed and remembered. A few instances I will give, and let others make what they please of them.

I was on my bed in a tent at camp meeting. Quietly turning my eye within, I saw an excellent breaking-up plow standing on its handles and beam's end. I saw it to be made of the very best material. But it had stood so long as to completely cover the wood with a thin skin of mold, and the plowshare was perfectly covered with a very thin rust.

I saw a land of prairie partly plowed, and what was plowed was laid in perfect order. I saw too that the land was not nearly plowed, and the plow stood at the last finished furrow, which furrow was as straight and perfect as anything of the kind I had ever seen. I then in spirit asked, "Is not this plow usable?" The answer came back that once round the land would make it as bright as ever. I saw that though the woodwork was rusty [sic], it was as sound as ever.

I then in spirit asked, "But where is the team to draw it? For I see no one near, nor any team." I then saw a chain come down out of a cloud, and I saw that the chain looked like one just made. The cloud came down close to the plow, and the chain came out of the cloud and touched the plow, and I said, "But where is the power to move this breaking-up plow?" And it was said, "The power lies behind the cloud."

Then an impression came to me, "Go and tell sister B. what you have seen, and she will know what it all means." I did so, and as I related what I had seen, she said that means [i.e., relates to] me, and by the help of God I will do my first works. [She] then related to me in substance the following narrative:

"When I lived in the East, God's Spirit led me into great light and showed me how far the church is behind what it ought to be. I finally reached a spiritual state where I was led to pray for the sick and lay my hands upon them, and they would recover. I was thronged with visitors who sought /373/ my aid. But I was opposed and [so] finally moved west. When I came here I found the churches very dead, and of course they could not bear the strong doctrines of holiness, let alone the gifts of the gospel. And," said she, "I began to excuse myself from the strong and aggressive cause of pressing the gospel upon them, and I have stopped and am rusty. God sent me here as a breaking-up plow, and I see my work is not done, and I will go at it again."

One more instance I will relate. I was, as able to do so, at the meetings in St. Charles.[690] There were a number who with me staid at the house of Father F. Before going to rest, they [would] sing the beautiful hymn called "The Sun-bright Clime."[691]

I went to rest, and in the night I heard it being sung as distinctly as I ever heard it. And what was singular, I heard the voice of Sister C. [probably Coon or Cooke] from M. [Marengo], who was in another part of the house, as distinctly as though she were singing alone. And I heard the voice of a great multitude singing with her, and I was impressed that they were a company of angels.

When they had finished the hymn, [I had] an impression that a

---

690 Probably Redfield is referring to the 1861 St. Charles Camp Meeting. Terrill in *The St. Charles' Camp-Meeting* reports that Redfield attended in 1861 and 1863 but does not mention him in his account of the 1862 gathering. In 1861, Terrill reports, "Mr. Redfield comes palsied [i.e., paralyzed] and almost helpless. He attempted to preach once; but the indiscreet conduct of a young enthusiast, who was determined to have him healed in the midst of the sermon, broke up the service" (18). It was however at the convention session held in conjunction with this camp meeting that Redfield was elected to deacon's orders and ordained (22). In his report B. T. Roberts wrote, "Two preachers, Rev. J. W. Redfield and Rev. Joseph Travis, were elected to Deacon's orders and ordained;... The ordination service was held on the Camp Ground the last day of the meeting" (B. T. Roberts, "The Western Convention of the Free Methodist Church," *The Earnest Christian* 2, no. 7 [July 1861]: 225). In 1863, Terrill reports, Redfield was "present but unable to labor" (*St. Charles' Camp-Meeting,* 33).

Terrill however records that, surprisingly, in the spring of 1861 Redfield had recovered sufficiently to preach some and "to travel quite extensively." In April Redfield conducted a revival at the Second Free Methodist Church in Buffalo, New York. From Buffalo he wrote to his friend Samuel Huntington at Burlington, VT, on April 17, "My health is gradually improving. I can walk about the house a little by using a cane, but I still have to be lifted in and out of a carriage. We are now holding meetings in the Second Free Methodist church, in this city. At the rate I am improving, I hope to be able to get in and out of a carriage during the summer" (JGT, 454). Instead, however, his health deteriorated further.

691 Cf. S. J. Oslin, "Over in the Sun-bright Clime." The song (based on Revelation 22:5), consisting of four stanzas, is found in E. V. Halt, *Spiritual Life Hymnal* (Indianapolis: Pilgrim Publishing House, 1948), no. 401, and appeared in Joe S. James, ed., *Sacred Tunes and Hymns* (1913). See http://fasola.org/love_lodef.html. Another, apparently unrelated, hymn or poem titled "The Sun-Bright Clime" by Rev. John Scotford is printed in *The Earnest Christian* 50, no. 2 (Aug. 1885): 48. It consists of six stanzas and is in a different meter from Oslin's hymn.

very essential part had been left out—for where are those bright ones whom John saw before the throne? Then instantly I saw through a partition of the clouds, high up and at a great distance and with the sound of distant voices, and yet clear. They sung to me word by word, and I remembered and copied it in the morning:

But far, far above this countless throng
I hear a wilder note of song;
'Twas out of great distress we come
Washed in the Blood of yonder Lamb
    Who dwells in this sun-bright clime.

The impression then came with force that the particular ones are not yet described. They have here many persecutions. But from whence came these? Then the same voices in musical sentences struck up again and sang,

Prophets, Angels, Martyrs all,
From mountain cave or lion's stall,
From Hebrews' furnace dreadful fire,
/374/ Raised by that whirling tempest higher
    To dwell in the sun-bright clime.

Again the impression came: There are many who would be martyrs if the law permitted it, and Sister C. is one. And yet I do not see as this song describes the state of such. The voice then sang this last verse, and all stopped:

Ten thousand, thousand, thousand more
From every age and every shore
Who battled till the war was o'er
With God shout on forever more
    To range through that sun-bright clime.[692]

[692] As Redfield's text implies, these additional stanzas were not part of the original song but were revealed to him in his dream or vision. "Auntie" Harriet Coon, who apparently had access to Redfield's manuscript, quotes these stanzas (with some minor variations) in her autobiography, *Life and Labors of Auntie Coon*, ed. E. E. Shelhamer (Atlanta: Repairer Office, 1905), 89–90. Coon recounts Redfield's last days and death (87–93), noting that most of this account was left out of Terrill's book on Redfield.

L. Pentecost: God's Ideal for the Church

After this I had another terrible spell with the enemy of all righteousness. I felt very much cast down at my very crippled condition when so much was to be done and so few to do it. We had more than twenty efficient men in the field and new places opened to us, and we in want of laborers.[693]

But here I had a lesson to learn that I least expected. One was suggesting one thing and one another as the probable cause. Then one of our preachers told me I must consecrate the Free M. Church [to God] and cast off my concerns. I then saw what a burden of care I was carrying. In attempting to give it up so that my only concern should be to stand by Jesus under all fears[?], I found I had hit one of the grand difficulties in my way. But when I had reached that point, I saw that any church where Jesus was owned [i.e., acknowledged] and honored is just as much a matter of interest to me as the F. M. Church. When that was reached, "Now," said the young preacher, "you must give up all the Free M. preachers."

I had no thought that I was doing a wrong to love and prefer these to all others. But as they came up one after another [to my mind], I was compelled to put them in the same spot where I put all other ministers and to think no more of them than of other gospel ministers who are equally pious as are ours. I lay for hours in /375/ agony, and I think I must have felt something as a father would feel to see his whole family die before his eyes. I never dreamed that I would do a wrong in loving them, and many were the bitter pangs I felt in making the surrender. But when it was done, if I could have met a minister of any denomination equally pious and zealous to spread the pure gospel, I should not know the difference between them and a Free M. preacher.

About this time Sister M., the wife of one of our preachers,[694] was suddenly seized with a disease which I knew in all probability under the best mode of medical treatment would require not less than three weeks [to recover sufficiently for her] to get about the house. She desired the pious to pray for her, and they did. A good sister saw her and to comfort her said, "We hope you may be able to sit up in a few days," and then went into another room and prayed so loud that Sister M.

[693] Twenty-one preachers were appointed at the 1861 Western Convention, including J. G. Terrill, E. P. Hart, J. W. Dake, and Redfield himself.

[694] Probably the wife of James Mathews who in 1861 was assigned to the Belvidere, Illinois, circuit.

heard her: "O Lord, bless Sister M. and raise her up."

Sister M. on hearing this cried out, "What, I lay here for days or weeks? No, never while Jesus lives!" Then her faith so took hold for herself that she was instantly healed and in the afternoon went out to church and testified to the healing power. I felt greatly rebuked, for God had shown me over twelve years before that Pentecost was heaven's ideal of a church on earth, and all that then took place was yet to be repeated.[695]

I resolved to put the healing power of Christ in my own case to the test. I did try, but an impression again came, "God has His own reasons for delaying your case, and when it is done, you and all shall see why it was postponed till then."

Then came up before my mind again one of those strange signs which used to guide me in going to places of labor, and that hung over S. [Syracuse]. I had been there ten or twelve years before and well knew what a desperate conflict we must have [if I returned there], and my heart shrunk from it. Then came the fact as clear as words, "You once went over that place with the breaking-up /376/ plow, and now you must go with the subsoil plow. It was then that God opened your mission on the subject of redemption."

But my reason revolted. "Here I am paralyzed in one half of my body and obliged to be lifted in and out of my carriage. But then to meet this," [I thought]. There was Bro. O. J., who declared that he felt called of God to take care of me and grant me all of that kind of assistance which I needed in lifting me. But again I well knew how hard a conflict I had when I was there [at Syracuse] and the conflict I might expect to meet again. And worse than all, [to] go and in my state, begin where I left off, and preach the full Pentecostal power as a thing to be looked for in our age! Will not the people say, "Physician, heal thyself"?

Now as soon as I gave way to these reasonings, I was thrown into spasms in which it seemed to me that I must lose my breath. I saw, as I used to see in such times, that I must yield to obey what my reason revolted at as fanaticism, or die. I was led to it, and with such spells of suffocation that it did seem sometimes I should never be able to breathe again. This was the first time that I ever passed through one of those spells in the presence of anyone.

When I yielded to go [to Syracuse], I was at perfect rest. But I felt too that it would in all probability be spring before I should be called to go, and yet I have had to keep myself in constant readiness to go. Oh, if

---

695 An important passage for Redfield's theology.

my persecutors could only know what it costs me in suffering before I can consent to go at all in my peculiar calling, and then the contests while in the field! It does seem [that] if they possessed one particle of humanity, they would not make my case any harder by opposition and slander than it is.

LI. Entering into Jesus' Sufferings

I was asking the Lord why I must be thus punished and goaded along, and why I could not be dealt with more like a reasonable being, for I knew that I would not knowingly oppose the will of God. I said to the Lord, "I am not a brute to need this awful chastening and compulsion to move me."

Then one said to me, "You know not what consequences rest on your doing your /377/ duty." And now came with force to me the saying concerning Christ, that He was made perfect through suffering. I had said I would accept of His cup and baptism, and I was now partaking of that cup. Now my mind was turned to the fifty-third [chapter] of Isaiah, and my track shown me.

"And must I pass that?" [I asked].

"You said you would."

The church did esteem Him "stricken, smitten of God and afflicted." Here too I saw that Job passed the same route, and now I must pass it ~~also~~.

If the world and the dead church only had entered [i.e., made] their accusation, I would have borne it as a persecution. But even many of our best pilgrims who had not as yet received this light and knew not the meaning said they thought my whole affliction was a judgment of God against me, and if I had not faith to get out, I must be badly backslidden. I saw [that] one after another, though not one word was said, were dropping this confidence in me. They knew not that I read their thoughts, and I could not tell them, but [must] let it all pass, and consent to be misunderstood.

But soon it was revealed to me that I must be as thoroughly cut loose from the best[?], and from their sympathies, as though there were but just two beings in the universe, myself and God. But I saw too, faintly shadowed but as a certain fact, that they must in another form pass just what I am now passing. Then they will see how unjust was their judgment in my case.

I asked the Lord why I must suffer so much and be misunderstood when I knew I could put my hand on my heart and look the great Father in the face and say, "Thou knowest, O God, that my motives and acts of my whole life in the ministry have been guided and moved by honesty and by sincerity. Are there not other resources within the power of the Almighty by which to accomplish my thorough development?"

Then the answer came, "There is but one way to save the world, and that is to /378/ bring the Almighty down and in contact with the world."

"But," I said, "man cannot comprehend, grasp, or span the Almighty."

"Well, but the attributes of God can be exhibited, and men may gaze on them singly. Christ came to manifest God in the flesh. When He bore the guilt of the world, this showed God's abhorrence of wrong and the severity of justice, which demanded a victim. The submission to this cost exhibited the promptings of divine love."

Then came in great clearness to my mind, that since Christ has left the world, His life of sufferings must be repeated in every age. And where [it is] repeated, though men understand it not, yet the converting power of God is felt.

I now had a key to many of the to me mysterious burdens I had seen people endure in different places, and could see this fact, that when they were in the greatest distress on account of this work, that then the work of salvation would move. I would almost judge to a certainty about the success of a meeting by these signs. And now I saw that this was indeed the fellowship of His sufferings.

I knew not of three persons in all the West, and not more than a half a dozen in the East, who had any clear light on this strong subject. And I knew full well that besides them there were none who were out enough into the light to know where to place me. Of course I must suffer on and be still and let God, if He will, vindicate. And if not, let me go misunderstood. But this much I could see: That every dark place through which I was called to pass led me in spirit out into a place, beyond words to express, of elevation and glory. Yet I could not talk of it to others. If I did, they could get no clear understanding from words.

I went one time to rest but not to sleep, and there appeared to my inner eyes a clear view of the road I had chosen to take. I saw it as a highway running upwards on a gentle slope. On each side I saw briers, thorns, and every kind of obstacle to arrest our progress. Yet in the path there was ample room to pass, in spite of /379/ all impediments.

I saw that I had reached a very high point of elevation and had so far passed as to be able to see out of the woods. I looked between the trees through, which the floods of light were shinning on my path. As I stopped to gaze, I saw the light be coming from the center of heaven. Then I learned that the path on which I was walking led directly to the very center of glory.

I stopped, and being shocked at the sense I had of my own unworthiness, I said, "O Lord, I never can go there. I am so unworthy, and what will the universe think to see one so utterly vile and unworthy as I am to go to such heavens? No Lord, Thou must excuse me, for I never can consent to be elevated to so high a point of dignity in the palace of God." Then I commenced a search to find a path off from the one I was on which would lead me to some obscure place in the realms of heaven.

Then the word came back to me, "It is too late now. God must be God, and [He] has laid out this path for all who take it as the one that leads to the center of glory. There is no such [other] path, for you entered this road at the other end when you knew it to be beset with difficulties and [that it] would cost you all things to walk in it. Now you must consent to endure it."

O, how this view did overwhelm me and renew my energies and courage to continue on in the way I had adopted. But still it is my prayer, if God can permit it, to allow me at least some secluded place in the realms of peace where I can be alone with God forever. I don't want nor ask any other distinction in the world of spirits than to be permitted to dwell alone with God, little and unknown, loved and prized by God alone.

Now I am quite sure that many on reading these things will at once conclude that my brain is turned, and that these things are but the offering of a disordered mind. Think as you please. I am positive that I see and reveal but a faint /380/ shadow of the reality. But I will risk the truth of what I here state in this prophecy: That in less than ten years God will have a great many living witnesses to the truth of what I here declare. Then they will know that I speak forth words of truth and salvation.

Another revelation I have had, and that is that this new uprising is indeed the John [the] Baptist to prepare the way for the second coming of Christ, and is of the same type as that which has blessed Ireland and other parts of Europe within a few days, and is also the angel flying through the midst of heaven and having the everlasting Gospel to preach [cf. Revelation 14:16].[696]

---

[696] An important passage for Redfield's eschatology. This entire several-page section of visions and revelations is omitted by Terrill. Instead he includes several Redfield letters and reports of Redfield's final meetings.

LII. Suffering and the Plan of Redemption

Chapter [35][697]

Standing upon this point and looking over the past, I can see and understand as I never could before the plan of redemption. Many of the mysteries of my experience now come to light. I see that the gospel is designed to reinstate us to where we were in the Eden where God looked upon and approvingly disclosed that all was not only good, but very good.

I never could know what had been done for me till I had passed to it, for I needed the light of the newly gained grace to see what was done. Standing on each new acquisition, I could see that all previous [ones] were distinct and clear. Standing where I do, I can look back and see that my justification is yet complete. No condemnation, and [I sense] the cleansing power of holiness, which has remodeled my tastes and given me a tendency to aspire after God's will. So justification takes away guilt, and sanctification wipes out the stain of Adam's taint.

Spiritual discernment comes of opening an existing eye in the spirit, rather than creating an eye. And so of the internal ear, and the unfolding of the intellect. And after these, we enter the field of suffering with Jesus. We suffered for Him when we took the consequences of identifying ourselves with Him. We suffer a tithe of the remorse which but for pardon would be eternal.[698] When we are penitents, we suffer an instructive loathing of our corrupt nature. When we reach after holiness and expect [it], /381/ we suffer the pangs of restoring our spiritual sense, for every advance is preceded by suffering. And last, we suffer with Christ and for the cause of Christ's sake [sic].

A given amount of suffering is necessary in redeeming the world. Christ's [sufferings] only are vicarious. But it became the Captain of our salvation to be perfected through suffering and to be tempted in all points like as we are, to make Him practically acquainted with our state. Acting on this practical knowledge, he became a faithful High Priest. If then Christ, not content to act in our case by virtue of the divine ~~prescience~~ comprehension, but must bring up the human in Himself and compel an acquaintance by actually suffering, so we to become acquainted with Him must partake of His sufferings.

I have read the story of Christ's sufferings till my heart strings

---

[697] Redfield here begins a new chapter, but this material is not included in JGT.

[698] The word here could be "a tithe" or "a little."

would stretch and my eyes were fountains of tears. And yet all the time I knew that a realization of the sufferings of anyone would produce the same emotions, in less or greater degree. But had I not felt this terrible disease of paralysis, with its concomitants, I never could have had the most distant idea of fellowship with Christ's sufferings. I have by this learned that mental or spiritual suffering can distort and distress the body. And never did or could I know the power of temptation as I now do had I not felt it under those most aggravating circumstances.

I must fail to communicate any just idea [of my sufferings] to the comprehension of anyone who is not practically acquainted with the disease in any form. But I will do my best. Let the reader if he can imagine how much he must endure to feel one half of his entire being shut up in a vise, the feelings a hundred times more acute than [on] the other side. One half of the brain feels as if shut up in a vise. One half of the tongue cannot bear heat, salt, or acid. One half of the face feels as if double its size, as if swollen. A desire to move the limbs, but [you] cannot; /382/ only as you move [a limb on one side] with the other. A kind of a sense of eternal nightmare in one half [of the brain]. Then add to this drawings and crampings which will pass over, and as they reach the highest pitch of agony you feel like taking your own life and really do bruise[?] yourself and tear your clothes.

Right here let the devil enter and accuse you of doing great wrongs, and that this is the judgment of God against you. Then [hear the devil say], "Review your whole life and look, item by item, [at] every act of your life which you can remember. Then see further the [publicly] known fact that you laid the whole foundation in the sufferings you endured in trying to advance the cause of God.[699] You have been followed up by the chastening rod of God, [just] as you supposed, [pushing you] to do just what you have done, and have met the terrible opposition from those who ought to sustain you. In a word, God stands behind you and goads you on, and the professed ministers of the gospel who do not see that God is behind you and goading you, they meet you with every weapon in their power. The word from God comes, 'March,' and you say, 'Lord, I can see only one step more and then they will stop me, for they don't know that Thou has sent me. And if I tell them so, that my commission is from God, that will be to them good evidence that I am insane and ought to be opposed the more.'"

In the midst of this strife and effort to please God your spirit sinks, and the terrible premonition[?] settles upon you. Your only relief from

---

699 I.e., people knew that Redfield claimed the sufferings he endured were due solely to his determination to advance God's cause.

the otherwise-pushings of conscience is in the bare fact that you have taken the last step that is possible.

Then comes in the devil and asks, "If you had a child so anxious to please you that in obeying your order he tried to do a little more than you asked him to, would you ~~kill him~~ cripple him for life?" Then the same evil spirit, who never has for a moment accused me of dishonesty or one selfish motive in my whole life (for that could not affect me, as I know better) [says:] /383/ "But you have broken a law in nature, and the penalty must be endured."

But I would ask, "Cannot God, Who is He [who] knows everything [and] knows I was only doing what I honestly thought was required of me, and [that] I have lost all in doing it, hear?"[700]

[Satan would answer,] "Either He has not the power or [the] will to help you." And next would be argued before me this as a possible fact, that God made men with all their propensities, and [the devil would tempt me to think,] "You war upon that as money[?]." Then I would plead and supplicate the Almighty to consider my ignorance and my weakness, and the fact that I was honestly trying to do His will when I met with this terrible affliction. Then the devil would tell me as clearly as words could express it, "God don't care a straw for you. He has the power, and it would not cost Him anything to help you out. Certainly you would not, if you had it in your power, suffer a day to [pass, allowing someone to] endure what you are now suffering. What can you think of such a God?"[701]

The blasphemy became too palpable by this time, and I saw the old cleft foot protruding.

I now knew a little of the sufferings of Jesus, and saw clearly that I was just now passing the identical garden where Jesus cried, "My God, my God, why hast Thou forsaken me?" Nothing ever opened my eyes to see and appreciate the sufferings of my Jesus like this. But O, how much ashamed I did feel of myself before God when in the flood of light which now burst upon me, I could see that what I endured was nothing worth to speak of. I saw too that God the Father treated Jesus in the same way, and under far worse circumstances. For He had all

---

[700] This sentence is convoluted in form, but the meaning is fairly clear. The words and punctuation I have added bring out the evident meaning.

[701] Some of this paragraph is obscure due both to the near illegibility of Redfield's script and the lack of punctuation. But the general sense is clear enough. If "You war upon that as money" is the correct rendering, the meaning would be: You have been profligate, wasting the resources of God's gifts and talents to you, to your own hurt.

perdition unmasking their brothers[?] and shelling his bleeding heart while it was yet breaking with the load of guilt which like monsters[?] did not only paralyze Him but pressed the blood from every pore of his tortured frame. All Earth was clamoring for /384/ the blood. His own church were the witnesses against Him, and the priests had [conspired] in giving verdict against Him.[702]

And as if earth and hell, with the church, could not make the last tender heartstring feel all that [a person's] anguish could endure, just in this dark moment—O God, how I see Him, while I record the sight, writhing in agony. His body groaned as drip, drip, drip, drip, the blood drops seek each other, till the agonizing frame writhes in a pool of blood. I almost smell the fires of hell. I hear the clamorous tongues of this world. I hear one after another the heartstrings snap. He is now passing the last great agony that shall decide whether the grand plan shall be finished of building the New Jerusalem, and whether the plains of paradise shall be dotted with mansions of the redeemed.

And right at this moment, when the problem looks [?] to settle, the sun of God's countenance is veiled. Christ could endure all else. He could bear[?] and not murmur. He must groan and writhe, and this He could endure as long as He could see God's face smiling and His great finger beckoning Him to hold on for one more turn upon the garrote. But now a cloud of mourning hides the face of God. "My God, My God, why hast Thou forsaken me?"

Just now an angel hastens to the spot to fan his pale brow and raise His fainting spirits, and point Him to the new earth and heaven and the untold retinue of a redeemed race where gladsome strains of joy should yet reverberate through all the hills and dales of the world of light. If Jesus had only come to save the rich, He could have had all the practical knowledge He needed while surrounded with all that wealth could do. But He comes to save all, even the lowest. He must save thieves, and is therefore killed with them. It is enough to be buried with the rich to reach them. So all conditions of society are covered by His personal interest and ministrations.

So now, if I am to be a partaker of Christ's sufferings, I too /385/ ~~must pass the same track~~[703] must pass unhonored and even mistaken so that even my worst agonies induced by my conflicts to maintain God's

---

[702] One or two words in this sentence are indecipherable, but the meaning seems to be something like "conspired."

[703] Redfield began page 385 with these words, then crossed them through, turned the paper 180 degrees, again wrote "P 385," and started over. So on page 385 these words appear at bottom of the page, upside down.

rights are the very testimonies used against me. So then my reward can only be on high.

But when I think of the fact that my sins have done the deed, my sins have had a part in wringing every drop of blood from His body and figured in every token of agony, I am confounded, and oh how utterly vile appears the murmuring of which I have been guilty while passing the [mere] shadows of what Christ passed as a dreadful reality. In this light I see I am only tasting a trifle of the cup of anguish which my sins merited, and which Christ has drunk for me, or I should have been compelled to drink it forever.

There is a fitness in this, that I should know a little of what my sins have cost the Redeemer in sufferings, and standing on this elevated point to view the very little I have ever known of suffering. I feel to loath myself, feel rebuked by the memory of the fact that I ever thought my fate a hard one. What if the world, the flesh, and the devil should contend with me at every step? I knew when I enlisted that a savage war had been practiced against God and right. I knew the fact that Satan had run up the black flag, the ram head and bloody horns a sign of no quarter. I knew that more than one hundred million of God's soldiers had been destroyed. I knew that to enlist for God was to enter the quarrel with God against the most daring, cruel, malignant, powerful and wicked foe in the universe.

I did not join the army to wave palms, wear laurels, or walk into the senate chamber unless I first [would] do some of the hard fighting and by my valor, fidelity, and conquest I can take them [i.e., the laurels] lawfully. To be sure, I had not the least idea that there were any traitors in God's government, living at the expense of God's government and laying their secret plots by means of secret golden circle societies to overthrow the government, stealing God Almighty's theology[?], /386/ [stealing] the naval and military stores as Floyd did that of our states.[704]

But when I found that whole departments of the church, or a large majority of them, [were] bringing the whole force and power of their

---

[704] U.S. Secretary of War John B. Floyd, former governor of Virginia, was charged with attempting to ship U.S. military equipment to the South at the beginning of the Civil War, though the charges were never proven. He resigned as Secretary of War on December 29, 1860 and shortly thereafter became a Confederate officer. He died on August 26, 1863, about two months before Redfield's own death. It is unclear whether Redfield was writing before or after Floyd's death. See E. B. Long with Barbara Long, *The Civil War Day by Day: An Almanac 1861–1865* (New York: Da Capo Press, 1985), 16–17, 933.

position to bear against primitive Christianity, I had no right to abandon God's cause but greater reason for remaining among the loyal armies of God and contending the harder for the exact right. Many a voice called upon me to moderate my zeal and used all kinds of epithets against me, threatened and tried to put me to silence, or at least to cry quarters before the real cause of the quarrel was put away. I had deliberately said, and above board, "You may do with me what you like. But I shall never surrender and never capitulate till you acknowledge God's right. You may send in your white flag, but I never [shall]. As long as I have a bone to stand upon, a nerve to move with, and the grand old arsenal of God's military stores at command, I shall contend for the exact right.[705]

I had no right after this to complain. I entered with my eyes open, and "Right or nothing" is my battle cry. But after enumerating my woes and trials, I [still must say that I] have abundantly more friends than I deserve, and all of them are choice. Not one of them is friendly only because they honor the right and they have nothing else to honor or love me for. And such ones I would prefer before a thousand who would only honor and love me because I was compromising. Such are as fickle as the wind and demand too many bribes to keep them, while the honest ones will never be changed by any cost or reverses.

I have always admired the spirit and decision of Moses who, though poor and of low origin, being the son of a slave, was taken into court but [yet] would go off and keep company with the slaves. Highly educated in all the learning of the Egyptians, yet [he] left the high and wise Magi for converse with the lowly. Was offered the throne and wealth of Egypt, but chose to suffer affliction /387/ with the humble outcasts [rather] than to enjoy all of these emoluments, and even prized the reproach of Christ higher than the treasures of Egypt. In this respect Moses has been a model after whom I have tried somewhat to copy.

LIII. Redfield Assesses Early Free Methodism

I am at present unable to preach but very little, and am frequently the subject of severe temptations. At these times I try to review my whole life and all the motives which have contributed to urge me into the field—only to be reassured that my motives in every instance have been purely to do the will of God. Then I get new assurances that I shall yet be healed and recommissioned to go out again and do more

---

[705] Redfield's language here and throughout this section reflects the context of the Civil War, then being fought.

than I ever have done in the cause of Christ.

As I am able, I go to visit the societies which God has raised up. When I witness their spirituality and the numbers of sinners coming home to God, as likewise the faithful labors of God's young ministers who have as by a miracle been raised up to man this infant church, I can only weep tears of gratitude to see [that] the very thing I have so long desired, wept, and labored for is really a living fact, and I live to see it. I had labored and wept, groaned and suffered till my load paralyzed me and I was compelled to stop. My agony was too great to bear, to see so much to be done and the work increasing, and then the few who were engaged so unable to attend to the mighty harvest whitening all over the land. And last of all, I am cut down and my enemies think it is a judgment upon me for interfering with the dead formality of the churches.

But now I see that God has taken the thing in hand and has raised up a goodly number of men from among ourselves who prove by their labors and successes that they are chosen instruments that God has chosen, taught, and fitted for the work. And I feel assured they under God can do much better than I could, [even] if I had the best of health to do with. Self-sacrificing young men whose hearts are in the work and whose diversities of talents fit them for the /388/ multifarious phases of our ever-enlarging, pressing fields of labor.

One peculiar feature in this work is that, like unto the first beginning of the gospel, a large number of women are evidently commissioned of God to take the vanguard. In Rochester six women led off, and so at nearly all places where we have churches or societies.[706]

I sometimes relieve myself from the tediousness of my crippled condition by counting over the number of our societies and preachers, and praying for them and calculating that in long years to come they will increase in number and stature and in favor with God and man. Then, looking forward to the day of final reckoning when death shall deliver up the dead, I feel so assured that a host will accumulate, and our number shall help to swell the vast retinue from every age and clime to witness the grand coronation and sing the refrain in the unearthly chorus, "Crown Him, crown Him, Lord of all."[707] And then my whole soul is dissolved in tenderness and gratitude for a sight of the

---

[706] An important passage in understanding Redfield's views on the role of women in the church.

[707] This passage is important for understanding Redfield's eschatology. He expected "long years to come" in history and the church's ministry, apparently, not an imminent return of Jesus Christ.

prospect.

I am strongly impressed that God has had one grand design in raising up this people, and that is to bring the church back to that type of religion which had its inauguration on the Day of Pentecost—that is, to give to the world an abiding specimen of what the gospel is to do for men. As long as the world sees only the moral change produced by the gospel, they will soon learn to parry its claims. Seeing the deficiency of the gospel to meet the wants of mankind, they will hardly feel to give full credit to the doctrine that sin has been the cause of all moral and physical evil, and that Christ is a restorer every way capable of completing the task of mending all our derangements. But let an occasional evidence, as on the Day of Pentecost, be given that Jesus can heal our sickness, cast out devils, and call upon the resources of infinite power in pressing need, and then the world will have a perpetual testimony before it that God is God and that the Christian religion in its purity has God's special care and protection.[708]

LIV. The Bible versus Rationalism and Spiritualism

One strong reason why God /389/ has (I believe) allowed the spiritualists to bring to light the wonders of their craft is to rebuke the Saduceean churches who have reduced even Christianity with all of its miracles to a system of moral philosophy whose only potency consists in moral suasion and a system of discipline. They may indeed assent to a qualified faith that what we supposed to be miracles were once believed. But our wise age has outgrown all of these appliances, and reason now can guide far more satisfactorily and can come down to the caviling infidel with a pure rational system of Christianity backed up by philosophy, metaphysics, and mathematics. I have even heard the confession of one Methodist minister to the fact that German rationalism was to a great extent the foundation of his faith. Said he, "Had I been questioned as to my faith in the casting out of the devil from the lad who often fell into the fire and water, I should have said that he was probably afflicted with epileptic fits. The witch of Endor I should have regarded as a relic of superstition."

I saw when this strange affair [i.e., spiritualism] was being disseminated that it was most sure to make great desolations with genuine religion. So instead of standing back and crying "Humbug" and in my ignorance denying the facts, I felt I might and ought to look the thing

[708] An important passage for understanding Redfield's theology, especially his ecclesiology.

full in the face. So I took a turn around and went to visit quite a number of the circles where spirits were consulted by various modes, though I was cautious not to become entangled by any unknown influence connected with it till I could satisfy myself concerning the moral character and tendencies of the influence. After satisfying myself that there was an unseen intelligent force acting (and, as far as I could learn, it did really communicate facts, for it did reveal some facts of which the operatives were entirely ignorant), [I concluded however that] there was about it a species of petulance, rashness, roughness, and especially in some cases what I should call blasphemy, and a very great tendency either /390/ to forgetfulness or downright untruthfulness.

Some said, "Do you not find that spiritualism is a great fact?" I said, "As an abstract fact, it certainly exists. But I never can link my doctrines with it unless I find it right and pure as a moral science, as well as a simple truth." I saw much of the moral tendencies to be wrong. I did not like so much assumption as some of the self-styled spirits were prone to. So when the spirits of some of the first [i.e., most prominent] men of the age who had passed away not long before had already forgotten how to spell their own names, [I saw it was a fraud. This was further confirmed] when another credible name of someone who had passed away asserted that T. [Thomas] Payne, one of the most filthy, loud-mouthed blasphemers, had gone directly to the paradise of God while men like John Wesley, who had devoted a whole life for the good of man and the glory of God, was in hell and damned. (The reason given was that he had afflicted mankind so long by preaching to them the securities of the law of God.) To hear that John Bunyan was keeping tavern[?] in the spirit land, and that the Apostle Paul was boarding with him! Next, to hear that the Spirit of the Almighty should take possession of a man and declare that this man was the only medium through which He had ever communicated, and then to learn that the professed spirit of the great I Am should violate the simplest rules of grammar and utter sentiments worthy only of some of the lowest of human minds. And last of all, to learn that one professed spirit should come up and complain of the terrible hell in which he had been suffering for five hundred years, and next comes up a spirit saying, "Don't believe that last spirit, for he has been lying to you and [has] taken advantage of your credulity, for there is no hell, but the lowest and meanest and vilest of earth, as soon as they pass away, begin a life of bliss and of /391/ development and progress to untold heights of blessedness! [With all this,] I could not but see, if I had any correct idea of "what things soever are of pure, lovely, and good report," that the religion I possessed was infinitely superior to spiritualism.

But I have learned a valuable lesson as far as spiritualism is concerned, and that is this: That the blessed old Bible is redeemed from the scoffs of infidels who have boldly asserted that, inasmuch as it is easier to see and believe that the Bible narration of miracles was a narration of impositions, therefore they were [in fact] impositions. Spiritualism may come out of the mouth of the beast, the false prophet, and of the dragon [cf. Revelation 20:2–10], and may do such wonders as even to deceive the very elect of God who allow reason rather than the Spirit and [the] Bible of God to govern their faith. I now take the Bible with increased confidence that I may trust its historical facts and theological statements, and feel assured that I have a better idea of it than I could have had before I saw the phenomena of spiritualism. For the [Bible's] whole statement of events stands out as unquestioned facts. [It is] beyond my philosophy to tell how, but these facts are now unquestioned. I can now see that there is a power behind the curtain to open prison doors, to take off the manacles from the prisoners. To produce a hand writing on the wall. In sort, to throw a favorable light on the strong probabilities of every supernatural effort spoken of in the whole word of God. And how much more precious does that Bible become to me when, in addition to all this, it is so securely [or: severely] pure in its teachings.

I have a collative [i.e., collateral] evidence to strengthen my faith in the fact that I am attended by my guardian angel wherever I go—especially when on any mission for God. In this light I can account for many of those strange signs by which I have been directed to fields of labor, and /392/ through these same influences and angelic agencies have so many who had never [yet] seen me been led to believe that God would send me to them to labor for the salvation of souls.

This confession may be a good text for my enemies to take, and from it put me down as at least a fanatic, crazy, or a fool. Have your own way, Gentlemen. I honestly believe and rejoice in the faith that the veil between me and the spirit land is very thin, and that my whole course, persecutions and all, was just right. I don't mean that it was right in men to do what I knew then, and do now, was wrong; they must settle with God for all the injury they have done—not [to] me, but [to] the cause of God. But it was just right that I should be made to feel this heavy hand of opposition. I should not have known the need of reestablishing from the foundation the cause of Christ had I not however seen and known that the legitimate guardians of God's cause had proved untrue to their charge. I needed the whole course of persecution to cut off my confidence in men whom my charity would tolerate while in reality they were retrograding from God and carrying the churches with them to the same ruin. It has cost me dreadful suffering to meet at every turn slander of the vilest kinds from ~~ministers~~ enemies in the guise of professed Christians. How could I know the depth of corruption to be cleansed away, had it not been raised to the top and brought to light? But it has done me much good in testing the qualities of my religion and it has pressed to me that I could love and pray for them.

Some will say, "If they did do wrong and you forgave them, why should you make a record of their acts to injure them?" I do not desire to keep in memory anything that will cost them a single pang one half as bad as a thousand they have caused me. But they have had their say of me, and when, time after time, a respectable number /393/ of good men's names have been appended to a respectful petition that they should do the favor of correcting their own wrong statements, this they refused to do. In one instance [they] turned away their [own] printer and got their agent removed, as was believed, for allowing us the use of their mail-book to send our correction of their misrepresentations printed in another paper.[709] And I suppose their stories will pass current and have their influence against the real work of God. Now, when after-generations shall ask why we have become a separate denomination, they can find one of our answers here and aplenty more in the trials of Bro. Roberts, McCreery, and Stiles.

LV. Methodism, Slavery, and the Civil War

I had for more than twenty years seen that the M.E. Church, which I loved and venerated, was trying by a course of human policy to win its way to favor. By a laxness of discipline [Methodists] were lowering their standard down to the acceptance of those who in heart were unwilling to pay the whole cost of being saved. I saw with grief that someone must do something to stop this downward tendency and to bring the church back to its original state of purity and of power. I never had an idea that I should have anything [more] to do in the matter than to exhibit a few specimens of the workings of old Methodist power, and then that capable men, seeing the results, would with an ability and good will set about a reform that would tell. And when I saw that B. T. Roberts and J. McCreery and W. C. Kendall had actually begun to look and act with the design to make their acts a permanent thing, no language can tell how my heart went out after them.

---

[709] See manuscript page 361, above. This passage suggests, more explicitly than the earlier one, that Redfield himself was involved in mailing out the "corrections" to the *Central Christian Advocate* notice about Redfield.

I had thought that when Bro. Kendall passed away, our principal reliable spirit had gone to the better land. But God seemed then to put a double portion of Bro. Kendall's spirit on Bro. R. [Roberts] and McC. [McCreery]. Although they delayed so long to act with a decisiveness that would inspire confidence that they were moving as fast and as firmly as the necessity /394/ of the case demanded, I saw that what they were failing to do, this opposing party were doing to hasten the final avalanche which constituted the F.M. Church. I did deeply regret that necessity compelled us to take a denominational stand outside of the M.E.C., and we should not [have done so] had we not been positively cut off from all power or liberty to do anything at all within said church.

Chapter [36][710]

In this present lamentable state of war between the North and South, I clearly see that the time to organize a new church had come. God raised up the M.E. Church not only to spread scriptural holiness over these lands, but gave to it the key to the house of bondage and bid her break every yoke.[711] The fathers of the American Methodist Church went to work in their day in good earnest to carry out the design, and God owned their labors. Many poor slaves were set at liberty. But by and by, some claimed rights to defer the manumission of their slaves for a length of time. This tolerance [allowed] to some was used as a precedent, and others demanded as a right to extent that lenity. One claim after another was demanded until to say a word against the sin of slavery at all was an annoyance not to borne with.

[Thus] church and state went hand in hand together. [Since] the tardy North [was] not growing wicked and cruel fast enough to suit the tastes of the South, the state [i.e., the U.S. government] passed the fugitive slave law, which compels all northern men to turn out and, like hounds, chase, run down, and catch the panting fleeing fugitive. The M.E. Church, to keep peace with the slave-owners, passed stringent conference edicts forbidding her ministers or members to agitate the subject. Some were tried and expelled [from] the M.E. Church for their sympathy with the poor downtrodden brethren of Jesus.[712]

So much humanity still tainted the northern church, [however,] that the southern people could endure it no longer. A split occurred and the

[710] Redfield here begins a new chapter, but this material is not included in JGT.

[711] I.e., God had give Methodism the commission to end American slavery.

[712] I.e., the slaves.

Southern M.E. Church was organized [in 1844–45]. Then /395/ they with commendable consistency expunged all prohibitory rules on slavery and commented on the old rule to mean a prohibition of the foreign slave trade [only].

The state took a farther advance step and fought for the conquest of territory to make more slave states where other nations had abolished slavery, and where remaining slaves could find an asylum. For many years no man could be President of the U. S. who could not give satisfactory assurances that he would use that high position to help the South bind, whip, and work his slave and help to gag the humane [impulses] of the North. If anyone from the North [who was] supposed to be tainted with antislavery sentiments should venture to cross Mason and Dixon's line and show or sell a page of a plea for God's poor lowly ones, they of the South could and did imprison, mull,[713] and hang them without redress.

Matters were moving rapidly to a crisis. It was demonstrated time after time that the slave power should have a peace offering by the grant of newly acquired territory, or they would split the Union. Mexico was taken to give them room, and California was created out of it. But the gold dust made it a free state—nothing else did. For white men would not allow one man to take on his slaves and monopolize the digging.

Texas had been taken years before and given to them. Florida was bought for the slaveholders, and then the Indians [were] driven off by northern men and money to clear the country for these men-stealers, these woman-whippers, and extend the great territory of ill fame—as the whole South is but one great bastardy.

The church follows in the wake. Men, money, and blood of the North have been banished from the North to keep peace with these cruel taskmasters. Plots [have been] laid in Congress to bully or kill senators for daring to speak their honest sentiments in favor of humanity. The North had long been drawn upon for treasure and blood to benefit the South by paying /396/ their postage. They [i.e., the Southern states] too demanded and gained a numerical power by being allowed to vote according to the number of their bondmen. And now our country dared to vote in a northern man [Abraham Lincoln] as president who, as far as we could learn, had not satisfied the South that he was ready to put his whole power in requisition to pacify about two hundred fifty thousand slaveholders. There are said to be not as many respect-

---

[713] Mull, here in the figurative sense of grinding to powder. This reading is conjectural, however; the word as written is nearly indecipherable.

able slaveholders as there were voters in the single state of New York, and yet this number of men must have the power of our whole government laid at their feet or split the Union.

The newly-elected president [Lincoln] in route for Washington to be installed into his office was followed by a mob who declared him a dead man if they could get at him. He however evaded the Southern chivalry and was protected in his office. Then the South Methodists and all [other Southerners] regarded this [as] so great a trespassment on their rights that they began war upon the North at once. They had previously seconded for office the right kind of men who stole the military stores and began to use them [i.e., these stores] against the great North—and then demanded of the North the privilege to carry slavery where they wished, and the payment by the North of all the expenses of their own rebellion.

Thousands of our northern men have fallen already in the contest. The North at last, thank God, are having their eyes opened to the fact that this great nest of vipers must now be wiped out. For the question now to be settled is not whether African slavery shall continue, or whether northern white people shall remain free.

This may appear as a diversion from my history, but I see it is in perfect harmony. [It] opens up the first great and wicked cause of our country's distraction and our churches' ruin. No kind of argument or trick of oratory can stave off the legitimate conclusion that our country is distracted [now with this great war] because the Methodist Church did not with fidelity to God and humanity perform her great mission.[714] /397/ Once the great wickedness of slavery with all of its loathsome beastliness was tolerated and shielded by the M.E. Church, it was but a legitimate step to ignore its pure and holy form of doctrine. When the spiritual phases [i.e., emphases, distinctives] of Methodism are turned out of doors, [and then] beautiful edifices, metropolitans, fiddles, and the whole claptrap of worldly policy and appliances substituted, ruin is the result.

In this state [of affairs], we look for the appliance [i.e., application] of Methodist power to undo the heavy burdens and let the oppressed go free. But her whole picket guard are standing as sentry to guard the vile slaveholder in his unholy grasp upon the blood, bones, and souls of God's image done up in a sable skin.[715] We looked for the sons of Wesley and listened for the thunderings against dazing, whipping,

[714] This is Redfield's key thesis and conclusion.

[715] Redfield picks up on the biblical and Wesleyan emphasis on the image of God in all people, including slaves.

bruising, and embittering[?] the conquered race of poor Ham. But they are preaching up the grand missionary advantages gained by opening again the slave trade, and now their whole artillery, once used against the downright loathsome wickedness of the southern brothel, is unmasked and is pouring its only and deadliest broadsides at the only ones who have not and will not be prostituted to believe and call evil good and good evil.

I do not say but there are, and were, many honest men who held in reserve a genuine spirit of philanthropy and [who], through their fear to meet the perils, have stood aloof from decided action against the evil. But these men have proved a powerful auxiliary to those whose rashness (they might call it) pressed them out into the forefront of the contest to begin in earnest to rebuild the walls of broken-down Methodism.

I am aware [that] it will by some be called uncharitable and wrong thus strongly to describe the existing evil. But if the narrative of murder be thought unkind and wicked, what mark of morality can we in charity put upon the murderers? I know (and so do these men who have become my /398/ enemies, because I have and will pull off their mask) that if they this moment were stirred by the deafening note of the resurrection trump, and saw the bones getting up, the world dashed to fragments and the heavens on fire, and the God of nature with the whole train of angelic myriads—I say, not one would then for one moment think or say that I was uncharitable or wrong in throwing what little influence I may possess right across their path to stop them if possible from committing one single insult more against God or Christ in the person of one of the least of His servants. Call me by what name you please; brand my sayings by what epithets you can—You know I am right, and if the great God would be here in five minutes to settle with the world, you would gladly exchange places with me, and I know it.

I venture the prediction that not many years hence there will not be found ten apologists for slavery where there are a hundred now.

LVI. Last Things

I have nearly lost my life, and quite all of my character, in the long-contested battle for right and God. Now as I look across the Jordan between me and my home, I am filled with comfort and rejoice that God has counted me worthy of having a hand in the battle for right. As I now look over the past, instead of feeling one single regret for what I have tried to do, [I can say,] could I live my life over again I would be more desperate and thorough in carrying out the great plan of reinstating the old doctrines of apostolic religion. For I feel to say I am sure that this kind of religion is right, and I would say with Martin Luther, if our religion ain't right, what kind is? If our organization is not a true church of God, where is there one? Men do stop sinning; become happy, kind, pure, and die in triumph. And when we see all of the fruits of genuine Christianity which have ever existed, how can we but be confident that we are right, and [are] in favor with God and all honest men.

/399/ On the eighteenth of March, 1862,[716] [I] went to visit the family of Brother Best, who with his wife had obtained the blessing of holiness four years before at a meeting we held in Woodstock. Sister B. obtained the blessing on the ninth of March [1858] and of course had professed it four years and nine days when I saw her on my late visit.

Sister B. is a lady of about fifty years of age, of good constitution, and had never known poor health. Had been brought up an Episcopalian. She was a member of the M.E. Church at the time she obtained the blessing of perfect love, and had been for at least twenty-one years, but said that she never before knew anything about the heart work of holiness. When the Free Methodist Church was organized and was compelled to take an independent stand as a separate denomination, Sister B. and her husband cast in their names with us.

During the last part of the summer of 1861, while Sister B. was praying for the salvation of sinners, the question came to her, as she believed from the Spirit of God, a number of times: "If God will answer your prayers in the conversion of sinners, are you willing to go with Christ into the wilderness and suffer as He suffered? Could you fast forty days?"

"O," said she, "my heart revolted at this, fearing fanaticism. But it continued to follow me, until I so long refused to take the cross that it entirely left me and passed from my memory. Shortly after this I began an ordinary fast, and [resolved] to continue it with prayer until I should see sinners saved. I did not suppose I should fast but a very few days. But the word came to me, 'If that is what you want, you must fast forty days, or fail in your answers to prayer.'

"The cross was so heavy that for five days I could not get the consent of my mind to say, 'I will take the whole cross and fast forty days.' I was fasting during all the time I was debating in /400/ my mind whether I would accept of the proposal. And yet during all this time, through an inner eye I saw Jesus holding out a glittering crown to me and saying to me, 'If you will bear the whole cross, this crown shall be

[716] One of the few times that Redfield in his manuscript gives a specific date. In this case, it helps to fix the date of the Woodstock revival meetings.

yours.'

"On the fifth day I got the consent of my will to promise I would take the whole cross. And then I felt I had great access in prayer for the salvation of sinners. I continued day after day to fast and pray till the twentieth day of my fasting. On that day I attended divine service twice, and became a little exhausted in body. And then I thought I could not go through, and as soon as my faith failed, I fainted and was taken to the door. But while standing there, I began to gather up my faith and to look to God for help, and soon felt quite well. I had seen that if I did not fail to go through, that God would give me thirty souls from among my neighbors who would be saved, and five hundred souls in Woodstock.

"On the thirty-fourth day of my fasting I felt a great prostration, which was due to the pressure of company which diverted my mind from Jesus to business. Then came the most severe temptations to distract and to draw away my mind from God. And now I began to know the fellowship of Christ's sufferings for a lost world. I felt too that I was suffering to prepare me to reign with Christ, and O, how it overwhelmed me to be counted worthy to suffer with Him.

"On the thirty-fifth day of my fasting I felt as well as ever, except [for] my weakness. But great was my triumph in Jesus.

"During all the time of my fasting I felt no inconvenience except my weakness, and no desire to eat, but rather a loathing. Once I touched my tongue to an apple, but it was loathsome to me. I have often dreamed that I saw various kinds of food and felt such a hankering after it that once or twice /401/ I dreamed that I had eaten, and O, what distress of mind I did feel, till I awoke and found it only a dream. Then my heart rejoiced that it was only a dream.

"I am impressed" (said she to me) "that when the forty days are ended, that I can eat a full meal without injury.[717] In this state I have a very clear view of the spiritual condition of people. I see too that this kind of religion so much spoken against is the nearest right, and the only kind that God approves. And I see too that we as a people (Free Methodists) are not ready to receive what God has for us and desires us to have. And I see that all other churches are ~~perfectly~~ dead, and unless they return to God He will spew them out of His mouth. I see too that Bro. Redfield is God's chosen instrument in this place."[718]

---

[717] Here Sister Best's narrative shifts from past to present tense. Apparently, however, the reference is still to her fast in the summer and fall of 1861.

[718] This sentence is written in between the lines, beginning above the words "His mouth." The name looks something like "Riddle" but perhaps may be

This far Sister B. I shall get a record of the balance of her history soon* and will add to this.

*Numbers of sinners are already powerfully converted.[719]

I examined her three days running, on the thirty-fourth, thirty-fifth, and thirty-sixth day of her fasting.[720] Her mind was very clear, eye bright, face flushed and full for her. Pulse about normal. No sign of fever or nervous irritation, nor any derangement of any function whatever. A little wasting of flesh and considerable weakness of body.[721] She had attended to her whole household affairs till about the thirty-fourth day of her fasting. When I saw her on the thirty-sixth day, she was quite joyful in God and full of faith that Christ would carry her through.

I ought to say that when we first saw her on the thirty-fourth day of her fasting, she was suffering most intensely from the power of temptation, which greatly distressed her. She told me she was suffering all her body could possibly endure. The enemy of her soul had a dreadful power over her to distress her. "But," said she to my wife, "when you and your company came into my room, I felt that a legion of evil spirits left and a band of angels came in, and Jesus so enabled [me] to lay hold by faith that my bodily strength was greatly revived." /402/ Myself and wife often felt while in her room that the heavenly world had come down to earth. A brother came in in the evening of the first day I was there, and she saw at a glance that he was quite depressed by temptation.

On the fortieth day I called again upon her, and then learned that on the thirty-seventh day she continued alternately to contend with temptation and then to triumph. On the thirty-eighth day her husband became fearful for her, and she felt it greatly to add to her depression. About eight o'clock in the evening she was nearly overcome by the force of temptation, which was greatly added to by the character of the unbelieving company who crowded around her. We at the house of

---

"Redfield," which one would expect, in context. The parentheses in this paragraph are Redfield's.

[719] This line, corresponding to the asterisk at the end of the previous line, is written in between the lines of handwriting and apparently referred to the promised five hundred conversions.

[720] Presumably Redfield means that, as a physician, he examined her to be sure her health was all right as she was fasting.

[721] This is the fullest "medical examination report" found in Redfield's manuscript (reflecting his medical practice), though he occasionally earlier commented on the physical and mental condition of persons who were ill to whom he ministered both spiritually and physically.

Bro. O. J., nine miles distant, [at that time] became so suddenly distressed about her, as we were strongly impressed that she was then passing a very severe conflict—so much so that we had a little family prayer meeting for her, and soon felt we had a perfect victory for her and were confident that she was having triumph. On comparing notes we found that our impressions were perfectly correct.

On the thirty-ninth [day] we felt that she was peaceful, calm, and happy all day. On the morning of the fortieth day, after prayers at Bro. J.'s I felt I must go and see Sister B. But [I] thought I would say nothing, and see if my wife was not led the same way, too. I went to my room, and she soon followed and then, said she, "I have felt all this morning that we must go and see Sister B. this day."

"Well," said I, "that has been my impression all the morning. But let us not say anything to Bro. J., and if he speaks of it, let that decide us."

Soon Bro. J. came in and, said I, "Bro. J., what is the thought just now uppermost with you?"

"Why," said he, "that I must go and see Sister B. And as the roads are so bad, I thought you could not go, so I had made up my mind to go on horseback."

But we all concluded to go and take along a shovel to clear away the snow banks, and by crossing three fields and shoveling snowdrifts, we /403/ were able to reach her house about give o'clock. We found her quite comfortable and peaceful. Said she, "This is the first day of my fasting that I have felt any faintness or desire for food."

We waited until she had fasted forty days and about two hours over, so as to be sure that the utmost limit of time had expired. Her last and strongest temptation that day, to a short time before we arrived, was that she should now die, and she distinctly saw an open grave which the devil, as she believed, had power to cause her to see. "Then," thought she, "what will be the injury done to the cause of Christ if I should die?"

"O," said she, "I had all I could possibly endure. But Jesus finally gave me the victory, and the comforting thought was applied to me that if Jesus had need of an angel to comfort Him, God will not fail in accomplishing in me what I knew He had begun, and I shall not sink."

"Well," said I, "Sister, as near as I can judge, you have now fasted forty days and about two hours over."

"Well then," said she, "I have suffered God's whole will in the matter, and now I am hungry, and wish for something to eat."

Supper was now prepared, consisting mostly of well-beaten egg and sweetmeat[?] and some codfish. Before she took a single teaspoonful of prepared egg, a goodly company gathered around her bed and sang the doxology. Then the awful glory of God rested down upon the whole company, who shouted and ~~leaped~~ and one fell under the power of God. I think I never knew a time in my life which could much exceed this season of glory and power.

She then took the first teaspoonful in the name of the Father and Son and Holy Ghost. The room seemed filled with angels and it seemed more like a sacrament, thus simply partaking of food. She said, after supper, she thought she had eaten in quantity /404/ about what she would at an ordinary meal for her, and then went to bed and rested well.

In the morning at family prayer each one who prayed besought God that He would instantly remove the prostration which was due to her long-continued fasting. She was instantly raised up and, said she, "I now feel that I can be dressed, and God would now for the first time allow of it." She sat up some time, and rapidly recovered strength.

Sister B. has now a very clear sight of the moral state of people while [they are] in her presence. [She] sees much more land to be possessed than we as a people have yet dared to hope. And, said she, "though my sufferings have been just all I could with God's help endure, yet such is my view of the value of souls that I could willingly suffer it all [again] to be the means of saving one soul."[722]

I just now finished reading the life of John Nelson, and O how rebuked I do feel to see the very wide contrast between him and myself.[723] He was pursued and even put in prison at the instigation of one of the ministers of his own church.[724] He was mobbed and bruised, and his life in jeopardy. Yet he was faithful, zealously striving to do all he could for God, and that too without repining—while I have only endured slander. Like a child I have grieved and wept before God and often enquired, "Why must I suffer all this, O my Lord, for my conscientious endeavors to serve Thee?" I felt so deeply humbled before God at my poor, timid, shrinking heart that I felt like blotting out all the memory of what I had done and suffered, and to begin anew and at the bottom of the hill.

---

722 Terrill omits this account from his book.

723 In Redfield's manuscript, this account begins about half-way down the page. Someone (perhaps Terrill) has drawn a large rather faint X through this whole lower half of the page of script.

724 John Nelson (1707–1744), "the Yorkshire mason," one of John Wesley's earliest and most effective "lay" preachers. See Simpson, *COM,* 640–41; W. H. Withrow, *Makers of Methodism* (New York: Eaton and Mains, 1898), 98–112.

But it is with me a serious question whether God will ever permit me to be trusted again with my mission. I thought I had done and suffered some things of which God approves. But O, what hard work I have made of it. I indeed have done my best to keep my sorrows to myself. But then I have suffered, nonetheless. I honestly /405/ believed I was doing the will of God, for I felt the divine approval, and never so richly as when I was contending and yet suffering for God's cause.

It now sometimes seems just—that I should be laid aside as a cripple, see the work to be done, and feel such an anxiety to be in the field as almost crushes me, and yet must be hid[?].[725] I feel I am utterly unworthy of a place in the gospel field. Now that I am crippled and cannot go, my enemies let me alone. Some dogs have too much principle to fight a crippled dog. Were I out again, I have no doubt but that the contest would be renewed, and I fear if God should venture to let me loose again, I should again weep and grieve over their opposition.

In reading some little of John and Charles Wesley's labors, travels, and successes, I saw as never before what a poor drone I have [been]. But I have made [a] vow, and here I will record it, that if God will once more allow me the privilege of laboring and suffering for the cause of Christ, I will try to redeem my misspent time. Instead of grieving at tribulation, [I will] try to get the grace that will thank God if I am permitted to suffer shame for the cause of Jesus. I have often complained of the want of courage and daring in the cause as manifested by those who would not shut the doors of God's house for naught. Withhold from them a good name and salary, and they would abandon the walls of Zion.

But before God I now feel to ask myself, in what am I better than they? 'Tis true, I go unpaid and get a plenty of ill will and slander, and now I see I go only because I must, and not because I love to. Paul said, "If I do these willingly I have a reward" [cf. I Corinthians 9:17]. Now, the fact that I grieved over it, and felt to wish I might be permitted to go untrammeled by opposition, shows /406/ a shrinking, and that shrinking proves that my will is not completely harmonized with God's will. O, when shall I if ever reach the point [at] which I see, not when I shall be past suffering, but when the will of God and not my own ease or comfort shall be the ruling motive of my heart?

---

[725] Redfield's meaning here is unclear. Does he mean that he now sometimes sees his present circumstances as "just" (as I have interpreted it)? Or did he perhaps intend to write "unjust"? Or is "just" to be taken as an adverb modifying "that," so that it should be rendered, "It now sometimes seems just [i.e., merely] that I should be laid aside as a cripple"?

I do not count suffering as a kind of price to pay my way to the favor of God. But [I seek] to be so absorbed in consulting God's will that I forget suffering—like the man who fell overboard and [was] so fearful of drowning that he struggled with all his might to reach the shore, and when he had gained the shore he for the first time found out the fact that one of his limbs had been broken.[726] So absorbed was he in the effort to save life that he did not know that he was maimed till his fright was past. So would I be so intent on doing the will of God, and that too regardless of all reward, but do it because it is right.

O, to love truth and right for the sake of truth and right! This to me is the highest point of perfection to which one can possibly aim. I love and serve God then not because He is great and infinite in His perfections, but [because] God is right or, in Bible phrase, God is Holy. I love holiness for its sake, purity for its sake, and not for the happiness and glory it will bring to me. The one great central quality in God which demands my veneration and love is that God is infinitely right. The mercy of God has its attractions for the guilty. The power of God commands the attention of the weak. The love of God comes home to the forlorn. But the exact justice of God. in all the severity of his holy exactions, is to me the richest quality of the Most High. Is God right? Then He is eternally the same, and I know just where to find Him. <u>Right</u>, <u>Right</u>, <u>Eternal</u> <u>Right</u> is the unchanging quality of the Lord of Hosts.[727]

/407/ Chapter [37][728]

In a former chapter, I intimated that I saw my error of grieving over the persecutions through which I have been compelled to travel. I now at times see that I am in error to take my crippled condition so hard. I might know that God can do better in the cause of Christ without than with me, and yet somehow I cannot shake off that feeling which hangs about me that, if I could once more get at liberty to go out, I could do so much more than I ever could do before.[729] O, when shall I be cured of my stupidity? Can I not in this condition do all that God

---

[726] Someone (perhaps Terrill) has drawn a large, very faint X through the lower two thirds of this page, beginning at about this point.

[727] This passage perhaps gives some sense of Redfield's preaching style. Theologically, it distances him somewhat from John Wesley, for whom God's love was the ultimate of his perfection.

[728] This chapter also is not included in JGT.

[729] Here again Terrill or someone else has drawn a large faint X across the page of manuscript. These markings likely indicate material that JGT had decided to omit from his book.

requires of me? My temptations are most distressing and infidel, for they all keep calling in question the need or the right of God to allow me to suffer what I do suffer, and all for trying to do the will of God. If I allow my reason to hunt for the cause and the justice of my suffering, as well as the motives which prompt me to wish to recover, I am always compelled to come to the conclusion that if my sufferings are just, [then] I have yet to change almost all of my former ideas of justice.

But notwithstanding all of this severe conflict, I have times in which I have revealed to me such a mine of divine truth as almost overwhelms me. Then [I] see that this very affliction has the effect to subdue and bring me down to a level where I can see things all unearthly. I cannot tell the bearing which suffering has upon my greater development. But I feel the application of the words, "What I do thou knowest not now, but thou shalt know hereafter" [John 13:7].

One thing I do know, and that is that my spiritual eyesight is very much cleared. There is a depth, height, length, breadth, and value to the science of redemption which I never before had any just conception of. I see, not /408/ by the contrast merely, the difference between my present state and the state in which I shall be placed by redemption, but [also], aside from this, [I see] an untold glory which defies words to utter. But O, how little did I realize it when I pledged my word that I would take the cup, the baptism, and the track of Christ. I have passed thus far through, but to my great dissatisfaction; yet my failures are humbling me somewhat and I deliberately forget the past and count it as nothing, and now begin anew resolving to take the whole cross and by the help of God get the grace which can joy in tribulation also [cf. Romans 5:3].

I begin to see a track where, if I can once set my foot, I can stand on a firm foundation—fearing, knowing, and caring for nothing but Jesus Christ and Him crucified. Then if I fully follow the Lord in all things, I shall know what it is to aspire with Paul after the fellowship of Christ's sufferings, and if by any means I may arise unto the resurrection of the dead [cf. Philippians 3:10–11], or reach translation. Enoch did not shut up the way [cf. Hebrews 11:5]. I may never reach it. But if I don't, I can see no earthly reason why I may not aim as high as that, and then reach as high as it is for me possible to reach, without being regarded as a fanatic or held up as a warning to others not to try to be too right with God.

What I now see as attainable to the aspiring zealous disciple is beyond words to express. Nor could it be understood if it could be expressed, except by those to whom it has been revealed. Now I see that

Pentecost, with all its wonders and miracles, is the lowest point from which to rise.[730] If the gospel is the plan by which men are to be restored to what they have lost, I see not why we are not authorized to take our standpoint on Pentecostal ground, and from that rise to our highest ideal of paradise, as led by the Holy Ghost. Only we should not assume to be advanced beyond our /409/ real spiritual state, and [should] keep in mind the fact that no spiritual state of advancement is gained by any fanciful or imaginary route; by no self-instituted set of means which we may desire. But remember that all advance is in the track after our Captain Jesus, who was made perfect through sufferings, and we too shall find that sufferings precede each and every advance ~~state~~ step.

Why we should be chosen in the furnace of affliction—what the need of any suffering preparatory to our advance—may not be made patent to us. But it is enough to know that all who do advance reach the end through suffering, and never otherwise. Whether the rasping of our sensibilities renders them sensitive to existing facts seen under no other circumstances, or whether like the astronomer we need to be put into the dark vale to render our stars which we would examine more legible, we may reason, guess, and imagine all we please. But our conscious uncertainty as to the exact facts in the matter will leave us with just enough doubt to shake our confidence in our conclusions.

Nor is it a matter of any importance to us whether we know an iota about the philosophy of the whole matter, any more than it is a matter of any moment to the famished beggar to know the exact chemical components of bread or be skilled in agriculture before he shall venture to appropriate a piece of bread to meet the wants of his famished nature.

The Bible said that Christ did suffer, and that He was perfected through that process. The same Word declares that it is "through much tribulation" that we must enter the kingdom [cf. Acts 14:22]. We do not regard tribulation as possessing any value or price for which we are compensated by being advanced, but only as an incident. Health is not the reward for the pains endured in amputating the gangrenous limb, but a result. Tribulations are the scalpels which /410/ cut away the proud flesh from our disordered spirits and without which we could not even know the need of purification, or the disease to be eradicated.

March 30th, [18]62[731] —[I] have has this day just all I could possi-

[730] Compare the earlier references to Pentecost, especially on manuscript pages 376–77 and 388.

[731] This specific dates fairly certainly establishes that Redfield had completed

bly endure of spiritual conflict in trying to reconcile my state with the justice of God.[732] Why I am left in my deplorable condition, or why God in mercy or justice could even allow me to be thus afflicted, is more than I can discern. I thought I had gained the victory over all my questionings and griefs, but no. The facts rush home upon me with great clearness. I know I was conscientious and honest to the last degree In my going out into the field at all. Never did I take the first step until I was driven by the butt end of the whip, [and then,] when thus compelled to go out at the cost of all things, to be met by such a formidable array of enemies who of course would not appreciate my motives or know that I took step after step only because I must. But after getting reconciled to my fate of trying to keep in with God and to endure the misunderstandings of men, and then to meet with the calamity which holds me yet with a sense of a perpetual nightmare. And worst of all, to know that I am suffering the legitimate fruits of my zeal in overtaxing my mind and body to do what I honestly believed to be the will of God.

The question will force itself upon me: Is God a being of mercy and of love? And if so, how does my affliction comport with all my previous notions of justice, love, and mercy? I may look forward and hope that I shall be made good by compensation in the world to come, and this hope may make my condition more bearable. But amid it all will spring up the question of the right or designs of God to permit this calamity. Then the worst and most distressing infidel conclusions distract me and leave me /411/ a prey to grief and helpless agony. I feel to say like Job, "Oh that I knew where I might find Him!" [Job 23:3]. I would order my case before Him and fill my mouth with arguments. I would say, "Do not condemn me, but show wherefore Thou contendest against me [cf. Job 10:2]. Am I a sea or a whale that Thou shouldst magnify Thyself against me? [cf. Job 7:12]." And in these spells, before I am aware I find a spirit which if it dare would find fault with God. Then I am grieved to know the depth of iniquity and the blindness of my nature.

I have often admired Job's fidelity and confidence in God, and felt that in much he was a model to imitate. But now I see, if the devil had put the question to the Almighty of me rather than of Job—"Does he serve God for naught? Just put forth Thy hand and touch his flesh, and he will curse Thee to Thy face" [cf. Job 2:4–6]—I should fail.

Oh, I have great reason to humble myself in dust and ashes before

---

the bulk of his manuscript by the winter of 1862.

[732] Here again Terrill or someone else has drawn a large faint X across most of the page.

the God of heaven—not because I must, but of choice. Job said to his wife, "You are very willing to receive good at the hand of God. Shall we not equally receive evil and trust that He is doing well by us?" [cf. Job 2:9–10].

In reviewing my past history, and my complainings, I see as I could not otherwise do without these calamities. How little I understand or harmonize with the will of God. And now in this light I see that, though I have been and still am regarded as a disturber of the peace of the church because I have insisted that God's Word was not an idle letter, but that its holy counsels must be strictly obeyed, on pain of eternal loss—but I now see that I myself have never had a clear, full, and exact idea of the severity and purity of the holy law of God or of the exceeding corruption of the human heart to be purified. Restiveness under suffering and disappointments /412/ shows as nothing else can, and where nothing else can, how stubborn, self-willed, and opinionated we are, and how much it costs to be cured of our rebellion to existing circumstances. Were God, who has the power, to be no more forbearing than we are, this world long ago had been demolished, and with it every hope which now animates and inspires the noble daring of the most exalted specimens of human nature.[733]

I have just finished reading a short history of Ulrich Zwingli, one of the great reformers. When I learn what a stormy time he had of it, and with what valor and fidelity he finished his mission, I am again humbled at the view I have of my own timidity and fearfulness, and see a deeper degree of degradation than I ever supposed existed in my poor fallen nature. Had I lived in his and Luther's day, I am quite sure that I should through faint-heartedness have quit the field and allowed God's cause to go by default. The corruptions of our church have by no means reached that degree of downright opposition to the true doctrines of the gospel as the Romish [Church] had. But all that belongs to vital godliness is by many in as bad reports in the M.E.C. as were the cardinal doctrines of the gospel in the time of Zwingli and Luther in the Roman church. But thanks be to God, we are now beginning to see a genuine revival of primitive Methodism, and I am positive that it will rise to efficiency and power and yet do a work that, but for him, would be left undone.[734]

I see, too, from this standpoint [in] which my very severe affliction places me, that the form of religion which we have adopted falls im-

---

[733] Someone has drawn a faint X through the lower two-thirds of the page.

[734] The "him" here apparently refers back to Zwingli, but Redfield could rather have in mind B. T. Roberts.

mensely short of what it should. Our aim has been too low, and still is, although we are regarded as fanatics. Our aim should be to reach the highest ideal type of Christianity as the only /413/ valuable or saving kind of religion, and our motto should be, "Right or nothing." This should be the great and all-absorbing idea, for any and every form of religion which does not meet the utmost longings of our spirit is just defective enough to be of no value.[735] Most [new religious] forms do no more than mitigate our most urgent demands, rather than to supply our spiritual wants, and it is due to this defect that every new form of vagaries, like spiritualism and Mormonism, makes so easy a prey of the masses.

There is in all men an instinctive sense of want which clamors for supply. All possible expenditures of misnamed charity with which we lavishly try to cover up the defects of formalism, and pass it off to the acceptance of those upon whom we must urge it with vehemence, and press our arguments upon the selfish motives to secure their acceptance, does not and cannot mend the defect. What form soever of religion which man adopts, if it meets his wants, is not changed for another. Am I hungry? Give me just what I want, and I cannot be persuaded to change it for something else. Give me all I want, and I ask no more nor seek to supply deficiency by the use of something else.

Now, every man has an internal regulator which truthfully responds to any form of religion, and sets its true value upon it. Disguise the real value by words as we will, Truth will out in spite of him[self]. He may declare his religion to be a satisfying portion. But we feel sure he has overstated its real qualities and value when we see him making up the deficiency by the use of the world.

Now, strip our argument of all side issues, prune our theme of all worldly interests, and allow nothing to be appended or form any part of our religion which cannot by the most natural and easy effort be made to serve a specific use or meet a special want in our present or future state, and we are reduced to the simple question: What must religion /414/ do for us, to be of any practical value? And our natural answer is: It must stop all wrong, stimulate to do right, supply all spiritual wants, and more. It must at least give us an earnest of its adaptation to correct all the evil brought upon us through the effects of sin, and [through which we are] so far remodeled that we spontaneously harmonize with

---

[735] This passage is significant for understanding Redfield's conception of what the Free Methodist Church was and should be—though Redfield is here writing under great stress with views that are more extreme than those he expressed earlier. (Here again a large faint X has been drawn across most of the page.)

the providence and will of God and can truly say, "Good is the will of the Lord." Obedience to God is then no longer a task which we compel ourselves to do. As soon as the contest ceases between us and God, there is an end of all drudging in obedience so that with our Redeemer we can say, "I delight to do Thy will, O God."

The church of this age does not meet the necessities of our nature. We are compelled to seek a form which meets our wants, and [to] continue to contend for some unimportant side issue to keep up a distinction between ourselves and others who are called by the Christian name. Who don't see that a most desirable end to be gained is to bring mankind to an ultimate and happy brotherhood?—and to an extent that God may once more look down and see that all selfish ~~distinctions are obliterated~~ lines are abolished, and that we have all things ~~in~~ common. One family, one interest, and all men are our brothers.

This happy zenith is a point so far exalted above our highest expectations that we have only to announce it as a guiding start to win the name of madman. Yet this is but the zero from which to rise to the measure of the fullness of the stature of Christ, and through this to win back our forfeited state of righteousness and wisdom and true holiness.

LVII. Final Return to Syracuse

Chapter [38][736]

In February 1862, at St. Charles, Illinois, one of my special revelations opened to me, and that was that I must return to Syracuse, N.Y. and repeat my efforts for a special revival of religion after the type of Pentecost.[737] I had labored in /415/ a revival in that city about eleven or

[736] This chapter also is omitted by JGT.

[737] Rather than including this passage, Terrill inserts more Redfield letters. He reports also that Redfield preached on the first Sunday in June (apparently), 1861, at "Ogle Station, now Ashton," Illinois (about eighty miles west of Chicago) at a quarterly meeting. Terrill was the preacher on this new circuit. He reports, "On Sunday morning [Redfield] preached from the text, 'It is finished.' His wife was obliged to sit by his side, and prop him up by holding her hands under his left elbow, while he held on to the pulpit with his right hand" (455–56). Terrill recounts the sermon and its remarkable effect on the congregation. "Before he was through with his last point, the benefits of redemption, more than twenty persons were on their feet, with eyes closed, clasped hands, and streaming faces, gazing by faith upon the wonderful provisions of grace." He adds, "Several times, I now recollect, I was lost with the rest" (457).

Accompanied by his wife and by Terrill, Redfield over the next week or two preached at Crystal Lake and Belvidere, then went to the St. Charles Camp

twelve years previous, and so well was I acquainted with the religious elements of the city, and the desperate conflict which must be met, that my whole heart shrank from the task. Nothing could appear more preposterous than the idea that God could send me in my paralyzed state to Syracuse, one of the hardest of all places to labor, with any hope of success, and I instinctively cried out, "Oh God, I cannot think of so impossible a task!"

Upon my refusal to comply, I was seized by an unseen power which nearly stopped my breath and pressed the question, "Will you go, or not?" As soon as I could get breath, I cried out, "O God, don't demand this of me, but release me, for I never can go in this condition to labor in that hard, hard place, for I can see nothing ahead but toil and agony and final failure in the enterprise. And besides all this, no one can understand me, and my best friends will feel confident that all of this is only a result of my very nervous and weak state of body."

At this another and another spell would seize me, more and more severe, and I thought I might never breathe again. My agony and cries betrayed the cause of my conflict to all around. Again my breath left, and I felt all the distress of strangling. And just to save my life, I answered, "Yes, Lord, I will." Then I was instantly relieved.

"Now," said my friends around me who had witnessed my conflict, "you must prepare to start right off."

"No," said I. "I know I have not to go now, but wait for the door to be opened."

I was now quite easy, and thought and said, "I shall probably have to go sometime during the next summer or fall."

My friends who had witnessed the severity of my agony could

Meeting (458).

Terrill reports that though Redfield about this time "began to entertain hopes that God would restore him," this did not happen. Redfield struggled with this, as the previous pages show. Terrill reports, "He visited the quarterly and camp meetings, gave advice, counseled with the young preachers, and did what he could in the public services. He sometimes tried to preach, but his thinking powers seemed paralyzed; and at last he gave up trying altogether" (458). His attempt to preach at the 1861 St. Charles Camp Meeting, noted earlier, came a few weeks after this appearance at Ogle.

Terrill then includes a February 10, 1862, letter from Redfield to Mrs. Ellen Roberts. Terrill says the letter shows Redfield's "state of mind at this time. Some of it evidently tokens the breaking down of his magnificent mind" (459). Where in the letter Redfield refers to his "commission to preach redemption," Terrill inserts the footnote, "Mr. Redfield held to the idea of a redemption of the mental faculties, to be experienced by the faithful in this life" (460).

hardly believe, after all this, that I would dare to postpone my journey for a week.

I could now in spirit see Syracuse, and the dreadful state of death which must be met and contended against. But with the same inner eye I could see a vast cloud, and a voice to my inner ear saying to me that "Syracuse is the Jerusalem of America, and from that point must salvation go forth to save the nation." Then said that /416/ voice to me, "You visited that city about twelve years ago, and there saw the first dawning rays of that type of religion which must usher in the Millennium, and after the pattern of Pentecost.[738]

"But," said the voice, that has nearly all been squandered and is now in disgrace in the eyes of the people. And now I send you again. And as you went through with the breaking-up plow, I now send you with the subsoil plow. Though you will have severe conflict, and must stand alone nearly, yet I will stand by you."

A providential door was opened about the thirtieth of October, 1862, to go to Buffalo.[739] I then said to my wife, this is the time for me to obey my call to go to Syracuse." Then she told me she felt so, too. But, [she said.] "Bro. J. [Joslyn] is all out of the order of God to go to Buffalo at all."

In due time, however, we reached Buffalo, and finished all we had to do to there.[740] When Bro. J. was for our immediate return to Illinois, my wife too seemed to favor our return and to doubt the propriety of our visiting Syracuse in my very feeble state, believing that labor with me was entirely out of the question.

At this decision the old agony seized me again, as it did in St. Charles. [I] went to my room and poured out my complaint to Him who alone could understand or pity me. "O God, why dost Thou thus deal

---

[738] The eschatological Pentecostal themes are significant here.

[739] Some months before this, in the summer of 1862, Redfield "purchased forty acres of unimproved land near Geneva,...and about three miles from St. Charles" where hoped to establish "a pilgrims' home," according to Terrill (460–61).

[740] Terrill records a spring 1861 trip in which Redfield, having recovered somewhat, "visited the East, and held meetings a few weeks in Buffalo, in the Free Methodist Church" (454). Then later Terrill notes, "During the winter of '62 and '63, a visit was made to Buffalo, and then to Syracuse, where were pilgrims of mighty faith, and he hoped for restoration in answer to their prayers. Here he began to show evidences of the breaking down of his mind; which led many of his friends to distrust his personal convictions of duty. This caused him great pain" (462). It is this visit to Syracuse that Redfield next describes.

with me? Must this project be abandoned? And if so, what confidence can I ever have after this in these impressions which have been my guide all my life? And now if this proves a failure, I must regard all former impressions as equally groundless, and I have been the victim of hallucinations."

When they all saw how much this counsel distressed me, they decided as best for my sake to bring me down to Syracuse, as the only means of satisfying me that I was mistaken in my notions of duty to visit Syracuse, and then I might be willing to go back. Bro. J. conversed freely with others of my best Christian friends about the propriety of hazarding the experiment of going to Syracuse in my feeble condition. Bro. R. [Roberts] thought it all /417/ wrong and only a whim which was due to my weak and nervous state of mind, and a project wholly preposterous. My wife too was quite sure that my notions were all wrong. But Sister R. [Roberts] thought it best to humor the thing, and she gave some hints that there might be more of God in this matter than could be seen by all.[741] O how much her advice did relieve me, for I had to bear it all alone thus far.[742]

I was now decided that I might come to Syracuse. I could not say positively amid all these hindrances that I was not mistaken in my convictions of duty. But [I thought,] "What can I believe hereafter of all previous impressions, and what confidence can I ever repose in any future impressions, if this proves a failure?" I could but cry out, "O God, what will become of Thy great name if this is a failure? For I have published the fact to others, and they are looking for and expecting a failure."

When I turned my thoughts back to Illinois, I could see nothing but thick darkness and gloom. And I felt, "If I go back, it is only to die, and all my hopes of ever doing anything more publicly in the cause of Christ [will be dashed]. My bursting heart was writhing in agony, and

---

[741] B. T. Roberts and his family were at this time living in Buffalo.

[742] This is part of the background of Redfield's February 10, 1862, letter from Marengo, Illinois, to Ellen Roberts, reprinted in JGT, 459–60. In this letter Redfield speaks of "gentle and sweet intimations that I must soon go to Syracuse" and also about some of the struggles he records (above) in his memoir. He also notes, "I am now writing my life, and shall bring it with me, to see about getting it published" (460). Redfield had probably begun the manuscript in 1861, if not earlier, and may have hoped that B. T. Roberts would publish it. This reference suggests that Redfield was probably well along in the writing. The content suggests that he was in fact nearly done, though he never brought it to a proper conclusion. It is worth noting that he intended that it should be published.

my heart sunk like a stone.

At this juncture Bro. T., a man of God and of a deep experience to whom all gave heed, spoke hopefully and advised I should go to Syracuse. This was as a soothing balm to my almost despairing heart, and Oh how thankful I did feel to find one precious saint of God who could sympathize with me and bid me Godspeed.[743] It was like the first rays of morning after a night of storm and darkness.

We finally reached Syracuse about the fifteenth of November and called on Bro. Hicks, at whose house the very few who are alive meet together for religious meetings. And though [Hicks was] glad to see me as an old friend, and sincerely sorry to see me in such a crippled condition, yet when Bro. J. informed Bro. H. of my object in visiting Syracuse, the most discouraging aspect was put upon the whole affair. Bro. H., who had suffered much financially in previous efforts to advance the cause of God, said he could not on any conditions think of assuming any /418/ farther responsibilities. So now I saw that God alone could or would stand by me.

I was now advised to go out to Bro. Stearns, and get him to help me by prayer to get my health. Bro. J. said he was sure that if God had anything to do in the matter of sending me East, it was for my own spiritual benefit, for [he] thought what I most needed was to get reclaimed. So said and thought my wife. Bro. J. finally became so tired and discouraged with me that he told me he had no hope of my ever getting well, and that the great trouble with me was that I was so far from God that I could [but] with difficulty get back.

But I felt that I knew my own case and that he did not, and I must be content to pass along unknown and to be misunderstood. Both he and my wife, when I would talk of praying for my health in conjunction with the work of God, would tell me pertly, "You had better get saved yourself before you talk of getting your health or seeing others saved through your labors." Then Bro. J. was for having me go back to Illinois, and when my wife would complain of ill health, he would say he knew the whole difficulty, and that it was because she was out of the order of God.[744]

---

[743] Redfield may mean Terrill, though it is not clear that Terrill accompanied the Redfields to New York. "Bro. T." may have been a Christian brother in Buffalo.

[744] Clearly the ongoing strain of dealing with Redfield in his pathetic semi-paralyzed and depressed condition had gotten to Bro. Joslyn and Mrs. Redfield. They were exasperated and had completely run out of patience with him, and unfortunately interpreted Redfield's struggles more in spiritual than in psycho-

I now saw if my impressions are right, Bro. J.'s were not, and I was greatly distressed as I saw him so set to go back. And then I knew my wife would be greatly discontented, and this added to my pain. Finally my wife told me she should go back and leave me alone, for she could not stay East.

And now my distress was beyond endurance, at the thought of leaving Syracuse unredeemed.[745] Again I would talk to Bro. J. and my wife about the work of God, and they would tell me, "You better get saved yourself, first." This I had heard so many times and from so many with whom Bro. J. had conversed that I felt, "No one knows my case, and I must submit to pass along as though I heard not." "Who is deaf as my servant, and blind as he that is perfect?" [cf. Isaiah 42:19].

One more effort was made at this house of Bro. H. to get me saved, and the prayers were by no means flattering as to my religious state. But I felt /419/ forbidden to utter a word or try to explain one single item, for if I am to pass over the path of Christ, I must be content to be misunderstood and to bear it without opening my mouth.

We finally went to visit Bro. Stearns. As I went I was thinking that Bro. S. would request me to get down in the dust before God and confess and struggle and groan, and possibly I might before morning begin to get some relief and hope. But no, Bro. S., who seemed to have a clear view of my real state and needs, began to offer hope and [to] prompt faith in Jesus as my great Physician by singing songs of faith and hope to help my sinking faith. Now I began to get a glimpse of hope for my health. Sister S. too took a strong hold for me, as did also the wife of Bro. M. S. who, while praying for me, became greatly enlisted in my behalf. To appearance, with her eyes shut and led by the Spirit, she came and laid her hand upon the exact spot on my head where all my trouble is seated, and prayed thus: "O Lord, bless and correct this place. Heal this spot, and the paralysis will all cease."

This I knew to be the real seat of all my trouble, and I have felt great relief in that spot ever since.

Bro. J. seemed to think they were mistaking my case by praying for my body rather than for my soul. But I seemed not to notice this and kept my mind upon my body. Then my faith rallied, and I began to feel decided relief in my body. I felt too [the] arising of the old power of God in my soul. And now for the first time in my life, I found that God would show His approbation of my asking my health in the name of

---

somatic terms.

[745] I.e., leaving Syracuse in its unredeemed state. "Unredeemed" here, in context, refers not to Redfield but to the city.

Jesus by blessing the soul at the same time. In this light I saw where I had lost the freshness of my former power and peculiar unction, the absence of which, together with the dumbness of my bodily powers caused by disease, led my friends to account me backslidden. I lost this power by ceasing to follow the light of former days which was leading me to endure and hold up the redemption of the body as a part of the fruits of the gospel.[746]

Again Bro. J. was greatly distressed about going back [to Illinois], and wished me and my wife to go back immediately. At this all the agony of my former distress came back /420/ for the redemption of Syracuse, and it did seem almost too hard that God should press me so hard to come and then to allow so many obstacles to stand in my way.

Bro. J. had had a very distressed state of mind [just] about every day, and [was] anxious to go back West. We now returned from S. to Bro. Stearns to Syracuse.[747] When Bro. J. was so greatly distressed about going home, I now became clear in my own mind that there was no use of trying to comfort him. I had so great a burden on account of my mission that his trouble, added to mine, put me in agony both in body and mind.

I now went to God and asked for relief, and I felt that I got a strong hold on the arm of the Lord, and was heard. On the same day, Bro. J. received a letter from home requesting him to return immediately, which he did. And O, how greatly relieved did I feel when he was gone. My wife took his departure quite hard, and I began to fear that she might never be reconciled to go out and labor with me as in former years. All I had on which to hope that she might be contented was that God might give some omens of good.

We now took up our abode with Bro. G. at Salina [New York], and I had hopes that we might get a chance to labor in the M.E. Church where I attended a meeting eleven years ago.[748] I was allowed to preach only once, and that was by the earnest request of my former friends. I heard that quite a number desired that I should be allowed to preach again. But it was quite evident that my preaching would not be at all welcome by the preacher. So I had to content myself with attending the class and prayer meetings at private houses. And in those meetings God began to revive the work and fan up longings for the state of grace

---

[746] Here again is the redemption of the body theme.

[747] Meaning unclear. Perhaps Redfield means they went from Syracuse back to Bro. Stearns' residence, then back again to Syracuse. Or he may have meant simply to say, "We returned from Bro. Stearns' home back to Syracuse."

[748] Salina, a village near Syracuse. See page 271, above, and note there.

which some of them enjoyed eleven years ago.

On Sabbath afternoons [in Syracuse] I would go over to prayer meetings at the house of Bro. Hicks. Such was the distress of my soul on two occasions that I could not help sobbing aloud, and was scarcely able to speak more than /421/ a word at a time. It did seem that unless God should redeem Syracuse, I could not find relief from my distress. The Lord now gave some tokens of hope, and my wife, though often greatly tempted about our stay in the city, now began to take hope, and this gave me a little relief.

December 20th [18]62[749]—Just two years and one month today since I was smitten with paralysis.[750] I am not healed, though much better than I have been since my affliction. No way [has] opened for us to labor yet in any church, so what we do must be done in the houses of the people. Even this much of labor I hear is publicly denounced as evidence of a want of fairness—to labor so slyly, and to go hawking religion about the streets. I see if I am to be healed and the work of God is to go on, some desperate effort must be put forth. I know it is useless to ask the use of the churches to preach Jesus and the resurrection. So I have resolved to hold a season of prayer and fasting and lay my whole case before the Lord. For I can do with God what I cannot hope to do with man.

I start with this prayer:

O Lord, Thy kingdom come. Thy will be done in Syracuse as in heaven.

First petition. O Lord, make me every whit whole.

Second petition. Send the Pentecostal baptism of the Holy Ghost in all its power, glory, and extent, and with all the accompaniments of Pentecost.

Third petition. Send us a revival in depth, breadth, and extent, and power such as this nation has never known.

Fourth. Put it in the hearts of the people to make an offering of a church as a memento of gratitude to God, to be used for the purpose of perpetuating this type of religion in Syracuse.

Fifth. Grant to usher in the jubilee of freedom to every man, woman, and child within this broad nation. And for these, God helping me, I will /422/ fast and pray till the token or answer comes.

First day of fast, [twenty-]first day of December, 1862, Sabbath.[751]

---

[749] From this point Redfield's manuscript becomes essentially a daily diary.

[750] Redfield may be mistaken here as to the date, as earlier evidence his stroke occurred on November 2, 1860, not on November 20.

[751] December 1, 1862, was a Monday. The date references before and after this

Went to church in morning and heard a sermon, dead, dry, and powerless. I am certain that such soulless preaching can never make men to seek God. The preacher betrays deep subtlety in trying to disguise his real spiritual state and make the people satisfied with their dead condition. I have no doubt the preacher would do all in his power to prevent his church from being used for a genuine revival of religion. My heart instinctively asks, while my heart is all broken up, "O Jesus, is this all that can be expected of Thy professed ministers? A few very commonplace references to philosophy and history, betraying his ignorance. Then a strong commendation of the existing state of death, a few thrusts at those who weep over the desolations of Zion and who pray for a return of primitive Bible religion. Then a performance by the choir accompanied by the melodeon, and the congregation is dismissed.[752] Nobody saved, nobody convicted of sin, and the people go to come again in due time to a similar repast. Nothing done, and in this state the people under this treatment will live and die and be lost. Oh my God, what will they do in the end thereof?"

Afternoon, went to Bro. H.'s house, and was obliged to keep my mind off from the moral state of the city or I should be unable to control my emotions and should disturb the meeting with my sobbing. At the close of the meeting one soul was powerfully saved. Thank God for this token of good. What adds encouragement is that many just now feel that something might now be done.

December 22. Second day of my fasting. Some part of the day [I] feel some tokens of healing power upon me. I am fearful that unless the work breaks out soon, Bro. G. may get discouraged, and then we shall be a burden if we stay here.

Third day of fasting. Early this morning before rising [I] felt very painful sensations of hunger. I asked the Lord to remove it and was so far relieved that I felt no special inconvenience till about /423/ three o'clock. I then felt such a sudden sinking that I was satisfied I had fasted as long as God required, and so I stopped it. I now found that I had been benefited in my body in a number of particulars.

Fourth day—Tried and tempted. All looks dark. My wife so tempted that she thinks she can stay no longer, and after a letter comes from the West urging her to return, and this makes the matter much worse. Altogether I have more than I can stand up under. But when I

---

suggest that Redfield was referring to Sunday, December 21.

[752] The reference to a choir and melodeon indicates that this was not a Free Methodist congregation. A later reference identifies it as the M.E. Church in which Redfield conducted his earlier revival effort in Syracuse.

look over the circumstances which have brought me here, I dare not leave. If no one can appreciate my motives and my wife should leave me alone, I must obey God at all cost.

I this day read over a short history of the toils and travels of St. Paul. My soul was all broken up in floods of tears, as I could trace the parallel of our cases. Did he go called of God? So did I. Did he travel at his own charge? So have I. Did he meet with perils and disasters, and the worst among his own countrymen? Was he an outlaw to his own Jewish church? Had he a thorn in the flesh? So have I. And now the thought overwhelmed me that I too am called to plant churches.

December 20 and 21. Some tokens of hope that God will yet save the M.E. Church in this place.

On Sabbath [December 28, I] went to church again, and O my God, is such stale and vapid talk to pass for gospel preaching? Eleven or twelve years ago my heart was almost broken, and my spiritual sufferings for this place were almost unbearable, till God sent us a specimen of Pentecostal power. But now, how is the gold become dim, and the most pure gold changed! [cf. Lamentations 4:1]. The preacher appears to be little better than a parrot.

On the thirtieth [I] went to visit a few whom I knew twelve years ago, and was quite refreshed to find them still gasping for life. My wife, with Bro. and Sister G., went out to visit a number of families, and God gave tokens of hope to their efforts.

Thirty-first. Went to a watch-night and heard a young man of promising talents. But what a need of a baptism was manifest!

I now learned that the preacher was going to have a series of meetings and has engaged four preachers besides himself. To me it was evident that the object was to furnish an excuse for not allowing me to preach at all. I was tempted, and feel grieved as I looked over my past labors, now about twenty-six years. [I] have labored without reward and can count up /424/ over thirty M.E. churches which had been built or redeemed through my labors. And now there are young men who were in their swaddling clothes while I was going forth amid scorn and opposition and at my own expense, weeping and bearing precious seed. Now many of them occupy the very pulpits which God helped me to build or redeem, and I must not be allowed to labor in them, though I do it for nothing and the people desire it.

For a few moments I felt quite grieved, and the more so as I saw that these men were void of the life and power of religion. But before this amounted to a murmur, the blessed Spirit of God spoke to me this: "Well, Christ came to His own, and they received Him not. But He made Himself of no reputation, but took upon Himself the form of a servant."

I felt rebuked in a moment that the thought should enter my head, and God helped me to banish it from my heart. And then I was overwhelmed at the thought that God counted me worthy of following in the footsteps of Jesus. I then became quite satisfied with my lot and the further fact that there were many families who would not be ashamed of my chain [cf. II Timothy 1:16] but would gladly welcome me to their hearts and listen to my counsel.

What further adds to my comfort is that my wife is getting the victory over these things. She seems willing to be slighted herself. But the temptation has been rather hard upon her, to see me turned off by those who ought to be like grateful sons in the gospel.

January First, 1863. This morning God gives a token for good. My companion seems ready to shoulder the cross anew, and as she has helped me to bear the burden in the heat of the day when my health was good, she seems now ready in an obscure way and unappreciated to renew her labors and leave the great settlement day to adjust all wrongs.

January Fourth. Quarterly meeting. While listening to a very dull and dry sermon, I was meditating on the state of grace this people were in twelve years ago, and now so dead. That verse in Revelation 18, seventeenth verse, was powerfully applied to my heart: "Alas, alas, for in one hour is so great riches come to naught."[753]

/425/ Monday, Fifth [of January, 1863]. My grief is too great to allow of my eating, and my cry is, "O Lord, either release me or clear away the obstacles in the way of my labors." I am greatly tempted that if all I have endured in coming to this place and the strong and agonizing impression to come here proves a failure, I must conclude that my whole life has been a failure, and all my impressions which have guided me all my life are only an invention[?] of the imagination, and I can never again trust to impressions to guide me. Now, in this light, my whole life appears a blank and failure. I have suffered all these things for more than twenty years for nothing. Oh God, do come to my relief, for I suffer all this for Thee.

January 6. Last night I attended church and found nearly all of the Spirit which had been gained in our neighborhood prayer meetings all quenched. The preacher plays deceit by appearing friendly in word, when I know it is all fake. God gave me to see he is only a whited sep-

---

[753] Cf. Revelation 18:16–17a KJV: "And saying, Alas, alas, that great city, that was clothed in fine linen, and purple, and scarlet, and decked with gold, and precious stones, and pearls! For in one hour so great riches is come to nought."

ulchre.

On my way home I felt I must soon see a change, or give up the place and with it abandon all confidence in impressions. My heart feels almost broke, and I ask in deep distress of soul, "Oh Lord, do give me relief. Release me, or open a way for me and give me some token on which to hope."

I am fearful and feel that God may come in judgment if the people do not learn righteousness, and this church and people will be rooted out. As for a revival, they will have none. But death and ruin will fill up their cup of agony, and [they will] repent, but too late. For God has been rejected and He will reject them, to the confusion of their own faces. "Behold, your house is left unto you desolate," will soon be applied to this people. And yet there is mercy with the Most High, and if they will return, God will yet show mercy.

January Seventh, [1863]. Some better in body and mind, and some very consoling evidence that our feeble efforts have been owned of God in reestablishing a goodly number in the old paths of life and power and salvation.[754]

---

[754] Redfield's manuscript ends here, near the bottom of page 425. The next page (the reverse side of page 425) is marked at the top, "P 426" but the page is otherwise blank. Redfield was still in Syracuse, or nearby Salina, when he stopped writing his document.

Shortly after this entry, it appears, Redfield and his wife returned to Illinois. Terrill writes, "At last he turned his face toward the West again, weeping as he went. He said but little now in public gatherings. He attended the annual session of the Illinois Conference. The love-feast Sunday morning was truly blessed, and none enjoyed it more than Mr. Redfield. When the bread and water were passed, he tried several times to drink from the cup, such were his overflowing tears, and the convulsive joy of his heart. Little did some of us think that it was the last we should see him alive. He returned to the home of Brother Joslyn, who had so long cared for him" (462).

Redfield had attended the Illinois Conference at Aurora, which met October 21–27. The love feast Terrill mentions was probably on Sunday, October 25; on that day also the new Aurora F.M. Church building was dedicated, with B. T. Roberts preaching. Redfield was listed in the conference appointments as "Conf. Miss." [Conference Missionary]. Report on the Illinois Conference, *The Earnest Christian* 6, no. 6 (Dec. 1863): 187–88.

On Thursday, October 29, Redfield wrote his last letter, to a "Brother F.," challenging him to be faithful in his ministry (JGT, 462–63). He suffered a final stroke on Sunday, November 1, and died the next day.

Bibliography

Allen, Ray. *A Century of the Genesee Annual Conference of the Methodist Episcopal Church 1810-1910.* Rochester: By the Author, 1911.

Asbury, Francis. *The Journal and Letters of Francis Asbury.* Elmer T. Clark, ed. 3 vols. London: Epworth; Nashville: Abingdon, 1958.

Barclay, William Crawford. *History of Methodist Missions.* Vol. 1, *Missionary Motivation and Expansion.* New York: Board of Missions and Church Extension of The Methodist Church, 1949; Vol. 3, *Widening Horizons 1845-95.* New York: Board of Missions of The Methodist Church, 1957.

Barnhart, Clarence L., and Robert K. Barnhart, eds. 2 vols. *World Book Dictionary.* Chicago: Field Enterprises, 1976.

Bassett, T. D. Seymour. *The Gods of the Hills: Piety and Society in Nineteenth-Century Vermont.* Montpelier: Vermont Historical Society, 2000.

———. "'The Mightiest Revival That Burlington Ever Saw' And Its Consequences. The Pine Street Methodist Church 1855-66." *Chittenden County Historical Society Bulletin* 30, no. 2 (Spring 1996): 7-12.

[Brooks, Joseph.] "Anti-Methodism." *Central Christian Advocate* 3, no. 15 (13 April 1859): 2.

[———.] "Ebenezer Church, St. Louis." *Central Christian Advocate* 3, no. 14 (6 April 1859): 2.

Burrows, Edwin G., and Mike Wallace. *Gotham: A History of New York City to 1898.* New York: Oxford University Press, 1999.

Canon, Charles. "B. T. Roberts' Supporting Cast: Rev. William C. Kendall (1822–1858)," *Free Methodist Historical Society Newsletter* 2, no. 1 (Summer 2001): 1.

Castle, C. A. *A History of the Methodist Episcopal Church in Burlington, Vermont.* Burlington: Free Press Association, 1903.

Chapman, Mary Weems. *Mother Cobb or Sixty Years' Walk with God.* Chicago: T. B. Arnold, 1896.

Chiles, Robert E. *Theological Transition in American Methodism: 1790–1935.* New York: Abingdon, 1965.

Clark, D. W. *Life and Times of Rev. Elijah Hedding, D. D., Late Senior Bishop of the Methodist Episcopal Church.* New York: Carlton and Phillips, 1856.

Cohen, Paul E., and Robert T. Augustyn. *Manhattan in Maps, 1527–1995.* New York: Rizzoli, 1997.

Coon, Harriet A. *Life and Labors of Auntie Coon.* E. E. Shelhamer, ed.2 Atlanta: Repairer Office, 1905.

Cullum, Douglas Russell. "Gospel Simplicity: Rhythms of Faith and Life among Free Methodists in Victorian America." Ph.D. Diss., Drew University, 2002. Especially "John Wesley Redfield and the Primitivist Impulse," 26–36.

Currier, A. H. *The Life of Constans L. Goodell, D.D.* New York: Anson D. F. Randolph and Co., 1887.

Duberman, Martin, ed. *The Antislavery Vanguard: New Essays on the Abolitionists.* Princeton: Princeton University Press, 1965.

"Experience of Joseph G. Terrill," *The Earnest Christian* 3, no. 2 (Feb. 1862): 53–57.

Gravely, William. *Gilbert Haven, Methodist Abolitionist: A Study in Race, Religion, and Reform, 1850-1880.* Nashville: Abingdon, 1973.

Grodzins, Dean. *American Heretic: Theodore Parker and Transcendentalism.* Chapel Hill: University of North Carolina Press, 2002.

Hambrick-Stowe, Charles E. *Charles G. Finney and the Spirit of Evangelicalism.* Grand Rapids: Eerdmans, 1996.

Hampton, Vernon Boyce, ed. *Newark Conference Centennial History, 1857–1957.* Historical Society of the Newark Annual Conference of The Methodist Church, 1957.

Hart, Edward Payson. *Reminiscences of Early Free Methodism.* Chicago: Free Methodist Publishing House, 1903.

Historical Records Survey, Division of Professional and Service Projects, Works Projects Administration. *Inventory of the Church Archives of New York City The Methodist Church.* New York: Historical Records Survey, 1940.

History of McHenry County, Illinois. Chicago: Inter-State Publishing Co., 1885.

Hogue, Wilson T. *History of the Free Methodist Church of North America.* 2 vols. Chicago: Free Methodist Publishing House, 1915.

Holdich, Joseph. "Revival in the Wesleyan University." *Christian Advocate and Journal* 20, no. 33 (25 March 1846): 130.

———. *The Life of Willbur Fisk, D.D., First President of the Wesleyan University.* New York: Harper and Brothers, 1842.

Huffman, Samuel. "Special Request." *Central Christian Advocate* 3, no. 11 (16 March 1859): 2.

Hunt, Sandford. *Methodism in Buffalo From Its Origin to the Close of 1892.* Buffalo: H. H. Otis and Sons, 1893.

Jones, Marsh Wilkinson. "Pulpit, Periodical, and Pen: Joseph Benson and Methodist Influence in the Victorian Prelude." Ph.D. Diss., University of Illinois, Urbana-Champaign, 1995.

Kverndal, Roald. *Seamen's Missions: Their Origin and Early Growth.* Pasadena: William Carey Library, 1986.

Long, E. B., with Barbara Long. *The Civil War Day by Day: An Almanac 1861–1865.*

[M'Anally, D. R.] "Our Northern Brethren." *St. Louis Christian Advocate* 9, no. 12 (24 March 1859): 3.

Marston, Leslie R. *From Age to Age a Living Witness: A Historical Interpretation of Free Methodism's First Century.* Winona Lake, Ind.: Light and Life, 1960.

Matlack, L. C. *The Antislavery Struggle and Triumph in the Methodist Episcopal Church.* New York: Phillips and Hunt, 1881; reprint New York: Negro Universities Press, 1969.

Methodist Episcopal Church. *Minutes of the Annual Conferences of the Methodist Episcopal Church,* 1836-61. New York: T. Mason and G. Lane. (Imprint varies according to names of book agents and assistant book agents.)

Nicolson, Frank W., ed. *Alumni Record of Wesleyan University.* Centennial (Sixth) ed. Middletown, Conn.: Pelton and King, 1931.

Oden, Thomas C., ed. *Phoebe Palmer: Selected Writings.* New York: Paulist, 1988.

Olin, Stephen. *The Life and Letters of Stephen Olin, D.D., LL.D., Late President of the Wesleyan University,* 2 vols. New York: Harper and Brothers, 1853.

Peck, Jesse T. *The Central Idea of Christianity.* Boston: H. V. Degen, 1856.

Price, Carl F. *Wesleyan's First Century: With an Account of the Centennial Celebration.* Middletown, Conn.: Wesleyan University, 1932.

Programme of the Celebration of the One Hundredth Anniversary of the Organization of the Methodist Episcopal Church, Burlington, Vermont, October 20, 21, 22, 1923 (1923). 8 pages.

Reid, Daniel G., ed. *Dictionary of Christianity in America.* Downers Grove: InterVarsity, 1990.

Reinhard, James Arnold. "Personal and Sociological Factors in the Formation of the Free Methodist Church 1852-1860." Ph.D. Diss., University of Iowa, 1971.

"Rev. Joseph G. Terrill." *The Earnest Christian* 69, no. 5 (May 1895): 160.

Roberts, B. T., ed. *The Earnest Christian* (monthly periodical) 1-64 (1860-1892). After Roberts' death in 1893, the periodical continued under other editors until the end of 1909. (Several articles pertaining specifically to Redfield are noted below.)

Roberts, B. T. "Death of Dr. Redfield." *The Earnest Christian* 6, no. 6 (Dec. 1863): 184.

———. "Dr. Redfield's Labors." *The Earnest Christian* 7, no. 2 (Feb. 1864): 37-38.

———. "Rev. J. W. Redfield, M.D." *The Earnest Christian* 7, no. 1 (Jan. 1864): 5.

———. *Why Another Sect: Containing a Review of Articles by Bishop Simpson and Others on the Free Methodist Church.* Rochester, NY: "The Earnest Christian" Office, 1879.

Roberts, Benson Howard. *Benjamin Titus Roberts, Late General Superintendent of the Free Methodist Church.* North Chili, N.Y.: "The Earnest Christian" Office, 1900.

Rosell, Garth M., and Richard A. G. Dupuis, eds. *The Memoirs of Charles G. Finney: The Complete Restored Text.* Grand Rapids: Zondervan, 1989.

Scharf, J. Thomas. *History of Saint Louis and County, from the Earliest Periods to the Present Day: Including Biographical Sketches of Representative Men.* 2 vols. Philadelphia: Louis H. Everts, 1883.

Simpson, Matthew, ed. *Cyclopædia of Methodism,* rev. ed. Philadelphia: Louis H. Everts, 1880.

Terrill, Joseph Goodwin. *The Life of Rev. John Wesley Redfield, M.D.* Chicago: Free Methodist Publishing House, 1889.

———. *The St. Charles' Camp-Meeting, Embodying Its History and Several Sermons by Leading Ministers, with Some Practical Suggestions Concerning Camp-Meeting Management.* Chicago: T. B. Arnold, 1883.

Weiss, John. *Life and Correspondence of Theodore Parker, Minister of the Twenty-Eighth Congregational Society, Boston.* 2 vols. New York: D. Appleton, 1864.

Weld, Theodore. *American Slavery As It Is: Testimony of a Thousand Witnesses.* New York: American Anti-Slavery Society, 1839.

Wheatley, Richard. *The Life and Letters of Phoebe Palmer.* New York: Palmer and Hughes, 1884.

White, Charles Edward. *The Beauty of Holiness: Phoebe Palmer as Theologian, Revivalist, Feminist, and Humanitarian.* Grand Rapids: Francis Asbury Press/Zondervan, 1986).

Zahniser, Clarence Howard. *Earnest Christian: Life and Works of Benjamin Titus Roberts.* Circleville, OH: Advocate Publishing House, 1957.

Index

Abbott, Benjamin, 95, 119, 195
abolitionism, x, xi, xiii, xxiii, 46–64, 199, 257, 267, 326–28, 369–70
Africa, xxiv, 135
African Americans, xxiv, 43, 50–54, 116–17, 151–52, 175, 178, 231, 261–62, 314–15, 333
Albion, New York, 258–62, 269, 285, 328
Algeria, slavery in, 53–54
Allen St. M.E. Church, New York City, 72, 82, 144
American Anti-Slavery Society, 50, 54
American Colonization Society, 49–50
American Missionary Association, xxiv
American Slavery As It Is, 50–53, 55
amusements, popular, 234, 347
angels, 4, 13, 15–17, 21, 24, 143–45, 156, 203, 247, 248, 351–52, 357, 360, 371, 374–75; guardian, 366
animals, concern for, xxiii
annihilation, 27–29
antislavery movement, x, 49–64, 368–69. *See* abolitionism
antislavery societies, 49–50, 54, 64; opposition to, 49–50
Apostles, 1, 25, 365
Appleton, Wisconsin, 300, 307
Asbury M.E. Church, New York City, 93
Asbury, Francis, 56, 126, 194–95
atheism, 27, 28, 247
atonement, 90, 163, 226–27, 354–55, 359–60; substitutionary, 163; universal, 360
Auburn, New York, 285
Aurora, Illinois, 297, 299, 340, 344–45, 346, 396
Austin, Joseph, 289
awakening, 80, 138–40, 148, 204
backsliding, 24, 115, 118, 123, 199, 243, 250, 257, 277, 355, 390
Baker University, 322
Baltimore, Maryland, 326
bands, Methodist, 306
Bangs, Heman, 158–60
Bangs, Nathan, 158
baptism of the Spirit, xxii, 196, 392, 394; Pentecostal, 392
Baptists, 130–33, 178–80, 185–86, 211, 218, 227–28, 257, 258, 263, 265, 304–5, 334, 340–41
Bassett, T. D. Seymour, 288
Bath, New York, 275, 277–79
Beaumont, Gustave, 202
Bedford St. M.E. Church, New York City, 71–72, 79, 91, 93–94, 101
Belvidere, Illinois, 352, 384
Benjamin, Walter W., 196
Benson, Joseph, 104
Bergen (New York) Camp Meeting, 293, 338
Bible, meaning of, 263–64; authority of, 366
Bible Society, 217
"Bible standard," 120, 219, 258, 264, 277
Bigelow, Noah, 75
bishops, M.E., 119, 121, 157, 172, 271, 281, 283–84
Black River Conference, M.E., 234, 236
blasphemy, 179, 187–88, 360, 365
Boardman, William E., 334
Boston, Massachusetts, 126, 181, 183–86, 212–14, 257–58
Bowen, Elias, 271
Bramwell, William, 95–96, 119–20, 194–95
Bridgeport, Connecticut, 180, 206–12, 215–16, 262–63, 267
Broadway Tabernacle, New York, xxv

Brooklyn, New York, 289
Brooks, Joseph, 313–14, 321, 323, 326, 342
brotherhood, 384–85
Brown, John, 342
"Buffalo Regency," 281–83
Buffalo, New York, 259–60, 280–83, 300, 307, 344, 350, 387–88
Bunyan, John, 365
Burdick, Chester F., 286–87
Burlington, Iowa, 311
Burlington, Vermont, xiv, xxi, xxiv, 285–90, 297, 351; 1855 revival at, xxi, xxii, 286–90

Calvinism, x, 173–74, 176, 200, 226
camp meetings, xxiii, xxiv, 5, 83–92, 105, 126, 134, 138, 150, 187–93, 196–201, 223–27, 234–36, 249, 290, 293, 298, 300–301, 338, 341–43, 349, 385
Campbellites, 314
Canada, refuge for slaves, 62, 64
card playing, ix, 208, 304–5
Carlton, Thomas, 282
Castle, Cassius, xxi, 288–89
Caughey, James, 107, 164–65
Caughlin, D., 318
character, 202, 209, 320, 335, 343; of God, 347
charisma, 76; of Redfield, 76
Chelsea, Massachusetts, 181–83
Cheney, Laban, 101
Chicago, Illinois, xxv, 294, 304, 326, 385
choirs, 94, 275, 392
cholera, 35
Christianity, primitive, 362, 371, 392
church, 128, 167, 264, 361, 364–65, 384–85; form of, 326; and Pentecost, 262–64, 364–65
church buildings, ix, 93, 109, 173, 193–95, 206–7, 210, 214, 220–21, 231–32, 237, 247, 250, 253–54, 265, 285, 288–89, 294, 329, 371; ornate, ix, 63, 157, 206, 288, 371; plain, 341–42; and social status, 206, 221, 288–89
church government, 326
church growth, xxiii, 314. *See* membership statistics
Church St. M.E. Church, Boston, 183
Cincinnati, Ohio, 172, 327
Civil War, U.S., xiv, 282, 362, 369–71
clairvoyance, 30, 349
Claremont, New Hampshire, xxi, 267–68
Clark, D. W., 213–14
Clarke, Adam, 103–4
class consciousness, 185. *See* social status
class leaders, Methodist, 24, 25, 47, 67, 80, 125, 127, 139, 162, 183
class meetings, 80, 93, 98–99, 109, 126, 162, 211, 325, 391
Cleveland, Ohio, 48–64; antislavery activity in, 48–54, 57, 62, 64
Clintonville, Illinois, 339
Clute, M. V., 258
Cobb, "Mother," 303
Coleman, Seymour, 286, 337–38, 341
colonization of slaves, 49–50
Combes, Clement, 208
common sense, 28
community of goods, 384
confession, 63, 89, 127, 243, 252, 256–57, 269, 270, 272, 280
Congregational Church, xxiv–xxv, 178, 185–86, 196, 199, 250, 254–58, 287, 304–5
conscience, 25, 42, 45, 58, 65, 72–73, 108, 207, 226, 269, 272, 324, 329, 347–48, 359
consecration, xxii, 88, 90, 264
consumption (tuberculosis), 124-25, 143, 317
contemplation of God, 237
conversion, ix, xi, xiv, xxiii–xxv, 4–7, 56, 80, 91, 93, 100, 109, 115–17, 125, 131, 139–41, 146–52, 155–56, 162–70, 176–77, 182, 185, 189–91, 195, 197, 200–203, 210, 223–24, 227, 232, 246, 254, 262–66, 270, 276, 279,

287–88, 300–5; radical, xxv, 287, 301; of slaveholders, 56; of the world, 95; testimony to, 109, 223–25, 262, 270, 276, 279
Coon, "Auntie" Harriet, 327, 346–47, 351–52
Copeland, John, 269
Corning, New York, 275–76
covenant, 88
cross of Christ, 178, 380
Crystal Lake, Illinois, 385
culture, xiii
Currier, A. H., xxii, xxiii, 287

Dake, J. W., 352
damnation, 21, 117
dancing, ix, 94, 162, 208, 211, 219, 296, 305, 347; spiritual, 241–42
Davis, Werter R., 322
death, accounts of, 142–45, 177, 192; as judgment, 170–71, 174, 187–88, 209–10; triumphant, 372
Dickey, William, 52
discernment of spirits, 243, 266–67, 357
discipline, 127, 202, 211, 364; M.E., 207, 210–13, 258, 273, 294, 297, 307, 315–16, 320–21, 325–26, 331, 339, 368; F.M., 329, 344
dreams, x, xiv, 4, 13, 20, 21, 26–27, 96–97, 118, 172, 175, 333, 347, 373
dress, issue of, ix, 83–84, 189, 211–12
Duane St. M.E. Church, New York City, 78
Dutch Reformed Church, 114, 169

East Genesee Conference, M.E., 269, 278, 284, 293–94
Eaton, William, 53
Ebenezer M.E. Church, St. Louis, Missouri, 312–24, 327–28, 330–32, 348–49
Eddy, Thomas M., 337
Edmonds (Edmunds), Mrs. George F., 287
Edmunds, George F., 287
Eighteenth St. M.E. Church, New York City, 72, 75, 79, 91–94, 97–98, 101
Eighth St. M.E. Church, Philadelphia, 168
election, doctrine of, 226–27
Elgin, Illinois, 301–2, 309, 312, 338–39
emotional manifestations, ix, xiv, 27, 132, 159, 168–69, 180, 238–49, 335. *See* spiritual manifestations
Enoch, Patriarch, 379
entertainment, popular, 219, 347
episcopacy, 326. *See* bishops, M.E.
Episcopal Church, 114, 140, 146, 179, 187, 212–13, 297, 372
Erie Conference, M.E., 49
eschatology, 102, 356–60, 363
eternal life, 27–30
eternity, 344
evangelism, xxii, xxv, 2, 6–8, 20, 93, 107, 211
exhorters, exhortation, 108–9, 126, 176, 192, 211, 242, 246

Fair Haven M.E. Church, New Haven, Connecticut, 220
Fairfield, Connecticut, 223
faith, 66–67, 82–84, 88–90, 227, 263, 284, 373, 375, 390; for sanctification, 136–37, 234–35; for healing, 353, 355
faithfulness, 211, 266, 272, 362, 382
Falley Seminary, 199
family prayer, 176, 211, 269
fanaticism, x, 147, 155, 197, 231, 255, 308, 315, 343, 353, 366, 372, 379, 383
fashion, fashionableness, ix–x, 94, 100, 112–13, 118, 133, 177, 189, 197, 212, 219, 234, 250, 271, 281, 289
fasting, 15, 18, 65, 81, 258, 372–76, 391–93
Fifth St. M.E. Church, Philadelphia, 168

Fifth St. M.E. Church, Quincy, Illinois, 333
Fillmore, Daniel, 214
Finney, Charles G., xi, xiii, 107, 254–55, 295; meets Redfield, 295; in Rochester, New York, 295
First Congregational Church, Burlington, Vermont, 287
First M.E. Church, New Haven, Connecticut, 214, 220
First M.E. Church, Rochester, New York, 293–95
Fisk, Willbur, xxi, 5, 9–10, 21, 83, 95, 267
Fletcher, John, 21, 95–96, 104, 119, 182
Floy, James, xxii
Floyd, John B., 361
Fond du Lac, Wisconsin, 298–99
forgiveness, 366
formalism, formality, x, 105, 113-14, 116, 211, 217–18, 231, 238, 250, 268–69, 338, 362, 383
Fort Edward, New York, 286
Fox, G. H., 299
Francis, Lewis, 287
Free Methodist Church, x, xi, xix, 63, 153, 236, 258, 280, 285, 297, 302–3, 317, 329, 339–45, 350, 352, 362–63, 367, 372–73, 392; founding of, xiv, xvii, xxv, 342–44, 367; mission of, 364
French, Charles, 311
Fugitive Slave Law, 56, 368
Fuller, James, 259–61, 281

gambling, 48, 298, 304, 347
Garrettson, Catherine, 171
Garrettson, Freeborn, 56, 171, 200–202
General Conference of 1860, M.E., 329, 340
General Missionary Society, M.E., 281
Genesee College, 292
Genesee Conference, M.E., 156, 258–59, 280–82, 293, 295, 300, 302, 328–29
Genesee Wesleyan Seminary, 78
Geneva, Illinois, 296, 387
George, Augustus C., 293
German Methodists, 334
gifts of the Spirit, 349
glory of God, ix, 129, 237, 345–47, 356, 365, 376, 380; "unearthly," 110, 283, 316, 347
God, attributes of, 355, 378; sovereignty of, 174
Goodell, Constans L., xxiv–xxv, 287
Goshen, New York, 146, 172–78, 187
government of God, 361
grace of God, 223, 264–65, 377, 379, 384
Gravely, William, 56–57
Green Bay, Wisconsin, 307
Griffin, Benjamin, 101
Grimké, Angelina (Mrs. Theodore Weld), 50
Grimké, Sarah, 50

Hageman, John, 322
hallucinations, 15, 18, 25, 27, 46, 142, 144, 243, 387
Hamline, Bishop Leonidas L., 106, 118, 172, 337
Hamline, Melinda, 106
Harroun, Charles Elliott, 296–97
Hart, Edward Payson, 302, 347, 352
Hart, M. L., 302, 347
Hart, Martha Bishop (Mrs. E. P.), 347
Hathaway, J. W., 318
Haven, Gilbert, 56–57
healing, 66–67, 123–24, 350–51, 353–54, 363–64, 388–92
Heath, J. W., 318
heaven, 28, 88, 128, 142–44, 166, 186, 201, 203, 237, 247, 270, 355–56, 360, 365; new, 360
Hedding, Bishop Elijah, 108, 212–14
hell, 24, 28, 105, 174, 193, 201, 225, 229–30, 245, 247, 253, 268, 274, 360, 365
Henrietta, New York, 268–74
Herrick, E. E., 287

Hicks, Charles T., 237–39, 248–49, 261, 271, 284–85, 388–93
Hicks, Elias, 163
Hicks, Mrs. Charles, 248
Hicksite Quakers, 163
higher life teaching, 333
Hogue, Bishop Wilson T., xv, xxi
Holdich, Joseph, xxi, xxiii, 155
holiness, and Christ's atonement, 90; as cleansing, 357; debates over, xxii, 94–95, 98–99, 106–7, 118, 135, 167–68, 182–83, 194–95, 199, 232–35, 293, 316; decline in emphasis on, 94; doctrine of, ix–x, xxii, 81, 92–95, 167, 195–96, 232–34, 263, 275, 282, 314, 342, 350, 368; experience of, xxii, 65–66, 92–95, 107–8, 122, 128, 132–36, 153–54, 168, 182, 187, 191–92, 218, 234–35, 243, 263, 277, 282, 288, 301, 304, 340, 358; foundation of church, 265, 385; of God, 378; preaching of, xv, xxi, 93, 99–101, 105–7, 132, 143, 145, 150–52, 158, 168, 182, 188, 193, 217, 231–33, 243, 301–5; and revival, 99–100, 104–6, 111, 117, 137–38, 150–2, 155, 177, 184, 190, 277, 287; as second blessing, 182; seeking, 133, 227–28, 232, 239; testimony to, 92, 181, 182. *See also* sanctification, entire; perfection, Christian
holiness movement, xiii, xxiv, 196, 281
Holy Spirit, xxii, 16, 27, 63, 66, 77, 85, 89–92, 115–20, 125, 129, 131, 139, 161, 166, 176, 193–96, 200–202, 236, 246, 262, 266–69, 278, 293, 299–301, 311, 325, 328, 340, 350, 365, 380, 390–95
Home Missionary Society, 113, 172
horse racing, 48, 115, 123, 280, 305
Howard, R. H., xxiv, 287, 289–90
Huffman, Samuel, 322, 331, 335–37, 340
Huntington, Samuel, 286–87, 297, 351
hymns, hymnody, ix, 20, 57, 77, 78, 127, 131, 133, 180, 326, 351–52
hypnotism, 238
hypocrisy, 240, 246, 259, 299, 347
hysteria, 244, 252

Illinois Conference, F.M., 395
Illinois Conference, M.E., 333
image of God, 203, 370; in slaves, 370–71
imagination, 67
immortality, 27–30, 115
"impressions," 4, 8, 10, 14, 16, 18, 26, 27, 28, 31, 44, 46, 66–69, 87, 100, 110–11, 115, 142, 202, 236, 242, 315, 325, 335, 344, 350–54, 375, 387–89, 395; evaluating, 67; false, 278
Indians (Native Americans), 6, 27–29, 45, 223–25, 298, 369
infidels, 26, 28, 68, 70, 82, 116, 122, 130, 134, 146, 169, 173–74, 177–78, 182–83, 187, 209, 231, 233, 247, 254, 257, 269, 305, 365–66. *See also* atheism
influence, Christian, 212, 219, 236, 371
intuition, 67, 247

Janes, Bishop Edmund, 281
Jefferson, Thomas, 52
Jefferson, Wisconsin, 299–300
Jerusalem, New, 360
Jesus Christ, deity of, 89; as Great Physician, 389; as healer, 123–24; humanity of, 87–89, 92, 357; incarnation, 355; as model, 63, 267, 360–2, 380, 393; second coming, 103, 356, 363; sufferings, 1, 86–88, 112–13, 273, 354–61, 379–80
jewelry, ix, 211, 219, 271, 274, 279, 281, 316
Jews, 313; conversion of, 225–26
Job, Patriarch, 27, 345, 354, 381

John the Baptist, 356
John, Apostle, 351
Johnson, Andrew, President, 286
Jonah, Prophet, 16
Jones, Marsh Wilkinson, 104
Joslyn, Mary, 346
Joslyn, Osgood, 309–10, 346–48, 354, 375–76, 386, 388–90
Jubilee, 391
judgment of God, 179, 187–88, 229, 355, 363, 395
Judgment, Day of, 1, 2, 8, 21, 22, 25, 31, 73, 75, 79, 135, 161, 203, 212, 216, 230, 272, 316, 321, 348–49
jumping, ix, 168–69, 240, 262
justice, 55; of God, 367, 379, 381–82
justification, 91, 235, 243, 358

Keeseville, New York, 291
Kendall, Martha (Mrs. William), 297, 300, 307, 310–11
Kendall, William Case, 155–56, 258–61, 269, 272, 282, 285–86, 289–90, 293–302, 306, 368; death of, 156, 261, 302
kingdom of God, 380, 391
Knapp, Jacob, 254–55

Lansing, Dirk C., 254–55
Lawrence University, 300
Laymen's Conventions, 328, 330, 342
Lee, Jesse, 126
Lee, Luther, 63
Leslie, Charles, 30
Lima, New York, 78, 269, 292–93
Lincoln, Abraham, xxv, 286, 370
Lindsay, John, 267
Lippincott, Caleb, 160–62
Little Chute, Wisconsin, 300
"Live while you preach," xxii, 73–77, 102, 119, 145, 165, 259, 299, 333, 345
Livingston, Robert, 171
Livingston, W. W., 287
Lockport, New York, xxii, 38, 40, 45, 64
Long Island, New York, 125, 138, 169, 180
love, 163, 204, 246, 267; of God, 356, 378, 381; holiness as, 182, 379. *See* perfect love
love feast, 75, 93, 213, 395
Luckey, Samuel, 78–79
Luther, Martin, 1, 295, 372, 382

Mackinaw Island, Michigan, 297–98
Maffitt, John Newland, 108, 163–64
magnetism, 30, 238
Marengo, Illinois, xxv, 302–4, 309, 327, 342, 346, 348, 351, 388; revival at, 302–4
Marine Hospital, New York City, 201–2
Martyrs, 1, 351
Mason and Dixon Line, 369
Mathews, Ellen (Mrs. James), 352
Mathews, James, 352
Matlack, A. C., 49
Mattison, Hiram, 198–200, 234
McCreery, Joseph, 78, 156, 293, 295–96, 306–7, 328–29, 340, 367
McKendree College, 323
Mead, Judah, 344
means of grace, 211
mediums, 365
meetings in homes, 133, 169, 288, 296, 309, 390–91, 394
membership statistics, xiv, 178–79, 210, 220, 269, 276, 287, 303, 305, 321
Merrill, A. D., 267
Mesmer, Franz, 238
mesmerism, 237–38, 258
Methodism, "primitive," ix, xxiii, 108, 114–19, 184, 195, 216, 220–21, 238, 268–69, 278, 283, 294, 307, 337, 382; revival of, 382
Methodism, as a movement, ix–x; structure of, ix
Methodism, British, ix, xxiii
Methodist Episcopal (M.E.) Church, ix–x, xiii, xxi–xxiv; growth of, ix; mission of, 118, 368–70; Redfield denounces, 55–56, 62–64, 268, 369–71; reform of, x, 145, 307–8, 339–40, 368–69; revival of, 268,

271; toleration of slavery, xiv, 55–56, 62–64, 368–71; transitions in, xiii–xiv, xxi; urbanization of, ix, xiii, xxiii
Methodist Episcopal Church, South, 107, 312–13, 326, 336, 338, 369–70
Methodist Missionary Society, 108
Methodist Protestant Church, 94
Methodist Tract Society, 259, 281
Mexico, 369
Michigan Conference, M.E., 300
Middletown, Connecticut, xxiii–xxiv, 152–58, 280
Middletown, New York, 146, 172, 178–79, 187
millennium, millennialism, 103, 386; Pentecost and, 386
Millerites, 103
ministry, apostolic, 121
miracles, 364–66
missions, evangelical, xxiii, 225, 370; Methodist, 108, 217
Missouri Conference, M.E., 312–32
moral reform, xiii, 363
moral sense, 204
morality, 29, 371
Mormonism, 383
Moses, Patriarch, 362
music, ix, 78, 94; heavenly, 145, 351; instrumental, ix, 94, 392

Napoleon, 120
Natchez, Mississippi, 326
Nature, 27, 41; harmony of, 6
"Nazarites," 78, 196, 281, 283, 295–96, 327
Nelson, John, 194–95, 376
New England, xxii, 108, 183–86
New England Conference, M.E., 108, 267
New Haven, Connecticut, 213–20, 222
new heaven and earth, 360
New Jersey Conference, M.E., 160–62
New London, Wisconsin, 299
New Orleans, Louisiana, 326
New York City, xiv, xxii, 42, 71–81, 92–95, 107, 112, 140–44, 149, 158–59, 166, 171–72, 187, 192, 194, 199–202, 236, 283, 289, 336
New York Conference, M.E., 75–79, 93–94, 102–3, 107, 138, 146, 158, 178–79
New York East Conference, M.E., xxii, 158, 180, 208–10, 220
Newburgh, New York, 187–92
Niagara St. M.E. Church, Buffalo, New York, 280–83, 300, 328
novel reading, ix, 208, 211, 347

Ogle, Illinois, 338–39, 384
Olin, Stephen, xxiii, 153–56, 171
ordination, x, 107–08, 341
organs, church, ix, 250
Osborn, Thomas, 138
Oslin, S. J., 350
Ossining, New York, 202

Paley, William, 28, 30
Palmer, Phoebe, xi, xiv, xxii, 65, 72, 82–83, 87–88, 91, 136, 143–45, 151, 172, 177–78, 187, 195–96, 198–99, 208, 234, 292
Palmer, Walter, 83, 87, 91, 143, 151, 172, 177–78, 208
Palmyra, New York, 249
paranormal phenomena, 236–49, 365
Parker, Theodore, 257–58
Paul, Apostle, 25, 74, 310–11, 365, 377, 379, 392
Payne, Thomas, 365
Peck, George, 79
Peck, Jesse, 167
Peekskill, New York, 200–201
Pekin, New York, 306–7, 341, 343
Pentecostalism, xi; proto-, xi
Pentecost, 168, 285, 384–86, 391, 393; and healing, 352; as ideal for church, 261–65, 351–54, 363, 379
perfect love, 89, 95, 112, 122, 132, 133, 142, 144, 150–54, 168, 191, 218, 243, 263, 293, 297, 304, 307,

328, 372, 378. *See also* holiness; sanctification, entire
perfection, Christian, xxii, 103, 106, 378, 380; in relation to suffering, 380. *See also* holiness; sanctification
persecution, 2, 209, 351, 353–54, 366, 378
pew rental, 94, 254, 340
Philadelphia Conference, M.E., 167–68
Philadelphia, Pennsylvania, xiv, 163, 167–68, 172
philosophy, xxii, 27–28, 264, 364, 380, 391
plainness, 233, 285, 289. *See also* simplicity
poor, ministry to, xxv, 63, 175, 214, 252, 340–41, 360; Redfield's concern for, xxiii, 63, 260; revival and, 159–63
popularity, "popular churches," 1, 159, 195, 215, 308. *See also* respectability
populism, ix–x
Port Byron, New York, 284
Port Jefferson, New York, 180
Poughkeepsie, New York, 171
power of God, 131–33, 138, 148–52, 157, 161–69, 181–90, 195, 209–10, 216–23, 232–33, 237–41, 246–47, 253, 255, 258, 261, 264–69, 276, 278, 283–85, 291–93, 298–99, 305, 308–9, 313–16, 345, 347, 354–55, 363; Pentecostal, 284, 353, 365–66, 375, 378, 382, 389–93; "unearthly," 6, 77–79, 132, 282–83, 285, 316
praise, 227, 244, 345, 360
prayer, for healing, 349, 352, 388, 391; for revival, 68, 391
prayer meetings, 68, 91, 93, 125, 128, 146, 154, 162, 166, 193, 211, 235–37, 254, 280, 295, 300, 304, 308, 374, 390, 394
preachers, F.M., 351–52, 362–63
preachers, M.E., 95, 118–22, 130–39, 146, 155, 162, 167–68, 173, 181–200, 206–22, 230–34, 247–62, 268–72, 280, 285–97, 301–41, 347–48, 364, 393; oppose holiness preaching, 118–20; salaries of, 259
predestination, 109, 226
premonition, presentiment, 10
Presbyterian Church, 48, 87, 129–30, 132, 173–77, 185–87, 196, 211, 255, 285, 304, 333; New School, 255
presiding elders, M.E., xxii, 25, 102–3, 112, 121, 125, 157–58, 187, 199, 231, 234–35, 250, 269, 271, 274, 285, 293–97, 299, 301, 303, 314–16, 321, 323, 336, 339
pride, 84, 159, 264, 296, 308
Primitive Methodists, ix
Princeton, Illinois, 311
Prindle, Cyrus, 63
prisons, 202–5
prophecy, 63–64, 66–67, 267, 299, 337, 357, 371
prophets, biblical, xiv, 8, 307, 351
proselytism, 113–15, 140, 174–75, 185–86, 206, 209, 211, 218, 270
providence of God, 383
psychology, 238, 244
Purdy, Fay H., xxi, 195–99, 208, 235, 238–39, 249–53, 261, 269, 271, 277, 284–85, 286, 288–90; conversion of, 197–98
purity, 116, 271, 37, 37, 378, 380

Quakers, 162–63, 299
quarterly conference, M.E., xxii, 25, 79, 102–3, 159, 297, 306, 309, 315, 318–19, 334–36
Quincy English and German Seminary, 333
Quincy, Illinois, 328, 331–34, 343

rationalism, German, 263, 364
reason, 5, 9, 14, 25–28, 88–89, 130–31, 353, 364
Red Mills, New Jersey, 160, 162

redemption, of body, 389; of perceptive powers, 264, 385; plan of, 249, 264–65, 356–60, 379, 384; suffering in, 356–57. *See also* salvation

Redfield, John Wesley, as abolitionist, xi, xxiii, 46–64, 314, 326–28, 368–69; birth, early life, 3; call to preach, xxi–xxii, 3–4, 9–20, 26–48, 70–79, 108, 110–12, 358, 380–81, 392–93; as class leader, 47, 93, 98–100; conversion, xi, xxi, 4–7, 83; death, xxv, 150, 395; decline of, 384–95; divorce, xi, xiii, xxii, 41, 75, 158–59, 290–91; education, xxi; eloquence, 153, 288; experience of holiness, xxii, 65–68, 80–92, 111, 235–36, 357; finances, xxii, xxv, 2, 34, 36–37, 40, 65, 70–74, 102–5, 128, 150, 157, 160, 164–65, 248, 253, 255, 259, 269, 275–76, 290, 299, 302–4, 311–13, 324, 331, 377, 386, 392; helps slave escape to Canada, 57–62; illness, xxii, 35, 40–41, 71–80, 141–42, 145, 165, 325–26, 343, 349–50; influence, xxiii–xxiv; lay (local) preacher, xix, 46–48, 64–65, 72, 75–77, 106–8, 133–34, 151, 159, 194, 321; licensed to preach, xxii, 46–48, 72, 75–77, 102–5, 159, 309, 315; marriage, xi, xiii, xxii, 31–45, 66, 71, 75, 80–81, 110, 121, 157–59, 290–91, 381; medical practice, xi, xiv, xxi–xxii, 30, 34, 71–74, 123, 262, 290, 348, 373–74; motives, 102, 354, 358–59, 362, 380–81, 392; oratory, xxii, xxii, 153; ordained in F.M. Church, 342, 350; parents and family, 3–4, 8, 17, 18, 26–29, 38, 42–45, 264, 268; personality, xiv, 76, 81, 215; physical description, 9; as portrait artist, xxii, 13, 34, 42, 48, 73; preaching, xxiv–xxv, 22, 47–48, 64–65, 93, 153, 188–89, 202–3, 288, 302–3, 317, 338, 347–50, 362, 378, 384; prison ministry, 201–5; remarriage, xxii, 289–92, 295; reputation, xxii, 157–58, 162–65, 253, 265, 275–76, 279, 282, 289–90, 298, 304–7, 366; revival ministry, xxii–xxv, 22–23, 48, 70, 93–94, 112–41, 145–49, 232–33; stroke and paralysis, xxv, 2–3, 344–51, 353, 357–58, 362–63, 376–78, 384–91, 395; theology, 264–65, 351–58; writing autobiography, xxv, 387

Redfield, Martha (Mattie) (Mrs. John), 291–92, 296, 299–300, 306–14, 318–19, 325–39, 341–42, 345, 374–75, 384–88, 390, 392–95

reform of world, 1, 285

reform, movements of, xiii, 382

religion, joy of, 7; nature of, 382–83

reprobation, 171, 226

respectability, ix–x, xxiii, 94, 115, 118, 133, 173, 177, 180, 206, 220–21, 245. *See also* popularity

resurrection, 203, 272, 379

revelations, x, 30, 78, 236–37, 333, 346, 351, 354–56, 378–79, 384

revival, assessing, xiv; hindrances to, 116; opposition to, xiv, 1, 94, 146, 169–70, 187–88, 281, 286; phenomena of, ix–x, xxiii, 284–85, 294 (*see* emotional manifestations, spiritual manifestations); in relation to holiness, 100–101, 105, 118, 137–38, 150–51, 155, 168, 171, 177, 184, 190, 277, 287; results of, xiv, xxi–xxii, 68, 113, 118, 129, 150–55, 162, 167–71, 174–79, 183–84, 190, 200, 208, 210, 218–23, 231, 233, 254–57, 271, 275, 280–81, 284–88, 290, 303–5, 333–34, 371, 393

revivalism, ix–x, xi, xxi, 22, 25, 68, 93–94, 100, 271, 279, 301–2, 356, 382, 391, 394

Rice, Phineas, 75, 102

Richmond, Virginia, 326
Roberts, Benjamin T., xiv–xv, xxi, xxv–xxvi, 3, 78, 87, 153–56, 196, 258–60, 280–84, 293, 295, 302, 306–7, 328–30, 337, 339–41, 343, 350, 367, 382, 386–87, 395; expulsion from M.E. Church, 282, 295, 306, 328–29; Redfield's assessment of, 280, 283–84, 306; trial of, 295, 302
Roberts, Ellen Lois Stowe (Mrs. B. T.), xiv, 65, 87, 280, 307, 384, 387
Robie, John, 283
Rochester, New York, xiii, 40, 78, 268–69, 278, 293–95, 343, 363
Rock River Conference, M.E., 302–5
Roman Catholic Church, 115, 122, 298, 382

sacraments, 187, 193, 375
sacrifice, 226, 363
Salina, New York, 236–37, 243–47, 390, 395
salvation, 7, 90, 92, 355; based on Christ's merits, 92; as Edenic restoration, 356; plan of, 249, 264–65, 356–60; of world, 7, 25, 95, 107, 113, 119, 285, 354. *See also* redemption
sanctification, entire, ix–x, xxii, xxiii, 81–85, 134, 150–52, 190, 197, 216, 227–28, 234, 263, 316; progressive, 234–35. *See* holiness
Satan, 1, 25, 71, 84–85, 90, 112, 119, 129, 133, 149, 182, 191, 193, 217, 223, 239, 255, 257, 259, 263, 267, 278–79, 309–10, 332, 344–46, 351–52, 358–61, 365, 374–75, 381
Schurman, William, 318
Scott, Levi, 326
Scott, Orange, 63, 267
screaming, 129, 132, 138, 170, 238–44, 258, 35–46
Seamen's Bethel, 48
Second F.M. Church, Buffalo, New York, 350
senses, spiritual, 264, 348, 357
Sherman, David, 294, 296–97
shouting, ix, xxiii, 6, 89, 129, 132, 168–69, 180, 187, 255, 262, 271, 315, 375
sight, spiritual, 264, 376, 379
signs, 14–19, 22–23, 171–72, 237, 249, 306, 308, 353, 355, 366, 384. *See* impressions; revelations
signs and wonders, 365
simplicity, xxiii, 63, 108, 195, 280, 281, 285
Simpson, Matthew, Bishop, xxi, 78, 223, 340
sin , 92, 201–4, 264, 360, 368; effects of, 363, 383; slavery as, 368
Sing Sing Prison, 202–3
Sing Sing, New York, 87
singing, 133, 142, 146–47, 180, 216, 262, 268, 275, 350–51, 375, 389; heavenly, 350. *See also* hymns; music
slave narratives, 57–64
slave trade, 368, 370
slaveholding, 312, 326, 329, 336, 338
slavery, x, xiv, 43, 49–64, 326–29, 368–70; extension of in U.S., 369; inhumanity of, 51–52, 368–70; profiting from, 43; slave codes, 50–51
slaves, emancipation of, 329; image of Christ in, 370–71
slaying in the Spirit, ix, x, xiv, xxiii, 81, 89, 99, 129, 132–33, 157, 161–62, 168, 180–82, 188–92, 208, 222, 237, 246, 253–59, 270, 274, 294, 375. *See also* emotional manifestations; spiritual manifestations
social conformity, ix–x, xi, 211–12, 219
social reform, xi, 1
social status, xxiii, 115, 173, 175, 185, 197, 233, 245–46, 288, 308
Southampton, New York, 138
spirits, demonic, 2, 266–67, 278–79, 298, 363–64, 374
spiritual manifestations, ix, xiv, 180, 182, 187–90, 237–49, 251–52, 285. *See* emotional manifestations

spiritualism, xxii, 30, 238, 334, 364–65, 383
St. Charles (Illinois) Camp Meeting, 300–302, 306, 342–43, 349–50, 385; revival at, 301–2
St. Charles, Illinois, xxv, 294–96, 300–302, 310–11, 338–41, 349–50, 386
St. George's M.E. Church, Philadelphia, 168
St. John's St. M.E. Church, New Haven, Connecticut, 214, 220
St. Louis, Missouri, xiv, xxiv, 172, 306–32, 334–45, 347–48
Stamford, Connecticut, 220–23, 226, 230–32
Staten Island, New York, 201–2
Sterling, John M., 54
Stevens, Abel, 281–82
Stiles, Loren, 340, 367
Stocking, David, 101, 103
Stratton, J. B., 108
suffering, xxiii, 32, 76, 89, 103, 110–13, 127–28, 134, 141, 152, 192, 243–44, 350–59, 372–82; of animals, xxiii; as God's judgment, 354, 358; of Jesus, 353–57, 373, 379–80; Redfield's, 109–10, 243–44, 262–64, 269, 326, 333, 345–48, 353, 357–59, 362, 366, 377–79, 385–95; and revival, 244
Sullivan St. M.E. Church, New York City, 93–94
Sunday schools, 288
Syracuse, New York, 236–37, 247–48, 254–58, 271, 284–86, 290, 307, 353, 384–95

Taylor, William M., xxv
Temperance Movement, 165
temptation, 267, 278–29, 309, 332, 345–47, 357, 362, 373–75, 378, 392–94
Terrill, Joseph G., xiii, xviii–xix, 3, 6, 7, 296, 305, 308–9, 325, 338–39, 351, 384, 387
theology, 26, 27, 264–65, 356–58
Theresa, New York, 234
Tinkham, Joseph K., 268–69, 284
Tocqueville, Alexis de, 202
Torrey, H. A. P., 287
Torrey, John P., 287
Townsendville, New York, 284
Transcendentalism, 257
translation to heaven, 379
Travis, Joseph, 350
Trinity M.E. Church, New York City, 199
Trinity, the, 119, 375
Troy Conference, M.E., 287–88
True, Charles, 184
truth, 30, 103, 208–10, 215–16, 258, 272–74, 378
Tuesday Meetings for the Promotion of Holiness, 82
Twenty-seventh St. M.E. Church, New York City, xxii

Underground Railroad, 56–57
Underwood, C. H., 317
Unitarians, 182–84, 213, 220, 238, 245–47, 255, 257–58
Universalists, Universalism, 8–9, 20–22, 125, 140, 162–64, 182–83, 210, 227–30, 246, 266, 304–5, 340–41; debates over, 228–30
University of Missouri, 312
University of Vermont, xxiv

Vernon St. M.E. Church, Quincy, Illinois, 333
visions, xiv, 23, 124, 142–45, 242, 262–64, 282, 309–01, 328, 344–51, 355–56; of heaven, 142–44, 355–56
visiting in homes, 126–27, 132, 138, 147, 192, 219, 334
visiting the sick, 66–67
Vosburgh, Peter, 282–83

Wallace, John H., 300
warfare, spiritual, 351, 361
watchnights, 15, 18, 65, 81, 393
Watts, Jonathan, 294
Waukesha, Wisconsin, 300

Weld, Theodore, 50–51, 55
Wentworth, John B., 282
Wesley, Charles, ix–x, 344, 377
Wesley, John, ix–x, 1, 3, 30, 91, 95–96, 104, 106, 112, 131, 149, 181, 212–13, 279, 315, 344, 365, 370, 376–78, sermons of, 212–13
Wesleyan University, xxi, xxiii, 9, 153–56, 184, 267
West Falls, New York, 261
Wickersham, Joseph, 329, 331
Wilbraham Wesleyan Academy, xxi, 9, 267
Wilbraham, Massachusetts, xxi, 9
will, of God, xxii, 134–36, 191, 359, 362, 376–78, 381, 383; human, 265
Williams, Thomas, 312–26, 330–31, 335–36, 347–48
Windsor, Vermont, 10
Winkler, Johann, 131
Wisconsin Conference, M.E., 299
women and dress question, ix, 189, 219, 317. *See* jewelry
women's issues, xi, xiii, xxi, 201, 363
women, preaching of, xiii, xxiii, 363
Woodstock, Illinois, 302–5, 371–73
Woodward, Charles M., 302
worldliness, x, 114, 118, 206, 208, 211–12, 219, 253, 273, 281–82, 370

Yale College, 215, 218
Youngs, James, 72, 75, 97, 102

zeal, 361, 379, 381
Zwingli, Ulrich, 382